8/16

D1566894

Brand Command

Communication, Strategy, and Politics

Thierry Giasson and Alex Marland, Series Editors

Brand Command

Canadian Politics and Democracy in the Age of Message Control

ALEX MARLAND

UBCPress·Vancouver·Toronto

25 24 23 22 21 20 19 18 17 16   5 4 3 2 1

Printed in Canada on FSC-certified ancient-forest-free paper
(100% post-consumer recycled) that is processed chlorine- and acid-free.

Library and Archives Canada Cataloguing in Publication

Marland, Alexander J., author
Brand command: Canadian politics and democracy in the age of message control /
Alex Marland.

(Communication, strategy, and politics)
Includes bibliographical references and index.
Issued in print and electronic formats.
ISBN 978-0-7748-3203-8 (hardback). – ISBN 978-0-7748-3205-2 (pdf). –
ISBN 978-0-7748-3206-9 (epub)

1. Communication in politics – Canada. 2. Branding (Marketing) –
Political aspects – Canada. 3. Democracy – Canada.
I. Title. II. Series: Communication, strategy, and politics

JA85.2.C3M37 2016   320.97101'4   C2015-908482-2
                                                        C2015-908483-0

Canadä

UBC Press gratefully acknowledges the financial support for our
publishing program of the Government of Canada (through the Canada Book Fund),
the Canada Council for the Arts, and the British Columbia Arts Council.

This book has been published with the help of a grant from the
Canadian Federation for the Humanities and Social Sciences, through the
Awards to Scholarly Publications Program, using funds provided
by the Social Sciences and Humanities Research Council of Canada.

UBC Press
The University of British Columbia
2029 West Mall
Vancouver, BC V6T 1Z2
www.ubcpress.ca

A century ago the Swiss historian Jacob Burckhardt foresaw that ours would be the age of "the great simplifiers," and that the essence of tyranny was the denial of complexity. He was right. This is the single greatest temptation of the time. [Simplification] is the great corrupter, and must be resisted with purpose and with energy.

> – Daniel Patrick Moynihan, Assistant to the President
> for Urban Affairs, excerpt from farewell speech to Nixon
> White House (1970)

We need to be extra-careful with our messaging. We can't afford any slipups. So, no emotional outbursts, no off-the-cuff remarks: the brand comes first, alright? Most importantly, it means that everything, and I mean *everything*, goes through this office first.

> – Prime Minister's Office Chief of Staff to party MPs,
> "Just Watch Me," *The Best Laid Plans*, CBC TV (originally
> aired February 3, 2014)

Brands are no longer limited to sitting on paper. Today, brands fly across computer screens and leap off of iPads.

> – *Advertising Standards Guide*, Canadian Wheat Board
> (c. 2012)

Contents

Appendices, Figures, and Tables

Preface:
Branding, Message Control, and Sunny Ways

In the digital age, communications technology is dramatically and irrevocably changing how people and organizations interact. This is particularly true for parliamentary democracy in Canada. As connectivity intensifies, political communication orbits around party leaders, coalescing to fuse the brands of the prime minister, the governing party, and the government. This empowers the ferocity of a top-down chain of command that is not only at odds with growing expectations of public involvement in policy formulation but also, as is argued in this book, undermines democracy itself. It is an unedifying proposition.

In this new era of politics, political elites repeatedly blur what is partisan, political, or impartial, despite promises of being different. On the first day of the 2005-06 federal election campaign that installed Conservative leader Stephen Harper in the Prime Minister's Office (PMO), he repeated the word "change" more than fifty times in his address to reporters. He further argued that the Conservative Party would "make government more honest, more accountable, more democratic" after the sponsorship scandal, which had occurred because of an abrogation of centralized power in Jean Chrétien's Liberal government (discussed in Chapter 7).[1] Initially, Conservative marketers portrayed their leader as a crusader of good governance, while Liberal marketers framed him as a Republican with a sinister agenda. However, the longer Conservatives were exposed to pluralism, the more they were convinced of the importance of cohesion and scripting and the less they were interested in democratic principles. They proceeded to turn the media's glare on opponents' weaknesses and mounted exacting message control to keep their own independent thinkers in check. All available resources were steered in an Orwellian-like manner to project an image of a decisive commander-in-chief who prioritized the economy. Invariably Prime Minister Harper was lampooned as the evil Darth Vader, overseeing an army of clones (see Figure 1.1).

The Conservative leadership circle agitated norms and pushed the boundaries of political correctness. Years of treating the legislature and traditional media as inconveniences, combined with a partiality to negative advertising and disparagement of critics, turned the Conservative brand into a nasty one. During the 2015 election campaign, they stirred debate about imposing restrictions on the wearing of niqabs, with nearly two-thirds of Canadians agreeing that the face-covering veil worn by some Muslim women should be removed at citizenship ceremonies.[2] The xenophobic dimension generated by this issue strayed from the brand's core promise of economic security (see Figure 2.4) and evoked negatives associated with conservatism that are unpalatable to the median voter. Lessons from the party's 2004 election loss were forgotten when, in an internal post-campaign memo, political marketers warned that "with tight messaging we can win or neutralize the debate on specific social conservative issues (which split the Liberals' base as well as ours), but we lose when the debate shifts to the emotive, patriotic symbolism" of the Charter of Rights and Freedoms (see Appendix 3). As the party's marketers foretold, the wedge favoured the Liberal brand's unwavering strength, namely national unity to reconcile division.

During the 2015 election campaign, the contrast between pugnacity and positivity was stark. The Liberal slogan of "real change" was punctuated with the trope that the Harper Conservatives operated "the most centralized, partisan, self-serving government in Canadian history."[3] The Grits' platform argued that the reason Canadians were turned off politics was "more a symptom of what is wrong than the cause of the problem itself: the steady weakening of the work of Parliamentarians, as power is increasingly concentrated within the Prime Minister's Office."[4]

On the face of it, today's Liberal Party distances itself from any craving for concentrated power. In his autobiography, Justin Trudeau mentions that, although his father Pierre was portrayed as autocratic, they both practise(d) a decision-making style that absorbs perspectives from a variety of voices.[5] Cue the Liberals' resurrection of the "sunny ways" mantra of Wilfrid Laurier, the early-twentieth-century prime minister who was often judged more by his dashing persona and optimism rather than by his policies or methods. The Laurier myth, shaped by a debonair appearance and decades of Liberal propaganda, pertains to a statesman who embodies all things good about Canadian democracy. Such a leader is held up as a conciliator who navigates the political tensions of English-French dualism while promising Canada can become an even greater nation. Dig deeper though and we find that power was more concentrated in the prime minister's circle than revisionism lets on. The centralization of federal government communications can be traced to the Laurier PMO's creation of the Canadian Exhibition Commission (see Chapter 8). He did not hold formal news conferences and demanded obedience from his MPs.[6] Laurier's right-hand man, Minister Clifford Sifton, headed a propaganda factory dishing out patronage to newspapers that published stories praising the Liberal government, sometimes authored by Sifton himself.[7] Nearly a century ago, former Sifton employee and *Winnipeg Free Press* editor J.W. Dafoe reflected about Laurier and Canadian politics:

> A prime minister under the party system as we have had it in Canada is of necessity an egoist and an autocrat. If he comes to office without these characteristics his environment equips him with them as surely as a diet of royal jelly transforms a worker into a queen bee ... It is in keeping with the genius of our party system that the leader who begins as the chosen chief of his associates proceeds by stages, if he has the necessary qualities, to a position of dominance; the republic is transformed into an absolute monarchy.[8]

Dafoe was prescient that the political environment envelops anyone who climbs to the top. *Brand Command* builds on this by arguing centralization is fuelled by shrewd political actors interacting with the forces of communications technology. The theory submits it is inevitable that prime ministers will demand message consistency from their agents. In politics, the desire to control permeates all.

Early indications are that the Trudeau Liberals know how to play the Ottawa game and are particularly adept at treating politics as show business.

On his final evening as PM-designate, an email in the leader's name titled "Before I put the kids to bed" was sent to the untold number of Canadians in the Liberalist database (discussed in Chapter 5). The message began:

> Friend, as I write to you, evening is falling outside our new home, Rideau Cottage, on the grounds of Rideau Hall in Ottawa. A few minutes from now, Sophie and I will put Xavier and Ella-Grace to bed (Hadrien is already fast asleep), but before I go, I want to share a few thoughts with you to mark this moment. Tomorrow, we take the next step in our journey together. I will be sworn in by the governor general, and become Canada's 23rd prime minister ... I [have] made a personal commitment to bring new leadership and a new tone to Ottawa. Sunny ways.[9]

On the day of the swearing-in ceremony, the Canadian Broadcasting Corporation documented Liberal PMO personnel reviewing plans to get the media visuals they wanted. The new cabinet would walk together in solidarity to meet the governor general, in front of cheering supporters to whom the Liberals had put out a call to attend. The CBC has among the best journalistic standards in the business and secured the unprecedented backroom access by testing the incoming government's commitment to transparency. Nonetheless, *The National* aired a fluffy montage. I happened to detect the following in a televised exchange between the PM-designate and a strategist, which was not remarked upon and inexplicably edited out of the CBC's online version:

> COMMUNICATIONS DIRECTOR (TO TRUDEAU): I think it will be a little bit chaotic at the [Rideau Hall] gates as you start walking. Because even though there are hold positions earlier, everybody's going to want to be there as you're walking just outside the gates, so that they get the shot ...

> J. TRUDEAU: But that's where we're tricking them a bit, because they think the buses are dropping us off at the gates, and getting off a bus is such an ugly shot that we're making sure that they get the walk over from 24 [Sussex drive].[10]

Trudeau goes on to plan that his children will wait by the fountain in front of the Rideau Hall façade, where he ended up greeting them with outstretched arms. The picturesque assembly of ministers on the Hall's steps, standing in unity behind the new PM delivering a presidential-style inaugural address, offered the sound and image bites that are the currency of digital media. He proclaimed "government by cabinet is back" and explained away prioritizing ministerial genotype over phenotype by saying he assembled "a cabinet that looks like Canada ... because it's 2015."[11] Ensuing visuals of PMJT – as Trudeau is now known in social media shorthand – hugging ministers and kissing his wife were mused to be "calculated facets of the Trudeau brand, intended to feed the notion of a kinder, sunnier government," as one columnist put it.[12] Days later, delegates, mostly women, sought selfies with the new prime minister at his first international events. Journalists in Manila chased him. "He's so hot and intelligent and he just took all our stress away," relayed a Filipina reporter.[13] Whether a head of government is portrayed as a simpatico prince, a calculating curmudgeon, or something else, it is the role of academics to see past personalities, especially when everyone else is preoccupied by them.

For political strategists, charisma like Trudeau's is marketing magic. The difficulty that Conservatives experienced vilifying him (see Chapters 4 to 6) followed a wave of adulation for Jack Layton, the telegenic New Democratic Party leader, indicating that positive messaging alone is not enough to rebuff negativity. But charisma is its own problem. It increases deference to the leader, and charismatic figures attract followers whose judgment is clouded by their emotional connection. Celebritization and tabloid-style coverage of the prime minister and his family are now trending. There is world media interest in Canada's handsome leader, about PMJT's and Sophie Grégoire-Trudeau's fashion and their Kennedyesque Camelot story, and about photo shoots in entertainment venues. Even TMZ, the American purveyor of low-brow celebrity gossip, treated the Trudeaus' post-election Caribbean vacation as newsworthy, adding to the Canadian media's story arc of international fame.[14] The prime minister maintains that his public performance is "not about image, it's about substance" because he connects with ordinary people,[15] and he rationalizes that global exposure, such as sensual photos in *Vogue* magazine, are a way to reach citizens in other countries.[16] Impartial observers will be frustrated when fans of the Trudeaus are ambivalent or defensive about valid criticism. Conversely, just as the spectacle and celebrity of the Obama presidency were eventually confronted by powerful forces resistant to change,[17] the domestic idealism associated with the Trudeau prime ministership will fade as promises are broken and controversies pile up.

The initial easy-going image of the new government both supports and challenges this book's thesis. Ministers' public musings about policy options, including comments that contradict the party platform,[18] belie some tenets of centralization, agenda setting, permanent campaigning, and branding. There is more to it than a third-place opposition party trying to find its legs after unexpectedly winning a majority of seats. The Liberal brain trust has obsessed with projecting an image of leadership that is the antithesis of the Conservative command-and-control approach. The Trudeau brand is built on message themes of transparency and a respect for institutions, wrapped in amorphous leanings towards policy centrism and a yearning for publicity. Communication breakdowns during the government's honeymoon period, such as repeated backtracking on timeline commitments concerning the arrival of Syrian refugees, were forgivable because they conveyed a democratic turn rather than weak leadership. Such amateurism is partly an outcome of an understaffed PMO taking months to vet and appoint the political personnel in ministers' offices who enforce the centre's bidding. On a microlevel, evidence of a branding philosophy is found in new staffers using @canada.ca email suffixes in lieu of conventional departmental nomenclature such as @dfo-mpo.gc.ca.[19] At a macrolevel, central control is prone to intensify as public frustration with the Harper foil dissipates and when bungling by Liberal ministers is framed by the media and opposition as incompetent leadership.

Concentrated power in the parliamentary system of government is a phenomenon strong enough to withstand proposed reforms. More time for questioning in the House of Commons, more independence for parliamentary committees, more power for the Speaker, ending the abuse of omnibus bills and prorogation, greater independence for the parliamentary budget officer, and the addition of a code of conduct for political staff in the guide for ministers are all positive inside-Ottawa initiatives promised or initiated by the Trudeau Liberals. Tinkering matters little if members of Parliament toe the party line. To this end, Liberal MPs are promised whipped votes "only" on matters concerning the party's election platform, major confidence matters (e.g., throne speech, budget), and issues evoking Charter values. Past attempts at decentralization have suffered under the weight of controversy and drama brought about by media reports of dis-symmetry, exemplified by the Canadian political right until Harper's team imposed rigorous controls (see Chapter 6's discussion about brand discipline). If free votes are to be viable it is because each new Parliament is more prone to fall in line with brand orthodoxy. Self-censorship and public loyalty are cultural norms instilled during modern election campaigns. Political parties obsess about screening out independent-minded candidates and they impose tight communications discipline to ensure conformity. Chaos swirls when party representatives make controversial remarks and when the disgruntled use the media as a venting outlet. Anyone on the perimeter who causes public embarrassment is ruthlessly banished. During governance, harmony is emphasized by requiring ministers to attend caucus meetings,[20] and MPs must relinquish mobile phones at the door.[21] The ambitious and the anxious find safety in approved messages. The emergence and treatment of discordant voices that derail the centre's agenda will test the thesis of brand supremacy.

Reforming PMO control is perhaps best described as *plus ça change*. Ministers and caucus are told PMJT's chief of staff and principal secretary speak on his behalf.[22] Posting mandate letters – the marching orders issued to a minister upon appointment – on the prime minister's website confirms that ministers are foremost "brand ambassadors" (see Glossary).[23] Releasing the Privy Council Office (PCO)'s revised guide for ministers further codifies expectations of public solidarity, which is a longstanding collective responsibility norm of cabinet.[24] Both instruments emphasize subservience to the PM and establish expectations that ministers coordinate their public statements with central agencies, particularly the PMO and PCO. There may be fewer ministers in the new government, but dozens of parliamentary secretaries continue to channel the government's message. A weekly Prime Minister's Question Period will add to the first minister's superstar status and eliminate any remaining doubt of who is in charge, while reducing expectations of the PM being present in the House on other days. In public administration, the Liberals look to Britain's New Labour government – which obsessed over spin and control freakery – for inspiration about cutting through layers of bureaucracy. PMJT's senior advisors reportedly sought to restructure the upper echelon of the public service around delivery units so the PMO can stealthily ensure progress is made on priority files.[25] Meeting policy targets and being directly accountable to "the centre" rather than to ministers would mark a further drift towards New Public Management (Chapter 8) and New Political Governance (Chapter 9). This is a reality of modern governance.

The Liberals' more respectful tone in terms of media relations, while welcome, must not be confused with abandonment of distorting truth through spin or ceding ground to advance an agenda. After being sworn in, ministers scrummed with reporters, offering variations of identical message lines about looking forward to getting to work.[26] The prime minister and ministers take questions in the National Press Theatre, sweeping aside the dark cloud hanging over the Canadian Parliamentary Press Gallery during the Conservative years (discussed in Chapter 6). The Liberal PMO sends a steady stream of media advisories about Trudeau's events, pledging to release his itinerary daily, all the while drumming up publicity for some activities while downplaying and concealing others.[27] Journalists are once again notified of cabinet meetings, so ministers can be asked questions immediately afterwards (known as "cabinet outs"). Yet the third floor mezzanine, where ministers walk out of cabinet, is off limits. Instead, media advisories specify that designated ministers will be available downstairs in the House of Commons foyer.[28] This allows other ministers to escape the media's glare without their evasiveness being caught on video. In the digital age there must be no surprises.

Media manipulation was on display as the Trudeau government sought to put climate change action on the public agenda. Public opinion polls find that other issues, notably the economy, are of greater concern to Canadians,[29] indicating that the Liberals are sales-oriented (a concept discussed in Chapter 2) and cherry-pick research to suit their political ideology. Scientists in the rebranded Department of Environment and Climate Change were made available to the media to emphasize the urgency of action. The practice of having their public comments vetted by communications personnel (see Chapter 6) was ended to serve Liberal purposes – though the party's manifesto does stipulate there will be "limited and publicly stated exceptions" to what scientists can speak about.[30] The return to first ministers' conferences, dispatching Harper's preference for a one-on-one style of executive federalism (also Chapter 6), was structured to advance the file. Early on, Trudeau served notice that the premiers would be invited to join him at a United Nations climate change gathering in Paris. Weeks before the event, PMJT hosted them in Ottawa to, in his words, "discuss the kind of strong and cohesive message" to be delivered in France.[31] The meeting of first ministers, mostly Liberals, was light on policy specifics and high on showmanship; grandstanding to advance regional interests was contained, for now. The prime minister asserted the need for unity and Quebec Premier Philippe Couillard stated that Canada "needs a serious effort in rebranding."[32] Turning the premiers into brand ambassadors was vital given the best laid plans are at the mercy of external events, including Paris terrorist attacks that killed 130 people. During the Paris conference, news releases promoted the PM (rather than the minister) announcing billions in government funding for climate change initiatives, and photos were tweeted of him with the premiers. Afterwards, another first ministers' conference on climate change was announced. These are among the many publicity devices available to the PMO to set and control the agenda.

This book impresses that, more than ever, *everything* political elites do involves communication calculations. This includes the actions of a new administration promising change and transparency. The Liberal election platform proposes to improve access to government data, including a pledge to "ensure that Access to Information applies to the prime minister's and ministers' offices"; however, the Treasury Board mandate letter adds the qualifier "*appropriately* applies,"[33] and those in power will find ways for their internal communication to evade detection.[34] The Liberals plan to increase reporting about parliamentary expenses but have not pledged to generate annual reports on the costs of government photo-ops, as recommended in Chapter 11. The electronic distribution of behind-the-scenes moments has expanded from official government channels to the PMO photographer's Instagram account, conveying an illusion of authenticity of shots planned in advance, sometimes at the behest of the PM's principal advisor.[35] The Treasury Board Secretariat is updating the government's communications policy to "reflect the modern digital environment," as the ministerial mandate letter puts it.[36] Yet there is no such policy for political parties, leading to suspect activities, such as Liberal database marketers circulating electronic fundraising messages in return for an opportunity to mingle with ministers or dine with the finance minister.[37] Transparency is even suspect depending on who the PMO authorizes to speak to the media. The prime minister's mother, Margaret Trudeau, stayed away from the media during the election campaign and when she became available post-election it was to justify the multi-million dollar expense of renovating 24 Sussex Drive. How cabinets shape government advertising is more nefarious. To convey non-partisanship the Liberals plan to appoint an advertising commissioner to advise the auditor general. This is another positive action that is handcuffed, given who controls the appointment process and defines partisanship. Moreover, cabinet will continue to deploy public funds for advertising to sell policy, and the Liberals will balloon spending on public opinion research to advance their interests, which they will frame as evidence-based decision making.

There is no easy fix to calming partisan opportunism. Incivility in the Trudeau government's first House debate led interim Conservative leader Rona Ambrose to quip that sunny ways lasted all of 25 minutes.[38] The Senate holds the most promise for the people's representatives to challenge the PMO's influence (see Chapter 11). Regrettably, the upper chamber houses *party* representatives, and meaningful Senate reform is caught in constitutional quagmires. Liberal plans to reduce senatorial partisanship are largely cosmetic, and changing the system for electing MPs has been deemed a greater priority. Conversely, given that Trudeau has withstood negativity and preaches positivity, the minister of democratic institutions could address the most sinister elements of debranding (see Chapter 6), particularly when personal affronts are subsidized with public funds. Reducing inclinations to stamp the governing party's brand on public administration is quite another matter. Some Liberal changes to eviscerate the memory of Conservative-associated iconography are logical, such as the prompt removal of links and images associated with the Economic

Action Plan from the government's websites.[39] Other branding decisions are unsettling, such as quietly removing the portrait of Canada's head of state from government buildings.

The so-called natural governing party's embodiment of the state is conveyed through a post-election penchant for proclaiming that "Canada is back." Within days of the swearing-in ceremony, some civil servants – reportedly mostly women with smartphones, again – mobbed Prime Minister Trudeau in the foyer of the Global Affairs building that is named after Liberal icon Lester B. Pearson.[40] Ministers were greeted by cheers; a reporter who asked a difficult question was jeered. Government employees circulated photos on social media of similar occurrences in other locations. This reflects more than an expression of liberation from Conservative politicization: it speaks to an underlying political culture within the Government of Canada, especially within Global Affairs whose personnel previously expressed disloyalty to the Conservative cabinet.[41] Perhaps some federal civil servants believe open expression of opinion in the workplace about political leaders is acceptable. They are wrong. They must uphold the Values and Ethics Code for the Public Sector, which states that they are to carry out duties "in a non-partisan and impartial manner," and behave "at all times with integrity and in a manner that will bear the closest public scrutiny."[42]

As explained in Chapters 7, 8, and 11, the public service's apparent favouritism of one political party is connected to the overlap between the visual identities of the Government of Canada and the Liberal Party of Canada. In Canada the main symbol of the state – the maple leaf flag – and its official colours are principally associated with one major political party. These visual bonds contribute to a sense of party-state normality and the commandeering of patriotic constructs. Brand overlap is inevitable when the Liberals are in power, such as with the Trudeau cabinet authorizing online ads featuring a stylized maple leaf reminiscent of the party's logo circa 2008,[43] and the integration of red colours on government websites.[44] The guide for ministers echoes other policies of the Government of Canada stating that "party symbols and identifiers and partisan content should not be present in department-supported communications, events and social media channels."[45] The intent is sound, but the execution is implausible when the official colours and symbols of the governing party run parallel to the official colours and symbols of the government. Appropriation of state semiotics is much less a problem in the United States or United Kingdom, where tricolour flags complicate political ownership of state colours, and where party emblems feature animals or vegetation.

The lure of brand management adds to the centralization of power no matter which party or individual is in charge. That the same communications practices plied by the world's largest corporations and most famous celebrities are penetrating politics and government has implications for parliamentary democracy. Observers like the Public Policy Forum are cognizant that digital media enables the synchronization of messaging and behaviour in ways never possible, warning that "tightening political control and the imperative of real-time government responses to unfolding events, reinforced by media and the Internet, leads to a concentration of power that profoundly impacts four of our most important institutions, namely: parliament, the cabinet, the public service, and the emerging 'political service.'"[46] Branding is addictive, it is circular, and it is a seemingly unstoppable force. It has a tightening grip on our leaders, on our elected representatives, on political staff, and on the civil servants who work on our behalf. There are persuasive reasons why the efficiencies offered by public sector branding are a positive development in the age of instantaneous 24/7 communication, microtargeting, and social media. In fact, a branding philosophy is essential to advancing an agenda, given the stark reality that those who do not preach consistency will flounder. However, branding requires message control and simplicity, and political power centralizes when communications converge. *Brand Command* lays out compelling evidence that the nature of parliamentary democracy has changed.

Acknowledgments

There are many people who helped make *Brand Command* possible. First and foremost, the interview respondents generously gave their time to share information and perspectives. Some of them offered documents, and some even proofed draft content to catch errors and omissions. Thank you – I am grateful.

Along the way, a number of discussants and attendees offered feedback at academic conferences in political science and public administration, including Paul Barker, Tom Bateman, Louise Carbert, Ian Stewart, Christopher Stoney, Linda Trimble, and Dominique Trudel. Special thanks are extended to Jim Armour, Susan Delacourt, Anna Esselment, Matthew Kerby, Mireille Lalancette, Meredith McDonald, and Jared Wesley for their assistance with aspects of this project. Many scholars such as Patricia Cormack, Ken Cosgrove, David McGrane, Jennifer Lees-Marshment, Tamara Small, André Turcotte, Paul Wilson, and colleagues in the Memorial University Department of Political Science have offered support and perspectives along the way. It is a special privilege and delight to work with Thierry Giasson generally and on the Communication, Strategy, and Politics series specifically. His thorough review of an earlier draft improved the quality of the manuscript. The detailed comments that were conveyed by the external academic referees via UBC Press similarly led to some conceptual tightening and wordsmithing. Their time and enthusiasm are appreciated.

I owe a debt of gratitude to two individuals in particular. Tom Flanagan opened doors to political elites for this and some co-authored projects. His assistance presented an extraordinary opportunity to access senior partisans. Because of his introduction and referral, they shared information in a less guarded manner, sometimes in interesting settings. Among the most memorable was a forthright interview with Senator Doug Finley in his corner East Block office on Parliament Hill. Finley delighted in sharing the history of his office's antique furniture used by Prime Minister John A. Macdonald, including a spittoon. The site was a sharp contrast with my budget hotel room in Calgary where I interviewed Flanagan, though the conversation was equally flowing and hospitable. Some interviews were held in ministers' offices within government departments in Ottawa. The fierce partisanship of political staffers was evidenced by the photographs of Stephen Harper, campaign paraphernalia and the like that adorned their office walls. Flanagan equally advised whom *not* to contact, cautioning in his colourful way that certain former colleagues might "declare a fatwa" against the research and instruct others not to participate. To ensure arm's-length research integrity of data collection and analysis, Flanagan played no further role in the interviews. He was purposely not privy to any plans for, or any drafts of, the book manuscript. He was not offered, and nor did he ask.

Flanagan also graciously offered up copies of internal party files. Soon after I spent time at the University of Calgary reviewing the Flanagan fonds, two boxes containing nearly 2,500 pages of documents arrived at Memorial University. While I was writing, Flanagan fell victim to the message discipline that he once preached, an experience that became the basis for *Persona Non Grata: The Death of Free Speech in the Internet Age.* The insights in that monograph underline the risky world that political operatives and public figures operate in now. Even Patrick Muttart, the Conservative strategist whose pioneering work is mentioned in this book and in studies of Canadian political marketing, was jettisoned following a campaign controversy.[1] In the branding age, those who live by the communications sword are more susceptible to dying by the communications sword. The Flanagan fonds and other sources of data all point to the conclusion that protecting the sanctity of a political brand is more important than hurting the feelings of its ambassadors.

The other person to whom I am indebted is a civil servant who shall remain nameless. She was inspired by a presentation that I delivered in

Ottawa about the prime minister's media management. From that point forward, she acted as a self-appointed media monitor who regularly sent me news stories. Near the conclusion of the project, she helped to secure some interviews with colleagues in central agencies, and she later brainstormed ways to generate awareness about the finished product.

I wish to acknowledge the financial assistance that has made the production of this book possible. *Brand Command* has been published with the help of a grant from the Canadian Federation for the Humanities and Social Sciences, through the Awards to Scholarly Publications Program. As well, over the years, Memorial University students provided capable research assistance with various components of this project, made possible by funding obtained through the university's Career Development and Experiential Learning programs. Ajbaili Ali, Lori-Ann Campbell, Russell Cochrane, Mark Drover, Sean Fleming, Brandon Gillespie, Charlotte Kumarasingam, Bryinne McCoy, Michael Penney, Stephen Power, Anwesha Roy, Subhajyoti Saha, Katie Walker, and Matthew Yong capably helped with matters such as collecting literature and media stories, preparing interview transcripts, and/or obtaining and cataloguing access to information files. Former graduate students John Samms, Dylan Stephenson, and, especially, Sarah Stoodley kindly offered constructive suggestions for how to publicize the book. Budding journalist Laura Howells coordinated the index.

UBC Press deserves special recognition for its enthusiastic support of the study of communication, strategy, and Canadian politics, and for demonstrating high standards of professionalism at every stage of the considerable work involved in the publication of a manuscript. Senior editor Emily Andrew and manager of production and editorial services Holly Keller stand out and played an important role in the creation of this book. Emily and Holly would be the first to point out that they are members of a capable team that includes Laraine Coates, Kerry Kilmartin, Melissa Pitts, and others, including members of the Press editorial board. The excellent work of copy editor Dallas Harrison, interior designer and typesetter Irma Rodriguez, and cover designer Jessica Sullivan also greatly enhanced the final book. All of these brand ambassadors are a credit to the UBC Press organization.

I am confident that the theory presented in this book has merit and can be supported by empirical testing. However, I alone am responsible for any errors and omissions, including unintentionally excluding anyone from the acknowledgments. Thank you to everyone, named and unnamed, who has assisted with this research undertaking, as well as to those who, after reading this book, grow inspired to delve more deeply into how branding and message discipline are changing Canadian politics and government.

PS: Inserting a postscript is a standard technique in direct mail to draw attention to a key message, sometimes in <u>underlined</u> and *italicized* typeface to really attract attention. This book argues that many Canadians spend too little time evaluating political choices and their government. <u>*For readers in a rush who want to get to the juicy bits, jump to Chapter 9's discussion of the politicization of the government of Canada.*</u> Hopefully, this will pique sufficient interest to begin with Chapter 1, which sets the context for why this is happening.

Abbreviations

ABCs	agencies, boards, and commissions
CAC	caucus advisory committee
CI	communications intermediaries *(label used for certain interview respondents)*
CIMS	Constituency Information Management System
CM	communications messengers *(label used for certain interview respondents)*
CP	communications principal *(label used for certain interview respondents)*
CPPG	Canadian Parliamentary Press Gallery
CRA	Canada Revenue Agency
CS	communications strategists *(label used for certain interview respondents)*
DFAIT	Department of Foreign Affairs and International Trade (subsequently rebranded as Foreign Affairs, Trade and Development Canada; then as Global Affairs Canada)
DND	Department of National Defence
EAP	Economic Action Plan
EDA	electoral district association
FIP	Federal Identity Program
GAC	Government Advertising Committee
GOL	Government On-Line Initiative
GOTV	get out the vote
MEP	Message Event Proposal

MINO	Minister's Office
MoD	message of the day
NPG	New Political Governance
NPM	New Public Management
OLO	Office of the Leader of the Official Opposition
PCH	Department of Canadian Heritage
PCO	Privy Council Office
PMJT	Prime Minister Justin Trudeau
PMO	Prime Minister's Office
PR	public relations
PWGSC	Department of Public Works and Government Services Canada (since rebranded as Public Services and Procurement Canada)
Q&A	question and answer
QP	Question Period
SO 31	Standing Order 31 members' statements
TBS	Treasury Board Secretariat
WOG	whole of government

Brand Command

1

The Centralization of Communications in Government and Politics

By most accounts, Canadians have been unhappy in recent years with their system of government. One public opinion study found that their foremost dissatisfaction is a perception that too much power rests with the prime minister.[1] Another found that making government accountable to Parliament is among the most important political issues.[2] The displeasure appears to be connected to a new style of disciplined communications management known as branding.

Branding is increasingly practised in politics and governance worldwide.[3] Branded communications save time for both the sender and the receiver by simplifying information for a disparate audience. Complex topics are distilled into message themes. A strategy of repeating visuals and core messages delivers efficiencies in a digital society bombarded with stimuli. However, branding threatens idealized notions of democratic government and party politics. It harmonizes and dumbs down. It requires strict message control and image management. Above all, public sector branding contributes to the centralization of decision making within the prime minister's inner circle.

Complaints about centralized power are chronic in Canada. Portrayals of the prime minister as an autocrat date at least to Richard B. Bennett. In 1930, Bennett was simultaneously prime minister, minister of finance, and secretary of state for external affairs. The Conservative PM was caricatured as a one-man show. In one joke, he was spotted talking to himself and thus holding a cabinet meeting; in cartoons, cabinet was comprised of his clones.[4] Nearly a century later, Canada's head of government is still lampooned as overly powerful, but the matter has reached a point of serious concern. Notwithstanding the optimism that accompanied the ascendancy of Liberal prime minister Justin Trudeau, an ominous turn has occurred, one that draws power from the manipulation of information and new communications technology. Among the countless examples of Conservative Prime Minister Stephen Harper's adversarial approach to communications are the following media depictions:

> Controlling the message, that's the communications strategy the prime minister has banked on ... Scrums have been cut back, or eliminated; bureaucrats can't talk without an okay from the Privy Council Office; cabinet ministers need PMO approval before talking to reporters ... Reporters looking for more than a photo are kept outside.[5]

> There's a whole infrastructure at every level of every department, of people whose job it is to manipulate and massage media. Highly paid people ... hundreds of people. Their only job every day is to manipulate a message.[6]

> Stephen Harper is famously scripted. News conferences are rare and tightly controlled. His answers in Question Period are deliberately repetitive, and often aimed at not saying anything interesting at all.[7]

> The Conservatives know how to craft a message. Keep it simple. Keep it short. Reinforce everything all the time. Make the party's four themes lock together: balanced budget, low taxes, smaller government, personal security. Mix in a little patriotism and Stephen Harper as a tried and trusted leader, and you have the Conservative campaign long before the election is called. All parties try tight messaging; the Conservatives do it best. That's the macro-campaign. Then there is the micro-campaign: the targeted pitch to specific slices of the electorate backed by domestic and foreign policy signals.[8]

The narrative of the democratic toxicity of central authority combined with political marketing extends to bookshelves. Popular press books by Ottawa journalists (including *Party of One: Stephen Harper and Canada's*

Radical Makeover; Harperland: The Politics of Control; Kill the Messengers: Stephen Harper's Assault on Your Right to Know; and *Spinning History: A Witness to Stephen Harper's Canada and 21st Century Choices*) depict Harper as a political overlord whose power was derived from information control.[9] Former Conservative MPs vex about the central influence over the legislative branch in *Sheeple: Caucus Confidential in Stephen Harper's Ottawa* and *Irresponsible Government: The Decline of Parliamentary Democracy in Canada.*[10] The perception of a communications puppeteer is fuelled by popular culture, which stereotypes politicos as self-interested actors who will stop at nothing to further their own ambitions. Harper was often portrayed as animatronic in comedy sketches and editorial cartoons, including as Darth Vader, the merciless cyborg of the anti-democratic evil empire from the *Star Wars* film series (Figure 1.1). The frame fits Harper's personal brand as well as the broader trends of presidentialization and centralization. The label of *The Friendly Dictatorship*,[11] which refers to Liberal Prime Minister Jean Chrétien's top-heavy style of governing, has darkened. The same fate awaits Justin Trudeau and his successors.

This sort of image is inevitable given that a prime minister is concurrently the head of a governing political party and the head of the non-partisan permanent government. As a partisan, that individual brings a political ideology and an agenda to governing. As the head of government, the prime minister must respect the rule of law and institutional processes and the apolitical public service bargain. Wearing either hat involves constant effort to manipulate the machinery of government to generate support for a political agenda. Communications management leads to partisan elites attempting to steer policy in directions contrary to the advice of civil servants.[12]

In Canada and elsewhere, the centralization of communications feeds worries about the politicization of an independent civil service.[13] Unlike political personnel, permanent staff members are hired through a merit system that rewards formal qualifications and public administration expertise. They are seen to prioritize evidence-based decisions that follow documented processes and embody professionalism. In theory, their neutrality upholds a greater good and is not tinged with the stain of politics. However, civil servants toil in obscurity. They are not elected, nor are they

FIGURE 1.1 Common frame of Prime Minister Harper's personal brand | Reprinted with permission of Michael de Adder; originally appeared in the *Hill Times,* October 3, 2014, 43.

directly accountable to the public whom they serve. Their worldview may differ from that of elected officials. This intersection of ideas, values, and norms constitutes a cultural divide between civil servants and their political masters.

Public administration specialist Paul Thomas explains that "there have always been planned, concerted, and extensive efforts by the PMO to maximize favourable publicity, to minimize bad news, and generally to enhance the image, credibility, and favourable approval ratings for the prime minister of the day."[14] Nevertheless, the political management of government communications has become such a serious matter that it contributes to the defeat of the government. In 2005, after the release of the first report of the Commission of Inquiry into the Sponsorship Program and Advertising Activities (the Gomery Commission), Paul Martin's Liberal minority government fell over revelations of the illegal funnelling of public funds to Liberal-affiliated advertising agencies during the Chrétien era. That episode, discussed in Chapter 7, demonstrates how strategic communications become embedded within government. Once embedded, they become institutionalized within the public service and then centralized.[15] In 2011, Harper's Conservative minority government refused to disclose spending breakdowns to the opposition regarding corporate tax cuts, crime legislation, and fighter jet purchases. It claimed that the principle of cabinet confidence shielded this information, which the opposition wanted to use to inflict maximum communications damage. The government was found in contempt of Parliament and then fell. The Conservatives nevertheless won a majority of seats in the ensuing election, an episode that implies that the fundamental tenets of responsible government are waning against the supremacy of brand control and political marketing tactics. Conversely, an anti-democratic image contributed to their election defeat in 2015, proving the limits of a brand command.

Much of what is treated as new in Canadian political communications is borrowed from Australia, the United Kingdom, and the United States. American politics in particular is the world's laboratory for political marketing. This has featured the rapid response unit in Bill Clinton's campaign war room and its thematic messaging strategies.[16] The George W. Bush White House reduced the number of media spokespersons and pursued narrowcasting with target groups. Public relations (PR) staff obsessed with photo-op set design, highlighted the president's common values, and avoided visuals of protesters in the name of security.[17] Political scientist Ken Cosgrove's observations about the American conservative movement during that era reads like a description of recent party politics in Canada:

> The brand strategy's use has let Conservatives produce a consistent message about themselves to their audiences, to reposition that message when necessary, and to build lasting relationships with their audience targets ... to produce politics and politicians that fit a consistent brand story, with limited two-way communication featuring a lot of emotion, strong language, and potent pictures but little discussion of substance.[18]

Branding information and lexicon began appearing more often in academia and the media when Barack Obama ascended to the US presidency.[19] The Obama brand was built using Web 2.0 and ushered e-politics into the mainstream. The website my.barackobama.com, commonly known as MyBO, acted as a social network while providing a controlled engagement platform that bypassed the mediation of the mainstream media. His campaigns collected information from millions of supporters regularly sent electronic messages and links to online videos.[20] As president-elect, Obama's brand converged with the communications infrastructure of the executive office. His political team has been tweeting from @BarackObama since 2007; his administration tweets in his name as president from @WhiteHouse. Obama's digital presidency has encompassed a number of firsts. In 2009, the White House began issuing a digital photo of the day featuring the president, and in 2010 it began producing a weekly video called *West Wing Week* posted to YouTube and the White House website. In 2012, Obama participated in online Twitter Q&A sessions live streamed, and he fielded questions on the social news website Reddit. In 2014, the White House created infographics to present information online as visuals, including the use of emojis (moving character pictographs).[21] Today's objective is to communicate with citizens on their mobile phones and encourage sharing of simplified information via social media such as Facebook, Instagram, and Twitter. Recipients are encouraged to provide their email addresses and zip codes to receive more infographics. Other examples point to trends that public sector elites face strenuous communications situations and use digital media to engage followers with controlled simplicity without relying on the press gallery. Along the way, senior political strategists such as James Carville, Karl Rove, and David Axelrod become household names, as do White House press secretaries.

Pivoting toward the latest communications tactics and spinmeisters is reflected in popular culture. For instance, the public administration satire of minister–deputy minister relations in the classic 1980s BBC sitcom *Yes Minister* was reinvented for the 2000s. *The Thick of It* revolves around the tirades of Malcolm Tucker, the unseen British PM's cunning and foul-mouthed director of communications. A typical backroom scene in government is depicted as follows:

[8:30AM DAILY COMMUNICATIONS MEETING]

TUCKER: "Morning, morning, morning. Alright, I wanna have a little bit of a think about some of our presentation issues with regard to yesterday. There seemed to be a bit of a problem with Liam on *Newsnight*. I would like to know: why did we have a minister on last night who did not appear to know the lines?"

COMMUNICATIONS MANAGER: "It's not all his fault, Malcolm. We grilled him beforehand. He's got a new baby. He's not getting enough sleep."

TUCKER: "I don't care if he's got a new baby. I don't care if he's tired. He looked like he didn't know what he was f**king talking about! Now, I *know* he doesn't know what he's f**king talking about, but he's got to appear as if he does, right? And that is your job! [points to communications personnel in turn] And yours, and yours, and yours, and yours! With all your respective ministers! Give them the lines, right?"[22]

Disrespect for parliamentarians is rampant. In one scene, Tucker (played by Scottish actor Peter Capaldi, of *Doctor Who* fame) tells a minister that a letter of resignation has been prepared, and that a news conference has been booked for twenty minutes at 10 Downing Street, so that the minister can say that he is resigning even as the press is told by Tucker that the minister is being forced out. In another, a member of Parliament wants to start a policy debate, which Tucker dismisses out of hand because the MP is "so backbench that you've actually f**king fallen off." The character is loosely based on Prime Minister Tony Blair's director of communications and strategy, Alastair Campbell, and satirizes New Labour's control freakery (discussed in Chapter 4).

When research about marketing in the 2015 British election becomes available, it is likely that Australian political consultant Lynton Crosby will figure prominently. Crosby helped to guide John Howard's Liberal Party of Australia to multiple election victories, leveraged that experience to manage the campaigns of London Mayor Boris Johnson, and strategized for David Cameron's British Conservative Party. News reports indicate that Prime Minister Cameron became convinced that only Crosby could instill the implacable message control needed to achieve election victory.

With the leader's authorization, two years before the campaign started, Crosby set about drawing on polling data and microtargeting to focus the Conservatives on core messages. Everything else was dismissed as a distraction. Crosby maintained a grid of daily announcements – a practice that was employed by the Blair government[23] – and ensured that the Conservative prime minister's communications aligned with a weekly theme. He periodically addressed parliamentarians and urged them to stay focused on approved messages. Issues and remarks that deviated from the script were dismissed as "barnacles on the boat" that needed to be scrubbed off, backbenchers were told that their job description did not include acting as political commentators, and whenever someone went off message he or she was reprimanded with an acerbic "not helpful" text message.[24] "One Vision" by Queen was the party war room's campaign song ("One man, one goal, one mission. One heart, one soul, just one solution. One flash of light, yeah, one god, one vision"). Crosby has also periodically offered strategic counsel to Canada's Conservative Party, including during the 2015 election campaign.

The influence of the Australian Liberal Party on the political marketing and message discipline of the Conservative Party of Canada is identified in Chapter 5. The point is that public remarks made by an Australian, British, or Canadian MP or candidate who holds a formal association with the party – whom we can refer to as "brand ambassadors" – are expected to stick to an approved script. The path-breaking marketing practices plied in US politics become partisan glue when deployed in the parliamentary system of government.

As in Britain, Canadians are fed a diet of news decrying how their government obsesses over communications management. This is framed as subversive to democracy and against the public interest. It is far easier for people to believe that political power is concentrated in elites than that political power is diffuse and elites face constraints. Neither approach is absolute. We are all predisposed to the former because political communications inflate the importance of political leaders, especially the head of government. A leader is a central actor whose role as the organization's primary spokesperson magnifies his or her perceived authority. This crescendo infuses a perceptual bias about politics and government: principals and their agents are purportedly micromanagers who inflict their will upon the rest of us.

The study of such institutional and perceptual biases has long been upheld as necessary to understand opportunities for, and limits on, political power. The challenge is to differentiate reality from imagination. Researchers must navigate the hyperreality of images and signs, as French philosopher Jean Baudrillard would put it, along with figuring out where the genuine ends and simulations begin.[25] A further challenge is that communications decisions are secretive, presenting researchers with the puzzle of finding ways to measure the unmeasurable.[26] This is especially true when examining the communications behaviour of public sector elites in Canada.

We lack a focused study of how political communications work in Ottawa. We need a theory for why they create a contagion of pulling everything toward "the centre" – a term with so many different and sinister connotations that in this book it refers to a transcendental concept, usually encapsulating the Prime Minister's Office (PMO) and Privy Council Office (PCO). We do not understand the requisite components of media management and political marketing, including the use of "symbols and brands to convey a positive image of the prime minister and the government."[27] The processes of government communications and the relationship of those processes with executive power beg attention. In particular, we need to comprehend the role of senior partisans and mandarins in the congelation of messaging. We must understand the extent of orderly control over information disclosed to the Canadian public.

An underappreciated reason for power gravitating toward the leadership circle of government and political parties is how elites are responding to disruptive communications technology. The growth of digital media is speeding up the news cycle as the number of platforms and voices increases. Informed and ill-informed critics subject the government to a relentless barrage of questioning in an atmosphere in which public officials are presumed guilty.[28] Public administration operates in an environment "more congested, complex, turbulent, intense, unpredictable, and risky" than ever before.[29] The changes have been so profound that they are characterized as digital media shock (see Chapter 3). A consequence of this technological revolution and abundance of open sources is the emergence of intense information control and image management techniques.

A brand-centric approach to power involves the strategic unification of words and visuals. At the most basic level, a branding philosophy holds that communicating disjointed messages in a haphazard style is less likely to resonate with intended audiences. Conversely, core information repeatedly communicated in an uncomplicated, consistent, and efficient way to targeted subgroups is more likely to secure support for the sender's agenda. Branding strategy positions the sender as unique, reassures audiences, and communicates aspirational, value-based, and credible messages.[30] Repetitiveness and symmetry are crafted to pierce the clamour. A "less is more" approach to communication reinforces information and messages and does so in a resource-efficient manner that accentuates visual imagery.

Branding balances the information demands of the impassioned and the uninterested. It communicates cues and signals to distracted audiences while stoking emotional connections with those who are most loyal. It involves marketers maximizing their communications investments by promoting messages designed to differentiate the brand and to resonate on an emotional level with target audiences. It understates or ignores the brand's flaws. It turns a humdrum interaction into a memorable experience. The resulting brand loyalty felt by the most ardent supporters is such that they can be impervious to missteps and to courting by competitors. An organization requires tenacious leadership to assert branding objectives over the demands and criticisms of other actors. The more fractured that media become, the more that party strategists and senior public servants seek to standardize and centralize their messages. The more that message cohesion, discipline, and centralization are practised, the more that society makes political choices based on images of politicians rather than on policy details. In politics, the brand unifies everything. The rest of us need to look at political leaders, party politics, the media, and public administration through a branding lens to understand this.

This book's theory of public sector branding follows American media scholar John Zaller's contention that political battles are waged primarily through media management. It accepts his premise that "the form and content of media politics are largely determined by the disparate interests of politicians, journalists, and citizens as each group jostles to get what it wants out of politics and the political communication that makes politics possible."[31] This jostling is responsive to a fragmented media landscape and to audiences with shortening attention spans. It also accepts American political scientist Samuel Popkin's concluding remark in his seminal study of political communications: "Ask not for more sobriety and piety from citizens, for they are voters, not judges; offer them instead cues and signals which connect their world with the world of politics."[32] Or, as Zaller puts it, those who follow politics and government must recognize that most citizens do not wish to invest much energy in monitoring political events. The general public's overriding messages to elites are "Don't waste my time!" and "Tell me only what I really need to know!"[33] The likes of Zaller and Popkin recognize that we live in a society in which visuals can dramatically reinforce or shift public opinion and public policy.[34]

In Canada, for all the attention paid to political communications, and to the concentration of power in the centre of government, there is no comprehensive resource that interprets both through a branding lens. Canadianists write about communications control by the executive branch. They pay heed to the message uniformity that pervades the legislative branch through party discipline. They touch on the consistencies between the brands of the governing party and the government. Canadian political parties and first ministers are treated as brands, as are Canadian cities. Some scholars look at Canada's international image and at the branding of public policy. Public sector advertising attracts much more interest, absent of branding theory. The idea that communications play a formative role in the centralization of political power has not yet been explained as a branding phenomenon. The relationship between branding strategy and technological change is also poorly understood.

An overarching research objective for *Brand Command* is to consider the digital communications environment for political parties, public ad-ministration, and journalism at the federal level of politics in Canada. It builds on *Political Marketing in Canada* and *Political Communication in Canada: Meet the Press and Tweet the Rest* by seeking to address three overarching questions.[35] First, *what is public sector branding?* Subsidiary questions include: Does public sector branding differ from long-standing practices of communicating? Why are visuals so important in branding?

How is branding different from framing, image management, and political marketing? Which forms of public sector branding exist? What does it hope to achieve? Why does it appeal to public sector elites?

Second, *how is branding and communications control practised in Canadian party politics and government?* Among the areas of enquiry related to this overarching question are how is control of information and media practised by political and government communicators? Which instruments are used within the federal government to achieve brand image consistency? How does branding hasten the concentration of power and decision making within central agencies? How does branding contribute to the fusion of political government with permanent government? How is branding a tool of the concepts of New Public Management and New Political Governance? Does branding constitute propaganda?

Third, *what are the implications of a branding lens for Canadian politics and government?* This theme encompasses an array of questions. What does a branding philosophy mean for electioneering and governance? What are the implications of the centralization of decision making in government? How concerned should we be about the hypermanagement of public officials' interactions with the media? Are targeting and narrowcasting better or worse for democracy than mass communication was? Is all of this a net positive or negative for Canadian democracy? What can be done about it?

To understand Canadian public sector elites' communications behaviour in the twenty-first century is to understand branding. How the media treat the political class, and how politicians treat each other, have implications for Canadian democratic government. Alarmism about the centralization of power and communications deserves to be balanced with an empirical attempt to recognize the circumstances and institutional factors that motivate elites' actions. There are concerns about the challenges facing professional political journalism and the implications for a healthy democratic society.[36] The withholding of information leads interest groups to issue open letters calling for reduced micromanagement of government communications.[37] Media coverage of political strategy is thought to increase mistrust of public officials and generate disdain for the media themselves.[38] These vexations contribute to the so-called spiral of cynicism

FIGURE 1.2
The Savoie thesis and branding lens thesis

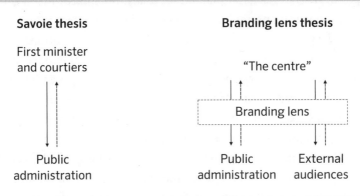

hypothesis that describes citizen disengagement.[39] It is only by attempting to uncover the alleged justifications for political actors' attempts to control communications that we can arrive at pragmatic remedies. *Brand Command* submits that the reasons increasingly centre on the supremacy of the brand in an accelerating media environment.

The idea of a branding lens extends what is known as "the Savoie thesis" (Figure 1.2). Public administration specialist Donald Savoie is a proponent of the centralization of power thesis, as expressed in a number of works.[40] By his account, cabinet is foremost a sounding board for the prime minister, who pays more heed to an inner circle of handpicked courtiers. The government is beholden to the cadre of influential ministers and senior political staff who dispense orders with the weight of the prime minister's authority. The Savoie thesis is a popular model that fits with the so-called presidentialization of the Westminster system of government. This holds that institutions revolve around the first minister rather than cabinet or Parliament. The waning relevance of parliamentarians leads to the abandonment of the *primus inter pares* ("first among equals") principle in favour of a cabinet headed by a commander-in-chief.[41] The presidentialization thesis itself builds on the notion of an imperial presidency. This describes the growth of the American president's staff and how power exceeds that executive office's constitutional authority.[42] The Savoie thesis is also consistent with the unitary system of command espoused by New Labour Party architect and political strategist Philip Gould.[43] Finally, it captures the negativity and fear-mongering promulgated by critics about "the centre."

Not everyone is convinced by the Savoie thesis of centralization or arguments about the presidentialization of the parliamentary system. Political scientists Herman Bakvis, Graham White, and others bristle at the suggestion that Canada's federal ministers are little more than conduits. Bakvis makes a compelling case that powerful regional ministers act as both enablers and constrictors of the prime minister's power.[44] White enumerates the many components of "a constricting web" of forces that limit executive power, among them international agreements and a less deferential public.[45] J.P. Lewis suggests that in reality Canadian cabinets operate within a hybrid autocratic-collegial decision-making model.[46] Furthermore, Matthew Kerby demonstrates that the prime minister faces considerable constraints in cabinet formation and reshuffling.[47] Even though premiers are sometimes political overlords, there is no consensus on the Savoie thesis at the provincial level either.[48] Moreover, the idea that the Westminster system is becoming presidentialized is challenged. Keith Dowding argues that we must not equate it with the personalization of politics (discussed in Chapters 3 and 4) and the decline of political parties, phenomena present in both presidential and parliamentary systems of government.[49] For his part, Harper maintained that the notion of him as a one-man band was overblown.[50] Chrétien echoes this position, writing in his memoirs that "prime ministers cannot – must not – get bogged down in the details of government or try to micromanage the business of the nation. Rather, it is their job to establish priorities, develop strategies, supervise crises, handle the toughest problems, *communicate the complicated issues in simple ways,* and delegate as much as possible to their ministers."[51] There is more truth to these comments than critics think.

The Savoie thesis needs updating. The many other Canadianists who write in this area do not examine with any rigour the important role of political communications, which I argue here play a formative role in centralization. Writing before Web 2.0, Savoie comments on the "enormous pressure" that television places on government, prompting complaints from political elites.[52] More recently, he observes that the media have "changed substantially" and that the advent of permanent campaigning has "shifted" where power is located.[53] In his latest book, he muses that social media has "strengthened" the power of the prime minister and agents, and that politicians believe that reacting quickly is necessary to be "in command of the situation."[54] White notes that "seasoned Ottawa watchers" believe that Savoie *underestimates* centralized power because the "centre's control over government communications and 'issues management' – the polite term for political firefighting – is even more pronounced" than it is over most matters of policy.[55] In the provinces, even weak premiers gain control from the growth of central agencies and from the executive oversight of "communications and legislative agendas."[56]

This book does not seek to test the Savoie thesis. Rather, it is concerned with establishing that changes in communications technology are enabling the centre to enforce communications control and to implement branding strategy. This examination will provide both believers and disbelievers of the Savoie thesis with a basis for further assessment of whether the centre has too much power – and in particular a better understanding of the institutional conditions and processes related to political communications and elite behaviour. *Brand Command* argues that the causes of centralization are systemic, not individualistic. In this light, Trudeau's pledge to empower cabinet and buck the forces of centralization seems idealistic. Branding strategy seeks to influence public impressions and to set and advance agendas. It is accompanied by an organizational willingness to exploit opportunities to penetrate a communications cyclone and a motivation to achieve resource efficiencies. In interviews conducted for this book, many respondents pontificated, unaided, along the following lines: "Disseminating a message in the clutter or bombardment of information that you get today is a huge challenge ... One of the solutions to that is consistency of messaging, which probably explains to a large degree the centralized approach that government has taken to its communications" (respondent CS 20).

A branding "lens" borrows the term from the public policy lenses that train analysts' focus on a topic. A memorandum to cabinet in the government of Canada requires that government officials treat public policy with a privacy lens, a bilingualism lens, and a gender lens. Perspectives such as legal risk assessment, horizontal policy impacts, environmentalism, regionalism, private and voluntary sectors, and international considerations must be considered.[57] Unlike those formalities, a branding lens does not exist on paper. It is an evolving yet consistent and unifying approach to communications. Like an ideology, the brand is a state of mind, and its conduits share a purpose that they might not be able to articulate. It is a point of view and a way of being held by those closest to power. Above all, as a strategy, the priority is staying true to the "master brand," a macroterm used throughout this book to refer to a core philosophical stance as distinct from the many microbrands that are components of the brand writ large.[58] The master brand should be constant over time. That umbrella must be supported by specialized and changing sub-brands. Internal exchanges between the centre and the civil service pass through a branding lens, as do external exchanges between government and its audiences. This is more than just the prime minister's entourage – it is an unspoken mentality that envelops the entire upper echelon of government.

This book submits that branding-related considerations play a prominent role in the business of government and politics and offer analytical value. A political observer who unlocks the governing party's desired master brand has a tool to decipher and perhaps even anticipate the behaviour of public sector elites. A branding lens is thus potentially a good theoretical tool because it meets the criteria of simplicity, predictive accuracy, and importance.[59] It is also a foundation for figuring out what must be changed to improve the democratic nature of Canadian government. The Reform Act – discussed in Chapter 2 – is a good start. However, a branding philosophy is so powerful that more must be done.

This matters because branding theory offers a new avenue to interpret the centripetal behaviour of elites. Throughout this book, as in public administration, politics is found at the intersection of partisan and non-partisan actions. "Political elites" are the partisans who work among the upper echelons of political parties and/or government. "Public sector elites" expands the concept to include the non-partisan senior mandarins subservient to cabinet within the confines of the law and the subjectivity of communications ethics. Likewise, a "political brand" refers to a partisan entity, while a "public sector brand" encompasses parties and government.

Whether decisions made at the top of the government pyramid are excessively partisan, and whether implementation of those decisions contravenes expectations of political neutrality within the public service, are often grey areas. I argue here that we are heading toward a single brand that unifies the government, the governing party, and the first minister in the public eye. Those who doubt that the first minister is all powerful must confront the adage that perception is reality.

Interest in studying public sector branding is growing with its practice. Margaret Scammell of the London School of Economics argues that "branding is the new form of political marketing. If market research, spin, and advertising were the key signifiers of marketed parties and candidates in the 1980s and 1990s, 'branding' is the hallmark now ... The brand concept has analytical value. It is not simply a fashionable term for image."[60] Establishing that branding is a tangible and important phenomenon in Canadian politics and government requires a philosophical and theoretical foundation. Theory will provide the basis for understanding the nature of enduring relationships between public sector elites and democratic institutions in a changing media environment, regardless of who is in power.

However, documenting the internal processes of branding is fraught with difficulty. The extensive access to internal government operations enjoyed by the authors of *The Superbureaucrats: Structure and Behaviour in Central Agencies* is a relic of a distant era.[61] Their 1970s observation of the inner workings of central agencies of the government of Canada peeled back layers of bureaucratic structure that is beyond reach today. The communications control and secrecy encouraged by branding strategy inhibits researchers' ability to obtain data.[62] Trade secrets are rarely divulged. Invisible processes by communications principals, strategists, and messengers cannot be easily uncovered. This research obstacle is an unfortunate if expected outcome of a branding philosophy that espouses that those on the inside should not talk freely, or at all, with outsiders. Those who do so will be guarded about what they disclose.

In Canada, monographs about elites' role in political communications tend to be atheoretical. Reflections authored by practitioners, such as *The Way It Works: Inside Ottawa* and *Harper's Team: Behind the Scenes in the Conservative Rise to Power,* offer one-sided accounts that would otherwise not come to light.[63] No Canadian political insider has written about elite communications since *Close to the Charisma: My Years between the Press and Pierre Elliott Trudeau,* with the possible exception of *Kicking Ass in Canadian Politics.*[64] Participant observation is limited to *Inside the NDP War Room: Competing for Credibility in a Federal Election,*[65] though here *Harper's Team* warrants a second mention. Journalists' works, such as *The Friendly Dictatorship* and *Harperland,* tend to be descriptive and selective, weaving together what has already been reported along with a spattering of new information. A pleasant exception is Susan Delacourt's *Shopping for Votes: How Politicians Choose Us and We Choose Them,* which traces the evolution of commercial and political sales tactics to argue that the political class treats electors as consumers.[66] For the most part, we must turn elsewhere for theory, such as American studies *Image Bite Politics: News and the Visual Framing of Elections* and *Branded Conservatives: How the Brand Brought the Right from the Finges to the Center of American Politics,* which argue that political communications are trending toward management of consistent, simple visuals.[67] An important Canadian study is *Making "Pictures in Our Heads": Government Advertising in Canada,* wherein Jonathan Rose documents the persuasive nature of government advertising in a mediated democracy, under the pretense of information campaigns.[68] In all instances, writers are confronted by data limitations.

There is no agreed way to study public sector branding. Methods for studying and measuring private sector branding are a source of debate in marketing literature.[69] Although there are efforts to quantify brand value, for the most part brand research tends to be a qualitative undertaking because of the need to understand layers of information.[70] Examining the ways that branding pervades an organization begins by recognizing its orientation toward a branding philosophy. In Canadian politics and government, the unanswerable question looms of whether principals impose branding on agents and organizations or to what extent branding is thrust upon principals. Researcher access to a sitting prime minister is implausible. His or her public comments are of limited value because of strategic calculations and selective reporting. As a result, assessing the prime minister's role in communications is "necessarily speculative," as media scholar Fred Fletcher once observed.[71] This begs a study of organizational behaviour, including information about human resources, management structures, internal processes, and hierarchy, at the top of which we find the prime minister. We must be satisfied with qualitative data obtained from avenues other than the principal, necessarily supporting theory with description.

Brand Command focuses on Stephen Harper's leadership of the Conservative Party of Canada. This encompasses the first five federal election campaigns contested by that newly constituted party and its first permanent leader between 2004 and 2015. Studying Harper's tenure is rather pertinent to research about public sector branding. As a government, the Conservatives imprinted a neoliberal policy agenda underpinned by a master brand comprised of strong economic stewardship and tough-on-crime measures. Public administration scholar Peter Aucoin remarked that the first term of the Harper administration is an exemplary case of New Political Governance (discussed in Chapter 9).[72] Delacourt describes Harper as "Canada's first marketing prime minister,"[73] and Tom Flanagan refers to his former colleague's "razor-sharp intellect, cunning strategic sense, and ruthless determination."[74] Historian Allan Levine, author of *Scrum Wars: The Prime Ministers and the Media*,[75] opines that "Harper is as skilled a politician who has ever been prime minister. He understands completely the way in which power has to be exercised in the age of social media and how errors of judgment and personal foibles can be costly. In short, he knows control-freakish behaviour can be rewarded."[76] Studying the Harper era matters because the early twenty-first century has been a period of profound innovation in information and communications technology. In the television age, repeating key messages was necessary because the media reduce long interviews, lengthy speeches, Question Period discourse, and other exchanges to succinct sound bites of less than ten seconds.[77] In today's hybrid media environment, communicating simple visuals is necessary because the media and citizenry diminish complex events to image bites – short clips of visuals without original sounds.[78] In this respect, Harper's tenure encompasses a formative time period and a leader deserving of study.

This forms a grounded theory case study. Theory is developed through asking new questions and documenting events not readily explained by existing theory, which leads to the formation of generalizations that have broader application.[79] *Brand Command* employs a descriptive method of examining past work and capturing events of historical value, with an element of storytelling. As the works of theorists ranging from Sun Tzu to Machiavelli and Maurice Duverger to Savoie show, the value of the descriptive approach rests with its identification of principles as an origin for categorizing observed phenomena.[80] Deductive reasoning is applied to those phenomena to develop enduring theories about elites and their relationship with political institutions. The methodological risks of oversimplification, ivory tower assumptions, and inability to account for infinite variables are tempered with experienced observations and mixed methods research. The deductive approach raises important questions about ethical interpretations of political conduct, and it advances the words and concepts of politics (see the Glossary).[81] A formative study of public sector branding must also be concerned with a practical approach to research. A practical approach involves the study of people or groups who seek power, or its smooth and effective operation, and who enlist technical experts to achieve their objectives.[82] Observations must be detached and tempered. This limits overstating the assumed effects of practices by winners and undervaluing those employed by losers.

In *Brand Command*, theory is built on mixed-method data that reveal internal communications processes and planning instruments. The first source of data is internal political party documents, principally those associated with Harper. Files were obtained through the Thomas E. Flanagan Fonds at the University of Calgary library archives (see Appendix 1). Flanagan is a prolific professor who, alongside Harper, held a senior role in the Reform Party of Canada from 1991 to 1993. He managed Harper's successful leadership campaigns for the Canadian Alliance Party in 2002 and the Conservative Party of Canada in 2004. Flanagan was the Conservative campaign manager in the 2004 federal election and the party's senior communications adviser during the 2006 federal campaign. He is among a select group of senior political elites in Canada who has made his personal records available for public access, joining stalwarts such as John Diefenbaker (via the University of Saskatchewan) and Keith Davey (via the University of Toronto). The Flanagan fonds comprise internal party memos, planning documents, minutes of party meetings, as well as printouts of private emails among party executives, including a small number authored by Harper. The research value and limitations of these records, as well as verbatim examples, are found in Appendix 1.

The fonds are an unfamiliar resource to students of Canadian politics, except those who are aware that they were mined by Flanagan for *Harper's Team*. Documents associated with communications were retrieved from the fond categories of election planning and leadership campaign planning. Some of them were manually reviewed at the University of Calgary library, after which nearly 2,500 pages of photocopied files were examined off-site. The socio-anthropological nature of this ethnographic review included reading private emails that capture how people operated in their environments at certain moments. They are an exceptional source of historical data that provides a window to the hidden world of political elites' exchanges on the windy road from fringe party to official opposition to government. They reveal that managerial time is mostly spent sorting out daily minutiae and that communications deliberations are top-down, horizontal, and/or bottom-up. These party files were supplemented by a search for information available on the Conservative, Liberal, and New Democratic Party (NDP) websites in 2014, which uncovered a handful of relevant internal files concerning election readiness.

The second main source of data is a large body of email exchanges in English and French between federal public servants and associated internal government documents. In 2012, requests were submitted under access to information legislation to fifteen government of Canada departments and agencies, totalling 109 submissions. The searches ranged from seeking any information about branding to specific requests concerning use of the Canadian flag, images of hockey, colour schemes on websites, design of photo-op backdrops (i.e., portable background decor), involvement of celebrities in media events, and the Economic Action Plan. This generated over 4,000 pages of internal emails and documents that were manually examined. Not available is content deemed by government censors to be confidential, including anything requested from the PMO, exempt from the Access to Information and Protection of Privacy Act. Details of the search are provided in Appendix 2. Additional government files were located in 2014 via searches of the government of Canada website for content about branding and marketing and through the Open Government initiative (data.gc.ca) to obtain other applicants' completed access to information requests. This procured additional information about communications policies, media relations activities, reports on advertising and public opinion research, the Federal Identity Program (see Chapter 8), and the Economic Action Plan. This quasi-systematic historical research was supplemented by a smaller number of government documents provided by some of the political staff and public servants interviewed, including some files that originated from the PMO and ministers' offices (MINOs). As well, hundreds of pages of PMO emails, which were presented as evidence in 2015 during Senator Mike Duffy's trial, were reviewed. This was a pragmatic if imperfect way to document internal processes and trends.

The third main source is data obtained via in-depth interviews with political party and government insiders. Between 2010 and 2015, I conducted semi-structured interviews with seventy-seven federal political party representatives, federal civil servants, federal political exempt staff, journalists, and communications consultants.[83] Sometimes I spoke with them more than once, other times as dyads and triads, and on occasion I followed up to clarify points. Given the difficulty of identifying and accessing public sector elites, I used a combination of convenience, purposive, snowball, and quota sampling. Greater access to members of Harper's entourage who had held varying ranks within the Conservative Party of Canada and/or its forebears was possible because of vouching from Flanagan. Invitees who declined to be interviewed communicated a preference not to speak while Harper was in office or did not acknowledge the request. I observed no commonality among those who agreed or declined to be interviewed. Discussions began with broad, open-ended questions – such as, "If you were to pick up a book about branding in Canadian party politics and government, what would you expect to be in it?" – before moving into a conversational format. This wide net enabled a search for information about political communications circumstances and about known and unknown processes. Each interview was transcribed, and key themes were identified by reviewing the transcripts.

Given the possibility of political retribution, such as the backlash experienced by a respondent identified in *Harperland*,[84] I have chosen not to associate names with quoted information, other than party leaders and a handful of public figures. Similarly, the authorship of most emails deposited in the Flanagan fonds and those obtained through access to information legislation have not been disclosed. Savoie took a similar approach concerning the unstructured, in-depth interviews that formed the basis of *Governing from the Centre,* rationalizing that "it would have been entertaining to attribute particular quotes directly. It would also have been inappropriate."[85] A list of interviews is found at the back of the book. When information is attributed to respondents, they are identified by the corresponding assigned acronym and number (e.g., CP 1, CS 5, CM 2, CI 6) to denote a communications principal, strategist, manager, or intermediary (see Figure 2.9).

The final main source of data is a manual review of over 900 news items from 2006 to 2015 in English media about political communications in Canada. They were collected through a wide-ranging initial capture of news stories from 2006 to 2008 using the Factiva news search engine. Keyword combinations included at least one of Conservative or Stephen Harper and at least one of advertising, branding, communications, or image. Specific searches for media reports about Message Event Proposals and the Economic Action Plan were conducted in 2014. They were supplemented with casual online scanning and archiving of relevant stories appearing in major Canadian news outlets and the *Hill Times* from 2009 to 2015. In addition, communications-related blog entries by Ottawa-based journalists with the CBC, the *Globe and Mail,* and the *National Post* authored between 2009 and 2011 were collected. This captured a number of additional details that did not receive mainstream news coverage.

In this book, I take a broad conceptualization of branding to bring together many aspects of political communications and to provide the basis for further study. *Brand Command* offers the basis for a theoretical framework that can be applied to other cases. Readers are asked to prioritize broad theory and institutional processes over personalities, events, and minutiae. They should also consider that everything intensifies under the microscope of an election campaign and political scandal.

The book deals with theory before delving into an enumeration of communication practices within Canadian political parties and government. Chapter 2 introduces the concepts of political marketing and branding alongside centripetal tendencies in Canadian politics and parliamentary government. Chapter 3 argues that recent changes in communications technology are of such a seismic scale that norms of political communications have been shocked. It then reviews an array of journalism concepts. These concepts serve to establish that political communications involve intense jockeying between political and media elites, all of whom have their own motivations. Chapter 4 theorizes that a number of types of brands exist in the public sector. A short case study looks at the special characteristics of the Trudeau brand. Chapter 5 serves as a wake-up call to those who pay close attention to the political sphere. It emphasizes that the majority of Canadians really are not that concerned with daily political minutiae and engage only in surface information processing of public sector issues. Chapter 6 summarizes ways that political parties engage in media relations and practise political marketing, with growing consideration given to branding. Chapters 7 through 10 train attention on the government of Canada by presenting an inventory of federal government communications policies and practices, last published in 1995.[86] Chapter 7 itemizes the communications functions of central agencies and communications actors within government. This itemization provides a foundation for Chapter 8's summary of the components of communications and branding in government, for instance by examining government advertising and public opinion research processes as well as corporate identity. In Chapter 9, the inner workings of the political coordination of government communications are revealed. The fusion of political priorities and public administration is laid bare in Chapter 10, bringing together branding architecture within government. This includes cataloguing planning instruments such as the Message Event Proposal and communications calendars. A short case study of the Economic Action Plan demonstrates the outcome of government-wide coordination steered by central agencies and their planning instruments.

The book concludes by examining the implications of top-down communications congealing into publicity and persuasion, under the auspices of branding strategy. Chapter 11 presents thematic findings and opines about the positive and negative implications of public sector branding for Canadian democracy. It positions the implications of a branding lens and offers some regulatory suggestions before presenting areas for future study. All told, this comprises an assessment of public sector branding that considers the perspectives of both the permanent government and the political government in Canada's parliamentary system.

2

Marketing and Branding in Politics

Debate over the image of Stephen Harper, Justin Trudeau, and other leaders is best left for political talk shows and coffeehouses. The institutional structures that channel so much attention on the prime minister and his or her inner circle are what really matter. Political strategists are enamoured with whatever marketing ploys will give them a competitive advantage, and more often than not that shines the spotlight on leaders. We need to unpack the branding concept if we wish to ascertain how marketing bolsters centripetal forces in Canadian parliamentary democracy.

MARKETING AND POLITICS

Political marketing is a growing area of practice and study in Britain, the United States, Australia, Canada, and elsewhere. It involves the use of market intelligence by public sector elites to inform their decisions, particularly those on communications. Before I can describe the components and objectives of branding, or its practice in the public sphere, we need to understand its foundations in persuasive communications and marketing.

Branding is as old as the ancient practice of marking livestock with symbols, yet in its modern sense it has only been around since the late twentieth century. The modern consumer origins of branding can be traced to the mid-eighteenth century, when businesses sought to differentiate commodities such as cocoa, coffee, soap, and tea.[1] Products were sold in an undifferentiated manner, giving customers little reason to prefer one manufacturer over another. The packaging of commodities and their promotion with hyperbole translated into improved competitive positioning in consumers' minds. This salesmanship evolved with opinion research techniques honed in the mid-twentieth century, when businesses had new tools to understand consumers' needs and wants. Rather than bombard the masses with persuasive advertising, they created goods and services to meet consumers' preferences. They tailored their communications to existing and prospective customers. It was the dawn of marketing: the design of a product or service that responds to consumers' desires, as identified through research, and the strategic selection of communications to promote its availability. These philosophical evolutions are known in business literature as product-oriented, sales-oriented, and market-oriented.[2] The latter two establish a philosophical basis for branding.

The evolution of motor vehicles is a good way to illustrate the three different approaches. Ford's Model T is known for its assembly line innovation and accessibility to the middle class. Like many industrial revolution products, the car enjoyed consumer demand despite its availability in just one colour (black). Communications in that era sought to generate awareness of its mechanical features and dependability as well as information about where to buy it. "Don't experiment, just buy a Ford," was the primary message of one 1905 print advertisement. It featured straightforward information about maintenance, the price, an award, and a photograph of the empty car.[3] Such an awareness campaign is a product-oriented approach to the marketplace.

As consumer interest subsides, and as competition intensifies, there is a need for businesses to stimulate demand. Competing motor vehicle manufacturers began to adopt assembly line production to keep costs down. New designs and colours were offered, giving consumers more choices. The Ford Motor Company and its competitors were faced with a need to persuade consumers to purchase their products. A sales orientation took hold as the subjective features of vehicles, such as styling, performance, and social prestige, were trumpeted in advertising.[4] "Smoother than ever – it's a new ride! There's a Ford in your future" proclaimed one 1945 print ad. Rather than focus on the vehicle, the visual emphasizes a smiling mother and her relaxed children. Small print describes a stylish automobile with a "velvety ride that's smooth."[5] This marked a move from objective to subjective information. It tapped into the aspirational features and lifestyle benefits that goods and services profess to offer. This persuasive communication is a sales-oriented approach to the marketplace.

Competition intensified with technological change. Executives drew on consumer research to inform them of which product features mattered most to their prospective customers. Manufacturers embraced a market orientation as they sought to offer products that fulfilled consumers' desires as expressed in market research. All sorts of cars, trucks, and crossovers became available. Each came with an array of standard features supplemented by a range of ways for the company to personalize the purchase to meet the individual customer's tastes. A 1974 advertisement for a Ford Mustang exemplifies the company's attempt to be persuasive while responding to diverse customer preferences. The Mustang is positioned as "the right car at the right time" and is accompanied by photos offering the choice of a two-door hardtop, a two-door hatchback, and a top-line model.[6] The advertisement's copy itemizes standard equipment and a variety of available options among which consumers could choose. This research-informed effort to appeal to defined segments of the marketplace is distinct from persuasive communication because it responds to customers' wants and needs. A marketing philosophy stimulates demand and reduces risk. However, it weakens the resolve of leaders to support creativity and innovation compared with when they follow their intuition.

The application of these sorts of business-style strategies to Canadian politicking dates back at least to the early twentieth century. Political strategists approached electioneering with a business-like philosophy more often than is popularly assumed. This philosophy includes a disciplined approach to campaign preparations, interelection campaigning, and the use of advertising agencies.[7] Today, in addition to working with marketing firms, political parties have their own marketing experts. They consort with domestic and international political consultants and draw on the Internet to monitor trends.

The dawn of retail marketing in Canadian party politics occurred during the 2006 federal election campaign.[8] The Conservative Party pledged to reduce the maligned Goods and Services Tax (GST) from 7 percent to 5 percent. The policy responded to the Conservatives' public opinion research, irrespective of economists and the intelligentsia who

FIGURE 2.1 Visual of GST campaign announcement (Stephen Harper, with Jim Flaherty) | Canadian Press / Frank Gunn.

believe that reducing a consumption tax is poor public policy compared with an income tax cut. The Conservatives staged a photo-op at a retail electronics store in Toronto. They held the event in the morning in a bid to set the day's news agenda. The event planners' intended visual made the news: party leader Stephen Harper was depicted placing a 5 percent blue markdown sign over a 7 percent sign on the side of a computer monitor (Figure 2.1). He was accompanied by Jim Flaherty, the former Ontario finance minister running to become a Conservative MP and the future federal finance minister. Harper then addressed the media, with the backdrop of a display of televisions broadcasting a 5 percent sign, saying that it would be a "tax cut you see every time you shop."[9] The event was smart communications strategy and was executed with precision.

The announcement was supported on the ground by local representatives across Canada. In marketing speak, campaign ephemera are known as marketing collateral. Collateral materials provide salespersons with mechanisms to reinforce the organization's corporate identity and advertising. Conservative candidates were provided with a shopping mall handout that featured a photo of a gift wrapped in blue. The other side of the handout proclaimed that "the Conservative GST cut means more change in your pocket. Happy shopping!" A postcard featured a girl with a computer, accompanied by the text "a computer for her, a tax break for you." On the reverse were a photo of the local candidate and the message "[candidate name]'s GST cut means a tax break on computers for school." Other postcards contrasted the Liberals and Conservatives, using a stylistic technique associated with upscale brand advertising. On the left side, against a bold red background, was a photo of Prime Minister Paul Martin and the number 7 percent; on the right side, against a bold blue background, was a photo of Harper and the number 5 percent. Issue-based lawn signs proclaimed "Cut the GST," with the party name, logo, and colours. There was no room for the candidate's name. Brochure templates featured a photo of a woman holding keys to her new car, under the text "Cut the GST," accompanied by a 5 percent markdown sign. A choice of template cards was available for candidates to pass out when they met with students, seniors, or families, each of which included a group-specific message about the GST. Markdown stickers like the ones used at the Toronto photo-op were available for placement on candidate lawn signs and as bumper stickers. This was supported by broader publicity. Behind the scenes, top advisers worked out ways to explain in a simple manner how families would save money.[10] For the next decade, the Conservatives' policy message of low taxes and a communications style of meticulous event planning would be repeated. They would form the basis of the separate yet connected brands of Prime Minister Harper, the Conservative Party, and the government of Canada.

The GST announcement fits many of the sales and marketing concepts discussed in this book. As a philosophy, marketing must envelop the executive levels of an organization that intends to fulfill the demands of the marketplace, as opposed to an organization that pushes executives' preferences for consumers. Political marketing scholar Jennifer Lees-Marshment advocates that, in theory, marketing is a boon for democracy. It increases political elites' concern for the citizenry. This generates public support for a political party's agenda and helps government to respond to public preferences.[11] Her typology of the product-oriented party, sales-oriented party, and market-oriented party is both path-breaking and controversial.[12] Its application of the aforementioned business approaches to politics is an

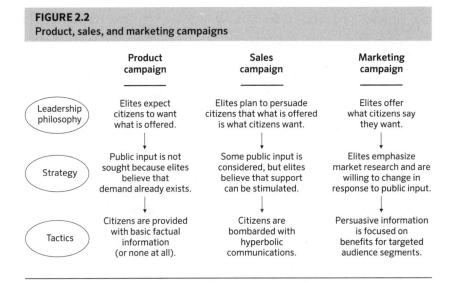

FIGURE 2.2
Product, sales, and marketing campaigns

	Product campaign	Sales campaign	Marketing campaign
Leadership philosophy	Elites expect citizens to want what is offered.	Elites plan to persuade citizens that what is offered is what citizens want.	Elites offer what citizens say they want.
Strategy	Public input is not sought because elites believe that demand already exists.	Some public input is considered, but elites believe that support can be stimulated.	Elites emphasize market research and are willing to change in response to public input.
Tactics	Citizens are provided with basic factual information (or none at all).	Citizens are bombarded with hyperbolic communications.	Persuasive information is focused on benefits for targeted audience segments.

innovative way of looking at political parties. Like all typologies, it is shackled by the difficulty of pigeonholing. A less ambitious application of these stages would look at all manner of public sector communications, not just from political parties during election campaigns. Notifications of party nomination meetings, Elections Canada's voter information cards, and Canadian Food Inspection Agency food safety advisories are product-oriented communications. They present statements of fact in an informative and objective manner, with an aversion to hyperbole. The sales-oriented approach dominates Canadian politics. Leading the way are spin, news releases, media events, and advertising, discussed throughout this book. Indications of a market-oriented philosophy are found in election manifestos, throne speeches, and government budgets. They are not wholly market-oriented because policy is a combination of partisan ideology and elector preference. Marketing cannot exist in an idealistic form in the public sector because nothing political is divorced from persuasion. These different strategic approaches are outlined in Figure 2.2.

The astute observer of politics will be aghast by now at any notion that marketing principles can be seamlessly applied to the political realm. There are indeed differences between product, sales, and marketing campaigns in the private and public sectors. This goes beyond the obvious points that consumers and electors do not behave identically or that businesses have a profit motive. Marketing in politics is unique for many reasons. Ideology limits political elites' flexibility to respond to electors' preferences. Free-speech provisions exist within a legislative chamber and in the Charter of Rights and Freedoms. Political advertising is excluded from the Canadian Code of Advertising Standards. Elections have a winner-take-all outcome, and the speed at which parties win or lose market share is much faster than that for a product. There are limited implications of low elector participation for political actors; there are electoral system considerations; there are different ethical and moral considerations; the media actively monitor the activities of public sector leaders; and so on. Above all, a politician is a human being concerned with societal issues, not malleable like a product, and government exists for the public good. A Conservative political marketer adds that

> one of the things I always tell corporate people is the difference with political marketing is the timelines are much shorter, and the stakes are much higher ... Imagine having to execute your entire marketing strategy and spend your entire marketing budget in forty days, and the entire strategy and the entire expenditure comes down to a single one-day sale where the doors open at 8:00 a.m., they close at 8:00 p.m., the entire marketplace decides, and at the end of the day only one company is left standing, and everyone else is basically out of business. Those are the stakes with political marketing. And it's why you have to get it right at the time when you need to go to the people ... if you have a bad day before that day, it can dramatically alter the results. (CS 4)

For all of its theoretical merits, sadly, the practice of political marketing is a Frankenstein of persuasion techniques. Political elites cannot communicate anything without factoring in the potential media implications. Journalism professor James McLean's study of the NDP's campaign war room led McLean to observe that all political communication is calculated and viewed through a strategic lens.[13] Ivor Gaber, another journalism professor, describes the phenomenon of a "political communications paradox" whereby public sector elites are incapable of communicating without assessing how to maximize the interaction for their own gain.[14] As will be discussed in Chapter 5, political marketers prioritize the concerns of "the base" (i.e., core supporters) and branch outward by isolating policies. They use digital communications technologies to contact supporters in an attempt to build and maintain loyalty. Research is used to design persuasive communications to sell public policy and political choices. This provides political elites with the opportunity to implement an agenda that prioritizes the concerns of target audiences over those of the broader population. Their methods do not represent a democratic ideal. The gravitation toward branding muddies matters further.

Sales, marketing, and branding are interrelated concepts that substitute communications technology for personal interactions between public sector elites and citizens. British political communications specialist Darren Lilleker has summarized the key features of media-centred politics. He lists them as limited face-to-face interactions with electors between elections; a majority of communications spending dedicated to television advertising; the celebritization of leaders to emphasize personalities; telegenic skills essential for spokespersons; media management prioritized by political elites; and an augmented role for communications professionals.[15] In this environment, public appearances are tightly scripted affairs. For instance, PR personnel are authorized to manage journalists' questions and to exert control over visuals, such as restricting the ability of the media to choose camera angles.[16] This gives rise to the related concept of public relations democracy. Lilleker explains that this is when information available about a political system is designed to persuade audiences that the correct course of action is being taken.[17] In a public relations democracy, the state embodies the governing party and its leader. PR tools are used for the organization's benefit, and elites are concerned about perceptions rather than facts. Government communications are primarily mechanisms to persuade electors of the righteousness of the governing party's agenda and to influence their vote choices. Canadian communications scholar Kirsten Kozolanka prefers to refer to the mixing of party and government communications as a publicity state, which she links to business-like approaches to public affairs.[18] In the publicity state, political and government elites recognize that communicating the minutiae of public policy is irrational in the face of demand for information tidbits and visual snapshots. Public policy is reduced to a prop in image management.[19] This sets the stage for sales-oriented and market-oriented organizations to unify communications under the umbrella of branding.

BRANDING AND POLITICS

Branding strategy is an evolution of marketing. It is a philosophy that envelops an entire organization and becomes a way of being. A brand is a more fulsome concept than an image. An image is the evoked impression of an entity formed from the recall of all communications impressions. A brand evokes emotional connections to specific images and stimulates loyalty among target audiences. Brands are complex concepts comprised of a multifaceted combination of tangibles, such as a logo, and intangibles, such as emotional attachments.[20] This interplay can be found in the American Marketing Association's definition of a brand as a "name, term, design, symbol, or any other feature that identifies one seller's good or service as distinct from those of other sellers" (the tangibles) and "a customer experience represented by a collection of images and ideas" (the intangibles).[21] The Canada Public Service Agency similarly notes the composition of tangibles and intangibles: "A brand is a promise made to clients to deliver clearly stated benefits that are valued and that set it apart from its competitors – it is much more than a logo, a tagline or a slogan."[22] Even more succinctly, a marketer at Canada Post (CS 15) remarked that a brand is a "collection of remembered touch points" (intangibles), and a communications consultant (CI 16) viewed branding as "repeating the same message over and over again" (tangibles). Whatever the definition, the attributes of a brand should work in unison to favourably differentiate it from competing brands. This should contribute to targeted consumers preferring it over other choices. A brand is part state of being, part visual identity.

The tangibles of a brand are straightforward: they concern public recognition. Brand communications generate awareness and appeal through the repetition of core messages. At the core of a brand is the actual product or service offered to consumers. In a consumer's mind, the nature of that offering changes when a label is attached, more so if the visual identifier is recognized. The design and colour of corporate and product logos simplify communications, project an organization's values, and exude a subliminal connection with consumers.[23] Lesser-known brands are comprised of an unfamiliar logo and name and a tagline that blends into a sea of information. The epitome of brand tangibles is the instant public recognition of a logo that does not even include the company name, such as the Nike swoosh or the Starbucks mermaid. As labels become successful, these visual cues become heuristics that allow busy consumers to quickly process information and make decisions.

An essential component of a brand's tangible communications is that all words and visuals ought to be interconnected and mutually reinforcing. This generates operational efficiencies and creates value. The logo appears everywhere. All images draw on the same colour palette, with tones consistent with the message (e.g., warm versus cool hues). A slogan is repeated, as are variations of central messages such as core values and promises. Together, they form the basis of a brand story that engages audiences. As a branding philosophy takes hold, the ability of journalists to obtain insider details from unsanctioned sources declines, which stabilizes the ability of the organization's leaders to pursue their communications objectives. With repeated exposure to consistent brand communications, it takes less time for audiences to recognize the brand.

The intangibles of a brand are more multifaceted: they concern consumer perception. The public image of a well-known brand becomes a social construct that connects on a psychological level with consumers. The benefits of a successful branding campaign are manifold and related to theories of information processing. If successful, branding will add value to a product or service so that a consumer develops a preference for it, even when the attributes of other brands are better. Brands establish legal ownership of a title. They are the basis of visual differentiation. They act as a shorthand device for consumers, and they reduce perceptions of risk by acting as a marker of consistent quality. Brands nurture identity systems and promote clusters of core values, becoming socially constructed realities. They project a human-like personality in the minds of consumers, who in turn form relationships with brand constructs.[24]

Studies find that branding is smart strategy. It improves strategic positioning and marketplace differentiation to meet targeted consumers' preferences, providing a competitive advantage.[25] Synchronized communications provide greater opportunities to increase familiarity with the brand, to generate favourable consumer attitudes, and to spur purchases.[26] This is particularly true for consumers who invest little effort into a purchase decision because they prefer the brand that they are familiar with, even if it is of lower quality than alternatives.[27] Branding brings people together in social relationships based on their attachment to the brand. Some consumers develop an unwavering loyalty based on their personal experiences, values, and expectations; however, others reject the brand, are indifferent to it, or lack sufficient information to form an impression of it.[28] To grow the brand's market share, marketers must appeal to identified markets in a manner that continues to satisfy the most loyal customers.

For brand strategists, integrated communications throughout the organization are essential because reputation is based on many touch points, including consumer experience.[29] At the epitome of intangibles are the brand's becoming part of a consumer's identity and lifestyle, and the forming of brand communities. Apple is a case in point. It was judged by consulting firm Interbrand to be the world's most valuable brand in 2015, with an estimated brand value of nearly $170 billion, of its market capitalization of approximately $600 billion. Its brand premium exceeds that of runners-up such as Google, Coca-Cola, and Microsoft. Customers line up overnight to be among the first to buy Apple products. It matters little to them that the newest model is marginally better than the one they already have or that it is more expensive than competing products that might better fulfill their needs. Through creative advertising and innovative product development, Apple instilled such an emotional connection with its brand that a counterculture formed. Owning the company's latest product addresses other aspects of customers' desires, including fulfillment of social prestige. Apple ascended to the most valuable brand status because of its meticulous attention to detail and technological innovation that "created a seamless omnichannel experience."[30] Visionary leadership and a passion for branding are central variables in its success. The demanding style of management of Steve Jobs did not care for market research, proving that marketing is not required to become a market leader. As CEO, he pushed for product innovations while micromanaging the aesthetics of the entire consumer experience. Under his direction, the company strove for communications simplicity and consistency. Consumers had an identical experience with advertising, retail stores, and packaging, as they did with the product and its aftermarket online tools. Even aspects of the brand that the consumer is never exposed to were painstakingly branded. Apple's workspaces and manufacturing equipment followed visual design principles of minimalism. The company centralized control in core team members and tightly integrated its divisions.[31] Painstaking work went into ensuring that the layout of the circuitry inside Apple's products would be aesthetically pleasing, no matter that a product's casing is designed to prevent opening. At Apple, Google, Coca-Cola, Nike, Starbucks, and other successful ventures, the brand pervades the upper tier of the organization and becomes an identity construct among its customer base.

As Apple's obsession with its brand suggests, how a brand is perceived is an important paradigm for organizations. The coordinated repetition of basic messages on multiple communication channels increases the likelihood that consumers will become aware of those messages.[32] Priority is placed on visuals because of their importance in recipients' memories and their implicit heuristic value. People who exert mental effort to process information about available choices seek to understand the meanings and implications of what is being communicated. Everyone else pays fleeting attention and expends minimal effort to comprehend. As discussed in Chapter 5, they take shortcuts by relying on their impressions of the source of the information, or on visual cues, which act as substitutes for deeper thought. Heuristic processing is an efficient if less reliable method. It saves people time and energy. However, they place greater weight on the superficial than if a systematic analysis is applied. This can result in errors of judgment.[33] Superficiality can be an ominous downside of branding.

In politics, brands have value because they help to advance agendas. Brand architects cherry-pick from a party's ideological positioning and package connected policy stances. They bundle ephemeral communications within a bigger picture that reinforces messaging. Brands influence the impressions of the many voters who make judgments based on snippets instead of deep assessments. The intangibles of a public sector brand include a name, a symbol, a set of policy positions, and other distinctive attributes of a political actor or public entity. The tangible elements are comprised of the evoked synthesis of information associated with visual impressions and personal experiences. How a public sector brand is perceived depends on what information people have, how they process that information, and whether an emotional connection is formed. It is a mental image that is an imagined reality – a psychological construct created through exposure to political communications. Public sector brands are real only in people's minds. Brands are artificial, manipulated, and open to interpretation. A brand is not a thing; it is a compilation of information and impressions.

The many components of public sector branding strategy and communications tactics are illustrated in Figure 2.3. Strategic communications include a variety of components. Among them are advertising and marketing, public opinion research, internal communications, corporate communications, regional media, risk and emergency communications, public outreach, social media, and general advising. Tactical positions include correspondence, publications, media monitoring, and media relations support. Insofar as understanding how public sector branding works, it is important to appreciate the difference between controlled and uncontrolled media. Controlled media refer to communications shielded from change by others. Advertising, direct marketing, internal communications, media relations products, personal communications, and Web 1.0 are all controllable. They can be re-enforced with the same messages promoted via a mix of media. In comparison, it is not possible to exert complete control over people's experiences with a brand. Nor can brand strategists control news media treatment, what opinion leaders say, opponents' communications, what happens on Web 2.0 and other participatory media, or word of mouth. How controlled and uncontrolled media converge to shape the different types of public sector brands is the subject of Chapter 4.

All of this comes together as permanent campaigning, also known as constant or perpetual campaigning. It is a theory that the strategies and tactics practised in the heat of an election campaign persist during governance and that all available resources are leveraged to maximize communications advantages. Political scientist Anna Esselment observes that permanent campaigning means that "every action, decision, and

FIGURE 2.3

Public sector branding strategy and communications tactics

Communications ➤	Branding strategy ➤	Controlled media +	Uncontrolled media =	Brand image
Ideology/agenda • beliefs, values • objectives	*Positioning* • core messages • core policies • core values • name • slogan/tagline • themes • value proposition	*Advertising* • print, posters, flyers • radio • transit, billboards • TV, video	*Audience experiences* • word of mouth *News media* • broadcast • online • print	*Audience attitudes* • brand awareness • brand liking • brand loyalty • brand reputation • brand satisfaction • brand trust
Research • consumer data • election data • focus groups • opinion surveys • oppo	*Visuals* • colours • images • logo	*Direct marketing* • email, text messages • letters, mail-outs • telemarketing	*Other political actors' communications* *Participatory mainstream media* • letters to the editor • open-line radio	*Corporate identity* • brand equity • brand personality • brand positioning
Segmentation • behavioural • benefits sought • demographic • geographic • lifestyle	• look and feel • people, attire • symbols • templates	*Internal communications* *Media relations products* • image bites • news releases • pseudo-events • spin	*Public forums and events* • protests/ demonstrations • Question Period, committees	
Strategy • differentiation • emotional resonance • media planning • relationship marketing • reputation management • target markets • triage • wedge issues		*Personal communications* • door to door • private meetings, events • telephone *Web 1.0 (static posts)* • banner ads • social media broadcasts • websites, blogs, videos	*Required information disclosure* • access to information • reports to Parliament and its agents *Web 2.0 (interactivity)* • file sharing • microblogging • social networking	

communication by government has been strategized, tested, and deliber-
ately conveyed according to an overall theme or message designed to win
public approval."[34] This has significant implications for government. For
one thing, the politicians and political staffers who direct the civil service
are keen to leverage tools to push forward an agenda and to get re-elected.
It brings into question how public resources are used. Moreover, though
constant campaigning provides media with plenty of news to report, they
are drawn to the drama of controversy and negativity. Permanent campaigning was at the fore throughout the three minority governments that
began soon after Harper became the Conservative Party leader. It persisted
once the Conservatives formed a majority government and visibly intensified as the scheduled election approached, as exemplified by the following
CBC News remark:

> While NDP and Liberal ads make scattered attempts at criticizing the
> governing party, the Conservatives are able to take full advantage of their
> position as governing party. By syncing both the content and timing of
> party ads with government ads, a much clearer, more integrated, more
> memorable message is delivered to pre-election taxpayers. And, the
> governing party can achieve all this synergy using significant quantities
> of taxpayer dollars.[35]

Examples of permanent campaigning appear throughout this book. They
include the use of ten percenter flyers, pseudo-events, public policy branding, and advertising, a discussion that climaxes with the mini case study
of the Economic Action Plan in Chapter 10. The concept of permanent
campaigning is particularly topical given the extraordinary seventy-eight-
day duration of the 2015 contest.

Even brand architects recognize that identifying the components of
an organization's brand strategy is a subjective undertaking prone to
fluctuation. For instance, the master brand of the Conservative Party of
Canada and Stephen Harper evolved over time while preserving some
underpinning characteristics. As opposition leader, Harper was branded
by his party as a straight shooter who would clean up Ottawa after the
sponsorship scandal, whereas his opponents promoted the image of a

radical conservative with a hidden right-wing agenda. A Conservative strategist recalled that the communications objective was to project an image of Eliot Ness, the law enforcement agent who took down prohibition gangster Al Capone, and create a ballot question on which leader could be trusted to fix corruption and mismanagement (CS 7). At the time, the party's master brand was accountability, supported by five subbrands of cleaning up government, cutting the GST, providing child care payments, reducing patient wait times, and getting tough on crime.

Once the Conservatives were in government, the brand relinquished vestiges of enthusiasm for social programming in favour of economic liberalism, until the 2008–9 recession and coalition crisis jolted the party to become a big spender under the auspices of the Economic Action Plan. By the onset of the 2015 campaign, the Conservative Party emphasized sub-brand messaging related to families and security, as it had in 2006, only now the economy replaced accountability. The party's main messages were jobs, growth, and long-term prosperity; keeping streets and communities safe; and supporting families.[36] These messages were intermingled with select symbols of conservatism, nationalism, and populism, such as traditional nuclear families, British connections, the Canadian flag, and hockey. A snapshot of how the party projected its desired brand is illustrated in Figure 2.4. The master brand of strong conservative leadership, supported by a core message of economic security, came through in all manner of government and party communications. Budget goodies included income splitting (dubbed the Family Tax Cut), a bevy of tax credits, funds for the Armed Forces and border protection, and money for the manufacturing sector. Government publicity promoted messages and visuals of the prime minister and cabinet championing tax breaks and economic growth. The Conservative Party sent missives to supporters that the government was building a stronger economy for families that stood to be undermined by Justin Trudeau's tax-and-spend agenda. During the ensuing election campaign, the leader's bus was wrapped in a photo of Harper next to the slogan "Proven leadership for a safer Canada, stronger economy." As the campaign climaxed, the shorter "protect our economy" became the rallying cry in all of the party's communication. Many would contend that the Conservative and Harper brands accumulated many negative attributes, chief among

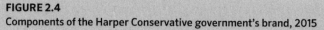

FIGURE 2.4
Components of the Harper Conservative government's brand, 2015

them a penchant for anti-democratic practices and a lack of accountability. Moreover, NDP leader Tom Mulcair assumed the role of Ness as he grilled Prime Minister Harper about the Senate expenses scandal, while Trudeau's team promoted the image of a unifier in contrast to Harper's divisive style of politics. By the time this book is in print, the brands of individuals and their parties will have shape shifted yet again. They will continue to do so under the Trudeau government as impressions and recollections of the Harper era fade.

In *Branding in Governance and Public Management,* public administration scholars Jasper Eshuis and Erik-Hans Klijn explain that the connection between branding and governance indicates how public policy problems and solutions are framed and managed; how actors are mobilized and become bound to the governance process; and how information is communicated.[37] Canadian studies theorist Richard Nimijean adds that political branding is comprised of three dimensions in Canada. First, branding strategy is used to create an emotional connection with audiences. The bases of this connection are political values and national identity. National symbols are appropriated by political parties as they seek to associate their political agendas and partisan symbols with patriotism.

Second, political marketers draw on public opinion research to adjust their branding techniques. Data on citizens' attitudes and perceptions inform the permanent campaigning that seeks to influence public opinion. Third, and of particular interest, Nimijean theorizes that branding strategy is highly concentrated in central agencies:

> The brand state requires the centralization of power within the government in order to effectively direct the cohesive implementation of the brand in all government [media] "products." The growing role of central agencies in managing communications allows the domestic brand state to flourish, as the centralization of power requires and cements a close relationship between the political (PMO) and the policy (PCO) spheres of the state thus allowing for more direct influence and direction on the national brand.[38]

Paul Thomas likewise subscribes to "the premise that communications has become a strategic and dominant preoccupation at the centre of the governing process within the government of Canada."[39] All three dimensions – the morphing of political identity and partisan communications, the appropriation of public resources for political marketing, and especially the role of branding in hurrying along the centralization of power – are explored throughout this book. A key theme is the democratic repercussions of a publicity state obsessed with coordinated brand control.

BRANDING AND PARLIAMENTARY DEMOCRACY

Democracy is founded on the idea that government rulers derive legitimate authority from the approval of the people whom they govern. This approval is conveyed through elections, formal mechanisms for citizens to render judgment on the representatives who act on their behalf. Legitimate consent is also rendered through plebiscites and referendums, policy tools rarely used in Canada.

Democracy might well be a bloodless way to resolve policy differences. However, the democratic process, like sausage-making, is messy. Democratic theorist Robert Dahl touches on some of the many philosophical dilemmas.[40] Is the ideal form of government a democratic republic? What of constitutional monarchies and oligarchic republics? What is the common good? Can it be identified through reason? Must we draw on intuition and experience? Who decides how to pursue it and in what manner? How do we adjudicate conflicting interests? What are the appropriate forums and processes to air and adjudicate disputes? To what end is majority rule legitimate? We must also ask questions such as, how should people participate in the democratic process and in public policy discourse? How do we ensure equality of access to those who hold a position of influence? What kinds of social training do citizens need? Is increased engagement necessarily positive, given that some groups are more willing and able to participate than others? These are questions for which there are only subjective answers.

At issue here is that the parliamentary system of government gives rulers so much tacit approval that the democratic legitimacy of their authority must be questioned. The placement of the executive branch (the rulers) within the legislative branch (their subjects' representatives) does not sufficiently pull the former toward the latter. Rather, communications technology combined with institutional structures provides rulers – chiefly party leaders, senior cabinet ministers, and particularly the prime minister – with growing opportunities to have their way with parliamentarians.

Traditionally, it is up to the people's representatives in the legislature and journalists to monitor government. In theory, representative government hinges on elected officials who speak up for their constituents. Responsible government adds the principle that government decisions must be supported by a majority of the people's elected representatives. To fulfill their responsibilities, those representatives must deliberate public policy and other issues without fear of reprisal from the executive. The notion that MPs can publicly stand up for their constituents refers to a distant, idealized era. Advocates of constituency representation underappreciate how forcefully communications technology shines the spotlight on party leaders and on any hint of group division. If party considerations and leadership prevail in the public mindset, which they do, then they will matter to parliamentarians and marketing strategists. Pierre Trudeau once said MPs are nobodies away from Parliament Hill. In reality, MPs are vital regional sales reps.

Advancing an agenda and maintaining a united public front require unrelenting centralized media management, both inside and outside the legislature. So it follows that criticism of the democratic functions of the House of Commons has deepened over time.[41] Party whips ensure that MPs vote along strict party lines, irrespective of constituents' concerns. Majority governments place time limits on speakers and invoke debate closure on controversial bills. The relevance of Question Period is waning, for it has become a national stage for theatrics and scripts and generates non-answers from cabinet ministers. These are not new issues. Cause for concern is that the partisan games and the government party's disregard for the legislature – both the institution and the opposition – appear to be worsening as communications technology emboldens tribalism.

The decay of the House of Commons is startling. The number of annual sitting days is in decline, from a mean of 153 in the 1980s, to 120 in the 1990s, to 111 in the first decade of the 2000s.[42] Attendance by the prime minister and opposition leaders is spotty, with Prime Minister Harper appearing at just 37 percent of QP sessions in 2014, in a year in which none of the three main party leaders was present at 45 of the 125 sessions (mostly absent on Mondays and Fridays).[43] The party centre issues directives to caucus via the house leader and party whip on matters ranging from who can speak to how parliamentarians are expected to vote. MPs are urged to communicate party lines during members' statements (known as SO 31s) in lieu of constituency matters,[44] and opposition MPs use designated "opposition days" to promote party messaging rather than to engage in parliamentary oversight.[45] Parliamentary websites tend to follow a party template, and MPs who author blogs or comment in social media forums are warned not to criticize or contradict the party's position. When faced with a recalcitrant MP, a party removes that individual from its list of scheduled speakers – or worse.

It is not just debate in the House of Commons that is under stress. Legislative committees and the parliamentary budget officer experience serious difficulties in obtaining financial data and documents from the government. Efforts are made to stonewall and destabilize the committee process. Parliamentary and government witnesses are prepped in pre-committee meetings about desired messages. A leaked Conservative handbook reportedly outlined instructions for how chairs should "favour government agendas, select party-friendly witnesses, coach favourable testimony, set in motion debate-obstructing delays and, if necessary, storm out of meetings to grind parliamentary business to a halt."[46] At times, legislative committees are boycotted by the governing party. Conservative ministerial staffers were no longer allowed to act as witnesses. Uniformity extends beyond political staff in the PMO and MINOs to Parliament Hill staff, who must now sign a lifetime conflict-of-interest and confidentiality agreement.[47] The people's house appears to be in disarray as parliamentarians routinely comply with the wishes of the party leadership.

Increasingly, from the moment of entry into party politics, there is an understanding that everyone must put party and national interests ahead of local and personal interests. Partisanship is an existing institutional condition that deepens with technology. It is a long-standing practice in parliamentary systems that a candidate must affirm loyalty to the party and its principles. Political parties have always vetted prospective parliamentarians, who enter "a voluntary and contractual relationship that essentially confers a series of obligations upon the individual to support the party."[48] By agreeing to represent the party in an election, candidates signal that they are followers who will obey the wishes of the leader and accept that there will be consequences for defying commands. They face considerable social pressure to exhibit loyalty. Limited dissent is enabled by the human tendency to side with the majority on matters that do not involve moral issues.[49] Most calculate that it is in their best interests to go along with what the party wants if they wish to gain more responsibility and/or avoid sanctions. Party cohesion and group conformity are thus much more of a two-way contract than people realize. Nevertheless, the primacy of party interests brings into question the role of an elected official. To some, the communications discipline required by a branding strategy is incompatible with principles of representative and responsible government. The notion that a party whip or other agent of the leader can dictate what can and cannot be said in public, let alone how elected representatives must vote, seems to be irreconcilable with constitutional protections of free speech, conscience, religion, thought, belief, opinion, and expression. To others, it is essential to portray the party as a strong and unified alliance. Executive control secures the votes needed to get elected, to achieve high office, to influence public policy, and to survive in the rough-and-tumble worlds of politics and governance. Outward-facing symmetry is essential because a single controversial remark or tweet is a source of immediate titillation for the media and provides opponents with an opportunity to pile on. As discussed in Chapter 6, "bozo eruptions" generate pressure on the leader to cut ties with the perpetrator in order to protect the brand. The sharp rejection of the remark and its author reinforces to others that the brand is sacrosanct. At other times, the leader publicly stands by colleagues embroiled in controversies because dismissal is calculated to inflict more communications damage than holding the fort.

It is in private where the people's representatives have a duty to flex their political muscles. The parliamentary system is predicated on members of the same political party expressing conflicting opinions *in camera* but presenting a united front in public. Compromises are worked out away from public view, reducing the pressure to act with urgency while conveying a sense of elitist stability. This is embodied by the principle of cabinet solidarity. Ministers are collectively tasked with setting the policy direction for the government of Canada and do so in secret cabinet meetings. They are individually responsible for overseeing matters in their assigned departments, and many of them have incentives to maintain low public profiles. Ministers who stay away from media controversy are prized by the PMO,[50] so they are saying less in post–Question Period media scrums.[51] By convention, ministers who make public statements inconsistent with the government's decisions must resign. That principle of public unity now extends to backbenchers. It is in private settings that they must lobby to influence the party's stance, such as during impromptu policy discussions. Caucus meetings are the one forum in which MPs are consulted and backbenchers are somebodies. But caucus is only as strong as the sanctity of secrecy. If dissenting opinions are leaked, then participants will start clamming up, and the leader will abandon the meetings, particularly the prime minister, who cannot afford to convey caucus discord with cabinet.[52] The overriding *modus operandi*, as Lynton Crosby would put it, is to stick to the script by avoiding political commentary and by scrubbing off unwanted message barnacles. The average member of Parliament is left to spew the party line in public and champion constituency services. Public advocacy is risky, especially during a minority government, when height-ened importance is placed on a member's durability and discretion.[53]

We will never know how much influence caucus or individual MPs have in private. All we see is an outward-facing unified stance, one pro-moted by party apparatchiks and assumed to have originated from the party hierarchy. On occasion, such as with private members' bills, public policy originates with individual MPs and winds its way through Par-liament. The Reform Act is a pertinent example. Michael Chong, the Conservative MP and a former minister of intergovernmental affairs, led an ambitious effort to take power away from "the centre" and give it to MPs. Parliament passed his private member's bill, Bill C-586, An Act to Amend the Canada Elections Act and the Parliament of Canada Act (Candidacy and Caucus Reforms), in early 2015.[54] The legislation amended the Elections Act to remove party leaders as the agents who must authorize election candidates. The veto power shifts to one or more designated in-dividuals, other than the leader, authorized by the party to endorse pro-spective candidates. Revisions to the Parliament Act empowers caucus – defined as a party's members of Parliament, not its senators – regarding the dismissal and re-entry of a member of caucus, a matter that has been the purview of the leader. In either case, the leader must receive a written request signed by at least 20 percent of caucus members, and the decision must be endorsed by a majority of party MPs in a secret ballot vote. The same process applies to the removal of the caucus chair and – significantly – the removal of the party leader. This provides caucus with a mechanism to initiate a party leadership review and to select an interim leader. The Reform Act promises to alter the context of many of the branding issues raised in this book and elsewhere. Its passage is significant for more than its substance: it is an indication that private members can wriggle out from under the thumbs of leaders. Prime Minister Harper was one of a number of members of cabinet who did not vote on the bill. Some Conservative senators attempted to block its passage. It went through nevertheless. According to Chong, "the passage of the Reform Act is a victory for democracy ... [and] addresses a long-standing problem in Ottawa: the concentration of power in party leaders, including the prime minister. It will give individual Members of Parliament more power to represent their constituents and Canadians."[55] Those concerned about the pervasiveness of branding philosophy might not be so optimistic. For instance, there is no legal requirement that party caucuses follow these processes. They must only hold a vote in their first meeting after a general election on whether or not to follow each process. The outcome of the vote will be binding on that caucus until Parliament is dissolved and another general election is held. Chong's success notwithstanding, on the whole the ability of members of Parliament to influence public policy and build a personal following appears to be declining as the authority of party leaders grows. The idea that MPs "need to stand up and show that they can maintain a connection to the constituencies they represent"[56] is trampled by branding's unitary command maxim. This is a problem if we believe that parliamentary democracy must empower elected officials to prioritize the wants and needs of constituents over those of the party. Conversely, the Reform Act's placement of more power in the hands of caucus takes it away from rank-and-file party members. Should a party caucus install its own leader, we would come full circle back to a practice done away with nearly a century ago because it was seen as elitist and undemocratic. Either way, it will be interesting to see how the dynamics of party cohesion and central control are affected.

The combination of party discipline and communications technology is ripe for branding strategy. An enduring puzzle is the extent to which socio-economic and socio-political factors spur technological innovation or whether innovation pushes forward social, political, and economic factors. Political economist Harold Innis and media theorist Marshall McLuhan were Canadian pioneers of a school of thought that communications technology is more influential than its content. Innis theorized that societies that rely on durable media such as clay or parchment are prone to be decentralized and headed by hierarchy.[57] Non-durable media such as electronic communications are subject to expansion, enabling the mass coordination of society necessary for the centralization of power while spreading information and democratic values. McLuhan believed that technology is the driver of social organization and that visual communications are especially potent. The full adoption of digital communications technologies is measured because society needs time to adjust to new cultural norms. His adage that "the medium is the message" was spawned from electronic media, specifically television.[58] It continues to apply to Internet media.

The theory of technological determinism helps to explain why strict message discipline is more prevalent in Westminster systems than in presidential systems. Western societies have reasonably similar exposure to communications technology, but only parliamentarians operate in comparable institutional arrangements in which party unity is so acute. It is thus the combination of political system and potency of communications technology that sets the table for a branding doctrine. Along these lines, constitutional scholar Peter H. Russell argues that the foremost reason for the existence of prime ministerial government is both institutional and technological. He blames

> the emergence of disciplined and well-financed political parties whose leaders employ the techniques of mass advertising to win and retain power. This development is aided and abetted by the techniques of public

FIGURE 2.5
PMO alerte-info-alert talking points for brand ambassadors

From: Alerte-Info-Alert <Alerte-Info-Alert@pmo-cpm.gc.ca>
To: Alerte-Info-Alert <Alerte-Info-Alert@pmo-cpm.gc.ca>
Sent: Sunday January 10, 2010
Subject: Ignatieff Liberals Renew Attack on Canadian Soldiers

Michael Ignatieff, unseen in Canada until Thursday night, when he arrived on a flight from Europe after an extended vacation, has launched a small-budget ad campaign intended to distract attention from his lengthy absence.

The ad campaign renews the Ignatieff Liberals' claim about a "cover-up" of "torture" of Taliban prisoners. Mr. Ignatieff persists in this attack even though the allegation that torture was covered up represents a direct attack on the men and women of Canada's Armed Forces. The Ignatieff Liberals like to pretend that their wild allegation bypasses the soldiers who captured and handed over Taliban prisoners – but that's just not logical. The rest of Mr. Ignatieff's ad campaign is more of the same – idle chatter that is out of touch with the real priorities of Canadians – including Canadians' number one priority, the economy.

Our Government is hard at work and remains hard at work on the things that matter to Canadians, in particular the economy. This includes completing implementation of our Economic Action Plan, returning to balanced budgets once the economy has recovered, and building a strong economy for the future.

Source: Taber (2010a).

management that downplay the deliberative role of elected representatives and Parliament's role in holding government responsible for its decisions. Between elections, the citizenry participates in parliamentary democracy primarily through brief exposure to sound bites and talking heads on the electronic media. On top of all this is a cult of celebrity that focuses political interest on the accomplishments, failures, and personalities of leaders.[59]

Short electronic messages exemplify how communications technology simplifies a parliamentarian's understanding of what should and should not be said publicly. This includes private messages, news releases, messages issued from the prime minister's social media accounts, and the Conservative PMO's Alerte-Info-Alert emails sent to brand ambassadors (Figure 2.5). Recipients repeat the prime minister's public comments and/or the party's position on an emerging issue. In various forms, the same core messages are sent simultaneously to all government MPs and the party's spinners, who debate on political talk shows. A former PMO chief of staff explained how smartphone technology enables communications conformity:

> You could prepare a message that today the prime minister in Question Period was asked some question, and here are the three points he made in a response. Type that up, email it to everybody – ministers, chief of staff, all the political staff, PCO for distribution to deputy ministers, ADMs of communication or whoever the appropriate person is ... The rest of the message discipline takes care of itself. (CS 31)

THE COMMUNICATIONS "CENTRE"

Public sector branding leans more toward institutionalism than technological determinism. That is, the executive dominance and party discipline found in Canadian politics and government are furthered by communications, not caused by them. Various institutional factors coalesce to cause power to gravitate to the centre, beginning with electoral laws that turn the party leader into a kingmaker who reigns over individual candidates. In this light, communications technology is a far-reaching contributing factor hurrying along an existing trend. At worst, the command-and-control ethos associated with branding is a sign of a diseased political system. Branding is not the exclusive reason that centralization of political decision making occurs.

It is generally agreed that the "centralist orthodoxy" that has long described Canadian party politics and government far outstrips its decentralized characteristics.[60] The prime minister and cabinet are responsible for strategic decisions within government. The political executive's directives are supported by an interwoven cluster of powerful central agencies. At the top is the Prime Minister's Office and the Privy Council Office. Academic debate swirls around the extent of central authority and even around what constitutes the centre of political power. The Treasury Board Secretariat (TBS) and the Department of Finance are normally included in conceptualizations of central agencies. Some scholars include Intergovernmental Affairs and its predecessor, the Federal-Provincial Relations Office, and the Public Service Commission.[61] Thomas adds that the Department of Public Works and Government Services Canada (PWGSC), rebranded as Public Services and Procurement Canada by the J. Trudeau government, deserves to be considered in studies of government communications.[62] White takes the broadest view, with the "core executive" encompassing cabinet, central agencies, supporting institutions, political staff, and deputy ministers.[63] If we consider the PM's advisers, this extends beyond government to political consultants (e.g., pollsters, lobbyists, communications professionals), senior personnel in the extraparliamentary wing of the party, select members of caucus, and others, including the PM's spouse. In short, there is no one way to define "the centre."

One reason is that not all ministers are created equal. Trustworthy ministers with a stronger media presence have more influence and hold greater sway as courtiers. These high-profile brand ambassadors are prone to agree with PMO requests to make announcements and to act as government spokespersons.[64] As they prove that they require little micromanagement, the PMO grants them further leeway to communicate with the media and interpret the brand. This independence sets them apart from ministers who are incapable of suppressing firm belief systems, who long for philosophical discussions, who have weak media management skills, or who linger as unknowns. The government's highest-profile brand ambassadors – historically mostly middle-aged white anglophone men in suits – act as extensions of the leader's and party's brands. They have the leeway to speak publicly and to choose their own staff. The reverse occurs for trouble-prone ministers, to whom the PMO assigns communications agents to protect the brand. Bev Oda (see Chapter 3) and Julian Fantino (see Chapter 6) are among the ministers discussed in this book who were demoted after their actions caused media controversy.

The government personnel and institutions that ministers oversee have interconnected communications responsibilities (Figure 2.6). Generally speaking, the Treasury Board cabinet committee sets the government of Canada's administrative policy, administered by the TBS, while PWGSC coordinates the contracting processes. Discussed in Chapter 7, the PMO and cabinet, including key committees, guide the government's communications strategy. The implementation of that strategy is coordinated and managed by the PCO. A more cynical view is that synchronicity is the basis for "ongoing and robust, yet flexible, connections and patterns of reciprocal identification" between the centre and government institutions.[65] Within departments, communications are directed from the exempt staff in the minister's office and by permanent staff led by a director general of communications. They liaise with a team of communications personnel as well as policy advisers, program managers, and various specialists. The Department of Finance plays no extraordinary role in communications beyond its leading role on major policy files, in particular the budget. Service Canada provides front-line communications, and Library and Archives Canada files information for reference purposes. The Office of Protocol, housed in Global Affairs, follows a manual of procedure and etiquette when engaging in international communications, including official events and visits. Although the permanent government is separate from party politics, the distinction is not so absolute in communications. Parliamentarians and political staff working in the legislative branch, as well as extraparliamentary advisers, perform formidable functions as strategists, brand ambassadors, and/or media relations practitioners. The roles of these politicos climax during episodic events, such as election and by-election campaigns and political crises. As with government personnel, their engagement in central processes fluctuates.

FIGURE 2.6
Communications actors in the government of Canada

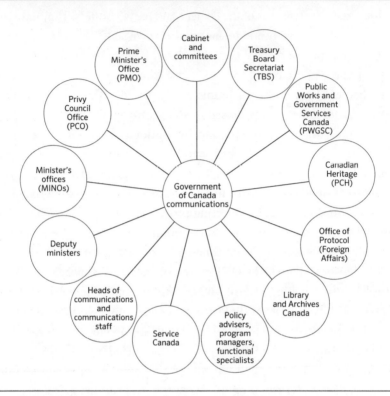

Source: Modified from Treasury Board of Canada secretariat (2012a).

Not all members of the core executive are involved with setting the government's strategic direction or administering its communications harmonization. At the heart of communications decisions are the political actors in the PMO, the senior civil servants in the PCO, and the political personnel in the MINOs that head up departments (Figure 2.7). A rule of thumb is that communications rules and institutionalized processes are more formalized when they involve the bureaucracy. This contrasts with the flexibility and urgency of processes concerning mainly political issues. In other words, matters that involve planning, public tendering, and/or evaluation assign formal roles to civil servants, whereas issues management and media relations are politicized. Thus, TBS and PWGSC perform essential roles in government advertising. However, their involvement

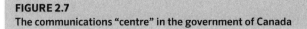

FIGURE 2.7
The communications "centre" in the government of Canada

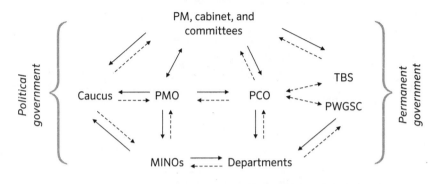

with news media functions is perfunctory. Information exchange and delegation of duties are constantly cycled between these central actors. There is one important exception: communications personnel in the Prime Minister's Office do not routinely interact with civil servants in departments. Instead, the PMO's wishes are conveyed through the intermediaries of the PCO and MINOs. A study of branding in Canadian politics and government should pay attention to the prime minister and cabinet, PMO, PCO, TBS, and PWGSC. Some consideration ought to be given to Canadian Heritage (PCH) in light of its role in government symbols and Canadian identity. Furthermore, describing communications operations within political parties will offer important context, in particular with respect to understanding the role of caucus as a limited two-way channel of communications.

As this conceptualization of the centre suggests, at the head of the communications pyramid is the prime minister. The blending of messages and unification of brands turn public perception of institutions and individuals into a monolith, regardless of rules and separate processes. If party leaders are becoming commodified entities marketed in place of policies, then a Canadian prime minister warrants special study, given that he or she is at the summit of what is supposed to be an apolitical organization (Figure 2.8). This is different from political marketing conceptualizations that give equal weight to the person/leader, ideology/policy, and party/organization while sharing a commonality that components cannot be autonomous.[66] The branding of the prime minister is explored throughout

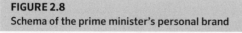

FIGURE 2.8
Schema of the prime minister's personal brand

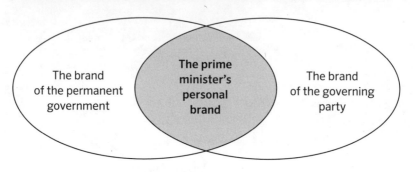

The brand of the permanent government

The prime minister's personal brand

The brand of the governing party

this book in a manner intended to be relevant regardless of which individual holds that title.

Those working with the leader have privileged access and insights that make them a superb data repository. Reflecting on public sector branding, Jonathan Rose observed that "the intersection between political party marketing and state marketing suggests that ... a study of modern politics cannot be divorced from an understanding of the role of symbolic handlers who routinely organize, plan, and manage the communications of political actors."[67] In this book, handlers in the communications centre encompass a wide network of actors, with eroding spheres of influence (Figure 2.9). These categories of communications personnel are used to inform a research design. A parallel centre exists within political parties, comprised of the parliamentary and extraparliamentary wings, of which some aspects come alive only during election campaigns (not shown). This conceptualization of principals, strategists, messengers, and intermediaries submits that brand discipline and centralized communications emanate from many people.

Whether in government or in party politics, the common thread is that the *communications principal* (CP) is at the top of the hierarchy and is surrounded by agents. The principal is the brand's lead spokesperson and has the final say on strategy and messaging. In a political party, this is the leader; in government, it is the prime minister. Our understanding

FIGURE 2.9
Public sector communications actors (labels used for interview respondents)

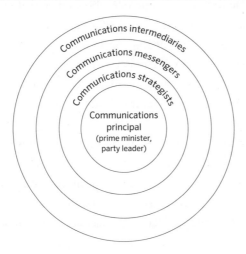

of the PM's and PMO's roles must extend to considering how party communications operate. Doing so will allow us to grasp the partisan influences of the political government.

The fluidity of communications is a constant to-and-fro that percolates throughout a public sector organization. Leaders draw counsel from, and delegate authority to, an array of people. We can conceptualize a *communications strategist* (CS) category to encapsulate senior ministers, the party brain trust, and well-placed employees who negotiate high-level communications decisions with, or on behalf of, the principal. They hold senior positions across government, particularly in central agencies and MINOs. Some have held senior posts in the party's election campaign(s). As the Malcolm Tucker caricature suggests, their authority is based as much on the force of personality as it is on the rank of position. Some PMO directors of communications are notorious for their aggressive style, whereas others are more conciliatory. This is a wide conceptualization that ranges from anyone who regularly interacts with the prime minister to departmental communications personnel involved in media strategy. It does not pretend to equate a minister on a powerful cabinet committee with a weak minister or the clerk of the Privy Council with a department's director general of communications. There is a chain of command in government. Rather, it is an indicator of the wide swath of people who strategize about communications without the prime minister's explicit involvement.

The directives of the principal and communications strategists are expected to be implemented by a *communications messenger* (CM). This eclectic group of people prepares communications products and/or publicly communicates authorized information. Again, this is categorized not so much by job title as by sphere of influence. This ranges from the party pundits who promote key messages on political talk shows to the junior staffers who write news releases and conduct media analyses. Messengers do not ordinarily become involved with communications strategy. They are implementers rather than decision makers, though from time to time they do contribute to strategic decisions. They are conceptualized here as mid-level political or permanent staff. Messengers include individuals whose job titles suggest that they hold sway with a minister but whose roles in the machinery of government serve other functions. Differentiating between communications strategists and communications messengers is a subjective undertaking that requires an understanding of the responsibilities and sway of each individual as opposed to her or his job title.

The immediate recipients of messages are external *communications intermediaries* (CI). These are mainly journalists as well as unaffiliated media consultants treated as independent communications experts by contemporaries. They are at the front lines of information exchange with a variety of external groups and publics. As will be discussed in the next chapter, their roles as gatekeepers and mediators are evolving and shrinking under the weight of digital communications technologies. An argument could be made that bloggers and citizens with social media followers are intermediaries who deserve study, but that extends beyond the scope of this book.[68]

3

The Tumultuous Digital Media Environment

Marketing and branding contribute to online chatter that the Canadian prime minister rules over trained seals in Parliament. The hyperbole is based on some truths. The sameness expected of all agents of a public sector brand is a fundamental characteristic of parliamentary politics, one bolstered by marketing strategy. In the political sphere, media scrutiny and public commentary are acerbic, and branding is the safety valve. The more media are democratized, and the more the public demands transparency, the more we should anticipate that public sector elites will say that they are pursuing openness while simultaneously seeking to control communications. Media biases and varying standards of journalism are contributing institutional factors.

DIGITAL MEDIA SHOCK AND THE FOURTH ESTATE

In a short time, mass communications have become faster and more pluralistic than most of us imagined possible. Digital technology is bringing more media, more participants, more sources of information, more content, more visuals, and more speed. There are fewer gatekeepers, less verification of claims, more gossip, more noise, and less time to think. Communications scholar David Taras refers to "the magnitude and jolt-like force of media change" in this digital environment as "media shock."[1]

The constant drumbeat of message delivery in the public sector is accelerating. Stephen Harper was the first prime minister to practise communications discipline in the turbulence brought about by social media.

In 1998, just 23 percent of Canadian households regularly used the Internet, a number that stood at 51 percent by 2002. In 2012, it had reached 83 percent of households, by which time broadband had displaced dial-up access.[2] Of those using the Internet at home, email is the most popular activity (93 percent in 2012), followed by personal and lifestyle activities such as searching for weather reports or road conditions (75 percent). Downloading videos and web streaming are growing. Just 8 percent reported doing so in 2005, and by 2012 the proportion viewing television online had increased to 25 percent. Internet communications are a popular way to interact with the public sector. In 2012, 57 percent of Canadians with Internet access searched for government information, and 27 percent communicated electronically with government. New platforms and devices emerged during Harper's tenure as Conservative leader. Facebook and Flickr were launched in 2004, YouTube in 2005, Twitter in 2006, Tumblr in 2007, Instagram and Pinterest in 2010, Google+ and Snapchat in 2011, and Vine in 2013. The portability of social and visual media coincided with the launch of the Apple iPhone in 2007, followed by its App Store in 2008, the iPad in 2010, and the Apple Watch in 2015. In 2004, 59 percent of Canadians had a cellphone, a proportion that reached 71 percent in 2007, when smartphones (handheld portable Internet-connected phones equipped with digital cameras) were emerging.[3] By 2013, more than half (56 percent) of Canadians had a smartphone, a percentage that is rising. The portability of Internet-enabled devices is every bit as influential as the consumer-friendly software that makes them indispensable. Many smartphone owners always bring their devices with them. They use them to regularly access the Internet and applications (apps), and they do so while engaged in other tasks, including television viewing.[4] Owners become dependent on the devices, with many engaging in the obsessive behaviour of checking for new information throughout the day, including at work and during social situations. One study estimates that postsecondary students spend approximately nine hours daily on their phones, mostly for social communications via email, texting, and social networking sites.[5] Media reports invariably mention that people take their phones to bed, check them while driving, obsessively take selfies, and document their surroundings. The transportability of information has profound implications for public administration, for political communications, and for

Canadian society. Moreover, smartphones are furthering a culture of simplified communications. Text messaging, chat acronyms (e.g., 2nite, GR8, LOL), and emoticons (e.g., ☺) speed up social conversations. As bandwidth expands, the sharing of photos and video clips in lieu of writing or talking becomes more popular. The public's expectation of instant replies is wildly disconnected from the ability of organizations to keep pace.

As a result, more than ever the digital workplace is a cacophony of urgent demands. Virtual meetings occur through group emails and electronic conferencing by telephone, video, or the web. Work hours are not confined to the office. The growing number of staff assigned mobile devices are expected to respond on demand whenever and wherever. Colleagues working across the country and beyond, including when they are travelling or on vacation, interact through instant messaging and collaborate on documents stored on "the cloud." Briefing notes and information notes are becoming more succinct. Detailed cabinet memorandums are replaced by bulleted lists of information.[6] The evolving environment hastens the need for departments to operate on horizontal platforms managed by centralized processes instead of within autonomous silos.

It is easy to overlook the fact that today's norm was science fiction when Jean Chrétien led the Liberal Party to power in 1993. Internet communications were emerging then. Canada's first twenty-four-hour television news channel, CBC Newsworld, was in its infancy. Public relations personnel were tethered to their desks waiting for phone calls and documents. Desktop computers, fax machines, and pagers were becoming common, with computing power primitive by today's standards. Long-distance phone calls and cellular phones were prohibitively expensive. The journalists travelling with a party leader or minister often filed their stories by land-line telephones. In their hotel rooms, they developed photographs that they scanned and submitted over phone lines. Obscure political happenings reported in one area of the country took days to be noticed elsewhere, if ever. Political parties used email mostly for internal purposes, and they did not yet have websites. The mobilization of supporters and activists relied on telephone trees and volunteers. The official list of electors was compiled by door-to-door enumeration. The computerized customization of direct mail letters was a burgeoning industry. Announcements of government decisions followed a protocol: cabinet made a policy decision; a media advisory was faxed to editors' desks with details of a news conference's location and PR contact information; a PR staffer would call around to drum up awareness; and the next day the PM or a minister went to a room operated by the Parliamentary Press Gallery to read a prepared statement and field questions. Ottawa journalists took notes and reviewed the paper copies of the media kits circulated. Significant developments were phoned in to the newsroom. News of an announcement broke on the radio, followed by the evening television news. The item appeared in the next day's newspaper and perhaps in a weekly magazine. If they needed more information, reporters sought private interviews, or they thrust a microphone at ministers in the hallways of Parliament Hill or in the press gallery's media facilities.

Since that time, the expansion of specialty television channels has increased the flow of information about current events, entertainment, lifestyles, weather, sports, business, and politics. Digital-only video platforms such as Netflix are causing cable and satellite TV operations to rethink their business models. The stubborn popularity of hyperlocal radio adds to competition for audience attention and advertising dollars, even as people subscribe to satellite radio and download audio files. Free daily transit newspapers like *Metro* have emerged, while subscription newspapers offer less news in print form. Internet communications put further pressure on traditional media, which increasingly require web-exclusive text and audiovisual content. Inexpensive or free information that can be easily reproduced is wanted more than ever, particularly visuals, as newspapers cut down on the written word and as websites and smartphones become scrolling canvasses. Suddenly, all news media are in the business of communicating with both visuals and written words. Audiences expect a constant stream of fresh material. A CBC executive summarized the new reality of digital media shock:

> You talk to a reporter now, and it takes about ten minutes for it
> to be splashed on websites across the country. [In the past], if
> you wanted to get news out, you'd have to issue a press release
> at 7:00 a.m. so that it would get to the newspaper outlets in time
> for their meeting at 10:00 a.m. ... They would call you by the next

morning, and the story would be in there. That's not how it works anymore, not even by a long shot. Everything's changed because of the Internet, the timing of things. News comes out 24/7. Now I go to the *Globe and Mail* website, and the headline hasn't changed, and you go, "What's going on over there, are they sitting on their hands?" You expect new news to come out every ten minutes or so. (CS 20)

Now add the dynamism of online interactivity and file sharing, known as Web 2.0. Visitors post their comments and react to others' remarks. Audiences are invited to upload their own digital content that can be reused by news organizations, both online and offline. Personal information that used to be private is now shared on social networking sites such as Facebook and LinkedIn. Visuals can be manipulated through graphics editor software such as Adobe Photoshop. Content communities such as Flickr and Instagram allow photos to be shared. YouTube is a major video platform. Microblogs such as Tumblr and Twitter circulate information in short bursts of characters (140 in the case of Twitter), photos, and links to videos. Citizens get their news from each other, and news consumers together decide what is trending.

Consider further that the ability to create, upload, and view digital media is still growing with advances in computing power and bandwidth. Wireless transmission and the sophistication of mobile phones are so affordable that tablets, smartphones, and phablets are rapidly displacing stationary computers, telephone land lines, and cable television. People can view and contribute to realms of mediated and unmediated communications nearly anywhere, anytime. Phone calls, emails, texts, user-to-user messages, photo sharing, and video downloads reach people across time zones and work/personal divides. Instant communication and access to powerful portable devices to search for archived information are the new reality. There is no turning back.

The nature of news production and consumption has changed irrevocably. Professional news organizations are up against people's desire for free information, and they are flanked by citizens who generate free content about current events. The media are pressured to attract and retain audiences who are time shifting with satellite media and PVRs and turning to web streaming on their smartphones, desktops, laptops, tablets, television units, and gaming devices. The gatekeeping role of news editors is diminishing, and journalists' behaviour is evolving, including an increased penchant to opine without verifying facts.[7] Tweets are suddenly the de facto source of breaking news and public commentary. Reporters live-tweet while a media event is in progress. News stories are posted online while event participants are still delivering their remarks.

The print industry's business model in particular has been turned on its head. Television still dominates as Canadians' primary source of news and information.[8] Traditional news media websites are next in popularity, and learning of news first through social media is increasingly common, especially among younger Canadians. But newspaper and magazine outfits are in a downward spiral. Subscriptions and sales are dwindling, as are advertising revenues, forcing consolidation and closure. In contrast, advertising sales are increasing on television and radio and rapidly so in digital and interactive media.[9] The written word is no longer even a priority on websites as text becomes clickable graphics and photo tiles and as news stories are filed as video only. Byte by byte, technological change is nibbling away at the written word's ability to command revenues to fund the delivery of details and contextual perspectives in a world of breaking news and episodic coverage.

Public sector hacks and flacks are devising ways to capitalize on the changing circumstances. News and information travel so quickly that it is difficult to keep up. The online sphere pressures politicians to make rapid decisions, which are instantly judged. The social media mob demands the immediate disclosure of information from government and publicly shames alleged wrongdoers. Politicians are expected to comment on issues trending in the Twitterverse. They fret about an off-the-cuff remark or visual that goes viral. "You used to be able to wait for a news story to develop. Now it's not even a matter of it happens and then you respond. It's just constant. It's just absolute constant. I sound like a whiner, but that's just the way it is," expounded a seasoned communications staffer in government (CS 25). A former Harper chief of staff observed that political journalists used to prepare a report based on Question Period. Now a story cycles two or three times before QP begins, and three or four times once it finishes, a process that extends late into the evening. "That's a generational change from the early Chrétien years. I'd say we were the first government – well, Martin and us – were the first who came in with this kind of 'no longer having daily news cycle but having a continuous news cycle'" (CS 31). A former PMO staffer added that

> it used to be that during the election it was the war room thing where you had to have [a] quick response to stuff. But now it's all the time. It's at night as well as during the day. It's on the weekends. I don't think that's the politicians creating the permanent campaign; they'd probably be delighted if it wasn't that way. It's that the media and the speed of the culture have made it such that politicians have to respond, because if they don't then they're seriously at risk. (CS 14)

Finally, aggressive opposition and dirty tricks are omnipresent and cloaked in anonymity. Party researchers and citizen agitators scrub the web for salacious information about opponents that can be released at an opportune moment. At every event lurks the possibility of a citizen proto-journalist or party operative who will capture a gaffe on a phone camera and upload it to YouTube. Search engine rankings are manipulated. Control is assumed over opponents' Internet accounts. Fake websites and social media accounts appear. Bogus online identities are used when posting comments to online feedback forums. Wikipedia entries are manipulated. Robocalls spoof caller identification labels and communicate falsehoods. It is within this information technology cyclone that media and public sector elites are forced to adopt new approaches to survive and thrive.

The downside of free and fast is that news is a mile wide and an inch deep. This worries the journalists who cover Ottawa. The "fourth estate" is a term that refers to the important democratic function performed by professional journalists who monitor the executive, legislative, and judicial branches of government on behalf of the broader populace. As an institution, the fourth estate gathers, processes, and communicates information about public affairs. Its members' way of thinking, as explained by the president of the Association of Electronic Journalists Canada, is that journalists "should doubt everything that we do not know to be true" (CI 7). Its ideals are embodied in the news division of the CBC, the state-funded public broadcaster whose journalistic mission is "to inform, to reveal, to contribute to the understanding of issues of public interest and to encourage citizens to participate in our free and democratic society."[10] Standards of professional journalism decree that a reporter needs to obtain proprietary information from insiders. This requires direct communication with spokespersons authorized to speak on the record, normally ministers or designated civil servants with specialized knowledge. Alternatively, information can be mined from well-placed personnel on the condition that these sources are not publicly identified. For organizations such as the CBC, government is a significant source of information, and at the core of a political journalist's work is her or his relationship with government officials.[11] Members of the general public and their elected representatives draw on the fourth estate's outputs as they render judgments about government and political choices. Among the many questions explored are: What is the political executive doing? Are its decisions in the public interest? Is government behaving in an ethical and accountable manner? How is it raising and spending money? The importance of unfettered media in Canada is such that section 2(b) of the Charter of Rights and Freedoms recognizes the fundamental freedom of the news media and other forms of communication. However, the quality of journalistic output is a reflection of media economics. The production of news is related to profitability and audience statistics and, in the case of the CBC, limited government funding. What political journalists uncover about the public sector is related to what their employers will bankroll. This sets up an opening for information subsidies, discussed later in this chapter.

Most media organizations that monitor federal governance and politicking belong to the Canadian Parliamentary Press Gallery (CPPG). Membership provides them with accreditation for special access in the Parliament Buildings, including the legislative chambers. Members operate out of the National Press Building, situated across from the Centre Block on Parliament Hill, and manage press conference rooms in those buildings. Even a casual look at the variety of accredited members of the

CPPG sheds light on the intensity of information demands and scrutiny of political life in Ottawa. National newspapers (e.g., *Globe and Mail, National Post, Le Devoir*), city newspapers with a national reach (e.g., *Toronto Star, La Presse*), and specialist newspapers (e.g., *Embassy, Lawyers Weekly*) belong. Television news is comprised of national (e.g., CBC TV, CTV, Global, Radio-Canada), regional (e.g., City, TVA), and specialty channels (e.g., APTN, OMNI). Radio and magazines have a smaller presence (e.g., CBC Radio, *Maclean's*, Radio-Canada) than the many news agencies (e.g., Canadian Press, Postmedia News Service, QMI) serving traditional media across Canada as well as a growing number of online news agencies (e.g., Huffington Post, iPolitics, Rabble.ca). A multitude of international media are CPPG members, such as Agence France Presse, Bloomberg News, *People's Daily of China*, the *Economist*, and the Vietnam News Agency. There are also freelancers. But the fourth estate is much more than the press gallery. Outside Ottawa exist hundreds of regional, local, and community and specialist media outlets that pay attention to national happenings, particularly when there is a dimension relevant to their audiences. Some of them, such as *Corriere Canadese* (Italian) and *Ming Pao* (Chinese), communicate in languages other than English or French. Countless web-only outfits have sprung up, among them the citizen proto-journalists who author blogs. The assortment of CPPG and non-CPPG media results in an array of perspectives and processes for reporting news. All have various needs for visuals.

Government representatives must prepare themselves for exposure to a barrage of questions from media that pursue assorted angles and controversies. Since the 1960s, there has been a bias of media skepticism toward the political class in Western liberal democracies. Pre-Watergate, the media were more deferential to political elites. The fourth estate employed many political scribes who provided a favourable account of government and politicians in return for privileged access. Post-Watergate, the media have been critical of the public sector, particularly political elites. This slant is found among even the most apolitical, dispassionate, professional, and objective journalists.

Today's political actors must grapple with the inevitability that news coverage distorts reality and favours one side over another.[12] The production of news is bigger than a single journalist's work. Journalists' reports must pass through editorial filters, and whatever is reported is interpreted differently by audiences, depending on socio-cultural contexts.[13] News selection decisions prioritize simple information that will be attractive to audiences and easy to report.[14] As a result, the complicated details that contextualize the story are prone to be cast off. These institutional conditions are ideal for branding strategy. However, rather than label the media as biased, we should think of political journalists as narrators of political stories.[15] They operate in a competitive marketplace in which business models are turning upside down and facing economic pressure to respond to consumer demand.

A hybrid news system of traditional and digital media is becoming the norm. Power struggles are taking shape as media gatekeepers' role at the centre of news production adapts to new realities.[16] In the public sphere, political communication is changing from centripetal (drawn toward the centre) to centrifugal (drawn away from the centre) as the CPPG and others relinquish their monopoly over mass media technology. At the turn of the century, British scholars Jay Blumler and Dennis Kavanagh theorized that the retrenchment of centripetal media results in audiences who are more selectively exposed to information.[17] There is an increased role for identity politics and political agendas and widening cultural gaps in society. Centrifugal forces are putting journalistic power in citizens' hands. However, though political elites have responded through greater grassroots interactivity (i.e., centrifugal activities), they have not relinquished centralization (i.e., centripetal behaviours), which appears in fact to have solidified. The democratization of government in the digital media age has not taken shape as anticipated. The responsibility of monitoring government is trickling down from the fourth estate to the masses, causing public sector elites to shift tactics to maintain control.

Even as mainstream media become democratized, such as by journalists interacting with audiences, this is occurring as electronic media and economic forces impose changes. News gathering is consolidating through wire services, syndicated columnists, and the sharing of cameras on trips. Media conglomeration results in news reproduction across outlets and platforms. Social media are intensifying pack journalism and groupthink, which see reporters from different news organizations converge on the same story as they race to break the news. They assemble archived information online that heretofore has been unnoticed, and sometimes uncovered by non-elites, which is homogenized into shared knowledge. Internet media specialist Andrew Chadwick refers to this as "assemblage in an information cycle," whereby loosely connected people cluster online, wading in and out of fluid conversations to offer details and perspectives in real time.[18] Issue publics convene through comment opportunities on news media websites and via social media such as the Twitter hashtag #cdnpoli. The finding that as a topical issue attracts more attention its treatment becomes similar across media outlets[19] is likely escalating as a greater number of people share information electronically.

Canadian journalists express exasperation with digital media shock. In an interview, Susan Delacourt recalled spending days sitting in the *Globe and Mail* library in the early 1980s going over Department of Employment and Immigration files obtained through access to information legislation. When the deputy minister found out what Delacourt was doing, he invited her into the department to personally observe how things worked. She relayed that this was not unusual at the time. That approach is nearly impossible today because of the combination of journalists' need to meet multiple daily deadlines and the guarded nature of the public sector. "You'd never be given that much access, you'd never be given that much time," Delacourt reflected. "Today the deadlines are something happens, file while it's happening, file right after it happens, and then file again. So three or four deadlines a day, which is ridiculous ... You're constantly looking for a shiny object to throw up onto the Internet" (CI 18). She is one of the many experienced journalists who do not have the time and space to engage in academic-like research. Instead, they work in hurried circumstances with an overwhelming number of people and topics competing for their attention.

The news industry's market-oriented approach to giving consumers what they want is resulting in a race to be first and popular, at the cost of upholding a fourth estate principle of investigating matters in the public interest. The number of page views and comments received by online news stories are metrics that guide assignment editors about which stories to pursue. Social media comments and retweets act as a barometer of audience engagement and interest. Some Canadian news organizations employ sophisticated data analytics to assess repeat visits, how long people linger on stories, how much scrolling they do on a page, which devices are used to view sites, and whether referrals originated from social media. This comes at the cost of offering context and understanding. The strange and superficial compete with the serious and important. Funny pet tricks, pranks, cute babies, Super Bowl commercials, music videos, mundane posts by friends and family – these are just some of the many sources of online content with which news producers and public sector PR personnel are contending.

The media's response to market forces means that breaking news and visual storytelling dominate. In the early 2000s, the BlackBerry changed the way that media and political elites interact by enabling portable email communication. Currently, smartphones such as the iPhone allow journalists to break news with photos and video rather than just audio or text. Jennifer Ditchburn, a Canadian Press reporter, relayed that, when the War Memorial and Parliament Hill shootings occurred in October 2014, she instinctively ran out the door, yet still had the tools to generate video content that circulated worldwide: "I didn't grab a video camera, it was happening so fast. I ran all the way down there. My iPhone was all I needed. I took pretty clear video, very close up, of the paramedics trying to revive [shooting victim] Nathan Cirillo. And then I just cut it down a little bit and emailed it so our video people had it almost instantaneously" (CI 19). Meanwhile, Ottawa's fetish with message control was evident in real time as public officials sought approval for the public release of information about the crisis.

There are many advantages and disadvantages associated with the media's messy journey of becoming decentralized and democratized. Journalists can locate and share much information about the public sector from an affordable device that fits in the palm. Informal conversations between media and political elites are publicly visible on social media. News spreads across the country and around the world, and non-elites can uncover and circulate it themselves. The distance between media elites and audiences is shrinking, and the quality of journalism is improved by access to different perspectives and accountability. The volume of information is expanding even as the number of beat reporters is declining. But the urgency to get information out the door means that multitasking journalists miss details. They tell of entering a half-conscious state in which they are so focused on one of their multiple duties that they become oblivious to what is happening around them. For instance, getting the right camera angle at a news conference, as opposed to taking notes, and then catching up by checking Twitter to see what their peers are presenting about the event just documented. This digital media environment makes branding strategy an appealing mechanism for controlling communications.

A concluding remark about the implications of digital media is warranted to put centralized control in perspective. Every day, organizations around the world issue clampdowns on the media behaviour of their representatives. Stories abound of employees being disciplined or fired for their public remarks and actions, even during their personal time. We can use February 4, 2015, as a random example. In the news that day, the Seattle police announced that changes to its social media policies were pending after one of its officers posted a racist comment on Facebook. A National Hockey League (NHL) referee received a one-day suspension for being photographed drinking tequila with a sports blogger in a bar. Toronto Transit Commission workers removed a map of a bus platform when a photo went viral and the map was mocked for its phallic shape. There were stories of insurance companies combing social media to find evidence to prove insurance scams and of lawyers using information gleaned from deactivated accounts in litigation. Parents were urged to warn their children about the lasting effects of social media posts. A sexual encounter in the workplace caught on video and posted online led to the employees' suspension. Protecting brands is a global phenomenon. Whenever a private situation becomes public for the wrong reasons, the employer faces pressure to take immediate corrective action as an online mob bombards the employer's social media accounts and damages its reputation. In the digital age, all representatives of all organizations are potential brand ambassadors.

MEDIA LOGIC

To understand why branding is attractive to "the centre," we need to delve more deeply into the jostling between media elites and public sector elites in a hybrid news system. Public sector elites are conditioned to play by the rules of the media realm. This is termed "media logic" because the news business's way of thinking is more likely to accommodate those who adapt to the media's norms, routines, and news values.[20] PR personnel learn to present information as new, even when it is not. They seek to fit information into an existing narrative rather than to treat it as an isolated event. They understand the need to communicate simple solutions in lieu of the complex and to turn boring processes into dramatic events.[21]

An example of media logic is PR staffers' awareness that events will be reduced to image bites. Visuals are processed by the human mind more rapidly and with more durability than verbal or written content. Image bites glorify triumphs, magnify mistakes, and capture moments that become seared in political memories. Canadian political strategists are unequivocal in their conviction about the importance of visuals in political communications. The usual clichés are trotted out: "A picture is worth a thousand words. Nobody looks at the written content of everything. It's all about image" (CS 3); "visuals trump words" (CS 4); "if you win the pictures, you're gonna win the election" (CS 28); and so on. The ideal is for image bites to reflect a controlled and strategic reality that gives the illusion of authenticity. Images of Chrétien racing up stairs and of Jack Layton waving a walking stick in front of cheering crowds are calculated visuals repeated so often that they became part of each man's personal brand. Image bites are staged, packaged, and repeated in anticipation that the media will opt for simple visual storytelling underpinned by the same visuals over time.

Recognizing the intense, confrontational, and manipulative nature of political communications is essential for understanding why branding is smart politics. Some of the interrelated theories of how media logic shapes the dissemination of political information are summarized in the following pages. The allure of branding to public sector elites is influenced by dynamics that include agenda setting, framing, information subsidies (including pseudo-events and digital image bites), politainment, celebritization, the strategy frame, and pseudo-scandal. A brief review of each of these concepts is supported by contemporary Canadian examples.

Agenda Setting

Political actors are in a constant struggle to influence which issues should be prioritized by the government and how those issues should be resolved.

Agenda setting involves persuading journalists to pay attention to certain topics and influencing how those topics are prioritized in their reporting. It requires that political strategists be familiar with the media's needs and which packaged information is reasoned to generate a favourable response. The pathway is as follows: agenda building via media coverage leads to the public agenda being set, which results in items being placed on the formal agenda of government for decisions. Agenda setting is predicated on the assumption that issues prioritized by the media in turn matter to the public, who will spur legitimate action by government.[22]

The communications strategies and tactics that public sector elites deploy are evolving as they attempt to lasso an array of media voices to control the agenda. Opposition parties, interest groups, think tanks, lobbyists, pundits, and other political actors perpetually advocate what they believe the government must do about a given issue. They seek to achieve their objectives via private meetings, and they apply pressure by publicly calling into question the government's action or inaction.[23] Their agitation begins by drawing attention to general grievances. Pressure builds through the articulation of specific demands. Advocates attempt to attract the sympathies of the attentive and general public as they seek to expand the number of supporters. The grievance and accompanying demand constitute part of the public agenda when many people are aware that a problem exists and want it resolved. At this stage, decision makers are confronted with a need to consider their options. Meanwhile, within government, the cabinet via political agents pushes its own agenda on the civil service. Despite their duty of loyal implementation, units and personnel within the bureaucracy do not always support the requested course of action and can resist it by dragging their feet or getting hung up in process.

"You're either driving a message, or you're getting run over by a Mack truck. Take your pick" is how a former PMO strategist rationalized the need for the centre of government to advance a communications agenda (CS 14). The Conservative government's use of communications to push the Canada Job Grant is a good example of how agenda setting converges with branding and permanent campaigning. The 2013 federal budget unilaterally declared that, when Labour Market Agreements were up for renewal, the government would change the terms with provincial and territorial partners. It proposed a reduction in funds for the byzantine

mix of programs primarily targeted at workers receiving Employment
Insurance benefits. Instead, a single national-based program would comprise much of the budget envelope. The Canada Job Grant would direct
up to $5,000 in federal funds per eligible worker to upgrade skills, with
other levels of government and employers also committing funding, so
that approximately $15,000 in total training funds would be available to
eligible Canadians. The proposed program was dependent on getting the
provinces and territories on side.

The Conservative administration proceeded to use publicity tactics
to pressure its subnational partners. Within two months, the Canada Job
Grant was touted in television advertising during NHL playoff coverage
as well as in radio and online ads. The creative design of the videos followed
the same colour palette and style as the Economic Action Plan (EAP; see
Chapter 10). Labourers were portrayed going to work as the announcer
relayed the benefits of the program. A closing blue screen featured the EAP
logo. When CBC News sought comment from Employment and Social
Development Canada about the multi-million-dollar advertising campaign, a spokesperson stayed on a master script by responding only that
"the government of Canada's top priorities are creating jobs, economic
growth and long-term prosperity."[24] The adage that all publicity is good
publicity applies because news stories criticizing the advertising generated increased awareness of the proposed program, moving it up on the
public agenda. But there is a limit. If controversy drowns out the message,
then this is problematic because it eats away at the government's agenda
and brand, painting it as anti-democratic and politically incorrect.

The media and opposition parties decried the Canada Job Grant publicity campaign as propaganda. After all, the government was promoting a
program that did not exist and relating it to the governing party's main
brand messages. Advertising Standards Canada ruled that the advertising
was misleading because of the suggestion that the program was accessible,
when in reality it would not be available for months, if ever. The Canadian
Taxpayers Federation designated the advertising campaign as the winner
of a mock award for wasteful spending. After a brief hiatus, the advertising
and news coverage returned, putting the federal government's preferred
policy back on the public agenda and framing the intergovernmental
negotiations in the federal government's favour. Within a year of the budget

announcement, all subnational governments except Quebec signed on, with each government set to finalize the details with the federal minister of employment. The advertising campaign continued, with a small text disclaimer that alternative arrangements were available in Quebec. This is among the many ways that government communications were used to prop up the Harper government's master brand about taking action on the economy and to limit federal-provincial bickering in national media.

A hidden aspect of agenda setting is the daily battles within government among departments and individual units to advance files. As they compete for attention and resources, government personnel use public communications as a mechanism to pressure and box in the centre. Departments and units have a constant urge to make premature announcements, such as publicizing the design of a project before the project is vetted or funded and years before it will come to fruition. The competitive environment is fuelled by political staffers who are constantly trawling for good news announcements. A former PMO chief of staff argued that the political government is always fighting to control the agenda against the permanent government:

> You have people [within government] making announcements
> and statements seeking to win a place in the approval process. So
> they raise a matter publicly and in a certain way, by rallying the key
> stakeholders who are seeking to move themselves up the queue in
> the policy approval and cabinet approval process. A very obvious
> one is people seeking to win resources. Materials written by
> officials very often contain thinly disguised kinds of advocacy
> for additional funds for those departments, quite outside of the
> budget-making process. (CS 30)

As we will see, internal and external wrangling to set the agenda can be better contained by branding.

Framing

Political actors compete to shape how the media and public think about organizations, individuals, and issues. Strategic messages are designed to inform the criteria used by journalists and citizens for evaluating political debates and public images. Selective information is promoted in a manner thought to influence receivers' evaluation criteria while meeting the sender's objectives. This purposeful presentation of selected information is known as framing. It is a technique that attempts to draw more attention to certain schemata than others. Framing occurs in a manner that succinctly identifies a problem, assesses options, and presents solutions.[25] It manipulates which information we are exposed to and the way in which we interpret it. For instance, when political actors author a tweet, their foremost intent is sometimes to influence how journalists and others analyze a topic.[26]

Framing is narrow, whereas branding is all-encompassing (i.e., a brand results from the entirety of all frames and other communications impressions). Both emphasize a perceived reality. The debate over the prohibition of marijuana is a classic case of framing. Some call for it to be legalized, whereas others take a zero tolerance stand. In 2001, the Chrétien Liberal government passed a bill allowing Canadians suffering from severe illnesses to apply to obtain marijuana through Health Canada. The legislation authorized the licensing of marijuana production for medicinal purposes. In contrast, a key plank of the Conservatives' brand is getting tough on crime. Upon forming government, the Conservatives initiated bills to increase penalties for drug dealers and organized crime. In 2012, Liberal Party delegates adopted a policy resolution to legalize and regulate *all* marijuana. Public discussion was ignited when new Liberal leader Justin Trudeau announced that he had smoked pot since becoming an MP. His admission came days after the Canadian Association of Chiefs of Police advocated that police should be able to issue tickets for possession of thirty grams or less of marijuana instead of filing criminal charges.

The resulting public discourse provides a snapshot of how political actors compete to frame policy options and personalities while staying true to their master brands. The Conservative Party promoted the following frame: the Conservatives are tough on crime; Trudeau wants to legalize marijuana and make it easier for children to access drugs; he also lacks a plan to strengthen the economy and is in over his head; PM Harper is a competent economic manager. Conversely, the Liberal Party sought to frame the matter this way: Liberals are a forward-thinking team of progressives who consider scientific evidence and listen to Canadians; marijuana laws that give criminal records to Canadians who possess it for personal use are excessive; cannabis should be legalized and regulated to keep it out of the hands of organized crime; by disclosing that he smoked pot, Trudeau was transparent, unlike the secretive and ideological Conservative government. The New Democratic Party's frame was as follows: the party has been saying for decades that nobody should go to jail for marijuana possession; legalization needs to be studied, including the implications for public health; the real issue of concern to Canadians is that Harper is leading a tired government mired in scandal and out of touch with ordinary Canadians' values; only Tom Mulcair and the NDP can be trusted to offer a progressive government. It was in the Conservatives' interest to put this policy issue on the public agenda as long as the framing created a wedge between the Harper/Conservative and Trudeau/Liberal brands. It was in the Liberals' interest to control the timing of the public revelation of their leader's illicit behaviour and to connect its marijuana policy to a broader brand of social liberalism. The NDP would generally prefer to advance a different agenda altogether, such as affordable child care or Senate reform.

The Conservatives' ability to access government resources was a framing advantage over the opposition parties. In late 2014, Health Canada launched a TV and Internet advertising campaign warning that marijuana is harmful to youth. It spent $7 million over a ten-week span, which exceeded the $5.2 million that the department spent on health-related advertising during the entire previous year.[27] However, the government failed to secure endorsements from medical organizations, which thought that the communications were partisan volleys. Furthermore, they did not like that they were expected to sign a confidentiality agreement limiting their ability to speak publicly about the advertising or issue.[28] This permanent campaigning converged with Conservative Party radio advertising critiquing Trudeau's marijuana policy. It was reinforced by Conservative MPs who distributed flyers through their parliamentary office budgets that disparaged Trudeau and featured a photograph of a boy lighting a joint. This too met some resistance (see Chapter 5),[29] and raises questions about the use of public funds for partisan gain.

Visuals are so potent that framing need not occur through words or ideas. Public sector elites are cognizant that a single negative visual in the mass media can derail a political agenda, alter framing, and reduce their power. The most famous Canadian case of framing and media subjectivity occurred during the 1974 federal election when Robert Stanfield, the Progressive Conservative Party leader, tossed around a football during a refuelling stop on the North Bay airport tarmac, in an effort to refresh his staid public image. The Canadian Press took so many photos of the leader catching the ball that his press secretary helped the photographer to ship the film to editors for circulation on the newswires.[30] The next day newspapers across the country publicized the now iconic photo of Stanfield with a defeated look at the one moment that he happened to fumble the football. The video clip of Chrétien throttling a protester and Canadian Alliance leader Stockwell Day arriving at a news conference on a jet ski are among the image bites that shape the brands of Canadian political leaders. Canadian politicos are ever mindful of these and other incidents and of the biases of news production. A former prominent journalist, now a Conservative senator, summarized: "A photographer goes to an event and takes 150 shots, and the paper decides which one to use" (CM 3). The new reality is that the masses create and distribute photos and videos. Concerns about selection bias have become centripetal anxieties about controlling every angle and every message all the time.

Public reactions to visuals educate a politician about the need to exercise strict image management. As opposition leader, Stephen Harper was photographed at the Calgary Stampede wearing a leather vest, string tie, and cowboy hat. This was culturally acceptable for the stampede. However, the snap became known in Ottawa circles as "the gay cowboy" photo and is thought to be "the low point of image management for the party" (CM 2). When Harper became prime minister, the media publicized images of him shaking hands with his son, adding to a frame of Harper as cold and aloof (Figure 3.1); participants in Conservative focus groups continued to evoke the visual nearly a decade later. That year Ottawa officialdom also guffawed at a photo of the new prime minister wearing a traditional Vietnamese tunic at the Asia-Pacific Economic Cooperation summit. Ministers must likewise take precautions to avoid unflattering images. Bev Oda, Harper's minister for international cooperation, evaded the media and questioning in the legislature. This evasion added to the controversy over her decision to reject funding to a humanitarian group, fuelled by a visual of a government document on which she

FIGURE 3.1 Media photos that frame the images of Canadian politicians: PM designate Stephen Harper dropping his son Ben off at school, 2006; Minister Bev Oda on Parliament Hill, 2011 | Canadian Press / Fred Chartrand; Canadian Press / Sean Kilpatrick.

had written the word *not* to deny the request. Then Oda was caught in a gotcha moment that framed her as a mobster. She was photographed smoking outside the Parliament Buildings while wearing sunglasses that made her look as if she had something to hide (Figure 3.1). From the point of view of Conservatives, the Canadian Press captured Oda in a private moment, making it a "predatory photo that was designed to deepen her problems" (CM 4), even though they accept that the minister left the media with little choice. Harper chose to defend Oda and her policy decision. However, news the following year that she stayed at a luxury hotel in London and billed taxpayers for a sixteen-dollar glass of orange juice were too much. This cut to the core of the Conservative brand, and Oda's political career was soon over. These are only some of the many examples of visuals and simple matters that can advance or damage a politician's brand and the party's agenda, resulting from mediatization of democracy.

Information Subsidies

The media and PR personnel are dancing partners who both want to lead. Consider the following email from a staffer on the Conservative Party leader's tour during the 2006 campaign:

> The pool crew is pissed with our/Stephen's refusal to give them on/off plane shots ... They will be rolling the camera the whole time we're in flight as a result. This means any awkward shot of the boss getting up, sitting down, bending to tie his shoe, is fair game. They're going to look for bad visuals ... We've been getting great visuals, and the pool guys have actually worked with us on fine-tuning shots, including letting us look through their camera. If they were just print journalists, I wouldn't care, but these guys can really screw us with bad shots.[31]

The parasitic-symbiotic relationship between political and media elites leads to institutional accommodation. Unpaid mass media coverage is earned by providing journalists with information formatted to speed up its processing, for instance press releases, photo opportunities, and digital content. This responds to the media's desire for economic efficiency and generally makes life easier for reporters. Information subsidies comprise a considerable volume of reported information,[32] and they are more prevalent today than ever before. This is a circumstance of media economics. "Newsroom budgets are shrinking everywhere, and people are looking for cheaper options," rationalized the editor of an alternative magazine (CI 5), while the president of the Canadian Association of Journalists conceded that, "as newsrooms shrink, there are fewer people to send. In a way, governments are filling a need" (CI 8).

Information subsidies are prevalent in war. Since 1990, the Canadian Forces has offered high-quality photos and videos of military operations that otherwise would be off limits and expensive to obtain. This has evolved into the Combat Camera website (combatcamera.forces.gc.ca), which allows users to perform searches for photos, videos, b-roll supplemental footage, and archived footage intended for reproduction. Media agencies can sign up for email alerts to be notified when fresh content is available for downloading. Of course, using controlled information goes against the fourth estate creed. However, media organizations are left with no alternative source. "It's just the reality. We can't have a guy taking photos everywhere," points out an *Embassy* magazine journalist (CI 9).

The information subsidy that involves the most planning effort is what historian Daniel Boorstin labelled a pseudo-event.[33] By this he meant the coordinated public relations occasions put on for the media, such as the GST announcement (Chapter 2) or the prime minister's photo-op in a Saskatchewan wheat field (see Chapter 4). Boorstin and others harbour deep suspicions about pseudo-events. They believe that media accommodation replaces the business of news gathering with news making. The fourth estate should not participate in manufacturing an illusionary reality.

A sharp contrast between pseudo-events was on full display one weekend in March 2010. The Liberal Party held a three-day policy conference in Montreal. It brought together prominent non-partisans and past Liberal leaders to discuss ways to improve Canada by the time the country celebrates its 150th year. Canada at 150: Rising to the Challenge convened international and domestic academics, business leaders, journalists, public servants, and Liberals. Among the luminaries were the president of the C.D. Howe think tank, a past international chair of the Inuit Circumpolar Council, and the director of the New York–based Global HIV Vaccine Enterprise. Bloggers were given accredited media status, and social media offered updates in real time. Keynote speakers' presentations were archived on a conference website. Satellite town halls were held in ridings across Canada to engage those who could not attend. Liberal leader Michael Ignatieff, who left his job as a prominent Harvard professor to enter Canadian politics, positioned the event as part of "a national dialogue about the future" and a "serious discussion" about major policy issues.[34] If scholars were to design a thoughtful public policy exercise, then the Canada at 150 event would be it.

That Friday the Conservatives used the machinery of government to coordinate a competing media event in the small Quebec community of Stanstead. The prime minister announced Economic Action Plan infrastructure funding for a hockey arena. The facility would be named after Montreal-born Pat Burns, one of the top coaches in recent NHL history. Burns had terminal cancer and made a rare public appearance at the event, emceed by another former Montreal Canadiens coach, then-Conservative Senator Jacques Demers. Among the attendees were NHL alumni and executives and politicians from different levels of government. It was the kind of retail politicking and permanent campaigning that frustrated the Conservative administration's critics.

The announcement of the Pat Burns Arena came a month after the PMO released photos of Harper with Wayne Gretzky. They were depicted cheering on Team Canada together at the Olympic men's gold medal game in Vancouver. In comparison, Ignatieff penned a thoughtful op-ed reflection on the significance of the game that appeared in the *Globe and Mail*. These juxtapositions of information subsidies fed into the broader branding frame that the Liberal leader was elitist, whereas the Conservative leader was in touch with common values. There are many examples of the PMO prioritizing an image of catering to small local markets. One that stands out is the mini furor that erupted when Harper returned from the United States to attend the grand opening of a Tim Hortons facility in Oakville. To do so, he skipped a speech by the recently elected President Obama at the United Nations General Assembly in New York.[35] This calculated prioritization of pseudo-events is anathema to the Canadian intelligentsia. It does not sit well with members of the CPPG and the so-called Laurentian consensus residing in Toronto, Ottawa, and Montreal enclaves.[36]

The dancing duel extends to treating the strategy behind information subsidies as news. A media kafuffle surrounded the revelation that six Citizenship and Immigration employees pretended to be new Canadians taking the oath in a citizenship ceremony, an event staged at the request of Sun News. Another case was Ottawa pundits' admonishment of a government junket to Israel during which Conservatives clamoured to get photographed in front of Old Jerusalem's Western Wall. One MP, whose riding is home to thousands of Jewish Canadians, urged a PMO staffer to include him in a photograph with the prime minister. The MP was recorded pleading, "It's the re-election – this is the million-dollar shot!"[37] Other episodes arise to become major media topics for days or weeks. Consternation emerged about an international media centre built for the G8/G20 summits in Toronto. Within it, Muskoka chairs were placed in front of a pool of water against a backdrop screen of images of Ontario lakes. The government hired a company specializing in the creation of "cultural capital" to promote Canadian business and tourism to the over 3,000 journalists visiting from around the world. Opposition politicians derided the $1.9 million spent on a "fake lake," actually the cost of the entire media pavilion, of which the pool cost $57,000. The higher dollar figure stuck. The prime minister defended the decision as an opportune "marketing project"[38] and was correct in that the pavilion and fake lake delivered an excellent payoff in international media coverage. The G8/G20 was a major public event and communicated a non-partisan message to promote the region and attract economic investment, notably tourism. The contract was awarded following a non-partisan tendering process. This did not matter to critics, who saw an opportunity to project a counterframe of the Harper administration as image control freaks and frivolous spenders.

Not all media organizations can or do assign representatives to attend pseudo-events. Digital media are a great equalizer. A number of Canadian public sector information subsidy firsts occurred in rapid succession during Harper's prime ministership. In 2010, the Department of Finance tweeted information about the federal budget as the finance minister delivered it to the House of Commons. The prime minister's response to the Speech from the Throne was streamed live on YouTube, and the PM participated in a YouTube interview with questions submitted by Canadians. In 2011, the PMO began making announcements by Twitter prior to an official news release being issued.[39] In 2013, Tony Clement, as president of the Treasury Board, hosted an interactive video chat on Google Hangouts. The budget speech was live-streamed so that those watching the online version would see supporting graphics and videos. The information was shared via Twitter, and budget materials were designed to be compatible with smartphones and tablets.[40] Within months, the prime minister's Twitter account unveiled each change of ministry in real time an hour *before* the details of a cabinet shuffle were officially announced. One by one, the ministers took to Twitter to issue short remarks of enthusiasm and humility. A comedic outtake of Harper doing impressions of politicians was leaked to the media via YouTube. Laureen Harper, sometimes portrayed in government and party images as a presidential-style first lady of Canada, maintained a blog during the prime minister's annual summer tour of the Arctic. The PMO now live-streams announcements so that anyone with

Internet access can watch the video in real time via pm.gc.ca/live (e.g., Figure 8.3). There are countless such examples of digital information subsidies that respond to the endless need for fresh content while satisfying the sender's desire to control the frame.

Elsewhere I have described a new form of information subsidy, namely the electronic distribution of controlled visuals by public sector actors.[41] From 2010 to 2012, the PMO issued a so-called photo of the day. The photos were taken by a member of the PMO's photography unit who was given backstage access and were posted on the prime minister's website almost daily. Photos were emailed to list subscribers and distributed via Facebook, Flickr, and Twitter. Aside from presenting subjects in a favourable light – usually the prime minister – the information subsidies present a business-as-usual image on days that the media are swirling with controversy. "A lot of this is pro forma, things you do as a prime minister," explained a PMO staffer, before granting that "sometimes the message of the photo is designed to counter the external media coverage" (CS 4). Small news outlets are believed to be the most likely to reproduce digital image bites. Journalists reason that the demand for visuals is driven by the Internet, in which there is a constant need for new content. Lower thresholds exist online, and photos generate greater click rates. "Life is a lot easier for reporters with digital photos. We've got all these photos coming in all the time," relayed a Transcontinental columnist (CI 13). Mainstream media use the digital handouts if they determine that there is a justifiable need, for instance a photograph of a backroom staffer who ends up in the news for whom there is no other official visual.

As bandwidth increases, the manufacture of digital image bites is shifting toward the distribution of video as a component of branding strategy. The PMO began producing a weekly video newsmagazine. *Stephen Harper: 24 Seven* offered a behind-the-scenes look at the prime minister's activities, accompanied by a voiceover. This provided voyeuristic access to government officials in the style of an unfiltered reality TV documentary. Although *24 Seven* was one-sided, free video is a tempting information subsidy, given the exclusive nature of the content, such as footage of Joe Oliver being sworn in as finance minister. The PMO's digital photos and videos reinforced message consistency among brand ambassadors. The visuals acted as quick updates on which sorts of things the prime minister was doing, what the message of the day was, and what slant the PMO wanted to apply. This extended to potentially turning reporters into unwitting brand ambassadors. "When we receive a photo from the PMO, even if we delete it, we are informed about where he is and what he's doing," offered a *Metro* editor (CI 12). Even those who snicker or frown at PMO image bites acknowledge that they might be susceptible to framing bias.

The exclusivity of PMO videographers is unsettling to the most principled members of the fourth estate. A press relations dispute in Nunavut stands out. In 2009, the PMO photographer was granted exclusive access to the prime minister and top ministers dining together on seal meat. It was such a compelling image that mainstream media reproduced the handout photo.[42] The journalists sent to cover the ministerial junket were seething. The episode did more than exhibit a lack of respect for professional journalism and the considerable expense incurred by the media outlets that sent the journalists to gather news: it challenged the values of independent journalism and presented a threat to their chosen vocation. Six years later the two-tiered access came to the fore when journalists touring with the prime minister in Iraq and Kuwait were warned not to communicate images of Canadian soldiers' faces. As well, they were required to sign documents attesting to the restrictions.[43] The PMO's *24 Seven* production crew overlooked this protocol. A mini furor resulted over the double standard and the resulting security issues for military personnel. Faced with an onslaught of criticism, the PMO was initially defensive but then quickly removed the videos and apologized.

Another fashion of digital image bites was the tweets issued by Prime Minister Harper's account (@pmharper) in 2013 that documented his day in photos, treated as newsworthy by the mainstream media.[44] His Twitter followers and subscribers to the #cdnpoli feed were invited to "follow my tweets to see what a normal day for me looks like." The prime minister was shown eating breakfast, with the family cat nearby. He then commuted from 24 Sussex to Parliament Hill. He met with senior staff. He worked in his office and ate at his desk. He met with parliamentarians and then participated in Question Period before meeting with military veterans. His day concluded with working at home in the evening, accompanied by his wife. Even though it is controlled, such an information subsidy has research value, given that the details of a Canadian PM's workday are closely guarded. Opposition parties are denied access to the prime minister's daily agenda book, and the Supreme Court of Canada has ruled that the PMO and ministerial offices are not subject to the Access to Information Act.[45] Justin Trudeau has pledged to make the PMO more transparent. Regardless, the "day in the life" Twitter exposé turned the humdrum into entertainment, while adding to a calculated frame of the prime minister.

Politainment

Today's journalists are pressured by audience ratings and click statistics to treat politics as entertainment and pique the public's interest.[46] Prior to the 1970s, MPs who participated in a legislative debate were all but assured of mention in a Canadian Press story, which might be picked up by local media.[47] The practice wound down as media economics demanded more captivating theatre and as political parties imposed greater communications conformity. In *The Newsmongers: How the Media Distort the Political News,* Mary Anne Comber and Robert Mayne identify ways that Canadian journalists construct the news to make it more controversial and captivating. Storytelling is more interesting when audiences are captivated by dynamic personalities and tragic characters. Speculation and controversy are encouraged. Pending cabinet shuffles are treated as "who's in, who's out" mysteries. Opinion surveys generate excitement and are used to pass judgments. News stories point out flip flops and use metaphors for conflict. Journalists create artificial polarities, such as by integrating comments from street interviews and experts, and they wrap up with parting shots. The authors explain the nature of politainment:

> In any story some politicians have lead roles and others are cast in supporting roles. They give performances and the spotlight tracks them across the political stage ... [This] allows journalists to play the role of theatre critic. Each day's performance can be reviewed and rated as successful or unsuccessful. Politics becomes a series of one-act plays with a new story almost every day. The role of the audience is to sit back and enjoy the show.[48]

Brand strategists are acutely aware that multiple political plays are on offer throughout the day in the digital media world. The formerly passive audience becomes an active participant through critiques and content generation. The proliferation of market-oriented journalism means that news is crafted based on a business model and that members of the public are consumers who must be pleased, not educated.[49] The idea of politics as theatre has been examined by media studies scholar Liesbet van Zoonen. She believes that politics is trivialized as a TV genre. Politicians are presented as serial characters and celebrities. Issues are tracked in story arcs, with attention paid to scandal, conflict, incompetence, and spin control. Stories are framed as a quest for a political objective, as bureaucratic ineptitude, as conspiracy theory, or as soap opera drama.[50] It is as though politics and government are comparable to a reality TV program filled with protagonists and antagonists, on whom the viewing audience passes judgment along with pundit judges.

Politicians respond to the media logic of politainment. Prime Minister Harper's appearance at a National Arts Centre (NAC) gala is a case in point. His criticism of elitist galas angered the Canadian artistic community during the 2008 election campaign. At the next year's G20 summit in Pittsburgh, Laureen Harper spoke with celebrity cellist Yo-Yo Ma about staging a pseudo-event and proceeded to work out the details with the NAC's chief executive officer.[51] The audience watching a performance by Ma at the NAC was stunned when the prime minister unexpectedly walked on stage toward a grand piano. In a stark contrast to his sombre image, Harper revealed a hidden talent by playing the piano while singing the Beatles hit "With a Little Help from My Friends." The witty selection referred to his minority government's tenuous hold on power, and the performance received a thunderous ovation. What was different from past turns of prime ministerial cool were the speed with which the pseudo-event became news and the number of media platforms on which it appeared. Moments after the performance, the PMO circulated a digital photograph of Harper playing piano during a rehearsal. The handout photo was reproduced on the front page of the *Globe and Mail*, under the impression that the photo had been taken at the live performance. Audience members with phone cameras uploaded their videos to social media. One YouTube video attracted over 500,000 hits that week alone, and it was an information subsidy for TV news programs, which aired it for days.[52] It was also posted on the homepage of the government's Economic Action Plan website, which caused some consternation among Ottawa watchers.

Building on this, over the years Harper played piano privately and publicly with journalists, political staffers, and Canadian musicians. One Conservative strategist reflected that "if you are sitting with him at his place ... he'll start playing the piano" (CS 7). The Conservatives sought to evoke recall of the NAC event through the congelation of other communications. Photos and videos issued by the PMO showed a Beatles coffee mug on the prime minister's desk. He drank from the mug in a Conservative Party TV ad. A *Maclean's* photo essay depicted the Harper family visiting the London recording studio of the Beatles and the prime minister playing music with his son at 24 Sussex. The cover of the Conservative Party's 2010 calendar, sent to select supporters, featured a photo of the Harpers crossing Abbey Road, in the style of the iconic cover of the Beatles album of the same name. Years later Harper sang the Beatles tune "Hey Jude" while playing piano at a Jewish fundraiser in Toronto, followed by an encore at a dinner with the Israeli prime minister during a visit to Israel in 2014. When he played with his band the Van Cats (a play on the French pronunciation of 24) at the Conservatives' Christmas party, the rehearsal was documented in *24 Seven* and became one of four scrolling photos on the government of Canada's homepage (Figure 3.2).[53] There is

FIGURE 3.2 PM's band featured on Government of Canada homepage | Screenshot by author, December 2014, www.canada.ca/.

such a yearning for new digital content that the PMO got into the business of creating information subsidies and politainment for the government itself. As with the fourth estate, the government is facing market pressures to deliver information in an entertaining manner, such as through emphasizing personalities and pop culture. Public and media fascination with Trudeau masks that the star treatment of the PM is cause for concern.

Celebritization

On Hallowe'en 2015, major news outlets, including the CBC, the *Globe and Mail*, and the *Ottawa Citizen*, filed tabloid stories of a smiling Justin Trudeau going trick-or-treating with his glamorous wife and three young children. It was a sharp contrast with how his predecessor was publicly depicted at the same stage on the path to the PMO (Figure 3.1). It was also a harbinger of the celebrity-style treatment of Canada's twenty-third prime minister.

As an extension of politainment, attention is paid to the personal character and public presentation of politicians, as the individual aspects that reveal the human side of political elites are discussed and debated. The personalization of politicians is understood to be a trend that arose because of a combination of media technologies and political strategies.[54] In particular, television focuses on individuals instead of the abstract collective of a political party, cabinet, or caucus. A result is that audiences become intrigued by the personal lives of political actors. In focus groups conducted for the Conservative Party, participants were less interested in the leader's policy remarks than in his persona. The party's pollster reported that people wanted "to understand what makes Harper tick" and that they liked his mentioning his family because "moments of candour were appreciated as an insight into his soul."[55]

The personalization and celebritization of public figures are partly a function of market-oriented journalism and partly a response to media logic by political elites. They teeter into areas that raise ethical questions. Should the media report that Harper made a late-night trip to the hospital because of a chest cold?[56] That Layton visited a massage parlour or, as the *Toronto Sun* framed it in the waning days of the 2011 federal election campaign, that years prior to his entry into federal politics he was allegedly found naked by police in a bawdy house?[57] That Mulcair and his wife remortgaged their home eleven times?[58] That Trudeau earned over $1 million in fees for giving speeches at charity events? Conversely, perhaps politicians open the door by talking about their private lives and by including their spouses and young children in public photographs and videos. The traditional role of the fourth estate in judging which private information is in the public interest is under stress against the values of a social media culture in which favouriting, friending, following, liking, and sharing selfies are norms.

To understand the branding of politicians, we need to recognize that there are different types of celebrity. Sociologist Chris Rojek differentiates between achieved, ascribed, and attributed forms.[59] People with achieved celebrity earn fame in recognition of their achievements in politics or other fields. They include first ministers and party leaders. Ascribed celebrity entails heightened public status and media fascination predetermined by biological descent. It encompasses the descendants of royalty or famous politicians. Ascribed fame is no longer a social norm. Aristocracy has been displaced by meritocracy as a social structure and by commoners who achieve notoriety by virtue of their perceived talents in open competitions. This leaves ascribed celebrities vulnerable to being attacked and ridiculed as elitist or being associated with the vapidity of untalented people who vie for public attention on reality TV or social media.[60] Such flash-in-the-pan phenomena allow people to build attributed celebrity by virtue of their temporary positions. Attributed celebrity includes those who hold jobs in the media business as well as some public office holders. Rojek's classifications are useful for interpreting types of personal brands and in particular Trudeau's candidacy (discussed in Chapter 4).

By far the main celebrity on the federal scene is the prime minister. That office holder is the de facto head of state in the eyes of the public – the person whom Canadian politics and government revolve around. The PM is at the centre of extensive communications resources of both government and the party in power. That figurehead is the focus of public demands made by international and domestic political organizations and individuals. As the NAC pseudo-event illustrates, prime ministers leverage their achieved celebrity to cross into the realm of pop culture celebrity. For instance, Prime Minister Martin appeared on an episode of CTV's *Corner Gas* in a cameo role. This caught Harper's attention and stoked his desire to do the same.[61] As prime minister, he played himself on an episode, an opportunity that did not exist as opposition leader. In it, he spoke to a captive scrum of journalists, blaming the former Liberal government for poor decisions. Next he appeared on *Murdoch Mysteries* as a policeman who jokes about hockey and does not know who the Liberal prime minister is. In another episode, he was credited for the plot idea. Harper also appeared on ethnic media programming, such as on the Mumbai-based *Dance Premier League*. He was regularly interviewed during live hockey programming, including on days that he shunned the press gallery. These are among the many non-political forums in which a prime minister has privileged access and avoids being drawn into policy banter.

Celebritization draws celebrities to the PM and the PM to celebrities. In this century, the most active engagement of a celebrity in a Canadian political pseudo-event occurred at the 2003 Liberal leadership convention when U2's Bono celebrated Martin's ascendency. There has also been celebrity activism such as indie rock band Arcade Fire speaking out against the Conservatives and musician Neil Young calling for an end to oil sands development. The stars really seem to come out when there is an opportunity to generate soft publicity. Courtesy of Conservative PMO digital image bites, we know that the prime minister mingled with Canadian hockey stars such as Sidney Crosby, Wayne Gretzky, Gordie Howe, Connor McDavid, and Bobby Orr; Canadian musicians such as Bryan Adams, Jann Arden, Justin Bieber, and Nickelback; celebrity senators such as Jacques Demers, Mike Duffy, and Pamela Wallin; select premiers and mayors; international stars such as Bollywood actor Akshay Kumar; international dignitaries ranging from Governor of California Arnold Schwarzenegger to members of the Royal Family; and Olympic and Paralympic athletes. Government communicators sometimes draw celebrity power to attract media attention. The Canadian Tourism Commission's (CTC) Brand Canada campaign saw Kumar participate in the Olympic torch relay and sprinter Donovan Bailey and actor Gordon Pinsent appear in domestic tourism advertising.[62] Celebrating famous Canadians is a regular occurrence at Canadian embassies in major international cities. As well, political parties recruit homegrown celebrities to run for office, and backbenchers are catapulted into the spotlight when they are appointed to cabinet.

These types of mutual exchange reinforce the stardom and brand lustre of both host and participant. The publicity helps politicians reach less politically engaged voters through entertainment magazine programming such as *ET Canada* and daytime talk shows such as CTV's *The Social*. The primacy of the brand and office requires that the prime minister have the upper hand. The following message was posted to Harper's Facebook and Twitter accounts on May 2, 2010: "Played 'Run to You' with Bryan Adams at 24 Sussex http://twitpic.com/1kbmrn." The link led to a photograph of Harper sitting at a piano and a jovial Adams holding a guitar. Reporters filed stories in mainstream and specialty media about how the PM with an economist image mingled with rock stars in his official residence.[63] "We invite people over to jam and you know, Bryan Adams or Jann Arden or – like whoever, it doesn't matter," Laureen Harper said in an end-of-year interview.[64] Two years later Adams revealed that the purpose of his visit was to urge the reform of copyright laws. "The next thing you know, we're playing music in his living room and I realize it's a photo op. The only publicity the story got is that Bryan Adams got to play with Stephen Harper. It was quite disturbing," the musician lamented.[65]

Strategy Frame

As Adams experienced, political elites seek to control information and perception. Disciples of Sun Tzu and Machiavelli, and anyone working in the political arena, can attest that democratic politics is a figurative blood sport. Political participants practise war games, such as surprise and deception, in order to gain an advantage.[66] It follows that reporting about politics invokes language of sports and war to describe elections, government, and public policy.[67] Identifying winners and losers in an endless series of mini contests provides the dramatic story arcs and politainment that make for captivating storytelling. Interest in disclosing political strategy grows with the controversy stemming from certain branding practices.

Aside from elections, the most pervasive tool for treating politics and government as a contest is the public opinion survey. Opinion polls and horse-race coverage, as well as bloggers' analyses of seat projections, are rising in Canadian media.[68] Polls are used by journalists to guide the subjective treatment of serious matters. Opinion research offers a shroud of detachment from the politicians being covered.[69] At best, polling data provide an objective measure of the public mood and inform political analysis; at worst, they are an inaccurate predictor of who will win an election, leading to fiasco situations.[70] Some media underplay a poll's margin of error[71] and inaccurately interpret data, to the point that "media coverage of election polls deceives more than it informs."[72] This deception is compounded by the popularity of unscientific online straw polls, for instance a "question of the day" on news websites, an easy way to encourage audience engagement while creating an information subsidy subject to political manipulation.[73] This leads to less than ideal news coverage. As a civil servant observed, "it's easier to cover the horse-race in polls than to do a detailed analysis of what's in the Budget Implementation Act" (CM 20).

Polling data are politainment that frames politics as a fierce battle between adversaries and gives a dramatic flair to political news. The media's agitation extends beyond horse-race speculation about winners and losers. Political elites are judged through a game lens on almost any topic – votes in the legislature, cabinet shuffles, floor crossings, scandals, court verdicts, public policy positions, interest groups' critiques, and so forth. The media are relentless. Was a knockout punch landed in the leaders' debate? Who was on the ropes in QP? Who gains and who loses from this morning's policy announcement? Who is leading in the latest quarterly fundraising results? The desire to compartmentalize multifaceted matters into the storytelling simplicity of a scorecard is relentless.

These forms of media logic tap journalists' interest in political strategies and media tactics. Digital media expand what presidential observer Colin Seymour-Ure calls "tertiary communication" – the incessant and uncontrollable media speculation pertaining to the head of government.[74] The thinking behind political decisions is interpreted by pundits. Guesswork ensues about a leader's feelings or state of mind. Journalists disclose attempts by non-media elites to manipulate the media. They report on politicians' efforts to outmanoeuvre opponents and to curry the electorate's favour. They reveal how PR staff behave, and they dissect the marketing strategy behind negative advertising. The strategy frame is an outcome of a number of converging dynamics, among them communications technology, the political system, and the media industry.[75] News is personalized on the basis of a reporter's first-hand experiences. For some, the strategy frame is an assertion of media independence in response to stonewalling and spin doctoring. Faced with restricted access to public officials, and frustrated by feelings of shabby treatment, journalists report on process and insider minutiae.

The quality and execution of political strategy are treated as a barometer of professionalism and, by extension, act as an indicator of the suitability of a political leader or party to govern. This assessment is temporal, for what is state-of-the-art becomes outdated and amateur. Acts of centralization and image management that inhibit the media's ability to investigate are critiqued for being anti-democratic. A moment later the same behaviour is cited as evidence of a well-oiled machine. Political strategists become conditioned to the media logic that requires meticulous attention to communications details. In the summer of 2005, the Conservative Party identified fifty-one news stories about its advertising. Of these stories, five negative stories resulted from the misspelling of an MP's name, and two negative stories critiqued the ads for not being enabled for the hearing impaired.[76] After that formative period (see Chapter 5), political observers credited the Conservative team for their strategic and tactical prowess. During the 2006 election campaign, the *Globe and Mail* reasoned that the party's lead in opinion polls was related to its astute media management. It was one among many stories praising the strategy of setting the daily agenda by announcing policies in the morning, such as the GST pseudo-event described in Chapter 2.[77] One Conservative respondent believed that Harper's "greatest contribution" was turning the Conservative Party "into a professional organization" (CM 2). Often this coincided with the dominant party's framing of an opponent as not being ready to govern. The trotting out of a Liberal Party brochure about home care that inadvertently included a photo of a man holding a cigarette[78] is one way to encourage a contrast between strategic amateurism and superiority and sustain an atmosphere of pseudo-scandal. The tables turned in 2015 when blunders made the Conservative campaign seem amateur compared with the well-run Liberal campaign.

Pseudo-Scandal

Today's voters are more educated and critical than ever before. They nevertheless become gripped by sensationalist media coverage, with the newest salacious details of minor indiscretions travelling quickly.[79] Media chatter about real crises – natural disasters, armed conflicts, health epidemics, labour shutdowns, cases of corruption – is interspersed with comparatively trivial issues such as an off-colour remark or a choice of clothing regarded as outrageous and deserving of mockery. Even the most stable of governments are portrayed as fluttering from problem to problem. Pseudo-scandal is constant and feeds the gossipy world of social media.

The personalization and celebritization of public figures make them particularly susceptible to being caught in a media firestorm. Ever since the Stanfield fumbled football incident, Canadian politicians have been acutely aware that even a minor blunder can damage their careers. In his seminal study of public performances, sociologist Erving Goffman referred to unmeant gestures as gaffes observed at ill-timed moments. They lead to "performance disruption."[80] The need to prevent performance disruption increases with the possibility of inopportune intrusions. In a digital society, minor indiscretions caught on video are repeated and dissected ad nauseam, particularly during slow news periods. This happened when Harper allegedly pocketed a communion wafer at the funeral mass for former Governor General Roméo LeBlanc. Public furor ensued as grainy video of the prime minister at the altar was replayed in slow motion, frame by frame. Did he consume the wafer or not? Witnesses were interviewed, and pundits debated the severity of the reported transgression. Later it was revealed that inaccurate details were reported about "Wafergate" by the New Brunswick *Telegraph-Journal*. The erroneous information was repeated as fact by other media. The newspaper issued a front-page apology and sanctioned its editor and publisher. Harper called the affair "a low moment in journalism."[81] The media quickly moved on.

The Wafergate episode illustrates why the political class is preoccupied with communications control. Those at the top of the communications pyramid suggest that it requires incredible resolve and energy for the leader and courtiers to stand their ground during moments of penetrating pressure. "Don't underestimate how difficult it is to stay focused on message when your press office and everyone around you is shivering because of a pseudo-scandal," advised a former PMO strategist (CS 4). Stockwell Day added that "it's almost unbearably fatiguing" to push back against communications advisors and colleagues recommending a different course of action. "There's a constant to and fro, and a good leader will invite that. But it takes phenomenal emotional and intellectual strength to stick with a message that you, as leader, believe is absolutely requisite and to stick to a few key points that you want driven home" (CP 4). Day was referring to the barrage of negativity that awaits almost every decision made by a member of cabinet or party leader. When communications are slipshod, they expose new flanks upon which opponents can pounce. Conversely, a leader who has the fortitude to stick to a brand strategy and figures out how to play the media logic game will limit unpredictable pseudo-scandals. Even so, media controversy will still follow a leader's decisions, including over the very management tactics invoked to inhibit any hullabaloo.

POLITICAL ADVERTISING

Finally, the most important tool in the branding and image management toolbox is advertising. It encompasses controlled communications purchased in print, radio, television, online, and other media such as billboards and conference kiosks. Advertising should reinforce all other communications and vice versa. Public sector advertising is purchased by political parties (discussed here) and by the permanent government at the direction of cabinet (discussed in Chapter 8).

Political advertising has many objectives. It seeks to improve party morale and to encourage supporters to donate. It tests creative and strategic messages. It stimulates voter interest and knowledge, changes impressions of candidates, and keeps contestants accountable. A Conservative strategist explains that "the reality about political advertising is it doesn't need to work while it's running. What it needs to do is accurately predict behaviour by your opponent that will reinforce the message that you are delivering."[82] Whatever the advertising message or theme, it must be consistent with all other communications, as another Conservative advertising expert explained:

> To be effective, your advertising has to be connected strategically, and on the same message, and vice versa. You could create the best ad in the world. Hit it with a thousand GRPs [gross ratings points], be all over the air, well, that thing will fall flat on its face, and it'll be a waste of dollars if you say something completely different

when you're on the campaign trail. So if your media is done well
and it aligns with the ad campaign, it's like double the size of your
ad buy in terms of how effective it could be. (CS 7)

As well, with a large media buy, there can be a quid pro quo expectation
of better news treatment and/or opportunities for op-eds and punditry.

Drawing on media behaviour statistics from sources such as
ComScore and Numeris is essential to reach targeted elector segments in
a cost-efficient manner. This is more science than art because of the fragmentation of media into specialty programming and the growth of Internet media. For instance, it is intuitive that the best way to reach a market
segment of active sportsmen is through The Sports Network (TSN) or
Sportsnet or any other sports programming. In fact, media analysis indicates that reaching them by advertising on *The Simpsons* animated sitcom
delivers better value.[83] During the 2006 campaign, Conservative Party
media planners prioritized programs watched by Canadians 25 to 54 years
old (skewing 35 to 54), adults 55+, and women 55+.[84] This resulted in
media buys on the CTV network and on specialty cable stations favoured
by target audiences, namely Bravo, CBC Newsworld, HGTV, History,
Prime, TSN, and W. To reach men 18 to 34 years old, advertising was
purchased on Discovery, Space, Sportsnet, and TSN. The party advertised
on Channel M, Fairchild, Omni 1 and 2, and Telelatino to reach ethnic
markets. Advertising on the main CBC network, or on specialty channels
such as MuchMusic and the Business News Network, was dismissed as not
having the potential to offer good value for reaching targeted audience
segments. The party employed a flighting strategy whereby the impression
of a constant presence is given through intermittent advertising (i.e., some
blackout days). This technique stretches the media buy because people
remember seeing the advertisement and forget that they were not exposed
to it the previous day.[85] Political parties also experiment with innovative
ways of matching the medium with the message. The Conservatives painted
their logo on a stock racing car and later purchased fifteen-second audiovisual advertisements on fuel pumps equipped with small screens to drive
home a message that the Liberals would increase gas taxes.

Given that the objective of most advertising is to persuade rather than
inform, and to change opinions and behaviours, its practice has long

troubled communications scholars. This harkens back to outdated theories such as the hypodermic needle model, which alleges that messages are injected into a receiver's mind. More sophisticated, and troubling, strategies use psychology to trigger an emotional response, including images and sounds that alter how a message is received.[86] The extent to which political advertising constitutes propaganda is a matter of debate. Propaganda is a loaded term that involves biased communications as part of a controversial power struggle.[87] At its worst, it attempts psychological conditioning and brainwashing for violent purposes, as with the promotion of falsehoods and anti-Semitism by the Nazi Germany regime.[88] More commonly, propaganda involves peaceful yet provocative messages repeated to persuade target audiences about a public policy position. This involves the systematic communication of emotional images in an attempt to shape public opinion. Video propaganda is prized because it can trigger an emotional response among members of various cultures and demographic cohorts. Thus, feel-good advertising that stirs nationalist or patriotic feelings is more propagandist, and more effective, than straightforward information.

Confusion reigns over whether the morphing of political government and permanent government communications results in propaganda. Rose demonstrated that the analysis of advertising entails figuring out the sender's intent. This requires a thorough dissection of planning documents and an examination of the advertising itself by studying rhetoric and semiotics.[89] More often than not it is a grey area. Take the Conservative Party's *Rising to the Challenge* video of 2011 that depicted Harper working late on Parliament Hill. The pre-election ad shows him walking along a hallway and up some stairs in the Parliament Buildings. The camera passes by a brass doorplate inscribed "THE PRIME MINISTER." The scene shifts to inside Centre Block Room 309-S. Harper is busy working at his desk attending to paperwork, surrounded by Canadian flags, and pausing to drink from a Beatles coffee mug. A voiceover coos about the Conservative government's economic policy achievements and how we Canadians are in "safe hands" with Harper, who cannot stop working for us. The closing scene shows the outside of the Parliament Buildings, with a tagline that the Conservative Party is "here for Canada." To some, there is nothing untoward about communicating the reality that a party leader is the head of government and seeking credit for public policy achievements. To others, Room 309-S is funded by all Canadians, and the government party must not exploit it for partisan advantage.

Advertising plays a profound role in Canadian political life and public sector branding. It sets agendas; frames political debate and a leader's image; is an information subsidy for news reports about political strategy; is a source of politainment; celebritizes party leaders; and, in the event of a particularly offensive ad, becomes a pseudo-scandal. A review of the theories and strategies of political advertising is beyond the scope of this book. Suffice it to say that one widely cited schema differentiates three types of advertising that seek to damage an opponent's brand.[90] Comparative ads contrast negative information about an opponent with positive information about the message sponsor. Negative ads deride an opponent's policy positions, drawing on public remarks, actions, and proposals. The most aggressive form is attack advertising, which targets an individual's character, lifestyle, and/or appearance and highlights comments out of context. The style and tone are every bit as important as the claims. The worst of them mimic the aesthetics of a trailer for a horror movie: dark background colours, unflattering or scary images of an opponent, grainy footage presented in slow motion, sinister background music and sound effects, snippets of provocative text. The goal is to provoke a lasting emotional response, whereby audience outrage at the perceived nastiness of the message sponsor is fleeting compared with the enduring negativity attached to the targeted brand. Ideally, the advertising will be treated as newsworthy and influence how journalists cover the news.

Judging by news stories and punditry, Canadians decry negative ads as unwanted American-style politicking that undermines an otherwise healthy democracy. They fail to consider that negative advertising is indirectly subsidized by the Canadian public through party financing regulations, such as the tax-deductible eligibility of political donations and post-election spending reimbursements. Many Canadians also overlook how competitive and nasty politics can get, a topic explored in Chapter 6.

4

Public Sector Brands

In politics, a crisis mentality is common; in the digital media environment, the urgency is magnified. The hoots and wails of social media exacerbate the intensity of political issues management. Branding introduces a sense of calm and confidence to counter the communications maelstrom. Government entities that compete in the consumer marketplace, such as Crown corporations, are long-time subscribers to marketing principles. Branding strategy now pervades other areas of the public sector. Places, tourist destinations, sports, products, corporations, public policies, political parties, and politicians are all branded.[1]

PLACE BRANDS

Branding is a component of international image and reputation management. Place branding pertains to communications designed to create an emotional impression of a country, city, or some other destination.[2] It extends to awareness, opinions, and stereotypes of the place's icons, residents, economy, geography, history, products, culture, celebrities, and politics. Place branding is an important component of tourism marketing, sports marketing, product marketing, and international diplomacy, to name some of the more prominent topics (another is pop culture). In theory, promoting a strong place brand generates economic growth. It stimulates interest in natural resources and tourism. It can attract specialized labour and immigration, encourage the relocation of business operations, and so on.

To Jonathan Rose, place branding and its subtypes (e.g., tourism branding, sports branding, product branding) represent the commercialization of statecraft. Logos and brands are mechanisms to reimagine a nation. Branding enables a place to forget its unfortunate past or undesirable present and to overcome negative stereotypes. The results are a "commodification of citizenship and a reinforcement of shallow nationalism."[3] He suggests that place branding can be an exercise in futility. It is up against the power of international news media to shape public opinion and faces the considerable difficulty of communicating with global audiences.

Rose is correct that place branding is difficult to execute. For Canada, a significant challenge is an absence of what Timothy Grayson, a strategic advisor with Canada Post, refers to as "the master brand."[4] The way that Grayson sees it, the master brand is the agreed upon core of the country's character. Canada lacks the national myth and cultural homogeneity present in other countries, and it has a conflicted sense of its national character. There are strong regional and Indigenous identities, and Canadians are thought to be ambivalent about their national history. The domestic media perpetuate that national unity is frail and that the country has an international image problem. A serious nation-branding exercise, he reasons, requires generating public awareness of Canada's past and the Canadian identity.

Grayson understates that Canada's place brand tends to be congruent with the values of the party in power. Richard Nimijean posits that Canadian values are framed by the governing party, most often the Liberal Party.[5] The Chrétien and Martin governments promoted "the Canadian way" to market their party's view of civic values and global citizenship. They and other Liberals frame Canada's brand as synonymous with the Liberal Party's self-image as unifiers. Trudeau conveyed this ideology during the 2015 campaign by arguing that

> Canada is a country that has succeeded because we look at diversity and differences as a source of strength, of resilience within our communities. We're there for each other as a country. And when [Conservative] leadership chooses to highlight differences and exploit those differences for

political gain, we start turning away from what has made Canada successful in the past. This openness, this understanding, this generosity.[6]

To Liberals, Canada is a nation of communitarianism, dualism, and multiculturalism. Canadians are portrayed as peaceful brokers of human security
who are better than Americans. This portrayal instills patriotism and
identity attachment and occurs irrespective of Canada's policy record or
that of Liberal administrations. Nimijean urges caution, concluding that
"the conscious effort to equate partisan political issues with national values
is one of the dangers of national branding strategies."[7]

Even if the political will exists to create a master brand, doing so is
fraught with difficulty. Aligning brand tangibles is challenging, even more
so coordinating the intangibles. An official flag is the main brand symbol
of nations, whereas organizations such as the National Capital Commission create a logo. The difficult part is that government departments and
units have their own agendas and cultures. Some of them unilaterally
promote their own view of the master brand in a manner not unified by a
core set of messages. The Canadian Tourism Commission positions Canada
as an emotional destination experience. Not long ago the Department of
Foreign Affairs and International Trade (DFAIT) promoted Canada as a
high-tech brand, and it recently partnered with provincial departments of
education to support an Imagine Education in Canada brand. Agriculture
and Agri-Food Canada emphasizes natural quality. And on the dis-
symmetry goes.

In *Branding Canada: Projecting Canada's Soft Power through Public
Diplomacy,* Evan Potter explains that nation branding was once the concern
of government tourism boards.[8] This function gravitated to foreign affairs
as part of the soft power diplomacy concerned with the country's brand,
because how nations see each other is a persuasive mechanism in international relations. Projecting a consistent image on the world stage communicates economic stability. It promotes policy interests and values and
shapes international alliances. Nation branding also involves stickhandling
around diplomatic controversies. When DFAIT introduced its Brand
Canada strategy in 2001, the objective was to increase Canada's profile
and image at industry trade shows. Coordinated communications included
the redesign of pavilions, timed cultural events, and the use of common

graphics and promotional materials.[9] Notwithstanding PMJT's initial frays (see Preface), even coordinated efforts cannot change the fact that Canada has a low public profile on the world stage. Potter reasons that low awareness of Canada in global affairs is related to the country's limited presence in international broadcasting. Resources are spread across federal government departments and agencies, and confusion results from provincial paradiplomacy, especially by Quebec. He suggests that Canada would benefit from "a more strategic, whole of government and whole of Canada approach" to public diplomacy and its international brand.[10] Whole of government communications are discussed in Chapter 9.

The challenges of place branding on the global stage are indeed significant. Place branding is rooted in political identities and institutional processes, and this makes recalibration difficult when there is a change of government. Global audiences are exposed to a barrage of information beyond the marketer's control, ranging from schooling and reference groups to the arts and news media. Moreover, international controversies derail branding. Participation or lack thereof in military campaigns, international accords, regional initiatives, leaders' summits, and other international organizations and events creates an international position that might be incongruent with the brand. Take the Canadian seal hunt.[11] Each spring disturbing photos and video clips are circulated of seal pups being killed on pristine ice floes. International interest groups label Canada a haven for bloodthirsty barbarians. Nude protesters covered in red paint descend on Canadian embassies, with media in tow. Boycotts are coordinated against the country's seafood and tourism industries. Suddenly, Canada warrants attention in global media centres, but such attention conflicts with a soft diplomacy image of a communitarian country with natural beauty and a modern economy. In such circumstances, civil servants are obliged to communicate the official position of the government of Canada and to correct misinformation. This must occur regardless of departmental interests or civil servants' personal worldviews. A communications manager in DFAIT emphasized the pragmatism of message consistency throughout government in controversial situations. He relayed that the public service must ensure that "there's one message, and there's no confusion, so that journalists don't get one message, then phone another department and get a different message" (CS 19). When the flood of media controversy subsides, the policy controversy is all but forgotten. Work resumes on promoting a Canadian place brand inconsistent at times with some nationalist policies that play to domestic audiences.

TOURISM BRANDS

A subtype of place branding connected to political identity is tourism branding. The marketing of tourism destinations is thought to constitute an outcome of neoliberal new governance models. National and subnational government tourism agencies promote what is unique about a destination. They seek to connect on an emotional level about the experience that awaits potential visitors.[12] At the forefront of tourism branding is tourism advertising. It is thinly veiled propaganda that attempts to win over audiences exposed to a fanciful version of reality. Idealistic visuals, icons of landmarks and natural beauty, distinctive slogans, and information about special events are communicated. Disciplined and repetitive communication in tourism campaigns "introduces order, certainty and coherence into an unruly urban landscape," for instance through a consistent style of street signage.[13] The leading spokesperson is normally the head of government, whose public image might be too close to the tourism brand (suggesting an excess of concentrated power) or too different from it (creating marketing problems).

Tourism branding is typical of public sector branding in that it features collaborative and exclusionary processes. Happiness and unity are conveyed to prospective visitors, but behind the scenes political power struggles emerge as stakeholders exert their authority and persuasive skills to achieve policies that reflect their values and interests.[14] Internal debate occurs over whether tourism campaigns envelop competing senses of place identity. Area representatives lobby for their locales to be promoted as preferred destinations for tourists to spend money. Elitism is prevalent as senior decision makers preside over an otherwise pluralistic undertaking. This is particularly true in cities.[15]

The politics of tourism marketing comes through in strategic efforts to reposition Canada's colonial and pastoral image into a branding muddle of "a progressive, vibrant nation full of people, culture, colour, nightlife, art, architecture, shopping, music, culinary traditions, fashion and stunning scenery and adventure" worth exploring.[16] To this end, the Canadian Tourism Commission introduced its aforementioned Brand Canada campaign. Its version of Brand Canada should not be confused with similarly named but different strategies launched by other government departments and agencies. The initiative aligned with the commission's objective of communications uniformity and clarity:

> Brand consistency is critical to positioning Canada as a premier tourist destination. The brand essence must remain the same across all communication mediums – advertising campaigns, consumer websites, visiting journalist programs or promotional activities with the trade. Coordinated and consistent branding and marketing will clearly define for customers the experiences that Canada offers and move Canada from a destination of consideration to one of choice.[17]

Among those tourism experiences are athletic pursuits, which themselves are branded.

SPORTS BRANDS

Another subset of place branding that is deeply connected to political identity is sports branding.[18] At international competitions, athletes display unity by wearing identical patriotic uniforms and waving the flag. They and their fellow citizens rally around a cohesive national identity brand. The opening and closing ceremonies of sports events celebrate the heritage of the host jurisdiction. Contests between rivals take on political symbolism: victories project an image of success and modernity, whereas losses and embarrassments wound national pride. Athletes become heroes and even icons whose personalities and stories epitomize an idealized national character.

Branding is a strategic tool for the Canadian Olympic Committee, concerned with integrating "the digital space, graphic design, elite photography, hard research and overall content planning and capture" throughout the organization.[19] In Canada, sports branding conjures up images associated with the maple leaf and Team Canada. Hockey is the identity sport of choice and is part of Canadian culture. It, along with sports such as

FIGURE 4.1   Prime Minister Harper's CANADA jacket and hockey imagery |
Prime Minister's Office (2015a); PMO photographer Jason Ransom, Kingston, January 10, 2015.

curling and Canadian football, is commodified by the tourism industry[20] and economic sector, notably event sponsors and patriotic brands such as Tim Hortons.[21]

The nationalism and patriotism of sports drew the Conservative Party to associate the brand of Stephen Harper with hockey and other winter sports (Figure 4.1). As opposition leader, he took a calculated image management risk by tossing a football with Peter MacKay on the front lawn of Parliament Hill in 2005. A more controlled winter sports strategy was advocated by Republican political consultant Frank Luntz, who reportedly urged the party to emphasize visuals and images of hockey as a slice of Canadiana that appeals to the Conservatives' base.[22] The Harper Conservatives initiated hockey-themed pseudo-events, issued digital image bites with hockey personalities, and ensured that the prime minister was seen by sports media at live events. This fanaticism extends so far that the government supported naming a new international bridge connecting Detroit and Windsor after NHL star Gordie Howe. Other examples are mentioned in this book, including that Harper published a book on hockey while prime minister. In the words of one Conservative strategist, the party targets "high school, middle-income, average Canadians. Hard-working people generally who have families or want families, many of whom are faith-based, with two or three children, trying to get ahead, worried about paying off their mortgage. Those are all the people that love hockey, right? They don't love the opera" (CS 12). Party insiders say that it was an easy sell because their boss was a bona fide hockey fan, which brings authenticity to the projected brand image.

PRODUCT BRANDS

The maple leaf is prominent on Canadian athletes' uniforms as well as on Canadian product labels. The branding of goods and services, particularly commodities, with national images is emblematic of a product orientation becoming a sales orientation. Governments seek to increase the purchase of domestic products by requiring that the country of origin be specified on the packaging. This labelling raises or lowers perceptions of quality and safety assurance on imports and exports, depending on the country's image.[23] Applying a country of origin marker is a low-cost, free-rider marketing strategy with potential upside for smaller ventures in particular.[24] Geographic labelling is a successful differentiation mechanism, albeit one not free of risk. It is branding by symbiosis, for the domestic firm's reputation is harnessed to the country's reputation. Commercial brand managers are therefore confronted by the lack of control over a shared brand symbol and the effects of the country's image on the product. This poses a problem during periods of political uproar, for instance international boycotts of Canadian seafood to express outrage over the seal hunt.

In Canada, the federal government regulates country-of-origin claims. The Consumer Packaging and Labelling Act requires that statements indicating that a product was made in Canada must be truthful. To reproduce the Canadian coat of arms, manufacturers must obtain permission from the Treasury Board Secretariat, and the Department of Canadian Heritage must approve reproductions of the official version of the Canadian flag. Manufacturers can display the maple leaf without government permission as long as it does not appear with one bar or both bars found in the government of Canada wordmark (Figure 8.1). The leaf is the primary symbol promoted by the Department of Agriculture and Agri-Food's Canada Brand strategy that differentiates Canadian-made products. The strategy offers producers access to simplified supports that include a photo bank, branding graphics, and messaging for product labels and promotional activities. This is intended to ensure a common visual identity under the "Made in Canada" label, associated with being trustworthy and of good quality (Figure 8.5). Nationalistic branding in the Canadian economic sector is all but certain to evoke the brand iconography found in public sector brands, principally a red maple leaf.

CORPORATE BRANDS

The application of private sector marketing practices to the public sector is particularly visible in corporate branding. It refers to the management of an organization's image, identity, and reputation through a coherent and repeated set of simple visual messages, including logos, slogans, and themes. The intended benefits of these identity cues include brand loyalty, improved employee recruitment and retention, and more capable issues management.[25] When a corporate image is not achieving its strategic objectives, decision makers put the organization through a rebranding process by refreshing its look and competitive positioning.[26] Minor adjustments to marketing aesthetics, such as a revamped logo, signal that something about the organization is new. Major change involves fundamental market repositioning and choosing a new name or possibly brokering a corporate merger. This is rare because it means the abandonment of years of communications that built the brand.

Observers of political communications should consider that financial institutions are among the most successful corporate brands in Canada. Interbrand compiles rankings of the top twenty-five Canadian private sector brands. It calculates brand value by analyzing the brand's financial performance, the role of the brand in purchase decisions, and the brand's competitive positioning. Canada's big five banks (BMO, CIBC, RBC, Scotiabank, TD Bank) hold most of the top positions and are buttressed by other financial services companies (Investors Group, Manulife Financial, National Bank).[27] Media organizations (Bell, Cineplex, Imax, Rogers, Shaw, Telus, Thomson Reuters), clothing retailers (LaSensa, Lululemon Athletica, Winners), retail outlets (Canadian Tire, Dollarama, Shoppers Drug Mart), the food/beverage category (Molson, Tim Hortons), and

transportation (CP, WestJet) round out the 2014 ranking. The safe bland-
ness and dollop of patriotism exhibited in many of these private sector
brands pervade the Canadian public sector. There is no Apple equivalent.

In public administration, corporate branding encompasses the government's international and domestic image and that of its many organizational units. The government of Canada's corporate brand, under the
auspices of the Federal Identity Program (see Chapter 8), has been consistent since the early 1970s, when central agencies began to unify the
government's many sub-brands under a master brand. The program is an
all-embracing if cumbersome undertaking. Many subcultures and identities exist in government, with shifting political values, such that government departments themselves wrestle with branding. The Canadian Forces
is a case in point. Faced with the need to attract recruits in the early 2000s,
the Department of National Defence (DND) ran Liberal-approved advertising that projected a peaceful career in the military.[28] The ads depicted
non-combat positions and concluded with the tagline "Think about it."
Focus group research found this to be at odds with media coverage of armed
conflict in Afghanistan and Iraq. But efforts to rebrand the Canadian Forces
faced internal identity resistance. It was difficult to agree on target markets
and to figure out how to overcome an array of public perceptions. DND's
recalibration of its recruitment advertising to promote a message of fighting
with the Canadian Forces aligned with a different philosophical approach
under the new Conservative administration. The first spots approved by
the Conservatives depicted on-the-ground scenes with a large maple leaf
in the background and the tagline "Fight with the Canadian Forces." From
mid-2005 to early 2008, DND spent more on advertising than any other
department as part of the Canadian Forces recruitment campaign, related
to service in Afghanistan.[29] Aside from the challenges of coordination
within the DND, there were media relations tussles with the PMO, which
clamped down on the DND's willingness to accommodate media access
to combat situations. The restrictions increased the media's reliance on
the Combat Camera website.[30] Communications control of the social
media era came to the fore in 2014 when the commander of the Canadian army sent a memo stating that soldiers who leak internal information to the media would be subject to disciplinary action.[31] Such internal

brand management difficulties occur within organizations throughout government at the same time as central agencies try to advance a master brand subject to change.

PUBLIC POLICY BRANDING

A major facet of public sector communications is the branding of public policy. Media strategy and issues management play a formidable role in the stages of public policy formation, from agenda setting to implementation. A Treasury Board exempt staffer said that heated exchanges within government rarely occur over a policy snafu; rather, communications lead to disputes.

> I've never heard the PMO call to dress down someone for a policy mistake. It's always been a communications thing. Because communications, it's hard to fix. If you make a policy mistake and it hasn't been communicated yet, normally you can fix it. If you're on the front page of the newspaper saying something incorrect, or not the party line, or not approved policy, it's out there, and you can't pull it back in. (CM 21)

Policy has time to evolve, whereas negative media coverage causes immediate tension. It is a truism in public administration that good public policy can be derailed by poor communications, but good communications cannot sell bad policy.

We can treat public policy branding as the evoked synthesis of policy information advanced by governments, political parties, politicians, interest groups, opinion leaders, and the media. Public policy expert Michael Howlett suggests that government communications tools revolve around front-end policy development and back-end policy implementation.[32] Information disclosed through access to information laws, whistleblower protections, the legislature's oversight offices, and program evaluation data can damage a policy's brand. Public policy can be shielded when the government does not release information. Furthermore, government seeks to persuade audiences through product labelling, e-government, advertising, and publicity. Howlett points out that even the simplest forms of policy branding are subject to communications slants. For instance, select information is leaked to the media, and expressions of social morality are found in the labelling of cigarette packaging. A broader trend that he does not delve into is the extent to which complex policy details are reduced to planned sound bites, image bites, and 140-character tweets.

According to an American activist, public policies must "have a brand name that can: simplify a complex issue; influence public and legislative opinion; be memorable and emotionally appealing; and help unify diverse groups around a common platform."[33] Positions and perceptions are clustered into an ideology (e.g., new right, third way). A tussle ensues over the framing and counterframing of a specific policy proposal (e.g., a green shift versus a carbon tax). The choice of words is calculated – *oil* becomes *energy, prostitution* becomes *sex trade work,* and so on. Occasionally, an established program is rebranded, such as the renaming of Unemployment Insurance as Employment Insurance. The branding of policy turns complex topics into understandable ones for the masses. Diverse interests are brought together under an umbrella of common vocabulary and shared policy objectives. Long names for legislation including omnibus bills are shortened, and bills are named in a consumer-friendly manner that fits the government's master brand message. The Economic Action Plan Act to implement the budget and the Canada-Honduras Economic Growth and Prosperity Act, which implemented a free-trade agreement, are examples.

The simplicity of branding is both a gift and a worrying development for public policy observers. Public debate is dumbed down as symbols act as cognitive placeholders for more complex information. Government waste is symbolized by the procurement of an expensive office item[34] or politicians invoicing the government for small items. Memorable examples are Bev Oda charging for her sixteen-dollar glass of orange juice and former Liberal minister David Dingwall testifying to a House of Commons committee while waving a pack of gum as a prop for whether he claimed the $1.29 item as an expense. Complexity is denied through the labelling of policies with patriotic words, which results in opponents being offside with public opinion, as when critics of Canada's role in Afghanistan were faced with an onslaught of political correctness to "support the troops." Doublespeak occurs, as with voting restrictions introduced in the Fair Elections Act.

The branding of public policy evolves with changes in media relations practices and the lifespan of a governing political party. Kirsten Kozolanka observes that policy making, media systems, political culture, and strategy became more sinister under the Chrétien and Martin governments, which "shifted focus from substance to image, from information to promotion, and from policy to communications."[35] The same trend was found in the Harper administration. When the Conservatives formed the government, their signature policy was to clean up Ottawa after the sponsorship scandal. The Act Providing for Conflict of Interest Rules, Restrictions on Election Financing, and Measures Respecting Administrative Transparency, Oversight, and Accountability sought to improve accountability and transparency. It was simply referred to as the populist Accountability Act. It is instructive to compare the standard media relations protocols at that time with the onset of social media. As PM designate, Harper held a news conference in the National Press Theatre, where he sat in front of a static backdrop of a row of flags while journalists lobbed questions. News releases were written in a story style. Text-heavy backgrounders, fact sheets, and the draft legislation were stored on a custom website (accountability.gc.ca). The media materials were available upon request by telephone or email. Further information about the proposed Accountability Act could be obtained by calling the desk phone numbers of Treasury Board Secretariat communications staffers. Compare this with the policy focus on the master brand when the end of the Canadian Wheat Board's protectionist monopoly was marked. In August 2012, Prime Minister Harper feted the coming into force of the Marketing Freedom for Grain Farmers Act by staging an outdoors media event in a wheat field near Kindersley, Saskatchewan. He and other speakers stood in front of a crowd of invited farmers and media, supported by a lectern adorned with a sign proclaiming, in capital letters, "MARKETING FREEDOM / LIBERTÉ DE MARCHÉ." The blue sign's white lettering was centred with a red maple leaf, a design theme that evokes the Conservative Party logo. The news release featured a large photograph of the prime minister at the lectern in the wheat field, with the sign clearly visible. In the release, his quotation began by promoting his administration's overall brand messaging about the economy before transitioning to a related frame of the policy itself: "Our government is committed to creating open markets that will attract investment, encourage innovation, create value-added jobs and build a stronger economy for all Canadians."[36] No communications personnel were identified as available to journalists for further information.

The scope of e-communications was more advanced too. Digital buttons were available for sharing the news release via email, Digg, Facebook, Google+, LinkedIn, Pinterest, Reddit, StumbleUpon, Tumblr, and Twitter. The photo gallery of the prime minister's website featured eight photographs of the event, all showing him in a favourable light. The "sound byte" section offered an audio player so one could listen to him speaking. The video remarks section linked to a YouTube video of his delivery. The Department of Agriculture and Agri-Food Canada's website reproduced one of the eight photos of the prime minister, followed by a photo of the minister, appearing under the heading "Prime Minister Celebrates Marketing Freedom for Grain Farmers in Western Canada." The photos were available via the prime minister's Flickr page and appeared on some Conservative MPs' websites. Communications synchronization was much more advanced than it had been just six years earlier. Even so, the prime minister's Twitter account that day congratulated Canadian athletes at the London Olympic Games and made no mention of the Canadian Wheat Board policy or pseudo-event. Such an inconsistency is unthinkable now. This is a reminder of how quickly we have come to expect sameness across media platforms, including a singular focus on the government's main policy messaging.

The thrust toward branding and the repetition of simplified policy messages are such powerful trends that they are blind to political idealism. In a 1989 internal memo, leader of the Reform Party Preston Manning advised that the fledgling party lacked a consistent way to answer a deluge of questions about its ideology and policy stances.[37] He recommended that a positioning statement be adopted that would be reinforced in all media relations activities. His suggested statement was nearly 100 words long, a jumble of messages on matters as varied as Senate reform and social entrepreneurship. Years later another internal Reform Party memo confronted the same need for policy messaging simplicity. A brochure listing fifty-six policy positions in a reader-friendly manner was deemed by the party centre to be overwhelming for most people:

> Our communications platform is too fragmented and cluttered. Our
> 56 reasons [to support Reform] creates confusion because we have ad-
> dressed many issues but not a single position. Consequently people
> have no context to understand our 56 reasons. People generally don't
> understand complex issues so we must go from the simple to the com-
> plex. Remember 24% of the population are functionally illiterate. Voters
> tend to rely on their impressions vs detailed information ... We must all
> speak with one voice and communicate one image.[38]

There are countless examples of policy detail losing out to communications
simplicity. As mentioned later in this chapter, the United Kingdom's New
Labour and Canada's Conservative Party both formed governments after
campaigning on five core election priorities. Pracademics[39] Jared Wesley
and Mike Moyes examined how the New Democratic Party adopted New
Labour's rebranding model of inoculation, moderation, and simplification.
They describe a coordinated federal-provincial effort to refresh the brand
by disassociating the party from its ideological fringes, by moderating its
policy stands, and by simplifying campaign pledges into "digestible
planks."[40] As NDP leaders made electoral gains, they built legitimacy
to pursue further rebranding. Policy simplification also involves curtailing
its analysis. Trudeau resisted calls to unveil Liberal policies prior to the
official election campaign, opting instead to provide candidates with a
twenty-five page document of policy talking points.[41] Another trend is for
election platforms to prioritize visuals over policy details. The Conservative
Party's manifestos have contained numerous photos of its leader, including twenty-two photos in a forty-one-page document in 2008,[42] and fifty-
four of the fifty-six photos in its 2015 platform.[43]

POLITICAL PARTY BRANDS

Political parties straddle a public-private world. As minders of government affairs, they are private organizations treated as public entities,
loosely comparable to some publicly traded companies and interest
groups. They face marketplace pressures to communicate professionalism
through uniform literature, logos, and consistent commitments.[44] The
electoral-professional party model sugests that a personalized leadership

is sustained by specialists who use digital communications technologies to appeal to public opinion.[45] Another party subtype, the business firm model, applies to entrepreneurial parties that contract out technical tasks, rely on political marketing, and treat electors as consumers.[46] These are by no means the only schemata – dozens of party models exist – but they serve to illustrate that political parties are similar to business operations that use the latest sales and marketing techniques. Canadian political party scholar R.K. Carty has advanced a theory that parties are akin to franchise systems, such as the McDonald's fast food chain, and unified by a strong brand. He explains that "the party embodies and sustains a brand that defines its place in the political spectrum and is the focus for supporters' generalized loyalties."[47] In the franchise model, the party centre is in charge of policy, leadership, national communications, organizational management, and fundraising. This gives parties flexibility to respond to changing situations.[48] The leader makes decisions that must be followed by the grassroots; on most other matters, members are reasonably free to run electoral district associations (EDAs) and nominate the party's local candidates. The centralization of communications, including common brand markers (symbols, logos, colours), creates a reliable consistency for citizens.

Treating a political party's label as synonymous with the brand is a common mistake about party nomenclature.[49] Just as brands are comprised of tangibles and intangibles, so too are political parties. A party brand constitutes an audience's emotional reaction to the sum of all processed information about a political party. This includes its name, history, leadership, policies, reputation, logo, colours, and the audience's voting behaviour and priorities. Branding strategy uses communications to nurture loyalty to voters' imagined construction of the party. This occurs whether or not there are changes in valence issues such as policy dimensions, leaders, or candidates (see the related discussion on consumer and voter behaviour theory in Chapter 5). The objective of branding a political party is to

> cultivate such a high degree of identification, trust, and loyalty that voters
> will be willing to let the party do the thinking for them. When voters
> enter into this relationship, they place their trust in a party to deliver the

best policies, thereby relieving themselves of the responsibility to stay informed and educated on public issues. If a party has marketed an effective image, this sense of trust and loyalty will carry on even after particular policy proposals become obsolete.[50]

Party brands are broad in scope. When a brand is ingrained in an elector's memory, exposure to an information node triggers any number of associations. For instance, exposure to media coverage of a party leader stimulates the retrieval of archived information ranging from personal characteristics to party policies.[51] The party logo and colour scheme become cognitive shortcuts, which help voters to "cope with the increasingly complex and over-communicated world in which they live."[52] Party brands are heuristic cues that offer voters easy alternatives to investing time and energy in evaluating political choices. In Canadian politics, the Liberal Party label is a more vacuous heuristic than the ideological meaning attached to the Conservative and NDP labels, but also the most familiar.[53]

Every so often, political parties introduce cosmetic changes to their logos. They can also make sharp, sudden changes that signal dramatic market repositioning. Party rebranding tends to coincide with a poor election result and/or the installation of a new leader. New leaders want to refresh the image of the party to differentiate it from the previous leader and/or public failures, to align it with new priorities, and to reposition the organization. The Liberal Party and New Democratic Party have opted to convey rebranding primarily through a change in leadership and policy shifts, accompanied by tweaks to the party logo. The one time that dramatic rebranding occurred among those parties was in 1961 when the Cooperative Commonwealth Federation (CCF) was dissolved in favour of the NDP moniker.

Parties on the right have been far more adventurous, with mixed success. What we now know as the Conservative Party has undergone many name changes in its history. At various junctures, it was known as the Liberal-Conservative Party (twice), the Unionist Party, the National Liberal and Conservative Party, the National Conservative Party, the National Government, and the Progressive Conservative (PC) Party. The dramatic fracturing of the PC Party in the 1993 federal election amid the rise of the Reform Party and the Bloc Québécois marked the beginning of a decade of brand introspection. In the late 1990s, Manning led a major rebranding exercise. His United Alternative movement culminated in the rebranding of the Reform Party into the Canadian Alliance Party. A leadership contest was won by the telegenic Stockwell Day. Nevertheless, the Alliance brand suffered from many of the same image troubles as its forebears, and PC Party leaders continued to resist overtures to merge. In early 2002, Day recontested the leadership, won by Stephen Harper. The details are too lengthy to describe here, but suffice it to say that Harper and new PC Party leader Peter MacKay agreed in late 2003 to merge their parties to become the Conservative Party of Canada, and Harper went on to win the new party's leadership contest in early 2004. During this interlude, his team of marketers shaped the new entity's brand by transitioning plans that Harper had approved to rebrand the Alliance.[54] They stayed on when he assumed the leadership and set about to introduce "a strong, simple, respectable, institutionalized brand that immediately communicated governmental experience, competence, and credibility" (CS 4).

The Conservative Party is an underappreciated case of party rebranding. To date, most political marketing scholarship has been directed to Tony Blair's transformation of the stodgy Labour Party of the United Kingdom into New Labour.[55] Despite their considerable differences, the two parties behaved in a remarkably similar fashion. Both undertook bold political communications directives under new leaders. They emphasized the gathering of opinion research intelligence and the importance of opposition research databases. They prioritized disciplined election campaigns with simple messages and speedy counterattacks. In the elections that vaulted them into government (1997 for New Labour, 2006 for the Conservatives), both parties promoted five policies, three of which were to get tough on crime, cut or maintain taxes, and reduce health-care wait lists. They targeted key seats and swing voters. Candidate screening became much more rigorous.

None of this is unique to party branding, to the political right or left, or even to those cases. Relevant for our purposes is that Prime Ministers Blair and Harper transitioned their disciplined style of campaign management to government. In Britain, Phillip Gould's unitary system of command – itself comparable to Lynton Crosby's edicts – operated in unison with communications strategist Peter Mandelson's mantra of "repeat-remind, repeat-remind, repeat-remind."[56] The command-and-control approach to media relations, spin, and illusions wielded by Blair's chief press secretary, Alastair Campbell, was so pervasive that the New Labour government was panned for its control freakery.[57] Both prime ministers reinforced centralized management through strict party discipline, the promotion of loyalists, and the public disparagement of critics – even civil servants.

The Blair and Harper approach to communications evokes harsh comparisons with the autocratic leadership and propaganda of fascist regimes. Theirs is a centralized style of government that invites similarities with totalitarianism and one-party rule. Political marketing scholar Nicholas O'Shaughnessy's conceptualization of the Third Reich as a brand implies just that.[58] The Nazi Party and New Labour (as well as the Canadian Conservative Party and, arguably, Canada's other major parties) feature leaders involved in propaganda decisions. Their images are dramatized. Solidarity, group cohesion, and unification of a regime are pursued through social conformity. A sense of normalcy is projected. Consumerism is encouraged, and audiences are segmented. Similarities notwithstanding, it is a gross exaggeration to suggest a direct comparison with the unspeakable horrors of the Third Reich. Which is exactly O'Shaughnessy's point: in a democratic system of government, there should be no basis for comparison. The wicked nature of the mass persuasion techniques practised by Joseph Goebbels, Hitler's minister of Nazi propaganda, are so unsettling that it is disconcerting that any similarities exist. It is the abhorrence of those methods that puts critics in liberal democratic societies on high alert about public sector branding.

PERSONAL BRANDS

Recognizing that audiences are shown only what is stage-managed is essential to comprehending public sector branding. George Washington was not defiantly standing in the boat crossing the Delaware River. Abraham Lincoln was a homely looking man who did not resemble the heroic figure depicted in invented surroundings in his many portraits. The media were so complicit in not documenting Franklin D. Roosevelt's need for a wheelchair that the extent of his physical disability was a secret from the public until after Roosevelt died. Likewise, the penchant of Canada's longest-serving prime minister, William Lyon Mackenzie King, for communicating with those in the afterlife was not widely known until he too was dead. So it should come as no surprise that today's political leaders seek to control how they are publicly viewed. Barack Obama smokes cigarettes in private. The Kremlin's photographs of Vladimir Putin convey machismo, from fishing while bare-chested to sitting in the cockpit of a fighter jet. In Canada, the Prime Minister's Office issued photos of Stephen Harper playing the piano and cuddling kittens at 24 Sussex. We do not see photos of leaders blowing their noses or arguing with their spouses. Harper once said when asked about being seen on a motorcycle with Laureen that "you've got to worry about image. I don't want to be on the back with my wife driving."[59] The public identity of a prime minister or an opposition leader is constructed in a strategic manner that attempts to project authenticity within social and cultural norms. This performance leads to an authenticity paradox.[60] Cultural theorists believe that the production of familiar images in political discourse, supported by persuasive rhetoric, conveys a sense of truthfulness. The mask of authenticity belies that the manufactured nature of the communication is unethical. The very act of constructing a projected lifestyle makes it inauthentic. Thus, the management of a leader's brand makes it difficult to discern what is real, causing citizens to form leadership judgments based on illusions.

Image management gives rise to the notion of a personal brand. It is now a cultural norm to manage one's online identity and to promote an idealized and inauthentic image.[61] For the public, self-commodification is motivated by idealized notions of rewards, including ego fulfillment, improved social status, and stronger labour market positioning. For organizations, much of the corporate brand is wrapped up in the images of executives and spokespersons as the entity's public face. In politics, personal brands – also referred to as human brands[62] – are comprised of the packaged public images of politicians. The construction of a personal brand is influenced by deeply rooted notions of society, ideology, and institutional norms. The trend toward personal branding is related to storytelling that emphasizes personalities over parties.

Although each situation is different, in politics a personal brand can be thought of as passing through stages on the way to becoming the head of government. Each marks a variation of the other. The individual's brand evolves from private citizen, to public figure, to candidate, to some combination of parliamentarian, critic, minister, leadership contestant, party leader, and/or opposition leader, and then first minister, and eventually ex-politician. For most backbenchers and election candidates, personal branding requires a level of expertise, resources, and independent control that they do not possess. Party discipline limits brand expression, and a personal brand is inextricably linked to the party brand. Those who manage to develop a personal brand that rises above partisanship do so based on their physical attributes, personalities, and policy stances.[63]

A personal brand is a modern take on Erving Goffman's concept of the "presentation of self in everyday life." Goffman theorized that human beings are akin to actors on a stage, conscious of their behaviour and appearance when others are present. Audiences seek further information about whoever is being observed and draw on clues and symbols, which he called "sign vehicles," to form impressions.[64] The presentation of self is important for political figures, obsessed as they are with reputation management as a means of advancing a political agenda and winning elections. In the digital age, aspiring politicians and public officials have more opportunities than ever to build public personas. Conversely, their critics have a greater ability to communicate negative sign vehicles. A result is that politics is often a carefully choreographed dramatic production.

Modern leadership is so image-centric that the source of political power is arguably a simulated character. That sphere of influence is heightened when a leader is charismatic and telegenic.[65] Charisma is a natural communication talent that is an attribute of the "great man" theory of heroes. It holds that people who exhibit transformative leadership have such enchanting personalities that followers see them as superhuman and form emotional connections.[66] Charismatic authority is worrisome; as sociologist Max Weber would point out, it is arbitrary and can be used to coerce devoted followers.[67] Charisma is such an ephemeral, ambiguous, ethereal, and above all human characteristic that such a captivating magnetism is difficult to define.[68] It cannot be manufactured by image handlers in a free media system. This is what makes leaders like the Trudeaus (discussed later in this chapter) so alluring for political marketers.

Whether a politician is charismatic or not, her or his packaging arguably requires more attention to detail than the branding of an inanimate product.

The physical characteristics and attire of politicians are scrutinized by the media and attentive members of the public. On television, close-ups of political actors magnify trivial details. Slight perspiration or hand fidgeting can be interpreted out of proportion, and the editorial switching between camera angles distorts a viewer's spatial comprehension.[69] Hairstyle, height, weight, tone of voice, gestures, facial hair, makeup, jewellery, eyeglasses, religious attire, and general demeanour are all on display. Politicians face some of the highest standards of physical decorum, and their clothing must adhere to cultural norms, lest it be a communications distraction. Expressive hair styles, provocative clothing, funny hats, lavish jewellery, visible tattoos, and body piercings are taboo. A dress code must be followed in Parliament and at formal events. In constituencies and on the campaign trail, it is more appropriate to wear casual attire, whereas at special cultural events it is important to don ceremonial clothing. At all times, politicians risk a performance disruption, one that can live in infamy online.

The political sphere tends to operate around the stereotype of a prime minister as a white-collar, university-educated, heterosexual, married, able-bodied, clean-shaven, white man who wears business attire. A gendered media lens pays attention to different characteristics and personal traits slanted in favour of a certain style of (male) politician. Women's personal brands, especially those of mothers, are comprised of the contradictory situation of fighting against feminine stereotypes while balancing authenticity.[70] Belinda Stronach's political career stands out in recent national-level politics in Canada. Stronach commanded a national stage for helping to broker the merger of the Canadian Alliance and Progressive Conservative Parties. She placed second in the Conservative Party's first leadership race, became a Conservative MP, and crossed the floor to become a Liberal minister, saving Martin's minority government from defeat. For these reasons and more, Stronach attracted considerable media attention and became a political celebrity. Her wealth and sex appeal were factors. Media coverage often discussed her looks, her wardrobe, and her personal life, including fascination about her relationship with MacKay.[71] A lesser known case is that of Allison Brewer, a lesbian who led the New Brunswick NDP. Her attempts to counter media stereotypes informed decisions about her wardrobe and public appearances. Brewer wore mainstream clothing. She ensured that she was accompanied by older conservative men, and she intentionally brought her children to campaign events.[72] Stronach, Brewer, and other female politicians must grapple with media logic. This includes greater attention being paid to marital status and age, referring to them by first name, and subjecting them to sexist remarks.[73]

Whatever a politician's socio-demographic characteristics, we tend to think that it is manipulative for that person to undertake a makeover. In truth, cosmetic changes are necessary to remove superficial distractions that encumber substantive discussions about policy. Preston Manning's voice and look resonated with westerners who wanted an anti-politician. When Manning sought to broaden his appeal to mainstream Canada, he took voice lessons, opted for a changed hairstyle, and had corrective eye surgery. As he explains, advisers convinced him to change his look on the basis that, "if how you speak or how you dress or something prevents people from hearing what you're saying, wouldn't it be worthwhile trying to fix that?" (CP 2). During Harper's preparations for the Canadian Alliance Party leadership, strategists reacted to an op-ed by political columnist Paul Wells, which critiqued his personal presentation. This prompted a strategy meeting to gauge audience reactions and recommendations about simple cosmetic changes for the aspiring leader. The strategists determined that Harper needed to be convinced that his clothing choices would become fodder for the media and public. In one email, Tom Flanagan urged him to accept that personal image management was necessary:

> Stephen, I have received a few [negative] comments and messages ... They seem rather petty to me, but nonetheless some people do seem to have these reactions. I think your haircut is fine, but you might want to review your wardrobe. Better to make any changes of that type early rather than later in the campaign, when they might become a topic of comment in their own right.[74]

Harper was reluctant. "I have not been packaged by an empire of pollsters and media managers. I have not been groomed by the experts and the influential," he said later on his way to winning the Conservative Party's inaugural leadership campaign.[75] Promoting an image of authenticity is a standard ploy by outsiders, something that is difficult to maintain once in power.

As prime minister, Harper underwent a series of visual changes. Upon assuming office, he employed a personal stylist on the public payroll before the revelation led to the Conservative Party paying her salary. In the 2008 campaign, he donned a light blue sweater to project a fatherly look, an appearance that sought to soften his intimidating and aloof image among women. That repackaging was seen as inauthentic. One memorable instance of its being mocked occurred during the party leaders' debates when Jack Layton quipped to the PM, "Where's the platform, under the sweater?" To those on the outside, the blue sweater was part of a master plan concocted by marketing strategists. In reality, according to a marketing consultant involved with the party's advertising, it happened to be the clothing that Harper showed up with on the day of a cobbled-together advertising shoot. He continued to wear the sweater at pseudo-events for visual consistency with the advertising. The consultant was emphatic that "it just happened to be the sweater he wore that day. It wasn't some sort of secret advertising plan to put a blue sweater vest on him ... We weren't even aware of whether the sweater was blue or whether he was wearing a sweater at all" (CM 10). The need to express a connection with ordinary citizens is especially important for prime ministers. Their brand personifies the seat of government and is subject to attack as being out of touch with citizens. The Conservatives found more success with Harper when he wore a Hudson's Bay Winter Olympics jacket with CANADA blazoned in white across the front in capital letters (the same one in Figure 4.1), which was part of his public image since the 2010 Winter Olympics were held in Vancouver. The jacket was a constant visual reinforcement of a marketing effort to position the prime minister as a patriotic fan of Canadian winter sports who shares the same values as ordinary Canadians. During the 2015 summer campaign he alternated between business attire and patriotic clothing. At the outset he stumped with his wife and teenage children[76] and later opted to appear at pseudo-events surrounded by supporters holding "protect our economy" signs, demonstrating that brand positioning varies depending on the context.

A novel way that leaders become commodified and shape their personal brands is by authoring books. The autobiography is a mechanism for spinning their versions of events and framing their images. Canadian politicians are finding that, as with their American counterparts, political memoirs need not wait until retirement. Chrétien's *Straight from the Heart* was a springboard to his becoming Liberal leader,[77] Layton wrote a book about homelessness, and Green Party leader Elizabeth May authored many works, including one about the degradation of Canadian parliamentary democracy, with claims such as "controlling the message is now the ultimate goal."[78] Justin Trudeau followed the model with *Common Ground*, in which his personal brand positions him as a progressive whose desire to become prime minister is motivated by a sense of duty and patriotism.[79] While in office, Prime Minister Harper released *A Great Game: The Forgotten Leafs and the Rise of Professional Hockey*, which cemented his credentials as a wonk and hockey fanatic.[80] His book is consistent with a broader brand narrative that he and his party were guardians of post-Confederation history and traditions. Not to be outdone, Mulcair's autobiography, *Strength of Conviction*, was released during the 2015 campaign, which provided a platform for NDP strategists to generate celebrity-style news coverage about their leader's brand story.[81]

Short Case Study: Justin Trudeau as a Brand Extension

The novelty of the Justin Trudeau brand provides an opportunity to explore the applicability of branding concepts to the public sector and politicians. We can treat him as a "brand extension," in which equity in the master brand (his father Pierre) is leveraged by attaching the parent brand name (Trudeau) to a new product line (the son) introduced within the same category (federal politics).[82] In marketing, awareness of and goodwill toward the parent brand create efficiencies when names, visuals, and slogans are consistent.[83] Extensions of brands capitalize on an existing market demand and a greater willingness among consumers to try the new product. A line extension revitalizes the brand. It allows it to enter new markets and taps customer loyalty. However, the strategy is constrained by the perceived credibility of the parent brand.[84] Extensions that are too dissimilar incur increased marketing costs and dilute knowledge of the original brand.[85] The spinoff risks damaging the parent brand, and likewise if the parent brand is damaged it has a negative spillover effect on the brand extension.[86] Furthermore, while consumers with deep attachments to the parent brand are likely to be more accepting of a lower-quality extension, those with limited familiarity are less willing to try the brand extension or be as forgiving of it.[87]

The brand extension framework offers broad theoretical application. In politics, it applies to a party brand with regional units, to the connection between the brands of the PM and government, to party candidates, to a politician whose offspring enters the political arena, and so on. Extending a personal brand involves associating a candidate with the mythical construct of someone else. When a politician leaves office, the strengths and weaknesses of that person's image are inflated or forgotten. This is compounded by fluctuations in how electors prioritize leadership traits at a given time.[88] Ken Cosgrove observes that American conservatives sought to build a brand extension between Ronald Reagan and George W. Bush by attempting to transfer the positive characteristics of the Reagan brand as a historical figure to Bush.[89] Canadian partisans leverage brand strengths by holding up past leaders as icons and ignoring others. Wilfrid Laurier, Lester Pearson, and Pierre Trudeau are favoured by Liberals over the images of other successful Liberal leaders, such as Mackenzie King, Louis St. Laurent, and Jean Chrétien, or less successful ones, including John Turner, Stéphane Dion, and Michael Ignatieff. They inflate the accomplishments of some (notably Laurier) and undervalue those of others (notably King). New Democrats hail the social progress achieved by Saskatchewan CCF Premier and federal leader Tommy Douglas, the values of Ed Broadbent, and the tenacity of Jack Layton. They ignore Audrey McLaughlin, the first woman to lead a major federal party, at the helm during the party's freefall in the early 1990s. Brand coherence is especially strong between the federal Bloc Québécois and the provincial Parti Québécois. Both use the powerful nationalist imagery of the fleur-de-lys and the Quebec flag. Moreover, the blue used by those parties symbolizes the embodiment of the Québécois people against the red used by federalists. The rise and fall of those separatist parties shows how federal-provincial party brands can operate in lockstep.

The brand of the Conservative Party is more selective, picking out certain aspects of the PC Party's history and its forebears. No mention is made of the many failures (recent and historical) of the Conservative family history or of Harper's past as someone who campaigned against the PC

Party. Kim Campbell, the country's only female prime minister, once rated by the National Geographic Society among the most important leaders in world history, is all but forgotten. There is scant recognition of the Reform or Canadian Alliance brand. Leaders such as John A. Macdonald and John Diefenbaker are trotted out, whereas a long list of others, notably Brian Mulroney, are not mentioned. The Conservative brand is unique in that it lacks official provincial cousins. This is an oddity, given the party's championing of communications synergy, until we consider that the master brand has limited control over provincial parties and leaders. As brand extensions, provincial parties can inflict damage on their namesake, for instance negative associations with Bob Rae's Ontario NDP government in the early 1990s afflicting the federal NDP brand. This marketing distance provides a federal Conservative administration with flexibility to pivot away from being drawn into provincial demands (see Chapter 6). It remains to be seen how long provincial PC parties will persist with their legacy brand's nomenclature, especially if provincial Liberal and NDP parties benefit from brand convergence.

As the Trudeau case implies, the concept of political brand extensions is applicable to personal brands in the form of family dynasties. Rookie candidates related to politicians have higher public profiles because of their familial relationships. Candidates with family ties leverage successful social and financial networks and access their relatives' political knowledge. They exhibit hereditary traits, such as an interest in public service, talent, ambition, and energy. However, political dynasties invite questions about the concentration of power, the ability of heirs with limited experience to be elected, and the lack of competition for a position.[90] Thus, political kinship in politics is interpreted as a signal of the lack of modernity of a democracy or political party.[91] This is a concern as the importance of brand equity grows in the political arena.

As the eldest son of Canada's fifteenth prime minister, Justin Trudeau is the latest offspring of a Canadian politician to seek elected office. An earlier instance was Paul Martin Jr., the namesake of his father, a prominent cabinet minister who contested the Liberal leadership three times. Other father-son leaders include the Premier Bennetts of British Columbia (W.A.C. and Bill), the Mannings (Ernest and Preston) in Alberta, the three Johnson premiers (Daniel Sr., Pierre-Marc, and Daniel Jr.) who governed

Quebec from three different political parties, and the Ghiz (Joe and Robert) premierships in Prince Edward Island. Family connections can broaden, as with the Laytons (Robert as federal PC cabinet minister, son Jack as NDP leader, and daughter-in-law Olivia Chow as NDP MP). There are many other instances of ministers, parliamentarians, and candidates drawing on their pedigrees. Brand extensions are not exclusive to the political arena. Stronach leveraged her businessman father's fame, and Al Gretzky, the uncle of Wayne, unsuccessfully contested a number of elections in the London area. The Trudeau brand is worthy of special attention because of its connections among the concepts of celebrity, image management, and marketing at the highest level. It informs us that the media offer favourable treatment to political leaders with media-friendly characteristics that embody their norms and ideals. Politicians change their images on the ascent up the political ladder in a manner that reflects socially constructed norms. Furthermore, it contrasts two eras of mediatized communications and offers some surprising similarities with former Prime Minister Harper's controlling style.

Pierre Trudeau's packaging as a debonair anti-politician and pop culture phenomenon spurred Trudeaumania in the late 1960s. Party strategists transported Trudeau by motorcade to waiting crowds and conveyed momentum by making visits to small events before proceeding to big ones.[92] They recruited young Liberal women to behave as obsessed fans in the presence of reporters. Trudeau was an intellectual and internationalist. As prime minister, he defended Canadian federalism in the face of Quebec separatism, and he was a visionary whose policies continue to profoundly shape Canada. However, as with other leaders who hold office for a long time, his image fluctuated, involved inconsistencies, and was ephemeral. He exhibited a consciousness that public images are illusions and that the media should not be trusted.[93]

When Pierre Trudeau and his team sought to control the media and public agenda, he went from being an anti-politician and a media darling to having a hostile relationship with journalists. At the midway point of the two-month 1974 federal election campaign – the one during which Stanfield fumbled a football – Trudeau became inaccessible to the media and avoided unscripted situations.[94] He held few press conferences, stopped phoning open-line radio shows, and dodged questions. His team pushed complex policy proposals without giving journalists sufficient time to analyze them. Media elites were up in arms about the slights. Nevertheless, electors returned a Liberal majority government. The press gallery soon squawked that they were only granted weekly audiences with the prime minister, which they proclaimed inhibited media freedom and was anti-democratic. Over time, Trudeau began cancelling news conferences, in part because of media fascination with his personal life. The media opportunities were moved out of the National Press Building to the Canada Conference Centre. This move provided the prime minister's press secretary with the power to select which journalists could ask questions.[95] Few Canadians today are aware that Harper's style of media management was a contemporary version of Pierre Trudeau's.

The political sphere has been pontificating about the political aspirations of Justin Trudeau since his stirring eulogy at his father's funeral. He grew up in the public eye, such that he is often referred to only by his first name, signalling a personal connection and perhaps an effeminate treatment, whereas opponents' use of "Justin" is thought to be calculatingly dismissive.[96] When he declared his candidacy for the Liberal leadership in 2012, people began talking about his personal brand as an extension of his famous father. "This is the age of the brand, and you can't beat the Trudeau brand," reasoned a pollster.[97] Trudeau's lineage, charisma, and ascribed celebrity catapulted him to the party mantle. In an interview, one of his closest advisers acknowledged the advantages of being associated with a Canadian icon, observing that "branding is all about presence and mindshare – and, if your last name is Trudeau, you have a brand" (CS 28).

On his way to becoming leader, Justin Trudeau leveraged and augmented his celebrity in many ways. He spoke at countless public events, defeated a Bloc Québécois incumbent to become the MP for Papineau, recruited thousands of online supporters for the electronic leadership vote, and, most bizarrely, won a charity boxing match against a Conservative senator. Trudeau is charismatic and telegenic, qualities that are valued in a mediated democracy and harken back to the "great man" theory. Many people who like and trust the Trudeau name, particularly Liberal partisans, have formed a parasocial bond with the dauphin. Others are averse to his father's policies and the son's fame. Treating J. Trudeau as a brand extension of P. Trudeau draws attention to the two men's surname, good looks, sense of style, cosmopolitan attitude, wealth, ability to draw a crowd, and confident playfulness with media. As with all brand extensions, J. Trudeau's public image is not identical to the parent brand. Whereas Pierre quoted Plato and exhibited a disdain for politicking, Justin displays an aversion to policy detail and a remarkable ability to engage people in person and online. He has a high likeability factor. He is the kind of leader that, according to one poll, Canadians would most like to vacation with or to hear sing their favourite songs.[98] In comparison, Harper was identified as the most likely to be the CEO of a large company and to offer the best advice on how to invest money. Embodying Canadian values is the enduring image of the Trudeau and Liberal Party brands; being an advocate of national unity is their core brand promise to citizens. For much of Canada's history, the Liberals were a pair of safe hands to confront the regional strife that threatened to pull the country apart. In recent times, demand for the party's brokerage politics approach waned as national unity threats fizzled. Justin Trudeau smartly leveraged his brand equity by projecting the image of a unifier who would bring Canadians together after years of market segmentation and divisive wedge politics practised by the Harper Conservatives. As prime minister he hugs the family brand of an internationalist, Charter defender, and big spender.

As with most politicians, J. Trudeau does not talk about wearing a public mask or mention that his image is a constructed reality. He says only that people draw conclusions about him based on his family ties. Upon becoming party leader, he positioned himself as an anti-politician as Harper had done, by vowing to avoid being packaged by communications handlers. "Canadians are tired of politicians that are spun and scripted within an inch of their life, [of] people who are too afraid what a focus group might say about one comment or [what] a political opponent might try to twist out of context," Trudeau said.[99] Evidently, there is political capital to be gained by presenting an anti-branding brand.

J. Trudeau benefits from his family fame, but he faces communications adversity in a manner that past leaders, including his father, did not. The battle to define the new leader's personal brand began as soon as the Liberal leadership contest was over. The Liberals ran positive but forgettable

TV ads in anticipation that the Conservative Party would attempt to smear the image of the young leader. Sure enough, the Conservatives launched a TV campaign of negative advertising that positioned him as a policy lightweight. The ads mocked his ascribed and attributed celebrity and raised questions about his qualifications to be prime minister. The attack came through in many ways: mention of his being born with a famous name, visuals of him disrobing in a sexy fashion show and sporting a goatee, the announcer's snickering tone, the use of merry-go-round background music, and the choice of a Tinkerbell-like moving font and sound in the closing moments. Conservative messaging repeated the tagline that Trudeau is "in over his head." A website, justinoverhishead.ca, archived the videos. Volleys in the media drew attention to his acceptance of public speaking fees from charities and his marijuana policy. Subscribers to the Conservative listserve were repeatedly told that Trudeau was a risk compared with the strong, dependable leader Harper. The line was publicly repeated by the party's brand ambassadors, such as in Harper's remark that, "we're not choosing the winner of *Canadian Idol,* we're choosing someone to lead our economy. The only trade policy Justin Trudeau's been working on is the marijuana trade."[100] This frame readied the media and punditry to pounce on any mistake or naive remark, particularly on economic matters, in the gotcha politics fashion that defines the social media era.

However, the Trudeau brand acts as something of an insulator. The media and public backlash against Conservative criticism of the aspiring PM demonstrated that he must be treated differently than Dion, Ignatieff, or Rae. Consequently, a 2015 Conservative ad dubbed "Justin Trudeau – just not ready" steered away from the nastiness of past missives. Instead, a group of Canadians huddle in the workplace around a stack of résumés and question Trudeau's policy statements. A remark by one of the women – "I'm not saying no forever, but not now," followed by the tagline "he's just not ready" – denoted Conservative strategists' recognition that many Canadians liked the Liberal leader and saw him as a prime minister in waiting.[101] In the battle to control his brand, J. Trudeau learned the necessity of communications control to avoid performance disruptions. Despite his initial opposition to being spun and scripted, he conceded a need to practise

FIGURE 4.2 Liberal Leader Justin Trudeau takes a selfie with a supporter following a campaign stop | Canadian Press/Adrian Wyld

message discipline, albeit with a positive tone.[102] This paid off during the long election campaign by reducing the likelihood of gaffes that the "not ready" frame depended on. Prior to each leaders' debate, an image-centric personal brand of vitality and tenacity was projected through photo-ops showing off his athletic prowess, including canoeing on the Bow River, thereby evoking the memory of his father's love of the Canadian wilderness and the country itself. The visual consistency of wearing business attire – without a suit jacket and with his shirt sleeves rolled up – conveyed professional maturity with a dollop of approachability. An image of spontaneity and of a "great man" was repeated through J. Trudeau's celebratory mingling among star-struck partisan crowds. Smiling for impromptu selfie photographs with fans (Figure 4.2) was a modern form of Trudeaumania and it contrasted with the rigid stage management associated with Prime Minister Harper. Trudeau 2.0's confidence around social media was a breath of fresh air that itself was a strategic image management calculation, harkening to the authenticity paradox of personal brands.

In opposition, leaders are not faced with the same concerns about branding and messaging as they are when they head up a government. During the campaign, Trudeau relayed in a CBC interview that "I actually quite like the symmetry of me being the one who'd end" the pattern of PMO control that emerged in the 1970s during his father's tenure. He vowed to reject the "discipline and message control" of the Harper era, beginning by "empower[ing] my MP's to actually be voices for their communities in Ottawa, and not just my voice in the community."[103] It will be interesting to see how the various brands associated with Justin Trudeau change the longer he is prime minister of Canada.

5

Communications Simplicity
and Political Marketing

The branding of organizations, public policy, political parties, and polit-icians involves the packaging of information in a persuasive manner. The strategic alignment of images and messages is based on thinking that citizens are not immersed in politics and governance. The simplification and dumbing down of political communications are not wrong or evil. They are largely a reaction to the lowest common denominator of elector interest.

COMMUNICATIONS SIMPLICITY

Political behaviourists focus on exploratory variables to identify how voters decide among candidates. Elisabeth Gidengil and colleagues recently formulated a multistage explanatory model that suggests Canadian voters' decisions are derived from a mix of social background, underlying beliefs and values, party identification, economic perspectives, issue opinions, and leader evaluations.[1] Their model is similar to many others in that it attempts to establish which factors are most important to electors when they make their decisions, including how information is processed. To political marketers, models of socio-psychological buying decision pro-cesses are of greater interest. In the preface to *Political Marketing in Canada*, Conservative political marketer Patrick Muttart is quoted as saying that

close campaigns are decided by the least informed, least engaged voters. These voters do not go looking for political news and information. This necessitates brutally simple communication with clear choices that hits the voter whether they like it or not. Journalists and editorialists often complain about the simplicity of political communication, but marketers must respond to the reality that undecided voters are often not as informed or interested as the political and media class are.[2]

Muttart is not alone in thinking about the path to purchase. Prevailing theories of consumers' information processing suggest that a branding philosophy of repeating simple, cohesive messages and of emphasizing consistent visuals is smart strategy. For instance, the cognition theory of awareness holds that a buying decision is dependent on how a consumer ranks available information against competing information.[3] This is a five-stage internalized process for which we can substitute a vote decision. First, an elector becomes aware of an election. Second, this triggers an internal information search to process known choices. Awareness of vote options is based on the sum of all external communications exposures up to that point. Political choices that an elector has even the faintest awareness of are positioned in memory within an internal "awareness set." Available options on which the elector has no information are relegated to an "unawareness set." Third, the elector renders judgment on these choices based on available information in the awareness set. Choices judged to be plausible vote options move along to the elector's "evoked set," options that will receive deeper consideration. Fourth, the elector assesses the choices in the evoked set and places them into categories. Political choices that the elector rates as favourable are slotted into the "consideration set." Choices that spur indifference comprise the "inert set." Those with negative associations are relegated to the "inept set." This internal ranking is repeated in reaction to new stimuli. The process of arriving at a decision is the fastest for brand-loyal durable partisans who habitually make the same choice without evaluating available information or other choices. It is the slowest for the volatile flexible partisans who engage in deeper decision making by seeking out information to assess and rank choices. Rankings continue until only one choice, including not voting, remains in the elector's consideration set. Fifth, the elector makes a decision about how to vote on election day. Although used in consumer behaviour research, the cognition theory of awareness is similar to the model of voter behaviour stemming from the 1940s Michigan University studies, in which Paul Lazarsfeld's team of sociologists proposed that there are four continuous steps in the activation of political predispositions: propaganda arouses interest, aroused interest increases exposure and awareness, selective attention reinforces predisposition, and a decision is made.[4] Those seminal studies, along with ones conducted at Columbia University, took a market research approach to analyzing voter behaviour. They revealed that voters are less informed about politics and public policy than is assumed.[5] The implication for political marketers is that communications must prioritize generating basic awareness before encouraging targeted citizens to rank favourably what is being promoted. It is also pragmatic to encourage people to discard other options to their inert or inept sets.

Political marketers supplement the cognition theory of awareness with hierarchy models of consumer response. One such five-step social cognitive model[6] holds that a citizen begins with "problem recognition": she recognizes a difference between the current and preferred state of being. To fix the problem, she conducts an "information search" to find a possible solution. Information is retrieved from memory, which graduates to external information obtained through personal or mass communications. Once her information search is satisfied, she evaluates the available choices in her awareness or evoked set, a process known as "alternative evaluation." Motives, evaluation criteria, and attributes are weighed to leave a single option in the consideration set, resulting in a "purchase" decision. However, the process does not end there. The last stage in the model occurs when the decision is assessed against information on whether expected or desired performance levels are being met. This "post-purchase evaluation" suggests that people reassess their decision actions, which can lead to problem recognition and so on.

Political marketers intuitively consider consumer decision models when crafting messages. They attempt to trigger problem recognition by pointing out inadequacies with current policy or representation. They select communications channels by understanding their target group's likely places to search for information. They provoke emotional responses that will shift awareness, internal rankings, and cognition-based decisions. They continue to communicate with stakeholders after the announcement of a new policy initiative in order to manage impressions. The extent to which political strategists adjust their communications strategies differentiates them from those who gamble with a hodgepodge of mass media. Other decision-making theories consider choice or decision criteria, such as economic or social matters. Theories of emotional processes exist, such as psychological theory. Behavioural influences are factors, such as motives and attitudes. The consumer model of voting of Hilde Himmelweit and colleagues recognizes that consumers and voters pass through comparable socio-psychological decision-making processes. A purchase occurs at the moment of voting, and "the same principles hold with regard to voting as those which guide the individual in purchasing goods for consumption."[7] Along these lines, customized political marketing models exist – such as political marketing scholar Bruce Newman's five-dimensional model of functional, social, emotional, conditional, and epistemic values[8] – that feature basic mental-processing concepts of awareness and behavioural decisions. Regardless of the model, communications strategists are interested in the common principles of creating problems and solutions in voters' minds, through the repetition of simple strategic messages.

The simplicity of communications is a key theme too in theories of economic utility. The rational choice model of economist Anthony Downs holds that electors exert only as much effort as necessary to identify which party or candidate is likely to best meet their needs and wants, including whether or not to vote.[9] Samuel Popkin builds on the work of Downs with an economic theory that people follow their instincts when they assess political actors.[10] Rather than embark on broad searches for information, citizens combine the knowledge that they obtain through personal experiences in daily life with what they learn from the media. This information satisfies their desire to make decisions on complex policy matters with limited effort. Popkin explains that this "low-information rationality" places considerable importance on heuristic cues or "information shortcuts." One of his more interesting illustrations is that politicians are judged by how they consume food in public. Food is a symbolic means of expressing culture and a staple of campaign stops. When the media recorded President Gerald Ford biting into a tamale in an unconventional manner, it became a visual symbol that the president was unable to relate to Mexican Americans' problems. The episode is referred to as "the great tamale incident." Political strategists who subscribe to this way of thinking, including those mindful of Stanfield's fumbled football, obsess about controlling every detail of public presentation. Image handlers are driven by a need to avoid performance disruptions by their candidates and to create conditions that will destabilize opponents.

The low-information rationality of voters expressed by Downs, Popkin, and others is supported by a number of studies of voter behaviour. The impression-driven model of evaluation suggests that electors draw on collective recall rather than memory of a specific issue to form an opinion of a politician.[11] The valence politics model refers to judgments by an elector on impressions of whether her values on a given issue are shared by leaders and parties.[12] The voter's assessment is not based on a detailed issue-by-issue analysis of a party manifesto or deep information processing. Rather, it draws on heuristic cues conveyed through the media. For instance, if a party or politician is framed as having a strong social conscience, electors who accept this frame will assume its broad application to all of that party's or individual's policy positions. They assess it against their own beliefs and values on the most pressing issues. This implies that the evoked public images of a leader and party are more important in vote choice than actual policy positions and certainly more important than the minutiae that matter to special interest groups. In developing the valence politics concept, Donald Stokes lamented that political observers are unwilling to concede that Madison Avenue techniques matter more than ideological positions.[13] Electors' attention is even more fleeting and image-centric today than when these models were originally developed.

In all of these models, busy electors are thought to rely on heuristic devices to arrive at political judgments, in lieu of investing efforts to make more informed decisions. This is pronounced if there is a perceived or real public crisis. People seek to calm their heightened anxieties by supporting a leader viewed as strong and competent, particularly on economic and physical security matters. Harold Clarke and colleagues synthesize the situation thus: "Voters use cues provided by party leader and candidate images, together with information stored in flexible partisan attachments and judgments about party performance on salient issues, to guide their electoral choices."[14] Electors who form enduring psychological attachments to a political party, leader, and/or candidate who quells their anxieties have little need to search for external information. They tend to be impervious to the persuasive efforts of other political actors. This constitutes anywhere from roughly a third to half of Canadian voters.[15] A higher proportion strongly identify with a political party. Partisanship is on the upswing with political marketing, with less than 55 percent of voters in the 2000 general election claiming a strong partisan identification, compared with 64 percent in 2008, a period that coincided with the perpetual campaigning of minority governments.[16] A difference between durable (immovable) partisans and flexible (movable) partisans is that the latter continue to self-identify as supporters of one party even after they vote for a different party. These floating voters are willing to reconsider their initial preference. For political marketers, this sizable proportion of the electorate constitutes the electoral battleground. This has significant implications for political branding, in particular for personal brands as attention is trained on leaders.

The cues mentioned by Clarke and colleagues tend to come from televised visuals, which figure prominently in voter recall.[17] The importance of leadership in politics and political communications bloomed with television and now digital media. Voters tend to consider a leader's attributes: the more media that they are exposed to, the more likely they are to prioritize leadership.[18] This is where low-information rationality and heuristics come in. Voter psychology literature demonstrates that, in experiments, electors prefer leaders most like them. This is especially true for flexible partisans and voters otherwise unfamiliar with a candidate.[19] Once people form impressions of a candidate's physical appearance, they are less likely to care about policy dimensions.[20] In experiments, photographs that convey a more favourable image of a candidate because of a better camera angle or a smile result in electors ranking the candidate higher on competence scores than when less flattering photography is used.[21] Studies of video arrive at similar conclusions, with the added component of emotional resonance with a politician's image, which changes some citizens' attitudes.[22] Popkin concludes that whether a politician's values are the same as an elector's is less important than whether a voter identifies with the public image of a politician and whether she projects her own policy positions onto that politician because of perceived similarities.[23] A leader deemed to share the views of an elector on a key policy issue is deemed to be the best representative on other issues. The elector's impression of shared values is what matters on election day, regardless of reality.

All of this suggests a stark reality. It has to be a concern for democratic theorists that manufactured images and physical characteristics are visual cues for voters to form impressions of a leader's competence.[24] Nevertheless, the electoral importance of leadership image should not be overstated. As recently as the 1990s, the primacy of leadership in vote choice in parliamentary systems was a contentious topic in academic circles.[25] Although Canadians tend to vote for the party whose leader they prefer, that dimension alone does not decide election outcomes. Leadership matters most when there are notable variances in how electors rate the different party leaders.[26] This is because leadership traits are associated with issue positions. That is, a voter is more likely to support a leader who shares similar socio-demographic, ideological, and/or partisan traits, regardless of other factors. This brings us back to the importance for a leader to maintain a public image that resonates with the electors and why something as trivial as properly biting into a tamale or showing interest in ice hockey is rather important.

These models of consumer and voter behaviour impress that most people do not exert much effort in extensive information searches and deep evaluations. Most Canadians say that they pay attention to the news[27] and can name the leaders of most of the major political parties.[28] However, those who pay close attention to federal politics are in the minority, estimated to be about 15 percent of the population.[29] These engaged citizens include "issue publics" – those electors with personal stakes in policy issues who spend time becoming informed about them and developing strong opinions.[30] They are more likely to consume print media,[31] and because media exposure reinforces their existing opinions they are more resistant to political persuasion. People with the lowest levels of political knowledge are also difficult to persuade because they are the least likely to receive or process information.

As Muttart and other political marketers know, electors who occupy the middle range of information exposure are the most responsive to political communications. These electors develop feelings about leaders of whom they know little, and their lack of knowledge means that they are more impressionable.[32] Canadians in this middle range are said to constitute "a large and receptive audience that evidently does benefit from learning simple pieces of factual knowledge."[33] Television is a good way to reach them because it communicates simple messages in an emotional manner and connects the engaged and disengaged alike.[34] So are Internet communications, given that people who use television and the web for entertainment are less exposed to politics and less prone to vote.[35] For these reasons and more, political strategists are thumbing their noses at political talk shows in favour of entertainment programming and narrowcasting.

The public's lack of interest in policy minutiae means that public sector elites are incentivized to emphasize big picture messaging. Much of the Conservatives' approach to political communications has been based on the treatment of voters as consumers, as with the GST photo-op (Chapter 2) and the Pat Burns Arena pseudo-event (Chapter 3). Political marketers are mindful that their targeted electors are not absorbed with Ottawa's politicking or the complexities of public policy. Conservative strategists believe that, in a sea of media choices, repeating clear and simple messages through the most efficient media platforms to targeted groups is the best route. It is a strategy that helps to penetrate the cacophony of uncontrolled media and the constraints of controlled media. Rules of thumb include that pictures matter more than words, that a thirty-second TV spot has room for no more than eighty-two words of copy, that humans spend about three seconds deciding whether to continue reading written material, and so on. Those on the inside relay that communications minimalism pervaded the Harper PMO:

> I'm a political marketer, and as a marketer my objective is to
> win an election. And here's the reality that we face as marketers:
> the people who decide elections, the late-breakers, tend to be the
> least informed, the least engaged, and the least intense voters ...
> Generally speaking, they don't watch national news, they don't
> read the *Globe and Mail,* they don't read the *National Post,* they
> don't go online looking for political information ... They're not
> political people, they're people living their lives. They're occupied,
> they're busy with other stuff ... You have to boil it down, you have
> to make it simple, and your message has to be compelling ...
> That's why so often campaigns come down to issues of character,
> and trust, and the person, as opposed to policies. Because the

voters who are making these late decisions in campaigns are less interested in ideas and are more interested in the personalities of the people who are seeking their support. (CS 4)

You want to make sure that the visuals of the event match the message that is being spoken. The idea is, if you turn off the [TV] volume, somebody's cooking supper, and they've got kids, they're playing, and they've got the news on in the background. They may not be listening to what's going on, but if you have a visual then the message will still communicate. Even if the reporter is doing a voiceover, or the reporter is contradicting what the MP is saying, part of the message will still come through. (CS 14)

The average Canadian spends eight minutes a week or something like eighty seconds a day thinking about the government or politics or the public sector. You compete very hard to grab their attention in that period of time. (CS 30)

The Conservative PMO repeatedly impressed that effective messaging combines visual and textual components. Political staffers were told that what audiences see in a photo or video must deliver the intended message regardless of explanation.[36] Other political parties caught on. After the Liberals ran a thoughtful campaign that resulted in a historic poor outcome at the ballot box, an aide to Michael Ignatieff reflected that Canadians are "too busy living their lives. They pay a little bit of attention to [politics], and if that little bit of attention is dominated by a particular message, effectively delivered and repeated over and over again, it's going to sink in."[37] By 2015 the Liberals ran a campaign of message simplicity and consistency, and won.

COMMUNICATIONS PRECISION

Within a political party, formative communications strategies originate in post-campaign reflections. A party must constantly evolve and embrace new approaches to politicking, perhaps under a different leadership team and/or after a series of shocks, including electoral setbacks. After an election, party strategists document a list of lessons learned and muse on preparations for the next venture. Their post-campaign evaluation, also dubbed a post-mortem, is a forensic blend of analysis of vote results and staff impressions.[38]

Post-mortems archived in the Flanagan fonds demonstrate that campaign strategists in the nucleus of a political party are concerned about unifying the hundreds of simultaneous constituency campaigns, or at least they were in the Conservative Party when Flanagan held a senior role in it.[39] They want a written plan and campaign script that all central actors endorse. The amateurism of local candidates is laid bare in the strategists' concerns about the need for training and scenario role playing because, to name one reason, many candidates are unable to distinguish between federal, provincial, and municipal areas of responsibility. Coordination at the centre of the party itself is essential. Attendees in senior management meetings must interact with the war room, the leader's tour, and regional units. Communications decisions must be reached by both the leader's tour and the war room and relayed to the regions. Collectively, the party apparatchik attempts to create a unified sales force.

In Canadian political marketing lore, it is thought that the post-campaign analysis performed in the aftermath of the Conservative Party's disappointing performance in the 2004 election was pivotal. Muttart is often credited with convincing Harper of the benefits of emphasizing targeted messages to audience segments and of using visual communications to do so.[40] One Conservative strategist referred to Muttart as "a trailblazer" (CS 3). Others made these observations:

> What is unique about Patrick was that he thought in comprehensive branding terms about linking policy to visuals. What should it look like? What kind of photographs, what kind of colours do we want? ... We regarded colours and pictures and so forth as just sort of peripheral things, whereas Patrick had a more integrated view of how you sell something. (CS 11)

> I remember Patrick used to say, "You have to tell somebody something fourteen times before they'll remember it." (CS 29)

> Mute the TV. That was a big thing. He always said, "When you're thinking of visuals, think of the housewives at home with the family around the kitchen table with the TV playing in the background.

They should be able to look at that TV and see a minister announcing something and pretty much be able to get what the announcement's about just by the visual." So the speaking backdrop was
huge, and so was the sloganing on it. (CS 22)

In reality, Muttart was not the only Conservative Party strategist pushing
marketing strategy. However, his sphere of influence magnified when the
party formed government and he joined the PMO.

The Flanagan fonds contain at least four significant communications
memos that Muttart authored or co-authored. The memo most referenced
in the media and literature, not publicly recorded until now, is reproduced
in Appendix 3. It reveals the groundwork for communications discipline
within the Conservative Party and the Harper PMO. It contains many
branding-related recommendations that were harbingers of what the
party would carry over into government.[41] There should be a scripted
message of the day, even on days that the leader is not working. Support
materials are needed well in advance of a media event. The centre must
be prepared to make quick rebuttals to attacks. All communications
products released to the media must first be approved by senior officials.
Aggressive communications must persist until the last moment. There
must be centralized control over local messengers. An ethnic outreach
program must be developed that segments and targets cultural communities. Advertising must be purchased where it will be seen by less informed
and floating voters. Finally, advertising messages must align yet allow for
some regional variation. Harper's willingness to adopt these recommendations transformed the Conservatives' approach to electioneering and
permanent campaigning.

A second Muttart memo reflects the centripetal pull of communications. In it, he relayed some opposition intelligence that the Liberals' senior
personnel, including Paul Martin, were directly engaged in all phases of
campaign advertising, from concept development through to media
buy. At the beginning of the campaign, Liberal advertising was designed
by committee, and as election day approached decisions were made by a
smaller circle of senior Liberals. Muttart observed that communications
symmetry occurred, with the party's advertising aligning with its communications via other media, and its national messaging was supported

by regional messaging. In the memo, he advised that, by employing a branding strategy, the Martin Liberals practised message coherence, even when different regional messages were communicated:

> The Liberals said the same things on television that they were saying on radio (or in print) thereby ensuring that various advertising mediums supported each other. In addition – and perhaps most importantly – the party ensured that Paul Martin's day-by-day messaging echoed – albeit in more nuanced tones – the new messages being delivered by the party's new television advertising. The Liberals ran a series of national ads, but supplemented their broad message with targeted regional messages in key battlegrounds (e.g., Ontario and BC).[42]

In a third missive, Muttart recommended that the Conservative Party follow the political marketing practices of the Australian Liberal Party outlined in *The Victory: The Inside Story of the Takeover of Australia*.[43] Tips were gleaned about researching voters in marginal seats to understand the emotional aspects of their desires and intolerances. Muttart urged the party brain trust to centralize its local campaign planning by providing signage and direct mail templates, while allowing flexibility to adjust paid media in marginal seats. A retail approach to advertising should be pursued, whereby template spots are developed with the same initial and concluding content, with room for new content in the middle (known as doughnut ads).[44] By reviewing polling data, Australian strategists had developed avatars of fictitious voters, named Phil and Jenny, to help party insiders think like targeted voters. As students of Canadian political marketing are aware, Muttart would soon do the same thing, developing profiles of Dougie the Nova Scotia tradesman and Zoë the Toronto yoga enthusiast.[45] These avatars helped strategists in the Conservative Party to visualize the decision to target rural tradesmen who rarely voted and to ignore young women who dined at Toronto bistros. Although not mentioned in the memo, another book influential in Conservative circles during this period was *The Unfinished Revolution: How the Modernizers Saved the Labour Party*, authored by the political consultant who pushed for top-down communications control in New Labour.[46] It too served as "a roadmap ...

on how you branded a party into a winning entity against an established competitor" and was "a treasure trove of information" (CM 2).

In a fourth memo, Muttart recommended a strategic approach that included conserving resources and fighting "message dilution" with "narrow" communications.[47] He advocated a focus on audience clusters, such as married women in suburban/exurban areas. Issues were grouped into narrow themes, such as opportunities for new Canadians. Subregions were targeted, such as suburban areas in Ontario defined by the telephone area codes 519, 705, and 905. Muttart advocated that core messages should be communicated by leveraging all avenues available to the Office of the Leader of the Official Opposition (OLO), including "supply day motions, headline speeches by the leader, free time broadcasts, members' statements, questions in Question Period, and material for householders and other direct contact pieces." Harper was advised to conduct one-on-one interviews about core message themes with regional media such as the *Barrie Examiner, Brampton Guardian, Kitchener-Waterloo Record, Mississauga News,* and *Oshawa News* that would reach targeted audience cohorts. These communications would be supported by pseudo-events in those locations. It was a tactical approach that extended to running "positive brand ads on appropriate policy themes in media markets when and where the leader visits. Ads will be much more effective if they mirror stories that the leader is creating on tour," added Flanagan in a 2005 pre-writ plan.[48] This was to be supported by the mailing of legislative newsletters on select policy themes to targeted ridings visited by the leader.

Doug Finley, at the time the Conservative Party's director of political operations and later its election campaign director, authored a provocative post-mortem. He likewise emphasized the need for written plans to enable pivoting in response to changing circumstances. Advocacy for a "roadblock" strategy of synchronization was one of his preferred recommendations. This sought to ensure that all communications were on message and delivered concurrently. Audiences would be exposed to the same information no matter where they turned. Finley explained it this way:

Roadblock is a method of achieving the rapid response and spontaneity required in today's rapid communications-type of election. It would allow the leader to be whatever he wants on any given day; it allows him to hit back at the opposition. Roadblock allows the leader's message to be the lead in on that day's talk shows, and it allows him to be the first to guarantee that his message will be one that opens the day and sets the daily agenda.[49]

Finley, Flanagan, Muttart, and other party brain trusts were determined to repeat-remind, a strategy proven to be successful elsewhere.

As Muttart's inside information about the Martin Liberals attests, from time to time these approaches are found in other Canadian political parties. Branding strategy contributed to the breakthrough of the federal NDP in 2011, and its front-runner status in some opinion polls in 2015. The party implemented a political marketing strategy that called for a centralized and professionalized approach to campaigning. It was a presidential-style approach that emphasized Layton's personal brand over the party brand.[50] In an interview, one of the architects of that strategy enthused about the benefits and necessity of branding in party politics. Brad Lavigne described how every experience of a target audience with a political brand must be consistent. This requires that everyone within the party become immersed in the brand, beginning with staff in the central party office. The NDP designated its deputy director of strategic communications as the person responsible for the brand. That person was tasked with monitoring all party communications, including events and materials initiated by MPs, to ensure brand compliance. All of the party's activities were subjected to a branding lens. As Lavigne explained,

> everything at your disposal needs to be branded in order for
> your brand to penetrate ... everything from your lawn signs, your
> literature, your website, your online presence, your social media
> platforms, your tour events, and obviously advertising. There's
> nothing that doesn't add to your brand. Even the internal colours
> of our office walls are renovated with the party colours. That acts
> as an extension of the brand for anybody and everyone. People
> are also part of that brand: who you put up on an issue, how you
> shadow the cabinet if you're the opposition, your cabinet if you're
> the government. Your spokespeople are your message ambassadors,

they will either add value or detract from your brand ... We never
left any event or communications material. Everything always had
the brand's lens through it. (CS 27)

Under Justin Trudeau, the Liberal Party regained its relinquished status
as a public sector brand leader. For a long time, the Liberal brand was
associated with the federal government's natural governing party. After
the shock of the 2011 election, the president of the Liberal Party authored
a memo arguing that communications coherence is essential during campaigns. Branding principles are omnipresent in an age of permanent
campaigning, he wrote, which pits message discipline against democratic
values.[51] Subsequent grassroots roundtables about the brand identified
the need for "clear, concise and consistent messaging."[52] The party's visual
identity standards manual stipulates that the Liberal Party is "focusing our
communications to deliver clarity, consistency and impact. It is crucial
that the brand appears correctly and consistently at every touchpoint."[53] In
the opinion of a top Liberal strategist, the party's image had become "a
party of deputy ministers" and intellectuals. Trudeau's challenge was to
"reconnect" the brand with middle- and working-class Canadians (CS 28).
This requires collection and analysis of market data.

Market Research and Segmentation

To pinpoint messaging, party elites draw on data collected through focus
groups, opinion polls, and other forms of market intelligence. Focus group
research is the preferred method for encouraging citizens to share private
feelings and associations. It is used to explore emotional levers and identify
messages that will resonate with targeted audiences. The perceived value
of qualitative data varies. Market-oriented New Labour found success from
a conviction in the leadership circle about the usefulness of focus groups.
Conversely, sales-oriented Apple became the world's most valuable brand
while shunning focus group wisdom. Stephen Harper and his inner circle
were likewise cautious about the ability of qualitative research to offer
meaningful insights. As leader of the official opposition, he was prone to
overrule qualitative data and advisers' associated recommendations. In
fact, even well into his time as prime minister, Harper and one of his senior
advertising consultants were outrightly opposed to testing party advertising

in focus groups, on the basis that what is vocalized is unhelpful and causes anxiety among weak-kneed strategists.[54] The method's main value is to differentiate the media-centred campaign from the voter-centred campaign, for there tends to be a "shocking discrepancy" between what ordinary people talk about in focus groups and what the opposition and CPPG talk about (CS 4). When they use group research, Conservative strategists prioritize researching the brand and using visual communications. They employ a "mood boards" technique to draw out participants' emotions. Photos of party leaders are distributed alongside cards with photos of military equipment, a family, or flags to see what these visuals evoke.[55] Other techniques in this vein include "concept statements," whereby participants jot down their personal thoughts before explaining them, and "game-type associations," such as asking what type of motor vehicle each party leader most reminds participants of.[56] Group discussions about what they would like to ask a leader, how they imagine the leader would respond to their questions, and what they imagine ideal responses would be is a role-playing conversation game that generates insights into a leader's brand image and how to reposition it.

For political strategists, opinion surveys offer a number of benefits over qualitative research. They permit the reliable identification of audience clusters and the sharpening of messages. Polls involve less coordination work, deliver results within a shorter time frame, offer statistically valid data, and are less expensive. In Canada, political parties primarily use opinion surveys to test messages and ideas to anticipate public reaction and interpretation. This sales orientation of figuring out how to persuade Canadians contrasts with the ideal of a market orientation that uses polling to seek out ideas and priorities. For all the talk of the age of "big data," the reality is that Canadian parties have less money for original research than their American or British counterparts. Canadian political marketers find resource efficiencies by subscribing to omnibus surveys and by monitoring polls reported in the media. Other quantitative data are available at little or no cost through Elections Canada and Statistics Canada. Among the evidence that political marketers consider are census data, elector identification data, and past election results. They are far less data driven than their American counterparts.

There is even lingering doubt about the need for professional public opinion research in Canadian politics. One senior Conservative strategist voiced serious reservations about the research biases of polling, and the social desirability of focus group settings, compared with the value of following "gut instinct" and phoning hundreds of contacts across the country to get a sense of the public mood (CS 5). A Conservative marketing consultant added that politics is so fast paced compared with private sector norms that the use of "intuition in a quick-speed environment" is necessary (CS 6). Another respondent contextualized that, even when copious amounts of public opinion research are available, it is still up to leaders to lead: "At the end of the day, sometimes you just have to make gut-level judgment calls on what the electorate wants, what the electorate is willing to believe in terms of your offering. It's not all science, right? It's a mixture of art and science, and sometimes the art is more important" (CS 4). This view might appear to lack scientific rigour, but political parties have the enormous tactical advantage of constantly receiving updated lists of electors from Elections Canada.

Leading up to the 2000 federal election, Canadian party strategists were "increasingly targeting discrete groups of voters with campaign messages designed specifically for the targeted group," based on polling data, and they were experimenting with targeted ad buys in specialty media.[57] Databases of supporters were under development and used for direct mail purposes. In Canada today, we are in the early stages of the data analytics that revolutionized American political marketing. Big data offer an unprecedented level of precision, sometimes based on information about electors that is gathered at little or no expense.[58] Such data inform which components of a brand to emphasize, how to position an opponent's image, and which messages to communicate. Data analytics guide brand positioning strategy and differentiation. They move beyond horse-race numbers to engage in multivariate analysis that includes demography (e.g., age, education, ethnicity, family, gender, income, language, occupation, religion), political culture (e.g., dualism, multiculturalism, social and cultural forces, social classes), and behavioural benefits (e.g., benefits desired, political engagement). Newer frontiers include loyalty reward program data (e.g., Air Miles), psychographic research (e.g., lifestyles, personalities, values), and monitoring of online behaviour (e.g., Internet cookies, video game biometric data). All of this is paired with statistical profiles of voters in party databases and can form the basis of sophisticated data modelling that uses algorithms to identify patterns among hundreds of variables.

Market segmentation uses research data to divide electors into groups with similar needs and wants. Since the 1930s, business marketing has held that a premium can be commanded from consumers when a product and its marketing are differentiated from those of competitors.[59] There are two basic approaches to becoming a market leader. One is that a product can be positioned to appeal to a broad spectrum. This is similar to the Liberal Party's traditional big tent strategy that brokers regional interests and searches for the median voter while ignoring the ideological fringe. The other approach is to appeal to a collection of narrow market slivers. This describes the marketing strategy of the Conservative Party under Harper, a global trend that vote maximizers must confront. When empirical data are used to turn "heterogeneous markets into homogeneous groups," the accumulation of these audience slivers accounts for a sizeable market share.[60] Promotional efforts focus on cohorts matched with the identified competitive advantage(s). Other consumers are ignored or, at most, tangentially engaged. The party uses communications precision to build a coalition by hardening the loyalty of its ideological base and by picking out like-minded members of mainstream society. However, it involves a risk of appearing to subvert democracy.

Audience segmentation and targeting operate in a manner comparable to triaging seats, only at a more precise level. The military concept of triage informs the allocation of limited resources on the battlefield.[61] Triage is also practised in emergency rooms, where medics must make quick decisions about how to prioritize medical attention. Patients are quickly clustered into one of three groups: those expected to survive without help, those unlikely to survive even with help, and those who might survive if they are provided with assistance. Attention is concentrated on the last group because this is the most efficient use of limited resources and will result in the greatest number of survivors. In party politics, triage strategy guides decisions about which seats to target, the transfer of party funds to local campaigns, the provision of organizational guidance, the intensity of advertising, a visit by the party leader, the coordination of a get out the vote (GOTV) program, and so on. It extends to beliefs that supporters' commitment must be reinforced, that those undecided should be targeted, and that opponents' partisans should be ignored. Floating voters in swing ridings are the priority, including those who pay fleeting attention to politics.

When a segmentation model is used, a form of triage is applied to a dataset, which generates a report of subgroups of electors and profiles. The results are analyzed to identify which cohorts should be targeted to meet the communication campaign's objectives. Segmentation helps strategists to identify how to position the party or candidate against competitors and which messages to promote. An NDP manager described how this works in that party. The New Democrats have a team of "people who understand regression analysis and math and modelling techniques" (CS 24). Those analysts identify different segments of the population that the party's communicators should be contacting "about a whole variety of things, whether it be just testing a message, or asking for money, or per-suading someone to support us." Segmentation occurs in stages. Initial segmentation employs basic geographic and demographic data, and deeper segmentation examines behavioural and psychographic data.[62] It is a process that increases the efficiency of political resources.

In Canada, dividing target groups through psychographic analysis dates at least to the late 1980s.[63] What is different now is the growing ability to isolate which cohorts to target and the diversity of narrow media to reach targeted citizens efficiently. This is how political parties are forming social relationships with electors and donors as they attempt to nurture brand communities not confined by geography. Take, for instance, Amer-ican presidential campaigns, in which the electoral battleground has been lower- to middle-class swing voters. Marketing in the 2004 presidential race targeted white men with blue-collar jobs. It is a cohort popularized in the media as NASCAR dads because of these electors' stereotyped pen-chant for stock car racing, working-class values, masculinity, and anger with the economy.[64] In the next campaign, the marketing of Republican vice-presidential nominee Sarah Palin was pitched at "Walmart moms." That is, the Palin campaign targeted mothers who shopped at the discount retailer and had lower education than the so-called suburban soccer moms favoured in the 1996 campaign.[65] Canadian media coverage attempts a local spin on this targeting, suggesting, for example, that "hockey moms" are the battleground cohort. For Canadian Conservatives, targeting these elector subsets must not deviate from the party's core messaging. Thus, communicating a master brand policy message of "tough on crime" is tailored as a sub-brand message of keeping drugs away from children and schoolyards (CM 8). In the Conservative Party, market segmentation is practised to identify which policies from the party's ideological canon should be promoted and which ones should be shelved.

By employing data modelling of electors' personal values and needs, party strategists can assess voters' social status, develop customized messaging, and offer insights on a variety of geographic scales. To persuade and motivate their targeted voter segments, they design policy and brand images around divisive wedge issues and ballot questions and employ microtargeting. The Conservatives have favoured specialized tax credits, such as the volunteer firefighter's amount, as a mechanism to curry the favour of targeted electors. This particular practice is multipronged because it simultaneously reinforces their master brand of economic stewardship and low taxes.

Some attention is paid in media circles to the Conservative Party's focus on select ethnic groups. A Conservative branding document demonstrates how political marketing is used to target ethic segments, such as Koreans and Hong Kong émigrés.[66] Party messaging has suggested that the Conservative brand shares the same values as members of select ethnic communities. On the ground, a traditional sales exercise dubbed "ethnic outreach" saw Minister Jason Kenney tasked with hobnobbing with cultural community leaders and speaking with ethnic media outlets. The party placed low-cost ads on specialty programs, such as during cricket games on Asian Television Network and Alpha Punjabi. This tactic reaches Chinese and South Asians who reside in key seats in the Greater Toronto Area and British Columbia's Lower Mainland. Advertising was purchased on websites visited by Chinese, multi-Asian, Punjabi, and South Asian communities. Seeking to communicate with ethnic markets is nothing new. For instance, Prime Minister Pearson's cabinet committee on advertising allocated funds to the "ethnic, religious and weekly press."[67] What has changed is the increased value of branding in a multiethnic society.

Branding's emphasis on the visual helps political parties to communicate, whatever the language of the audience. The ability of visuals to get past language barriers is an attractive proposition in Canada given that the number and proportion of allophones and "ethnic" voters are growing.

Direct Marketing

Related to market segmentation is direct marketing, a form of below the line personalized communication that supports the brand among niche audiences. It is also known as under the radar communication, or stealth campaigning, because technology is used to send messages without an intermediary to target audiences through phone, post, email, and/or newer avenues such as texting and social media. These messages reinforce other communications without competitors knowing who received what information. Direct marketing is a cost-efficient way to inform and engage people. It is a formidable component of permanent campaigning and branding.

Direct marketing is practised in three prominent ways in Canadian party politics, all of which invoke concerns about communications ethics. The first way involves harmonization of parliamentarians' communications. MPs are entitled to send letters, newsletters, calendars, and "happy holidays" cards to electors. Communications centralization is visible in their "ten percenter" flyers. A ten percenter is a leaflet prepared by an MP's office and mailed to up to 10 percent of the number of households in the MP's riding. They are intended to provide citizens with information on issues and events in Ottawa or the MP's electoral district. The costs are covered by the Parliament of Canada's budget. During Harper's tenure, his party's legislative research branch, known as the Conservative Resource Group, encouraged Conservative MPs to use templates to promote co-ordinated communications (Figure 5.1). Millions of Parliament-funded ten percenters promoting partisan, and often negative, messages were sent across Canada, including to households in ridings not held by Conservative MPs. The practice serves a dual purpose. The broad objective is to exploit public resources to promote central party messages. Less obvious to some is that mail-back forms are returned at public expense since no postage is required to send mail to parliamentarians. The information

FIGURE 5.1
Parliamentary office
"ten percenter" flyers
using centralized party
templates | Conservative
MP's Parliament Hill office
(c. 2009).

collected from mail-backs is entered into a party database for donor and volunteer prospecting. This enables further direct marketing. Conservative insiders explained the approach:

> Once you tell me you don't want to have anything to do with me, that's great information. I won't waste any more money trying to get you. I will never try to convince you to change sides. What I want to find is people who are open to our message, because they are the people that will give us money and vote for us. (CS 10)

> If they are against gun control, then we enter that into our database, into CIMS [Constituent Information Management System], and then we can do direct mail to that home talking about gun control, soliciting, asking for funds. But they are prequalified. And when the candidate knocks on that door, they know in advance what that person's views on several topics are because we make sure that they continue to get ten percenters on various other subjects. (CM 7)

Lassoing parliamentarians into supporting the centre's efforts to commandeer constituency communications entitlements is fraught with difficulties. It exposes the tenuous hold of party executives on the caucus. In 2004, a public affairs officer in the OLO emailed all Conservative MPs, their assistants, and their constituency offices with a request that they "donate" their ten percenter allotments to the party (Figure 5.2). The OLO wanted the MPs to use a template message critiquing the Liberal government to be distributed in non-Conservative ridings. At least one Conservative MP's assistant emailed all recipients to express disgust with the template's negative message about Prime Minister Martin. Tom Flanagan responded by warning that, if such an email were leaked, it might result in a news story about internal dissent. He relayed that her concerns should be expressed privately to OLO staff who had created the materials and that it was up to the Conservative MP whom she worked for to decide whether or not to participate. If her employer had a criticism, it was to be voiced in the privacy of a caucus meeting.

FIGURE 5.2
Request to centralize Conservative MPs' ten percenter flyers

From: *<name of OLO public affairs officer>*
Sent: Tuesday, November 23, 2004
To: Conservative assistants; Conservative constituency; Conservative members;
     Conservative research
Subject: OLO Collective ten percenters – November

To Conservative Party of Canada MPs and Assistants:

The OLO Public Affairs division is involved in an aggressive campaign to identify as many Conservative Party of Canada supporters as possible. As part of this program, we are asking Members of Parliament to donate their ten percenter allotments in order to send brochures into non-Conservative held ridings across the country.

Attached are the ten percenters that we have created for that purpose. Please note that these have been attached in Publisher format in case any Member would like to send them into his or her own riding. Please feel free to do so if you feel the topic would be applicable to your constituents. Should you choose not to use these ten percenters in your own riding, we would request that you would allow us to use them to continue this very valuable program.

Please review the ten percenters and reply by Monday, November 29th, letting us know which of them you wish to donate to the outreach program.

Source: Flanagan (2004e).

Occasionally, the Conservatives have pushed the ten percenter envelope too far. The negative messages in some flyers led to public pressure to end the practice. In 2010, the House of Commons rules were changed so that ten percenters can no longer be sent at public expense to households outside the member's riding. Negative ten percenters continue to be allowed in ridings held by the party. Another spat occurred when the Conservative Resource Group prepared templates portraying Justin Trudeau as inexperienced. Canadians' emotional connection with the Trudeau brand is such that many electors were reportedly upset with the flyers. In a rare public display of defiance, more than twenty Conservative MPs, including Minister MacKay, refused to circulate the material and declared that they would not participate in personal attacks.[68] Amid the controversy, Prime Minister Harper defended the practice as operating within the communications rules set by the House of Commons.[69] The rules still allow the Conservative Resource Group – or the NDP caucus services or the Liberal research bureau, for that matter – to urge MPs to mail letters with negative partisan messages to electors in other ridings in lieu of ten percenters. Other controversies surrounding the partisan co-opting of parliamentary mailouts include Liberal MPs mailing letters critical of the New Democrats in NDP-held ridings, the NDP coordinating 1.8 million pieces sent to electors in ridings immediately before by-elections were called, and some Conservative MPs sending leaflets with a Quick Response (QR) code that directed constituents to a party website.[70]

The second development in political direct marketing is the fervency with which Canadian political parties use email blasts.[71] They aim to frame the debate and to cultivate a brand relationship with supporters. Visitors to party websites are greeted by a splash page or homepage requesting a name and email address. For instance, at one juncture in 2014, the Liberal Party website collected names as part of a series of rotating petitions that urged policy change; the NDP's request for information was more discreetly nestled at the top of its homepage; and the Conservative Party website asked people to submit their contact details to declare that they would "stand with PM Harper." To view some areas of the Conservative leader's webpage, visitors were required to enter a password, available in exchange for an email address. Those who did so were granted insider opportunities, ranging from an advance look at party advertising to visuals of the prime minister's annual tour of the Arctic. The contact details submitted by site visitors were added to a party database, as with the ten percenter mail-backs. The email addresses become part of a customizable party listserve. The emailed messages include links to areas of a political party's website that solicit the collection of more information and donations. Some of the appeals are presented as having been authored by a member of Parliament and encourage recipients to read a related opinion piece on the party's website. Many emails feature hard-hitting remarks designed to provoke an emotional response, ranging from inspiration to fear (Figure 5.3).

Email blasts are now the preferred method of donor prospecting among all major political parties. The impetus stems from party financing rules that took effect in 2004 and 2006 and from termination of the per vote subsidy in 2015. This increases the need for parties to secure donations from ordinary citizens rather than from corporations, unions, or wealthy donors. The parties maintain databases known as CIMS (the Conservatives' software), Liberalist, and Populus (previously NDPVote) to archive

FIGURE 5.3
Email blast to the Conservative party listserve

From: Director of Communications, Conservative Party of Canada <info@conservative.ca>
Sent: June 26, 2015
To: *<Conservative Party listserve>*
Subject: Iran and ISIS

[Conservative Party logo]

[recipient's name],

On Tuesday, ISIS terrorists drowned, shot, and burned alive three groups of prisoners.

That same day, Justin Trudeau promised to stop all bombing missions against ISIS in Iraq and Syria.

When Trudeau was pressed by a reporter on when he'd support military action if he wouldn't support bombing a terrorist regime as ghastly as ISIS, he called the question "nonsensical."

That's not proven leadership.

Prime Minister Harper knows that ISIS is a genocidal death cult that must be forcefully opposed. And he has made Canada a leader in the international coalition against them.

Justin Trudeau has proven once again that he is just not ready to take on the serious job of leading Canada on the international stage.

Worse, he will undo all the hard work our Conservative Party has done to make Canada a moral leader in the world.

The world is a dangerous place – and the threat of terrorism is a present reality, not some future possibility. Justin Trudeau would ease up on terrorists who have named Canada as a target.

I know this sounds crazy – but click here **to see it for yourself.** Then let us know you agree that Justin Trudeau's just not ready for the serious job of protecting Canadians.

Thanks,
Director of Communications, Conservative Party of Canada

Note: Sender's name has been replaced by the author with the sender's position title.
Source: Conservative Party of Canada (2015b).

information on electors and donors. The basis of the databases is the national list of electors. The Canada Elections Act stipulates that the names and addresses of registered electors must be provided to registered political parties. Elections Canada provides the parties with data in electronic format for purposes of communication. This information is supplemented by data gathered through door-to-door canvassing, along with names collected at events, donor records, responses to mail-backs, and listserve signups. Canvassers are encouraged to bring their own smartphones or tablets and immediately to input data into the national database. They are trained to use database apps and follow a canvassing script. Collected information enters party databases via the CIMS to Go (C2G) app and the Liberalist app MiniVAN.[72] Liberal operatives repeat the refrain that, "if you don't put it in Liberalist, it doesn't exist."[73] Party, constituency, and campaign office staff as well as parliamentarians can access select areas of the database remotely through the Internet to enter new records and update data. The parties draw on this voter identification to target mailouts, phone calls, and meeting invitations to voters in swing ridings; to manage memberships, lawn signs, and volunteers; and to coordinate GOTV activities.

With CIMS, each voter record is assigned a number that stipulates current and lifetime support levels, and the party differentiates between supporters, potential supporters, and non-supporters.[74] The software is integrated with a server that enables personalized correspondence to be sent instantly by email. All local Conservative campaigns must forgo their ability to generate voter lists, a function now centralized in the national party office to ensure consistency of contact data.[75] Conversely, Liberal and NDP electoral district associations control their own lists. NDPVote/Populus has the dual function of comprising a political database and a case management database. A firewall setting prevents MPs and constituency office staff from inputting private information into the political database, and political office staff cannot view the case management data.

Database marketing is not primarily a political education service. There should be no mistake that the parties' motivation is to raise money and mobilize support. Long-time Conservative fundraiser Irving Gerstein explained that "we have created complex, leading-edge fundraising techniques such as data mining, segmentation, targeted marketing and relationship management, all in an effort to move our pool of identified supporters up the support pyramid, from supporters to members to donors."[76] An NDP database manager confirmed that moving supporters up the ladder is a priority in that party too:

Often you'll use your voter information, the information about people you've collected on the doorsteps, to move people up a certain progression of engagement. "Are you willing to support us? Oh, great, are you also willing to take a sign? Oh, great, would you

volunteer? Oh, that's amazing, now can I also have fifty bucks?" So
it's like you make time shifting people up that ladder. (CS 24)

The software is not cheap: the Conservative Party squandered over
$7 million on a new voter tracking program, dubbed C-Vote, in develop-
ment for five years before it was abandoned because it was not as user
friendly as CIMS.[77] To optimize their fundraising efforts, Canadian political parties follow the Obama campaign model by testing email messages
and subject line wording. They are assessed through constant monitoring
of which subject lines and messages generate the highest number of donations. Different messages are sent to different audiences for testing purposes. Customized messages are also sent to precise groups, for instance
only to party members, only to donors, only to residents of a certain province, and so on.

The real opportunity for using direct marketing to build a brand is
nurturing a connection with recipients. Relationship marketing theory
holds that communications efficiencies are achieved when long-lasting
personal relationships are cultivated with customers.[78] In this paradigm,
businesses and marketers change in response to public opinion research
and experiences with customers. Organizations seek to resolve short-term
problems in the name of maintaining long-term relationships with clients.
Trust and brand loyalty are built by engaging in a dialogue with supporters
about promises and then articulating that commitments are being upheld.
For their part, supporters are asked to make regular transactions as part
of an ongoing relationship of exchange. The NDP does this best through
its "day of action" Saturday canvassing events. People on the party's listserve
are encouraged to get involved in local door-knocking blitzes across
the country and to interact online with other volunteers and supporters.
The party sends email blasts asking for donations to help pay for clipboards
and lunches needed for canvassers. Data collected during the canvassing
become part of the party's list.

For the most part, Canadian political parties appear to treat relationship marketing as they do other communications: by putting their interests
ahead of Canadians' interests. Email blasts regularly ask supporters to
"chip in" as little as three dollars, to sign an online petition, to add their
names to show support for proposed legislation or policy, and so on. Party

messages are communicated through text, photo, and video. The emails are an information subsidy for the media, which at times treat the content as internal party communications that warrant strategy frame news treatment.[79] Signs of the commodification of leaders are visible in Liberal and NDP emails but not in Conservative messages. The Liberal Party invites donations in return for party swag, such as a sticker, a t-shirt, or mittens. Prospective donors have been invited to enter Win a Dinner with Justin contests, with all donors given a copy of the leader's favourite barbeque recipe and a chance at the runner-up prize of a limited edition Trudeau scarf. Donors are promised a "free" excerpt from Trudeau's book or a signed digital photo. NDP supporters are asked to vote on their preferred design of a bumper sticker, which they can receive "free" if they donate five dollars, or to contribute for a chance to win tickets to watch an NHL game with Mulcair. Emails give the illusion of a personal connection with the Liberal and NDP leaders, whose messages are written as though they are coming from a friend; in fact, "friend" is often the salutation used if not the recipient's first name on file. By comparison, Conservative emails have been sent from parliamentarians, senior party personnel (as in Figure 5.3), or members of the PMO, who sign off with their election campaign job titles. That party's email appeals have emphasized competing frames of the Conservative and Liberal leaders' brands and provided information on Conservative government accomplishments. They have expressed outrage at a provocative statement made by another party's leader or MP or an op-ed penned by a left-leaning media outlet. They have pointed out contradictory remarks made by Trudeau in different regions of the country. Emails from all parties convey some sort of urgency for the recipient to donate. In an act of personalized politics, each year the three major parties issue appeals asking supporters to "sign" a digital birthday card for the respective leader by submitting contact information. Desperation was palpable in the final days of the 2015 campaign when the Conservative digital crew sent emails from the prime minister, his wife, their son, and the party's top campaign strategists, pleading with recipients to vote.

The third noteworthy practice of direct marketing is more nefarious. Computerized autodialing and the delivery of prerecorded messages are so cost efficient that citizens are exposed to robocalls on a regular basis.

In politics, the communications technology is an excellent tool for getting messages out, for instance to invite supporters to a party event or to remind them to vote on election day. However, robocalls have a notorious place in Canadian political communications. A Conservative staffer was sent to jail for his role in the 2011 voter suppression scandal that saw thousands of voters receive automated phone messages on election day that spread false information that their polling stations had been moved. The calls were made to voters who, according to CIMS data, did not support the Conservative Party. After an investigation, the chief electoral officer did not find evidence to implicate the party itself. However, the party did admit to having organized robocalls in a Montreal riding to promote rumours that the Liberal MP was planning to resign and that a by-election was pending.[80] On a brighter note, citizen engagement occurs when voters dial in to tele–town halls and listen in to live conversations hosted by party leaders and local representatives. Even so, this excludes the mediatization of the fourth estate, and repetition of the party line is paramount.

6

Brand Discipline and Debranding

The practice of political marketing ranges from the cutting-edge dissection of data, to the more rudimentary practices of party discipline and spin, to the blunt instruments of opposition research and negativity. The so-called slicing and dicing of the electorate to find a communications edge is futile if brand ambassadors make unscripted remarks. Ruthless media management, uncompromising party discipline, and aggressive volleys are required on the political brand battlefield.

MEDIA MANAGEMENT AND COMMUNICATIONS CONSISTENCY

Between elections, personnel in the parliamentary and extraparliamentary wings of a political party are concerned with election readiness. As per Carty's franchise model, this encompasses communications, fundraising, policy development, candidate training, and so on. During an election campaign, there is a further layer of communications urgency. Partisans hone communications skills, learn to exploit opponents' weaknesses, and harden loyalties with their clan, including their leader. Members of the upper apparatus appreciate the importance of being able to trust each other to make smart decisions quickly in stressful situations. A war room is staffed with a rapid response unit. Specialists are brought in from advertising agencies, opinion research firms, boutique marketing shops, government relations firms, telemarketers, database marketers, and Internet specialists. The leader tours the country in a series of mini events under a media microscope that magnifies campaign gaffes. Media relations, polling, advertising, and other outreach intensify in efforts that centre on the leader and climax on election day. Afterward, a number of these party workers transition to parallel jobs in the PMO or a MINO (see Table 7.1) as well as in parliamentarians' offices, where the focus is on implementing an agenda while preparing for the next election. This requires communications planning and centralized coordination.

Media management and the packaging of politics must be cued. Media management – also known as news, reputation, or impression management – holds that political elites can influence public opinion if they can control how they and their opponents are projected.[1] Politicians and PR staff seek to manipulate so-called earned or free media (i.e., uncontrolled communications; see Figure 2.3) to promote a brand as part of their promotional mix. They attempt to satisfy the media's need for information without subjecting their brand(s) to unnecessary risk, through tactics that include pseudo-events and other activities described in Chapter 3. Macromanagement is concerned with controlling the overall brand image and reputation of the party and its leader. This includes ensuring that media messages are consistent with the operation's broad strategic positioning, such as through party discipline. Micromanagement is concerned with paying attention to details as part of an obsession with image and risk aversion. This sets the foundation for branding strategy as a basis of centralized control.

Communications cohesion begins at the centre of a political party. Every leader brings a different approach to delegating communications management. If politics is a battlefield, then the generals are located in the leader's office, and party candidates and front-line workers are the troops. The leader's inner circle must ensure that the generals operate as a unified whole, almost in a command and control manner, if they expect the troops to do likewise. Troops do not set strategy or make their own decisions. They must follow orders, or else face charges of insubordination. Those at the top are too busy battling to bother with the semantics that party members are the ones supposed to democratically set policies at party conventions. Top-down alignment requires copious internal communication through formal and informal meetings, telephone calls, and electronic media to negotiate agreement on everything from broad strategy to tiny details. Materials must pass through multiple rounds of internal editing.

Facts and statistics must be double-checked. The tiniest detail, such as a typo, communicates reduced standards of professionalism and can disrupt a communications agenda.[2] At the federal level, documents and tweets are translated into the other official language and, if applicable, into unofficial languages that must be proofed by native speakers. Translation can be tricky for slogans and catchphrases. For publicity materials, text copy must be provided to design and layout professionals, who labour over visuals and aesthetics. Electronic files must be sent in standardized formats to printers or web designers. Advertising preparation adds another layer of complexity given the need for creative planning and execution, the financial expense, audience testing, and organizing the media buy. Using closed captioning for the hearing impaired adds a day or two to the production cycle. Messages must then be synchronized with an array of other communications points of contact. This adds to timelines and pressures in a fast-paced environment. The tension peaks during the high-stakes time of an election campaign, when agents are trusted to carry out obligations with precision, when a myriad of committees meet daily to discuss strategies and logistics. Even after so many layers of review, mistakes happen.[3] Much of this occurs without involvement of the party leader.

Whenever a pressing issue emerges that requires an immediate public response, senior staffers convene and draw in others via a conference call. Tentative agreement is reached on advice to provide to the leader. Sometimes this advice is passed through a gatekeeper, such as a director of communications, who scrutinizes the information and proposed messaging. The proposed approach is presented to the leader as a means of encapsulating the party's position and making it comprehensible to the public.[4] Through private back-and-forth, over and over, the leadership circle becomes as one. It is then up to party elites to ensure that all brand ambassadors are prepared for situations with scripted comments vetted by the party centre.

Parliamentarians have more opportunities than ever to communicate and cultivate a personal brand. However, they lack the sense of loyalty to the institution of Parliament that they once held.[5] Instead, they profess an unwavering loyalty to the party and its leader. Conformity is sustained by a deepening belief that communications discipline is required for candidates to get elected, to access the perks of office, and to advance a political agenda. "If you can't run a disciplined, well-run election campaign strategy, then you make it very difficult to convince people that you can run the country," reasons an NDP strategist, who adds that parliamentarians and candidates must trust professionals in the centre to run everything (CS 27). A former PMO chief of staff agrees that most politicians appreciate the need for a consistent public voice led by the centre. "It's not that complicated. It's like being in the football huddle. I say, 'Here's what the play's gonna be.' You don't have to go around and somehow have some system for enforcing what the play's gonna be; everybody's on the same f**king team. I'm trying to score a goal," he observes. "There's a team mindset that takes over, especially when you're in the day-to-day political grind. If you don't socialize yourself and acclimatize yourself to that pretty quickly, you're not gonna have a very fun time in politics" (CS 31).

The sense of calamity that results whenever a party is off-message is held up as proof. Years of unauthorized remarks by Reform, Canadian Alliance, and Conservative candidates and MPs informed Canadian politicos everywhere, especially Harper, of the need for centralized communications control. A series of controversies framed those parties as having politically incorrect brand images. The right-wing parties were "viewed as marketed in a manner ignorant to issues of race, gender and the environment," as opposed to brands, such as Apple, with progressive images perceived to be sensitive to pressing societal values.[6] The evolution of communications technology and growing primacy of the brand can be seen in the declining tolerance that political parties have for wayward remarks. Today it is unimaginable that a party representative who makes unsavoury comments in a public setting could avoid stirring up a media frenzy followed by the party promptly disassociating itself from that individual. Nowadays everyone is indoctrinated from the outset that he or she is obliged to ensure that public messages are compliant with approved messaging. But in 1992, Kamloops newspapers reported that Keith Raddatz, a local candidate for the Reform Party nomination, made racist remarks at a public forum. He reportedly said that Indigenous people "don't want to work" before adding that people of Caribbean descent were "very heavy in the drug scene in Toronto" and responsible for a disproportionate share of that city's crime.[7] Today, within moments, such comments would rocket across traditional and social media platforms, and online trolls would pile on. Possibly, the information would be kept secret by opponents for optimal exposure at a future opportune time to inflict more damage. Either way the candidate would be abruptly expunged from the party. The media coverage would be intense but fleeting, and the culprit's political career would be over. In 2015, this happened many times with candidates of all parties. However, in 1992–93, the Reform Party did not distance itself from Raddatz. The grassroots party upheld a greater democratic principle that the people's representatives must be free to speak their minds and not be beholden to the centre. Raddatz went on to win the nomination in Kamloops and placed second in the ensuing federal contest. Privately, the party centre was concerned and conflicted. At the time, Flanagan urged a central response, which he penned in an internal party memo:

> The egregious gaffe made by Keith Raddatz in Kamloops raises important questions of political management. His remarks about Indians and Blacks are rattling around the country confirming the racist stereotype of the Reform Party, and neither the leader nor the national office has done anything to counter the bad impression. In my opinion, very quickly after Raddatz made his ill-advised statement, he should have been obliged to retract, or else we should have cut him loose. *The leader and national office cannot take a hands-off attitude towards candidates' statements that discredit the whole party or cast doubt upon important areas of policy.*[8]

Media frenzy over "bozo eruptions" in the Canadian right persisted for over a decade. Parliamentarians, candidates, members of EDAs, and party members were free to speak their minds in the spirit of grassroots engagement and decentralization. However, each controversial remark pulled the party centre into crisis mode and undermined its ability to advance an agenda. The negative publicity proved to be so significant that, as mentioned in Chapter 4, Preston Manning led a marketing movement to rebrand Reform into the Canadian Alliance. It was all for naught as long as party representatives had the freedom to make remarks that stirred media interest, leading to pseudo-scandals that necessitated damage control. Manning's successor, Stockwell Day, reflects on the hazards of leading a political party with a decentralized democratic spirit. In his opinion, it is impractical for leaders to pledge that MPs must be free to speak up in public on behalf of their constituents or to express their independent thoughts. If they expect to govern, modern political parties must emit tightly knit and centralized messages. Day posits that during his tenure at the helm of the Alliance Party

> freedom for all turned out to be a free-for-all. What may have been a noble intention to allow my MPs and their communication people to be freelancing with messaging that they thought was important to their constituents, that results in a disarray that leaves you vulnerable, as a leader, to all kinds of questions about policies – some of which you may have never articulated or even thought of ... [As a consequence,] I would say that most of the [Conservative] caucus is now convinced that the way to go is to keep the messages basic, only have limited and appointed spokespersons, and to disregard the wailing in the media about tight scripting because, in fact, tight scripting does result in people understanding where you're coming from, and that will get you support in the long run ... [Conversely,] it's a field day for media types and opponents when you've got so-called absolute freedom of MPs to speak their minds. (CP 4)

When an embattled Day stepped back as leader, Flanagan re-entered the Canadian political scene to help Harper seek leadership of the party. They brought an unwavering attitude to communications discipline. In one email to a campaign spokesperson about a contentious issue, Flanagan directed that Harper wanted no further comment offered to the media. If a public remark was warranted, then the leader would be the one to make it; everyone else was to be silent. When media enquiries persisted, and others chimed in by email with opinions about how to respond, Flanagan sent the following message using capital letters (to simulate shouting): "EVERYONE JUST KEEP THEIR MOUTH SHUT ON THIS. NO ONE TALKS TO THE MEDIA ABOUT THE TOPIC. THAT'S A DIRECT ORDER FROM STEPHEN. WE WILL HANDLE IT."[9]

This rare evidence in the Flanagan fonds of such a forceful tone illustrates internal communications management within the upper echelon of the political communications pyramid. As opposition leader, sometimes Harper dictated the content of a news release to staff,[10] and sometimes senior advisers directed that a document or message be prepared. He held morning communications meetings with eight to ten staffers of various ranks who looked to him for direction. After each meeting, they sought to interpret the leader's will and jockeyed for the authority to make decisions. At other times, an adviser overruled by Harper complained to more senior advisers, hoping that they would apply pressure on the leader to reconsider.[11] In a post-mortem of the 2004 campaign, a senior policy adviser remarked on the difficulties that emerged when the leader made decisions independently:

> Stephen completely took over the messaging for the campaign, and the war room often did not know what the message was until he actually delivered it. This severely constrained the ability of our communications team to spread our messages, which was never a problem up to that point. Part of the reason for this was that we had not scripted the final week. However, having these decisions made on the tour, often at the last minute, and especially when our events in the last week usually started later in the day, was a severe problem in the final week in terms of communicating our message.[12]

In a subsequent memo, Flanagan remarked on Harper's complaints that the party's communications personnel were softening or distorting messages. When he was touring the country, Harper sometimes reacted to the party war room's strategy by directing minions to make changes to messages approved by core advisers.[13] To his detractors, this is evidence of an obsession with micromanagement. Perhaps, but that is the party leader's role. Leaders must support everything that the party is communicating and how it is communicated.

Despite efforts to ensure communications discipline, under Harper's leadership the Canadian right continued to wrestle with the virtues of grassroots free speech versus centralized control. This was particularly difficult with respect to social issues. Perhaps the most costly off-message remark occurred in the waning days of the 2004 campaign. The Liberal

Party released earlier recorded footage of a Conservative MP saying "to heck with the courts" on the tenuous matter of same-sex marriage legislation.[14] This derailed the Conservative Party's momentum by adding to opponents' frame that the party harboured extremists and had a hidden agenda. Henceforth, Harper's team determined that anybody who represents the party brand must not be permitted to muse publicly about party policy and that the media must understand that comments from anyone other than the leader are not necessarily those of the party. Candidates and MPs were told that, if they wander off-message and embarrass the leader, at a minimum they will have to apologize immediately and publicly. This included ministers who were expected to issue a retraction if they said something inconsistent with the master message.[15] By relentlessly preaching message discipline, a party reaches its desired brand state, whereby, as a Conservative spinner explains, "it doesn't matter what some backbencher from some riding you've never heard of says, because everybody knows and understands that the leader sets the policy, and, if backbencher so-and-so says something, who cares?" (CS 9). Indeed, when a Conservative candidate talked about abortion during the 2011 federal election campaign, the party centre distanced itself from the controversial issue by dismissing him as a "backbench MP."[16] Message control was more pronounced in the next campaign when a number of Conservative candidates were unrepentant in their decision to avoid interacting with the media.[17]

The same discipline is expected of the party leader. Whenever a leader does not stick to pre-agreed messaging, he or she is drawn into punditry, which necessitates damage control to deal with his provocative comments.[18] The Conservative Party learned to insulate its leader and all brand ambassadors from unscripted situations, but even then off-message sound bites like Harper's impromptu comment in 2008 that the plunging stock market represented some "good buying opportunities" are problematic. As one Conservative strategist explains, the objective is "to have the consistency of a metronome" and "to consistently drive your messages until the end of the campaign."[19] A former Harper PMO communications director adds that this is necessary because the political class is "asked for reaction all day, every day, on every issue, at a moment's notice and with tight deadlines ... In the cluttered communications environment, messages have to be repeated endlessly before they punch through."[20] Planned messages are often provocative too. The Conservative policy that Muslim women ought to remove their niqabs during Canadian citizenship ceremonies, and possibly those employed in the federal public service too, is an example of how a calculated wedge issue risks tarnishing a party brand as politically incorrect.

Containment of off-message remarks in Canadian politics is now an art form. A case in point of how a bozo eruption becomes a top news story, is contained, and then dissipates occurred in 2014 when a Conservative MP advocated that fellow parliamentarians wear a body camera, in his words, to "prevent besmirchment." A news release issued from his parliamentary email account stated that he wore a digital camera as a form of "risk protection" against accusations of impropriety. This deservedly became news and was panned on social media and in televised punditry. Within *hours* of the remark, the MP issued a second release, this time through the PMO: "Earlier today I issued a press release that I now recognize was completely inappropriate. I retract that press release unconditionally and deeply regret it."[21] The PMO emailed a statement to journalists that the remarks reflected the MP's personal views only. Apparently, the MP was so worked up into a state of paranoia about inopportune encounters destabilizing his personal brand and the party's brand that his anxiety and poor judgment did just that. Even if we appreciate the reasons for containment, this practice raises questions about the influence of the executive branch over members of the legislative branch, and about the state of Canadian democracy in the digital age.

Control over brand ambassadors is possible mainly because of the scope and speed of digital media, combined with the leader's control over candidate nominations. Communications centralization has been fuelled by changes made to the Canada Elections Act in 1970, which required that party labels must be included on election ballots. Doing so reduces a voter's search for information and the potential for confusion and increases the primacy of party affiliation and branding. Also introduced was the requirement that the party leader must sign every candidate's nomination papers. Ever since, leaders use their power to shut out undesirables and to usher in preferred candidates, including incumbents. It is a tool for "the centre" to exact stringent discipline over its agents. Passage of the Reform Act (see

Chapter 2) shifts that power from the leader to one or more designated representatives of the party. It remains to be seen whether party agents will do the centre's bidding.

All major Canadian political parties demand rigorous background checks of anyone seeking to represent them. Questions on candidate nomination forms assess whether applicants are likely to toe the party line, such as if they disagree with any party policies or principles or have ever held extremist views. Considerable scrutiny of the applicant's personal history is performed. A prospective Conservative must provide a certificate of conduct from the police and authorize the party to perform a credit check and criminal record check. Consent is sought to gather information on any offences or infractions held by the Canada Revenue Agency, the Canada Border Services Agency, Citizenship and Immigration Canada, and the Department of National Defence. A New Democrat is asked about citizenship, associations with groups, and anything that the applicant thinks might result in public embarrassment. A Liberal must disclose information on matrimonial or custody proceedings, suspension from postsecondary studies or a job, tax liabilities, charges of plagiarism, or breach of trust. That party asks its prospective candidates the following, which by now surely places more emphasis on the individual's social media footprint:

Have you ever written anything that has been published or widely distributed through the Internet or other means? Without limiting the breadth of this question, this includes academic or professional papers, books or textbooks, newsletters, newspaper reports, op-ed pieces, columns, letters to the editor, magazine articles, short stories, novels or other fiction. If so, copies of all such writings must be provided herewith or, if the volume of your writing or other obstacles makes that impractical, ten representative samples must be provided (extracts from a book will suffice if a copy is not readily available) along with a comprehensive list of all such publications. NO/YES (if Yes, provide details).[22]

If an applicant passes the screening process, the Conservative Party's nomination rules stipulate that a $1,000 good conduct bond must be submitted. This is refunded if the party is satisfied that the contestant followed the nomination rules.[23] Applicants must sign a confidentiality agreement not to publicly reveal information on the screening process. Brand control does not stop there. During election training sessions, candidates are warned to stay on script and always be on the lookout. At one session, a former Conservative PMO communications director advised that, "even when out shopping, or you're at an event, you're always on, people always listen to you, they may be tape recording you, they may be videoing you."[24] We know this because the Liberals leaked a secret recording of her remarks.

Irrespective of the changes associated with the Reform Act, nominated candidates will be expected to act as brand ambassadors. They are no longer free agents. Local campaigns are provided with communications templates to avoid the look and feel of a "curate's egg," as Doug Finley put it.[25] Candidates are fed messages of the day and news releases for local distribution. They are told to follow party office instructions for marketing collateral (campaign ephemera). The party centre commissions a professional agency to create brochure and signage templates that enforce a common design and consistent messages. The candidate's name, photograph, riding, and/or contact details are added, with perhaps some room for a personal bio. Postcards are almost exclusively party messaging, with some room on the back for candidate information. During the 2006 federal election, Conservative candidates received a thirty-two-page catalogue of party marketing collateral.[26] The catalogue included a template for a required general introduction brochure. They were given a choice of prepared issue flyers regarding agriculture, child care, crime, accountability, seniors, tax credits, small business, or sports. Templates of posters, flyers, and hockey pucks were recommended for distribution at local hockey arenas. As mentioned in Chapter 2, the catalogue included materials to support the party's GST message. To avoid leaving anything to chance, candidates were asked to review proofs provided by the party centre. A central party worker submitted the electronic files to a local printer in the required format to ensure consistency of ink colours, card stock, and dimensions. Website design templates were similarly prepared. Requests from candidates for special design elements were fed up the line for consideration, such as placing the candidate's name above her or his photo rather than below it.[27] This central coordination of communications creates resource efficiencies, with limited flexibility for candidates to respond to local circumstances.

It is a support service that addresses the needs of the many constituency-level operations that request assistance with all manner of promotional activities.[28] Having one's electoral communications managed from the centre reinforces that candidates, local campaign personnel, and electoral district associations are not the ones in charge.

Party discipline and top-heavy management are more difficult to implement in the parliamentary arena. The threat of pushback and pressure from caucus and individuals is ever-present. When elected officials are not allowed to speak out on hot-button issues, their disputes escalate into broader principles of free speech and parliamentary representation. The reasons for insubordination vary and include some combination of thwarted ambition, ideology, principle, and emotion. During the Chrétien years, backbencher frustrations with the centre were symbolized by the catchphrase "it's who you know in the PMO," a rallying cry in the Liberal caucus, which wanted more involvement in government decisions. They pushed out Chrétien in favour of Martin even though the prime minister had led the party to three consecutive majority governments and continued to fare well in the polls. The Martin PMO turned out to be just as centralized as its predecessor but less successful.

From time to time, Conservative MPs have publicly resisted brand control. One instance was the aforementioned unrest when many refused to participate in a coordinated ten percenter scheme against Justin Trudeau. Another visible test of Harper's leadership occurred when a number of Conservative backbenchers publicly voiced their support for a Conservative MP who wanted to speak on female gendercide, a matter that includes abortion, a debate that Harper vowed he would not reopen.[29] When the party whip denied the MP an opportunity to raise the issue as an SO 31, the MP complained to the speaker of the House of Commons that this was an affront to his parliamentary privileges. The speaker, himself a Conservative MP, agreed that members have the right to speak in the House without their party's permission. When the member was finally granted the opportunity to do so, he opted to speak instead about a talent contest in his riding. Other cases of brand incongruence are not resolved so amicably. Parliamentarians who cause public embarrassment are removed from cabinet and/or caucus, and some leave of their own accord. When Conservative MP Brent Rathgeber opted to sit as an independent, he cited frustration with the PMO's micromanagement of communications: "When you have a PMO that tightly scripts its backbenchers like this one attempts to do ... we have to take a stand that we're not going to read these talking points that are written by PMO staffers, that we're not going to vote like trained seals based on how they tell us."[30] Referring to "trained seals" predates Harper and digital media. It is the central scripting that is more pronounced now.

As in any large organization, some people recoil at being told what to do unless they accept the rationale. A branding imperative means that the leadership circle must ensure that brand ambassadors understand why communications consistency is necessary. Parliamentarians are anxious to know about preparations for the next campaign and to be engaged in decision making on matters that concern their constituents. Caucus pushes for communications templates, slogans, and advertisements to be vetted and for strategic plans to be divulged.[31] While in opposition, the Conservative caucus decided to form its own committee to preview and vet campaign radio and TV ads. One MP pitched the plan for a caucus elections committee to the party centre as follows: "The [caucus] group will sit as any other focus group does to provide comment on the ads. It is expected that the ads will be presented to the group well in advance of [the] final version so that the group's input can influence necessary changes. Caucus hopes to be of significant assistance to the developers of such ads."[32] It is unclear how Harper responded to this demand. Needless to say, there are many reasons that caucus in control of communications strategy is an unworkable proposition for professionalized parties. It is one of a number of incidents that impress upon a leader that message control is stronger when there is organizational buy-in.

Message discipline is possible only if caucus is given meaningful opportunities to engage with the political executive, in particular with the leader. Harper expressly engaged the Conservative caucus in regular closed-door meetings in which they were invited to share their concerns with him in front of their colleagues. MPs were expected to mount well-prepared arguments. Often their concerns and demands were rationalized and rebutted. But if they made compelling cases, Harper sometimes announced to the room that a decision would be delayed or changed. In contrast with his public persona, this demonstrated that he was listening and willing to adjust policy in response to caucus concerns. Another mechanism for MPs to voice opinions is the Conservative caucus advisory committee (CAC) system introduced in 2010. Day relays that he spoke with Harper about how Alberta Premier Ralph Klein set up standing policy committees made up of ministers and government backbenchers. His ministers were required to vet legislation in those committees; this inspired the importation of a similar system by BC Premier Gordon Campbell.[33] Borrowing from the Alberta model, and mindful of the internal uprising that led to Chrétien's ouster as Liberal Party leader, CACs were created for backbench MPs and senators to provide policy input to ministers. The committees were chaired by the parliamentary secretaries to the ministers and made up of five other government MPs, who tended to belong to the relevant House of Commons standing committee, and three government senators. Their meetings were normally attended by the minister and a senior political staffer. Such a large number of CACs was possible in part because so many parliamentary secretaries existed (thirty Conservative MPs had the title in early 2015) and acted as trusted spokespersons for their ministers, including in the House. The prime minister expressly told ministers to take a cabinet proposal to the CAC, and he expected a full report at cabinet on the remarks or concerns raised. The parliamentary plan section of a memorandum to cabinet specified that the minister's office was to provide a summary of consultations with caucus, including the CAC, and if not to explain the rationale for not doing so.[34] Proposals lacking such formal consultation or pointing to dissent at the CAC level were unlikely to advance in cabinet. The forums enabled mutual exchanges. Backbenchers gained an opportunity to express their points of view from across Canada about topical issues and policies and to validate their ability to connect with cabinet and the prime minister, who benefitted from greater awareness of MPs' perspectives. The inputs assisted political staff and were used by party strategists to determine which issues to probe in market research.[35] The caucus advisory committee system was an underappreciated outlet for backbenchers to communicate with the centre, though as Rathgeber points out members lacked any authority to overrule ministers.[36] This sets up the paradoxical scenario of a process that "provides an important counter narrative to the image of an all-controlling Conservative government enforcing discipline to compel caucus cohesion" yet "further serve[d] to centralize and consolidate power with the prime minister at the expense of individual ministers."[37] Regardless of the intent, the result is that CACs solidified the brand construct by providing an institutional mechanism to keep brand messaging in line with brand ambassadors, who in turn are more likely to fall in line.

With the existence of CACs, and whatever parallel mechanism the Trudeau Liberals intoduce, frustration about the constant reminders and expectations of sameness tends to be external to the caucus. Government and party elites learn the value of taking measures to avoid the possibility of others applying a slant to their message. Just as a baseball pitcher twists the ball in such a way that makes it difficult for the batter to prevent it from reaching the catcher, politicians and communications aides spin messages (the ball) to reach audiences (the catcher) with as little interference from journalists (the batter) as possible.[38] On the surface, spin pertains to how information is publicly spoken and written. Words and phrases are used to frame the issue in a manner favourable to the speaker. Unfavourable information is withheld or twisted. When a journalist asks a direct question, a politician uses a bridging phrase, such as by saying "the real issue is" or "what you need to remember is" (CI 16). At a deeper level, spin requires that all brand ambassadors repeat the same messaging established by strategists at the centre, without necessarily knowing the reasoning behind the messaging. According to Lilleker, spin lingers from the pre-political marketing age. It is now part of the entire packaging of communications. He writes that "there is no truth. Realities are a matter of perception, they are created and destroyed and only exist at an individual level ... The reality that is constructed is one of imagery, packaging, designer politics and aestheticization."[39] He cautions that spin involves underhanded attempts to obscure truth and hide bad news. This becomes the story when politicians are critiqued for evasive manoeuvres and when journalists are counterblamed for treating brand ambassadors unfairly.

In Canadian party politics, message discipline, spin, and brand control are practised in so many ways that even those working in the Ottawa bubble lose track. Depriving the media of uncontrolled situations limits journalists to complaining about a lack of access instead of mining information for the story that they are pursuing. This inhibits a communications snafu or gaffe by messengers, and though it does not prevent a negative story it might reduce its news cycle. When a political organization drives the news agenda, journalists' questions focus on that issue. If there is a solitary, unified message emanating from all spokespersons, then there is little else about which the media can talk. Otherwise, journalists have opportunities to make the news, and they are prone to ask about process and controversy. Likewise, if given the chance, political opponents and protesters will mobilize to disrupt the government's agenda. Not only will considerable preparation and financial outlay for a positive news story be wasted, but also the interruption will make for bad news and visuals that damage the master brand.

The Harper Conservatives shared another commonality with Blair's New Labour: brand control becomes the story if it appears to be subversive to democracy. Limiting and controlling media access to Conservatives was so regimented during the 2011 federal election campaign that pundits dubbed it a "bubble campaign." Reporters on the leader's tour were permitted five questions a day – four from the national press and one from a local outlet. Attempts to receive further information from communications personnel resulted in a terse response: "What the prime minister said stands."[40] Across Canada, representatives from all parties – particularly Conservatives – refused invitations to participate in all-candidates' debates and opted to knock on doors instead. Heading into the 2015 campaign, the party announced that it would not participate in the traditional leaders' debates organized by the broadcasters' consortium in an attempt to exert control over the high-stakes forum. The growth of digital media allowed the Conservatives to break the consortium's monopoly on leaders' debates that had lasted for a generation. By that time, the limit of five questions per event was routine and no longer a news story in itself, though it continued to add to an anti-democratic narrative.

In the midst of that campaign, and beyond the party's control, hundreds of PMO emails were made public during the Mike Duffy trial. They offer further insight into the centre's fixation with media management and communications consistency. Recall that the PMO is exempt from access to information requests, so the messages provide a unique opportunity to peer into real-time issues management practices. The emails surround a period in 2013 when Senator Duffy's expense claims were under scrutiny, which culminated in Prime Minister Harper's chief of staff, Nigel Wright, personally repaying $90,172 on Duffy's behalf.[41] The media pressure and opposition questions at the time were relentless, and the emails reveal how the centre leads the charge on a file at the top of the public agenda. However, it is not clear to what extent if any the prime minister was involved with the communications planning; it is only clear that his inner circle wielded significant clout. Three noticeable communications themes are present.

First, the PMO plays a central coordinating role in the stickhandling of a major controversy. Wright requested that the leadership circle "coordinate every move,"[42] and he directed other senior members of the PMO that "nothing [happens] without our prior approval. We will not set anything in motion without knowing where we want it to end up and how we will make that happen."[43] In another message, he relayed that "we'll have to do this in a way that does not lead to the Chinese water torture of new facts in the public domain; that the PM does not want."[44] At one point, Wright suggested that it is not the role of a chief of staff "to be micromanaging files,"[45] an indication that such a level of central engagement is atypical. The prime minister's principal secretary was often included in email exchanges but not the director of communications.

Second, the PMO moves in lockstep with senior government senators, expected to be brand ambassadors. "We have to ensure that further statements by our senators on this ... are coordinated with PM," Wright relayed.[46] He requested that actions from the office of the leader of the government in the Senate, Marjory LeBreton, be subject to "pre-clearance"[47] by the PMO, and he conveyed to her that "as long as you and I stay together on this we can minimize the damage already caused."[48] Wright and other prime ministerial staff were also in contact with the two Conservative members of the Senate subcommittee on internal economy, budgets, and administration. Those senators worked with the PMO to soften language in the subcommittee's report on the audits of expense claims. One of the senators was Carolyn Stewart-Olsen, a former PMO press secretary and director of strategic communications, praised in the emails for her communications management efforts in the upper chamber. She felt that receiving instructions from the centre without being part of the strategic deliberation encumbered her ability to deliver. "I am always ready to do exactly what is asked but it would have been a great help to know in advance what the strategy was. I can only do so much without background ... Some personalities take a bit of management," Stewart-Olsen wrote to Wright.[49] The exchanges indicate that certain point persons are PMO conduits in the Senate and that backbench senators are not under the thumb of their party's leadership circle to the extent that backbench MPs tend to be.

Third, we live in an increasingly litigious society in which the remark of a public official is subject to instant analysis and can be treated as a policy statement with legal implications. Top members of the PMO as well as legal counsel cited the need for communications symmetry. Included within Wright's infamous "we are good to go from the PM" email was a remit from those working on the file that "the PMO will take all reasonable efforts to ensure that members of the Conservative caucus, if they speak on this matter, do so in a fashion that is consistent with the agreed media lines."[50] Wright concurred, on the basis that "the media lines are accurate, and we do not wish people to make inaccurate statements." He initially authorized media lines for Conservative senators; these lines went through a round of revisions and further review by solicitors.

The high-profile and evidentiary nature of the Duffy-Wright emails begs the question of whether henceforth political and government actors will be more cautious in their written exchanges. More broadly, it is proof that PMO staff seek to spin and control information, which raises questions about how involved the prime minister is in overseeing their actions.

COMMUNICATIONS CONTROL

Regional strife is arguably the greatest risk to a federal government's message agenda. Bakvis argues that the most significant inhibitor of a Canadian leader's authority is federalism.[51] To curtail this threat to brand messaging, Prime Minister Harper eschewed the defining image of executive federalism by refusing to participate in first ministers' conferences or summits. He opted instead to exchange letters with premiers and to hold private one-on-one meetings. This came with the condition that, if the meeting was to proceed, the media would not be alerted without PMO approval. Asymmetrical federalism is calculated to be a useful tool when dealing with temperamental premiers and ones who campaign for a federal opposition party. Premier of Ontario Kathleen Wynne – an enthusiastic supporter of PMJT and a fascinating study of personal branding in her own right – agitated for media attention when she publicly complained that her requests to meet with the prime minister were being referred to federal ministers. The premier publicly released letters to the prime minister in which she remarked that it took two months to receive a response to her previous letter and that it was nearly a year since the two first ministers last met. Wynne proclaimed that she wanted to discuss agenda items ranging from infrastructure to violence against Indigenous women and girls.[52] Harper was silent, further fueling anti-democratic anxieties. His communications gambit was that this type of pressure would recede as the media lost interest without new information to report. However, Wynne succeeded in placing her demand on the public agenda. This became a problem for Harper when media and pundits connected it to a negative framing of his strict style of media management. When the prime minister finally agreed to meet with Wynne, the PMO took pains to point out that he would do so immediately prior to the world junior gold medal hockey game in Toronto. The exact location of the meeting was not publicized, and the photograph released by the PMO suggested that both participants were jovial (Figure 6.1). A throng of media would have pounced had the location been revealed. Instead, TSN interviewed the prime minister – wearing a Team Canada hockey jersey – in the stands about hockey, without mention of politics. Journalists followed up with Wynne about the meeting and to find out why, unlike the PM, she did not attend the game. Without national media forums attended by the PM, it is more difficult for a premier to develop a national profile and agitate for regional de-mands. The diminished sense of regional cleavages increased the Con-servative's ability to control the agenda. The difficulty for premiers to command a national audience brings into question the future of first min-isters' conferences, even as Trudeau promises more amicable relations.

In the right circumstances, ordinary citizens have the power to derail an agenda. Prime Minister Brian Mulroney's notorious confrontation with a senior citizen illustrates why leaders are normally kept away from engaging with electors in uncontrolled circumstances. In a bid to reduce

FIGURE 6.1 PMO photo of Prime Minister Harper meeting with Premier
Wynne | Prime Minister's Office (2015b); PMO photographer Jason Ransom, Toronto,
January 5, 2015.

overspending, his Progressive Conservative government planned to de-
index old age pensions, breaking a promise not to do so. Seniors were
outraged. Some of them protested on Parliament Hill and spotted Mulroney
chatting with tourists. One senior proceeded to scold the prime minister
in front of news cameras, calling him a liar and concluding with "goodbye,
Charlie Brown." The media repeated the clip over and over. Within a week,
the policy was abandoned. Reflecting on the matter, Savoie observes that
"the best-laid plans by the 600-person-year strong department of finance,
including hundreds of senior economists, came crashing down all because
of a 15-second sound bite."[53]

Astute observers of Canadian politics will notice that protesters have
had no such success ambushing Prime Minister Harper. The Conservatives
screened attendees at his events to deny entry to undesirables. They were
removed in the name of security and to prevent interruption; it was spun
as a room capacity issue. Controversy erupted during the 2011 campaign
when two youth were told to leave a party rally after it was discovered that
one of them had posed with Ignatieff and posted the photograph to her
Facebook page. Minister John Baird defended the controls: "This is the
middle of an election campaign. You don't invite the public to come in
here and ask questions at your press conferences."[54] Screening of attendees

at Harper's pseudo-events tightened further in the 2015 campaign. Only party supporters received an invitation to attend. After registering online, pre-screened invitees received an email advising them that they would be notified later about the exact location of the event, sometimes with twenty-four hours' notice. They were issued a ticket with a QR barcode, which presumably connected to the party's Constituency Information Management System database. Upon arrival, guests were denied entry unless they presented the barcode and proved their identity, and then they were given a wristband. Everyone else, including journalists who had to wait in a separate area, were told that it was a private event. As well, in addition to the normal RCMP detail assigned to protect party leaders, the Conservatives hired their own security personnel to enforce the practice. However, the party backtracked on a policy that attendees other than accredited media must agree not to circulate information about the event.[55]

Caution about interacting with the public extends to ministers, who risk Mulroney-like performance disruption. Upon assuming office, the Harper PMO instructed the Privy Council Office to ensure that personnel were aware that all communications, including those by ministers, had to be vetted by "the centre."[56] There is good reason. Julian Fantino was appointed as minister for international cooperation in 2012 upon Bev Oda's exit. The following year the Canadian International Development Agency (CIDA) held a town hall meeting with Fantino. The media reported that complaints were fielded from employees about political micromanagement. There was frustration about limited access to the minister's office, self-censorship, and bottlenecking. Staff were annoyed that they were not permitted to talk publicly about their observations and experiences. One CIDA employee argued that political masters did not comprehend the workplace difficulties that result from the lack of "agility of the system" to allow employees to make decisions "without having to always go back and forth [through] 17 versions of a memo."[57] Within six months, CIDA was subsumed into the renamed Department of Foreign Affairs, Trade and Development. Fantino's star waned in 2014 when, as the minister of veterans affairs, he arrived over an hour late for a meeting with veterans, who wanted to voice concerns about the closure of regional offices. In front of cameras, ex-soldiers berated the minister, who chirped back before leaving the room. Months later cameras recorded the minister walking away as the wife of a soldier called out for help with her husband's post-traumatic stress disorder. The media replayed footage of both episodes over and over. This fuelled a view that the government was not providing enough support for veterans, which struck at a Conservative sub-brand. In an effort to control the minister's poor communications, the PMO's director of media relations was appointed Fantino's chief of staff, and a new deputy minister was assigned to the department.[58] Still unable to shake negative media coverage, Harper's first order of business in the new year was to protect the brand by demoting Fantino to associate minister. The announcement came after another defence minister was already sworn in.

Controlling media access to members of cabinet was at the forefront of Harper's relations with the Canadian Parliamentary Press Gallery in particular. The PMO agitated the norms and demands of the gallery by curtailing journalists' access.[59] As Pierre Trudeau did before him, Harper wanted his staff to vet which journalists could ask questions. When CPPG members unanimously voted to ignore the PMO's list of approved journalists, Harper responded by ceasing to attend events at the National Press Theatre. Conservative PMO media advisories often invited only photojournalists to photo-ops (Figure 8.2), signalling that no questions would be fielded, and finally sidestepped the fourth estate altogether by live-streaming pseudo-events (Figure 8.3) and holding controlled Q&A sessions (Figure 8.4). The PM and a number of ministers, including some with responsibilities for major portfolios, avoided interviews by not returning journalists' phone calls. They escaped the visual of being attacked in a scrum by not walking through publicly accessible areas of Parliament Hill. The PMO ceased publicizing the times of cabinet meetings and ordered the removal of microphones in the hallways of rooms where cabinet meetings are held. Sometimes Harper went for long stretches without speaking to the media. He did not take questions in the summer of 2010 during the rancour over his administration's decision to discontinue the long-form census, leaving Minister Tony Clement to be the government's spokesperson on the issue. More than a month passed until, after a mini cabinet shuffle, the PM took four questions. None was allowed about the census. "We do not do first come first serve. We never have," said Harper's deputy director of communications in reference to the PMO's selection of which reporters could ask questions.[60] In the days of longer media cycles, the media were exasperated when Louis St. Laurent and others were unavailable for extended stretches. At times opposition leaders also limit questions from journalists, such as Mulcair's refusal to take any media questions in the period immediately before he was elected leader of the NDP and on the first and last days of the 2015 election campaign. There is little that journalists can do about being shunned once political figures have ascended to the heights of power.

Jostling with the press gallery is not restricted to Parliament Hill. Unlike Martin, Harper held half of his media events outside Ottawa.[61] "A lot of previous prime ministers seem to make all of their announcements only in Toronto, Montreal and Vancouver and I have made a point as prime minister of trying to travel regularly across the country to a wide range of communities, not just east and west but south and north as well," Harper explained.[62] On visits to foreign countries and on his Arctic tours, he similarly accepted no more than four to six questions during his daily media availability. On one occasion, media on the PM's airplane wanted to speak with him about Senate appointments. When the plane landed in Canada, the opening of the second staircase for journalists to disembark was delayed, while Harper got off into a waiting car.[63]

Aside from disputes about access to government officials, there are concerns about how the release of information is controlled. One of the countless examples occurred when the prime minister waited until the day before New Year's Eve to ask the governor general to prorogue Parliament for two months. Another was picking budget day for the chief electoral officer to make his first public statement about the Conservative-linked robocalls that spread false information on polling stations. Officials invoke secrecy about the government's operations, such as by barring reporters from access to military conflicts or documenting the repatriation of soldiers' remains. The Conservative government refused to provide information to the Military Police Complaints Commission that investigated Canada's role in transferring Afghan prisoners. As mentioned in Chapter 1, its refusal to provide financial information to the legislature led to its falling on a motion of non-confidence.

The national media and opposition became furious about these blocking tactics. Their outrage is justified given their responsibility to monitor government on behalf of Canadians, yet there was little that they could do.

The Canadian Association of Journalists called upon its members to stop putting up with emailed responses when an interview was warranted. The organization urged journalists not to reproduce handout photos or videos and whenever it occurs, to mention in their stories that the government refuses to provide information.[64] After years of seeing access decline, the CPPG unanimously passed a motion that members have the right to ask questions "in all photo-ops, and availabilities with the prime minister, cabinet ministers, and all parliamentarians, to fulfill our function as journalists in a democratic society."[65] These efforts did not result in any significant changes. They did spur an image of the Conservative brand as anti-democratic, contributing to the public's galvanization around the sunny ways of the Trudeau Liberals.

A branding strategy that deprives journalists of information assumes that they will eagerly snap up whatever is offered to them. Controlled leaks, practised by all parties, reveal information in a manner suggesting that it is not intended for public consumption. While in opposition, a Conservative MP wrote in an internal party email that Harper requested that some information on campaign preparations be leaked,[66] though some interview respondents suggested that he was more averse to leaking tactics as prime minister. This is not to say that controlled leaks do not happen. A long-standing practice is to float policy options as trial balloons to test public reactions to contentious policy proposals. One such instance involved a leaked presentation to cabinet by the heritage minister. The presentation outlined a proposal to amend the Copyright Act so that news clips owned by the media would be fair game for use in political advertising.[67] The leak was a shot across the bows of major broadcasters. It appeared to be a response to a letter sent to political parties warning that political ads that use source material without the content creator's authorization will not be aired on their networks.

Some leaks undermine the role of Parliament. The sanctity of government budget making has been usurped by political staffers who divulge information in advance of its delivery in the House of Commons. This occurred during Prime Minister Martin's tenure and persisted under that of Prime Minister Harper.[68] In 2008, the PMO chief of staff authorized a leak that the government would be reducing funds for artistic and cultural programs.[69] The next year a PMO staffer anonymously unveiled the budget deficit figure.[70] Other leaks are designed to discredit opponents. For instance, a Conservative PMO communications officer quietly offered the media details of Justin Trudeau's public speaking fees and asked to be identified as an unnamed source.[71]

Sometimes uncontrolled leaks occur despite the best brand control efforts. Information is released by accident, such as when the wrong email address is used,[72] and there is the ever-present concern that confidential information will be made public by a disgruntled employee. Preston Manning points out that "all it takes is one secretary or volunteer with an iPhone or a camera, and by nightfall they can show the world that this is what you are inside and this is what you are outside" (CP 2). At other times, it is unclear whether a leak is intentional, as with a Conservative dossier of controversial statements made by Harper and obtained by the Liberals, which media outlets made available online in searchable format.[73]

The rebuffing of requests to disclose information carries over to the government's compliance with the Access to Information Act. In recent years, the number of access to information requests has increased significantly. So have the number of complaints.[74] An overarching concern is that responses are delayed and/or redacted.[75] Moreover, political interference occurs: the Office of the Information Commissioner identified improper screening by political staffers in Public Works. The Conservatives also put a stop to the PCO's tradition of releasing federal cabinet documents after thirty years, which had provided the media with opportunities to report on past administrations' decision making. At the same time, proactive disclosure by government is increasing. In 2011, the government of Canada initiated a pilot launch of its online Open Data Portal (data. gc.ca), which made over 260,000 government datasets publicly accessible. Later that year the government announced that departments would be required to disclose online whatever is released under access to information requests. Depending on where you sit, the Harper administration was either more transparent or more secretive than any government in recent memory. Either way, the attempted politicization of an Open Government logo (discussed in Chapter 10) is evidence of a permanent campaigning mindset even on matters of government transparency.

Although it is tempting to direct all blame at the principal, it is important to understand that agents themselves promote spin and brand control.

Political communications staffers, or at least the ones around Harper before he became prime minister, offered to torque information. One volunteered in a group email to party strategists that, "if you feel this analysis needs spin-doctoring, please let me know."[76] After the Conservative Party's inaugural leadership campaign, journalists pressed for turnout data, provincial results, and riding-by-riding breakdowns. Internal discussions ensued about which numbers to release. Party strategists knew that dissection of voting data would prompt opinions and questions about regions in which the party was the weakest. In one group email, a partisan asked "why should we give strategic info on our strengths and weaknesses?" and remarked that releasing only select figures "for spin" would draw attention to the positive angles.[77] As mentioned at the end of this chapter, Stéphane Dion likewise found that political communications personnel are eager to engage in subterfuge.

COMMUNICATIONS SWORDS AND SHIELDS

To influence media frames, political actors use communications "swords" and "shields." This is Conservative communicators' lingo for the identification of issues that require aggressive actions (swords) or defensive manoeuvres (shields).[78] Sword issues are the ones that the party wants to advance. Proactive and aggressive communications tactics are required to push a point of view. Shield issues are matters that the party does not want on the public agenda and is vulnerable to. When under communications attack, strategists must avoid going into a communications bunker. Doing so would allow others to frame the debate and put the brand under siege. Rather, the adage that the best defence is a good offence applies. They attempt to change the topic of conversation to a sword issue. If that does not work, then they proceed to discredit the shield issue. In the age of branding, it is not enough to deconstruct an opposing argument: damaging the opponent's personal brand is a staple. This is done with the repetition of simple phrases and visuals calculated by the centre to reinforce the party's preferred wedge.

Many believe that it is a stain on democracy that political communications are disposed toward negativity. Positivity and cooperation stir uplifting emotions such as hope, optimism, and pride among supporters. A common criticism of adversarial politics is that it is difficult to determine the precise causes for Canadians' declining trust and engagement in the political process, but it is hard to imagine that shallow, negative campaigning ... does anything to inspire increased participation in the democratic process. Worryingly, it is more likely to produce a largely uninformed and disengaged electorate who become more susceptible to branding, marketing and personality driven campaigns and increasingly base voting decisions on emotion rather than evidence or careful policy analysis of the major issues. Those looking to engage in more substantive, policy driven political debate will instead become increasingly cynical and disillusioned which may also result in further disengagement.[79]

Others would point out that negativity is a sign of healthy democratic competition and pluralism in a society that values freedom of speech. Political debate inherently involves criticism, polarization, and negativity. Moreover, conflict and negative messaging stir the attention of audiences, arouse them, and increase their recall.[80] The ruthless nature of democratic politics, and political strategists' own use of the game frame, are laid bare in the following excerpt from a post-campaign memo by Doug Finley:

> To be successful in tight races, there has to be a win-at-all-costs mentality. One has to have a killer instinct. When your opponent is in trouble, you have to stand on his toes so he can't escape, then bludgeon him into submission. You don't step back into a neutral corner and allow him to regain both his feet and his breath.[81]

To exploit weaknesses, political parties have long recommended that campaign managers maintain "a nice fat file" on opponents to inflict damage.[82] "Oppo," short for "opposition research," is the practice of gathering information about opponents for strategic communications purposes. It involves monitoring news reports and conducting online searches, and speaking with sources in opposing camps to extract inside knowledge. To protect their brands with swords and shields, political actors must constantly self-research to anticipate what their opponents will uncover.[83] They must obtain information to pre-empt, defend, or otherwise limit potential damage. Oppo is even conducted against colleagues. In an email, Harper claimed, "I know that, under [Preston] Manning, the party was collecting extensive files on me, even while I was still an M.P. Good use of public money, eh?"[84] All manner of oppo is seen as anti-democratic and un-Canadian. The publicity associated with the revelation that Day met with a private investigator to scrutinize his opponents contributed to a caucus revolt that ousted him as party leader.

The internal scrutiny of party nomination candidates is a reflection of political operatives' awareness of the value of oppo. Political party staffers scour the web for digital footprints. E-communication provides a treasure chest of data, including statements made on social media, news media archives, public comments, publications, legislative voting records, campaign finance disclosure, court files, property tax records, driving histories, work histories, and personal lives.[85] The media's appetite for strange and sensational free content is exploited by encouraging people to seek and distribute gotcha videos to provoke pseudo-scandals.[86] Political parties assign workers to monitor their competitors' functions. At party conventions, members of other parties are granted observer status to acknowledge and control their presence. On the hustings, party leaders grow accustomed to being followed by opposition partisans. By the end of the 1997 campaign, Jean Chrétien invited one opposition shadow to join him in a round of golf. During the 2004 campaign, the Conservatives resurrected a Diefenbaker-era technique by sending high-profile MPs to Paul Martin's events to promote their party's point of view.[87] In 2008, the Conservatives sent trackers to compile videos of Stéphane Dion, and the Liberals responded by posting a video to YouTube of one of them following Dion's movements.[88] By 2014, trackers were *agents provocateurs* – undercover agents who incite their marks to behave in a dubious manner. Conservative legislative assistants working after hours attended public events in which Liberal candidates and MPs were speaking. They provided video footage of controversial remarks to the Conservative Party centre, which in turn distributed it to journalists. The media played a video clip of one Liberal MP remarking that Trudeau was having a "bozo eruption" for requiring that all Liberal candidates must be pro-choice and that the party centre had "no political sense whatsoever."[89] The remarks were obtained when the MP was asked to speak about the policy in private and was secretly recorded by a Conservative staffer.

Changes in communications technology make discoveries easy to disseminate. Strategists (sometimes comprised of the candidate and family members[90]) consider which information should be emphasized or minimized. Sourced facts and quoted remarks are archived in databases so that the information can be retrieved as part of rapid response and reality check communications rebuttals. Campaigns aim to have arsenals of "destabilizers" at the ready to release to derail an opponent's agenda. A common tactic is to destabilize a leader's visit to an electoral district by unveiling embarrassing details about the local candidate whom the leader is endorsing. Surreptitious information achieves maximum exposure and brand damage if its release coincides with existing media and public interest in a subject.

Control over brand ambassadors reached new heights in the 2015 campaign. The volume of publicly accessible comments by candidates, the ability of electors to act as online *agents provocateurs*, and the number of candidates who were quickly dumped by their parties stands in sharp contrast to the Raddatz incident of 1992. Between them, the three major parties fielded over a thousand candidates, but their screening methods proved to be imperfect. When news stories identified candidates whose personal opinions were at odds with their party's position, the candidates soon afterwards issued public statements of apology and retraction and dodged media requests. Opponents and journalists also pounced as digital footprints demonstrating poor judgment were publicly revealed, sometimes by unaffiliated Internet sleuths. In many cases, the parties quickly cut ties with their candidates. As well, the trend of some candidates not attending all-candidate debates or speaking to media persisted. Most were Conservatives who apparently did so at the request of party headquarters, which did not want to risk a local gaffe becoming national news.[91] There appears to be a higher threshold for disciplining a party staffer who has close ties to the leader than there is for someone more distant or who is seeking public office. Controversy embroiled Harper's chief of staff about his role in the Duffy scandal and, to a lesser extent, Mulcair's director of communications for making derogatory remarks on Twitter about the Catholic Church and the Pope two years earlier. Lesser actions felled candidates, but both leaders stuck by their staff members. At each election, all of this increases the propensity for the House of Commons being filled with MPs who parrot the party line, and for political staff to fearlessly relay the centre's directives to elected officials and civil servants.

Destabilizing an opponent is a symptom of the ferocity of communications leading to more zealous efforts to harm political brands. One academic study uses the term "anti-branding" to describe "intentional attempts to nurture and communicate negative impressions, thoughts and feelings for an entity."[92] Finley and the Conservatives preferred the term "debranding" (CS 5). In commercial marketing, it refers to the removal of brand labels, as with the Loblaws No-Name line of products. Finley meant it in the sense of ruining a competitor's brand. Methods vary from high-profile planned forays (e.g., negative advertising) to the cut-and-thrust of political discourse (e.g., accusations in QP) to the surreptitious (e.g., coordinated cyberbullying).

As mentioned already, the brands of Canada's right-wing parties were so damaged that they were rebranded and relaunched. The debranding was helped along by the Liberal Party. It provoked pseudo-scandals by drawing attention to politically incorrect remarks made by MPs and candidates in an effort to prime the media with a radical frame. It used the media to frame Canadian Alliance leader Day as a religious ideologue, which demonstrated the importance of defining a leader's brand image as soon as possible. It routinely reminded the media of the rebranded parties' pasts, such as by referring to the Conservative Party as the "Reform Conservatives." The Liberals experienced debranding of their own as a result of the sponsorship scandal and, as will be discussed, when their leaders were debranded. All cases suggest that it is not enough for political parties to exert excruciating brand control: they must undermine the brands of their opponents as well.

The debranding employed by the Conservative Party is more assertive than anything seen before in Canadian politics. Following a conference call within the PMO, and immediately prior to a cabinet shuffle, a member of the PMO's issues management division requested that each minister's office compile a blacklist for inclusion in ministers' transition binders. Among the requests was for political staff to identify "who to avoid: bureaucrats who can't take no (or yes) for an answer" in the department and "who to engage or avoid: friend and enemy stakeholders."[93] This included environmental lobby groups, non-profit organizations, civic and industry associations, public servants, and journalists unfriendly to the Conservative government's agenda. The request met some internal resistance, after which the PMO sent a follow-up email stating that troublesome bureaucrats need not be named. In the past, warnings about unfriendlies were exchanged in passing between outgoing and incoming ministers and their political staff. During Harper's tenure, the centre rooted it out in a coordinated manner to shield the brand.

Communications swords and shields are exhibited through passive-aggressive techniques, such as delaying action in areas of responsibility and shutting out those who obstruct a political agenda. Government scientists present a particular threat to the brand. Scientists are unique because of their ability to be framed in the media as purveyors of impartial evidence that can delegitimize the government's action or inaction. The Conservative administration limited the ability of these civil servants to publicly critique policy. Government scientists and other staff were put through communications training,[94] and they were not free to speak with the media. Departmental practices of routinely releasing scientific information were curtailed. One civil servant explained that a tug-of-war existed as new norms were established, because superiors within the bureaucracy insisted on following established practices of disclosing statistics and financial data, until MINO staff intervened (CM 19). In some areas, spending on scientific research was significantly reduced and subject to oversight. For instance, the research of Department of Fisheries and Oceans scientists was reviewed to identify the implications for government policy, raising the spectre that they would be prevented from publishing their findings.[95] Scientists were asked to sign confidentiality agreements when participating in international forums, where they were more guarded. An environmental activist reflects that in the past "we'd hang out together just because we were all Canadians, even though we were working on opposite sides of the issue. Now (in the Harper era) when I go to an international conference, the Canadian delegation won't even look at you or acknowledge you" (CI 17). This alarmed advocates of good government, who seemed impervious to the realities of political communication. Advocacy groups Democracy Watch and Evidence for Democracy called on the federal government to permit scientists to speak freely about their research in a timely manner, to express their personal views, and to have final say over media products.[96]

Critics positioned the Conservative policy as a "war on science" against progressive policy. The Public Service Alliance of Canada (PSAC), the Canadian Association of Professional Employees (CAPE), and the Professional Institute of the Public Service of Canada (PIPSC) coordinated protests against what they framed as the muzzling of scientists and an affront to the integrity of the public service. The journal *Nature* also voiced its concern:

> Since Prime Minister Stephen Harper's Conservative Party won power in 2006, there has been a gradual tightening of media protocols for federal scientists and other government workers. Researchers who once would have felt comfortable responding freely and promptly to journalists are now required to direct inquiries to a media-relations office, which demands written questions in advance, and might not permit scientists to speak. Canadian journalists have documented several instances in which prominent researchers have been prevented from discussing published, peer-reviewed literature. Policy directives and e-mails obtained from the government through freedom of information reveal a confused and Byzantine approach to the press, prioritizing message control and showing little understanding of the importance of the free flow of scientific knowledge ... Rather than address the matter, the Canadian government seems inclined to stick with its restrictive course and ride out all objections.[97]

The government countered that scientists are not different from other public servants who must be authorized to speak with the media. It maintained that the anti-science narrative was overblown. In the case of Environment Canada (now Environment and Climate Change Canada), the media relations group fielded more than 725 media enquiries about science in 2012, of which 561 requested an interview with a scientist, and 478 of the requests were granted.[98] Environment Canada scientists published over 700 articles that year, and considerable information is available on the department's website.

Communications swords and shields elevate to aggression and debranding. The reasoning is that, regardless of culpability, the cloud of suspicion that will result for the accused is worth the gambit. Name-calling, mudslinging, stunts, and negative communications attempt to exploit the perceived weaknesses of opponents and influence public sentiments.[99] For instance, the president of the Conservative Party filed a complaint with the CBC ombudsman about a paid pundit on CBC's *Power and Politics*. It was an attempt to curtail further criticism from Ekos pollster Frank Graves, whom the party alleged was portrayed by the public broadcaster as impartial, despite his Liberal Party ties. By recommending that the Liberals incite a "culture war" with the Conservatives, Graves purportedly compromised his ability to offer non-partisan insights.[100] To apply further pressure, the Tories sent a message to supporters questioning the CBC's impartiality. Later that year the party's director of political operations resurrected the tactic by writing to the ombudsman to complain about the CBC's "blatant agenda-driven reporting."[101]

The levers of government were pulled to undermine the credibility of opponents. Ministers publicly disputed the believability of a diplomat who testified to the parliamentary accounts committee about the torture of Afghan prisoners.[102] The 2012 federal budget set in motion tougher monitoring and enforcement of registered charities' political operations and foreign fundraising efforts. This was interpreted as a move to curtail environmentalists' objections to natural resource development. It soon extended to audits of government critics, including Pen Canada, an organization that opposes censorship and promotes freedom of expression.

Government appointees were not spared the communications sword. Unhappy with the parliamentary budget officer's critiques of their budget forecasts, Conservatives questioned his judgment and suggested that the officer was sympathetic to the Liberal Party.[103] The chair of the Canadian Nuclear Safety Commission was fired just hours before she was scheduled to address a parliamentary committee. She had publicly criticized cabinet's decision to overrule the commission's recommendation to shut down a nuclear reactor for safety upgrades, during which time it would be unable to produce much-needed medical isotopes. But judges cannot be so easily disparaged or removed. The Supreme Court of Canada (SCC) is the ultimate check on the executive and legislative branches of government. The Conservative government abandoned its process of all-party review of SCC judicial nominees because it gave a forum to the government's critics. After a number of unfavourable SCC decisions, Harper and his minister of justice, Peter MacKay, publicly alleged that Chief Justice Beverley McLachlin behaved inappropriately when she attempted to speak with the prime minister about an appointee. Besmirching the personal brand of the presiding chair of the SCC was unprecedented.

The ultimate form of the communications sword is legal action. Statements made in the legislative chamber are shielded by the principle of parliamentary privilege; comments and allegations made outside the chamber are not. The Conservative Party sued the Liberals for defamation and misappropriation of personality regarding Harper's role in the alleged bribing of independent MP Chuck Cadman. The parties settled the matter out of court, casting a chill on opposition criticism. Legal issues that damaged the personal brands of party insiders resulted in the requirement, stemming from the party centre, that all brand ambassadors put distance between the party and its castoffs. Prime Minister Harper installed firewalls against a number of party stalwarts who ran into legal issues, among them Senators Patrick Brazeau, Mike Duffy, and Pamela Wallin; his parliamentary secretary, Dean Del Mastro; and Minister Helena Guergis. The so-called fatwa against Brian Mulroney during the Oliphant Inquiry was particularly difficult.[104] PMJT will do the same to protect his personal brand, his party's, and his government's.

Among the most maligned forms of communications swords is political advertising. Two formative uses of advertising for debranding stand out in Canadian politics. First, political elites learned in 1993 that mocking an opponent's physical characteristics is beyond the pale. The Progressive Conservative Party attack ads that implied Chrétien was unsuitable to be prime minister because of his Bell's palsy were met with such a public backlash that strategists dare not repeat the debacle. They have come close, including in the next election, when Reform Party ads derided party leaders from Quebec; however, rarely do party communications explicitly criticize people for their physical appearance. When a video on the Conservative website showed a digital puffin defecating on Dion's shoulder, Harper immediately apologized and ordered that the ad be removed. "It was tasteless and inappropriate ... I think belittling images are not fair game and not acceptable, and obviously I'm not pleased that that happened. I offer my apologies for that, and we'll make sure that we stick on a substantive level," the Conservative leader said on a campaign stop.[105] The party's subsequent "Justin Trudeau is just not ready" advertising, which ended with a dismissive voter's parting shot of "Nice hair, though," shows that debranding on the basis of physical traits comes in many guises.

The second formative use of advertising for debranding occurred in the early 2000s as the Conservatives straddled the fine line between the fact-based aspects of negative advertising and the personal affronts levelled in attack advertising. Within a month after Dion became Liberal leader, Conservative advertising portrayed him as indecisive and unfit to be prime minister. It turned a communications shield into a sword by deriding his climate change policy as a carbon tax championed by someone who was not a leader. The Conservatives persisted with the frame through all manner of communications until election day nearly two years later. Michael Ignatieff faced a similar missive when he was framed as a power-hungry American elite who was "just visiting" and would raise taxes. Next their messaging focused on interim Liberal leader Bob Rae's poor economic record as Ontario premier. The "in over his head" label was applied to Trudeau, followed by the "not ready" campaign. A senior Conservative advertising consultant explained the debranding strategy:

> We agreed that the minute they got elected as leaders, we would brand them before they got a chance to brand themselves, or allow themselves to glow, because as soon as they got elected they'd go up ten points because they'd glow in the bask of the Liberal brand. So we'd say let's tell the public the truth about these guys before they get away with it. As soon as Ignatieff got in power, the media got in bed with him, it was like a honeymoon. "Oh, he's back from Harvard, he came back to save us." The media rolled out the red carpet for him. So we knew we had to act immediately to let everyone know, hey, the truth is X ... We had to rebrand him accurately and correctly, while we were branding our guy that the public saw in a positive way. (CS 7)

Promoting a consistent critical frame of a personal brand from the moment that a leader is anointed, and feeding this into a broader brand narrative that causes a contrast with the master brand, is a new norm in Canadian politics. When debranding, Conservatives understand the efficiency of choosing a frame that simultaneously augments their own leader's brand strengths. This occurs through an implied contrast. Framing Dion as a weak leader reinforced their positioning of Harper as decisive and strong. The Conservatives' framing of Ignatieff as a self-interested American aristocrat coincided with efforts to pivot Harper's image to that of a Canadian patriot with common values. Criticizing Rae's record as premier of Ontario contrasted with the prime minister's brand as a capable economic manager. Branding Trudeau as a pretty boy out of his depth concurrently reinforced the frame of the incumbent as a steady and experienced, if inimical, head of government. The downside is that, by authorizing negative advertising, Harper offered his opponents ammunition to counterbrand him as calculating, aloof, and nasty. Moreover, negativity debrands the vocation of politics and undermines public confidence in the democratic system of government.

Given his experience as the target of a ruthless debranding campaign, it is interesting to consider Dion's opinion about negative advertising. He believes that the primacy of free speech and the legal tools of suing for libel and slander preclude the need for regulating political communications. What concerns him is that, if a spokesperson's brand is damaged, audiences and the media will think that his or her causes are wrong. It is also disconcerting to him that political marketers advocate debranding over positivity. As he puts it, political strategists' ingrained view is that "an emotion of fear, an emotion of anger, is easier to create in a few seconds than an emotion of hope and happiness" (CP 3). Dion found that the leader takes over a party organization that already has strategists and PR staff on the payroll, and conflict ensues if their recommendation to "go neg" is not shared by the party's primary spokesperson. Thus far, the only antidotes to the poison of debranding are charisma and celebrity. Debranding is a symptom of a diseased system. To find a cure, we must recognize that there is a deeper pathology at work in the Canadian democratic system of governance.

7

Central Government Agencies
and Communications

The abrupt and unyielding nature of political communications must seem barbaric to civil servants. As administrative officers, they are trained to follow the orders of political masters; as employees of a non-partisan public institution, they are conditioned to rise above the political fray. To varying degrees, many of them become cogs in the government publicity machine. Our understanding of public sector communications will be stronger if we can visualize what kinds of positions exist within public administration and how they interact. The purpose is not just to compile an updated inventory of centralized communications processes in federal public administration. The underlying objective is to impress that, all things being equal, government communications are consolidating no matter who happens to be the prime minister of Canada. The public administration principle of "let the managers manage" within departmental silos is evolving into "managers must promote the brand."

POLITICO-BUREAUCRATIC SPIN DOCTORS

In his seminal treatise on public administration, Woodrow Wilson, the future American president, observed that politics and administration operate in two different realms. He argued that public servants must be trusted to interpret whether the partisans running the government reflect the priorities of the broader populace. Wilson reasoned that "the idea of the state is the conscience of administration" and that "wherever public opinion exists it must rule."[1] If we accept these claims, then it is the responsibility of political elites to consider public opinion when they issue directives to government employees, who in turn act as self-appointed custodians when they uphold the state's interests.

The Wilson paradigm sets a high standard. Civil servants ought to be non-partisans hired on merit who embody the core value of political neutrality in the operations of a democratic government. They have a duty to identify the most prescient ways to implement political decisions.[2] Or, as is commonly suggested, they should offer fearless advice and loyal implementation. They should be anonymous, for it is the minister who takes public credit or responsibility for their actions. A senior executive in Citizenship and Immigration Canada explained the role of executives in the permanent government:

> The role is to advise, to give our best advice and recommendations. The minister in the end has to make the decision, and government has to decide where they want to go with that. In proper terms, it's sort of like the cliché "fearless advice, loyal implementation" ... The sillier cliché is "truth to power," and the problem is that it assumes that civil servants have the entire truth, and the minister has no truth ... I had a number of discussions with the minister and his staff on different issues, and sometimes I prevailed on my point, sometimes I didn't, but in the end at least I made the minister and his staff aware of the risks. (CM 20)

The Canadian public service exists for the betterment of Canadians' socio-economic well-being and strives to carry out business in a trustworthy manner.[3] A code of values and ethics articulates that the bureaucracy should uphold principles of exhibiting respect for democracy, respect for people, integrity, stewardship, and excellence.[4] Employees are told that they must serve the public interest, promote transparency, embody impartiality, make responsible use of public resources, and strive for high standards of performance. To achieve public service excellence, policies and programs must deliver value for money, and the workplace culture must be one of satisfied employees who follow plans developed by upper leadership.

As neutral actors, civil servants, as declared by Treasury Board Secretariat policy, have the responsibility to "uphold the Canadian parliamentary democracy."[5] This is the normative way of looking at government in Canada: cabinet should not unduly politicize the administration of government affairs. Civil servants seek to defend what they interpret to be neutral standards and formal processes, while political personnel advance an agenda that requires speedy turnaround, even if that means eschewing norms. The most strong-headed among them assure that the two divides are in a constant state of agitation.

The need for speed compromises the public service's ability to resist politicization. Employees are pressured to act quickly in a deliberative system designed to question haste and an organizational culture not equipped to adapt to rapid technological change. Public administration scholar Jeffrey Roy summarizes the internal effects: "In short, the Internet's explosion of information and mobilization externally has also fueled a reinforcement of hierarchy and control internally – due to the powerful inertia of traditional structures and culture of government. Bureaucracy is thus both challenged and fortified, often simultaneously."[6] The stress and shortened deadlines associated with digital media shock that confront politicians and PR personnel are passed along and encounter processes unable to cope. A former PMO chief of staff indicated that journalists and the public have unrealistic expectations of the ability of the political government and PR personnel to provide information quickly:

> There are brand-new media inquiries coming in at seven o'clock, eight o'clock, nine o'clock at night, and journalists expect answers that same night and are grumpy if you can't give them an answer ... That has had a huge impact on our organizing, because the public service day, that sort of starts at 8:30 a.m. and wraps up at 4:30 p.m. So you're looking for public service input on answers to questions that crop up at seven o'clock at night, but there's nobody working on the public service side at that time. Then at 5:30 a.m. Ottawa time, you're trying to get questions answered for stuff that's cropped up in the Newfoundland cycle at seven o'clock in the morning there. There's just nobody around, all of the public service

support for communications is built around Question Period at
2:15 p.m. Public servants will say, "Yeah, we'll get you an answer
by the time Question Period comes around." Well, that's not what
we're looking for. (CS 31)

Another former PMO employee relayed that bureaucrats have difficulty
meeting firm deadlines without considerable notice. They are so hung up
on following the approvals process that they insist on proceeding even
when a deadline passes and when the information is no longer needed.
"The thing with the civil service is it's process before outcome every time,"
he lamented. "They persist in letting it go through the approvals process
and then handing it to you twelve hours late when you have no need for
it" (CS 22). He was among a number of political respondents who relayed
that they experienced difficulty speeding up the process, even when civil
servants are told that the prime minister specifically requests the information by a certain time. Even so, they praised the ability of public servants
to mobilize massive amounts of communications supports and ancillary
materials when advance notice is available, such as with the throne speech
and budget.

From the permanent government's perspective, non-partisan civil
servants must uphold what they have been trained to do. In Britain, the
civil service is said to embody the three values of permanence, impartiality,
and anonymity. All three values are under stress in one way or another in
Canada. Senior public servants serve at the pleasure of the governing party,
and they are expected to act as political allies.[7] They must defend political
decisions, and doing so proliferates a "culture [that] is infested with the
norm of promiscuous partisanship."[8] They are instructed to put a subtle
partisan slant on government communications products, particularly
advertising, interpreted by audiences as having been authored with neutrality.[9] Anonymity is eroding because of media inquisitiveness as well as
politicians who shift blame.[10]

These tenets, along with the government of Canada's code of values and
ethics, assume that the guidance provided by civil servants is apolitical
and unbiased. Policy advice cannot be neutral, no matter how well intended.
As one civil servant noted, "the public service is political by definition but
is not necessarily politicized. There's a big difference, and it's very hard to

get across" (CS 19). When there is a media furor, public servants might feel compelled to uphold principles of parliamentary democracy by acting in a manner consistent with what they deduce to be in the public interest, which can compromise the principles of cabinet authority and public service neutrality. Their ideals might align with another political party or ideology. They might be entangled with interest groups or caught up in social movements. Media and opposition criticism can convince them that the political government is wrong. They do not always provide information to public officials, and some agitate with the slow implementation of decisions that go against their values.[11] They do so even though they are not elected or otherwise held accountable to electors. They might resist that the political executive, not the civil service, has the legal authority to prioritize ideas and values as long as it enjoys the confidence of the House of Commons.

Some civil servants take their role as defenders of the public interest seriously, and they become disillusioned when they are rebuffed. There are indications in government of a number of incidents of executives subjecting staff to incivility, such as verbal abuse, a trend mirrored in other workplaces.[12] One Privy Council Office communications staffer confided that senior ministers hold such privileged positions that, whenever she questioned a detail of their speeches, her PCO supervisor forcefully stopped her intervention by saying "what the f**k are you doing?" (CM 22). In her opinion, the tone of workplace relations is set by the attitude of the prime minister's director of communications. She recalled that one such character made life intolerable at the centre of government, à la Malcolm Tucker:

> He knew what Harper wanted of him, and he would execute it at all costs. It didn't matter who he hurt, who he pissed off, this man had ultimate control. Grown men at PCO were scared shitless of him. And PMO was scared shitless of him. In meetings, he would just take 'em down. Grown men had tears in their eyes. If you're dealing with someone who has got the prime minister's ear, what are you going to do?

Another public servant told of an episode when, the day before a pseudo-event, a Conservative PMO staffer chastised him on the telephone: "Do you know who you're f**king talking to? Do you know you've essentially been pissing off the Prime Minister's Office with your misinformed morality play? This is what the prime minister wants, and we're going to have a word about it tomorrow morning. We're going to discuss whether you're going to still be working for this office" (CM 19). Such behaviour makes good theatre for Tucker's character in *The Thick of It*. In real life, it has serious implications for employee morale, and the chain of command.

Changes in political communications are adding to blurred lines and stresses. Bureaucrats are under great pressure to avoid mistakes that risk embarrassing the government. The anticipation of spin and the fear of repercussions lead some to provide advice and information slanted toward what they think partisans want.[13] This raises the spectre of a public service that politicizes communications because it assumes that this is what the political executive wants. Government of Canada employees believe that their work output is increasingly assessed against identified objectives, which suggests that professionalism is trumping politicization. However, their frustration grows over the many approval stages, and their sense of empowerment and job satisfaction declines.[14] They overthink what should be routine matters, imagine the worst, and eventually learn to play the game. One civil servant put it this way:

> There's a huge amount of self-policing, because you never know when you're going to get into trouble ... There's a certain fear in the public service, everywhere. These are risk-averse institutions to begin with. It's pretty dangerous to take initiative. It's hard to get into trouble for being too careful ... If you keep getting rejected, you start to think you're not doing your job right, or maybe I'm getting fired or whatever. So you try to please the customer and try to figure out what they would like. (CM 17)

The melding of strategic communications with administrative pre-science similarly results in a clash of cultures and values. Communications-related jobs within a political party also exist in the PMO and a minister's office (Table 7.1). Many political staffers in government arrive fresh from the campaign trail, where they worked in a winner-take-all pressure cooker. The adrenaline that climaxed in the euphoria of winning is transitioned

TABLE 7.1

Communications-related job titles in political parties, the PMO, and MINOs

Political party	Election campaign	Prime Minister's Office (PMO)	Minister's Office (MINO)
• Campaign technologies manager • Communications adviser • Director of communications • Director of finance • Director of outreach • Director of political operations • Director of volunteer mobilization • Election readiness • Electoral district association member • Executive director • Field organizer • Graphic designer • Manager of membership services • National policy chair • Regional media officer	• Campaign manager • Communications director • Debate preparation • Director of fundraising • Director of research • Director of war room communications • GOTV coordinator • Graphic designer • Local campaign manager • Media bus coordinator • Media buyer • National campaign chair • Pollster • Rapid response researcher • Senior communications adviser • Tour advance • Voter contact organizer • Wagon master • Web designer	• Chief of staff • Deputy chief of staff • Director of communications • Director of issues management • Director of media relations • Director of policy • Director of stakeholder relations and outreach • Director of strategic communications • Director of tour and scheduling • Manager of appointments • Manager of new media and marketing • Manager of strategic communications • Principal secretary • Press secretary	• Chief of staff • Director of communications • Director of issues management • Director of policy • Director of parliamentary affairs • Executive assistant • Policy adviser • Press secretary • Regional affairs director • Regional communications adviser • Regional press secretary • Senior policy adviser • Senior special assistant

Note: Not intended to be a definitive list. Not all positions exist at all times.
Partial sources: political party websites; Treasury Board of Canada Secretariat (2011c); Flanagan (2009a).

to running the machinery of government. The long hours, crisis management, rapid response, triage, and quick thinking endure, as does the partisan ferocity. Working on weekends, and making and receiving calls in the middle of the night, go with the territory. One former member of the PMO explained: "The thing that unites all political staffers in the PMO is fatigue. It's not ideology, nothing. It's fatigue, they're all tired" (CS 8). Stress and anxiety are normal. There is a looming fear of being on the wrong end of a tongue-lashing from a superior. The possibility of being fired is ever-present. Although difficult workplace relations exist everywhere, senior politicos learn on the campaign trail that barking orders at subordinates is tolerated and even rewarded if results follow. Working at the centre, "you wouldn't be surprised to hear that one of the people with these really poisonous personalities had made someone cry," relayed a former PMO employee (CS 29). In contrast with the civil service, political exempt staff work in a non-unionized atmosphere, and rude behaviour is tolerated. Perceptions that a minister's agenda must align with the government's, and thus that all personnel must be onside with the PMO, run deep.[15]

Civil servants in central agencies, particularly in the Privy Council Office, feel a sense of urgency and anxiety about making mistakes that is shared by executive-level employees in departments. Compared with routines in the PMO, those in the PCO experience more gyration. Some days PCO personnel work standard 9 a.m. to 5 p.m. hours in the office. Other days an emerging issue rockets to the top of the public agenda, such as a natural disaster or the passing of a public figure, and staff are pulled in to prepare communications products for the prime minister. For instance, if news breaks at 11:30 p.m. about a matter of significant public concern, then a PCO staffer will prepare materials until 1:30 a.m., at which point a supervisor takes over. This way the PMO has draft materials available by 7 a.m. Political personnel ready the prime minister to deliver public remarks as the country is waking up to the news.

Compared with "the centre" or a minister's office, life for most members of the bureaucratic wing of government is more about routines periodically interrupted by urgent matters. The unionized environment, obsession with process, and complexity of public policy do not cope well with the fleeting urgency of political communications. Bureaucrats are risk-averse. They prefer the security of intra- and interdepartmental meetings, information searches, and standard planning documents. Consultation, rules, and conformity dominate their thinking. If working in the nucleus of a national campaign or in the PMO is a kaleidoscopic communications experience, then in comparison the bowels of public administration are a morass of drudgery.

Nevertheless, the public service is not immune to the faster pace brought about by advances in communications technology. In the early 1990s, departments lacked formal directors of communications. By 2003, ministers each had a two-person communications staff.[16] Between 2006 and 2011, the number of Information Services employees increased from 3,118 to 3,824, before declining during austerity measures to 3,325 in 2014.[17] Most of them are based in the Ottawa area, including approximately 100 communications personnel combined in the PMO and PCO. Employees based outside Ottawa have been losing their autonomy to the centre since the emergence of the telephone.[18] Recent technological innovations are increasing the frequency and intensity of interactions among political staff, government PR personnel, and other public servants. The "political overload"[19] experienced in the PMO and MINOs trickles down to impartial administrators. Before email or smartphone technology, the normative master-servant relationship in a hierarchical chain of command was already evolving. It has become a collaborative system in which bureaucrats are politicized and politicians are bureaucratized. This distortion of roles into "politico-administrative hybrids" encourages backbench MPs to seek out detailed information on policy nuances and produces administrators below the deputy minister level who are concerned about the political implications of government activity.[20] The prioritization of delivery skills over analytics leads to a "politico-bureaucratic 'class' of spin-doctors" that nudges aside traditional public servants.[21] Branding strategy deepens this emphasis on communications at all levels of government.

Cabinet: Communications

At the top of the politico-bureaucratic pyramid is cabinet, responsible for directing the strategic communications of the government's agenda.[22] Over time, it assumes greater formalized coordination of government communications, even as the same formalities reduce the opportunity for partisan gain. The Mackenzie King cabinet was concerned about different public interpretations of procedures and laws, which led to the adoption of standardized practices in some government advertising.[23] Prime Minister St. Laurent secured cabinet agreement for departments to report their publicity costs in a uniform manner.[24] Diefenbaker personally approved government advertising contracts once he took office,[25] and the Pearson cabinet decreed that advertising of the recently created Canada Pension Plan should carry on during the 1965 general election.[26] Today the government of Canada's communications policy, authorized by a cabinet committee, makes it clear that the authority to "present and explain government policies, priorities and decisions to the public" is vested in cabinet.[27]

The prime minister is the government's chief spokesperson. That individual is directly involved with communications on a macrolevel; it is naive to think that the busiest person in Ottawa has time for micromanagement. Ministers must prove that they can be trusted to be the primary voices of the institutions that they oversee. They have the authority to choose whether to designate civil servants to speak to the media.[28] According to the 2012 version of the government's communications policy, ministers

> determine, together with their respective deputy heads, their communi-
> cation priorities, objectives and requirements; approve the corporate
> communication plans of the institutions they head; define the responsibil-
> ities of ministerial staff with respect to communications; and establish,
> together with their respective deputy heads, effective liaison between
> ministerial staff and institutional heads of communications to ensure
> that the communication of policy and operational initiatives is co-
> ordinated, with particular attention to media relations and participation
> in public events and announcements.[29]

This notion that ministers determine a department's communications priorities fails to mention the significant constraints imposed by the core executive. The prime minister and key cabinet committees set the government's overall communications agenda. Departmental communications are expected to follow established regulations and standards. Most ministers do not even set the policy agendas within their institutions: the mandate letters that they receive from the PMO do that. Prime ministers warn that members of their cabinets must not cause a communications distraction. In his first cabinet meeting, Chrétien advised ministers that to keep their jobs they had to be cautious with the media and minimize their public comments.[30] The first time that Harper assembled his cabinet, he reportedly cautioned that public embarrassments would not be tolerated: "I am the kingpin. So whatever you do around me, you have to know that I am sacrosanct."[31] By extension, years later, a former PMO staffer added that "you don't go freelancing. If you know what's good for you, you don't freelance" (CS 22). Likewise, in the civil service, "if you're not a spokesperson, you keep your lips zipped" (CM 18).

The importance attached to communications management is reflected in cabinet processes. Memorandums to cabinet and submissions to the Treasury Board must identify communications considerations.[32] A memorandum to cabinet includes a strategic communications plan, a standard annex. The plan is comprised of "objectives and considerations" to identify how the initiative is related to the government's agenda. The "analysis of public environment" section includes information about public opinion research findings, consultation outcomes, and media monitoring. "Anticipated reaction" estimates how specific groups will respond. The "storyline and core government messages" describe how the anticipated news story is related to government priorities and messages. Finally, the "announcement strategy" offers details of media outreach. The plans are drafted by political staff in the MINO, civil servants in the department or agency, and the PCO Communication and Consultations Secretariat. Some cabinet submissions are supplemented by a topline presentation, known as a deck, to cabinet or a cabinet committee. This features communications considerations such as stakeholder views, key messages, and strategies. Plans approved by cabinet are the basis for post-cabinet strategizing in the PMO and PCO.

Cabinet committees play a formidable role in setting the communications direction of government. The priorities and planning committee (renamed agenda and results by the J. Trudeau administration), chaired by the prime minister, determines the government's strategic directions, sanctions cabinet recommendations, and approves appointments. The cabinet committee on parliamentary affairs (previously known as operations) is focused on advancing the government's agenda through communications, issues management, and legislative planning. Once a policy is approved for public announcement, members of the parliamentary affairs committee identify communications themes and narratives of the issues put in front of them. "Those are the times when cabinet ministers sit around a room and really talk hard how to communicate, what to say, what the plan should be, how sustained the plan should be, who should be doing it, major themes and narratives, that kind of stuff," advised an insider (CS 30). It is notable that the prime minister is not a member of the parliamentary affairs committee but that the chief government whip is.

The Treasury Board is the cabinet committee with the greatest systematic influence on government communications. The Board establishes management norms in consultation with other cabinet committees and central agencies. It reviews budget proposals and promotes program evaluations. The objective is to achieve spending efficiencies while advancing the government's strategic priorities. Its communications role, enforced by the Treasury Board Secretariat, is discussed later in this chapter. The minister of finance and the president of the Treasury Board are members of all three of these committees, in either a standing or an ex officio capacity. It is a structure designed to ensure that office holders, not civil servants or political staff, set the government's communications agenda.

Prime Minister's Office

According to Prime Minister Harper, a cohesive and "disciplined" centralized organization is necessary in government, one in which political staff "act together to inform each other of what we're saying and doing, so we're not caught by surprise."[33] The PMO is "a central partisan agency" that sets the direction for coordinated government operations.[34] Senior members of the PMO provide strategic advice and logistical support to the prime minister. Its operations are guided by a chief of staff who, along with the principal secretary, belongs to an elite group who regularly interact with the prime minister. Others in that circle of influence include a handful of senior ministers who comprise the inner cabinet, the clerk of the Privy Council, the director of communications, and pollsters. Those "courtiers," to use Savoie's term, are the heavy hitters who steer the government.[35] Senior members of the PMO are go-betweens with political personnel across government. Teams of people set the communications strategy, and other teams busily coordinate and implement the strategy while managing emerging issues. Yet other PMO personnel are involved strictly with routine administrative matters. Handling correspondence, coordinating a demanding schedule, making travel arrangements, and ensuring the first minister's safety all require attention. The political and partisan behaviour of staff in the most powerful publicly funded central agency was explained by a Conservative strategist:

> The Prime Minister's Office, just like the office of the leader of the op-position, is a political office. The people who work there are political staff. Their job is inherently political. And what the PMO does, the communications shop in the PMO does, is communications on behalf of the prime minister and the government that extend the types of communications that the prime minister and ministers make in Question Period and in the House of Commons. And as a big part of that they are promoting the political positions of the government.[36]

Working in the Prime Minister's Office involves coping with the tyranny of the urgent to gain breathing room to advance a handful of agenda items. Tom Axworthy, Prime Minister Pierre Trudeau's former principal secretary, has opined that prime ministers must be strategic with their limited time if they wish to champion an agenda.[37] Writing in the 1980s, he estimated that a Canadian first minister can give individual attention to a handful of issues. The cabinet manages another twenty-five to thirty issues. A few core message themes must be selected from hundreds of choices and countless causes pushed by others, within and outside government. It is up to PMO staff to create process efficiencies to reduce the time demands placed on the political executive and minimize the potential for crisis. Axworthy maintains that, in a strategic prime ministership, the role of the PMO must be the promotion of partisan perspectives within government. It is the job of political staff to coordinate and align the neutral public service, the parliamentary wing of the governing party, and its extraparliamentary wing.

The need for central processes to liberate the prime minister to concentrate on strategic thinking is echoed by Eddie Goldenberg, Jean Chrétien's former senior policy adviser. To Goldenberg, perceptions of the PMO as "a powerful, fear-inspiring, mysterious organization" are gross exaggerations by uninformed outsiders.[38] He likens the PMO to the conductor of a symphony. People working at the centre coordinate government activities and provide oversight, for instance by issuing the mandate letters to ministers that outline the centre's policy priorities and delivery expectations.[39] Goldenberg adds that during the Chrétien era the PMO's director of communications blocked ministers from proceeding with public events unless they were synchronized with the government's broader communications agenda, a practice that flourished in the Harper era.

This central coordination imposes measures that limit ministerial autonomy. The requirement that ministers must seek PMO clearance to travel outside Ottawa is one such example. A two-page travel proposal must be submitted by a minister's office to the PMO. The proposal collects information on where the minister proposes to go and why, whom the minister will be travelling with, what the cost will be, and what the proposed itinerary is. The information is submitted to the corresponding regional desk in the PMO, where a desk officer crosschecks the information against the "rollout calendar" (see Chapter 9). For practical purposes, this ensures that cabinet can assemble in the event of an emergency, a problem when Canadian airspace was shut down in the wake of the terrorist events of September 11, 2001. When the legislature is open, the party whip's office is apprised of ministers' whereabouts so that the government does not risk defeat or embarrassment in the House of Commons. At any given time, the centre knows where ministers are and, if they are away from Ottawa, which activities they are undertaking. Some ministers find themselves on standby up to the last moment about whether they are authorized to travel. This is one of the many ways that oversight by the PMO is facilitated by communications technology and standardized processes.

Despite complaints about the growth of the centre's influence, it has not required an exorbitant growth in personnel. In 1978, there were approximately seventy people working in the Prime Minister's Office,[40] and in 2014 the number stood at ninety. The federal government's electronic directory of public servants identified five branches in the Conservative PMO that employed staff with communications-related job functions, including four special units.[41] In the Harper PMO, much of the brand management came out of two groups of thinkers: those involved in strategic communications planning (at one time led by Deputy Chief of Staff Patrick Muttart) and those dealing with daily media issues (led by the prime minister's director of communications). Past members of the PMO reflected on the importance of providing strategic planners with time and space, in contrast to the urgencies of the communications personnel who are under pressure to manage pressing situations. A former chief of staff put it this way:

> The two groups obviously talk to each other, but I tried to make sure that we had a team to manage the day-to-day shit falling from the sky and a team to manage the longer-term efforts we were trying to engage in. Otherwise, the day-to-day squeezes out the longer-term work. Keeping two different teams to manage the two different things I think is an essential part of political management and the abso-lutely essential part of running a Prime Minister's Office. (CS 31)

Within the chief of staff branch (n = 13 in 2014), the Conservative PMO's manager of government advertising and marketing reported to the chief of staff, and so did an employee dealing with regional affairs. The chief of staff is tasked with the management of political personnel and conveying the prime minister's directives. This involves liaising with ministers, PMO staff, and PCO representatives using the (perceived or actual) force of authority of the prime minister and strategizing about issues management. Dealing with human resources issues is a significant role, and finding experienced personnel is a challenge. In an interview, another former chief of staff (CS 30) enumerated the reasons that he, the PMO, and other mem-bers of the centre sought to coordinate government communications.

1 *Message consistency:* The PMO wants the government of Canada to have a certain tone, narrative, emphasis, and direction evident in com-munications. This means ensuring that messages originating from ministers' offices are not incongruent with the government's overall message or juxtaposed against other messages or what is happening in the news. For instance, if one arm of government announces meas-ures against mass illegal movements of migrants, the next day's message should not be an announcement from another department concerning initiatives to attract skilled immigrants. Likewise, a scheduled announce-ment is moved up, delayed, or cancelled if news coverage of a related issue is incongruent with the government's message.

2 *Populating the calendar:* Central coordination is needed to schedule announcements and media activities. If left to their own devices, ministries and the bureaucracy would follow the parliamentary/cabinet cycle, resulting in many days with plenty of announcements and other days and long periods with few announcements. Communications calendars are discussed in Chapter 9.

3 *Themes and emphasis:* The communications strategy and logistics of each public statement must be planned. Considerations include the authority to make the announcement, how it is positioned vis-à-vis the government's overall agenda, which aspects of the announcement should be emphasized, whether a pseudo-event should be held in Ottawa or somewhere else, which stakeholders should be involved, whether it should be delivered primarily in English or French, and so on. This includes identifying which people should speak at the event, a consideration that spans minister(s), parliamentary secretaries, backbenchers, government officials, and/or non-government spokespersons. For instance, on a matter of international armed conflict, message coordination is required because the minister of national defence, the minister of foreign affairs, and the minister of international development would all have something to say.

4 *Quality monitoring:* Civil servants prepare communications products using the language of officialdom, and young political communications personnel in ministers' offices tend to lack a suitable writing style. The PCO and PMO work to adjust wording, to consider the logic of statements, and to verify the accuracy of claims and facts. Effort is exerted by the centre to limit a tendency to make premature announcements.

5 *Avoiding policy making through communications:* The government of Canada is a collection of independent-minded institutions with their own legal frameworks, and the hierarchical approval process slows down as it reaches the apex. Departments seek to advance policy and bind the government by making commitments through all manner of communications, which requires central oversight.

6 *Encouraging communications innovation:* People at the centre encourage new ways of thinking creatively and communicating about how announcements are made. The former chief of staff put it this way: "Government's not a terribly innovative organization at all, it's quite

hidebound. Left to their own devices, their classic communications approach is a media release, perhaps accompanied by some official or some minister or MP standing behind two microphones and a podium." The PMO urges a different way of projecting communications, including a greater involvement of stakeholders as spokespersons and the use of different media channels.

Flowing from this, the Conservative PMO's communications branch (n = 22) managed the government's day-to-day media activities and its overall communications. It prioritized supporting the prime minister at media events. The branch prepared media relations products such as news releases. PR personnel negotiated the terms of the prime minister's interactions with journalists. Regional communications support was offered by advisers for the greater Montreal and Toronto areas, by English and French media officers, and by a translator. A manager of new media and marketing directed the PMO's Internet communications, a position created during the Harper era. Collectively, the branch ensured that departmental media outreach, including advertising and speaking events, communicated desired messages.

The tour and scheduling branch (n = 15) planned and coordinated the prime minister's travel, events, and appearances. Five employees, working under the manager of advance, assessed locations to gather logistical intelligence for planning a prime ministerial visit. A manager of visual communications prioritized the overarching imagery and overall look of public events. Event details were sorted out by event coordinators and a tour logistics coordinator. Members of the advance team took many digital photographs of the location, which they sent back to the PMO, where details and visuals of the planned pseudo-event were nitpicked.

The Harper administration created the issues management branch (n = 8) to deal with strategic situations.[42] Among its personnel were a director of issues management, issues managers, and a media monitoring officer. One of their responsibilities was the laborious process of preparing the prime minister and ministers for Question Period, which begins with early morning conference calls and meetings, as discussed in Chapter 9. During Harper's tenure, QP preparation featured daily meetings of cabinet.[43] The sessions involved role playing, with a senior member of the issues management branch putting questions to ministers while the rest of cabinet listened. This sometimes prompted the prime minister to urge a different response, which embarrassed the minister, who likely thought that, because the line was vetted by the PMO, it was supported by the PM. Afterward, politicos rush to prepare revised pages for their ministers' QP binders.

Members of the stakeholder relations and outreach branch ($n = 4$) were responsible for meeting with special interests, which must be disclosed in lobbying registry reports. Four subunits in the Conservative PMO were explicitly concerned with communications. The advertising and market research unit ($n = 1$) employed a director of market research. A manager and three speechwriters worked in the speechwriting unit ($n = 4$). The PMO's photography unit ($n = 3$) employed the prime minister's official photographers. The position of official photographer was created in 1981 to preserve historic moments.[44] Visuals are so valued that photographers/videographers accompany the prime minister to all official events (as do the official photographers of the other major party leaders). They enjoy extensive access to behind-the-scenes activities, even to the point that the PMO photographer had a seat reserved on rescue mission flights.[45] It is through their efforts that digital content is generated for image bites for the PMO website (see Chapter 3).

The correspondence unit ($n = 7$) employed writers who respond to inbound communications. In 2007, as smartphones were becoming common, on each day including weekends the prime minister received about 3,000 emails and 1,700 pieces of mail.[46] To manage this volume, apolitical letters to the prime minister are redirected to the PCO's executive correspondence unit. Other branches and units in the PMO in 2014 included policy ($n = 8$), appointments ($n = 3$), personnel and administration ($n = 2$), planning ($n = 1$), Quebec senior adviser ($n = 1$), and office of the parliamentary secretary to the prime minister. This suggests that the majority of personnel employed by the PMO are involved in communications management in some way or other.

The nature of political staff positions is that they attract young people. In Ottawa circles, the label "boys in short pants" is used to refer to the (usually male) inexperienced agents of the PMO who issue orders to parliamentarians.[47] The complaint reflects a long-standing resentment among political veterans exacerbated by overblown perceptions of PMO staffers' authority.[48] The boys in short pants were described by one respondent as immature megalomaniacs: "The rank and file people who go to work in the PMO, they're young, they're in their twenties. They're fresh out of school. Their dad is a constituent or a lobbyist ... They don't question anything" (CM 22). Another female respondent thought of them as "boys in their fathers' suits" who – as with a number of PMO "dragon ladies" – want to exercise their authority (CS 29). Personnel churn is inevitable, though it was especially noticeable under Harper. From 2002 to 2015, he went through fourteen senior communications aides, including nine directors of communications in the PMO. In comparison, Peter Donolo was Chrétien's director of communications from 1993 to 1999.

Privy Council Office

The PCO is at the intersection of communications of the permanent government and the political government. It employs non-partisan public servants who provide the PMO, cabinet, and cabinet committees with advice and support. The PCO is led by the clerk of the Privy Council. As head of the public service, the clerk is both secretary to cabinet and deputy minister to the prime minister. He or she plays a central coordinating role in government by issuing policy guidance and communications directives to departments. Strategic work flows from cabinet, including from the communications annex in a memorandum to cabinet and the records of cabinet decisions. The PCO liaises with civil servants, whereas political personnel in the PMO communicate with MINOs. This division of labour aligns exempt and non-exempt staff within departments. As one respondent put it, the "central monitoring supervision" process involves "PCO to departments, PMO to ministers' offices, and then some ongoing coordination between PMO and PCO to tie it together" (CS 30). As a central agency, it values individuals who have worked at "the centre" and who return to line departments with the mentality of prioritizing the needs of their superiors.[49] Its employees must understand how government works and need the political smarts to realize that the PMO is the decision maker. Members of the PCO's communications section summarized the central agency's functions this way:

Privy Council ... tries to get that complex machine [of government] to go in a specific direction, and it has to synchronize with ... the prime minister's agenda and the agenda that he or she gives to the different ministers. They have their particular marching orders, and those ministers have to meet their mandates, and their departments have to synchronize with those mandates. All those mandates together need some type of coordination, and that's where PCO is. So there's a fair amount of interactivity involved ... We have a hand in everything the prime minister does as far as announcements [are concerned]. (CS 26)

PCO communications tries, as best it can, to address and give direction to the rest of government. Based on the relationship that PCO has with PMO, it interprets that sort of political will, political need, into a direction for the various departments in government in terms of communication priorities ... It helps to steer communications that come out of departments that need to be approved at the centre, in a way that contextualizes it with the bigger picture of the broader government agenda ... Communications are very much controlled at the centre, because the government needs a consistent message and a coherent message, and that can only be done providing there's guidance from the centre so that it's all consistent with the broader government agenda. (CM 23)

PCO personnel in charge of strategic communications are concerned with written communications. They are in constant contact with departments to seek out information and to review submitted material, ranging from news releases to departmental progress reports. They want to ensure that government communications are accurate, clear, concise, and understandable to Canadians. This involves cleaning up government bafflegab and acronyms in materials submitted by departments. They proof departmental communications to identify red flags before sending the materials along to policy analysts in the PCO for review. Double-checking facts and statistics is prioritized because when a cabinet minister says something on the record it is interpreted as government policy.

The PCO seeks to ensure that whatever is stated publicly is consistent with the prime minister's message. This includes seeking uniformity with the tone of "the boss" (as some PCO employees refer to the PM), including his or her public personality where speechwriting is concerned. Considerable effort is exerted to avoid or address mistakes. The PCO wants to catch visible errors that would be detected by the attentive public and that require conferring with a member of the PMO. The PCO likewise aims to detect invisible errors that otherwise go unnoticed and need gentle correction.[50] Everything down to the spelling of names is verified. The importance of avoiding mistakes intensifies with the proliferation of digital communications technologies and the shortening of turnaround times for communications products. "We discussed every single issue and micromanaged every news release, everything," offered a PCO official.[51] All feedback is provided by the policy shop to the PMO, where the communications are subjected to a political lens.

The preparations that the Privy Council Office requires for cabinet and its committees are extensive and exact. Institutionalized central planning constrains the sovereignty of the prime minister by limiting ad hoc decision making. A special area of support provided by the PCO is comprised of government-wide communications and public opinion research. The variety of communications-related positions in the PCO is illustrated in Table 7.2, alongside comparable positions in the TBS and PWGSC.

The PCO Communication and Consultations Secretariat, headed by an assistant secretary to cabinet, coordinates government-wide communications concerning announcements, advertising, crisis management, digital media, strategic communications, and web strategies.[52] The secretariat was created to support the now defunct communications committee of cabinet, disbanded when Chrétien took office in 1993, but the PCO secretariat endures.[53] The secretariat's coordination functions include steering temporary initiatives, such as the Economic Action Plan, and leading the modernization of government communications.

Among the PCO's responsibilities is relaying difficult information to employees, such as when the PMO orders a change in communications plans. "If you have to deliver an unsavoury message, it is PCO's job to drop the hammer on the department and make that happen rather than that coming from the political office," reflected one former PMO staffer. "I see PCO as having to walk a very fine line between the notion of what the public service exists for and what the Prime Minister's Office politically

TABLE 7.2
Communications-related job titles in government of Canada central agencies

Privy Council Office (PCO)	Treasury Board Secretariat (TBS)	Public Works and Government Services Canada (PWGSC)
• Communications quality control officer	• Chief, media relations	• Communications and marketing manager
• Correspondence analyst	• Communications and promotion officer	• Coordinator, publications support services
• Director, advertising and marketing	• Communications officer	• Director, communications and corporate management
• Director, corporate and media affairs	• Communications strategist	• Manager, advertising advisory services
• Director, new media	• Communications and research officer	• Manager, media relations
• Director general, strategic communications	• Correspondence analyst	• Manager, strategic intelligence and marketing
• Executive adviser, engagement, outreach, and communications	• Correspondence and communications officer	• National manager, governance and communication
• Manager, public opinion research	• Director, communications policy and Federal Identity Program	• New media communications officer
• Media analyst	• Director, public affairs	• Regional communications adviser
• Parliamentary liaison communications officer	• Manager, publishing and corporate identity	• Regional webmaster
• Senior director, communications	• Manager, web and print publishing services	• Senior adviser, communications
• Senior multimedia monitoring analyst	• Manager, web content and communications	• Senior marketing adviser
• Tour coordinator	• Press secretary	• Senior media relations adviser
• Web communications senior analyst	• Senior communications adviser, public opinion research	• Web and multimedia developer
• Web publishing officer		• Web communications specialist
		• Web content coordinator

Note: Not intended to be a definitive list. Not all positions exist at all times.
Source: Public Works and Government Services Canada (2014a).

would like to happen" (CS 29). Even though the PCO has the reputation of being an obedient arm of the PMO, tensions exist among some of the most senior political staff and civil servants. This results in diverging opinions about what constitutes appropriate process, as noted by a former PMO communications director:

> There is just a vicious battle in PMO, there always is, between PCO and PMO staff. Because in PCO they have the cream of the crop, they have all the information. And they want to get in there, and they have their own agenda. They have the clerk's agenda, and they have the [agendas of] departments they represent. So they're always pushing those agendas. The political advisers have the party's agendas. And they're thinking "All right, this is what the party stands for, this is what we ran on, this is what we said in caucus, this is what's being said in the media, and my own personal thoughts." So all of those are combined into how they advise. So the prime minister ... sits in the middle and says "All right, then it's up to me to make all the decisions here, because I'm the only one that can synthesize." (CS 8)

The system stirs up tensions between the PCO and PMO, which add to an already stressful environment exacerbated by the egos and brashness of certain political staff in particular.

Minister's Office

As the political head of a government department, a minister has the last word on departmental decisions. Aside from falling in line with the normal regulatory constraints, the minister must negotiate matters with agents of the prime minister if not the PM. In each department is a minister's office, or MINO, in which exempt staff provide political support that the non-partisan civil service cannot. They are involved with political strategies and communications. Tasks include scrutinizing departmental materials, shaping public policy, speechwriting, and coordinating activities with their peers throughout government.[54] A minister's office staff lack legal authority to issue directives to civil servants, and they are expected to go through the relevant channels. In each MINO is a departmental liaison who acts as a link with civil servants in the department.

A department's media relations are led by a minister's director of communications. This individual is a political appointee who works closely with the minister. The official duties associated with the director's position make it clear that the minister's and department's communications must be consistent with those of the whole of government. The department must regularly consult with the PMO so that all government communications can be synchronized.[55] To this end, on weekdays an issues manager from each MINO across government participates in an early morning meeting with PMO staff. This is described in Chapter 9.

Minister's office exempt staffers apply a political lens to departmental affairs and handle communications matters.[56] They behave as gatekeepers whenever anyone wishes to meet or speak with the minister. They vet invitations in different ways, with a commonality of seeking to deal with the volume of unsolicited enquiries in an efficient manner. For instance, when a request is received concerning the president of the Treasury Board, the MINO completes a meeting/event request form. The document identifies all of the necessary details required prior to the chief of staff's comment and before it is submitted to the minister for review and a decision (Figure 7.1). The meeting/event form allows the minister's office to track which personnel have reviewed the request and what their opinions are. The minister's chief of staff reviews the input gathered, seeks out further information as required, and makes a recommendation to the minister. The minister considers information and perspectives offered by staff when deciding whether to accept the event invitation. If the minister agrees to a request to participate in a public event, this triggers a need for a Message Event Proposal (see Chapter 9) or some sort of equivalent.

The role of MINO personnel in government is growing in conjunction with the importance attached to media management and branding. In Environment Canada, communications strategists have been engaged from the outset in deliberations on how to cut spending as part of budget preparations.[57] This ensures that senior departmental mandarins consider the anticipated public and media reactions while policy recommendations are formulated. It provides the PMO with a channel to stay informed and to voice suggestions. It allows communications personnel both in the

FIGURE 7.1
Ministerial meeting/event request form

Ministerial meeting/event request form		*Date:*
Details		
Date:	Location:	Time:
Group/Organization:		
Contact Name:	Email:	Phone number:
Type: ( ) Meeting ( ) Event		
Details/Notes:		

MINO Comments

Item	Comments	Signature/Date
Policy		
Communications		
Issues		
Scheduling		

Approval:

Name	Comments	Signature/Date
Chief of Staff		

Action after approval	Comments	Signature/Date
( ) Approve		
( ) Regrets		
( ) Referred to:		
( ) Greeting/letter, including due date:		
( ) Optional/tentative:		
( ) Consider for future event or visit:		

Source: Provided to the author by a minister's office employee (2014).

department and at the centre to prepare for controversial announcements. Their involvement lays bare that communications influence public policy decisions in government. The need for a communications lens is irrefutable; to what extent policy and governance are politicized and branded is the issue.

Treasury Board Secretariat

The Treasury Board Secretariat supports the Treasury Board cabinet committee in its attempts to align government resources and achieve value for money. The secretariat's power resides in its ability to recommend to the Treasury Board that financial sanctions should be applied against a government institution that does not comply with the standards that the TBS oversees.

Among the recommendations of the 1962 Royal Commission on Government Organization (the Glassco Commission) was the need for the Treasury Board to develop and implement government-wide processes. A three-person communications division was created in the TBS to strengthen public relations coordination. Departmental managers became responsible for following and refining the central standards and policies. The cross-departmental nature of communications is embodied in the TBS-based government communications plan, which emphasizes cooperation and coordination:

> Communications within the Government of Canada is a shared responsibility involving officials and employees at all levels. Effective policy and program development and administration requires cooperation and coordination throughout the government: among ministers, senior officials, policy advisers, analysts, program managers, communications staff, specialists in human resources, information technologists, Web masters, graphic artists, researchers, marketing specialists, access to information and privacy coordinators, librarians, receptionists, call-centre staff and others. Cooperation and coordination between institutions are also necessary to better serve and inform the public. It ensures that government themes and priorities are clearly and consistently reflected in the information and messages communicated to Canadians at home and abroad.[58]

Ministers retain the prerogative to decide when an exemption to this policy is warranted. That power comes with the proviso that the decision is subject to review by the Treasury Board and the auditor general, and in practice it is difficult to secure an exemption. Administrative rules present so many constraints that the Treasury Board delegates authority to TBS public servants to screen departmental submissions.[59] At times, the Treasury Board responds to concerns that central rules are obstacles to efficient programming by relaxing its policies and by devolving decision making to departmental managers. For the most part, however, the central agency's policies are enforced, and ministerial compliance is expected.

By administering central rules, the secretariat unifies the government into a single service.[60] Among its concerns are ensuring that human resources are centrally managed, that government services are provided in both official languages, and that procurement processes are followed.[61] Chief among its integrated planning activities is the management frameworks program, which assists ministers in setting government-wide policy in areas such as information technology and communications.[62] It includes information about the maintenance of procedures for planning and contracting public opinion research, oversight of the Federal Identity Program (see Chapter 8), and the government's communications policy.

This policy, created in 1988 by the Treasury Board and updated in 2006 and 2012, aligns priorities through dozens of requirements. The scope of these standards illustrates the complexity, rigidity, conformity, and professionalism of government communications. As mentioned, according to the policy, public servants are expected to "manage communication design and presentation along common lines and in a co-ordinated manner" and to "reflect Government of Canada themes and messages in communication plans and strategies." In doing so, they are "expected to provide information services in a non-partisan fashion consistent with the principles of parliamentary democracy and ministerial responsibility."[63] Internal audits are conducted to evaluate whether departmental communications practices are compliant and align with government priorities. We can organize the communications requirements into the following themes of responsiveness, centralized coordination, public communications, innovation, service, and archiving.

Communications responsiveness. The government's communications policy details the requirements of reflecting diversity, official languages, regional operations, environmental analysis, public opinion research, and consultation and citizen engagement. These provisions outline guidelines for the use of electronic media monitoring services and opinion research. They stipulate the need to use the Consulting with Canadians website (consultingcanadians.gc.ca) and urge the involvement of regional offices in communications planning. They establish tools for identifying Canadians' program needs and expectations, and encourage a spirit of open and responsive communications. Applicable rules and norms include the Canadian Multiculturalism Act, Official Languages (Communications with and Services to the Public) Regulations, Procedures for Planning and Contracting Public Opinion Research, and the government's official newspaper, *Canada Gazette.*

Communications coordination. Communications policy requirements are identified for corporate identity, for management and coordination, for planning and evaluation, for memorandums to cabinet and Treasury Board submissions, and for internal communication. The policy expresses the expectation of maintaining a consistent brand image. It advocates the availability of communications resources and the establishment of communications links with core functions. Corporate communications plans must be provided with submissions to central agencies, and employees need to be engaged. Rules include the Federal Identity Program, the Policy on Internal Audit, the Policy on Evaluation, the Policy Framework for Financial Management, and the Official Languages Policy Framework. Deference to centralized communications is articulated throughout. For instance, government advertising must be "aligned with government priorities, the Government Advertising Plan, and government themes and messages, with advice from PCO and the Government Advertising Committee."[64] (For more on government advertising, see Chapter 8.) The PCO is responsible for coordinating regional communications that involve multiple government institutions.

Public communications. The communications policy outlines requirements for media relations, spokespersons, public events and announcements, advertising, marketing, risk communications, crisis and emergency communications, partnering and collaborative arrangements, and sponsorships. The requirements advise public servants on the need to anticipate public risks. PR personnel must recognize that they operate in a twenty-four-hour media environment. They are expected to deliver prompt and effective communications to restore public confidence or limit harms in the event of an urgent situation. The policy identifies ways to handle media enquiries and makes it clear that ministers are principal spokespersons. Communications personnel are required to support the minister's participation in news conferences and non-partisan special events, ensure that advertising is suspended during federal elections, develop marketing plans and strategies, encourage fair and equitable joint activities, and acknowledge sponsors. Rules include the Emergency Preparedness Act, the Policy on Government Security, the Policy on Reporting of Federal Institutions and Corporate Interests to Treasury Board Secretariat, the Framework for the Management of Risk, and the Procedures for Planning, Contracting, and Evaluating Advertising.

Communications innovation. Improving the quantity and quality of e-government and online services is a communications priority of the government of Canada. The government's communications policy stipulates requirements for technological innovation and digital media, for Internet and electronic communications, and for training and professional development. This encourages government personnel to adapt to digital technology. They are expected to maintain an active online presence, to promote the Canada website (canada.gc.ca), to familiarize new employees with the policy, and to participate in staff training to enhance their communications skills. Rules include the Privacy Act, the Policy on the Use of Electronic Networks, the Policy on Management of Information Technology, the Policy on Information Management, the Policy on Government Security, the Policy on Privacy Protection, the Standard on Web Accessibility, and the Standard on Web Usability.

Communications service. This policy theme includes the requirements of informing and serving Canadians, of providing information free of charge, and of using plain language. It promotes communications clarity and information accessibility in both official languages. Applicable rules include the Charter of Rights and Freedoms, the Access to Information Act, and the Official Languages Policy Framework.

Communications archiving. The federal government has policy requirements for publishing; copyright and licensing; film, video, and multimedia
productions; and cataloguing and securing information. Among the
guidelines are the need to maintain an index of published works in a central publishing database and the licensing of Crown copyright. Relevant
rules include the Library and Archives of Canada Act, the Policy on Title
to Intellectual Property Arising under Crown Procurement Contracts,
the Copyright Act, the Trade-marks Act, the Common Services Policy,
and the Contracting Policy.

The government's communications policy forms the groundwork of
public sector branding. This includes providing public assurances of responsiveness to the fourth estate, whose members observe that the policy
is not always upheld. One press gallery respondent mentioned that, when
she receives a non-answer from government officials, she sends back select
passages to point out that the policy is not being followed:

> When I get an unsatisfactory response from a government depart-
> ment to a quite clear question, I flip them back the Treasury Board
> Secretariat's communications policy, which is very explicit. So I cut
> and paste and say, "With all due respect, I think you need to review
> the government's stated communications policy." Sometimes I'll
> get a response. I feel like it actually shakes something loose. If I'm
> really angry, I'll copy senior bureaucrats in the department, saying
> "This is an unacceptable answer to my question." I talk [publicly]
> about this a lot, but I don't think people really understand why it's
> so serious. (CI 19)

In his mandate letter, Scott Brison, the new Liberal president of the Treasury
Board, was directed to revise the communications policy "to reflect the
modern digital environment."[65] However, the absence of an oversight
mechanism to assess the implementation and relevance of such an important policy is a weakness with the current system.

Public Works and Government Services Canada

Little was written about the Treasury Board or TBS until the 1970s.[66] The
same can be said about PWGSC until its communications function was

thrust into the spotlight during the sponsorship scandal. Public Works describes itself as the "treasurer, accountant, central purchasing agent, linguistic authority, and real property manager" of the federal government.[67] The organization provides support for government operations to achieve best value and sound stewardship, in particular through the management of procurement activities. This support includes public opinion research and advertising.

Government advertising contracts have always been something of a golden temple for political parties. The allure of patronage has motivated communications firms to contribute to a political party and to provide pro bono services during election campaigns. The governing party historically returned the favour by politicizing the process of awarding lucrative contracts. Leading up to 1993, the selection of advertising agencies was a political decision. The public servant who managed the advertising section in PWGSC – which employed two political appointees – reported to the cabinet committee on communications rather than to immediate superiors in the department.[68] Other departments seeking advertising services would request that the PWGSC hold a public tendering competition. However, only advertising agencies affiliated with the governing party were eligible to be shortlisted. When Chrétien became prime minister, his government directed TBS to revise the policy for the contracting of advertising, communications, and public opinion research services. The process did not become fully depoliticized because the redesigned policy no longer prioritized price. It also required that contractors must be 100 percent Canadian owned, which benefited Liberal-affiliated advertising agencies.[69]

From 1994 to 2001, advertising and other contracts related to the special projects and sponsorship program were issued under PWGSC's budget. The sponsorship program was an initiative of cabinet that aimed to increase the profile of the federal government in Quebec after the 1995 sovereignty referendum. Initially, the PMO's chief of staff directed the program and drew support from the Privy Council Office. These central actors worked in concert with the public servant who headed the PWGSC advertising group. That the head of the advertising group reported to the prime minister's chief of staff was an evolution of the aforementioned reporting to the now defunct cabinet committee on communications. This contributed to the abrogation of normal processes. Over time, central agents relinquished their involvement to the minister of PWGSC. The program became a front for government money to be siphoned into Liberal-friendly advertising agencies, some of which was sent to the Liberal Party via party fundraisers in Quebec. Its existence also reflected a culture of communications largesse and entitlement among government personnel, who sought perks such as tickets to corporate boxes at NHL games (CS 15).

In 2001, as the *Globe and Mail* and the auditor general were uncovering indications of wrongdoing, the sponsorship program was reassigned to the newly created Communication Canada, an agency of PWGSC. Henceforth, normal procurement standards were followed. In 2002, Communication Canada published the first annual report on the government's public opinion research.[70] It was followed in 2003 with the first annual report on federal government advertising.[71] As the fallout over the sponsorship scandal grew, PWGSC created a quick response team to prepare information for anticipated questions in the House of Commons.[72]

One of the first acts of the Paul Martin government was to cancel the sponsorship program. In 2004, it disbanded Communication Canada, and Martin announced the formation of the Commission of Inquiry into the Sponsorship Program and Advertising Activities. The Gomery Inquiry uncovered a litany of dubious and illegal government contracts. It sounded the alarm on the absence of rules and oversight that allowed the communications scandal to happen. An overarching conclusion of the inquiry was that there should be less centralized political control within government and increased accountability to Parliament.

As mentioned in Chapter 4, when Stephen Harper assumed office, his government introduced the Accountability Act (2006). The wide-ranging scope of that legislation included provisions to reduce political involvement in procurement, expanded access to information, and measures to protect whistleblowers. The act requires that all written reports on advertising and public opinion research be submitted within six months to Library and Archives Canada, which since 1995 has posted available reports online. This is subject to content restrictions such as national security and federal-provincial considerations.

Public Works continues to establish the terms of procurement for government advertising and public opinion research. It has a mandate to search for financial value, including efficiencies of scale in advertising buys. The

PWGSC's information services subprogram is concerned with the public release of information through publishing services, the dissemination of advertising and opinion research, the preparation of *Canada Gazette*, and electronic media monitoring.[73] How communications services are contracted and delivered is constantly examined. For instance, the government has sought to augment the consistency of service and further outsource its communications activities. The National Procurement Strategy for Communication Services, finalized in 2012, spells out a need for more standardized and simplified processes, including the ability to procure social media services.

Canadian Heritage

The sponsorship program was one of a number of federal government communications responses to Quebec nationalism. Over the years, federalism has been promoted through special government units, including Information Canada and the Canadian Unity Information Office, and through initiatives such as the Federal Identity Program. Canadian Heritage – Patrimoine Canadien in French, hence the acronym PCH – is the latest incarnation to perform a centralized political identity function through government communications. PCH promotes Canadian culture, history, heritage, and civic pride in any areas not prescribed to other ministries. It is the department that distributed free Canadian flags in the aftermath of the 1995 Quebec referendum. The Department of Canadian Heritage Act gives PCH residual jurisdiction over human rights; promotion of bilingualism and multiculturalism; the arts; national battlefields, museums, archives, and libraries; promotion of sport; state ceremonial and Canadian symbols; some aspects of broadcasting; and cultural policy. In 2013, the department became responsible for coordinating public events in the National Capital Region, such as Canada Day festivities. It is the guardian of state protocol, which includes organizing tours by members of the Royal Family.

Canadian Heritage attempts to foster Canadian identity and culture by funding and supporting the arts, cultural industries (e.g., film, music, broadcasting, books), history, landmarks, community participation, official languages, and sport.[74] The PCH initiative with the most visible connection to Canadian identity is its attachment to the Canada Program, which promotes national pride, celebrates Canada, and supports civic education. Between 2012 and 2014, PCH led a communications campaign to raise awareness of many select aspects of Canadian history. Among them were the bicentennial of the War of 1812, the queen's diamond jubilee, the Canadian Arctic Expedition, the centennial of the Grey Cup, Sir George-Étienne Cartier, the Charlottetown and Quebec Conferences, and the start of the First World War and Second World War. Other communications campaigns intended to recognize John A. Macdonald, Louis- Hippolyte Lafontaine and Robert Baldwin, Wilfrid Laurier, the Fenian Raids, women's suffrage, the Battles of the Somme and Beaumont-Hamel, the Battle of Hong Kong, the Battles of Vimy Ridge and Passchendaele, the Dieppe Raid, the Stanley Cup and NHL, and the Canada Games. The recognition of hand-picked aspects of Canadian history is occurring in the lead-up to the country's 150th anniversary celebrations in 2017, during which five years of integrated advertising intend to increase public awareness of Canadian history and patriotism.[75] The PCH-led Canada 150 campaign engages departments such as National Defence and Veterans Affairs and extends to agencies, boards, and commissions (ABCs), including Canada Post, the National Capital Commission, the Royal Canadian Mint, and national museums, as well as the governor general and RCMP.

The Canada 150 efforts are part of a broader communications campaign, authorized by the Conservatives and led by the DND, dubbed "operation distinction." It is a branding plan that proposes to unify government communications through to 2020, which will mark the seventy-fifth anniversary of V-E Day in the Second World War. Operation distinction was a directive from former Prime Minister Harper involving staff in DND, PCO, PMO, PCH, and Veterans Affairs.[76] We should anticipate that the tone and style of Canada 150 publicity will change at the request of Prime Minister Trudeau and his cabinet.

In addition to fostering patriotism, Canadian Heritage is responsible for managing state ceremonial and Canadian symbols. Initially, Canada used the Royal Arms of the United Kingdom as its official emblem and the Union Jack as its flag. As new provinces emerged, a mishmash of icons was integrated into the country's Great Seal. It authenticated official documents and became the arms of Canada. Beginning in 1904, Canadian Olympic athletes' clothing sported a red maple leaf on a white background. In 1921, King George V proclaimed that the Royal Arms of Canada would be comprised of lions, a unicorn, maple leaves, the Union Jack flag, and a fleur-de-lis flag. The king also proclaimed red and white as Canada's national colours.[77] The next year the Red Ensign was approved for Canada's international use, and in 1925 a cabinet committee began researching a Canadian flag without completing the task. In 1945, an order-in-council designated that a Canadian version of the Red Ensign be used on federal government buildings on Canadian soil. The next year a parliamentary committee called for submissions for a national flag, but it did not recommend a design to Parliament. In 1964, Prime Minister Pearson presented a proposed flag to be used to promote Canadian identity, patriotism, and national unity. The "Pearson pennant" was comprised of three red maple leaves on a white background bordered by blue sidebars. Instead of the pennant, a special parliamentary committee recommended a red-white-red design with a red maple leaf in the middle. The design was similar to the commandant's flag at the Royal Military College, and the maple leaf flag became official in 1965. In 1970, the Federal Identity Program was implemented. It continues to permit red as the only colour, other than black and white, in production of the Canada wordmark (see Chapter 8). The Liberal Party, whose own official colours are red and white, was in power at all of these junctures.

The creation of a national anthem followed a convoluted path too. "God Save the Queen" (or "King") was Canada's unofficial anthem for much of its history. "The Maple Leaf Forever" was composed in 1867 and resonated in English Canada given the references to Britannia's flag, the queen, and praise for English, Irish, and Scottish ancestry. In comparison, "O Canada" was written in French by a Québécois and first performed in 1880 in French at a Saint-Jean-Baptiste Day event. In 1967, at the urging of Prime Minister Pearson, a special joint parliamentary committee recommended that "O Canada" become the country's national anthem, with "God Save the Queen" designated as the royal anthem. That decision coincided with promotion of the "Ca-na-da" centennial song initiated by the federal government's Centennial Commission. A bill to formalize the Canadian national anthem was introduced in 1980. The Liberal Party was in power during these twentieth-century state-branding junctures as well.

The devolution of Canada's place brand from its British connection is by no means complete. The governor general, lieutenant governors, and territorial commissioners receive royal treatment, such as by reading the Speech from the Throne. The royal arms and portraits of the monarch appear in some public buildings, on currency, and on passports. The royal title appears in many Canadian institutions, including one of its most iconographic symbols, the Royal Canadian Mounted Police. The Conservatives attempted to resurrect a number of royal symbols and aspects of Canadian heritage from which past Liberal administrations distanced themselves. This rebranding of the state is discussed in Chapter 9.

Finance, Other Departments, and ABCs

As mentioned, the Department of Finance is treated as a central agency in public administration studies. It is a department unlike others. The annual unveiling of the government's budget is a major event. Its preparation requires dozens of communications plans, and the final document provides a year-long roadmap for spending announcements. Finance is a high-profile department whose central role is evident in its minister's membership in the three most powerful cabinet committees (agenda and results, parliamentary affairs, Treasury Board); as mentioned, only the president of the Treasury Board holds the same status.

A look at the department's consultations and communications branch can help us to understand how it organizes communications intelligence, strategy, and tactical functions.[78] The branch is organized into three divisions. The communications policy and strategy division gathers intelligence through media monitoring and public opinion research. It uses those data to inform communications plans. This is the basis for advice to policy personnel and department executives and for making strategic decisions. The division is responsible for the execution of activities that require strategic decisions: namely, advertising, backgrounders, news releases, question and answer (Q&A) documents, and speeches. Operational support in the branch is provided by the public affairs and operations division. It gathers intelligence in outward-facing ways that serve a publicity function, such as conferences, consultation exercises, and meetings. The division's only strategic function is media event planning. Most of its work concerns the delivery of communications activities, including editing services, media relations, ministerial correspondence, news conferences, photo ops, protocol services, publishing, translation, and website content. The branch operates a parliamentary relations division that provides legislative agenda advice to policy branches and departmental executives. Its communications functions involve responding to matters emerging from the legislature (e.g., parliamentarians' written questions, petitions, motions for the production of papers) and the tabling of annual reports. Work across all three divisions intersects and requires timely collaboration.

The way that the Department of Finance handles enquiries changes with communications technology. Before the Internet, it was difficult for Canadians to know where to address their handwritten or typed letters or even which order of government to contact. Now it is possible to send an email from anywhere and (unrealistically) expect an instant response. To cope with the deluge, Finance and other departments coordinate a standard response to inbound letters, emails, and other forms of enquiry. Replies must be approved by senior communications personnel and, if necessary, translated. Each boilerplate response to a given issue is assigned an internal number. The template reply that is used is logged for future analysis. Dozens of template replies are available for the most popular issues. For instance, Canadians contacting Finance about pensions or retirement income receive one of over eighty standard replies, ranging from reply PEN100 ("Pension reform – general") to more temporal concerns such as PEN130 ("Termination of CHCH-TV pension plan").[79] This is synthesized as a frequency count of contacts deemed to be in favour, against, or neutral. Data are provided to the MINO about which template replies are used the most, which indicates what the minister's key messages ought to be. This is a crude assessment of what issues are running "hot."

The involvement of other central agencies in communications activities, even when the Department of Finance is the lead, means that its functions are not as relevant for a study of public sector communications. Like other government departments, Finance feeds the centre information and receives direction and authorization about the substance and timing of announcements and pseudo-events. A former communications official in the department put it this way: "At the departmental level, all they're doing is implementing. They're not doing any strategic decision making. They're not deciding whether this is the best way to communicate this government policy. That's all coming from up top, and they're just organizing the news conferences, making sure the train runs on time" (CM 17). Finance is unquestionably a powerful department that plays a formidable synchronizing function in government. Yet where communications are concerned it lacks the institutional heft of the PCO or PMO or the central policy prowess enforced by the TBS and PWGSC.

Across government, each department employs executive managers who provide general communications direction to civil servants. As the permanent heads of government departments, deputy ministers operate at the intersection of politics and bureaucracy. Deputies lead a team of senior executives, including associate deputy ministers, directors general, regional directors general, and others who oversee strategic decisions and implementation. Among them is the director general of communications and marketing (or some such title), who heads up the media shop. In each department is a team of communications personnel recruited through the normal public service process. As illustrated in Table 7.2, growing numbers of them are employed in the areas of multimedia, social media, video production, website management, and web analytics. Departments employ discipline-related communications specialists, such as scientific communications in the Department of Natural Resources or labour communications in the Department of Human Resources, Skills and Development. Just as political communications staff must take their cue from the PMO, the public servants involved in advertising, communications, and opinion research are expected to follow directives received from the PCO and guidelines maintained by PWGSC and the TBS.

The coordination of communications in agencies, boards, and commissions is murkier given that such bodies are created to deal with the administration of government policies in a depoliticized manner. The thrust of ABCs is that agencies, including Crown corporations, report to a minister not involved with their day-to-day operations and/or to Parliament. In comparison, boards of appointed citizens guide and monitor an area of government, while commissions are struck to investigate a contentious issue and provide arm's-length guidance about the best way forward. Generally speaking, agencies and boards behave as agents of government, whereas commissions are created as short-term operations that operate with more autonomy. Communications personnel in ABCs perform a suite of job functions comparable to those of their peers elsewhere in government.

Departments and ABCs are required to have corporate communications plans. Such plans are developed to optimize organizational resources and align strategic activities within the institutions. Corporate communications plans synchronize participating actors and provide political staff with detailed information. Input can be obtained from the PCO, whose sign-off might be required. This type of central influence further steers the communications strategy and identity of a government unit to align within the broader confines of the government of Canada's brand. Institutions are responsible for ensuring that compliance analyses are carried out to see how their own communications measure up against the government's communications policy.

The Canada Revenue Agency (CRA) is a case in point on how sub-branding has taken off in the federal government and how it becomes a mechanism to reinforce the political executive's master brand. In 2005, branding was identified as a critical strategic project within the CRA. Its public affairs branch conducted an analysis of best branding practices in government. The next year it researched what clients and staff thought of the CRA brand. In 2007, it established a brand steering committee and committed to a "whole of agency" approach to adopt brand management as an ongoing business practice. The agency commissioned a marketing consultant to prepare a brand strategy. The consultant identified branding implementation issues common throughout government and resembling organizational culture.[80] Among the identified challenges was a need to generate buy-in from employees, including senior management; to adhere to the organization's core mandate; to tackle lingering public confusion about the agency's role; and to address a lack of control in a political environment in which negativity in one area of government sullies other areas. The CRA would have to confront a lack of organizational agility, staff fatigue with change, limited marketing resources (including low awareness of branding), and the multifaceted nature of an organization that operates in silos. Implementing the consultant's recommendations would face the constraints of TBS rules, the agency's close relationship with the Department of Finance, and public perceptions that included Orwellian concerns about the agency's activities.

The CRA's marketing consultant observed that building brand equity would require a commitment to unified communications that cuts across all points of contact with clients, including Internet, phone, and counter service, as well as correspondence and outreach, client relations, media relations, advertising, publications, and internal communications. An outcome of the consultant's report was that the CRA commissioner approved a brand strategy, comprised of a brand promise statement and an audience-centred approach to communications. This included establishing a visual identity that matched the agency's brand strategy, a corporate colour (blue-grey), and audience-specific colours (green for taxpayers and benefit recipients, taupe for businesses, gentle blue for employees and unions, orange for charities). Overarching corporate messages and core messages for each audience group were identified. A brand network was created to implement the strategy, led by the director of the agency's branding and marketing division.

In 2008, internal briefings were held within the CRA on the proposed branding initiative.[81] The focus was on building initial awareness of branding principles, for instance stressing that branding is not a synonym for logo. Employees were informed that the value of private sector branding practices as a reputation management tool is recognized within the public service and by senior government of Canada leadership. Brand modules were planned for employee training programs, and special workshops would be coordinated. A "CRA brand lens" (its wording) would track audience perceptions, agency performance, and audience behaviour to measure the brand. Among the plans for the 2008–9 fiscal year were brand learning events and the engagement of a brand steering committee. A "brand toolbox" (also its wording) of corporate messages was prepared for employees to access via the CRA Intranet. It sought to ensure clarity and consistency in all of the CRA's communications across the country. A graphic standards manual was created to promote a consistent visual identity, noting that Canadians in all regions, no matter how they interact with the CRA, must be exposed to the same corporate look.[82] The convergence of public administration with the marketing-savvy Conservatives set the stage for a WOG branding initiative in the form of the Economic Action Plan (see Chapter 10), which employed similar graphic standards manuals and colour schemes.

Crown corporations confront the greatest competitive pressures to engage in commercial branding. This branding ranges from a major overhaul of Canada Post as it reimagines itself as a courier service through to minor acts such as Parks Canada selling merchandise branded with its beaver symbol. Rebranding is brought about by an adjusted mandate. When the role of the Canadian Wheat Board changed (see Chapter 4), it communicated optimism through the launch of a new corporate logo and visual identity. Its advertising standards guide espoused the need for continuity and unified messages in language, tone, voice, tagline, visual identity, colour, photography, and typography.[83] The CWB brand was envisioned to have human attributes, such as being caring and efficient. An avatar named Trevor was even profiled as the desired brand in human form. The marketing board has since been sold and rebranded as G3 Canada Limited.

The arm's-length nature of ABCs was at the forefront when the CBC announced plans to rebrand its French-language platform from Radio-Canada to Ici. Minister of Heritage James Moore commented that he was not consulted about the proposed rebranding and had "no idea" about the announcement.[84] The minister publicly called on CBC management to justify the change. In a statement, Radio-Canada rationalized the rebranding as a visual necessity in a crowded multiplatform media environment, remarking that "our mediascape is rapidly evolving, driven by the proliferation of TV specialty channels and the rise of digital platforms such as the web and mobile apps. It is in this context that a consistent brand identity – a common denominator for all Radio-Canada platforms – was needed."[85] The CBC scuttled the rebranding plans after five days of public backlash.

The backpedalling came after *Strategy* magazine named CBC one of the brands of the year for embracing digital media.[86] The public broadcaster communicates the same content on multiple platforms, including mobile ones, while readying content for access through gaming consoles and building Canadian celebrities. The CBC wants to create a Canadian "star system" of homegrown national and regional personalities because it wants "people to associate those folks with the CBC brand" (CS 20). It is a strategy whereby the Mother Corp accepts that in a multichannel universe it must compete head-on against American show business. The development of CBC personal brands brings risks similar to those in politics: any brand ambassador's "bozo eruption" or contentious behaviour can damage the master brand. This is exemplified by the controversy that has swirled around the stars of some of its flagship programs. When faced with negative publicity, CBC sought to protect its master brand by firing the hosts of the *Q* radio show and the *Power and Politics* television show for conduct unbecoming and by ceasing its practice of allowing its on-air personalities to give paid speeches in the event of conflict of interest.

8

Branding in Canadian Public Administration

Government communications are a labyrinth of processes. The prime minister, cabinet, and political personnel are confounded by a complex maze of regulations and policies that inhibits snap political decisions. This is an important safeguard because a professional public service must be bound by norms of behaviour and operational efficiencies. It must also be insulated from excessive politicization. Yet internal controls approved by cabinet are often so rigid that public servants cannot complete tasks in a timely manner or respond quickly to political or fourth estate demands.

THE GROWTH OF MARKETING AND BRANDING IN GOVERNMENT

Years ago government had scant need or ability to coordinate its communications. In the nineteenth century, personal communications and print advertisements were the main forms of government publicity in Canada.[1] Politicians gave speeches in public places and hobnobbed with constituents. Lecturers were employed to drum up interest in immigration and annuities. Trade commissioners promoted Canadian exports. Information was mailed to farmers and businesspeople. Ads were placed in partisan newspapers. Pamphlets trumpeted the virtues of immigrating to Canada. Pavilions at exhibitions and trade fairs publicized Canada and its agriculture. All of this was rudimentary by today's standards.

The first significant attempt by the Prime Minister's Office to harmonize government communications occurred in 1901. Prime Minister Wilfrid

Laurier created the Canadian Exhibition Commission, a government agency with responsibility for coordinating all exhibitions. Over the years, the federal government's most prevalent communications functions shifted from the Department of Agriculture to the Department of Trade and Commerce. During the First World War, they became the domain of the Press Censorship Branch of the Department of the Secretary of State. Departments began to employ their own publicity staff, and the minister's executive assistant played a role in public relations activities. Ministers and their deputies shaped information policy.

Advances in government identity management accelerated during the Second World War. At the outset of the war, the Canadian army lacked a media relations unit. Such functions operated out of Canada House in London. A tiny organization called the Bureau of Public Information was created to disseminate select information about the conflict, and government censors prevented other information from circulating. As the war progressed, there was a greater need to stir up public support through positive publicity. In 1942, the bureau became the Wartime Information Board, which employed social scientists to measure public opinion and design propaganda.[2] The board was a cheerleader for the war effort, as was the National Film Board of Canada. After the war, the Wartime Information Board's domestic activities were wound down. Its international communications persisted as the Canadian Information Service. The communications functions of the Department of National Defence grew so much that its public relations activities were a source of concern to the 1962 Royal Commission on Government Organization. The Commission was wary of centralized control over communications, even though it otherwise advocated for greater harmonization of government activities.

The foundations of the government of Canada's corporate identity are found in the ensuing Task Force on Government Information. The Task Force was struck to report on the government's information services, advertisements, and communications. Its 1969 report observed that communications technology and the public's information needs appeared to be changing "by the hour."[3] Insufficient communications planning and research, patronage in the awarding of communications contracts, a lack of expertise and standards, an absence of testing, inadequate coordination, and other inefficiencies were common in government advertising.[4] Moreover, the Task Force raised concerns about the government's insufficient self-publicity. It vexed that, without publicity, Canadians were unable to distinguish federal activities from those of other levels of government. All aspects of the federal government's communications were characterized by one word: *disparity*.[5] Government of Canada vehicles were different colours, and buildings had varying styles of signage. Government publications and aesthetics were designed by non-experts in departments, resulting in haphazard communications. In comparison, the Task Force noted that Crown corporations such as Canadian National Railway were beginning to adopt private sector branding techniques. The company had hired a New York design firm a decade earlier, and the firm recommended that all of the railway's properties – rails, trucks, hotels, ships, stationery, menus, buildings – needed a single visual identity comprised of a consistent symbol and colour scheme.[6] A marketing ethos of message control and visual symmetry stood in contrast to the amateurism of communications disparity.

The Task Force recommended the creation of common communications policies in the federal government. Each institution needed to designate a head of information in a senior role within the organization. These individuals needed to work with central agencies to make far more efficient use of communications resources. Information divisions were to be renamed as public affairs divisions. The Task Force called for a coordinated graphic design program to be housed within a central agency, one that should be implemented by personnel in institutions. It urged that:

1 The government establish a general policy on design, incorporating systems for federal information and guidelines for both federal and departmental identification programmes.

2 The policy and guidelines be developed, and their implementation and review ensured, by a central design group in Information Canada working with departments, agencies and outside experts, with a view to attaining the highest quality at the least possible cost.[7]

This vision of centralized communications was realized when Information Canada was created in 1970 and put in charge of coordinating government communications campaigns. From the outset, the agency's work was undermined by the Task Force members' connections to the Liberal Party and the opposition's charges that Information Canada was spewing Liberal propaganda. In 1976, Information Canada was disbanded for reasons that mirror recent concerns about government communications. Critics disliked centralized control over information and were concerned about the partisan nature of government activities. In particular, they did not like the use of public resources to promote policy decisions for which the political government took credit.[8]

Information Canada's legacy endures in the institutionalized branding program created during its first year. The Federal Identity Program (FIP), discussed later in this chapter, has become a branding leviathan. It establishes the terms of the federal government's overall corporate identity and sets the parameters within which individual institutions must manage their own images. The objective is to promote a common corporate identity of the federal government in Canada and on the world stage. This is achieved by requiring the use of a standardized brand look, avoiding bureaucratese in communications, and following common graphic design standards.[9] Ensuring that all communications occur in both official languages is another central tenet. Some institutions, notably Crown corporations, are exempt because of their legal status, intergovernmental nature, or other cabinet approval. Still, the program has unified the communications of disparate government entities.

The Canada wordmark (Figure 8.1), with a Canadian flag positioned above the final letter in the word *Canada,* is the main visual marker associated with the FIP. It was designed in 1965 by Toronto's MacLaren Advertising, now MacLaren McCann Canada, as part of a tourism campaign for the Canadian Government Travel Bureau. When the brand signature was updated in 1971, it featured a graphic of a partial Canadian flag. The visual was of a red bar on the left of a red maple leaf, without a bar flanking the leaf's right side. It was comparable to the Liberal Party's logo of the time. The visual symmetry was an apparent outcome of close ties between the design agency and the governing Liberals. In 1987, the Progressive Conservative administration adjusted the wordmark to feature a full Canadian flag. The FIP also stipulates guidelines for use of the government's official symbols. The coat of arms is meant to be used in materials associated with the signature of the head of a government institution and

Canadă

FIGURE 8.1 Government of Canada wordmark | Federal
Identity Program, Treasury Board of Canada Secretariat.

by Foreign Affairs in its formal correspondence with other governments. A standard version of the Canadian flag must accompany the name of the institution in both official languages, unless an exemption is granted by the Treasury Board.

What is less well documented is that the public service itself has come to recognize that it has an organizational interest in branding. Kevin Lynch, as clerk of the Privy Council, encouraged this interest at the behest of the Prime Minister's Action Committee on the Public Service. In 2007, the clerk's annual report to the prime minister featured a commitment to develop a public service brand as part of a renewal plan that would situate government as a career of choice.[10] A public service brand was expected to fill the need for a master brand that cuts across departments and agencies. By year's end, the Canada Public Service Agency developed a brand framework. It argues that branding is "essential to compete for attention and retention of messages," and it stipulates that a master brand must "be flexible enough to allow for complementary sub-brands" (i.e., departmental/ agency brands).[11] The civil service's brand needs to tell a story that will complement the FIP's visual identifiers. Steering and working committees were struck, and they engaged representatives from central agencies and other personnel.

In 2008, the Advisory Committee on Senior Level Retention and Compensation delivered a report to the president of the Treasury Board about human resources management. The committee urged that branding continue to be a priority for the public service as a means to instill pride and engagement among existing employees and future recruits.[12] Presentations on branding and its benefits were made to senior executives throughout the government during this period. Public Works representatives met with directors general of communications, and debriefings were held on how branding factors into career fair preparations. This spurred departmental marketing and public affairs units to seek more information on branding. They set about to generate staff awareness of the strategy and to pursue rebranding of their units or organization.[13] Civil servants across government attended leaders' forums and professional development workshops. In Ottawa, the Centre for Excellence in Communications delivered public sector branding workshops that explored the basics of the branding process, how to create a public sector brand strategy, audience segmentation, and the brand implementation process.[14] This coincided with the Canada School of Public Service's training on Web 2.0. Videos were available for loan on topics ranging from communicating the government's desired message to how the Cirque du Soleil's business model could inform branding of the public service. News stories and practitioner resources on branding were circulated among staff, including tips from Interbrand's online resource (brandchannel.com) and a step-by-step practitioner resource *Guide to Branding in the Public and Not-for-Profit Sectors* by the Ottawa-based Centre of Excellence for Public Sector Marketing.[15] This built awareness of the benefits of brand strategy and planning within the public service at a time when smartphones and social media were becoming popular.

Public sector employees learned that branding supports a client-centred outlook on service delivery. Instead of defining a department by its programs and internal organization, communications personnel are trained to focus on reasonable outcomes for target audiences. They harmonize what the department does, what it says, and how it is perceived. To accomplish this, each organization must speak with one voice and portray a consistent image. This requires corralling diverse lines of business and media platforms within the department. It requires greater recognition that the brands of departments/agencies are subservient to a master brand set by cabinet and enforced by central agencies.

The government of Canada master brand was to be maintained by the Public Service Renewal Initiative, headed by the clerk. In 2008, the master brand was positioned as "serving Canadians with integrity and distinction."[16] It is a work in progress. Defining and communicating the public service brand, through action items that include building a strategy through online consultation, are features of the government's Destination 2020 (also known as Blueprint 2020) vision exercise. Despite these efforts, we must be careful not to overstate the pervasiveness of branding throughout the over 100 entities in the federal government. Statistics Canada, for one, has commissioned branding studies not acted on. StatsCan does not even have "any definite colours or looks or styles" or backdrops for its media activities (CM 12). Nevertheless, a trend within government is apparent.

NEW PUBLIC MANAGEMENT AND GOVERNMENT COMMUNICATIONS

Politico-administrative spin doctors operate in a business-like government workplace dubbed New Public Management.[17] The NPM framework is associated with neo-liberal changes in public administration in the 1980s driven by a business-like search for cost savings and by political sentiments that bureaucratic processes were too constrictive. A motivator of the philosophical shift was creating a government more responsive to citizens and constituents, treated as customers or clients. Characteristics of NPM include outsourcing, the negotiation of public-private partnerships, and a customer-centred operating environment. Government bodies are expected to develop plans of action to keep them focused on their core mandates and budgets. Mandarins cede ground as the main source of advice to political elites. The influence of outside consultants, party strategists, and interest groups, combined with accountability mechanisms, reduces the independent nature of public administration. Managers and front-line workers are given flexibility to respond to emerging situations, at odds with our perceptions of centralized control until we consider that NPM has morphed under the strain of political pressure.

Service Canada is emblematic of how New Public Management brings more business-like approaches to government communications. Created in 2005, Service Canada's objective is to simplify information provision by offering a single point of contact for citizens with enquiries, regardless of the medium of communication. They can visit one of approximately 300 service locations, dial 1-800-O-Canada to be served by a call centre, obtain information online via servicecanada.gc.ca, and be apprised of developments through Service Canada social media sites. Service Canada staff schedule visits in smaller communities; in the event of a crisis, they are mobilized to provide in-person service on a temporary basis. This requires unifying government institutions, in particular those dealing with the top information searches of jobs, taxes, passports, Employment

Insurance, and other benefits. It also requires collaboration with provincial, territorial, and municipal governments given that citizens do not always know where to direct their enquiries. The organization was branded with a visual identity comprised of the word *service* above the Canada wordmark. Internal and external signage was installed in its offices and outreach sites. This NPM approach to customer service further harmonizes the government's touchpoints with Canadians.

Under New Public Management, all government communications are prone to converge given that managers enforce the centre's will. The Treasury Board Secretariat groups government communications into six themes,[18] each of which is beholden to a variety of centrist policies and practices. As described in the following pages, government advertising, public opinion research, corporate identity, publishing, web communications, and social media all exhibit practices imported from the private sector and involve centralized processes. We begin with a seventh theme, media relations, not part of the TBS list, but which likewise involve centralization more prevalent because of digital communications technologies.

Media Relations in Government

Even in a democracy, the government's media relations activities should not prioritize delivering what journalists say they need. Rather, there is a balance of providing information and using the media as a communications vehicle. According to the government of Canada's communications policy, federal institutions "must cultivate proactive relations with the media to promote public awareness and understanding of government policies, programs, services and initiatives."[19] Environment Canada's media relations handbook illustrates that this requires careful planning and execution.[20] Managers and experts have a duty to keep Canadians informed, and it is in the public interest to develop positive relationships with journalists. The handbook cautions the importance of staying on message when confronted with off-topic or aggressive questions or those that encourage speculation. To avoid miscommunication, employees must deliver compelling messages with clarity and identify three key messages that will be repeated three times.

A sunny ways approach to government must nevertheless prepare for a media storm. Preparations for interactions with journalists draw in multiple personnel and diverse processes. Information notes are written to advise PR personnel about an emerging scenario and to provide media response lines. The structure of information notes varies among departments. Examples of headings include situation, purpose, principal spokesperson, and guidance. For instance, a public affairs guidance note might apprise departmental staff about the planned response to media enquiries resulting from the throne speech and the associated blackout period for ministerial announcements. "Holding lines" are to be followed by PR staff when the government wishes to direct media attention to a core spokesperson or not to comment on an issue. To block questions, designated spokespersons remark that they will not speculate on an issue, that it would be inappropriate to comment on a matter before the courts, and so on.

The government's communications policy states that institutions "must operate and respond effectively in a 24-hour media environment."[21] This involves interacting with journalists "on short notice" and responding to media enquiries "promptly to accommodate publication deadlines." To keep up with the volume of media enquiries, and to repeat and reinforce approved messages, government media relations personnel often opt to respond by email. Written responses allow government personnel to control how they spin information and avoid going off message. One journalist called the Conservative PMO with a binary question about whether or not the government has a policy on negotiating with terrorists. Foreign Affairs emailed her the following perplexing canned response:

> I am emailing you on behalf of the minister's office to follow up on your earlier request. I am sending you some comments. See below. You and your editors may already have this information but this is something we remind all journalists who call us on this issue. Regarding your precise question concerning a policy, we do not have any comments.[22]

Overthinking and delays in media relations are epitomized by the *Ottawa Citizen* asking the National Research Council (NRC) and the American National Aeronautics and Space Administration (NASA) about a joint study of snow.[23] A NASA representative spent fifteen minutes providing answers to the journalist's questions. The Canadian agency refused an interview and provided information to the newspaper by email on project equipment as opposed to the project itself. Through a subsequent access to information request, the newspaper learned that eleven federal bureaucrats participated in dozens of email exchanges trying to determine how to respond. The internal process had begun with an NRC analyst identifying the tone of the journalist's enquiry. A director general disagreed that an interview was warranted, so public servants turned their attention to negotiating the media lines. By the time a response was sent, the *Ottawa Citizen* had nearly completed its story. Afterward, an NRC staffer lamented that the paper's coverage understated the agency's role. This is one of the many predicaments that confront the fourth estate in Ottawa as well as government communications personnel.

Details of how the Treasury Board Secretariat deals with submitted questions seem to be even more painstaking than with Foreign Affairs and NRC. In the TBS, a journalist is required to provide a name, a media outlet, a phone number, an email address, a specific deadline, and finally the question(s). The request cannot be processed until all relevant details are received in writing. The following is a typical response from the TBS when it declines a request for an interview: "Thank you for your enquiry, we are, however, unable to provide you with an interview but should you wish to send us specific questions, we will endeavour to provide you a written response. Additionally, if you plan to provide questions, please provide a deadline for us to work with."[24] To outsiders, this is infuriating; to insiders, it is necessary to manage the high volume of enquiries and to protect the brand.

Documents obtained in 2012 via access to information indicate that detailed questions trigger a multistage vetting process in the TBS.[25] Once the supplementary information is provided, it is entered by a TBS staffer into a media request template email. The completed template message is sent to the director general of communications, to the assistant secretary of strategic communications and ministerial affairs, and to the chief of strategic communications. The message is copied to ten TBS staff, including three executive assistants, the director of parliamentary affairs, the manager of strategic communications, an adviser in the PCO, and other public affairs officers. A response is drafted by a communications strategist, who consults with the relevant policy sector within TBS and who must obtain approvals up to that sector's director level. The draft response is reviewed and approved by the department's director of strategic communications. It is now ready for further internal review in preparation for submission to the minister's office.

The draft response is sent to the TBS media relations team for inspection, which then submits it to the director of public affairs and the director general of communications. If the latter are unavailable to complete a review within one hour, the draft response proceeds regardless. It goes to the president of the Treasury Board's press secretary and the department's director of communications, and it is copied to six others in the TBS, including the ministerial liaison. The subject line of the email, in capital letters, is "FOR APPROVAL – MEDIA REQUEST: Journalist (MEDIA) – Subject." If the journalist's deadline is imminent and a response from the minister's office has not been received, the request is resent with "RED FLAG" added to the start of the email subject line. If a revised deadline can be negotiated with the journalist, the message is resent as "UPDATED DEADLINE." Once the response has been approved, nothing more than it can be provided to the media. Efficiencies are found when an approved response is reused, in which case the process skips to the director general of communications in the secretariat. If a question can be addressed by pointing the journalist to an area of the government's website, then the approval process stops at the chief of strategic communications. At all times, only the approved wording of information is released. One civil servant observed that this process "is a fabulous control mechanism" because "it takes so goddamn long to answer a routine question" that "there's no chance for the journalist to get anything extra or get any sort of a different twist on things" (CM 17). It is instructive that the PCO is involved from the outset. Engaging the PMO might occur at any given time as the coordinated response moves up the line.

In keeping with the NPM approach, the permanent government refers to media relations materials as "communications products." The terminology is absorbed by politicos, with the PMO's director of communications and cabinet ministers referring to news releases in this manner: "We issued a product."[26] A routine communications product is a media advisory. Media advisories provide assignment editors and reporters with basic information about the nature of an event, the people who will be present at it, the time and location, and whom to contact for more information. It identifies the level of media accessibility, such as whether a speech is open to media personnel, if there will be an opportunity for visual capture, and whether questions will be taken. If the intent is to generate attention, then PR personnel will contact journalists directly to encourage them to attend the event. Some advisories invite reporters to participate in a teleconference with a minister. On complex matters, a background not-for-attribution technical briefing held by senior public servants is offered. If the situation warrants, then the technical briefing is available by teleconference and/or held simultaneously in a number of major centres.

Media advisories concerning the prime minister are less inviting. Control was in excess with Harper but still exists with Trudeau. Public event notices often state that only photographers and videographers are welcome – meaning that no questions from journalists will be answered (Figure 8.2). Media are required to show identification to gain entry. Sometimes those who show up are corralled into a meeting point and bused to a secret location, away from uninvited guests and the theatrics of protesters. As alarming as that is, digital media further squeeze out the perceived need for traditional journalists. PMO media advisories transmit pseudo-events in an unfiltered manner to anyone who receives the advisory, including subscribers to the prime minister's listserve. Opposition political parties do the same, suggesting that the motivation is not to bypass the fourth estate so much as to broaden the reach. The difference is that opposition parties are eager for media attention, whereas the traditional media are eager for information on the prime minister and the government. Thus, the terms of control are different.

All forms of news operations, even radio, need a constant supply of fresh visuals in the digital media age. The media visually document the prime minister walking along the Hall of Honour in the Centre Block with another head of government, followed by a tête-à-tête; the prime minister departing from the country for international business on the Airbus CC-150 Polaris reserved for government dignitaries (Figure 10.1); meetings with members of a community; or perhaps delivering remarks at an association's awards ceremony. In circumstances in which media questions are permitted, the advisory specifies that the prime minister will make an announcement or that the event will be open to the media. Other times, the event is livestreamed (Figure 8.3), another example of how new

FIGURE 8.2
Pseudo-event media advisory, PMO

PUBLIC EVENT FOR FEBRUARY 27, 2014
Ottawa, Ontario
26 February 2014

Public event for Prime Minister Stephen Harper for Thursday February 27th is:

Toronto

4:30 p.m. – Prime Minister Stephen Harper will participate in the Prime Minister's Volunteer Awards Ceremony. He will be joined by Jason Kenney, Minister of Employment and Social Development and Minister for Multiculturalism.

> Acme Hotel and Conference Centre
> 500 Main Street
> Toronto, Ontario
> M1W 2A3

*Photo opportunity only (cameras and photographers only)

NOTES:

- Media should arrive no later than 4:00 p.m.
- Media are required to present proper identification for accreditation.
- Media should arrive at the east entrance of the building (via the general parking lot).

PMO Press Office: 613-555-5555

Note: Names, location, and phone numbers have been changed by the author.
Source: Prime Minister of Canada (2014).

FIGURE 8.3
Live-stream media advisory, PMO

From: PMO [pm@PM.GC.CA]
Sent: Thursday, June 18, 2015 3:40 PM
To: LIVESTREAM_E@LSERV.PMO-CPM.GC.CA
Subject: Livestream

From the Prime Minister's Web Site (http://www.pm.gc.ca/)

LIVE STREAM

June 18, 2015
Toronto, Ontario

Prime Minister Stephen Harper will make an announcement. He will be joined by Joe Oliver, Minister of Finance.
The live stream will begin at approximately 2:45 pm (EDT).
Watch the live stream at pm.gc.ca/live

The Prime Minister's Office – Communications

Source: Prime Minister's Office (2015b).

communications technology is used to expand reach. Afterward, the government issues a news release summarizing the event, which points journalists to associated information resources available online. This is controlled convenience for those who cannot or do not attend.

A growing trend in media relations and brand control is for political leaders to feign accessibility by participating in a staged Q&A conversation put on by a non-governmental organization. A moderator directs pre-screened questions to the prime minister, seated at the front of the room, before questions are received from members of the invitation-only audience – but not from journalists (Figure 8.4). Meanwhile, a government photographer/videographer documents private backstage moments and holds a monopoly on unique visual angles. Afterward, the PMO issues news releases with digital photographs and video clips. The prime minister is shown participating in Q&A sessions hosted by community groups. For instance, the Mississauga Board of Trade hosted a Q&A at a Brampton banquet centre, and the executive director of the Ontario Federation of Anglers and Hunters put questions to Prime Minister Harper about rural issues at a Sault Ste. Marie inn. The forums are more than information subsidies and ways to avoid the media's agenda; they provide safe havens for controversial announcements. At an event in New York, moderated by the editor of the *Wall Street Journal*, Harper said that he had not ruled out further military action in Iraq against the jihadist group that calls itself the Islamic State.[27] The chaotic nature of media scrums in Ottawa is supplanted by the visual of a calm conversation in front of an attentive audience. This media relations technique is a throwback to the 1930s radio "fireside chats" by President Roosevelt and Prime Minister Bennett.

A news release is issued when the PMO or another government entity wishes to make a formal announcement. The speed of communications means that releases must present information in a way that will be picked up easily and quickly. For ages, they were written in the style of a news story to encourage their verbatim reproduction by media outlets. Now news releases emphasize brief remarks and visual storytelling. Circa 2008, the government of Canada began circulating audio clips with its news releases. This was followed circa 2009 by photo releases and video releases, which attach visuals or announce the availability of digital content for media reuse.

FIGURE 8.4 Moderated Q&A session (Prime Minister Harper with moderator) |
Prime Minister's Office (2013); PMO photographer Deb Ransom, London, ON, November 8, 2013.

This is sensible given that text releases with a photo are viewed 1.8 times more often than text-only releases, those with video 4.3 times more often, and those with a photo and video 7.4 times more often.[28] In 2014, the government of Canada introduced a condensed format for news releases that reflects a media and news consumer movement towards simplicity. The new format instituted a snazzier headline style and adopted user-friendly formatting so that journalists can quickly locate and reuse information (Figure 8.5). A heading and subheading summarize the issue, followed by a few sentences of text. Subheadings such as "quick facts" offer some bullet-style content, "quotes" include a single quotation from the lead spokesperson(s), and "associated links" provide journalists with URLs to locate further information. Photos, audio, and video from a related event are distributed electronically and/or are available for download. As per the government's communications policy, news releases issued by the government must not include partisan remarks; nevertheless, partisan slants are sometimes detected.[29] Condensing information into key sound bites and image bites fits with a branding strategy of communications

FIGURE 8.5
Simplified style of government of Canada news release

Harper Government Prepares to Consult on "Made in Canada" Branding Campaign

▪ Economic Action Plan 2014 to enhance awareness of Canadian-made products

February 26, 2014 – Melbourne, Australia – Department of Finance

Finance Minister Jim Flaherty today met with representatives of the Australian Made Campaign Limited (AMCL) to discuss the organization's experience with its successful and long-standing national branding campaign, as the Government of Canada prepares to undertake a similar initiative.

Economic Action Plan 2014 announced plans to consult on a private-sector-led "Made in Canada" branding campaign to raise consumer awareness of the quality and range of Canadian-made products both domestically and internationally. Following these consultations, a private sector steering committee will be established to lead this initiative, which will strengthen Canada's competitiveness at home and abroad.

▪ Quick Facts

• The quality of Canadian products is recognized across the country and around the world. Branding products "Made in Canada" is a potentially powerful tool to encourage consumers – both in Canada and internationally – to choose such products. While other countries such as Australia have capitalized on their national brand as a competitive advantage, no widely recognized Canadian branding exists.

• The Australian Made campaign was launched in 1986 and is currently overseen by the AMCL. In addition to managing the Australian Made logo, the AMCL hosts a website [hyperlink to www.australianmade.com.au] that markets participating products and presents Australian companies' profiles. Approximately 1,700 Australian companies currently use the logo on more than 10,000 products.

▪ Quotes

> "Our Government is committed to fostering trade and Canadian entrepreneurship. A 'Made in Canada' brand will help advance both of these goals by raising awareness – both in Canada and internationally – of high-quality Canadian products. Learning directly from the Australians about their successful branding initiative is a first step in the process."
>
> – *Jim Flaherty, Minister of Finance*

▪ Associated Links

Economic Action Plan 2014 *[hyperlink to budget webpage]*

▪ Media Contacts

Jane Doe, Press Secretary, Office of the Minister of Finance, 613-555-5555
John Q. Public, Media Relations, Department of Finance, 613-555-6666

▪ Stay Connected

Email Alerts *[hyperlink to Department of Finance email alert registration form]*
Twitter: @financecanada *[hyperlink to https://twitter.com/financecanada]*
RSS *[hyperlink to XML file]*

Source: Finance Canada (2014).

control. This accommodates journalists who work in a fast-paced environment and often do not contact the issuer for further details, while allowing the government to frame the message.

A further way that information released by the government of Canada is simplified in the digital media age is by creating content exclusively for online audiences. Social media are discussed later in this chapter, but worthy of mention here is BuzzFeed, a source of daily diversions such as pet videos. BuzzFeed features news content contributions commonly presented as lowbrow quizzes and snappy lists accompanied by visuals. Posts use an informal style not normally associated with bureaucracy or diplomacy. In 2014, Foreign Affairs posted "12 Ways Iran Is at War with the Internet" and "11 Myths Putin Is Spreading about the Crisis in Ukraine."[30] One accuses Iran of wanting "to go full North Korea"; the other refers to Putin delivering a speech in which he "rambled through his conspiracy theories," followed by this provocative remark: "In case you actually believe your own story, Mr. Putin, your reality check is here." There is no fee to post information on BuzzFeed, and the Foreign Affairs posts conclude with a link to a French version. This is one of many examples of the burgeoning practice of social media diplomacy.

Government Advertising

Advertising offers much more message control than media relations, but it is pricier. It is used by the government to build awareness and support for public policy and to increase Canadians' confidence in public institutions. The federal government ranks among the top ten advertising spenders in Canada. As an accountability function, each year a summary of its advertising expenditures is detailed in the annual reports prepared by Public Works. The reports identify spending breakdowns by institution and campaign, types of media placement, and agency of record suppliers. As well, each quarter the TBS releases amounts approved by the Treasury Board for government-wide advertising plans. Media placements in fiscal year 2004–5, the last full year of the Martin government, compared with placements in 2013–14, show how digital media are displacing print media.[31] The proportion of federal government advertising devoted to Internet media has steadily increased, from 1 percent of all expenditures in 2004–5 to 27 percent in 2013–14. Conversely, the proportion of advertising spending on print dailies (4 percent, down from 17 percent), weekly/community newspapers (4 percent, down from 18 percent), and print magazines (1 percent, down from 3 percent) has plunged. Spending on television, radio, cinema, and out-of-home such as billboards accounts for the rest and has fluctuated, with television (46 percent, up from 44 percent) continuing to command almost half of all advertising expenditures. The movement away from print is more than a reflection of changing technology: it represents a strategic preference for visual media conducive to branding.[32]

Officially, the government of Canada purchases advertising to "inform Canadians about their rights or responsibilities, about government policies, programs, services or initiatives, or about dangers or risks to public health, safety or the environment."[33] This product-oriented approach is found in public notices concerning information sessions, requests for tenders, public hearings, job advertisements, office addresses, and so on. In practice, much government advertising is sales-oriented. Its purpose is not merely to inform or generate public awareness. Rather, it is quasi-propaganda that attempts "to seduce, cajole, or persuade through the manipulation of images ... [that] appeal to basic instincts."[34] Three years before the Canada 150 anniversary in 2017, Heritage Canada ran a video ad evoking similarities to Conservative Party communications. Images of the Fathers of Confederation, including Conservative Prime Minister Macdonald, transitioned into Sidney Crosby scoring the overtime winner in the 2010 men's Olympic gold medal hockey game in Vancouver. The ads were buttressed by a narrator who promoted the men's strong leadership and a concluding tagline of "Strong. Proud. Free." The ads were patriotic as opposed to informative. Variations of the tagline appeared in Conservative Party communications and in other government advertising and as a theme for Canada Day celebrations. This example of a sales practice is a component of permanent campaigning, the publicity state, and branding strategy.

Advertorials are another grey area. The pressures of media economics are such that "content marketing" is an option, whereby advertising staff in a media organization urge editors to prepare a news story that will appear next to the ad (CI 16). Some government institutions supplement their

FIGURE 8.6
Advertorial created by the Canada Revenue Agency

Children's arts now qualify for a tax credit

(NC) – No matter whether your children are inspired to be the next YouTube sensation, like Justin Bieber, or hope to pen a worldwide bestseller like Lucy Maud Montgomery, or dream to go Back to the Future like Michael J. Fox, the new children's arts tax credit will allow them to live out their dreams. In addition to fitness programs covered by the children's fitness tax credit, parents may now be able to claim a children's arts tax credit for the amounts paid for prescribed artistic, cultural, recreational, and developmental programs.

This new non-refundable tax credit allows kids the choice to focus on fine arts, music, performing arts, outdoor wilderness training, learning a language, studying a culture, tutoring, and more. When parents claim the children's arts tax credit – up to a maximum of $500 for the cost of eligible programs – they can save as much as $75 at tax time per child claimed. More information on this topic is available online at www.cra.gc.ca/artscredit. Pull out those paintbrushes and clarinets, and let's get creative.

Note: Original accompanied by a photograph of children (not shown).
Source: Canada Revenue Agency (2012a).

media relations activities with paid ads made to look like they were prepared by arm's-length journalists. During tax season in 2012, the Canada Revenue Agency prepared general interest news stories about personal finances. Text of between 130 and 230 words was packaged with a catchy headline, a photograph, and a website address. The CRA paid News Canada to circulate seven pseudo-news stories with headings such as "Tips for Buying That Perfect Home" and "10 Ways to Reduce Your Tax Bll" (Figure 8.6). News Canada is a clearinghouse for copyright-free syndicated features. The publicity agency's stories are offered for free reproduction without copyright. They are available in text, audio, and video forms, along with submitted photographs. The advertorials are created for easy downloading, tweeting, posting to Facebook and Google+, and emailing. The company pitches its services as "providing the media with ready-to-use, timely, credible and copyright-free news content. Editors, broadcasters, web and video content providers rely on News Canada for newsworthy content to effectively enhance their websites, newspapers and broadcasts. Content is made available to you, the media, in the format you need, when you need it."[35] The idea is that media organizations will avail themselves of the information subsidies and that audiences will attach journalistic credibility to them.

The advertorials are published by some traditional media outlets and are embedded in websites. Smaller media outlets use News Canada content as long as it "does not compromise our editorial integrity," explained an editor of *South Asian Focus* (CI 14). Access to information documents show that News Canada found that the CRA's write-ups appeared as news stories hundreds of times in transit newspapers, weekly community papers, ethnic publications, magazines, and websites ranging from newspapers to blogs.[36] Well-funded media organizations are more suspicious. The *Toronto Star* located News Canada material that trumpets the federal government's fresh food subsidy for residents in northern areas, even though the auditor general critiqued the subsidy for not conclusively contributing to reduced prices.[37] The advertorial practice was formalized in 2014 when Public Works issued a standing offer with News Canada.

For major advertising campaigns, a number of central agencies are engaged (Table 8.1). The Privy Council Office steers the campaign through a multistage process with Public Works, as described in the following pages.[38] The process differs in the event of an emergency or crisis because of urgencies and the potential need for coordination with provincial and/ or municipal governments. In normal circumstances, the time from conceptualization to assessment varies. In the case of the CRA's annual tax-filing season campaign, the presentation and approval of a creative brief and media strategies begin in September. Online focus group testing and media buys occur in October. Advertising production and PCO approvals carry on through year end. Advertising and social media activity runs into the first quarter of the new year. Finally, in April, the advertising is analyzed and evaluated by the PCO.[39] The considerable lead time for advertising campaigns stands in contrast with the tyranny of the urgent faced by media relations personnel. Nevertheless, both forms of communication are subject to extensive planning and internal scrutiny.

A federal advertising campaign passes through an extensive internal process. It begins with a proposal prepared by a department or agency using PWGSC's Advertising Management Information System. It must identify how the advertising aligns with government priorities and key messages. Twice a year advertising proposals are reviewed by working groups, notably the interdepartmental Government Advertising Committee (GAC), comprised of directors general of communications and chaired by

TABLE 8.1

Roles of central agencies in the government of Canada advertising process

Institution	Role
Cabinet committees	Parliamentary affairs (previously government operations) and the agenda and results (previously priorities and planning) Cabinet committees review and approve the advertising plan. Treasury Board sets broad policies and procedures, such as the Federal Identity Program, and must approve funding allocations.
Treasury Board Secretariat (TBS)	Coordinates implementation of policies and procedures on behalf of the Treasury Board. Prepares financial allocations for board approval.
Departments/agencies	Manage advertising campaigns and report on results.
Privy Council Office (PCO)	Develops the advertising plan and provides oversight. Chairs the government advertising committee (GAC).
Public Works and Government Services Canada (PWGSC)	Awards advertising contracts and work authorizations. Coordinates implementation of advertising campaigns and pre-testing/post-campaign evaluation. PWGSC teams include the Advertising Coordination and Partnership Directorate (ACPD), the Communications Procurement Directorate (CPD), and the Public Opinion Research Directorate (PORD). Internal tools include the Advertising Management Information System (AdMis) and the Advertising Campaign Evaluation Tool (ACET).

Note: Subject to change.
Partial source: Public Works and Government Services Canada (2014c).

the PCO. Collaboration among institutions is encouraged. All proposals must be assessed within the context of the PCO-managed Government Advertising Plan that enumerates current and proposed advertising expenditures. In the Conservative government, the plan had to be approved by cabinet's operations committee before being vetted by the priorities and planning committee. The Treasury Board then considered a request for funding.

The planning and approval stage is followed by the contracting stage. It engages PWGSC's Advertising Coordination and Partnership Directorate (ACPD) and its Communications Procurement Directorate (CPD) to review the advertising plan and coordinate procurement details. Public Works coordinates a competitive process to generate a list of advertising agencies eligible to be awarded contracts for the development of campaign planning and creative services. Large, complex campaigns call for proposals on buyandsell.gc.ca. Smaller campaigns are managed in-house and require some outsourcing, such as the purchase of stock photographs. Public Works designates a single advertising agency of record to prenegotiate rates for purchasing media time and space. The decision on where to place advertising remains with the department. The coordination of a central media buyer leverages the government's buying power while ensuring broader oversight.

The process enters the third stage of advertising production once a contract is signed with an advertising agency. The contracted supplier works with the client on aligning the strategic objectives, creative concepts, and media plan. The creative concepts must adhere to government policies, including its communications policy, the Federal Identity Program, and the Official Languages Act. This can include incorporating Service Canada points of contact, namely the 1-800-O-Canada information phone line, the government's primary website (canada.gc.ca), and/or its public service intranet website (publiservice.gc.ca).

The next stage is the pretesting of any major advertising buys involving $400,000 or more (dollar amounts are subject to change). The creative concepts are tested in focus groups contracted through the PWGSC's Public Opinion Research Directorate (PORD) and reviewed by the GAC. Data collected in the pretest, such as participants' responses to storyboards, are used to inform potential adjustments and provided to the PCO and PORD. The fifth stage is the media buy. The supplier develops a media plan with the client, which it submits to the PCO and ACPD. The purchase of media space is carried out by an agency of record selected by the CPD, and it liaises with the ACPD. The PCO analyst or GAC must sign off on the media plan.

The final stage is the post-campaign evaluation of advertising, required only for media buys that cost the treasury $1 million or more. The Advertising Campaign Evaluation Tool (ACET) is administered to assess project outcomes against the planned indicators of success. The ACET is an opinion survey consisting of standardized questions that track target audiences' recollections of the advertising. It identifies their reactions and behavioural responses. Among the standard questions are the following:

- Over the past few weeks or so, have you seen, heard or read any advertising about [X]?

- What can you remember about this advertising? What words, sounds or images come to mind?
- Did you do anything as a result of seeing/hearing this ad?
- Who do you think produced it; that is, who paid for it?
- How would you rate the performance of the Government of Canada in providing information to Canadians about [X]?

By administering such standard questions, the ACET generates pan-governmental comparative data. Privately, departments grumble that they lack the flexibility to make adjustments to meet their needs.[40] Political staffers are not always fond of the ACET either. A former chief of staff opined that the process "is stuck in the 1990s" and "really just wasteful and not very creative and, in the end, not very useful ... The government buys an enormous amount of market research that is of no use whatsoever. It's just 'make work' projects" (CS 31). The evaluation survey represents a New Public Management search for value through an attempt to ascertain communications impact and to inform better choices.

A completed report on the post-campaign survey is submitted to the PORD and the PCO analyst. A research presentation might be made to the GAC. The data are used to inform decisions in future campaigns. They also become fodder for the media to file stories about the limited effect-iveness of expensive ad campaigns.[41] To curtail the criticism, the Conserv-ative administration ceased administering ACET questions on whether audiences were inspired to take action and on the government's perform-ance. The PCO explained that the emphasis is now only on questions "most useful in assessing a campaign's objectives – notably recall, recognition and message retention."[42] This represents a clash between the civil service's interest in program evaluation and the political government's concern with publicity. This may change again under the Liberals.

Public Opinion Research by Government

The core function of government public opinion research is to assist in the selling of public policy as opposed to designing it.[43] Its communications value to the federal government ranges from taking stock of the general public's priorities to – as just discussed – assessing the impacts of adver-tising on targeted audiences. During advertising design, focus groups establish the forms of language that Canadians use and their emotional reactions to proposed messages, while opinion polls provide comparable evaluation data to assess the impact of a campaign. More advanced analysis offers an understanding of audiences' attitudes, emotions, lifestyles, and values. This invites the spectre of the politicization of government-funded research, a topic beyond the scope of this chapter. Health Canada communications personnel, at least, are steadfast that the department's MINO tends to accept the strategic approach developed from research findings (CM 16, CS 18).

Publicly, selected survey results are promoted in government news releases and ministers' speeches. This demonstrates that a policy decision is in line with what the citizenry wants and is a rational use of government resources. Behind the scenes, persuasive messages and arguments are tested. Reactions to possible courses of government action, including to the anticipated countermessages of opponents, are probed. Benchmark data and post-advertising evaluation are the basis for understanding whether media tactics changed target audiences' awareness of, and attitudes toward, a policy issue. Different reactions to the same messages in English and French are sometimes detected. Public forms and documents such as tax returns are reviewed in focus groups, as are telephone messages and websites. The budget speech is tested to pinpoint messages that resonate with audiences and to identify what should be repeated in media interviews. Emphasis is placed on assessing the awareness and attitudes of demographic subgroups.

The Treasury Board Secretariat maintains the government's procedures for planning and contracting public opinion research.[44] The procedures stipulate that the head of communications in each government institution is responsible for the planning, contracting, reporting, and monitoring of its data collection. The management process is delegated to a public opinion research coordinator. An annual plan must be prepared to identify anticipated research, including the testing and evaluation of advertising. A draft of the plan must be reviewed by the PCO's Communications and Consultations Secretariat, which receives a final version, as does the PORD at Public Works. The CPD coordinates procurement and contracting, ensuring that government funds are not used to measure party or voting preferences. There must be agreement on an appropriate methodology.

The disruptive nature of digital communications is heightening the need for mixed-mode surveys that use at least two of live telephone, automated voice response, email, and web communications.

Once a contract is signed, the PWGSC must receive draft research instruments before the research goes into the field. The PCO reserves the right to request any materials for review. As mentioned in Chapter 7, within six months of completing an opinion research project, a report must be deposited with Library and Archives Canada (LAC) and with the Library of Parliament. The PORD, CPD, and LAC are expected to relay any non-compliance issues to the TBS. As with the advertising process, the rigidity of the public opinion research process inhibits flexibility, resulting in senior departmental staff becoming frustrated.[45]

There are other ways that public opinion is monitored. Consultation and citizen engagement initiatives, such as online forums to submit feedback on strategy papers, are handled separately from public opinion research. Public invitations to participate appear in the *Canada Gazette*. They are publicized on the sponsoring organization's website and on Service Canada's Consulting with Canadians website (canada.ca/consultingcanadians). In 2007, the government began operating mystery shopper programs to collect data on the customer experience. Such quality assurance programs assess the front-line and online service of organizations such as Canada Post and Service Canada, and they are further evidence of NPM from a communications angle.[46] This is in addition to considerable monitoring of traditional, community, ethnic, and social media (see Chapter 9).

Corporate Identity (Federal Identity Program)

Within the government of Canada, there are over 100 government departments and agencies, each of which has its own subunits. They all have their own subcultures and policies that employees want to brand. Within the confines of the FIP, departments may create their own visual look and feel as long as they do not create any logos, even for short-term functions such as a contest. This recognizes an understanding of clients' information needs while ensuring that the government "doesn't end up drowning in logos that confuse the public and waste lots of money" (CS 13). Departments maintain some flexibility to develop their own branding strategies for specific activities. For instance, as mentioned in Chapter 4 (see also Figure 8.5), labelling food with "Made in Canada" is a unified effort to denote food quality, which fulfills the FIP objective of branding public policies in a consistent manner so that they can be easily recognized. Some organizations are exempt from the program, notably most Crown corporations. But make no mistake: the FIP is a central agency parameter that provides the foundation for branding and message control in the federal government.

The centralization of government communications is related to federalists' desire to promote national unity messaging. Branding has acted as a communications counterfoil to separatism because it harmonizes the national unity functions of the publicity organs of the state. The Bureau of Public Information and its successor, the Wartime Information Board, promoted the merits of the war effort in a tense environment of opposition in Quebec during the Second World War. Among federalists' responses to Quebec's Quiet Revolution in the early 1960s was a thickening of Canadian nationalism and a desire to improve Canadians' awareness of the federal presence. Federalists thought that Canadians, particularly Quebecers, did not recognize how significant a role the federal government played in their society. This led to the aforementioned Task Force on Government Information, its recommendation for a centralized corporate identity, and creation of the Federal Identity Program. The Canadian maple leaf flag, Expo '67, Task Force on Government Information, and FIP were all established during the throngs of debate over bilingualism and biculturalism. The Coordination Group of the Federal-Provincial Relations Office planned an information strategy after the Parti Québécois was elected in 1976.[47] An offshoot, the Canadian Unity Information Office, was created to publicize federalism during the 1980 Quebec sovereignty referendum and the 1982 patriation of the Constitution. Canadian Heritage's flag program and PWGSC's sponsorship program were created in response to the 1995 Quebec referendum. Many of these initiatives fulfilled public demands for information on the country and its government during anxious political times. They have done so by unabashedly publicizing the virtues of federalism. Once again, the Liberal Party of Canada was in power at all of these points.

A 1993 report on the federal government's corporate identity observed that the consistent application of corporate symbols contributes to the projection of "an image of the Government of Canada as a coherent, unified administration."[48] The FIP manual explains that a corporate image is continuously expressed through numerous media that form impressions among the public. Not only is the Canada wordmark (Figure 8.1) the single corporate logo used by federal government departments, but also all departments must include the word *Canada* in their names or be associated with the *Government of Canada*. For instance, the Department of Health is known simply as Health Canada. No abbreviations are allowed, though inevitably some departments become known by acronyms, such as the Department of Fisheries and Oceans, condensed to Fisheries and Oceans Canada, but commonly called DFO. A department's name must be in both official languages. All departments use a consistent corporate signature that contains the bar and leaf logo and the name of the department.

The Treasury Board integrated new requirements into the Federal Identity Program in the aftermath of the 1995 Quebec sovereignty referendum.[49] The revisions established that the government's visual presence is paramount and that any exemption to the branding program must obtain Treasury Board approval. Henceforth, all government of Canada institutions, even if otherwise exempt, are required to use the Canada wordmark. Government lease arrangements must accommodate the FIP, namely that the wordmark is to appear prominently on federal government buildings, with commercial signage prioritizing branding rather than direction (e.g., the signage must not emphasize the street number). The Canadian flag must be on visible display in public areas within the building. Uniformed employees must be identifiable as being on duty for the federal government. Furthermore, the Treasury Board directed that the government of Canada's logo prevail over institutions' own logos. The program

> helps project the government as a coherent, unified administration ... through clear and consistent identification. The FIP policy, in concert with the Communications Policy of the Government of Canada, helps shape the "face" and the "voice" of government ... It applies to a broad field of applications including stationery, forms, vehicular markings, signage, advertising, published material, electronic communications, audio-visual productions and expositions, personnel identification, awards and plaques, packaging and labelling, and identification of equipment.[50]

After the revisions were adopted in 1998, government institutions set about to install the Canada wordmark on high-profile buildings that they occupied, even when Public Works was not the owner. Lower-cost interior signage was an option when a building's architecture or visibility did not merit an exterior sign. The wordmark now appears on over 100 buildings across Canada, satisfying the program's original mandate. It is widely used on government marketing collateral. The program's website (tbs-sct. gc.ca/fip-pcim) has a password-protected area that provides departmental FIP coordinators with access to high-resolution files of the government's official symbols and information on how the symbols should be applied. When they are faced with a difficult question, FIP coordinators contact TBS representatives about compliance rules, such as co-branding initiatives with private sector firms and charities or cost-shared ventures with other governments. "The centre" is cautious about attaching the Canada wordmark to collaborative undertakings lest doing so be interpreted as implying the Crown's endorsement of partner organizations.

Policing the Federal Identity Program's standards is difficult and indicates that decrees issued by the centre are not summarily followed. As the Task Force on Government Information envisioned, each department and government agency is required to designate a staff member as its FIP coordinator. Coordinators often hold congruent positions; for instance, the director of corporate communications in the Atlantic Canada Opportunities Agency is also its FIP coordinator. Other coordinators have this responsibility tacked onto their unrelated duties, such as the director of case management services in the Canada Industrial Relations Board or a planning and reporting analyst in the Canada Intergovernmental Conference Secretariat. A senior adviser in the Treasury Board Secretariat explained that "the department's head of communications (and staff) is ultimately the first line of defence against unnecessary logos, and should provide alternative strategies. Such proactive efforts really pay off later, by avoiding unrealistic expectations, wasting your own communications time, and avoid[ing] engaging central agency machinery."[51] TBS staff field coordinators' questions, ranging from matters as innocuous as where to place the wordmark on stationary to contending with arguments for special treatment.

Public servants at the centre routinely exert their authority over government branding. There is general irritation within the TBS that line departments venture into graphic design and proceed without following central policy. A senior FIP adviser lamented that "I see it almost every day – people think they can make the wordmark. They have Times New Roman on hand and they just add a clipart flag. The next most common problem is they use the whole national flag and not the flag symbol."[52] Excruciating details such as using the required Baskerville typeface and shade of red (Pantone 032) are micromanaged by TBS. The most exuberant of TBS staff take photographs of non-compliant building signage and billboards for internal discussion and action. They even maintain an inventory of hundreds of non-compliant visuals dubbed "the logo wall of shame." In an internal email, one TBS staffer cautioned a Public Works employee that signage principles are outlined in "the wordmark sign program that WE control."[53] In response to another PWGSC enquiry, involving a request to brand government computer desktops, the TBS contact wrote that

> the policy on the identity of the Government of Canada is in place to do two things – regulate the official symbols, and control the creation or use of all others. The objective is to brand government as a single coherent organization with obviously many parts and many activities ... I can caution you now that there is zero support for program logos, particularly internal ones.[54]

However, many non-FIP symbols and logos persist, which the TBS attempts to reduce because they compete with the main government symbols. In yet another internal email, the TBS employee explained to a line department that "FIP is under constant challenge from institutions trying to distinguish themselves through unique identifiers, logos, symbols or entirely separate identities. This fractures government's identity, weakens the public's ability to clearly recognize federal institutions and access federal programs and services (e.g., Service Canada)."[55] For their part, heads of communications and FIP coordinators complain that the program is too complex and restrictive.[56] Agitation with centralized protocols seems to occur wherever such protocols exist.

At other times, the Treasury Board Secretariat recognizes that flexibility is necessary and only demands visual consistency among regions. A complication is that the FIP is silent in many areas, such as with respect to novelty items and apparel. The policy does not fully reflect changes brought on by digital media. Social media buttons such as Facebook and Twitter are displayed in government communications, and badges are developed for mobile applications. Iterations of the policy, including those stemming from interdepartmental consultations, provide more clarity while expanding the program's reach. When faced with an absence of policy stipulations, such as how co-branded signage can acknowledge funding from multiple levels of government, the TBS recommends "common sense advice to craft a clear, direct and efficient message ... that best serves all of the criteria."[57]

The Federal Identity Program is a standard-bearer of New Public Management and how branding is related to centralization. The program's manual states that the FIP is a "management technique" for the strategic communication of the "organization's unique characteristics" in a clear, accurate, and memorable manner.[58] It fulfills an NPM function in that ministerial discretion is removed in favour of a centrally administered policy "in the spirit of ensuring that government is visible, accessible, and ultimately accountable to the public for every single thing it does" (CS 13). The TBS rationalizes the FIP as communications expenditures that improve Canadians' ability to identify the government of Canada.

This branding protocol is positioned as a democratic undertaking because it increases accessibility and accountability.[59] An opinion survey administered in 1999 found that the Canada wordmark is a well-recognized government symbol that evokes a sense of Canadian patriotism and causes Canadians to place more trust in information.[60] It is a model for other levels of government too: the TBS periodically exchanges knowledge with counterparts in the private sector and other governments, for instance administrators of the Government of Ontario's Visual Identity System and the City of Toronto's Corporate Identity Program.

Government Publishing

Another way that digital media and branding are converging is through the move to put government publications online. Publications are information materials prepared for the public that have an extended lifespan, such as books, brochures, maps, and videos. In the federal government, publishing is overseen by each institution's head of communications, ex- · pected to ensure that all materials comply with central communications policies. As per TBS procedures, publications must reflect the diversity of Canadian society and regionalism.[61] The PWGSC maintains a central depository of published works, known as the Depository Services Program. It produces the *Canada Gazette,* the official source of new statutes, regulations, board decisions, and government appointments. Library and Archives Canada collects and stores certain publications, maintains a national database of publications, and issues serial numbers. It also preserves audio and video recordings.

Volume printing of reports and research studies is being phased out in place of on-demand printing and digital publishing. Advertisements, tutorials, and contests are available via video on government websites. Video streaming is now the standard for accessing archival materials such as National Film Board productions as well as recent productions, such as the PMO's *24 Seven* video newsmagazine. Raw footage of speeches, web-only video addresses, and video of government experts providing technical explanations are available to Canadians online via the web and internally via the government Intranet. Increased access to government information is the new normal. The movement toward digitization comes through in public demands for government transparency. Open Government (open. canada.ca) is a portal that makes federal government information available online. The portal has many objectives, including expanding e-commerce, posting completed access to information requests, creating a virtual library of government documents, using electronic record management, uploading datasets, disclosing spending information, and developing a citizen engagement platform. The various activities are grouped into subcategories of Open Data (e.g., publicly available datasets), Open Information (e.g., contracts over $10,000, access to information requests), and Open Dialogue (e.g., consultations, *Canada Gazette*). Unfortunately, Open Government is not above politicization (see the discussion surrounding Figure 10.2).

Government Web Communications

The standardization of government websites was a communications priority of the Conservative administration. Initially, central agencies were slow to take the lead. The 1999 Speech from the Throne pledged that by 2004 Canadians would be able to use the Internet to obtain information on all of the federal government's programs and services.[62] This became known as the Government On-Line (GOL) initiative. The government of Canada website, created in 1995, was relaunched in 2001 as a portal to a maze of department and agency websites. Government websites were rudimentary sources of information and warehouses of links to other sites. Over time, the details of programs and services expanded, and reports were uploaded. Departments took their own approaches, resulting in a government web presence where webpages reflected how a department was organized rather than what information citizens were seeking. It was a morass of information likened to a "wild frontier."[63] Unseemly domain names (e.g., cic.gc.ca rather than the more intuitive immigration.gc.ca or citizenship.gc.ca) were used, and photos were purchased from online databanks. The GOL targets proved to be too ambitious and were modified to commit to basic information availability by the end of 2005. Years of content accumulation resulted in tens of thousands of links to each department's website, tens of thousands of pages of content on each site, and hundreds of different sites. An NPM approach was initiated with the aforementioned launch of Service Canada, accompanied by the objective of offering one-stop service provision in person and online.

The 2013 budget announced the government's intention to fuse its 1,500 websites into a single access point. The idea is to organize information in the way that citizens look for it rather than how the government or departments are organized or how the bureaucracy thinks. Within a year, the canada.ca homepage was organized with a row of topical subjects across the top and scrolling photographs associated with recent government achievements. Observers noted the blue colour scheme and the prioritiz- ation of certain subjects, which had their own tabs (jobs, immigration, travel, business, benefits, health, taxes), whereas other content was lumped into a drop-drown menu.[64] Rotating photographs drew attention to political messages and public service information (see, e.g., Figure 3.2). This fusion is indicative of branding strategy and permanent campaigning, and it is built on the FIP model of central standards enforced by departmental representatives.

At a philosophical level, the whole of government framework (see Chapter 9) is connected with the movement toward e-government. This espouses that consistent government information is available 24/7 from anywhere with Internet access, encompassing service transactions and transparency. Technological advances in bandwidth, wireless, mobile devices, and platforms are having profound implications for the technological specifications. To keep pace, the government reorganizes its websites and makes content accessible via mobile platforms. Streamlining the leviathan of e-content is an arduous task. Among the complications are loss of search engine placement, changes to visual design, site redirection, purging of dead links, and reprinting of marketing collateral that contains old website addresses. Centralized leadership is required to overcome territorial issues within public administration and to simplify the user experience.

A branding imperative is found in the commitment to consolidate web services. This is promoted as the embodiment of democratic principles of openness, transparency, and information access.[65] The posting of text, photos, audio, and/or video increases the volume of accessible information, and consistent navigation and user experiences improve the ability of site visitors to locate it. This saves time and money by creating a single template for departmental web designers. Technological glitches are reduced, and solutions are shared in a pan-governmental learning community. As well, the TBS places tools on an open source website to encourage collaboration from private industry, leading to innovation while ensuring that "people aren't reinventing the wheel all the time" (CM 11). Technology advances so rapidly that central standards become outdated. Any summary of information technology architecture, including what appears in this book, should be seen as indicative rather than definitive.

The government's communications policy states that web conformity includes the repetition of messages and themes used offline. Web standards for the government of Canada have tried to create a common brand experience, such that until 2010 the guidelines were known as the "common look and feel" standards. They stipulate corporate identity conventions, for instance the naming format for email addresses and website domains. The applicability of broader rules such as the Federal Identity Program and official language requirements are mentioned.[66] The universal criteria are maintained by the Web Standards Office, located in the Chief Information Branch of the Treasury Board Secretariat. Agencies, as well as government initiatives (e.g., Service Canada) and marketing campaigns approved by the PCO, have some compliance flexibility. So do internal wikis and blogs, treated like emails.

Technology specialists follow centralized guidelines so that websites have a similar appearance. In 2014, the TBS administered four standards. In 2011, the Standard on Web Accessibility took effect. It recognizes that a parallel navigation experience is important for web content that can be readily viewed by people with physical disabilities. The standard requires that the government's websites follow international guidelines for improving the navigation of text, sound, and image content. This follows a ruling by the Federal Court of Canada that found in favour of a blind Canadian denied equal access to government of Canada services online. The court ordered the government to improve its monitoring of over 100 federal institutions to ensure compliance with accessibility standards.[67] Also taking effect was the Standard on Web Usability, which requires that websites conform to common design and layout principles.[68] Visual standardization and simplicity help people to locate accurate and current information in a minimum number of clicks, with limited reading or scrolling. In 2012, the Standard on Web Interoperability set the conditions for reuse of online content across the government's websites regardless of platform or device. For instance, syndicated content offered through news feeds is required to follow a common look. Departments retain some independence to reflect their target audiences' needs, such as Immigration, Refugees, and Citizenship Canada, which transcribes its online videos into Arabic, Mandarin, Punjabi, Spanish, and Tagalog. And in 2013 the Standard on Optimizing Websites and Applications for Mobile Devices was introduced. It stipulates that a consistent navigation bar must be used, comprised of the Canada wordmark and home, back, menu, search, and settings buttons. Websites must adhere to specific dimensions, alignments, and colours so that online content is accessible from small touchscreens.

The voluminous and technical nature of web communications makes for a breathtaking challenge of policing from the centre. As with other government communications, the TBS places the onus on senior executives in each institution to monitor conformity with central standards. Web specialists are responsible for ensuring content accuracy, functionality, and consistency. The secretariat promotes compliance by offering supports, such as web templates and education forums for web specialists.[69] It maintains GCpedia (gcpedia.gc.ca), an internal wiki launched in 2008 exclusive to the government network. GCpedia is an online forum for public servants to obtain policy information and share knowledge. Recommendations for how to manage compliance activities are available, along with a summary of tasks that government communications personnel should follow to ensure consistency with common look and feel standards for e-communications. This sharing of knowledge adds to communications consistency throughout government.

As in the FIP office, requests for clarifications and exemptions are received daily at the Web Standards Office in the Treasury Board Secretariat. Staff in the central agency adjudicate pleas that standards are too onerous, that they are technically infeasible, that the policy conflicts with a department's/agency's mandate, that it inhibits a richer user experience, and so on. A TBS employee explains to confused or frustrated personnel what the relevant standards are and what the institution is required to do to solve the dilemma. Compliance results in a myriad of logistical frustrations. For instance, in an email to the Web Standards Office, an IT director in a line department lamented that "the logic of having someone being able to navigate out of a form to another part of the site in the middle of filling out the form even for accessibility doesn't make sense. I'm obviously missing something." [70] In response, the team leader in the central office insisted that the TBS standard prevailed and suggested that the solution was to insert a statement on the webpage that, if a user were to navigate away from the form, all data would be lost. Some departmental web specialists who are aware of the conformity stipulations chafe against unrealistic demands for content creation placed by the PCO and PMO in support of media announcements. As one DND staffer relayed in an email to colleagues, "I will do my best to assuage fears [from the centre], but you must understand: we have a huge web presence with many, many different administrators, limited resources to implement the kind of changes you're asking for, and two weeks' notice that change would be required ... No one was aware that [website content] change was expected on this scale."[71]

As with the FIP process, if an institution is not satisfied with the web standards, then the minister can pursue an exemption, which can be granted by the president of the Treasury Board. An exemption requires the completion of an application, maintained by Public Works, accompanied by a cover letter signed by the minister. The applicant identifies which requirements cannot be met, provides details about the rationale for special treatment, performs a self-analysis of the risks (including the possibility of public embarrassment), and offers supplementary background information. The TBS performs its own risk assessment, which includes identifying any legal, policy, and liability considerations. It wants to know how many people will be exposed to the non-compliant information, how long it will take for the applying institution to ensure compliance with the government's web standards, and whether risk mitigation is in place. If the rationale is deemed to be sound, then the Web Standards Office seeks input from other TBS units, including the FIP, and if necessary from the PCO.

Requests for exclusion from central web standards tend to be denied, even those that appear to be innocuous. For instance, when demand for Canadian-based Research in Motion's BlackBerry smartphone began to wane against consumer interest in Apple's iPhone, Foreign Affairs sought a well-meaning exemption. It wanted to promote the BlackBerry by including "Sent by BlackBerry/Envoyé par BlackBerry" in emails sent by trade commissioners based in other countries. The practice was deemed to be inappropriate by TBS because it might prompt similar requests from other companies, and it would be unfair to privilege one over others. Exemptions are more likely to be granted if technology cannot comply with the web standards (e.g., integration of a Google map) or if there is a mandate-driven rationale (e.g., the ombudsman website).

As a branding philosophy takes hold, communicators want to promote key government initiatives and messages on all of the online access points. The government's website template includes standardized icons to advertise government initiatives that might bear little or no relevance to what a site visitor is seeking. On websites and social media, information technology specialists are told to reuse and repeat information. "It's all about repurposing information, repackaging it, and sort of rewriting things for different media. You can just repurpose it using different tools to reach different audiences," explained a communications analyst in a government agency (CM 11). The most visited government online property is the Environment Canada weather site. It registers over 1.5 million visits and 16 million page views daily. As part of the rebranding of government online properties, in 2013 the prominence of Environment Canada's name and corporate signature on its website was diminished in favour of "Government of Canada" and a Canadian flag.[72] Visitors to weather.gc.ca in late 2014, or to any other major website with the gc.ca extension, were greeted by three banner ads that had nothing to do with the weather forecast. The first promoted the expanded Universal Child Care Benefit, with a link to the budget page. The second urged parents to "Prevent Teen Drug Abuse," which linked to healthycanadians.gc.ca and the government's drug prevention advertising. The third photo tile asked "can we talk about cyberbullying?" and led to information on protecting children from cyberbullying at getcybersafe.gc.ca. These vanity URLs offer uncluttered user experiences in contrast to the navigational complexity of some department-specific pages. All of this fits a consumer-oriented NPM approach to communications while becoming a source of debate about the politicization of government and about Canada becoming a publicity state.

The macromessages in the banner ads (e.g., low taxes, tough on crime) reinforced the Conservative government's master brand, and the specific sub-brand messages allow departments to promote certain policy objectives. The government's strengthening web presence is becoming a formidable communications platform to build and set agendas. Within days of announcing plans to introduce an income tax–splitting credit, and before a bill to change the Income Tax Act was debated, the government's web presence was filled with visuals touting a "family tax cut." Government advertising featured images of suburban nuclear families that the Conservatives were targeting and followed the same colour palette as the Economic Action Plan advertising. Tweets using the hashtag #StrongFamilies were issued by the Department of Finance and retweeted by a number of departments. "Strong families" was a phrase associated with the Conservatives' electioneering, once again bringing into question to what extent a democratic government should be politicized. Web communications are ripe for infusing a brand command.

Social Media and Government

The Internet is a cost-efficient tool to send out unfiltered information. It continues to evolve from the static, one-way, 24/7 communication of text (Web 1.0) to the peer-to-peer exchange and co-production of content (Web 2.0). For corporate bodies, social media are important public engagement tools that present opportunities to disseminate information and solicit opinions about proposed courses of action. For the government, social media use repurposes a variety of content, such as repeating the core message of a news release, and has become an essential tool in crisis communications. Consolidation is palpable as digital information is shared via stakeholder websites. One Canada Revenue Agency PR staffer waxed enthusiastic in an internal email, summarizing the reposting of information across online platforms as "not much $$ spent, little effort for a good return."[73] At times, this might be nothing more than evidence of workplace productivity, rather than something more sinister. Whatever the motivation, the repetition of messages is a hallmark of branding, and social media is an increasingly prominent message vehicle.

Politicians took to social media ahead of public service personnel. Their adoption of Twitter was faster than the uptake of Facebook, which politicians experience difficulty with compared with the brevity and immediacy of microblogging. The @pmharper handle, maintained by the PMO, began tweeting in September 2008. Its first tweet urged followers to "check out the new Conservative Party website," five days before the governor general was asked to dissolve Parliament. The novelty of the technology is such that major party leaders issued only one to three tweets per day during that election campaign, and by its conclusion their followers numbered in the low thousands.[74] This stands in contrast to the 818,000 followers of @pmharper as of June 2015, the 658,000 following @JustinTrudeau, Green Party leader Elizabeth May's 151,000 via @ElizabethMay, the 132,000 followers of @ThomasMulcair, or the 85,000 following the @GillesDuceppe account of Bloc Québécois leader Gilles Duceppe. The @pmharper Twitter account is an instance of the predicament of the prime minister, who has feet in three worlds (i.e., as a party leader, head of government, and Parliamentarian). Followers of party accounts paled in comparison: 51,000 of @CPC_HQ, 138,000 of @liberal _party, 76,000 of @CanadianGreens, 86,000 of @NDP_HQ, and fewer than 10,000 of @BlocQuébécois. This illustrates that Twittter is no longer reserved for early adopters and that personal brands are trumping party brands, a pattern magnified in the post-Harper era. As well, social media contribute to the further conflation of government, party, and personal brands. An appeal to followers to join the Conservative Party's mailing list sent from @pmharper prompted media discussion on whether this violated the non-partisan covenant of government communications policy. Concern was expressed that the staffer who posted the message was on the payroll of the government rather than the Conservative Party.[75] The username continued to be updated throughout the 2015 campaign, while Prime Minister Trudeau continues to use @JustinTrudeau. This campaigning from the seat of government invites further questions about the convergence of the prime minister's brand.

Tony Clement, Conservative MP for Parry Sound–Muskoka, is one of the Canadian political pioneers of Twitter. In 2010, Canadian politicians began experimenting with Twitter, resulting in gaffes and newsroom mocking (CI 2). In March, as the minister of industry, Clement started microblogging from @TonyclementCPC. Consternation ensued throughout the PMO about what he was doing. His office staffers were told "what the heck is Tony tweeting that for, that's ridiculous; he can't tweet that" (CM 21) and "he's tweeting too much, we don't want him on that medium" (CS 29). Throughout government, permanent and political staff monitored what ministers such as Clement were tweeting. They frenetically performed Google searches to become literate in the acronyms now common in shortened electronic communications (e.g., IMHO is shorthand for "in my humble opinion"). A month before the 2011 election, Clement became the first minister to announce a policy directive via Twitter. He responded to a journalist's nighttime tweet about whether a Canadian Radio-television and Telecommunications Commission (CRTC) decision on usage-based Internet billing should be overturned: "True. CRTC must go back to drawing board."[76] Clement explained the background preparation with the PMO leading up to those eight words that came across as impromtu:

> We were breaking ground with using a new medium to create news
> ... [But] I can't just wake up in the morning and decide to do that. I
> have to follow a process, and the process involves collaboration

with the Prime Minister's Office so it's not a surprise to them. I
had full collaboration with the director of communications of the
prime minister to make sure that he was comfortable with it ... I
think he saw it as I did, as a very appropriate news item to break
on Twitter, since the people who were concerned about the issue
were people who were very much engaged in social media, and
who were very passionate about Internet policies. So to that extent
the medium and the message converged. (CS 21)

By June 2015, the @TonyclementCPC handle stood at 51,000 followers,
the same number as those following his party's Twitter account. As with
most politicians, his Twitter personality quickly became part of his personal
brand. In comparison, the government of Canada's foray into social media
communications, much like its experience with the World Wide Web, was
haphazard. Some departments launched accounts, seeking to present
themselves as innovators willing to communicate with Canadians while
reducing the number of questions received. Other departments held back
in the absence of direction from the centre and even blocked employees'
access to social media from government computers. In the PCO, social
media caused "a lot of stress" because it was unclear how the government
should deal with two-way written communications in a public online forum
(CM 22). Thus, Health Canada launched its Facebook and Twitter accounts
in mid-2009, whereas Public Works employees were unable to access social
media from their computers until early 2012. This goes some way to explaining why Canadian e-politics expert Tamara Small experienced such
difficulty locating departmental Twitter accounts around that time.[77] That
year the PCO drafted a preliminary inventory of government of Canada
social media accounts. It located 445 across seven platforms, of which
fewer than half had been approved by the PCO and PWGSC.[78] At the urging
of the PCO, risk-averse departments began unblocking employees' access
to social media on their government machines. A Public Works employee
explained the divide between departmental early adopters and laggards:

There were two schools in government. One school went the way
that they were going to block all social media, and the other group
of departments just sort of left access open ... We're talking about

all social media: Twitter, Facebook, YouTube, these types of software or types of networks. So, of course, at that time it was the big, bad social media. Now there's a little more understanding and a little more acceptance around it. The group of departments who had originally blocked access are going through the process, with help from Privy Council, to try and make it fair access to social media all across government. (CM 13)

Central agencies recognize that social media empower employees. The technology breaks down silos and encourages pan-governmental collaboration. It shrinks the workplace through vertical and horizontal integration, and it engages citizens.[79] Electronic communications also bring "the centre" closer to previously far-flung government units and staff. Nevertheless, after equalizing access across government, central agencies worried about relinquishing editorial control over content and design and negotiated terms of service agreements with social media providers. From the perspective of the Treasury Board, a leading role and standardization are necessary to provide the process-oriented public service with guidance. Clement explained that

> people in the public service will not engage in social media unless they know what the rules are. So paradoxically the absence of rules actually lessens the usage of these new social media tools, it does not increase it. It lessens it because people don't know what will be considered onside or offside, and so they are afraid that some invisible line will have been crossed by their department. The very act of establishing boundaries and rules, and appropriate versus inappropriate behaviour, actually does free up people who know what the rules are to then engage in a positive and constructive manner. (CS 21)

Communications personnel need guidelines for the rules of engagement in social media, such as what to do in the event of political posts or discriminatory language and expected response times to posts. The centre is concerned that virtual communities and discussions occur on third-party sites where standards of information conformity, privacy, and security are anathema. The TBS Guideline for External Use of Web 2.0 identifies communications threats associated with the government's use of social media. Its extensive legal and policy obligations, such as communicating in both official languages and respecting matters of privacy, are difficult to apply with fast-paced electronic communications. "Negative perceptions" resulting from harsh remarks, from political commentary, and from the "inability to fulfill reasonable expectations of timely two-way communication" are possibilities.[80] Social media users might see online comments from a public servant as synonymous with the official position of government, even if that person is communicating online as a private individual. The Department of National Defence is particularly concerned about its employees disclosing sensitive information. On a number of occasions, it has summoned the Canadian Forces National Investigation Service to investigate the unauthorized public release of information via electronic media.[81]

To cope with these problems, the Standard on Social Media Account Management promotes a "strategic and coherent approach" to Web 2.0.[82] As with the Federal Identity Program and web standards, the onus is on the head of communications in each government unit. That person is responsible for approving a department-based social media strategy. The strategy considers business value, resourcing, oversight, strategic approach and evaluation, as well as a risk management plan.[83] When public servants use social media, even for private use, they are expected to follow the Values and Ethics Code for the Public Sector, as they should with any unofficial communication. This goes some way to explaining why an Environment Canada scientist was suspended with pay in 2015 for posting a political protest song on YouTube that received hundreds of thousands of views as the election campaign wore on. In *Harperman*, the former prime minister is accused of controlling parliament, squashing dissent, being secretive, imposing a strict party line, promoting the politics of fear, being a control freak, muzzling scientists, and curtailing press freedom.[84] The video prompts questions about how far public sector brand control extends, how apolitical the public service should be, and whether the right of freedom of expression should prevail.

The Guideline on Official Use of Social Media outlines the multifaceted nature of coordinating a social media presence for the federal government.

TABLE 8.2
Roles and responsibilities in government of Canada social media planning

Role and/or function (add others as needed)	Area of responsibility
1. Drafting content	Identify departmental
2. Translating and editing content in both official languages	area responsible for each key function
3. Approving content	(head of communica-
4. Publishing content	tions must approve)
5. Managing the account (administering, monitoring, responding)	
6. Issues management (responding to issues related to the account should they arise)	

Source: Treasury Board of Canada Secretariat (2014c).

Considerations range from the need for bilingual postings to risk management planning. The variety of people and stages involved in generating social media content is illustrated in Table 8.2, a template used in social media implementation plans to organize the personnel who deal with an electronic medium. In practice, the approvals process for government social media posts is more onerous; for instance, Industry Canada (now Innovation, Science and Economic Development Canada) follows a twelve-step protocol of review, culminating in approval from the MINO.[85] Interdepartmental coordination occurs as departments arrange in advance for other departments to retweet messages. The Privy Council Office plays a coordinating role, maintaining a week-by-week blog calendar to schedule upcoming social media topics.[86] This includes its coordination of media "takeover days" to swarm coordinated social media postings on the home-pages of media organizations such as Canoe, Comedy Network, and MTV.[87]

The centre has assumed control over the government's social media presence. Government institutions must observe a formal procurement process for social media accounts. To open a Twitter account, a department/agency must submit a formal request to the PCO, which assesses the intended purpose, anticipated risks, planned mitigation strategies, and proposed measurement metrics.[88] Central agents corral a coordinated approach whenever the design and layout of an account are changed, such as when Facebook adopted its timeline feature or YouTube rebrands the look and feel of its channels. However, approvals do not apply to ministers and government members. Those individuals have leeway to create their own accounts and to issue their own social media posts, albeit at their own risk, and if they are announcing policy, as Clement has done, it must be cleared in advance. Clement pointed out that a benefit of social media for public officials is that they bypass the mainstream media filter:

> It really is a transformational technology in so many ways. It adds so many dimensions to political communication on the one hand, political dialogue. Quite frankly, it's a way to bypass mainstream media if one chooses to do so. You're not tethered to the mainstream media of what they consider newsworthy or important to comment on, and, as well, it's totally breaking down any remaining structure that separates the average Canadian citizen to the people who govern. You can have a direct dialogue with anyone in Canada if you so choose. (CS 21)

That is what David Taras means by media shock: the transformational nature of digital media. Political institutions are being turned upside-down. The power of traditional media gatekeepers – owners, editors, columnists, beat reporters – is fading. The political class is doing what it can to engage citizens directly more than ever before, yet this is happening behind an electronic wall of control. Politicians and political staff are taking advantage of new technologies to communicate directly with citizens while exercising caution to keep the brand sacrosanct. The politicization of public administration and government communications is as broad as it is penetrating.

9

Politicization of Government Communications

The public service, much like academia, has specialized skills that do not align well with the freewheeling, oversimplified digital media world. Experts in the preparation of research reports, the development of policy nuances, and the copious use of acronyms, they are impervious to the stark reality that the general public is not interested in obscure detail. This is where marketers and political communicators have an edge. Politicians can distill bafflegab into easy-to-understand messages so that the public and journalists can grasp what government is doing. This public accountability function is a safeguard that inhibits civil servants from pursuing policy pathways that are at odds with political priorities. However, the political management of government communications is controversial because of tendencies to centralize and sanitize. Institutionalized planning instruments and processes exert centripetal forces that contribute to the blurring of party and government communications. It is through political planning tools such as calendars and Message Event Proposals that the intersection of branding theory and political practice is found in Canadian public administration. To understand politics and government in the digital media age, observers of Canadian democracy must pay heed to these inner workings.

NEW POLITICAL GOVERNANCE AND WHOLE OF GOVERNMENT

The presence of central agencies in government communications runs deeper than New Public Management. Peter Aucoin's model of New

Political Governance (NPG) suggests that the emphasis in public administration is to ensure political control in all areas of government. The emergence of permanent campaigning concentrates greater decision-making power in the prime minister and his entourage. The PM is more involved in the appointment of senior government executives. A growing number of partisan staffers are entrusted to issue directives to the bureaucracy. Civil servants are expected to demonstrate enthusiasm for the prime minister's agenda. These human resource dynamics encourage them to compromise tenets of the Wilson doctrine of public service neutrality and "to provide a pro-government spin on government communications."[1] New Political Governance takes into account technological change and the pressure on government. Writing in the pre-Twitter era, Aucoin reasoned that media shock

> pressures governments to be more strategic in what they do and especially in what they say as well as the way they say it. Modern government communications, accordingly, have become perhaps the driving force behind the concentration of power, as the political leadership seeks to manage a constantly turbulent political environment, especially in relation to the mass media, which have vested interests in political turbulence.[2]

Although he does not mention branding per se, his NPG concept is consistent with branding as a contributor to centralization.

The convergence of New Political Governance and permanent campaigning fosters the expansion of a whole of government, or WOG, approach to communications. Broadly speaking, whole of government refers to any pan-governmental initiative that engages central agencies that align the over two dozen semi-autonomous departments as well as dozens of other government institutions. On an ongoing basis, the Speech from the Throne and the budget process are exercises that engage the entire government. WOG projects include the Government On-Line Initiative of the early 2000s (see Chapter 8) and that era's efforts to generate comparable financial data on government programs. What is changing is that special activities led by the PCO and PMO are gradually commandeering all forms of government communications.

In 2011, Public Works issued a request for proposals to adopt a mechanism to bring government communications together. Research found that the government's corporate identity symbols and advertising are not penetrating a cluttered marketplace. The bid document explains that

> there is growing evidence that this [existing communications] approach may no longer best serve the public in today's highly competitive advertising environment – in both the traditional media and the new and emerging communications environments. In the context of new technologies, where audiences are bombarded with a high volume of information, and based on findings from advertising pre- and post-campaigns research, it has become evident that there is a need to refresh how the Government of Canada applies its corporate identity to paid advertising.[3]

That year the Privy Council Office began developing a WOG framework. Every activity of government must be assigned to one of four program spending categories of economic, government, international, or social affairs.[4] This is used in the measurement of program outcomes. The WOG framework relates to branding as a unifying philosophy creeping into communications. Branding and WOG are found in the government of Canada's communications policy, which states that the government's corporate identity and visibility must reflect "key government themes and messages in information and communication materials so that overarching goals and the government's priorities for the country are consistently identified and communicated."[5] Some of the WOG communications projects in the Harper administration included the Economic Action Plan, the Vancouver Winter Olympics, operation distinction, and Canada 150. Such pan-governmental initiatives require considerable vertical and horizontal coordination. This common purpose is led by cabinet and its agents.

Morning Strategy Meetings

Branding, New Political Governance, whole of government, communications centralization, permanent campaigning – these and other related media management concepts are put in motion in the early morning hours of every workday. Communications harmony is espoused from the moment that government elites awake. After checking media headlines on their smartphones, they participate in conference calls and strategy meetings to discuss topical issues and news coverage. The planned message of the day (MoD) is connected to the message theme of the week. For instance, a narrow policy announcement about changing parole review would not interest the media or public, so it is boiled down to a message of "safer communities," which in turn feeds a broader government brand narrative of "tough on crime." All planned announcements and events are grouped so that they support the day's message theme. So, if the MoD is "getting things done for Quebec," it would be supported by publicizing that the party's French caucus is holding meetings that day and making a government spending announcement in Quebec.

Here is how the morning looks for personnel with communications-related responsibilities in the PMO, PCO, and MINOs, according to information obtained from, and checked by, a variety of interview respondents in the final year of the Harper PMO. All times are approximate. Processes change, and timelines fluctuate. As one respondent said, "sometimes 6 a.m., sometimes 6:30 a.m., sometimes 7 a.m. It is early. It is always before eight o'clock. I mean, you don't roll into the minister's office at nine o'clock, that's yesterday's news at that point in time" (CM 22). Respondents mentioned using their smartphones as they get ready for work – sometimes trying to figure out when to get into the shower because conversations are so intense – and then commute to the office. Some of the Conservative PMO's senior communications strategists required that the morning issues management discussion be attended in person at the Langevin Building, whereas other senior PMO personnel were satisfied with a conference call. The following description is illustrative rather than definitive, pulling back the curtain on the early hour coordination activities among communications managers at "the centre."

> *PMO preliminary media scanning (4:30 a.m.).* Before coming into the office, members of the PMO issues management group begin trolling through media headlines and social media chatter to identify issues and controversies since the end of the previous day. Information and impressions are circulated electronically.

PMO media review (5 a.m.). One of the two PMO press secretaries reviews news clips available online. The designated press secretary compiles information in preparation for a briefing of department heads in the PMO and the prime minister. The press secretaries alternate days of responsibility for the media review.

Department media review (5:45 a.m.). Senior communications personnel (political and non-political) throughout government scan media headlines to prepare for conference calls and their day.

Department conference call (6 a.m.). Department communications personnel participate in a conference call to discuss media clips. Department officials are on standby to answer questions in the event that further information is required. In some cases, the departmental liaison for the MINO (a non-political position) participates in order to advance information collected from the civil service. If there is overt political discussion, then the liaison is asked to leave the call or to just ignore the banter. Other civil servants from the department participate if the situation warrants.

PMO scripting meeting (6:30 a.m.). A representative of each MINO (normally the director or manager of issues management) participates in a discussion led by the PMO issues management group to go over news coverage, discuss the day's and week's agenda, and establish desired messaging. The purpose is for the PMO to be assured that each MINO is aware of an issue and can be trusted to handle it and to direct communications staff to do what is needed to turn negative media coverage into positive coverage. Several conference calls occur simultaneously and are clustered according to the handful of departments assigned to each issues manager in the PMO's management branch. The PMO issues manager reviews "hot" issues appearing in the morning news and how they should be handled. Media response lines are requested by a specific time, as is Question Period material if applicable. Sometimes the scripting meetings occur by conference call, with a periodic need to attend in person in the Langevin

Building; other times in-person attendance at all meetings is mandatory. No civil servants participate.

Meetings in MINOs (7 a.m.). Senior members of each department convene to brief the minister about which portfolio-related issues are in the news and discuss what the day's focus should be. In addition to promoting a message, this meeting establishes which media issues need to be quashed. Afterward, department media relations staff are expected to be ready to respond to journalists' enquiries, to initiate efforts to correct misinformation, and, in the case of political personnel, to spin viewpoints. On days that the House of Commons is sitting, the meetings are more intense. Conversely, on statutory holidays, interactions between political staff and journalists begin an hour or so later than normal.

PCO meeting with the clerk (7:30 a.m.). The clerk of the Privy Council, deputy secretaries in the PCO, and the assistant secretary of communications convene to discuss the day's agenda and communications issues. Direction is given on what work needs to be undertaken.

PMO department heads meeting (7:30 a.m.). All heads of branches and units within the PMO (e.g., issues management, strategic communications, media relations, policy stakeholder relations) convene in the Langevin Building. The meeting brings them together to discuss perspectives on the previous day's events and news, among a number of other agenda items. The main purpose of this segment of the meeting is to prepare answers to questions that the prime minister might ask that morning and to develop proposals for government actions and communications related to topical issues. Media review and issues management comprise one of the couple of dozen items on the meeting agenda, which entails reviewing pertinent news from the previous evening and that morning. A rapid-fire roundtable is conducted to gather top-of-mind impressions of communications coverage and issues concerning the departments that fall within a PMO staffer's responsibility. This includes challenging each other with pointed questions that the prime minister or any other relevant stakeholder might ask. A former PMO staffer explained that the meeting "is attended by department heads and some deputies such as deputy communications, press secretaries, PM's executive assistant, et cetera. It runs on a set agenda usually for an hour before the PM joins for his brief. Agenda items include communications brief, issues brief, PM note returns, follow-ups. A list is kept by the chief of staff's office" (CS 4). Another former senior PMO official advised that, though it should not be inferred that "media review and issues management dominate the agenda of the morning department heads meetings and PM briefing," it is reasonable that "an issues management mentality might loom larger than it should across the government's communications effort and a certain subset of its actions" (CS 30).

PCO communications meeting (8 a.m.). A meeting of the communications and consultations secretariat in the Privy Council Office is held to discuss the issues identified in the earlier meeting with the clerk and which matters need to be addressed. Flowing from this meeting, duties are delegated to PCO communications analysts who are assigned to different files in government and work with respective departments.

PM joins PMO heads meeting (8:30 a.m.). The prime minister enters the PMO department heads meeting (i.e., the heads of units within the PMO) to receive a communications briefing and go over the day's agenda. This includes such things as a caucus meeting, policy and cabinet agenda item discussions, preparations for Question Period, any travel plans, and so on. Sometimes the PMO department heads meeting resumes after the prime minister leaves.

Follow-up meetings (9 a.m. on). In the Langevin Building, senior PMO and PCO communications personnel meet to review failures and successes of the previous day, to identify communications issue that day, and to establish urgent needs for information from line departments. In departments, meetings are held to convey direction from the MINO about which issues to focus on and how to handle scenarios. Afterward, attendees relay the direction back to their units for implementation. When the House of Commons sits, there is the additional task of preparing the minister for Question Period. PMO and ministerial staffers liaise to agree on lines for QP binders, subject to change after the QP prep sessions with ministers.

All of this goes on before most civil servants arrive at the office. These morning events occur in addition to regular planning meetings, such as meetings of directors of communications across government, and the many conversations that occur through electronic messaging. This loosely aligns with one former PMO director of communications' description of a typical workday as being filled with constantly checking a smartphone for a deluge of emails, looking at private messages, and monitoring traditional and social media.[6] As communications technology advances, there is a greater need for early morning meetings to get ahead of emerging issues and media coverage. In the Chrétien-Martin governments, when exempt staff arrived at a minister's office at 8:30 a.m., it was then that they began discussing what news they had spotted, after which they perused the newspapers. Such a process is no longer viable.

Again it must be understood that the nature of these meetings is subject to change, including under the same prime minister. At the start of Harper's tenure, the PMO held a fifteen-minute media review meeting for all PMO communications staff in the Langevin Building. Attendees watched a recorded summary of the previous evening's English and French newscasts prepared by the PCO. To save time, the video compilation was viewed in fast playback, which one respondent described as "super-high chipmunk speed" (CS 29). This was discontinued when news videos became available online. Instead, as mentioned, a press secretary prepared a summary to brief others verbally. Other changes included changing the scripting meeting from a discussion about all MoDs to instead discussing the prime minister's events. The planning of MoDs became the responsibility of the deputy communications director in the PMO and a team of communications strategists, who had responsibility for assigned departments.

All prime ministers, even those vowing change when they assume office, will surely introduce a variation of this pan-governmental coordination to ensure that departments are communicating only what is authorized by the centre and are managing the message.

Communications Calendars

Calendars are an essential planning tool. During election campaigns, they are initially structured around Elections Canada's list of activities, such as when nominations close and when advance polls are held. In governance, timelines range from parliamentary calendars that track the status of bills to human resources calendars that list staff holidays. So it is not surprising that public officials create communications calendars to coordinate a symphony of media events.

Information fed into the centre is put into a global communications planning calendar. An annual calendar is maintained in the PMO to map out the government's policy agenda for the upcoming year. It incorporates the throne speech, the forward cabinet agenda, plans for the budget, and so on. The year-long roadmap provides central planners with guidance for steering government policy and communications. The PCO and PMO also maintain weekly calendars that allow the harmonization of MoDs and message themes. As plans for announceables are harvested, they are added to these central coordination devices.

The main function of a communications calendar is to organize the scheduling of communications events and announcements. Central agencies get involved to ensure that departmental preparation aligns with bigger picture messaging. This occurs for both pragmatic and political reasons. Without centralization, media events would be clustered on Fridays when ministers and parliamentarians can travel or are in their ridings. Aside from avoiding a glut of announcements, the PMO is cognizant that it is difficult to stretch good news issued late in the week compared with information released on a Monday, and vice versa it is easier to bury bad news late on a Friday. A member of the minister's office in the Treasury Board put it bluntly: "The aim of the communications is to get us re-elected. So why would we give two good news stories out on one day, when we can give a good news story out today and a good news story out tomorrow?"

(CM 21). Another logistical reason for communications calendars is that ministers and government MPs get upset if they are not informed in advance of a government announcement that affects their particular department and/or constituency. Finally, without political oversight, the bureaucracy would bombard the public with announcements during peak periods in the parliamentary cycle and communicate little during the summer months or holidays. The centre ensures that there is a steady and coordinated stream of media relations.

Within departments and agencies, certain communications campaigns are repeated on a regular basis no matter which party is in power, such as informing Canadians about the deadline to file income tax returns. Many other events are one-offs. The spreadsheet nature of these calendars represents an inventory of planned media events and the distribution of responsibilities (Tables 9.1 and 9.2). Departmental calendars span months. They are regularly updated to identify planned news releases, web postings, the minister's private meetings, receptions, ministerial travel, and so on.

Departmental calendars must be synchronized with the central communications calendars maintained by the PCO and PMO to coordinate the government's message of the day. Departmental communications personnel are required to provide the centre with information on their planned pseudo-events (Figure 9.1). They are also asked to identify independent events organized by outside interests. The compilation of all this information allows central planners to look at the big picture of government communications with brand objectives in mind.

Departmental calendar information is fed into a PCO weekly calendar of events. Another PCO calendar identifies the communications products that the PCO itself is working on, such as statements and announcements. These calendars allow personnel to understand what the prime minister is doing, what departments are up to, and what the PCO is preparing. An international dimension is integrated to reflect changing circumstances outside the domestic arena. The PCO is on standby whenever an international organization or head of government makes a major announcement that requires a response from the federal government. Thus, the calendar is populated with fluid plans subject to rescheduling around static events and emerging circumstances.

TABLE 9.1
Government of Canada communications management template

Ref #	WHEN	WHO	WHAT		WHY	HOW			
					SECTION 1: *Communication details*			SECTION 2: *Communication management*	
	Date	Target Audience	Info Item	Key Messages	Objective of Communication	Mode	Delivery Frequency	Tasks to Do	Office of Primary Interest (OPI) Name or Initials	Status (O)pen, (H)old, (C)losed

Source: Public Works and Government Services Canada (2014d).

TABLE 9.2

Communications implementation plan, tax filing season, Canada Revenue Agency

Communications products/activities	Advisors	November					December			
		1	7	14	21	28	5	12	19	26
Planning										
Draft of overarching messages	J. Doe, F. Dupuis, S. Smith	CR	PR	PR		CR	T/PE	CA	PA	
Guides, inserts, labels	S. Smith									
Strategies/plans										
Overarching national communications strategy	A. Chen, J. Doe, S. Smith		D	PR		CR	PR	CA	PA	
Implementation plan	S. Smith									
Children's art tax credit synopsis	A. Chen									
Media outreach strategy	V. Singh									
Regional communications strategies										
Products										
Tax tip on children's arts tax credit	A. Chen									
News release: Stay connected, Stay informed	S. Smith					D	PR	CR	CA	T/PE
News Canada contracting	V. Singh						D	D	D	D
Contact via email to media outlets	V. Singh								D	PR
Fact sheet: Tax filing season	J. Doe									
Web plan	J. Doe					D	PR	CR	CA	T/PE
Social media plan	L. Lewis					D	PR	CR	CA	T/PE
Series of in-house YouTube videos	S. Smith									
Ministerial event launch & proposal	A. Chen									
Media advisory	Ministerial Events									
Speaking points	Ministerial Events									
Media lines	A. Chen									
News release: Ministerial tour – Wrap-up	A. Chen									

Legend: D: Draft; AR: Annual review; P: Planning; CR: Client review; PR: PAB review; CA: Client approval; PA: PAB approval; C: Completed; T/PE: Translation/parallel editing; R: Release; WM: Working group meeting; CC: Conference call; PM: Post-mortem meeting

Note: Advisors' names have been changed by the author.

Source: Abridged from Canada Revenue Agency (2011).

FIGURE 9.1
Departmental media calendar prepared for the Privy Council Office

Tuesday, January 24: (Vancouver) Chinese Canadian Military Museum exhibit (Community Historical Recognition Program supported) MP Wai Young, Vancouver South on behalf of Minister Kenney.

Wednesday, January 25: (Ottawa) Launch of the MS St Louis Commemorative Project with Jewish Youth Library (CHRP supported) Parliamentary Secretary Dykstra on behalf of Minister Kenney.

Thursday, January 26, 11am: News conference in Calgary to announce results of Provincial Nominee Program evaluation.

Thursday, January 26, 7pm: Minister Kenney attends Besa Photographic Exhibit hosted by the Calgary Jewish Federation – speech and news release.

Friday, January 27: Statement issued on International Day of Commemoration in Memory of the Victims of the Holocaust.

Note: Abridged list of confirmed events. Because of space considerations, unconfirmed events are not included.
Source: Citizenship and Immigration Canada (2012a).

The master communications calendar is controlled by the PMO. For day-to-day management, the Conservative PMO used a "rollout" calendar that summarized details of the current day's events and the next day's activities. It was maintained by the deputy director of communications, responsible for the MoD and any other rollout scheduling matters. The rollout calendar acted as an inventory of upcoming events for the next six weeks. This provided personnel with a quick reference point about the MoD, the other communications activities for that day, as well as what was coming up next in conjunction with the weekly communications theme. Two former managers of the PMO rollout calendar recalled its purpose:

> I managed the rollout calendar, which had the prime minister's activities and messages, ministers, senators, everything. This included if there was a special interest group doing a press conference in town that day that we needed to be aware of that could trample on the government's message of the day. It would also have other parties on there like Liberal and NDP, such as if we'd gotten intelligence that they were planning a big news conference. The idea being that, if the prime minister had a big announcement, other ministers and senators, et cetera, should not be unveiling

their life's work, and on days when the prime minister was going to be down [i.e., not in the media] there should be a minister or senator up there trumpeting some kind of message. (CS 23)

I used to explain it as the job of an air traffic controller. You can't have two major 747s in the same airspace at the same time. I couldn't have Jim Flaherty giving an economic speech while John Baird was doing an environment speech in the same Toronto media market, for example. So you have to decide which one takes precedence there. That comes down to the brand, the messaging, what's the message of the day that we're trying to push. (CS 29)

Bearing in mind that internal forms and processes are subject to change, in the Harper administration's first term there were six categories of information for each day on the rollout calendar, maintained in a Microsoft Excel spreadsheet. The first entry at the top of the grid was "message." Underneath was "key event." They were followed by "minister's duties," "media issues," "house duties and news," and a catch-all "other." Everything was intended to revolve around the message of the day, congruent with the master brand.

A daily summary of the rollout calendar was prepared to offer a snapshot of all the day's anticipated communications events, both within and beyond the government's control. Initially, the rollout calendar file began with a "government communication daily backgrounder," a detailed grid of all known internal and external communications. The daily backgrounder was organized under the categories of MoD (subcategories: announcements/events), tactical issues (subcategories: opposition, premiers, third parties), and routine business (subcategories: announcements/events). Of those, the MoD was the most prominent. The tactical issues section identified what is known about the publicity plans of external organizations, such as the opposition parties' scheduled media events. The routine business category listed the many public announcements and pseudo-events planned by ministers and their departments. It enumerated the plans of other entities, such as officers of Parliament. Through advance planning, the PMO aims to reduce the clutter of competing messages that stem from routine business. By spreading them out on a rollout calendar, the topics can be grouped into message themes and support the MoD. This way items in the announcements/events category outshine the routine business.

Messaging and thematic grouping of events in the rollout calendar (or equivalent) are planned two or three weeks ahead of time, sometimes more. Every Thursday or Friday, a planning meeting of about twenty Conservative PMO staff would be held, including department heads, dubbed the "rollout meeting." The objective of this coordination function was to review and adjust the list of upcoming communications events. Rollout meetings also allowed the PMO to identify publicity items that could be co-opted by the prime minister. An immediate goal of each rollout meeting was to ready a calendar of upcoming communications activities. The list was distributed to senior-level personnel within the PMO by week's end. Assignments were divvied up among issue management personnel for follow-up with MINOs. At the rollout meeting, the identification of message themes was first influenced by uncontrolled events that would attract media interest. Commemorative public events were considered, ranging from civic and religious holidays to international observance of an issue, for instance the UN designation of March 8 as International Women's Day. PMO planners inserted information on the known activities scheduled by other organizations. This ran the gamut: the monthly release of consumer price index data by Statistics Canada, announcements by officers of Parliament, the travel plans of opposition leaders, pending provincial and municipal elections, international conferences, parliamentary breaks, and so on. The planners differentiated between time-sensitive government announcements and those with more date flexibility that could be moved around. As much as possible, announcements were plotted in a thematic manner in the rollout calendar, with the objective of message control. A former PMO staffer reflected that the purpose was to

> control all of the things that we know are going on, so that we understand the environment in which we are operating, and then let's look at what are the announcements that we have in the can ... Instead of just sort of throwing it out there, let's be intentional about how we're going to handle it ... so that it all kind of fits together. (CS 14)

The scheduling of events is pieced together as a steady number of messages that reinforce each other. Ottawa-based communications are supported by satellite events in regional locations and PR personnel are expected to ensure that all government spokespersons and communications products repeat the MoD. That way ministers across the country make announcements that deliver the same message, as opposed to conflicting messages that drown each other out. For instance, if major legislation was pending, the Conservative PMO selected a day not expected to feature any significant external activities to which the media will be drawn. If the bill was tabled in Ottawa at ten o'clock in the morning, then at eleven o'clock Eastern Standard Time ministers in different areas of the country participated in related pseudo-events, ranging from similar-themed announcements to scheduled meetings with supportive stakeholder groups. When a ministerial announcement was designated as the MoD, then personnel in the new media division of the PCO requested that high-resolution photographs of the event be provided for immediate posting on the government of Canada website (canada.gc.ca). The rollout meeting and equivalents are a rational planning exercise that takes on importance with branding strategy. A former PMO staffer argued that this is

> not nefarious, and it's not an indication of a heavy-handed central approach ... It's about how can we allow ministers to do the things that they want to do, and it's their job [to speak for government], but it's not helping anybody if there isn't central thinking about it. Otherwise, you end up having good messages that cancel each other out ... It's helping ministers do their jobs better because they don't have that central perspective. (CS 14)

To what extent the Trudeau PMO or ministers agree with this reasoning is unclear. However, with brand control pervading candidate recruitment, the mantra that the party leadership and central messages rule supreme will carry over to Parliament and governance no matter who is in command.

Of course, plans go awry. Pseudo-events are cancelled at the last minute when a greater priority arises or something has gone wrong and causes a postponement. This happens for many reasons. An initiative fails to get anticipated cabinet approval; house leaders or other circumstances such as an emergency debate cause a rescheduling of legislative business; a major news event commands public attention; and so on. As with other communications planning, the intensity of effort spent in preparing roll-out calendars and thematic messages is prone to ebbs and flows as personnel change or an election draws near. Another reason is that speeding up communications makes it impossible for central agencies to keep pace with the barrage of questions from PR personnel in line departments who want to double-check everything for fear of making a mistake. Cabinet and the PMO must have faith that departments will implement strategic directions and handle minor communications matters in a manner consistent with the master brand.

Pseudo-Event Plans (Message Event Proposals)

Government branding is predicated on the centre's trust in institutions to implement strategy and follow guidelines. So it follows that the centre seeks to control the look and feel of pseudo-events.

Memorandums to cabinet include a strategic communications plan as an annex, which summarizes the objectives and anticipated outcomes of a proposed announcement. Event plans consider public opinion research, stakeholder positions, and anticipated reactions. They are prepared by the MINO and department/agency personnel. The former applies a political lens to the background and analytical content authored by the latter, including how the announcement aligns with the government's broader agenda. Tie-in to the master brand occurs through the need to present "a broad overview of the storyline and core messages for the announcement, including the links to government priorities and the proposals' benefits for Canadians."[7] Another required annex to a cabinet paper is the parliamentary plan, similarly up to two pages in length. Among its communications considerations are how the government caucus will be engaged; during the Harper era this involved CACs (see Chapter 6). The parliamentary plan must identify anticipated reactions by opposition parties, explain how parliamentarians' questions will be addressed, and establish past positions taken by the governing party. This extends to the party's positions in election platforms and its time in opposition. Event plans must fit within the corporate communications plan maintained by the institution and align with the communications direction received from central agencies. Planning begins when the MINO, PCO, and possibly PMO establish that an announcement is needed and/or while a memorandum to cabinet is being prepared. The value of planning and coordination is captured in the following email remark from a departmental PR staffer as she exited a PMO strategy discussion: "Really, the meeting was all over the place, and we need to clarify exactly what is required of us and who the players are."[8]

Departments have their own styles of pseudo-event planning documents that bring together the expertise of media planners and policy analysts. The Canada Revenue Agency uses a communications synopsis template. The synopsis is organized around the headings of issue; background; strategic considerations; communications objectives; target audiences; key messages; communications approach; communications products and activities; roles and involvement (minister, commissioner, and spokespersons); budget; and evaluation. Conversely, the Department of National Defence develops a public affairs event plan (Appendix 4). Such department-specific mechanisms capture information that will be integrated into a central communications template. In the Conservative PMO, this was known as a Message Event Proposal, introduced as digital communications technologies were proliferating.

Message Event Proposals (MEPs) were prepared for "the centre" in anticipation of the media rollout of a pseudo-event. The forms required departmental event planners to consider a litany of communications details. It included the desired news headline, key messages, media lines, strategic objectives, desired sound bite, ideal speaking backdrop, ideal event photograph, tone, attire, rollout materials, and strategic considerations. MEPs are evidence of the professionalization of communications expected of the PMO, of permanent campaigning, and of NPM/NPG. They were a central control mechanism to ensure that departmental preparations were in place to achieve communications objectives. Above all, MEPs reflect the trend toward minimalism, synchronization, and visuals. They are thus an important brand management tool.

The origins of this planning instrument date to Harper's OLO in 2003. Leader's office personnel were influenced by a similar practice in Ontario PC Premier Mike Harris's office.[9] Message Event Proposals developed with the strategic thinking that occurred during the Conservative Party's election campaign planning. They were prepared during the 2006 campaign so that detailed event plans were available for each of the next number of days on the leader's tour. When Harper and key strategists moved into the Prime Minister's Office, they introduced the forms to the public service.

The initial intent of using MEPs within the government of Canada was to limit the possibility of communications mistakes at events involving the prime minister. The attention to detail dovetailed with a new way of thinking in the PMO. As Prime Minister Harper's deputy chief of staff, Patrick Muttart applied the retail marketing and branding strategy that was successful on the Australian and Canadian campaign trails. Within the PMO, he displayed photographs of demographic groups that the party was targeting so that strategists would focus on framing messages to those electors.[10] As indicated in Chapter 5, Muttart's insistence on visual communications is renowned in Conservative circles. One former member of the strategic planning shop in the PMO recalled that "we'd have weekly scripting meetings with Patrick, and we'd discuss the MEPs that we were working on, and he'd be saying 'What's the picture? What's the picture?' and would really push us on it" (C 22). As Conservative personnel became familiar with their newfound surroundings, they realized that ministerial communications required centralized coordination. In the absence of central planning instruments for pseudo-events, conversations between PMO and MINO personnel were not translating into desired media outcomes. The MEP was introduced to departments.

There was little fanfare when Message Event Proposals were first reported. In May 2008, buried on page 12 of a Monday edition of the *Toronto Star*, a story disclosed that the PCO was required to vet media requests submitted to the government of Canada. "No federal cabinet minister speaks to a journalist, gives a speech or makes a policy announcement until a 'message event proposal' has been vetted by a wing of the Prime Minister's Office," the story began.[11] Previously, non-exempt communications staff would prepare a media response vetted by an immediate superior, normally at the director level, unless a sensitive topic warranted escalation. The existence of the central planning instrument confirmed that the PCO and PMO were playing a greater role in screening not only the information released by departments to the media but also the manner in which it was communicated.

Two years later the *Hill Times* obtained a copy of a MEP, and by that time MEPs were ubiquitous in government communications offices. The story prompted the first-ever tweet about MEPs when the *Toronto Star*'s Susan Delacourt reacted with "'Message Event Proposal'?? This is a joke, right?"[12] Soon afterward, the Canadian Press conducted a review of MEPs obtained through access to information requests.[13] The templates were framed as tools to script media interactions on an unprecedented level. The story alleged that the instrument was politicizing the government in an anti-democratic manner, zapping morale in the public service, and adding more red tape. The MEP was responsible for stopping not-for-attribution background conversations with government insiders; for weakening relations with the news media; for reducing the public availability of information and spokespersons; and for journalists missing their deadlines. Civil servants and journalists alike were reportedly addled, with some communications staff allegedly quitting out of frustration. A Foreign Affairs source complained that public diplomacy tactics of creating a favourable international image of Canada were compromised. A former senior official in the Privy Council Office relayed that the objective was "hyper-extreme control" over government communications. "The existence of this draconian, Orwellian, unprecedented prerequisite to clear any and all public statements that might be picked up by the media reflects, in my view, a level of micromanagement in the public service, a lack of confidence, trust and respect, and a commitment of total control of the message the likes of which has never been seen before," said another civil servant.[14] In the story, a former director of communications in the PMO countered that message consistency across government is important, and that uniformity requires planning. The PCO's position was that the MEP is a tool that assists the PCO and PMO in their role of discussing policy and communications.

A completed MEP is presented in Appendix 5, using Muttart's template as it existed in 2011. Significantly, that version positioned a heading, "visual message(s)," *before* written messages were to be considered. The overarching consideration was to focus planners' attention on the desired visuals to be captured by photographers and videographers. Integration of the

MEP into government communications processes caused political staffers and public servants to think about the assortment of media considerations with a meticulous level of planning detail. The document was provided to the PCO at least three days before the proposed event. The PCO briefed the PMO, which provided direction relayed back to the institution. The completed template also allowed the PMO to integrate insights gathered from public opinion research paid for by the government and the party.

Introduction of the Message Event Proposal fulfilled its objective of infusing a change to organizational culture in the government of Canada. The permanent government became more cognizant of the importance that the political government attaches to communications planning and visuals. The details required in the MEP evolved as key personnel, notably Muttart, departed from the PMO. For those who remained, the potential for a MEP to be obtained via an access to information request caused a rethink. The revised structure of a Message Event Proposal, as it existed in 2014, is presented in Figure 9.2. Compared with the 2011 version, it seems that communications planning was curtailed. In fact, the original form was broken up into a number of instruments, meaning that pseudo-event preparations were spread across multiple planning documents. Information such as location details, invitees, visuals, sound bites, desired headline, and key messages were instead dealt with in a separate media plan. A social media plan was required as well as a cultural media plan. New content in the template included the event location's postal code for media products to facilitate locating the event using a smartphone. The revised version reveals that more emphasis was placed on the approvals process, ensuring that MINO personnel approved the MEP and obtained the PMO's blessing. In the final months of the Harper government, there was a "ten-day rule" to ensure that the centre had sufficient time for calendar planning. Government personnel were told by the centre that their institution would not be authorized to proceed if a MEP was not received a minimum of ten days before the proposed event, unless there were extraordinary circumstances.

Interview respondents offered further hypotheses for the shift to a simpler template. Staff turnover means that in a majority government fewer politicos in the PMO have experienced the intensity of a national election campaign. The threat of a snap election is ever-present in a

FIGURE 9.2
Message Event Proposal template (revised version)

Message Event Proposal

Date:	Media Market: (Please be specific)
Location: Name of Venue XX Street City, Province Postal Code	English Media Spokesperson:
	French Media Spokesperson:
	Multicultural Media Spokesperson:
	Media Plan & Social Media Plan Developed? (Yes or No)
	Cultural Media Plan Developed? (Yes or No)
	Priority Theme Week Message? (Yes or No)
	MRO contacted? (Yes or No)

EVENT

Description of event, including funding amount. Please provide as much detail as necessary to understand the event and/or announcement.

STRATEGIC OBJECTIVES
• List no more than three to four.

GOVERNMENT/PARTNER FUNDING (IF APPLICABLE):
• Federal/Provincial/Municipal/Other

OTHER PARTICIPANTS (IF APPLICABLE)
• Identify other speakers.

STAKEHOLDER ENGAGEMENT
• List all national, regional and local stakeholders that will be contacted for this announcement.

ACTUAL SPEAKING BACKDROP
• Describe actual backdrop and podium sign. Please provide picture, if possible.

WRITTEN MESSAGE(S)

NEWS RELEASE HEADLINE: (Insert what the Headline/Title will be)

MINISTERIAL QUOTES (Insert Ministerial/federal rep quotes)
• Insert quotes for each Minister or federal rep that will participate in the announcement.

ROLLOUT

COMMUNICATIONS PRODUCTS (check all that apply):

☐ Media Advisory   ☐ Speech   ☐ News Release   ☐ Backgrounder(s)
☐ Q&A   ☐ Talking Points   ☐ M.P. / Caucus Kit   ☐ Biographies
☐ Post-Event Media   ☐ Web Content   ☐ Photo Release   ☐ Props (describe)
    (Twitter, Facebook)

APPROVALS

MEP APPROVED BY (In the Ministers Office):
☐ Communications: (insert name)
☐ Policy: (insert name) - - - - - - - - - - → ☐ followed up with PMO policy (check yes or no)
☐ Issues: (insert name)
☐ Stakeholders: (insert name) - - - - - - → ☐ followed up with PMO Stakeholders (check yes or no)

Date:

Source: Provided to the author by a minister's office employee (2014).

minority government, minimizing the room for error, whereas anxieties are lessened in a majority government. Speeding up communications reduces the planning window, forcing emphasis on the most critical components. The advent of social media adds a further planning dimension. Finally, as a political template becomes institutionalized into government, it is depoliticized and bureaucratized. The MEP evolved from pitching a media event to describing one that already was tentatively approved, sometimes pulled together with twenty-four or forty-eight hours of notice of postponement of the event. As a former PMO staffer explained, "the original MEP was intended to be a 'political' document written by and for political staff/actors. The process quickly became bureaucratized when political staff outsourced the writing/thinking to civil servants" (CS 4). Another elucidated that

> over time the MEP, for want of a better term, morphed. [MINO] directors of communications, who have significantly less political staff at their fingertips than PMO communications, found that they were downloading the job of writing the MEP to the public service. So the public service took a look at their request to create a document that had strategic messages in it, that had a location proposal in it, and acted on it obviously as they should, from a non-partisan perspective. So the potency of the MEP as a document that proposes events to ministers, to leaders, was really watered down at that point. Today it's not a document that, at least at the minister's office level, they pay much time and attention to. Which I think is too bad because ideally that was the brand on paper ... Frankly, they bear no resemblance to one another, the MEP of 2006 versus the MEP of 2014. (CS 29)

Regardless of what template is used, or what party is in power, the level of detail in pseudo-event planning is exacting when international dignitaries and international media will be present. Preparations for media events not held on Canadian soil take on an added dimension and a loss of control. Photo ops involving the prime minister in other countries are scouted by PMO advance personnel. Preparations engage embassy and MINO staff. As part of an official visit, the embassy identifies cultural and educational activities and suggests photo opportunities that they think will align with the government's brand and/or prime minister's brand.[15] Whether an event held in Canada or elsewhere, communications planning crystallizes in the days leading up to a media opportunity. Pre-event briefings are offered in person or by teleconference to affected communities and individuals who might be contacted by journalists. Third-party stakeholders who might speak in favour of the announcement are identified based on their past media commentary, their positions within non-governmental organizations, their academic publications, their testimony as a legislative committee witness, and so on. The heads of external organizations are encouraged to prepare their own post-event media relations to register their support for the government's announcement.

The timing of pseudo-event activities is scripted in a sequence of events plan, also referred to as an event scenario plan. The sequence of events plan simplifies planning details into a minute-by-minute timeline (Figure 9.3). Included are setting up flags at the site, arranging for refreshments, determining the entrance location for guests, explaining ground rules to the media, the minister's speech, the placement of participants in a photo-op, and a post-event media scrum. The plan ensures that communications personnel work in unison and that the speakers are aware of the anticipated proceedings. The scenario outlines whether the event will be preceded by private interactions with the minister in a secluded area, dubbed a green room, and whether post-event one-on-one media interviews are planned. A separate list is prepared with the names and cellphone numbers of people who will accompany the event speakers, on-site government communications personnel, security, and photographer/videographer. As the event date approaches, internal deadlines are set and adjusted for draft communications products. Discussions about logistical details continue into the evening and resume early in the morning. Potential complications must be anticipated, such as learning about another media event scheduled for the same day or rescheduling airport pickup of ministers.

The sequence of events plan is detailed for media events that involve considerable logistical considerations. The audacious unveiling of Canada's polymer bank notes stands out in this regard. At a predetermined moment in his talking points, planned to the exact second, Finance Minister Jim

FIGURE 9.3
Departmental sequence of events plan

	Wednesday, April 18, 2012 Private Meeting: 8:30am – 9:00am News Conference: 9:00am – 9:30am Government Building (Canada Revenue Agency) 1 Front Street W., Toronto Knowledge and Resource Centre Room, Main Floor	
Event contact	• Jane Doe (cellphone: 416-555-5555)	
Special guests	• Kevin O'Leary will provide opening remarks and introduce Minister Kenney.	
8:25 am	• Minister Kenney and Mr. O'Leary arrive at 1 Front Street and are met by John Q. Public, CIC Communications. • Minister and Mr. O'Leary are escorted to side room for a private meeting.	
8:55 am	• Minister and Mr. O'Leary are escorted to press conference room.	
9:00 am	• John Smith, CIC Communications, thanks everyone for coming and introduces Kevin O'Leary, O'Leary Ventures.	
9:02 am	• Mr. O'Leary says a few words and introduces Minister Kenney.	
9:06 am	• Minister Kenney gives short speech announcing the start-up visa.	
9:15 am	• Minister invites Kevin O'Leary and Alex Kenjeev, President of O'Leary Ventures, to podium for photo op. • Q's and A's with media.	
9:30 am	• Minister Kenney (or John Smith as required) concludes Q and A session, and thanks everyone for coming.	
9:35 am	• Minister is escorted back to green room for one-on-one interviews as required.	
10:00 am	• Minister exits 1 Front Street.	

Note: Names of employees have been changed by author.
Source: Citizenship and Immigration Canada (2012b).

Flaherty paused to accept a live satellite call from Commander Chris Hadfield from the International Space Station. To prepare for best case and worst case scenarios of the pseudo-event, the Bank of Canada co-ordinated a twenty-nine-page briefing book.[16]

Pseudo-Event Visuals

In branding, all impressions should reinforce each other. The nondescript visual of a minister sitting at a table in the National Press Theatre, reading from speaking notes with a few limp flags in the background, no longer holds value. PR personnel scout out their own locations and bring portable and customized banners, podium signs, and panels if a natural or permanent backdrop cannot be used. The logistics involved with portable backdrops and flags are crucial to achieve the desired visuals specified in communications planning documents. Exhibit display signage includes colourful and transportable roll-up banner stands that are easy to set up. Plans concerning participants' clothing are shared, and VIP seating arrangements are negotiated. Simplicity on event signage is pursued; for instance, "cracking down" becomes "crackdown." Large text is used at the top of a backdrop sign for angles that show a headshot of the speaker (see Figures 9.4 and 9.5), while smaller "step-and-repeat" text appears on backdrop signs for camera close-ups. Simplification has even crept into legislative business, such as when Conservative ministers attempted to use signs as props at televised House of Commons and Senate committees.[17]

So much importance is attached to controlling visuals that some departmental communications directors refused to approve a MEP unless it was accompanied by a photograph of the planned backdrop.[18] The obvious reason is that they want to communicate their message no matter what voiceover or editorial copy is applied in news coverage. As well, controlling the background visual is intended to prevent performance disruption. An example is the "devil's horns" photo that ran in the *Globe and Mail* during the 1984 election campaign. That front-page photo depicted Prime Minister John Turner with the silhouette of two forks protruding from his head, courtesy of a crafty photograph that captured an unfortunate background sign at a luncheon event.[19] Even minor background gaffes must be avoided lest they are mocked in social media. Years after the fact, a PCH employee was aghast that the queen wore a red dress on Canada Day, causing her to appear on television as though she blended into a red stage backdrop (CM 15).

In concert with the Message Event Proposal, strategists in the Harper PMO spent a lot of time briefing communications personnel and micromanaging pseudo-events. In their first year in office, they wrote up detailed instructions for event backdrop materials. A two-page guidelines document shifted the public service's focus away from reusable tradeshow signage with large text and big pictures and toward thinking about MoD reinforcement. Signage more suitable for television coverage was adopted. A respondent from that era reflected that

> you couldn't see anything behind the speaker's head on TV. So we commissioned backdrop guidelines, which were incredibly exacting – like a grid of an 8 by 10 backdrop and exactly where the message needs to occur, what kind of fonts to use, how to set it up once it's created, all these types of things. The guidelines were needed so that the government side as well would start institutionalizing these changes and make it easier for these types of products to come up the supply chain. Without that, there was no chance that the ministers' offices would be able to execute these at all. (CS 23)

The public servants tasked with coordinating a pseudo-event feel the pressure of the lack of room for error. A diagram is prepared of the event scenario to locate the placement of the speakers' podium in front of the desired backdrop, where people will be seated, where flags will be positioned behind the minister, and where refreshments will be available. Ministerial personnel in Ottawa want to plan for media visuals and camera angles that public servants at the regional event site cannot accommodate. Coordination of visuals persists while a pseudo-event is in progress. A photographer emails photos in real time from the event location to personnel in Ottawa headquarters. Ottawa staff reply with suggestions for which other visuals or angles to pursue and proceed to transmit a selection of the initial photos to web specialists for posting online. Images taken by the photographer are quickly uploaded to an Intranet site. The photos, along with taglines, are used for the department's homepage and the minister's webpage.

Careful planning goes into thinking about visuals and props at pseudo-events for the prime minister. For major events, the entire site is drawn out like an architect's floor plan to show event planners where everything will be positioned. On stage, the distance between the podium(s) from the front-row chair and the distance from the backdrop are measured. The locations of flat-screen TVs, feed box tables, the audio tech table, question microphones, the mediator, media risers, broadcasters, the media entrance,

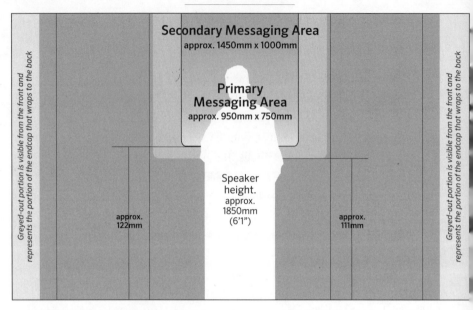

Greyed-out portion is visible from the front and
represents the portion of the endcap that wraps to the back

Secondary Messaging Area
approx. 1450mm x 1000mm

Primary Messaging Area
approx. 950mm x 750mm

Speaker height.
approx.
1850mm
(6'1")

approx.
122mm

approx.
111mm

Greyed-out portion is visible from the front and
represents the portion of the endcap that wraps to the back

FIGURE 9.4   Desired visual frame at government media events | Redrawn from Department of National Defence (2012b).

cameras, washrooms, a wheelchair-accessible ramp, interpreters' booths, the speakers' entrance, and other considerations are all identified using industry design standards. Even the distance between installed curtains and the room walls is stipulated. At the location, advance personnel role-play on stage to help them visualize camera angles and compile information for an event scenario plan. A former PMO media event planner argued that the painstaking attention to detail demonstrates that pseudo-event preparation is "as much design and metrics as art" (CS 23).

The event location must be assessed to help identify the necessary dimensions of signage and font so that the key message will appear within the desired visual frame. This requires estimating the speaker's height (Figure 9.4). PR personnel are encouraged by the centre to look at events with a 16:9 aspect ratio in mind, the rectangular dimensions of most television screens and computer monitors. If applicable, negotiation about signage ensues with another governmental or non-governmental organization. The right reusable signage must be located in-house, which staff identify by perusing photographs of past ministerial events. Otherwise, new signage must be preordered. Quotes from graphic designers and printers must be obtained, along with financial authorization. Assurances are needed that the vendor will deliver the materials on time and to the correct location. At the event, signage backups are needed in the event of non-delivery or other problems, for instance arranging for personnel travelling to the event to bring signage in case the courier is a no-show. If applicable, thought is given to where a post-event scrum will happen and/ or one-on-one interviews and whether additional signage should be placed in the scrum location. Sudden requests emanating from central agencies must be considered, such as a desire to integrate master brand signage.

A standard requirement for flags at the event location increased under the Conservative government. PR personnel perfected the art of flag visuals and the corresponding infusion of patriotism, related to their efforts to supplant the Liberal Party's embodiment of the state. In 2003, debate waged within the newly formed Conservative Party over the colour of the maple leaf in its logo. Marketing consultants recommended that the new party be associated with state symbols. Harper agreed, and supported a party logo with a red leaf, against the wishes of a number of caucus members who preferred the Reform-Alliance symbolism of green.[20] On the campaign trail, Conservative tour staff carried around thin nylon Canadian flags rather than the heavy waxed canvas ones used in government. Undeterred, they used paperclips and tape to affix the flags to coat hangers to give the flags a perfectly draped look on camera. As prime minister, Harper wore a Canadian flag lapel pin. Flags were installed along the Hall of Honour in the Centre Block of the Parliament Buildings so that cameras depicted the prime minister walking statesmanlike down the ceremonial hall, ac-companied by a visiting dignitary. Whenever ministerial staff complained that they did not have suitable backdrops, they were told by the PMO to bring a flag to the event, an inexpensive way to convey professionalism to viewers who pay fleeting attention. Whether in Ottawa or on the road, PR personnel used an iron to press the flags so that they appear crisp and used hidden flag spreaders. The Privy Council Office caught on and purchased a top-of-the-line set of eight flags with brass bases that roll up for storage in a portable case. Appearing at campaign-style events in front of an enor-mous Canadian flag affixed to a wall, as in Figures 4.2 and 9.5, makes for a powerful visual.

FIGURE 9.5   Typical visual at prime ministerial pseudo-events | Prime Minister's Office (2014a); PMO photographer Jason Ransom, London, ON, May 2, 2014.

Being surrounded by supporters is another pseudo-event practice. A standard visual is of the prime minister standing at a podium adorned with a concise message, with theme-related citizens standing behind him and/or a large Canadian flag (Figure 9.5). In the 2006 campaign, Harper delivered speeches using two raised paddle teleprompters, and supporters were lined up as a visual backdrop that matched the message. By the 2011 campaign, he stood on a riser wearing a wireless microphone and referred to speaking notes on a nestled television screen.[21] Supporters were placed all around him. Harper talked while pacing around the riser so that all possible camera angles would feature an attentive public in the shot. During the campaign, a leaked email from a local Conservative worker caused a minor kerfuffle over the nature of an invitation to multicultural groups to attend one of the prime minister's events. The email stated that

the opportunity is to have up to 20 people in national folklore costumes which represent their ethnic backgrounds. These people will sit in [the] front row behind the PM – great TV photo op. We are seeking representation from the Arab community. Do you have any cultural groups that would like to participate by having someone at the event in an ethnic costume?[22]

Event planners use this way of thinking to integrate different segments of the Canadian electorate in political communications. In the 2015 campaign, another leaked email revealed that the Conservative Party was looking to recruit veterans for television ads.[23] For all major political parties in that contest, the dominant daily visual was evocative of the desired visual frame for government officials: the leader addressing a partisan crowd from behind a podium decorated with a short key message, surrounded by flags and supporters as a backdrop.

As the leaked emails suggest, though planning minimizes risk, the unexpected still occurs. Complications occur when media liaisons interact with non-media personnel, for instance a communications manager who uses technical lingo with a baffled minister's executive assistant. For outdoor events, in case of inclement weather, a backup plan must be prepared, such as renting tents. On windy days at outdoor events, signs cannot be secured to the podium's stand-up microphone. Roll-up display banners are held up with impromptu materials such as sandbags and duct tape. Government emails indicate that public servants have coped with flags flapping behind the minister because of indoor venting and using the wrong podium signs. At one DND event, a ceremonial gun misfired and burned part of a flag, which had to be frantically replaced.[24] Moreover, scripted situations sometimes fall flat when a more human touch is called for.

Media Lines, the Spokesperson's Book, and MP Kits

Cabinet annexes, Message Event Proposals, and the like ensure that spokesperson messages are prepared and vetted before a public announcement and/or interaction with the media. These approved messages are readily accessible to brand ambassadors through the spokesperson's book and an MP kit. A spokesperson's book contains the media lines approved by the MINO. A public servant summarized the reference manual this way: "A spokesperson's book is essentially a reference/playbook. It's an aggregate of all the media lines and potential issues so that, when there are media calls or the ministers go out on the road to events, they have a book so that when an issue comes up they can quickly reference the book. It's basically a script" (CM 18). The basis of approved messages originates from the governing party's election platform and the department's historical position on an issue. Non-partisan civil servants develop key messages seldom micromanaged by the political class, which ensures some message consistency and conformity whenever there is a change of ministers. Anybody authorized to speak on behalf of the department is expected to adhere to this messaging. A spokesperson's book is similar in style to a briefing book, the detailed synthesis of current policy issues and activities prepared for ministers. Both are comprised of tabbed sections for ease of use. As well, electronic versions are maintained on an internal wiki page or some other platform that permits collaboration and requires authorized access. Ministers can view electronic versions of the book's contents on their computers or smartphones. The exact style and format of a spokesperson's book is left to each department. A typical page begins with an issue heading, followed by a brief summary of the issue and then the media lines. The subject-specific content is organized in a Q&A style. If a government spokesperson is confronted with a question not in the book, or faced with a persistent questioner, then the directive is to refer the journalist to the minister's office for follow-up. Given the delays caused by various approval processes, the spokesperson's book facilitates prompt, albeit mechanical, responses to routine questions.

Some spokespersons are masters at providing the media with information without deviating from the script. Others are not skilled in Ottawa-style media relations, and if they are faced with uncontrolled circumstances they stick to their rehearsed media lines. The following exchange between a CBC reporter and Peter Penashue, the Conservative minister of intergovernmental affairs and then-MP for Labrador, is an example of political brand control gone amok. At the time, Penashue was under fire for financial irregularities in his election campaign. This absurdist exchange illustrates the stonewalling that journalists face when politicians seek to control the soundbite, and how a branding mentality can convey anti-democratic values.

CBC REPORTER: What's the status of the loan right now, that you took out in the last election campaign?

MINISTER PENASHUE: Let me just say first of all that during the campaign we worked very hard to get elected, and I think we were very successful at that. And we made some errors, and we are working with Elections Canada to rectify those.

CBC: Do you take responsibility for the errors that were made by your campaign?

MINISTER: Well, as I've said, we've made a submission, and we are working with Elections Canada to rectify those concerns.

CBC: Do you take responsibility for what happened in your campaign?

MINISTER: As I've said, we've made submissions to Elections Canada, and we are working with Elections Canada to rectify those concerns.

CBC: Do you dispute their claims that your campaign overspent during the last election?

MINISTER: What I've said is that we've made a submission to Elections Canada, and we are working with them to find any errors that we have made.

CBC: What role did John Doe [who made an interest-free loan] play in your election campaign?

MINISTER: Again, as I've said, we've made a submission to Elections Canada, and we are dealing with any errors that we may have made, and we're working very hard to make sure that we have those rectified.

CBC: But we're not talking about errors here, we're just talking about Mr. Doe. What was his involvement in your campaign?

MINISTER: As I've said, we've worked very hard in this campaign, we've made a submission to Elections Canada, and we will be working with Elections Canada to rectify any errors that we have made.

CBC: But does that submission have anything to do with Mr. Doe?

MINISTER: As I've said, we are working with Elections Canada to rectify any errors that we may have made.

CBC: When do you expect the loan will be repaid?

MINISTER: As I've said, we are working with Elections Canada to rectify any errors that we have made.[25]

A stronger communicator would spin the message more elegantly. Within a year, Penashue resigned both posts. He was not elected in the resulting Labrador by-election and, somewhat perplexingly, was cleared by the Conservative Party to run again in 2015 but was not elected. Notwithstanding such bumps, party strategists reason that brand discipline is necessary given that media are drawn to controversy and drama. Journalists are unrelenting. Strategists fret that even the tiniest of unapproved remarks will force them into brand damage control.

The spokesperson's book is constantly updated. In some departments, there are regular meetings to review the content, and it is an ongoing duty of PR staff to scan the media for suggested updates. Information is integrated from recent events and departmental initiatives. Communications personnel speak with the relevant policy experts to anticipate which types of questions will be forthcoming. They draft proposed answers for the MINO. When public servants are provided with media lines from the PCO, there is confusion about whether these lines also need to be approved by the MINO. Jousting occurs between regional director generals and exempt staff when political messages are inserted, for instance the moniker "Harper government" (discussed later in this chapter). As well, sometimes the minister's approval indicator is removed from media lines in the book without explanation to lower-level departmental personnel.

Media lines are repeated in speaking notes. Speechwriters are provided with information from a MEP or equivalent so that they can identify key messages and understand the context of the event. This is accompanied by information on the intended duration of the speech and the proportion of official language content. Suppose that an event is being held at a location where English is the dominant language. Government speechwriters would be informed that 10 percent of the speaking time for anglophone ministers should be in French, whereas 100 percent of a francophone minister's speaking time should be in French. Draft speeches for major events are provided to the PCO for review and approval.

As brand ambassadors, members of the government caucus must promote the government's messages. Approved media lines are provided to government MPs who represent ridings that will be affected by a ministerial announcement. The lines are given to senior public servants in the region(s) as well as the regional minister's office. Information packages, known as

MP kits or caucus kits, facilitate sustenance of the desired message and prevent spokespersons from going off track. A scaled-back version of the MEP or equivalent is included with basic recommendations, for instance the desired photo that the MP should use. Some content in provided template communications products is left blank so that the MP's office can personalize them. A news release template features a suggested headline, suggested quotations, and background information. Full speaking notes are available for customization, with fill-in-the-blanks for the names of attendees: "Thank you *insert name* for your kind introduction. I'd also like to thank *insert name* for hosting today's event at *insert venue.*" A fact sheet comprised of a bulleted list of information is offered. A Q&A document lists anticipated media queries and standardized responses. MP kits and spokesperson's books are integral to the implementation of public sector branding. Despite such considerable preparations, there is no standardized evaluation mechanism for media coverage, and the government's media relations activities are not subject to the formidable assessment or accountability process required of its advertising campaigns.

Media Monitoring and Communications Assessment

To control the message, government personnel need to be aware of what news is reported and what the reaction is. Media monitoring is explained by the Privy Council Office as a useful tool for tracking important public policy issues and for assessing the effectiveness of government communications.[26] Government tenders for media monitoring add that this helps departments to identify trends.[27] Media monitoring within government occurs on an ongoing basis. The leading stories on major traditional news outlets get the most attention, supplemented by community newspapers and ethnic media[28] and what is trending in social media.

The prime minister relies on daily media summaries provided by PMO staff.[29] Within departments, staffers prepare and circulate media relations tracking reports that summarize, by region, which reporters placed enquiries, the nature of the question(s), and how the request is being handled. In the past, media monitoring involved "clippers," who started work in the early hours to peruse newspapers for relevant content. The clippings became part of photocopied packages by the start of the business day, and videotapes of television coverage were distributed. With the evolution of digital media, news is freely obtained online and shared via social media. Broadcast news stories obtained from electronic media monitoring services are circulated within government by email and/or uploaded to Intranet sites.[30] This includes media content that contains the names of government organizations and spokespersons, critics, provincial and municipal politicians, and journalists. Issue-specific keywords generate content about specific topical matters and are supplemented by public servants' monitoring of websites (e.g., news media, industry associations, think tanks), blogs, and social media posts. Creative ways of monitoring media are practised, such as setting up Google News alerts and circulating photo collages assembled by news aggregator PressReader. The number of times that a story is shared, liked, or commented on acts as an indicator of topicality. Technological innovations offer a variety of tools, from apps that display the areas of the country/globe where social media posts are originating to analytics that identify the key influencers on a given topic.

In the days following a pseudo-event, electronic files of associated media coverage are uploaded to an Intranet site for internal viewing. A "quotations" synthesis of what individuals said in the media about the event or announcement is prepared daily or even more often. PR personnel based in Ottawa and in the event location(s) prepare informal summaries of media coverage. These post-event reports go by the names public affairs assessment, public environment analysis, or media monitoring and analysis. They convey subjective impressions of the success of the pseudo-event, a list of the media present, and the tone of immediate media coverage. Sometimes a verbatim transcript of the event is commissioned. The post-event report is prepared for the minister's office and circulated among event organizers. For major events, the PCO asks departments to identify factual errors reported by the media and to lobby for corrections. Procedures vary among government institutions. A post-event monitoring technique used by the Department of National Defence is its "detect and correct" notifications, which identify reporting discrepancies (Figure 9.6). The PCO must approve the proposed corrective action.

There is such a volume of digital chatter that government contracts are awarded to provide "real-time monitoring and analysis of social media content including Twitter, Facebook, blogs, chatrooms, message boards, social networks and video and image sharing websites, and real-time

FIGURE 9.6
Detect and correct summary, Department of National Defence

Detect and Correct Summary
Issue: Historical Designation
Date: August 16, 2011 – Noon

Media Outlet(s): *La Presse, Radio-Canada, Agence QMI*

Journalist: N/A

Date/time: August 16, 2011

Issue: Initial reporting has French version of new name for Royal Canadian Air Force incorrect.

Correction: Corps d'aviation royal canadien

Proposed Action: Identified media will be provided with the correct version in French.

Outcome: French version of name will be reported correctly.

Source: Department of National Defence (2011c).

monitoring of Internet news sites."[31] Tracking of issues is simplified by monitoring the short bursts of information posted on Twitter in particular. For Budget 2013, the Department of Finance prepared in-house Twitter summaries comprised of a daily top-line analysis, examples of tweets (mostly from journalists and media outlets), the number of mentions that budget-related hashtags received, how many times a departmental tweet was retweeted, and changes in the number of followers of the department's Twitter account, @FinanceCanada.[32] Political communications occur so quickly on so many platforms that real-time media monitoring is practised by government employees. For instance, to stay informed about the Idle No More protest movement, government personnel followed tweets issued by @IdleNoMore4 and associated tweets grouped under the Twitter hashtag #idlenomore. The Government Operations Centre in Public Safety Canada, whose foremost purpose is to monitor domestic and international emergencies, monitored Idle No More protests, as it now does with any civil unrest mobilization. Federal departments and agencies are asked to provide details of upcoming demonstrations that pertain to their portfolios, based on information compiled from public sources, shared with applicable partners such as the RCMP.[33] This real-time monitoring function was at the forefront during the Parliament Hill shootings as the Government

Operations Centre monitored "open sources" and circulated information updates while security forces were trying to contain a violent situation.

Detecting and correcting are significant components of the workday for many government PR personnel. They tell of constantly skimming tweets, and not even clicking on links to news stories, whereas in the past they reviewed a news story in detail. In the digital media landscape, PR personnel have to contend with a much greater volume of information distortion, half-truths, rumours, and speculation. If an error is detected, they endeavour to contact the reporter or editor by the end of the next day's news cycle to urge a correction. It can take days to convince a reporter or other opinion leader to correct or retract a misleading posting. By that time, the misinformation has been shared over and over with others in the online sphere, heightening the need for rapid response.

This form of news management contrasts with that of the strategic planners in the PMO who pontificate upon whether a pseudo-event achieved its communications objectives. Particular interest is taken in judging the government's desired news photo or video against the actual outcome(s). During Muttart's time in the PMO, staff awarded impressionistic grades of A, B, C, or fail to news visuals. An example of a C grade is a photograph that depicts the prime minister, the premier of Ontario, and the mayor of Toronto surrounded by a row of flags from each jurisdiction. The image conveys intergovernmental cooperation. However, based on the photo alone, the audience has no way of knowing what was discussed. Moreover, the reporter's voiceover or written copy could emphasize something other than the desired message. The PMO would award an A+ if the prime minister were positioned in the centre of the shot in front of a blue backdrop that features clearly visible words on either side of his head and a podium sign that repeats the written message (e.g., "tackling gun crime"). The premier and mayor should be portrayed as supportively standing on either side of the prime minister. That exact photo appeared on the front page of the *Toronto Sun* in 2006, ideal because that media outlet reaches so many of the Conservative Party's target groups. Conversely, the PMO would be frustrated if the visual ignored the pseudo-event or conveyed the wrong message. For instance, a photo of the prime minister entering or exiting a government limousine was labelled "message failure."

A glaring weakness of brand control is an inability to pivot quickly when circumstances demand it. During the 2015 campaign, newscasts led with distressing photos and video of the lifeless body of Aylan Kurdi, a three-year-old Syrian boy, lying face down in the surf on a Turkish beach. Given that the Conservative Party brain trust obsessed over visual communication, it is telling that Harper's team was tone deaf about public concern for the European Union migrant/refugee crisis and was on the wrong side of public opinion when news broke that Kurdi's aunt had been trying to bring her family members to Canada. The process of tight scripting for planned events does not provide sufficient flexibility to respond to the unforeseen. Harper was reflective as election day approached: "I've seen issues come up before that get a lot of press attention. And sometimes a photograph or sometimes a side issue can move votes, but I always believe that the big votes are moved on the big issues. I don't believe that most people are attracted by the rabbit tracks of day-to-day media coverage. [Voters] go and they think, 'What's the best choice for my life and the broad community?' I actually think they make those decisions based on pretty big impressions, and those are not necessarily detailed policy impressions, but they're impressions of leadership."[34] A more nimble operation would have contained the issue by expressing humility and sensitivity to public opinion. More than ever, Canadian political leaders walk a tightrope of maintaining message control against the immense pressures of the wisdom of the crowd.

10

The Fusion of Party and Government Brands

If a political party and prime minister are in power long enough, their brands become synonymous with that of the government. Imprinting a political brand on public administration and the public requires that the government be divested of the outgoing administration's brand. To hurry along brand convergence, the Conservatives attempted to erase Liberal governments from the public consciousness, just as Liberal administrations impress their political values on the Canadian public sphere.

There are at least three general ways that the brands of the governing party, its leader, and the government are fused. We can synthesize them as brand evisceration (the selective elimination of the previous political government's brand), brand reclamation (the selective promotion of affiliated political governments' brands), and statecraft rebranding (the embedding of the brands of the current political government and its leader into that of the state). While some practices are commonplace, such as manipulating the colour scheme of budget materials, there is no methodical order to brand fusion. The governing political party simply uses whatever levers of publicity and marketing that "the centre" is willing to command.

BRAND EVISCERATION

When a political party and prime minister take power, they put their own stamp on government. Accomplishments of the outgoing administration are rescinded or ignored. Information is trumpeted about new policy directions. To set the stage, a new and improved brand label is communicated, and, if the governing party has changed, the government's colour schemes take on a partisan hue.

In the waning days of the 2006 election campaign, Stephen Harper remarked that the power of a Conservative PMO would be encumbered by vestiges of the outgoing Liberal government:

> I'm not sure there's such a thing as a true Conservative majority in the sense of a Liberal majority. The reality is that we will have, for some time to come, a Liberal Senate, a Liberal civil service – at least senior levels have been appointed by the Liberals – and courts that have been appointed by the Liberals ... We'll have checks on us and limits on our ability to operate that a Liberal government would not face.[1]

Upon the formation of a minority Conservative government, the PMO issued a verbal directive that all references to the government of Canada in communications products, including media advisories, news releases, media lines, speeches, and webpages, had to refer to "Canada's New Government." The idea was to erode the Liberal Party's stranglehold as the natural governing party and put a Conservative stamp on government. This label spurred some pushback within the public service. One scientist was fired, and later reinstated, for refusing to comply. At the behest of the PMO and PCO, after twenty-one months, the phrasing was altered to "Harper Government" (Figure 8.5). The rationale for the label was that people commonly refer to the government by the PM's surname. Critics decried it as a partisan move that goes against a covenant of the apolitical public service. Defenders of the phrasing pointed out that it did not contravene the government's official communications policy, which is silent on the matter. A Conservative strategist reasoned that "an essential component of branding is to establish an identity, and often in politics the identity falls around the leader – for good or for bad."[2] The confusion results from different interpretations of the prime minister in multiple communications worlds (Figure 2.8) and the lack of a written directive.

Internal government emails show that, when draft communications products were sent up to the PCO/PMO for review without the "Harper

Government" moniker, revised drafts were returned with it included. Sometimes departmental personnel decided to change it back to "Government of Canada" prior to releasing the materials, or they opted not to mention the absence of the political label in the French version. Political staff from the minister's office would then follow up to see what happened and avoid a repeat. The emails illustrate that some civil servants were incredulous and recalcitrant. One recalled the back-and-forth when the label was inserted by MINO exempt staff into the spokesperson's book and communications products:

> We had to go "No, we're not allowed to do that." It would be right up to the last minute: we would change it, [the minister's staff] would change it, we'd change it back, they'd change it back. Sometimes it got so close to the wire it would go out as "Harper Government," which was a clear violation of what was supposed to be done. (CM 19)

Civil servants who pushed back too hard were "cut out of the loop." They ceased being invited to planning meetings, their questions went unanswered, and their work received less feedback.

Some entities, notably the DND, negotiated an exemption from the practice. In the confusion, a battle of wills ensued. After a strategic communications analyst in the DND prepared a draft speech and news release for proofing, a DND manager wrote to a subordinate that "we don't use 'Harper Government.' Unless a directive comes down officially, my understanding is that we continue as per normal. If she [the communications analyst] wants to change it then she can, but we'll probably change it back without clear and specific direction."[3] The one time that the labelling practice was interrupted was from late 2009 to late 2010 following public controversy over Conservative MPs who used logoed ceremonial cheques (discussed in the next section). Internal emails show that this created a reverse scenario in which public servants using "Harper Government" phrasing were told at the approval level to revert to "Government of Canada" phrasing. When political staff instructed them to resume using the former nomenclature, the pushback re-emerged in some areas of the civil service.

Further communications subtleties sought to eradicate reminders of previous Liberal administrations. Liberal government policies received reduced attention in the revised *Discover Canada* citizenship guide. The Conservatives all but ignored the fiftieth anniversary of the creation of the Canadian flag. The twenty-fifth and thirtieth anniversaries of patriation of the Constitution and passage of the Charter of Rights and Freedoms went unrecognized, even as other events in Canadian history were being celebrated. The Thérèse Casgrain Volunteer Award, created by the Pierre Trudeau administration, which recognized the political activism of its feminist namesake, was renamed the Prime Minister's Volunteer Award. The visuals on Canadian banknotes changed: a transcontinental train appears on the ten dollar bill instead of an image of peacekeeping; the Vimy Memorial appears on the twenty dollar note where Aboriginal art was featured; a Coast Guard research icebreaker pushed aside the Famous Five and Casgrain Award from the fifty dollar bill.

Efforts to put distance between political brands stretch from pettiness to disrespect. A statue of Lester B. Pearson and his Nobel Peace Prize are displayed in the foyer of the Global Affairs building in Ottawa that bears his name. It was a Liberal administration that decided to commemorate one of its leaders in such a public and lasting manner. In 2007, the Conservative government held a trinational news conference in the building's foyer. PR staff installed curtains and rows of flags as a backdrop. A projector screen depicted a blue brick wall in front of the Pearson display, obscuring it from view. According to a Liberal MP, public servants were "apoplectic" that the photo-op preparations hid the statue.[4] Furthermore, Minister of Foreign Affairs John Baird obtained an exemption from the TBS rules to remove mention of the Pearson Building from his business cards. Public servants expressed that this was against TBS rules and responded by preparing a disclaimer form to be signed by Baird's chief of staff.[5] Years later a Pearson statue on Parliament Hill was the only prime ministerial statue encased in plywood during a prolonged phase of construction.[6] It is unlikely that a governing party would treat its own icons in such a manner.

Brand evisceration inevitably involves debranding the former governing party. Blame for current problems is attributed to the bad decisions made by the previous administration. This need not be limited to recent events. For instance, Chris Alexander, then–Conservative minister of immigration, retorted in Question Period to Liberal MP John McCallum that

> I would invite that member to apologize for decades of racism by his party under Mackenzie King blocking South Asians from coming to this country, blocking East Asians from coming to this country, blocking Caribbeans from coming to this country, the injustice of backlogs under the [Pierre] Trudeau regime and the Chrétien era. It is that party that has been the racist party in this parliament over decades.[7]

Such hostility requires the PMO's prior approval and can originate as talking points from the centre. There is irony in such commentary given the politically incorrect image of the Reform Party and the Canadian Alliance Party that Conservatives would sooner forget. Moreover, the Liberals are the ones who, like the NDP, promised to bring in thousands of Syrian refugees without delay, ultimately under Minister McCallum's tutelage. Such daily banter, coupled with the politics of forgetting, illustrates how party brands are constructs of slanted political communications.

BRAND RECLAMATION

The governing party lauds selected elements of past administrations with which its brand is affiliated. The Conservative Party, constituted in 2003, has sought to evoke hand-picked aspects of the Progressive Conservative Party history and to overlook its Reform-Alliance roots. Party communications convey a rich history by connecting with Macdonald (the country's first prime minister) and Diefenbaker (the prairie outsider), while Conservative prime ministers such as Robert Borden, Richard Bennett, Joe Clark, Brian Mulroney, and Kim Campbell go unmentioned. The Harper administration renamed a government property across from Parliament Hill the John A. Macdonald Building. The bicentennial of Macdonald's birth was celebrated. The Diefenbaker Defender of Human Rights and Freedom Award was created. Ottawa's old city hall was renamed the Diefenbaker Building, and an icebreaker was named after him. The webpage of Canadian Heritage was changed to feature information on Sir John A. Macdonald Day (January 11) but not on Sir Wilfrid Laurier Day (November 20). This Conservative sleight of hand occurred even though both days were recognized in the same legislation passed in 2002 during a period of Liberal majority government. The suggestion that Macdonald and Laurier are of comparable historical significance is itself a Liberal artifice. Laurier's time in government was less significant than is popularly imagined, as is mentioned in this book's preface; his iconic status is rooted in the superficiality of a dapper personal image combined with decades of propaganda. For their part, the Conservatives ignore Macdonald's role in the Pacific scandal and the harms of colonialism, nor do they mention Diefenbaker's shaky leadership.

Brand reclamation extends to reviving brand iconography. The Conservative administration changed the graphic design of the maple leaf in government communications to accentuate the leaf's finer details. This harkens to early- to mid-twentieth-century designs found in identifiers ranging from the Royal Canadian Air Force and old Canadian Olympic uniforms. Interestingly, the Liberal Party followed suit by tweaking its own logo in 2009 and 2014, likewise moving away from a simplified leaf to an etched leaf.

A special effort has been made to associate the Conservative Party's and the Conservative government's ties with the monarchy. A policy that photographs of the queen must be displayed in government offices was reinstituted. The Air Command and the Maritime Command reverted to the Royal Canadian Air Force and Royal Canadian Navy, respectively (see associated pseudo-event planning in Appendices 4 and 5). The maple leaf rank on officers' shoulder boards was returned to British and Commonwealth ranks and designations. The Conservatives' throwback to an earlier British era used "The Maple Leaf Forever" in the PMO's *24 Seven* videos rather than the dualist "O Canada." An attentive observer would link the Harper brand to celebrating visits by the Royal Family and an interest in The Beatles to this Britannic theme.

Conservative political marketers determined that a party that technically has no history can benefit from invented traditions. Conservative government communications promoted a more combative version of Canada etched in pre-Confederation history. Website and TV advertising recognized the War of 1812; a monument was installed on Parliament Hill. Blue lapel pins with a red maple leaf and two cutlasses commemorating the War of 1812 were worn by members of the Canadian Forces, bearing similarity to the Conservative Party logo. So did a War of 1812 design in commemorative flags flown by military units. This is connected to the reimagining of the Canadian military from peacekeepers to fighters (see Chapter 4) and was supported by micropolicies, for instance once again referring to the Canadian Forces as the Canadian Armed Forces. It interlocks with brand evisceration, given that 2012 was also the unrecognized thirtieth anniversary of the Charter.

STATECRAFT REBRANDING

A further means of brand fusion is to embed the iconography associated with the governing party and its leader in state officialdom. Civil servants are entrusted with "careful stewardship" to maintain "the trust, credibility, dignity, and longevity" of government symbols and try "to prevent them from being used as branding or marketing devices" (CS 13). However, the decision to create and shape such symbols is a political one. This is what the Liberal Party did with the creation of the original Canada wordmark, which looked like the party's logo. Sublimating the instruments of state is one of many ways that the Liberals created an enduring brand as the party most closely affiliated with the state. Under Liberal administrations, a red-and-white colour palette is used in government of Canada communications; that it happens to be the natural governing party's official colour scheme, not just the country's, is passed off as a happy coincidence. Under the Conservatives, government communications emphasized blue, the colour associated with toryism. For instance, Canada Day festivities in Ottawa shifted from reds to blues,[8] and will be red and white again under the Liberals. Only one is seen as normal and acceptable, but both are partisan.

Repainting the prime minister's aircraft exemplifies the alignment of brands of the government party, the government, and the leader. Leaders arriving or departing is a natural way for journalists to begin and/or conclude their stories. To capitalize on the optics, during election campaigns the major political parties paint buses and airplanes in party colours along with the logo and campaign slogan and perhaps the leader's name. The Conservatives noticed that the aircraft used by the Canadian Armed Forces to transport the prime minister, the governor general, and other dignitaries was bland and missed an opportunity for visual communication.

FIGURE 10.1   Prime Minister Harper and Canadian Forces VIP airplane | Prime Minister's Office (2014b); PMO photographer Jason Ransom, Ottawa, March 21, 2014.

The Airbus CC-150 Polaris sported the Canada wordmark, and its dark grey paint evoked connotations of the Cold War era. For four years, the PMO pushed the Department of National Defence for a new design.[9] Marketers wanted emphasis placed on visuals at the front entrance of the airplane, where cameras document the prime minister and other VIPs embarking or disembarking.

The resulting blue, red, and white airplane evokes Conservative Party colours and symbols. A prominent Royal Canadian Air Force logo – to which the Conservative Party logo is comparable – is positioned at the front of the aircraft (Figure 10.1). Under the cockpit window, in italicized script, is *"True North Strong and Free"* and its French equivalent. The phrase is taken from the Canadian national anthem and has appeared in Conservative Party messaging, such as the title of its 2008 election campaign manifesto ("The True North Strong and Free: Stephen Harper's Plan for Canadians"). It conjures up associations with the Harpers' Arctic visits, with the "Strong. Proud. Free." tagline that appeared at the end of government advertising, and with the strong leadership that the Conservatives emphasized as part of their core brand. One reason the iconography was permitted is that the Federal Identity Program details requirements for motor vehicles but not for aircraft. In any event, though the Department of Defence is subject to the FIP, the Canadian Armed Forces are exempt other than a requirement to integrate the Canada wordmark. As well, the design is similar to the one used on the aircraft's predecessor. In the early 1990s, a CC-137 Boeing similarly displayed an RCAF logo, though it lacked the blue underbelly paint and more visibly displayed the Canada wordmark. The logo disappeared under the Liberals. In the same vein, the Team Canada Olympic logo for the Vancouver Winter Games, developed by the Hudson's Bay Company, mirrored the Conservative Party's logo by featuring a blue letter C with a red maple leaf insert. During Liberal governance, Team Canada clothing evokes the brand image of the Canadian flag and equally that of the Liberal Party of Canada.

A further example of politicized statecraft is the heretofore unknown attempt to brand Open Government in a manner implying a Conservative Party initiative. Access to information requests reveal that, when the Open Government beta site was developed in 2011, it contained a logo provided by the PCO to the TBS. The draft logo is shown at the top of Figure 10.2. The semi-circle to the left, bordering a red maple leaf, was red. The remainder of the text and the semi-circle to the right of the maple leaf were in white, and the complete logo appeared on a blue background. Public servants in the Treasury Board Secretariat were struck by the similarity with the Conservative Party's logo. "Reminds me an awful lot of a certain political party's logo," wrote one TBS employee.[10] Another emailed, "has anyone made the link between the half red "O" and the shape of the "C" in Conservative?" to which a co-worker replied "Everyone who has seen it."[11] Given their positions in the government hierarchy they saw little choice other than to proceed. The logo did not go over well, however, when it reached an assistant secretary of strategic communications in the TBS. She flatly remarked that not only would using *any* logo contravene FIP policy, but also the proposed visual was "almost identical to the Conservative C." For these reasons she declared that the design submitted by the PCO was "not on."[12] A depoliticized logo deemed compliant with the FIP was available within a week (bottom of Figure 10.2). The Open Government logo situation is an egregious example of the many vertical and horizontal conformity issues that confront central agencies and the potential for politicization of the government brand. We are left to imagine how often statecraft battles occur within government.

FIGURE 10.2   Open Government politicized logo and final logo |
Treasury Board of Canada Secretariat (2011f, 2011i).

Short Case Study: The Economic Action Plan

As earlier chapters hinted, the EAP is a definitive case of branding public policy and statecraft rebranding. It is a hallmark of a whole of government and permanent campaigning approach to communications. From mid-2009 to mid-2015, the communications associated with the stimulus spending program were extensive, continuing years after the program's conclusion. Publicity arguably became the main product.

The EAP brand originated as a policy response to the global recession in late 2008 after the collapse of the American housing market and banking system. In a compelling display of Keynesian economics, governments worldwide calculated that they should borrow funds to finance major infrastructure projects as a means of stimulating economic activity. In Canada, the newly re-elected Conservative minority government was ideologically opposed to deficit financing. It proposed tax cuts as well as a number of contentious policies, including the immediate termination of political parties' quarterly financing payments. The per vote subsidy was the financial lifeblood of the opposition parties, whereas the Conservative Party had built a CIMS-based direct fundraising empire. All of the opposition parties rejected the government's fall economic update on the premise that it did not propose enough spending. They vowed to pass a motion of non-confidence and form a coalition government. As the drama of the ensuing coalition crisis subsided – itself a fascinating case study of political communications[13] – the Conservatives accepted the core demand attached to the Liberal Party's support for the government's budget. Parliament would be required to receive regular updates on the progress of considerable economic stimulus spending.

Budget 2009, branded as *Canada's Economic Action Plan,* proposed to inject nearly $30 billion into the economy.[14] The taps of government money were turned on for skills training, housing construction, industry bailouts, and shovel-ready infrastructure projects. Among the programs were energy efficiency upgrades to social housing, renovating and building community recreation centres, and infrastructure spending on roads and public transit. The reach of the EAP would be broadened through cost-sharing with provincial/territorial governments, municipalities, and other organizations. Budget communications initially positioned the spending as a continuation of the theme of the Conservative government's first budget, dubbed *Advantage Canada,* a long-term plan that trumpeted the competitive advantages of lower taxes, infrastructure investments, and training initiatives. *Advantage Canada* advocated the elimination of the government's net debt, whereas now the government was embarking on deficit financing. The stimulus spending and thus the EAP were intended to be temporary so that, as the economy improved, the government would return to a balanced budget. Even though the stimulus programs would come to an end in 2012, the communications campaign continued.

The Privy Council Office led a WOG approach through the Department of Finance. In March 2009, two connected advertising proposals were presented by the finance minister to the operations committee of cabinet. The first advertising proposal concerned the requirement that the government deliver scheduled reports to Parliament. A Finance memo from the deputy minister to the minister positioned the advertising campaign as meeting the parliamentary obligation of "reporting to Canadians." The partly redacted memo, obtained through access to information, advised that the advertising would comprise "an umbrella marketing strategy and overall design to be used by departments in their campaigns on particular aspects of the Economic Action Plan, so as to allow for cohesive messaging and efficient use of resources." The second proposal was to promote ActionPlan.gc.ca.[15] The memo envisioned the EAP site as "a single, integrated portal featuring and communicating all elements of the Plan," and it would "support and feature ongoing strategic communications and outreach initiatives with updates, pictures, lists of projects, announcements, speeches, etc." The seamless integration of digital media with traditional media is apparent, as are tendencies toward communications centralization and a marketing ethos.

Throughout mid-2009, representatives of the centre held meetings with departmental representatives to brief them on the whole of government branding approach. They were instructed that any related project or announcement had to use the Economic Action Plan corporate look instead of department/agency visuals. Federal Identity Program protocols were secondary.[16] Communications expenses, such as for the production of backdrops and podium signs, were to be covered by departmental budgets and project partners. All signage required for events attended by the prime minister had to be delivered to the PCO communications and consultation secretariat for provision to the PCO tour crew.

The creation of a thirty-five-page EAP visual style guide, also obtained through access to information, was an important process tool in the coordination of pan-Canadian and pan-governmental communications. The visual style guide was supported by a fifteen-page project signage style guide. The preambles in those documents remark on the PCO's responsibility for coordinating the implementation of communications. A brand command was made clear – even the word *brand* was used:

> The Government of Canada has developed a standardized and whole of government approach to communicating the programs and benefits contained in the Economic Action Plan, linking multiple initiatives and media. As part of this strategy, a number of communications activities ranging from paid media, national and regional announcements, an interactive website to signage on highways and infrastructure projects, have been undertaken in collaboration with departments ... [It will feature] consistency in Canadian government communications and maintaining the integrity of the brand (visual identifier, common messaging) for all communications products and activities including announcements, releases, advertising, marketing materials, websites, backdrop, and signage.[17]

The importance of consistency, plain language, and bilingualism were stated. Both style guides were filled with details and illustrations concerning the proper use of background imagery, typography, colour combinations, white space, minimum size requirements, letterhead, media documents (i.e., news releases, advisory notices, backgrounders), and print ads. Detailed specifications were provided for the use of the EAP logo for three seconds in the closing frame of television advertising. Templates for media event materials included backdrops, podium signs, roll-ups, and PowerPoint presentations. This level of instruction was deemed necessary to institutionalize and standardize the desired brand image.

In short order, the EAP publicity machine ramped up. In 2009–10, of the $136.3 million that the federal government spent on advertising, 39 percent was related to the EAP (Table 10.1). All visual communications featured the EAP logo: a formation of blue, grey, and green upward-pointing arrows, accompanied by a black maple leaf that later became red. It was a colour palette used in EAP advertising and on the website. Advertising blanketed the airwaves, including on high-profile and expensive TV programs such as the Academy Awards, Hockey Night in Canada, and the Super Bowl.[18] It extended to transit advertising, such as the exteriors of GO Trains in Toronto wrapped in the EAP logo.

Economic Action Plan branding penetrated areas of government that were previously models for impartial public administration and management, notably the Canada Revenue Agency.[19] The agency's structure blends guidance from an independent board with statutory responsibilities while remaining subject to ministerial oversight. It nevertheless became a hub for the Economic Action Plan by bundling communications about stimulus spending with tax reductions. A seventeen-second CRA video titled *Tax Savings Working for Canadians* was emblematic in that the visuals juxtaposed blues with a neutral colour scheme (e.g., white, taupe, black, grey, mauve) devoid of red.[20] The ad begins with a blue screen and the words *tax savings*. The screen transitions to "working for you" text over a head-and-shoulder shot of a man with a blue shirt holding a woman wearing a beige shirt. The next frame shows them wearing blue jeans and standing in a beige room adorned with blue trim and even a blue thermostat. As the narrator mentions the availability of tax credits, the man spreads white paint, while the woman wipes her hands with a blue towel. The next scene shows another woman, wearing a grey coat, stepping off a white-and-blue bus. She walks through a crowd of people dressed in neutral colours, except for a boy in a blue stocking cap. Next she is shown in a blue shirt while seated at her office desk. One respondent observed that the advertising is "actually funny. Everybody is wearing blue. The house is blue. The walls inside are blue" (CM 17). The video wraps up with the black leaf EAP logo on a white backdrop, accompanied by the Canada wordmark and, in a blue corner, the website address cra.gc.ca/TaxSavings in white font. Years later, the "Strong. Proud. Free." tagline became the final visual under the Canada wordmark. This harkened to the Canadian anthem as well as party campaign themes, as noted earlier. The first four notes of "O Canada" were added as a closing chime. A similar look and feel were employed in other departments' EAP advertising.

Advertising put out by the CRA fell outside its product-oriented norm, such as a flyer promoting the availability of "tax cuts" distributed with tax filing packages during this period. The flyer touted the Home Renovation Tax Credit, First Time Home Buyers' Tax Credit, Children's Fitness Tax Credit, Public Transit Tax Credit, Tradesperson's Tools Expenses, and Pension Income Splitting. Later, the wording was modified to "tax savings" in promotional material that appeared on the back page of the 2014 tax filing guide (Figure 10.3). Less prominent were the information brochures on topics such as Employment Insurance extensions. They were circulated at the height of the stimulus spending via Service Canada information sessions and via EAP kits distributed to employers.[21]

The Economic Action Plan advertising campaign was buttressed with thousands of green, blue, and white outdoor signs – which later became blue – omnipresent across the country at project sites. Large billboards were erected in front of construction and building locations (Figure 10.4) or on the sides of buildings or as window displays. They featured slogans of no more than five words, such as "improving community infrastructure," "road improvements," "investing in Canada's post-secondary institutions," "investing in sports infrastructure," and, eventually, the more generic and brand-centric "jobs, growth, prosperity." The PCO and PMO monitored the progress of the signage communications. Each month, departments were required to submit to the PCO lists of locations at which signs were installed and pseudo-events where podium signs were displayed. At a

FIGURE 10.3 Advertising on back cover of CRA tax filing guide | Canada Revenue Agency (2015).

microlevel, this enabled the tracking of infrastructure projects where signage still had to be installed. The centre monitored sign maintenance in terms of vandalism and storm damage. At a macrolevel, the list of signs allowed central agencies to ensure that cabinet's directive was implemented. The clerk drew on the list as part of his update briefings with the prime minister. To ensure that signs were in place, the government issued contracts stipulating that up to 20 percent of the funding would be withheld pending, among other things, receipt of a photograph of the sign and Global Positioning System coordinates of its location.[22] In early 2011, the PCO directed that outdoor EAP signage would stay in place until that fall.[23] As part of a phasing-out process, departments and agencies were to place a large sticker on signs to indicate that project work was complete. Nevertheless, unaltered project signs were still visible around the country many years later, including during the 2015 election campaign.

FIGURE 10.4 Economic Action Plan roadside sign | Photographed by author, St. John's, December 2014.

The style and tone of EAP communications persisted for years. Prime Minister Harper took to the road to promote spending initiatives, for instance to announce the Pat Burns Arena (see Chapter 3). A one-hour town hall Q&A event was put on in Cambridge, Ontario, where Senator Mike Duffy reprised his former occupation as a journalist with the prime minister.[24] Event planners did not permit the media to participate. The setting featured a multimedia presentation as a backdrop in front of a crowd of 300 invitees. The event attracted news coverage as well as criticism for being a taxpayer-funded partisan activity. It was one of countless pseudo-events put on by government officials across Canada over many years. Ministerial events used podium signs and background banner signs with concise messaging, such as "ECONOMIC ACTON PLAN / PLAN D'ACTION ÉCONOMIQUE." EAP branding was required even when program-related funding represented only a portion of an announcement.

When Conservative members of Parliament were engaged in thematic announcements across the country, including at buildings that received funds under the EAP, they were provided with what the PMO dubbed "an event-in-a-box."[25] The MP kits included a customized template for media advisories, news releases, and talking points for a speech and/or interaction with the local media. In some instances, a roll-up banner was provided. The imaginative nature of the MPs' ability to promote the distribution of government goodies took hold. One minister announced public funds for skating rinks while wearing a hockey jersey with the Conservative Party logo on the front and Harper's name on the back. Most prominently, many Conservative MPs participated in photo-ops with ceremonial cheques that featured the party's logo and colours. The props implied that the Conservative Party, not the government of Canada or the Canadian public, was funding stimulus spending. An investigation by the conflict of interest and ethics commissioner determined that a cheque template originated on the website of the party's caucus research bureau, the aforementioned Conservative Resource Group.[26] The commissioner ruled that it is inappropriate to apply partisan identifiers on government spending announcements because doing so can harm public confidence in government.[27] No codes of behaviour were deemed broken. Nevertheless perceptions of a publicity state were taking hold, even after the lessons of the sponsorship scandal.

According to the Privy Council Office, the objective of EAP advertising was to encourage visits to the program's website, ActionPlan.gc.ca (Figure 10.5).[28] In 2010, the PCO directed that all government websites must steer visitors to that site. The request, the prime minister's chief of staff explained, was necessary for "strategic brand building."[29] The integrated nature of off-line and online communications spurred criticism on a number of fronts. The site exhibited a different visual design than other government sites, and it used the "Harper Government" moniker. The TBS denied a request from the minister of finance, who, at the urging of the PCO, sought an exemption from the common look and feel policy for web communications. Exceptions were requested for page dimensions, column layout, background colours, fonts, navigation path, the use of third-party symbols (social media logos), the domain name, and an array of other technical matters. The following excerpt from the TBS denial letter illustrates how central agencies enforce brand standards, even among each other:

> After a thorough review of your exemption application for the Economic Action Plan website (www.actionplan.gc.ca) from Common Look and Feel Standard (CLF), I must inform you that your request is denied. The reason being that the exemption rationale for the EAP website would also apply to a number of other GC institutional websites; this could lead to other GC institutions to request exemptions with similar rationale.

The result could be a weakening of one of the CLF Standard objectives of ensuring trust and confidence in GC websites through the consistent application of appearance and navigation ... However, I acknowledge and respect the fact that PCO has a central role in coordination and management of government communications. In order to ensure that the CLF Standard evolves, I would recommend that TBS and PCO clarify and formalize their respective responsibilities for layout and design specifications in CLF 2.0 to ensure that PCO assumes ownership of the requirements and TBS assumes responsibility for supporting the GC community in implementing the PCO managed requirements.[30]

By the next year, the Department of Finance was granted an exemption for all of these areas on the basis that the Economic Action Plan was a temporary initiative. Later on, the manager of digital media in the Privy Council Office directed government institutions to insert code into their websites to produce an image-based link to the EAP site that would be managed by central agencies. Public servants expressed concern that Canadians would not be able to identify the website as a government of Canada product because it deviated from the consistent look and feel. The PCO countered that many EAP participants were agencies exempt from the web standards. Only the look of the site would be different, it advised. A further area in which an exemption was granted was permitting photographs of the prime minister on EAP webpages (for instance, Figure 10.5).[31] This exemption was deemed necessary because the website included a link to a video of Harper playing the piano at the National Arts Centre (see Chapter 3). Earlier the Canadian Press had documented over forty photographs of him on the website. When the press sought comment on the practice, it observed that most of the photos were removed, after which their existence was denied by PMO and PCO spokespersons.[32] The unspoken message to public servants was that their web communications and branding initiatives are expected to comply with excruciating micropolicies set by the centre of government, while politically motivated projects are granted exemptions.

Conservative strategists reasoned that it made no sense to abandon brand equity in the Economic Action Plan once the obligation to report to Parliament was met. Consequently, it became more than a short-term

FIGURE 10.5 Economic Action Plan homepage | Screenshot by the author, December 2014, www.actionplan.gc.ca.

stimulus spending program and a way to communicate spending progress to Canadians. What began as the label of Budget 2009, *Canada's Economic Action Plan*, became a frame for the government itself. The same theme continued in Budget 2010, titled *Leading the Way on Jobs and Growth: Canada's Economic Action Plan Year 2*. Transition of the EAP brand from the name of a stimulus program to the government's budget occurred in 2011, when "next phase" wording was introduced. That year the title of the budget was *A Low-Tax Plan for Jobs and Growth: The Next Phase of Canada's Economic Action Plan*. The 2012 and 2013 budgets used the identical titles of *Jobs, Growth, and Long-Term Prosperity: Economic Action Plan*, followed the next year by *Creating Jobs and Opportunities: Economic Action Plan 2014*. The fusion of brands continued in 2015 with its final budget title *Strong Leadership: A Balanced-Budget, Low-Tax Plan for Jobs, Growth, and Security*. In its messaging, the Conservative government used the EAP label as more than a synonym for the budget – the entire government budget became a policy tool within a bigger branding plan.

Because the moniker began as a label for the federal budget, the government could tinker with its brand meaning. The EAP was transformed into a pseudo–master brand that encompassed all manner of financial initiatives and government communications. By late 2014, a list of 379 budget items was featured on the EAP website. To put in perspective that all and sundry were included within this umbrella brand, consider the first ten items on that alphabetical list: the 150th anniversary of Canada's founding conferences; Aboriginal justice strategy; accelerating approval processes for Building Canada Fund major projects; access to broadband; an action plan to improve northern regulatory regimes; addressing prescription drug abuse; addressing violence against Aboriginal women and girls; the Adoption Expense tax credit; an advanced manufacturing fund; and advancing knowledge and treatment of spinal cord injuries. The initiatives were grouped into subthemes of trade and investment, jobs, business, infrastructure, innovation, families, communities, building the North, natural environment, and government.

This became more ominous with the budget bills, which contained all manner of legislative change. Take, for instance, the 2015 budget implementation act, which used the short title of Bill C-59, Economic Action Plan 2015 Act, No. 1. A two-pronged approach was used. The first prong was to bundle tangentially connected items as an omnibus bill, for instance a number of security measures that arguably had nothing to do with the economy. The practice allowed the government to push forward a number of matters by limiting the negative media attention that results from issue publics that mobilize if given the chance. This finagles parliamentary scrutiny of proposed legislation.[33] Omnibus bills package a wide swath of proposals as a strategic tactic that impedes parliamentary scrutiny and encumbers proper public debate. They box opponents into making a single choice to either vote for or against a compilation of things that they both support and oppose and perhaps have not had time to review. Omnibus bills are a reminder that what is in the political government's interest is not necessarily in the public interest.

The second prong of the budget was to brand public policy initiatives. Changes to the Income Tax Act, Universal Child Care Benefit Act, and Children's Special Allowances Act that lowered certain taxes and increased certain benefits were organized within Bill C-59 under the heading "Support for Families." An extensive advertising campaign ensued, propped up by pseudo-events and website content touting new initiatives, even though the bill had not been passed by the House of Commons. The requisite complaints ensued from pundits that this was partisan propaganda. Among the revelations was that Pierre Poilievre, the minister of employment and social development, was featured in departmental videos following him around his riding as he informed people about some of the budget goodies. The style and tone of the videos were a blend of *24 Seven* and election campaigning and concluded with the government of Canada wordmark. Media interest in the "vanity videos" revealed that the department maintains a small "creative production team" that produces content posted to YouTube and promoted via the minister's Twitter account.[34] To proponents, a minister speaking in plain language with constituents about government initiatives on social media is forward thinking and democratic. To critics, the commandeering of government resources – in this case, employees were paid overtime on a weekend – for a pre-campaign video is an unacceptable exploitation of public resources for partisan purposes. It is a general criticism levelled against all sales-oriented government publicity, in particular the EAP.

Elsewhere in this book, Canadian political communications are understood to be lagging behind those of other anglophone liberal democracies. Not so with the Economic Action Plan. It was an ambitious form of permanent campaigning that pushed the boundaries of publicity and branding. A comparative analysis of stimulus programs administered in Australia, Canada, and the United States concluded that "Canada stood out as having a concerted, centrally-planned advertising campaign that, at times, clearly blurred the lines between public and partisan interests."[35] The quasi-propagandistic nature of EAP communications and the shirking of Treasury Board norms generated complaints. The concern is synthesized in the following remarks delivered in the House of Commons by then–Liberal MP Martha Hall Findlay:

> Taxpayers across the country have paid for millions of dollars of self-congratulatory advertising by the government. Even worse, these millions of dollars of this self-congratulatory advertising have also blurred the

image of the Government of Canada with the image, the colours and slogans associated with the Conservative Party of Canada. That is in breach of several of our federal laws and guidelines ... in particular the Treasury Board guidelines of communications policy, [and] the Federal Identity Program.[36]

The advertising expenses associated with the Economic Action Plan became a favourite topic of the media and critics. Dollar figures were used to imply that the spending was a waste of money and a misuse of taxpayers' dollars for partisan purposes. The denunciation cut to the core of the Conservative brand of strong economic management. Critics could not grasp why millions of dollars were available for propaganda when there were myriad other ways to allocate the funds, especially during periods of fiscal restraint. This line of questioning was reinforced by dubious findings using the Advertising Campaign Evaluation Tool. Surveys provided evidence of the apparent ineffectiveness of the EAP advertising by finding low recall among Canadians and that few of them visited the website. On the other hand, a Finance spokesperson pointed out that website metrics had improved and that surveys had found increased awareness of the program over time.[37]

The media's game frame tendencies make the allure of ad spending an easy story in the vein of horse-race journalism on opinion poll results and party fundraising data. In 2009–10, the total spent (i.e., planning and production, not just the media buy) on EAP advertising was over $50 million (Table 10.1). The amount was much lower in the next two years, but it ratcheted up again in 2012–13, when it is estimated to have represented more than half (53 percent) of all of the government's spending. This increase is notable given that it occurred years after the economic crisis and *after* the EAP stimulus spending program was wound down. Money continued to be spent, including a $7.5 million EAP "umbrella advertising campaign," as PWGSC described it, to promote the 2015 federal budget.[38] The budget advertising was supported by publicity and direct marketing, such as letters from the Canada Revenue Agency to Canadians promoting proposed budget initiatives that had not yet been approved by Parliament.[39]

To put the size of the EAP media buy, and the sales orientation of the Conservative administration in perspective, the government spent in the

TABLE 10.1
Government of Canada advertising spending, 2009–10 to 2012–13

Advertising campaign	2009-10	2010-11	2011-12	2012-13*
Economic Action Plan (EAP)	$53,159,848	$22,776,043	$21,002,435	$36,239,202
• Agriculture	$291,186	$1,143,940	–	–
• CRA	$14,388,336	$6,067,934	$6,705,559	$7,020,497
• Finance	$16,498,667	$6,223,264	$7,226,521	$14,891,026
• HRSDC	$13,179,239	$9,340,905	$7,070,355	$6,098,973
• Infrastructure	$7,547,946	–	–	–
• Natural Resources	$1,254,474	–	–	$8,228,706
Biggest non-EAP campaign	$23,533,280 H1N1/ pandemic influenza (Health Canada)	$13,324,310 National recruitment (DND)	$10,710,366 2011 census (StatsCan)	$5,009,748 Health and safety (Health Canada)
Total spending on all government advertising	$136.3 million	$83.3 million	$78.5 million	$69.0 million
Proportion of advertising spending falling within the EAP umbrella	39%	27%	27%	53%

* Other than Finance, the 2012–13 annual advertising activities report ceased identifying major campaigns ($500,000+) that fell under the EAP umbrella. Assumes that all CRA, HRSDC, and Natural Resources advertising culminated with the EAP logo and website address during this period, as it appeared to do.
Sources: Calculated from Public Works and Government Services Canada (2011a, 2012b, 2013, 2014c).

neighbourhood of $5 million annually on public opinion research. This contrasts with the Liberal Party's approach to governing, which saw $29 million spent on public opinion research in 2004–5.[40] For further perspective, consider that in 2009–10 EAP advertising constituted spending comparable to the annual media buy budgets of prominent businesses such as Tim Hortons, Hyundai, Loblaws, and Ford.[41] Untold millions more are incurred in putting on pseudo-events. For instance, the bill for the aforementioned EAP town hall moderated by Duffy came in at over $100,000. Another event held in Truro cost over $46,000, including staff travel and webcasting by a Halifax media firm. Costs incurred by Laureen Harper to attend a pre-election party fundraiser in the area were paid for by the Conservative Party, however footage of her at the fundraiser appeared in *24 Seven*.[42] The prime minister's touring of the country is part of the expense, with the cost of flying the CC-150 Polaris estimated at more than $10,000 an hour.[43] The salaries of political and government staff comprise a fixed cost that nonetheless adds to the price tag. The publicity was perceived to be so egregious that the Liberal Party ran negative advertising during NHL playoff games criticizing the government for spending a combined $750 million on EAP advertising.[44] Conversely Harper spun the extraordinary length of the 2015 campaign as a way to save taxpayers money. "I feel very strongly ... that the [constant campaigning] money come from the parties themselves, not from government resources, parliamentary resources or taxpayer resources," he said.[45]

The Economic Action Plan is a harbinger of branded communications in the public sector. The Conservative administration managed to marshal disparate government resources and spending under a sustained umbrella message of economic growth and job creation. Aided by the convergence of communications technology, the WOG approach developed a look and feel that took on the identity of a Conservative Party campaign. It brought the master brands of the government of Canada, the Conservative Party of Canada, and the prime minister together in a message of strengthening the economy. The branding philosophy that took root with the Task Force on Government Information is flourishing. One indicator that WOG branding is the new normal is found in a redacted PCO presentation titled *Modernizing Government Communications: Branding*, obtained via access to information. The presentation identifies an objective for the centre to "build on the success of the Economic Action Plan brand by developing an overarching branding strategy for Government communications."[46] The promotion of initiatives by the new Liberal administration will surely draw on the communications experience of the EAP and the further institutionalization of a marketing mentality in the Canadian public sector. Public sector branding is a phenomenon that will persist regardless of who controls the government.

11

Public Sector Branding:
Good or Bad for Democracy?

This book uses the word *brand* as an amalgam of the outcome of marketing theory, image management, centralized decision making, and communications simplicity. The main finding is that the digital media environment combined with existing institutional conditions leads to political elites' enthusiasm for branding strategy. This increases the power of leaders, particularly the prime minister who simultaneously personifies the government and governing party (see Figure 2.8). Branding describes a trend that will persist regardless of who holds the keys to 24 Sussex Drive, Rideau Cottage, or Stornoway. The anti-democratic image of any head of government's obsession with branding is an opportunity for an unscripted populist or reformer to ride to power on a message of anti-establishment change, as Justin Trudeau did. Branding lens theory holds that it will not matter: the days of haphazard communications and MPs who speak freely in public are gone. The grip of message control pervades the online self, even sanctioning aspiring parliamentarians for a single off-colour remark made years before entering public life. For many people, branding and centralized communications are rational, and indeed necessary, responses to the unrealistic demands of the media and issue publics. For others, message management and permanent campaigning encourage the concentration of unchecked power and an unsettling use of government publicity resources for political purposes. Perspectives vary: branding and message control in the public sector must be fostered, or something must be done to stop it.

CONCEPTUALIZING PUBLIC SECTOR BRANDING

Public sector branding stems from the use of marketing practices in politics and a New Public Management approach to public administration. In theory, political marketing ought to embody the essence of democracy, since it holds that political elites are concerned with making decisions influenced by public opinion (Figure 2.2). Similarly, the use of marketing in government is a forward-looking practice that reflects new norms in the private sector and society and saves money. However, marketing and branding in the Canadian public sphere leave something to be desired.

Perspectives about voter behaviour lead to some triage rules of thumb for politicking. Reinforce the views of supporters and cultivate brand loyalty. Deploy a careful selection of policy positions and planned communications in order to persuade undecided voters and flexible partisans to support you. Identify potential supporters among the pool of floating voters, respond to those voters' needs without eschewing the ideological values of the party, and narrow your promotional efforts to focus on appealing to these segments of the electorate using simple messaging. Repeat messages ad nauseam because the point at which insiders tire of a message is when audiences begin to absorb it. Do not waste resources on steadfast supporters of your opponents. Debrand your opponents to relegate them to voters' set of inept choices. Bypass media filters. Spin and obscure information. Frame wedge issues. Collect oppo that can be used as a destabilizer. And on it goes. Against that exclusionary and uninspiring backdrop, branding strategy counters an intensifying maelstrom of media fragmentation. Branding espouses that less is more. It is comprised of strategic communications decisions and tactics that aim for an emotional resonance and loyalty among target audiences. It turns policy minutiae into easy-to-understand messages. As a strategic tool in the struggle to frame images and issues, it is used to shape public opinion and to set the agenda. Branding optimizes communications and imposes organizational standardization. All outward-facing activities become unified around uncomplicated, centralized, and repeated messages. The minimalism and symmetry espoused by branding are, in theory, efficient ways to deal with the media tumult.

FIGURE 11.1
Hypothesis of a branding lens

Issue 1

		Strengthens brand	Damages brand
Issue 1	Advances agenda	Action: Generate publicity	Action: Swords and shields
	Derails agenda	Action: Swords and shields	Action: Pivot and distract

A branding lens is a good theoretical tool because it offers predictive power and an explanatory mechanism beyond left/right ideology. As stated in Chapter 1, *Brand Command* seeks to advance the hypothesis that branding strategy is used by public sector elites for efficiency reasons as part of a broader attempt to control political communications and, by extension, to influence public impressions and advance agendas. It is a theory that connects and elucidates other ways of looking at the public sector in Canada, such as the centralization of government proposition (the Savoie thesis), the growth of the publicity state (a theme espoused by Kozolanka, Nimijean, Rose, Thomas, and others), and Aucoin's New Political Governance model. It sharpens our ability to anticipate how a political organization will behave if we can unlock its apparent brand strategy and agenda, in particular its desired master brand (e.g., Figure 2.4). The premise of communications strategy as an influence on policy decisions is presented as a schema in Figure 11.1. It submits that, as long as an issue is thought to strengthen the party's brand while also advancing the party's agenda, the party will likely seek to generate and sustain publicity on that matter, even in the face of dogged criticism. If an issue strengthens the brand but derails an agenda, or advances an agenda but damages the brand, then the party will initiate communications swords and shields (see Chapter 6) to battle the matter with critics and opponents, in an attempt to strengthen its position and avoid a weakened position. If an issue both derails the party's agenda and damages its brand, the leader will try to get out of the situation by distracting the media with something else or slightly alter course to diffuse the tempest.

A branding lens goes a long way toward rationalizing political decisions that are otherwise perplexing. Why did the Conservative government press forward on eliminating the long-form census in the face of public outcry? On proroguing Parliament? Introducing the Anti-Terrorism Act? Refusing to cave to the demands of the Idle No More or Occupy movement or to calls for a national inquiry into missing and murdered Indigenous women? Persisting with preventing government scientists from speaking their minds? Supporting pipeline development and dragging its feet on meaningful climate change initiatives? Reviewing the charitable status of certain organizations? Eliminating the long-gun registry? Overturning plans for a Federal Court building to be named after Pierre Trudeau in favour of creating a Memorial to Victims of Communism near the Supreme Court? Conversely, other polarizing issues are withdrawn. Why did the Conservative government back down on the Internet surveillance bill? Why were certain ministers demoted? Why were social conservatives unable to advance debate on hot-button issues such as abortion? Why did the government undo provisions that it introduced to the Temporary Foreign Worker Program? Why did it press forward with tough-on-crime legislation that seemed certain to be rejected by the courts as unconstitutional? Why did the party eventually adjust its election stance on refugees in the wake of the Syrian refugee crisis? As well, a branding lens can help explain why some political issues achieve all-party unity. Why did all parties support an NDP motion to eliminate the GST on tampons and other feminine hygiene products? A Liberal motion to apply sanctions against those responsible for the death of a Russian whistleblower? What about a Bloc Québécois motion to express "profound sadness" over how *Maclean's* portrayed Quebec in a corruption-themed cover story? More than ideology and gut instinct are at play. The fear of negative coverage in traditional media persists. But now political communications from countless commentators are non-stop. In the digital media age, political marketing and branding are part of the strategic calculus meant to confront a rabid online public sphere.

A branding way of analyzing government behaviour needs to be subjected to empirical tests. Intuitively, a branding lens seems to be sensible theory. Take, for example, the issue of decriminalization of marijuana described in Chapter 3. Because the Conservative government sought to generate publicity about the matter, we can deduce that party strategists believed that it strengthened their brand, boxed in their opponents, and helped the party to advance its agenda. When police associations called for the power to issue tickets for personal possession instead of laying criminal charges, the Conservatives uncharacteristically opted to change course and accepted this appeal. The presumed strategic rationale for backing down is that the debate threatened to derail their agenda and damage their sub-brand of getting tough on crime because the party would be offside with law enforcement.

A branding lens helps to rationalize many other examples presented in this book, from retail politics to efforts to control information. Of course, no theory can perfectly predict or analyze elite behaviour, and leaders base their decisions on a host of factors and information, including intuition. Nevertheless, this way of thinking can inform our ability to anticipate and understand a variety of political issues. It can help us understand why a government chooses to barrel onward in the face of intense media and public outcry and why at other times it abruptly changes direction. This sort of strategic game playing speaks to why, in the age of social media and proto-journalists, all political parties are hypersensitive about controlling communications. The details outlined in the preceding chapters make a compelling case that a branding lens fuels centripetal tendencies. Institutional arrangements in the government of Canada will ensure that this approach to governing prevails no matter who the prime minister is, subject to some variation. This has both positive and negative implications for Canadian politics and government.

PUBLIC SECTOR BRANDING: THE GOOD, THE BAD, AND THE UGLY

The Good

In Canada, the institutional conditions for branding strategy are favourable. The parliamentary system, party discipline, the electoral system, the leadership circle's control over candidates, and the media system provide a basis for implementing branding in party politics. In public administration, the foundation exists through central agency concern about corporate image, notably through the Federal Identity Program and a New Public

Management philosophy that trains civil servants in the art of marketing. The interoperability of executives and staff in the PMO, MINOs, PCO, TBS, and other areas of government is replacing departmentalism with centralism. Following central command is a reality of modern governance.

The reduction of independence and silo mentalities is fuelled by the swirling of digital communications technologies. Smartphones and social media have irrevocably changed the way that Canadians communicate. Digital media shock and the democratization of media, on the whole, are positive developments. They diminish the gatekeeper power of elites and increase their engagements with citizens. An undesirable side effect is that the news media industry is faced with an economic dilemma. Media consumers want a constant stream of digital information for which they do not have to pay and the role of journalists as arbiters is in peril. That demand is being partially fulfilled by citizen proto-journalists and PR personnel who generate content accessible at no charge on multiple platforms. To compete, the mainstream media race for new information and are under pressure to gravitate toward facile processing. The mile-wide, inch-deep characterization of news resulting from politainment, celebritization, game frames, and pseudo-scandals is altering the nature of public discourse. The demand for quick hits and interesting visuals influences the communications behaviour of people who hold senior positions in political parties and government. They need not rely on the Canadian Parliamentary Press Gallery, which is not the impartial mediator that it professes to be, because digital technology enables the rapid transmission of controlled information directly to followers across the country. Content is offered as packaged information subsidies, including hypercontrolled pseudo-events and image bites. The format of news releases – the staple of communications officialdom – has been simplified to compete with fleeting attention spans and 140-character statements issued on social media. The intellectualism of international diplomacy is reduced to lowbrow jabs on BuzzFeed. Government and political circles experience a paralyzing fear of making a mistake, one that will echo across social and mass media. Unscripted situations are *verboten* for all but the leader's most trusted lieutenants, and rushing to answer a journalist's question honestly is unadvisable. Protection from the performance disruption warned by Erving Goffman is prioritized above all else.

For these reasons and many more, public sector communications cannot be slapdash. Planning mitigates risk by providing the centre with an opportunity to screen communications and push spin. The political government aligns communications personnel in the PMO, PCO, and MINOs through morning strategy calls. Direction is given on the sub-brand messages of the day and week, which support the overarching brand. Communications calendars, strategic communications plans, Message Event Proposals, event scenario plans, and media monitoring are used in the development, deployment, and management of messaging. Ministerial announcements are centrally coordinated, and MPs are pressured to clear all public remarks with the centre. Style guides and backdrop guidelines provide instructions for consistent media relations. Media lines, spokesperson's books, and MP kits are provided to brand ambassadors. Meanwhile, the permanent government initiates its own brand enforcement. Government institutions are required to designate central agency liaisons. The Treasury Board Secretariat propagates guidelines concerning the government of Canada's corporate brand. Institutions must follow central policies that advance the standardization of communications and Internet use. Government advertising and opinion research follow detailed processes managed by PWGSC, and Heritage Canada takes on a quasi-propagandistic role by selling patriotism. The public service advances its own brand for recruitment purposes. All of this – the non-partisan and the political – is inching toward a whole of government visual identity that revolves around the prime minister. This is what the professionalization and politicization of government communications looks like.

Why is this good? One reason is that efforts by political staff and civil servants to scrutinize and harmonize departmental communications contribute to stable government that delivers on its election promises. By following a strategic narrative, the leviathan of government operates in an efficient and confident manner, with an ability to implement an agenda on which it will be judged and held to account. It is reasoned that slipshod media relations and chaotic government are far worse: a decentralized government that offers communications flexibility to departments and ministers is criticized as disorganized and weak. Its messages get lost, and the media chase inconsistencies as the government flutters from pseudo-scandal to pseudo-scandal. A civil servant argued that you may not agree with it, but it's far more problematic if individual departments aren't talking to each other, and aren't talking to the Prime Minister's Office, and crafting their own messages without regard to the overarching messages. It's about coordination. The bias of the press is to point out contradictions or to lament the centralization ... I don't see how centralization is de facto anti-democratic. (CS 19)

Public sector branding is good because a government with a recognizable master brand and evolving sub-brands stays on course with its mandate compared with one that panders and flip-flops. It is democratic because it improves the ability of citizens to judge whether a political party is staying true to the platform upon which it was elected. Governments must not chase every political wind, and branding is a tool to stick to a pathway as a collective whole.

The consequences of inadequate communications preparation and synchronization are learned by politicians of all persuasions. The democratization of party caucuses and decentralization of messaging is noble in theory but imprudent in practice. The Reform Party and Canadian Alliance Party, which held dear a grassroots ideology and allowed candidates to break free from party discipline, came to accept that the leader must insist on message coherence. All Canadian political parties learn hard lessons from bozo eruptions and pseudo-scandals that damage the brands of both party and leader, not to mention the personal brands of those emitting the remarks. As media convergence speeds up, there is an increased need to eviscerate surprises and off-message situations. Political parties of all stripes are adamant that the place for pontificating and rigorous debating among caucus members is in camera, not in the media. This includes public forums, where brand ambassadors might wander off message or say something controversial. Despite the democratic promise of social media, political figures must exercise extreme caution and aversion towards public commentary, given the propensity of an errant remark to put an abrupt end to a political career.

In a parliamentary democracy, message discipline is more two-way than critics allege. It works only if the principal and central agents engage caucus and if party representatives willingly take part. This is why the prime minister and senior PMO personnel attend caucus meetings, why a system of caucus advisory committees became an institutionalized mechanism to inform cabinet, and why so many parliamentary secretary positions are prone to exist. Conversely, to even be eligible to represent the party in an election, a candidate is subject to rigorous background checks. It is a process that weeds out people assessed as unfit for public office on the most frivolous of matters, a practice that appears to be widely accepted. A decisive leadership circle that listens to caucus, and political parties that field election candidates with clean backgrounds, should result in better government.

A democracy is only as strong as its ability to engage the electorate beyond the intelligentsia and the attentive public. On this score, in many ways, political marketing and branding are inclusive. The dumbing down of communications that accompany branding is driven by a desire to reach citizens who interact with government and/or vote but pay little attention to politics and public policy. Branding articulates core values and policies and allows supporters and citizens to readily form judgments on the top decision maker. Database marketing is a branding tool that provides a means to compile information on supporters in a manner more responsive and individualized than public opinion polling. Party elites build relationships with electors outside election campaigns by sending them customized information electronically. Email marketing and social media outreach promote awareness of political issues and encourage citizen engagement. Listserve members across the country are given insider opportunities, such as seeing a political ad before it hits the airwaves or receiving a link to watch a leader deliver a speech online in real time and unfiltered. On electors' doorsteps, door-to-door canvassers collect data that are inputted into smartphones and uploaded to central party databases. Such microlevel engagement is more frequent and tailored compared with political parties relying on the mass media and opinion leaders. Branding is salient as long as the political battle is fought over simple images that inform cognitive shortcuts among select electors in select ridings exposed to select media.

To enthusiasts, branding is a force for good because it encourages internal compromise on policy matters, which leads to outward-facing accord as opposed to public unrest. Audiences benefit from intelligible information that permits faster searches and processing. The organization profits from a better return on communications investment since wasted efforts are curtailed and messages pack more powerful punches. Within government, branding fits the NPM objective of seeking operational efficiencies. The Federal Identity Program increases Canadians' awareness of the government's presence and saves time and money by preventing micro-brands and mixed messages. The WOG framework is likewise motivated by cost savings in procurement and web publishing. Websites and other e-content catapult forward the synchronization of messages as well as the common look and feel of visual experiences.

Arguments against branding tend to be alarmist and are built on ideal-istic assumptions about how government and politics should work. Critics are content only if they get their own way, or they believe in a utopia where political debate results in unanimity, and in this fantasy the government must be wrong if it moves forward in the face of adversity. The PMO and political staffers are portrayed as pushing an illegitimate partisan agenda on virtuous public servants and noble journalists who are victims of the evils of centralization. Scientists are framed as impartial, evidence-based researchers prevented from revealing normative truths that poke holes in the official government position and agenda. These characterizations are exaggerated. Nobody in the political sphere is without bias, including social scientists, and impartiality does not normally describe those who seek media attention. Cabinet has the unequivocal authority to set the direction of government communications; as long as it enjoys the confi-dence of the legislature and obeys the rule of law its directives are based on legitimate authority. It is not the purview of a public servant to comment on government policy or express opinion about political leadership. That is up to a member of cabinet, or a designated spokesperson, both of whom should stick to media lines cleared by the centre. In the usual course of business, the minister is the designated public spokesperson responsible for explaining policy and passing judgment on its appropriateness. Min-isters and the centre recognize that a public servant or MP who issues a single dramatic tweet might derail the government's entire agenda, along with the considerable work invested in communications planning and corporate identity. Quite simply, brand control is warranted for the effective implementation of public policy and smooth operation of the state.

Histrionics about the politicization of government communications need to be reined in. If the public service is meant to be impartial and professional, then it has a duty to fulfill the directives of cabinet, which carry the force of law. Cabinet is designed to be political: it is comprised of partisan members of the elected legislative branch, and unlike public servants they are ultimately accountable to the electorate. Consequently, public servants must enact political directives in an impartial way, very different from the implication that unknowns should stand up to political decisions in the name of perceived impartiality. There is a fine line between unwarranted politicization and speaking truth to power. But critics imply that a professional bureaucracy that independently ignores the will of cabinet and its political agents is somehow more democratic or that rules and norms put in place by past political administrations are impervious to change by current masters. All policy decisions are inherently political, and the public service is innately politicized in some manner. What is at stake is not whether government is politicized, which it always is and ought to be, but at what point the politicization of government is excessive.

Politicization is impeded by many rules and practices of good governance. Political communications under Harper were clean compared with past administrations. The sponsorship scandal brought to the fore that government communications historically have been stained by patronage and skullduggery. The Accountability Act and the Lobbying Act, as well as a suite of process formalities administered by the TBS and PWGSC, are in place to inhibit unethical behaviour and limit the influence of people with party connections who seek access to government pork. The provisions of the Access to Information Act, including the recent practice of making completed requests available to others, ensure that reams of inside details about government are available, which were previously hidden. The Open Government initiative requires that all sorts of government information be proactively posted online, and internal controls prevented the potential use of a party lookalike logo for that initiative. The considerable reporting requirements of the Elections Act increase the transparency of party and election finances. Clearing messages through the centre instills a healthy anxiety that imparts greater awareness of the need for internal consultation and good governance. Despite their protests, journalists have enjoyed more equal access to more information on government and elected officials than ever before.

All told, there are strong arguments in favour of branding strategy and communications centralization in government. Branding promotes focus within public administration and brings together the asymmetry that results when the bureaucracy is left to its own devices. Inward-facing mentalities and technical speak are replaced by outward-looking whole of government and consumer-friendly communications. Government and party representatives refer media enquiries up the line, as we would expect of employees in any large professional organization, particularly in an environment in which minor gaffes are ruthlessly mocked by the media and online mob. Blaming the governing party ignores that, regardless of who is in charge, the upper echelon of the bureaucracy will champion the value of image management and push communications conformity. Pointing the finger at individual officeholders overlooks historical patterns of behaviour in a comparatively sluggish communications setting. Branding plays an integral role in governance and politics today, which is better than the problems that result from disparity.

The Bad

There are downsides to public sector branding. Reflecting on the publicity state, or what he and others call public relations democracy, Darren Lilleker points to a dichotomy between realists and pessimists. The former, he argues, believe that publicity is a mild form of propaganda. They argue that there is nothing to fear, because it is understandable that political actors try to persuade their audiences. The latter disagree. They maintain that persuasive communications practices "are wrong, they are anti-democratic, reduce civic participation and lead to an inactive public sphere, and create a cynical public disengaged from the democratic process."[1] They think that democracy is about listening, outreach, inclusiveness, and natural freedoms, and above all that power must reside in the people's elected representatives rather than the Prime Minister's Office. Similar vexations apply to the consequences of branding in party politics and governance.

Branding – along with marketing, journalism, bureaucracy, party politics, and political advertising – has an image problem. Government-commissioned research finds strong public support for design consistency and common identifiers on the web. Canadians say that this uniformity improves their navigation experiences and assures them that a website is maintained by the government as opposed to being a spoof site.[2] However, they are less convinced of the merits of a branding concept. When asked to rate actions that can be undertaken to improve government services, focus group participants ranked the option to "develop a trusted Government of Canada brand or identity with which Canadians can easily identify" as the lowest priority.[3] The presence of marketing in politics and government is derided as undemocratic and "un-Canadian,"[4] labels that debrand the strategy itself. When a political party is so enthused about message control, that anti-democratic behaviour becomes its brand. This whets the media's appetite for performance disruptions and strategy frames and stirs public anger. In short, public sector branding swirls with controversy, some of it deserved, and all of it linked to a top-down decision tree.

There is plenty of reason for concern. Whatever the theoretical optimism for marketing, or the need for central coordination, political elites tend to be peddlers who blend marketing with salesmanship to fulfill their own needs. A healthy pluralist society should allow room for deliberation of public policy and consideration of a full range of competing ideas. Brand control inhibits this, because everyone is terrified of making the tiniest of gaffes and especially of being derailed by a bozo eruption. Moreover, elites cater to like-minded segments of the electorate as a means of achieving their own goals, and they are unconcerned with the needs of the electorate as a whole, even when they profess otherwise. The concentration of marketing efforts and search for efficiency include ignoring – or at least not prioritizing – citizens who are not within targeted subsegments of the electorate. To its detractors, public sector branding invites manipulation, duplicity, and propaganda. The divisions between partisanship and a neutral public service are blurred. Morale is low and frustration high among civil servants who do not support the governing party and/or are opposed to what they perceive to be politicization of the public service. A branding philosophy contributes to permanent campaigning, the superficiality of external scrutiny, the personalization and celebritization of the political class, the use of the game frame, political echo chambers, and deepened partisanship. It adds to the importance attached to visual cues, at the cost of deeper scrutiny and analysis. Branding is nothing more than a modern variation of long-standing attempts by the political class to control their public image and manipulate public opinion. The fourth estate, opposition critics, academics, and pundits are correct to sound the alarm.

Monitoring political marketing behaviour is necessary where government advertising campaigns are concerned, as Jonathan Rose has warned. Advertising expenses for sales-oriented publicity campaigns warrant questioning, unlike product-oriented information campaigns. There is a constant stream of media coverage of the latest expense figures regarding government advertising and the limited effectiveness of that advertising as measured using the Advertising Campaign Evaluation Tool. Millions of dollars are said to be wasted or misused, against a backdrop of government cutbacks and budget deficits, not to mention interest groups' unrelenting pleas for resources. Hypocrisy was at the forefront with the Economic Action Plan cornucopia of quasi-partisan communications, which persisted amid financial restraint as the government sought to balance the budget, years after the stimulus spending was laid to rest.

In *The Problem with Political Marketing*, Heather Savigny warns of the manner in which political elites use marketing and argues that its practice contributes to democratic malaise.[5] Politicians become followers with a fluid ideology who pander to public opinion and sidestep difficult decisions. The citizens whose viewpoints are voiced through social media, reported in the news media, and solicited through focus groups are not necessarily indicative of public opinion. Political actors engage in preference-shaping and persuasion strategies to condition audiences to favour what political elites offer. Segmentation, targeting, and triage are anti-pluralistic and cater to narrow interests. Presenting a constructed public image and appealing to the lowest common denominator matter more to political elites than increasing elector interest and knowledge about politics. The result is centrally driven pseudo-events, sound bites and image bites, and style over substance. Marketing, Savigny believes, is practised by elites with the primary objective of augmenting their own power. She has a point.

Branding takes this control and self-interest a step further. Politicians and PR personnel need not rely on the press corps to communicate information, as they once did; but the media is still drawn to political news, particularly of the prime minister. This enables protecting the brand by limiting the media's opportunities to derail a political agenda and the chances of spokespersons to go off message. The resulting increase in access to information requests and MPs' written questions to ministers, both of which require a response within a specified time, ensure that information released on government is rarely impromptu. This recourse is not viable during an election campaign, when brand control goes into a hyper state. The media and critics complain, but the courted voters who pay cursory attention to politics do not seem to notice or care.

Frustration with centralized political management should be directed at the mobilization mechanisms that fuse the brands of the government, the leader, and the governing party. Kirsten Kozolanka suggests that the question for scholars on such matters is "when and where to draw the line."[6] The government's overall corporate identity structure is more entwined with that of the Liberal Party than with that of any other entity, something that the Conservatives tried to change in their favour. But formally referring to the government of Canada as the Harper government and using Conservative party colours in government communications imply party ownership and excessively politicize a non-partisan organization. For public sector entities, there is a significant risk/reward aspect to having brand equity invested in the leader, because the fortunes of their brands are so wrapped up in the image of a single partisan holding a statesman-like position. Significant rebranding and upheaval occur when that person leaves; think of the honeymoon enjoyed by new leaders. Political parties and governments are much more than their leaders, yet the leader is the face of the brand. The situation is more pronounced in public administration given that the prime minister is the embodiment of the government and of the political party that controls the House of Commons and – as far as image is concerned – as the brand head of state. Among the difficulties with government communications casting attention on one individual is that this is anathema to the many citizens repelled by his or her public persona and politics. The electoral system deserves some blame: the prime minister can be and is anointed with less than 40 percent of the vote, on ballots that do not ask which leader should head the government, and by votes cast by less than two-thirds of electors. Despite the pride of Canadians in democratic values, a majority of them are led by someone whom they did not vote for, and they put up with living in a publicity state.

Given that so much is riding on the leader, it is to be expected that government and party communications will be leveraged to develop the myth of a heroic figure and expand the base of loyal followers. Once ensconced in power, political parties use public resources and information subsidies as part of a permanent campaign to advance their agendas. The *24 Seven* video magazine is an example of how image makers attempt this as well as a reminder that charisma cannot be manufactured. Branding is of even greater concern when a telegenic figure like PMJT heads the government, particularly if that person is a populist who eschews norms. The personalization of politics diverts attention away from the serious and toward the superficial. It conditions electors to form intuitive impressions of politicians based on how they appear in the media as opposed to judging the quality of their arguments or discerning what is an act and what is real. In turn, political parties in a media-centred democracy are disposed to anoint people who can manage a positive public image. Branding theory invites apprehension that the celebritization of leaders has a centralizing effect, because power follows when attention is placed on individuals rather than on collectives. Branding increases the power of party leaders over party caucuses and members and undermines party politics.[7] It steers support within a political party toward the vision, personality, and image of the leader and away from the rank and file. It contributes to the presidentialization of the parliamentary system of government and to the Savoie thesis of centralization. Branding places more power in the hands of the first minister and his or her agents, in part because perception becomes reality. This is not absolute. Scholars such as Paul Thomas and Graham White are correct that the Savoie thesis must be nuanced. Canadian prime ministers simply do not have as much unbridled power as is popularly claimed or imagined. Nevertheless, centripetal forces are maintained by agents who promote the leader's brand and the compliance of media that trains the public eye on the head of government. This will persist with social media technologies that synthesize information into the bite-size "news snacks" described by media scholar Florian Sauvageau.[8] The future is not just Twitter, Instagram, or BuzzFeed – it is any number of rapid-fire texts, photos, and video tidbits that whiz around the public sphere and are herded with branding.

The Ugly

Long-time political marketing critic Nicholas O'Shaughnessy likens the practice of branding to propaganda.[9] In his view, political elites use opinion research and communications technology for subversion and manipulation. Rhetoric, spin, and hyperbole seek to persuade. Emotions are stirred to quell rational reasoning. Brand symbols become heuristics for myths. Values and beliefs are mobilized so that they become aligned with those of the propagandist. Enemies are socially constructed to define the similarities of those whose interests the propagandist seeks to unite and defend. To O'Shaughnessy, the communications instruments used by government, political parties, journalists, and special interest groups are all organs of propaganda. His view is that very little in the political arena is product-oriented or truthful. Other international perspectives are not nearly as pessimistic, yet we are cautioned that branding undermines democratic principles.[10] Public sector branding scholars Eshuis and Klijn identify the risks of branding to governance processes as anti-engagement, public manipulation, populism, and elitism. Attention is drawn to the tensions among branding, democracy, and public sector goals. Unlike O'Shaughnessy, their concern about the implications of a distorted reality is tempered by uncertainty about how brands influence perceptions.

Believers in the public information function of the fourth estate have particular cause for worry about the ascendancy of branding strategy. On some topics, the government practises information censorship as though it is facing insurrection. When journalists, as individuals or a group, pose a risk to a public sector brand, they are shunned. The sensationalist or slanted nature of news does not justify their questions being ignored by those in power, and yet the overly punitive nature of social media calls for defensive posturing. Somehow information processing in democratic government needs to keep pace with the fast-moving nature of news. The elongation of the internal media process that results from paranoia about making a communications mistake is incompatible with the accelerating pace of media demands. Citizen proto-journalists are joining the fray, but they lack the professional training and resources of accredited journalists and editorial oversight.

A problem with branding and permanent campaigning is the ability of the governing party to dip into the public coffers to finance its publicity initiatives, to choose the topic of that publicity, and to influence its tone. Advertising campaigns for the Economic Action Plan, Canadian Forces recruitment, War of 1812, Canada Job Grant, and Canada 150 contributed to the Conservative government's overall brand image while framing issues and setting the public agenda. For instance, over $11 million was spent promoting Canada 150 fully two years before the milestone anniversary. This expenditure included bundling advertising marking the anniversaries of the Charlottetown and Quebec conferences and the War of 1812, while the government ignored milestones linked to undesired political brands. Stéphane Dion's criticism of such ventures is common: "They blur the line between government information and partisan ads."[11] Another sinister practice is the wilful leaving behind of those cohorts who will never support the governing party. Dividing the electorate into cleavages of issue publics, and excluding opponents from political communications, arguably damage the public sphere, pluralism, and elections.[12] A further concern is that we have no standardized reporting mechanism for the considerable financial expense incurred by government pseudo-events.

The ugliest aspect of political marketing is debranding. The harshest and most personalized forms of negative advertising are symptomatic of the tendency for political actors to view voters as consumers who do not follow government business. It does not treat them as citizens who deserve quality political information. Fact-based critiques of policy and political leaders is the epitome of the democratic principle of the freedom of speech and can be the cornerstone of a thriving democracy. The opposite occurs: negativity seems to contribute to cynicism about political personalities and to lower voter turnout. The propagandistic nature of negative advertising is a scourge of democratic politics. It does more than draw attention to policy or leadership competencies; it purposely strikes fear and loathing. More jarring is when ministers publicly rebuke civil servants, including diplomats and chairs of administrative tribunals who speak up against the government, to say nothing of Prime Minister Harper's unprecedented volley against the chief justice of the Supreme Court of Canada – who, it should be said, willingly enters the fray when she expresses a political opinion in public speeches.[13] Canadian government depends on the relative anonymity of its civil servants to provide frank advice to ministers and a judicial branch that rises above politics. This system is inhibited if individuals fear that they will be publicly admonished, and there are concerns that bureaucrats are less inclined to keep records.[14] Arguably, debranding contributes to the erosion of an independent civil service and to lower civic engagement and flawed governance.

The hidden aspects of debranding are no less malicious. They range from secret strategies to eviscerate the personal brands of opponents to daily minutiae that only the attentive public cares about. The circulation of negative talking points for spinners is routine. Ten percenter flyers that call into question an opposition leader's provocative policy push the ethical limits of using parliamentary entitlements. Subversive actions in the legislature are unbecoming, including purposely agitating committee work and not producing financial details. Spreading rumours about an MP resigning, or *agents provocateurs* behaving under false pretences, are reprehensible. No justification exists for illegal acts such as the robocalls voter suppression scandal. The ugliness of political branding persists because too many areas of politics lack ethical guidance and oversight.

SUGGESTIONS FOR REFORM

The dark side of branding must be reined in. New rules are needed to contain nefarious behaviour and curtail the most despicable acts. In *Democratizing the Constitution: Reforming Responsible Government*, Peter Aucoin, Mark Jarvis, and Lori Turnbull argue that proposals for democratic reform in Canada must establish clear objectives, place formal constraints on prime ministerial power, provide mechanisms for the House of Commons to enforce the reform, and entrench the power of MPs in both majority and minority governments.[15] Within this framework, they present some specific suggestions for reforming the Canadian Constitution, the executive, the legislature, and political parties. Their ideas are concerned with curtailing the power of the political centre of government, such as increasing the threshold for dissolving the legislature by requiring the support of two-thirds of MPs. Further suggestions for reform are found in *Tragedy in the Commons: Former Members of Parliament Speak Out about Canada's Failing Democracy*, authored by the co-founders of Samara, a Toronto-based non-profit organization that seeks to improve Canadian democracy. Their recommendations surround the professionalization of what amounts to schoolyard behaviour. Written questions provided in advance of Question Period, orientation sessions and job descriptions for MPs, increased transparency of political party business, and an improved role for MPs as brand ambassadors are just some of the ideas mentioned based on their interviews with former MPs.[16] Inevitably, they concede that a cultural shift is required to set the stage for significant change. Both works are a good basis for initiating dialogue on what would amount to a seismic shift in Canadian political life.

The first attempts at curtailing the worst aspects of political branding must balance audacity with plausibility and look beyond partisanship and personalities. Above all, what must be limited is the publicity state's contribution to the fusion of party and government brands. The conflation of state and party symbols, and the use of public resources for political communications purposes, run counter to the democratic principle of detachment of party business from public administration. In comparison, little can be done to prevent brand evisceration or reclamation, part of the normal ebb and flow of changing administrations. A number of possibilities to curtail statecraft rebranding and other forms of public sector branding are identified in the following pages. They follow the advice of Aucoin, Jarvis, and Turnbull to identify the objective of the proposed reform and a mechanism to give power to the people's elected representatives to enforce it.

Increasing Professionalism: More Ethical Public Sector Communications

1 *Have Parliament regularly update the government of Canada's communications policy.* The government's communications policy should be regularly reviewed by Parliament to reflect changing circumstances and evolving communications technologies. A number of issues raised in this book

should inspire a further update, planned by the Trudeau Liberals. The government should not use advertorials. Government communications, including the promotion of public policies or programs for which parliamentary or intergovernmental approval is pending, should not proceed until a motion is passed by the House of Commons pertaining to the specific item to be publicized. Visuals of members of cabinet should not appear on government homepages, with some exceptions, such as pm.gc.ca. The government of Canada and its institutions should not be referred to by anything other than their formal names in communications products. Government buildings should not be named after former party leaders. Journalists should expect a response within a certain time period; however, it should be specified that faster responses are possible when questions are submitted with considerable notice and during normal business hours. The communications policy should be subject to scheduled reviews and approval by a multiparty committee of parliamentarians. An officer of Parliament should monitor implementation of the policy.

2   *Create a political communications code of ethics.* A voluntary code of practice about political marketing should act as a moral compass for political actors who have different interpretations of the boundaries of freedom of speech. Industry codes of behaviour, such as the Canadian Code of Advertising Standards and the Canadian Marketing Association Code of Ethics, are insufficient since they all but exempt politics. A political communications code of ethics would form the basis of stimulating dialogue on what is acceptable behaviour. It would spell out the privacy safeguards associated with database marketing, what sort of negativity is beyond the pale, when it is fair game for politicians to critique those who stand in their way, to what extent they should have access to media footage of opponents, when a controversial remark warrants sanction irrespective of the brand ambassador's position, and so on. Such a code would apply public pressure on political parties and interest groups to sign on. A code of practice would raise the bar while tempering the outcries of idealists, putting us on the path to more civil discourse. It would be the basis of a normative assessment of the actions of American-style political action committees, an emerging force in Canada.[17] The non-partisan code should be developed by a broad consortium of practitioners

and specialists who would work toward securing the endorsement of all major political parties. It would be periodically updated to reflect changing norms. Over time, Parliament would ideally come to recognize the code and participate in scheduled reviews of it.

3 *Eliminate financial support for debranding.* Highlighting problems with an opponent's candidacy, platform, and claims is one thing; denigrating leaders on a personal level is quite another. Excessive negativity and debranding are harmful to civic discourse and public engagement in a democratic system of government. Canadians should not unknowingly subsidize the worst forms of debranding. Political fundraisers ought to be legally required to obtain donor consent for a donation earmarked for advertising that is foremost negative.[18] Such donations should be subject to a less generous tax refund scheme. Post-election financial returns should itemize advertising spending associated with personal attacks, which should qualify for a lower rate of refund to the party or candidate. This would result in political parties maintaining two separate war chests and being choosier about negativity. Parliamentarians who distribute debranding materials with harsh personal slights paid for through their office budget allotments should be required to repay the amounts as well as receive a temporary suspension from the privilege. The adjudication of what constitutes unacceptable forms of debranding should be the responsibility of a non-partisan review board that reports to Parliament.

Depoliticizing Government Communications: Inhibiting the Fusion of Party and Government Brands

4 *Prevent political parties from using the official colours of the government of Canada.* The convergence of party, prime ministerial, and government brands is perhaps the most significant concern raised in this book. Brand fusion intensifies centralization, undermining confidence and trust in political and public institutions. The brand markers of the government must be state-like and above repute so that integrity is preserved regardless of which political party or prime minister is in power and irrespective of public opinion about personalities.

The provision in Ontario's Government Advertising Act that government advertising is partisan if it "includes, to a significant degree, a colour associated with the governing party" is a starting point in that it recognizes that colour schemes are loaded with political meaning. Regardless of which party is in power, all government of Canada visual communications should always be based on a red-and-white colour palette. This is practical only if the official colours and symbols of the government cannot be co-opted by any political party. To avoid perceptions of partisanship, the government of Canada and its institutions must have a monopoly on using the official colours of the government, the Canadian flag, and the red maple leaf symbol. No political party in the federal arena should use a red-and-white colour scheme in its marketing communications. Whenever a maple leaf is used in visual communications by political organizations, that icon should be any colour other than red.

The Elections Act should be amended to prohibit tax-deductible status and financial payments from the government to any political party whose logo, advertising, website, signage, or other visual communication uses mostly red and white. Funds should be withheld if any political party uses a red maple leaf. To help established political parties – particularly the Liberal Party of Canada – with the transition to new marketing collateral, a generous one-time financial payment should be extended to help defray costs incurred from market research, graphic design, and production of new materials. To the extent possible, these amendments should be approached in a non-partisan manner when they are debated in Parliament. Such provisions must be designed to withstand a Charter of Rights and Freedoms court challenge.

5 *Require that the official red and white colours of the government of Canada be used in its communications.* If steps are taken to depoliticize the use of red and white, then, for good measure, the communications policy of the government of Canada should be amended to prohibit government from using other colours, in particular the main colour(s) associated with the government party. Those colours are identified in the logo filed with Elections Canada and campaign materials in the preceding election. Materials sent from parliamentarians' offices, such as ten percenter flyers, householders, and calendars, should not be permitted to use colours normally associated with a political party. These amendments

should be part and parcel of a parliamentary debate about the role of colour use in brand fusion.

6 *Issue annual reports about government spending on photo-ops.* The federal government issues annual reports on advertising and public opinion research. To capture a fuller understanding of government communications spending on publicity, and as a measure of accountability, regular financial reports should be prepared concerning media pseudo-events. This includes proactive disclosure of costs such as signage, room rental, audiovisual equipment, travel, photography, and other extraordinary non-fixed expenses for special communications events such as photo-ops, speeches, or videos. In lieu of a customized measurement vehicle such as the Advertising Campaign Evaluation Tool, the financial outlay for pseudo-events should be balanced with an estimate of the financial value of the earned media. The reports should be presented by the minister of public works to Parliament each fiscal year.

7 *Create a checklist to assess government advertising.* There is a need to reduce the politicization of government advertising as well as unwarranted claims of partisanship, both of which erode trust in government institutions. There is no obvious solution to limiting the ability of cabinet to commandeer public resources for partisan-like communications. As long as the political government can originate advertising on policy priorities of its choosing, little can reasonably be done to turn a sales-oriented approach into a product-oriented one. The partisan nature of the creative content of the ads is also in the eye of the beholder, making the vetting process a potentially subjective rather than an objective exercise. As with EAP advertising, short of being able to spot a party logo, little explicit evidence of partisanship can be policed, and the WOG approach to advertising is not necessarily a problem.

In the short term, a non-partisan group such as Samara should research, create, and maintain a user-friendly and publicly accessible government advertising checklist. The checklist would enable anyone to readily assess whether a government ad is excessively political or partisan. It would expand on the basic framework of the Ontario Government Advertising Act. If this checklist were adopted by Parliament, it would perform a public accountability function and inject some objectivity into claims of partisan communication. It would pressure government to exercise greater caution while freeing it from opponents' constant alarmism. This would be a step toward adopting a more robust review process of advertising than has been proposed by the Trudeau government.

Turning Lapdogs into Watchdogs: Empowering Public Guardians

8 *Create media guidelines.* News coverage of Canadian politics involves too much politainment and precious little public policy analysis. There is brinksmanship between political parties and the media on all manner of topics. More broadly there is excessive celebritization, pseudo-scandal, and the treatment of politics as a sporting event. The media has its reasons, and not all journalists fall into this trap. In a democratic society, the freedom of the press is sacrosanct – and yet without intervention into media logic (discussed in Chapter 3) the quality of democracy in the branding age is suspect.

One mechanism to encourage good coverage is the creation of media guidelines by academics identifying what the political media ought to voluntarily prioritize. Guidelines might promote the ideal that the media should strive to deliver information about government and political parties without applying a slant and without the trappings of market journalism. Editorializing and politainment ought to be confined to forums such as panel shows and opinion pieces so they can be differentiated from news reporting. Journalists and news editors should be encouraged to see past personality politics and to periodically explain to their audiences how the Canadian system of government works. These sorts of ideals would require a collaborative effort between interest groups committed to good governance and media organizations in conjunction with service standards in the government's communications policy. Media guidelines passed as a non-binding motion by academic organizations could build on the CBC's journalistic mission and the Canadian Association of Journalist's ethics guidelines. This sort of rethinking is necessary to combat the message control of public sector branding by making it less likely for government officials to be fearful of media agendas.

9   *Empower and legitimize the Senate.* There is no getting away from the forces of branding that require message symmetry among members of the executive and legislative branches. Ideas to increase the power and independence of members of the House of Commons are problematic given the communications pressures on ministers and members of Parliament to act as mouthpieces for their political parties. It remains to be seen whether the Reform Act or reforms promised by the Trudeau Liberals (see this book's Preface) will have chops. A more ambitious way to limit the power of the prime minister and cabinet is to change the Senate itself so that it acts as a legitimate counterbalance to the brand discipline of the House of Commons. The theory that responsible government places power in the hands of the people's representatives in the lower house is antiquated in a world where communications technology enables and pressures conformity. Whereas only the attentive public concerns itself with the procedural nuances of the House of Commons, the average Canadian can instinctively recognize the undemocratic nature of the Senate. A democratized Senate would provide a second forum for representative government. The public demand for that outdated institution to hold the political executive and permanent government to account grows with the diffusion of communications technology.

Senate reform is such a long-standing issue in Canadian politics that in the 1960s the topic was written off as "merely a plaything of parties."[19] In recent years, the outrageous spending by a number of senators, in particular Mike Duffy, has galvanized public opinion that something must be done. However, the possibility of reform is slim as long as there is division over the most viable way to modernize Parliament. Academic discussion on restructuring the Senate has fallen out of favour as scholars and democracy advocates focus on the House of Commons and the electoral system. The ivory tower punditry seems to have little effect on political parties and MPs, with the important exception of Chong's bill. It is the Senate that a sizable majority of Canadians want to see changed, but there is no consensus on how to proceed.[20] Prime Minister Harper went through extended periods without making Senate appointments, and he required that new appointees support his efforts to limit their terms and require election. The Conservative administration referred the constitutional nuances to the Supreme Court of Canada, which ruled in 2014 that support from both federal chambers and seven provinces representing half of the Canadian population (known as the 7/50 amendment formula) is required for the federal government to implement senator elections and/or term limits.[21] The New Democratic Party's long-standing position is that the Senate should be abolished, a sentiment periodically advocated by some premiers, including Brad Wall of the Saskatchewan Party. This is implausible because the SCC ruled that abolishing the Senate requires the unanimous consent of both federal chambers and all provincial legislatures; moreover, doing so would only concentrate more power in the hands of the prime minister and courtiers. For his part, in 2014 Trudeau dramatically expelled all senators from the Liberal Party's caucus to create a symbolic division between members of the two chambers. As prime minister, he plans to depoliticize the appointment process. There is thus widespread agreement that something must be done about the Senate and disagreement about what must be done. Trudeau is unwilling to reopen constitutional debate, so it will be up to others to take a united stand on reform to turn the political plaything into a meaningful mechanism to limit brand power.

Suffice it to say that the brand's clutch means that, in addition to the old chestnuts of creating an equal, elected, and effective Senate,[22] there must be institutional measures to loosen the communications control of party elites. The Senate tends to be populated by some of the governing party's most active brand ambassadors. They are not sufficiently accountable, and members constitute an exclusive club of individuals with connections to the current or recent prime minister(s). The Senate must elevate the importance of regional/local priorities over those of a senator's party or its leader. Its members must somehow be elected on a staggered electoral cycle not always twinned with general elections of MPs, and perhaps not be permitted to campaign as affiliates of a political party. Only through such change will senators gain public legitimacy to act as a check on the House of Commons and constrain prime ministerial power. To ensure responsible government, reforms would need to prohibit senators from jointly being members of the executive branch and a political party's caucus. Parliamentary reformers such as Peter Russell, who argues that the House of Commons must take on the role that the Senate was originally intended to perform,[23] must establish consensus. Whatever the pathway, observers of Canadian parliamentary government should take a page from the public sector branding playbook and speak with a united voice to repeat a simple, consistent message of what must be done about the upper chamber. Divergence must become convergence on the matter of parliamentary reform if anything is to happen.

AREAS FOR FURTHER RESEARCH

These ideas should not be gauged as partisan or dogmatic but as a fitting reflection on the preceding pages' description of what goes on in party politics and government. The considerable presence of marketing in politics warrants greater scrutiny. A branding lens can increase our ability to analyze political phenomena and bring to the fore questions about how democratic government operates. It compels us to question our constitutional understandings of the political neutrality of the public service and the accountability of political staff and central agencies. It opens avenues for research in a variety of connected disciplines, including the evolving role of the fourth estate.

Branding theory adds another tool to scholars' ability to interpret politics and government. It adds to models built on the application of marketing and private sector approaches to the public sector, including the electoral-professional, business firm, franchise, and market-oriented models of party politics, and theories of New Political Management and New Political Governance. It needs to be tested against other theoretical constructs not discussed here, such as new institutionalism. It is unclear whether there are nuances in how branding is practised in French or in communicating with ethnic groups. First Nations communities have been encouraged by the government of Canada to think of their organizations as brands and to develop branding strategies,[24] which might result in different tactics than the ones described here. It is possible that the branding framework is more intense in the public sector in smaller jurisdictions, given that there are greater opportunities to concentrate power in the office of the premier.[25] For instance, there are indications that provincial tourism advertising, brand signatures, government websites, budget materials, highway signage, and even the colour of licence plate letters are

commandeered by partisan image managers.[26] There is no clear understanding of the influence of American political consultants in Canada or
even, for that matter, of Canadian-based consultants. Research is needed
to better understand image makers and brand ambassadors.

Trends in communications technology and their connections to information control deserve monitoring. Personal brand stories are built and
shaped via digital image bites shared on Instagram, a platform that is the
new frontier for brand management and negative video.[27] Citizen journalists are conducting online opposition research. Crowd-sourcing of video
ads remains in the experimental stages in Canada. Technologies such as
cable addressability are on the horizon, whereby digital cable providers
deliver different television advertising to viewers of the same program, and
they are among the new frontiers of marketing cost efficiencies. The political
landscape is further prone to branding tactics as different forms of media
sharing, microblogging, social news, and social networking emerge. Push
notifications via smartphone applications are growing in popularity. Apps
such as Snapchat represent forays into the emerging world of video messaging where users share visuals of up to ten seconds in duration, whereas
apps such as Meerkat and Periscope enable live video streaming. Short
looping videos on Vine are becoming popular. *Brand Command* aims to
provide a foundation from which to analyze emerging phenomena as a
subcomponent of brand strategy.

This book has attempted to advance a theoretical tool and to document
communications processes at the federal level of Canadian politics and
government, drawing foremost on Canada's first microtargeting prime
minister as a case study. Only Stephen Harper knows how much he prioritized branding concepts. Certainly, his public statements and actions
indicate a visceral desire to control information. Since his initial foray in
the Reform Party, he saw first-hand on many occasions how the media
themselves practise debranding and do so in a publicly acceptable manner.
He witnessed how the game changed with social media and smartphones.
Political parties and governments of all persuasions operate in an evolving
technological world of hourly communications battles. No matter who is
in power the centre will lean toward unifying all communications around
the prime minister.

Branding is an unstoppable force in politics and government. Its many positives come with downsides and unforeseen consequences. Given the connection between unity of communications and unity of command, it creates some serious problems for Canadian democracy. Public sector branding must be confronted.

Appendix 1:
The Thomas E. Flanagan Fonds

Reviewing information archived by political elites is an exceptional basis for inductive reasoning drawn from rare evidence. Researchers interested in studying the Flanagan fonds should bear in mind a number of methodological considerations. The parties that Tom Flanagan was involved with cannot be deemed representative of how things work in all opposition parties under all leaders at all times. We cannot know exactly what Flanagan was involved with in those parties. There is little point in coding the data because of the absence of a purpose for doing so as well as the logistical complexities (e.g., the files are not in readable electronic format). Furthermore, political staffers are often told that they should not put something in an email that they would not want to see in the news,[1] though in a fast-paced environment this can be impractical or overlooked. In one email archived in the fonds, a political strategist described Harper's concern that email communication could end up in the media:

> Stephen specifically mentioned to me his concern about the security of communications. That involves: (1) Minimizing the number and size of [email] communications we send, and the distribution thereof – i.e. only write something down if absolutely necessary. (2) Strongly self-censor your content. That means refraining from e-mailing very sensitive or potentially harmful material. Use the "leak test" – would it be damaging to Stephen or the campaign if the e-mail were leaked to the press?[2]

And sometimes confidential matters were explicitly not broached by email: "We are in crisis here. I will call with further explanation."[3] Conversely, evidence at the Mike Duffy trial shows that email messages are regularly used to reach people in diverse locations, including between offices on Parliament Hill. In the Flanagan fonds, there are plenty of emails demonstrating that the self-censorship directive was not rigorously practised:

> The call started with several expletives ... which didn't bother me. I just expleted right back for 60-seconds which has a wonderfully remedial effect on the caller ... We are quietly trying to broker a deal between the other three candidates ... I have no confidence that the party apparatus has the ability to foresee and plan solutions to these many problems ... I'm wondering, and seeking your advice, should I, for future plausible deniability, make such a suggestion in writing?[4]

When asked about the methodological limitations of the fonds, Flanagan asserted that he did not withhold any content and that the research value of the files deposited in the University of Calgary's library archives resides foremost with understanding how political party personnel operate:

> The biggest problem with using a collection such as mine is that the party leader did not use email. That was a sensible precaution, because anything with the leader's name on it is subject to being leaked. But it means that the collection lacks documentation from the most important person on "Harper's Team," namely Harper himself. As campaign manager and chief of staff, I communicated frequently with Mr. Harper, but it was usually through personal meetings, or phone calls when we were not in the same place. If I needed him to read something, I would usually print it and give it to him personally. Occasionally I would send emails to those who were with him all the time asking one of them to give the leader some bit of information or pose a question to him. So the Flanagan collection is useful for documenting the preparation and running of campaigns but doesn't give a lot of insight into the leader's thinking.[5]

The fonds, as Flanagan says, are a valuable glimpse into the inner workings of campaign planning. Most of the emails among the leader's advisers were transactional and often composed in rushed circumstances. Internal party documents reveal mock-ups of brochures and iterations of draft speeches and news releases as well as polling data. Image management and branding were rarely discussed, and given the time period there is little mention of Internet communications. Reviewing archived personal correspondence is a bit like time travelling. One moment we are reading about the grainy photograph quality on Harper's Canadian Alliance leadership webpage in 2001 and how there should be a "hits" counter; the next moment we are whisked into the tension-filled final days of the 2006 election campaign as Conservatives were on the cusp of forming the government.

EXAMPLE OF FLANAGAN FONDS ENTRY

The Flanagan fonds contain all manner of internal party documents and written correspondence, including email messages that capture deliberations between party strategists. The following example serves to illustrate what type of content is available. Sometimes the email printouts are accompanied by hard copies of emailed attachments, such as the campaign post-mortem memo that is reproduced as Appendix 3. Names of senders and recipients appear in the originals; all but Flanagan's are removed here.

University of Calgary Archives, Accession # 2002.032, File #44.01
Stephen Harper campaign [text]. – December 1-December 15, 2001. –
1 folder.
File consists of e-mail correspondence.

Subject: RE: [Fwd: Fw: latest letter with coupon revised]
Date: Mon, 03 Dec 2001 12:03:10 -0700
From: *<name #1 removed>*
To: *<name #2 removed>*, Tom Flanagan

I think using an exclamation mark is overcompensating ... No "!" suggests that Stephen will be "Getting It Right" as a foregone conclusion
...

> **From:** *<name #2 removed>*
> **To:** *<name #1 removed>*, Tom Flanagan
> **Subject:** RE: [Fwd: Fw: latest letter with coupon revised]
> **Date:** Mon, 03 Dec 2001 11:56:43 -0700
>
> Hello all
>
> Do [we] want the 'Getting it Right' (the exclamation point is removed
> on the latest copy I am putting up) that is below his name on the
> current comp removed then? What I was thinking, is something to
> replace the logo in the oval. I could replace the whole oval with the
> square (but I would need it in colour).
>
> http://www.fpp.ab.ca/election/comp01/comp01.html
>
> *<name #2 removed>*
> ---Original Message---
> **From:** *<name #1 removed>*
> **Sent:** Monday, December 03, 2001 11:45 AM
> **To:** Tom Flanagan, *<name #2 removed>*
> **Subject:** Re: [Fwd: Fw: latest letter with coupon revised]
>
> assuming it's in colour, it works for me ...
>
> *<name #1 removed>*
>
>> **From:** Tom Flanagan
>> **To:** *<name #1 removed>*, *<name #2 removed>*
>> **Subject:** [Fwd: Fw: latest letter with coupon revised]
>> **Date:** Mon, 03 Dec 2001 11:33:04 -0700
>>
>> *<name #1 removed>*, *<name #2 removed>*,
>>
>> We don't have a logo as such. What do you think about using the
>> "Getting it right" graphic from the top of this letter?
>>
>> Tom

Appendix 2:
Access to Information Method

Requests for information from the government of Canada were filed through Access to Information and Protection of Privacy (ATIPP) protocols to gather baseline data on branding and communications centralization. The Prime Minister's Office is exempt from such requests, which is why the PMO emails presented during the Duffy trial are of considerable research value. Sometimes departments withhold information pursuant to specific provisions of the ATIPP Act, such as records that involve recommendations to a minister, a summary of internal deliberations, negotiation plans, and information prepared for cabinet. As in party politics, in the public service there is some reluctance to put things in writing. One civil servant relayed that, if something is "in a grey zone," staff will speak in person to ensure that no written record exists (CM 19). Another mentioned that this was particularly true among exempt staff; as she put it, "they will not write emails that you can ATIPP. People are very cautious behind this kind of thing whenever they want you to do certain things that may be perceived as crossing the line" (CM 18). Civil servants also relayed that at times sensitive content is saved only on USB sticks to avoid ATIPP. Nevertheless, emails obtained through access to information demonstrate that some civil servants are less cautious than others, as some quoted passages in this book have indicated.

The purpose of the submissions was to cast a wide net to gather inside information on internal processes and tactics. Requests were submitted in September 2012. The total number of completed responses ($n = 49$) was less than the number of requests made (n = 109) because of submissions being redirected to another government institution that already received a request, no records being located, exemptions to the ATIPP Act being invoked, and interviews being granted in lieu of some requests. All records obtained for this project are accessible by searching the completed access to information requests portal at data.gc.ca. A list of organizations, the rationale for their inclusion, and a summary of the data collected are available from the author.

Each request was accompanied by a five dollar application fee that entitles five free hours of internal searching for records; any requirement to pay additional fees for additional data was not acted on. The wording of each request was normally as follows: "Recent communication and files such as emails, PowerPoint decks, and memos about the strategy, rationale, deliberation, and/or execution of [topic] since early 2006. Please include other records already released on this subject. Alternatively, I would be satisfied to interview someone about this." Central government agencies and the biggest advertising spenders were sent requests (CHP, CIC, CRA, DND, DFAIT, Finance, Health Canada, HRSDC, PCO, PWGSC, TBS) on a variety of connected topics in order to generate a variety of content related to public sector branding. Government agencies contacted were Canada Post, the Canadian Broadcasting Corporation, the Canadian Wheat Board, and a small agency that will go unnamed to conceal the identity of interview respondents. The requests generated a corpus of 4,067 pages of internal emails and planning documents that were manually reviewed. Requests were worded as follows:

- the terminology "branding" and its variants, such as brand, brand image, brand identity, et cetera (1,192 pages received);
- the use of graphic arts visuals, such as colours, logos, photos, and videos, that are commonly identified with the Conservative Party of Canada, such as blue colours, images of the prime minister, et cetera, on government Internet sites (758 pages received);
- the creation and use of portable signage, such as banners, podium signs, lectern panels, et cetera, that are visual props at photo-ops, such as media announcements, new conferences, et cetera (562 pages received);

- media publicity that featured people other than MPs with a significant public profile, such as pop culture celebrities, athletes, premiers, "ethnic" group leaders, et cetera (391 pages);
- the Canadian flag as a visual prop (243 pages received);
- the colour scheme of Economic Action Plan external communications, such as information explaining why shades of blue are often dominant, why there tends to be a limited use of the colours red and orange, et cetera (240 pages received);
- external public communications materials using the prime minister's personal name, for instance, but not limited to, any internal information discussing the government of Canada being called the "Harper Government" (237 pages received);
- internal emails with central government agencies concerning the Federal Identity Program, including in cases where the department was potentially not compliant with FIP guidelines (193 pages received); and
- visual images of ice hockey, curling, and/or other "Canadian" sports, such as lacrosse, skating, CFL football, et cetera, in external public communications (145 pages received).

In addition, some specific requests were submitted. Information concerning the prime minister's performance with Yo-Yo Ma was received from the National Arts Centre (thirty-nine pages), and information on the plain language policy requirement of the communications policy of the government of Canada was obtained from the TBS (sixty-seven pages). Attempts to obtain examples of PMO "Alert-Info-Alert" electronic communications (no records found) and "roll-out calendars" used by the PMO (not disclosed because of exemption) from the PCO were unsuccessful, as were efforts to obtain from the TBS cabinet records between 1970 and 1987 concerning development of the Federal Identity Program (no records exist).

These proprietary submissions were supplemented with additional internal government files collected in 2014 and 2015, as described in Chapter 1.

Appendix 3:
Conservative Party Election Campaign
Post-Mortem Memo

The following internal party memo marks a transformational way of thinking in Canadian party politics.[6] It captures the period when the Conservative Party became committed to the disciplined message scripting recommended by political marketer Patrick Muttart and others. The Conservatives brought this brand command way of thinking to government via the Prime Minister's Office, which was formalized as a Message Event Proposal (Appendix 5). Names of the authors and the recipient – which was not Stephen Harper – appear in the original; all but Muttart's are removed here.

MEMORANDUM
PRIVATE AND CONFIDENTIAL

To: *<name #1 removed>*
From: *<name #2 removed>*, Patrick Muttart
Date: July 9, 2004
Subject: Lessons Learned – Campaign 2004

Thanks again for providing us with an opportunity to work on the national campaign.

Here are some – in our opinion – "Lessons Learned" from Campaign 2004. The memo is broken down into three categories: (1) scripting, (2) the general campaign and (3) advertising.

Given that the memo is titled "Lessons Learned," it focuses on
things that we either did wrong or could have done better – a classic
post-mortem exercise.

One of the problems with post-mortem memos is that they often lead
the recipients of such memos to think that everything went wrong or
that everything could have been done better. This is most certainly
not the case.

You ran a tight ship and your achievement was particularly impressive
given how little time you and your colleagues had to map out and plan
Campaign 2004.

We were immensely proud to be a part of your team.

(1) Scripting

▶ **There must be a scripted message of the day – *every* day**
In a future campaign, there must be a scripted "message of the day"
every day. Even if the implicit message is momentum (e.g. "Conservatives
gaining ground in Quebec") there needs to be an explicit message (e.g.
"Conservatives to tackle fiscal imbalance") to complement it.

▶ **The message of the day must be delivered *early* – *every* day**
We need to have an early (before 10 am local, before 12 Eastern *at all
costs,* even if we are in BC or Alberta) policy message out every day. This
means more breakfast events, and more tour pre-positioning to the next
day's venue the night before.

▶ **Not enough "raw materials" were produced in advance**
All too often, we found ourselves spending hours upon hours preparing
raw materials for events that we knew far in advance we would be doing
(e.g. platform launch, defence policy launch, agriculture, etc ...) ... It is
difficult to forward plan when trying to package full policy announcements the day before such events.

▶ **The Leader's "down" day should never be a week day**
Too much happens on a week day – particularly during the latter stages
of the campaign. Sundays – and only Sundays – should be "down" days.

▸ **There must be a scripted message event *even* on days when the Leader is off**
A series of pre-scripted message events should be developed and planned for execution in Ottawa, Montreal or Toronto where significant national media are permanently located.

▸ **Responses to Liberal announcements should be planned in advance**
It is imperative that we script days – before the election – that would see designated spokespeople – with creative backdrops – attack the Liberal proposals.

▸ **Liberal attacks are predictable so our responses should be scripted**
As much as possible, there should be scripted, "turnkey" events available featuring appropriate spokespeople. When the abortion controversy erupted, for example, we should have had prominent pro-choice Conservatives put forward front and centre to say that a Conservative government would not introduce abortion legislation, and that there is a diversity of views in the Party and caucus.

▸ **Tour should be more strategic, Leader should not make unilateral changes**
Scripting and Strategy should drive Tour and not vice versa – ever. And, the Leader should not be able to unilaterally change the tour without at least some discussion of the senior messaging strategist or the overall strategy group.

▸ **The donut is the message**
Inserting a few lines into a speech that the media have heard dozens – if not hundreds – of times before is a recipe for the message to be lost. In order to pay attention, the donut must be more than just a few lines but a mini-speech – complete with an introduction, build up and conclusion. The donut should be clearly introduced (e.g. "Today, I would like to specifically talk to you about ... ") and be supported by an accurate news release.

▸ **A policy/messaging assistant should be on tour**
As noted above, the Leader will always make last minute changes. Therefore, it is imperative to ensure that somebody senior is on tour to ensure

that the Leader's changes do not cloud the message of the day and that all supporting materials (e.g. news releases) are adjusted accordingly.

(2) Overall Campaign

▶ **A sign off process must be in place for *all* released information**
Although it sounds bureaucratic, the campaign was severely hampered on two occasions by advisories/reality checks that should never have gone out ... No major company releases an advisory/news release/ backgrounder unless somebody at a VP-level signs off on it. And nothing should leave Campaign HQ unless somebody of correspondingly similar importance signs off before release/publication. A similar process should apply to all letters/questionnaires going out to interest groups.

▶ **The health care wedge should not have been allowed to reopen**
Keeping health care off the table as an election issue was fundamental to our campaign strategy for over a year before the election ... Like supply management and official bilingualism, the Canada Health Act is seen as a symbol, and we must assert our fidelity to the CHA and the five principles and pledge to work to uphold them as the federal government.

▶ **We completely failed to capitalize on Ontarians' anger at McGuinty**
While our opponents were featuring Mike Harris (and his distant record) in their ads, we were unwilling to go hard – via either advertising or through scripted messages – on McGuinty and his broken promises and higher taxes.

▶ **Specific social conservative issues did not hurt us, but the symbolism of the Charter did**
When debate took place over our position on abortion and gay marriage, there was little if any negative movement in the polls. In fact, the same-sex marriage issue seemed to be quite beneficial on the ground. However, in the last two weeks of the campaign, the Liberals shifted the debate from the specifics of abortion and gay marriage to the symbolism of the Charter and positioned themselves as the defenders of the Charter and minority rights. The Randy White comments fed into this beautifully. The lesson here is that with tight messaging we can win or neutralize the

debate on specific social conservative issues (which split the Liberals' base as well as ours), but we lose when the debate shifts to the emotive, patriotic symbolism of the Charter.

▶ **There should be no Western "victory lap"**
The initial tour plan called for the final week to move from West to East. This should have been adhered to, with the Leader flying home to Calgary only on the final Sunday night / Monday morning to vote.

▶ **The last weekend matters**
Conventional wisdom has long held that people's minds are made up at least four or five days before an election, and that voters claiming to be undecided on the final weekend of the election are in fact non-voters. This election disproved that conventional wisdom ... The war room saw its senior management, including policy and communications staff, move out to Calgary. Polling and advertising were on auto-pilot. There was no effort at getting an aggressive message into the media. Clearly, this cannot happen next time, and the war room must be "warring" until polling day.

▶ **We need a way of re-dramatizing our main message in the final week**
We were by and large unsuccessful in turning the focus back to our core message of "waste, mismanagement, and corruption" in the final week of the campaign ... A way of redramatizing the issue – perhaps with advertising, perhaps with messaging – needed to be developed.

▶ **The platform should be more modest and more thoroughly costed and third-party endorsed**
While overall the platform was not a major liability, clearly large-scale tax cuts are not that popular / important for the electorate, while fiscal credibility still is. In the next campaign, a more modest, more thoroughly costed platform, preferably endorsed by an independent economic forecaster, would be preferable.

▶ **Candidate recruitment in key ridings should be more centrally coordinated**
We lost a number of highly winnable ridings because of weak candidates or poor local campaigns, or in other cases had "sure thing" riding

nominations won by weak candidates which could have been held for stars. Without using the undemocratic power of appointment, there is still a great deal that can be done to control nominations more thoroughly. Provincial campaign chairs / committees, led by prominent individuals, should be struck early to identify candidates in key ridings. Clear rules should be established to prevent local riding associations from controlling nomination dates, etc., and establishing membership and candidate criteria which must be met before allowing a nomination.

▸ **We need to be able to respond to specific charges based on our generic promises**
... If our platform proposes measures that will or could affect specific local projects / companies / etc., we should develop specific local talking points to respond to the inevitable charges.

▸ **There needs to be a far more systematic ethnic outreach program**
Ethnic outreach has been pursued amateurishly for many years. We now need a systematic program which escapes from the patronizing rubric of the "Bridge Building Committee," which should be abolished. Specific campaigns should be developed for specific target communities. This means not simply lumping all ethnic groups together, but having separate Taiwanese and Cantonese campaigns, separate Arab Christian and Arab Muslim campaigns, etc.

(3) Advertising

▸ **Fight fire with even *more* fire or make their fire *the* issue**
... A "soft sell" response to Liberal negative advertising ... was insufficient to respond to the level of hatred and vitriol generated by the Liberal advertising. A rule of American politics is "A charge unanswered is a charge accepted." We should have had specific response ads out answering the false charges directly.

▸ **The air war is *the* war**
A general rule of thumb in contested political campaigns around the world is that 60% of the campaign budget should be spent on advertising, 5% to 10% should be spent on research and 30% to 35% should be spent

on everything else. Within the advertising budget, almost all of the
advertising budget should be directed to production – but mostly the
purchase – of television spots aimed at swing and undecided likely voters.
And generally speaking, news channels should be avoided as they are
watched primarily by super-informed decided voters. Radio is generally
only effective as a tactical "get out the vote" vehicle and print generally
works only as a tool to mobilize core voters.

▶ **All advertising mediums should be aligned**
Once the Liberals got their advertising message straight, they focused
everything they had – across all mediums – on demonizing Stephen
Harper. In contrast, there was a clear disconnect between our radio
and television campaigns ... We cannot control friendly fire nor can we
control what the media chooses to report, but we can – via our media
buy – do our utmost to keep our ballot question as the electorate's ballot
question.

▶ **The message should be more regionalized**
The Conservatives should learn from the Liberals who ran regionalized
messages in Quebec, British Columbia, and elsewhere ... The advocacy
of regionalized ads does not mean that we should have run as many ads
as the Liberals did but that there should be an element of regionalization
built into the plan so that we would have appropriate advertising in each
region.

▶ **Advertising structure should be re-visited**
The party – as the Alliance – made two decisions that, in retrospect,
should be re-visited. The first concerns selecting an ad agency to be
party's AOR [agency of record] rather than building a team of in-house
experts. The second was *not* to appoint a single member of the campaign
team to be responsible for advertising (and report through to the overall
head of messaging or campaign manager) ... With respect to the second
point, it is imperative that the Conservative Party – like any business with
a marketing budget or virtually every other party – have an advertising
manager – a professional whose sole responsibility is to serve as the
contact between the head of messaging and the in-house or external
agency. By not employing this approach, advertising gets designed

by committee and there is very little flexibility in changing tactics mid-campaign because the committee members are all too busy doing their day-to-day jobs.

▶ **Party leaders shoot ads on their days off**
This is simply a campaign fact. Each day off ... provides party leaders with an entire day to shoot new creative [content] as a response to opponent attacks or a deliberate change in messaging. During Campaign 2004, there appeared to be a strong resistance to filming new ads.

Note: Abridged for length by author.

Appendix 4:
Public Affairs Plan

The following internal planning document illustrates the preparatory organizational and logistical thinking that goes into a ministerial announcement.[7] A bureaucratic instrument like the public affairs plan or its equivalent fulfills an inward-looking public administration function, compared with the outward-facing political purpose of a Message Event Proposal (Appendix 5).

Department of National Defence
Public Affairs Plan

xx August 2011

Public Affairs Plan – Renaming of Environments
A. GoC Communications Policy
B. DND/CF Communications Policy

SUMMARY
1. On August 16, 2011, the Honourable Minister Peter MacKay, Minister of National Defence, will announce the restoration of the historic names of the three branches of the Canadian Forces: the Royal Canadian Navy, the Royal Canadian Air Force and the Canadian Army. The Vice Chief of the Defence Staff Public Affairs (VCDS PA) account, in conjunction with Chief Military Personnel

Public Affairs (CMP PA) account, plans to hold a ministerial announcement to inform the Canadian public of the name changes at HMCS *Sackville* in Halifax. This PA Plan outlines the way ahead for the ministerial announcement.

SITUATION

2. The Government of Canada has recently made the decision to restore the historic names of the three branches of the CF. This change recognizes a part of our heritage without in any way diminishing the capabilities inherent in our unified Canadian Armed Forces.

3. The Assistant Deputy Minister Public Affairs (ADM (PA)) is the lead for coordination and planning of communications to support the announcement to rename the environments. CMP as lead organization for the renaming of environments will lead the long-term communications strategy.

PUBLIC ENVIRONMENT

4. Lobby groups for Canadian Republicanism will meet the decision to restore the names of the Canadian Forces with resistance, as it will appear to embrace our Royal heritage.

5. In this time of strategic review, workforce management and cost cutting measures, this decision to make a change of this magnitude will be met with resistance.

STRATEGIC CONSIDERATIONS

6. *Cost Efficiency:* In these tight economic times, the Canadian public are tuned into government spending. Name changes can be expensive, especially in a department as large as Defence, impacting small items such as stationery, to large items such as equipment.

7. *Unification:* The department is continuing unification, and restoring historical names, which speaks to the richness of our Canadian military's history.

8. *LFAA Change of Command:* There is a change of command for the Land Force Atlantic Area taking place on August 16, 2011, in the morning. This is the same day and relative location as the planned MND announcement.

APPROACH

9. A proactive communications approach will be adopted and a Ministerial Announcement is planned to inform the Canadian public of the renaming of DND/CF's Environments. Public affairs products will be prepared to assist the formal announcement, including a backgrounder, fact sheets, news release, media response lines and media advisory.

10. All media queries regarding the name changes will be handled from the national level. CMP PA will handle all queries post announcement. Environment PAO's will be provided the approved messages below for use when it is directly related to their respective environment.

AUDIENCES

11. The following internal and external audiences will be targeted:
    External:
    a. Canadian public;
    b. Historians and other academics.
    Internal:
    c. Canadian Forces members and their families;
    d. Civilian employees of the Department of National Defence; and
    e. Veterans.

MESSAGES

12. The following messages will be communicated in the event of a media query:
    - The historic names of the three commands are those under which Canadians fought and died in the Second World War and Korea, and contributed to the defence of Europe and North America during the early days of the Cold War.
    - Restoring these names is an essential part of our government's commitment to acknowledge our nation's proud history, to celebrate our heritage and to honour the memories of so many brave Canadians who have sacrificed in service to Canada.
    - Bringing back the original names of the three former services reinstates an important and recognizable part of military heritage, along with a key part of our nation's identity.

- The restoration of the historical names is being done in a fiscally responsible fashion, and will have no impact on the capabilities, the organization or the operational effectiveness of the Canadian Forces.

EXECUTION

13. National Defence's Assistant Deputy Minister (Public Affairs) (ADM (PA)), through VCDS Public Affairs section, will provide public affairs support to the Ministerial announcement in Halifax. This will involve support from Maritime Forces Atlantic Public Affairs (MARLANT PA), Chief Military Personnel Public Affairs (CMP PA) and the respective ECS PAOs, and support to departmental subject matter experts.

VCDS PA will be responsible for the logistics of the Ministerial announcement, the coordination of public affairs products (backgrounder, fact sheet, and Q&As) through Chief Military Personnel Public Affairs (CMP PA), and the development of public affairs products (news release, media response lines, and media advisory).

The ECS's are responsible for the changes required to their respective website banners and content.

14. *Concept of Operations:* The following is the concept of operations for the Ministerial Announcement strategy:
   a. VCDS PA will coordinate the Ministerial Announcement for the Historical Designation at HMCS *Sackville* in Halifax, Nova Scotia. Media will be invited, and information on the Environments' renaming will be available.
   b. Following the Ministerial Announcement on August 16, 2011 (TBC), CMP PA will be responsible for handling all media queries.

- *Spokespersons:* The following spokespersons and subject matter experts will be available:
   a. The Honourable Peter MacKay, Minister of National Defence.

- *Invitees:*
   b. Chief of the Air Staff or representative of the Air Force;

c. Chief of the Maritime Staff or representative of the Maritime Staff;

d. Chief of the Land Staff or representative of the Land Staff;

e. His Excellency the Right Honourable Governor General, David Johnston.

Each organization of the above mentioned invitees is responsible to provide the formal invitation to attend.

- *Subject Matter Experts:*

  f. Acting Director and Chief Historian, CMP (TBC)

CO-ORDINATION

- *Contacts:*

  g. Jane Doe, Communications Advisor, ADM(PA) / DGPASP / VCDS PA, 613-555-5555

  h. Sally Smith, Account Manager, ADM(PA) / DGPASP / VCDS PA

- *Budgets:* The ADM (PA) organization is responsible if Policy PA personnel are required for travel if attendance is necessary. The Environments are responsible for the development and creation of visual aids, such as logos, if necessary.

- *Evaluation:* Media coverage and web-hits will be monitored, and an after-action report will be issued by VCDS PA.

CONCLUSION

- This communication approach is issued in accordance with the authority at Annex A. ·

Annexes

Annex A – Clearance Sheet

Annex B – Media Response Line (to come later)

Dist List

Note: Abridged for length by author. Some names changed by the author.

Appendix 5:
Message Event Proposal

The Message Event Proposal is indicative of the internal communications planning discipline that was imposed on government by the Conservative PMO.[8] As a political instrument, it builds on the Public Affairs Plan (Appendix 4) or some such equivalent preparatory matter that is authored by civil servants. The MEP imposes detailed step-by-step event planning, all crafted through a branding lens that calculates how to control media coverage by maximizing emphasis on the visual message. Over time, the MEP became shorter (see Chapter 9) as awareness of the importance of message control increased within the public service and as the pace of communications sped up.

MESSAGE EVENT PROPOSAL
Historical Designation Announcement

Date/Time: August 16th, 2011   Media Market: Regional, national
Location: Citadel Hill, Halifax,   English Media Spokesperson: MND
        Nova Scotia   French Media Spokesperson: MND
                                       Multicultural Media Spokesperson: N/A

THE EVENT

PROACTIVE EVENT OR INVITATION
• Proactive

EVENT

- [*not shown: content from the summary in the public affairs plan (see Appendix 4)*]
- Minister MacKay would deliver a speech flanked by Canadian flags, three Second World War veterans (Navy, Air Force and Army) and three serving representatives from the Canadian Forces (possibly the Chief of the Maritime Staff, the Chief of the Air Staff and the Chief of the Land Staff; otherwise, one representative each from the Army, Navy and Air Force). Historical flags (Blue Ensign, the Ensign of the Royal Canadian Air Force, Canadian Army Battle flag) would be raised following the speech. Minister MacKay would then be handed, one at a time, a folded version of each historical flag by the appropriate serving members. He would present each flag one at a time, in turn, to the appropriate veteran of the Royal Canadian Navy, the Royal Canadian Air Force and the Canadian Army (photo opportunity to occur as part of each successive presentation). The National anthem would be performed. Event would conclude with a bagpipe performance. A separate location on site would be used for a question and answer session with members of the media.
- Separate from the main announcement would be a series of three to six subsequent photo opportunities staged at various locations across Canada over the following weeks. The photo ops would serve to further underline the importance of the restored designations, and would be built around various historical locations, events and anniversaries. Government of Canada representatives to take part in the photo opportunities could include Associate Minister of National Defence Julian Fantino, Parliamentary Secretary Chris Alexander, and The Honourable Laurie Hawn.

GOVERNMENT OF CANADA FUNDING / PARTNER FUNDING (IF APPLICABLE):

- N/A

VENUE DESCRIPTION

- Atop Citadel Hill with the Armoury in the background

MEDIA INVITED?

- Yes

MINISTER'S REGIONAL OFFICE CONTACTED?
• Yes

OTHER PARTICIPANTS (MPs, PROVINCIAL REPS, STAKEHOLDERS, ETC)
• N/A

AUDIENCE SIZE AND DESCRIPTION / TARGET AUDIENCES
• International / national media
• Canadian Forces members and their families
• Veterans
• Historians and other academics
• Canadian public

VISUAL MESSAGE(S)

DESIRED PICTURE (STILL)
• Minister MacKay, in a historic setting surrounded by Canadian flags, presenting veterans from the Royal Canadian Navy, the Royal Canadian Air Force and the Canadian Army with historical flags from their respective services.

DESIRED PICTURE (VIDEO)
• [*not shown: repeated content from "desired picture (still)" above*]
• Minister MacKay speaking with veterans of three services.

ACTUAL SPEAKING BACKDROP
• Citadel Hill

WRITTEN MESSAGE(S)

NEWS RELEASE HEADLINE
• Minister MacKay announces restored titles of the Canadian Forces
• Royal Canadian Navy, Royal Canadian Air Force, Canadian Army names reinstated

DESIRED HEADLINE
• Canadian Forces reconnect with their history

DESIRED SOUNDBITE / KEY NEWS RELEASE SOUNDBITE
- "The restoral of the historical names of the services is an important part of celebrating our history and honouring the men and women who served Canada in World War II, Korea and beyond. I am very proud to be re-forging that link between our veterans and our serving soldiers, sailors and air personnel."

KEY MESSAGES
- Our government believes that an important element of Canada's military heritage was lost when, in 1968, the Canadian Forces Reorganization Act unified the Army, Navy and Air Force into a single service.
- [*not shown: same content from messages in the public affairs plan (see Appendix 4)*]

ROLLOUT

COMMUNICATIONS PRODUCTS
- ☒ Media Advisory
- ☒ Speech
- ☒ News Release
- ☒ Backgrounder(s) – Historical information on each of the three services / organization of the CF
- ☒ Fact Sheet – Information on each of the three flags
- ☐ Biographies
- ☒ Talking Points
- ☒ Q&A – To include
- ☐ M.P. / Caucus Kit
- ☒ Props (describe) – Flags (see below)
- ☐ Post-Event Media (Twitter, Facebook)
- ☒ Web Content – CF website content would be revamped to reflect the restored names
- ☒ Photo Release – Combat Camera photos/videos
- ☐ Other (describe)
- ☐ For information
- ☐ Comment

OTHER BACKGROUND INFORMATION:
- There have been several flags used by the Royal Canadian Navy, as well as at least two variants of the RCAF flag. Proposed historical flags for use at the announcement would be as follows:
  1 – The Blue Ensign – A traditional flag of the Royal Canadian Navy
  2 – Canadian Army Battle Flag – Approved in 1939 and used in WWII
  3 – The Ensign of the Royal Canadian Air Force – A traditional flag of the RCAF

MEDIA PLAN

PLANNING
☒ Live Coverage (check if yes) – Access to the Citadel would be negotiated with CTV, CBC, Sun
☒ Photographer booked (to distribute photos to media) – Combat Camera
☐ Readout

STRATEGY
- Maximize national coverage

PROMOTING THE EVENT
Media Advisory
- DND website (forces.gc.ca), MarketWire
Contacting Media
- TBD

FOLLOW-UP MEDIA (ONE-ON-ONES)
English Media Interviews
- List proposed interviews
French Media Interviews
- List proposed interviews
Multicultural Media Interviews
- List proposed interviews

MEP APPROVED BY:
John Doe (Press Secretary, Hon. Peter MacKay)

Note: Abridged for length by author.

Glossary

This glossary contains key communications-related concepts used in *Brand Command*. This list, partially derived from *Political Marketing in Canada* (UBC Press, 2012, 257–63) and *Political Communication in Canada* (UBC Press, 2014, 247–54), provides important contextual relevance.

access to information (or freedom of information): The legislated provision that citizens have the right to request and obtain records from their government within a reasonable time period, subject to reasonable limitations. Among the limitations are files received from other governments in confidence, files that might harm diplomatic or military activities, files that might injure a person, or files that might harm the jurisdiction's economic interests. Advice and recommendations prepared for senior government officials, including ministers, are normally exempt. Coordinators interpret the legislation to determine what must be released verbatim, what must be redacted, and what must be withheld.

advertising: Any controlled, mediated (print, television, radio, and Internet), and paid form of communication whose objective is to influence the opinion, choice, or behaviour of its destined audience. See also *attack ad.*

agenda setting: Agenda setting occurs when extensive media coverage of an issue increases people's perceptions of its importance. The more coverage an issue receives, the more likely people are to perceive that it is important. The amount of attention devoted to particular issues in the news can influence political priorities and policy responses.

attack ad: Negative advertising that emphasizes the personal characteristics of an opponent rather than just political or policy aspects. One notorious example in Canada was the Jean Chrétien "face" ads featured during the 1993 federal election campaign.

attentive public: The small proportion of citizens who follow political happenings, including issues and events not treated as leading news stories.

blog: A blog (short for weblog) is a low-cost, publicly available, single or multiauthored web publication that has limited external editorial oversight. See also *social media.*

brand ambassador: Any individual perceived as speaking on behalf of an organization. The greater the individual's power, the more the remarks are assumed to reflect the official position of the organization.

branding: Branding is the overall perception of a product or organization and often employs familiar logos or slogans to evoke meanings, ideas, and associations in the consumer. In politics, branding involves repetition of spoken, written, and visual messages that are determined by the strategists at the apex of the organization. A political brand is deeper than a political image because brands are comprised of tangible and non-tangible components including personal experiences, emotional attachments, and partisan loyalties. See also *image.*

celebritization: According star treatment to a person or group. This involves a style of media coverage in entertainment programming that elevates famous people and favours charismatic personalities. See also *politainment.*

centralization: The concept that information, power, and communications strategy are clustered around core decision makers. In the federal government, centralization normally refers to central agencies, such as the Prime Minister's Office, Privy Council Office, Treasury Board, and Department of Finance. Within political parties, it normally refers to a leader's concentration of power and inner circle. Centralization constrains the independence of line departments, junior ministers, parliamentarians, and election candidates.

database marketing: Information on electors stored in a database and used to create targeted marketing messages. In Canada, political parties begin with information obtained from the list of electors. See also *direct marketing; microtargeting;* and *relationship marketing.*

debranding (or anti-branding): The use of political communications to inflict damage to an opponent's brand. See also *attack ad* and *oppo.*

direct marketing: The communication of precise messages in a cost-efficient manner – via direct mail, telemarketing, direct dialogues, personalized emails, or texts to portable communications devices – directly to targeted individuals, thereby bypassing filters such as the mass media.

election platform/manifesto: A document identifying a political party's commitments and policy proposals that, should the party form government, will guide the government's agenda.

election turnout: The proportion of electors who voted in an election.

fourth estate: A term suggesting that the mainstream media play such a vital role in democratic government that they are accorded institutional status on the scale of the three branches of government (executive, legislative, judicial). The media are positioned as impartial actors who research political decisions and government behaviour while filtering and mediating publicity and propaganda. This accountability function occurs on behalf of the broader citizenry. See also *mass media* and *press gallery.*

frames: Frames are interpretive cues used to present and give meaning to social and political issues by emphasizing or excluding specific elements. The political elite as well as the media develop frames to define political debates. Frames provide targeted audiences with definitions of social and political problems or issues along with the agendas of political actors involved in the debates and their proposed solutions or potential outcomes. See also *framing* and *images.*

framing: Framing is both a strategic communicative process and an effect of the mediatization of politics. As a strategic process, it is the act of shaping or presenting issues, such as political ones, by using frames to reflect particular agendas and influence public opinion. As an effect, it is the in-direct consequence of exposure to media coverage of politics over public opinion. The public's understanding of political issues is therefore influ-enced by the dominant frames used to define them. See also *frames* and *image*.

game frame: The media's treatment of politics and issues as a game that reduces complex matters to an assessment of winners and losers. This extends to media analysis of the strategy behind political decisions, par-ticularly those involving political marketing. See also *horse-race journalism* and *strategy frame*.

gatekeeping: A process in which news editors select and favour certain types of stories over others, thereby controlling the flow and content of information, political or otherwise, and ultimately determining the news. Gatekeeping is highly influenced by the subjective attitudes or biases of journalists and editors and results in a hierarchy of news stories presented to the public. See also *agenda setting* and *fourth estate*.

get out the vote: Mobilization strategies designed to ensure that supporters turn out to cast ballots on election day. GOTV increasingly uses segment-ation and voter profiling to identify whom to target, and direct marketing (emails, mobile texts, or phone calls) is often employed to reach key seg-ments by drawing on information stored in party databases.

horse-race journalism: The tendency of news media to report predomin-antly on opinion polls, campaign events, or leaders at the expense of electoral issues. This results in media coverage of even routine political events becoming mini contests in which the focus is on winning and losing. As an election campaign climaxes, there is less coverage of contestants who are behind in opinion polls and thus cannot influence the outcome of the race, and a fascination with who is leading in the polls. See also *gatekeeping* and *politainment*.

image: The mental impression or perception of an object, being, or concept, such as a politician, political party, or public policy. Images are subjective because of the ways in which their target audiences receive, absorb, process, and evoke political communications. The public images of political actors are imaginary constructs shaped by information and visuals controlled and filtered by political parties, public relations personnel, the media, pundits, and others. See also *branding* and *framing*.

image bites: Visual snippets, often in the form of digital visual files (photographs, videos) whose brevity accommodates the media's demand for succinct visuals easily accessible at no cost. See also *information subsidies* and *sound bites*.

information subsidies: Newsworthy information designed to be easily reproduced by the media, such as a press conference or news release. Increasingly, this means low-cost information distributed electronically by political organizations, such as social media posts, digital photographs, and online videos. Newsrooms benefit from speedy information, and audiences have access to a wider variety of news. However, the objectivity and integrity of such controlled content can be suspect, especially if the source has political motives.

infotainment: The treatment of information in an entertaining manner to attract and sustain audience interest. See also *politainment*.

interelection period: The time between official election campaign periods. In Canada, the interelection period, unlike campaign periods, is not regulated by extraordinary limitations on fundraising activities, spending, or political communications. See also *permanent campaign*.

issue publics: Individuals and groups who actively wade into political communication when a pet issue is in the news.

market intelligence: Empirical data on the political marketplace and public views, also known as market research. Collecting market intelligence involves quantitative and qualitative methods such as polls, opinion surveys, focus groups, role playing, consultation, and analysis of existing public census data and election records. A political party relies on market intelligence to prioritize issues, develop and refine communications strategies, and present itself as the most competent party to address those issues.

market orientation: A willingness to use market intelligence and other data to assist in the identification and understanding of audience concerns and priorities, and to incorporate them into the design of the product or service. A market-oriented organization therefore engages in far more consultation and dialogue with the public than does an organization that is product or sales oriented, and is more responsive to audiences' needs and wants. See also *product orientation* and *sales orientation*.

mass media/news media: Print and broadcast news outlets that reach a mass audience, such as newspapers, magazines, radio, and television. They are also referred to as the mainstream/traditional/conventional media because of the growing presence of alternative information channels, including blogs, online media, community news outlets, transit publications, and social media. See also *fourth estate*.

master brand: The concept that an umbrella brand ties all sub-brands and communications together. This requires a central command that imposes message discipline on brand ambassadors and communications products.

media logic: The theory that institutional actors change their behaviour in response to how journalists gather and report news.

media management: The strategies and techniques employed by PR personnel in their interactions with the media, particularly tactics designed to control the message and frame.

media relations: Activities undertaken to manage and optimize interactions with the news media, such as news releases, pseudo-events, and fielding questions from journalists.

message event proposal: A policy instrument created by communications personnel in Stephen Harper's PMO requiring departments to provide the PCO and PMO with detailed plans for public events, such as ministerial announcements.

microtargeting: A strategic use of resources, uncovered through market intelligence, designed to focus communications on small segments of the electorate whose profiles indicate a propensity to support the sponsor. Sometimes called hypersegmentation, this process relies on complex voter profiling activities or databases. One such example in Canada was the Conservatives' use of micropolicies such as boutique tax credits targeted at construction workers and truck drivers.

narrowcasting: The act of selecting media, based on the nature of the communication, most likely to reach targeted market segments, for example communicating with target groups by advertising on sports or lifestyle specialty channels.

New Political Governance: A theory in public administration that political elites' desire to control all communications politicizes government. See also *permanent campaign.*

New Public Management: A theory in public administration that governments have been adopting private sector practices since the 1980s in an effort to modernize their relationships with citizens while achieving cost efficiencies.

oppo: Short for opposition research, oppo involves the collection of information on political opponents to discredit a target or defend oneself. Internet media have increased the ability to gather details and opportunities to disseminate findings. See also *debranding.*

partisanship: A person's psychological ties to a political party. Every party has a core of strong partisans who might or might not publicly self-identify as such.

party brand: All information that an individual has on a political party, including its name, logo, colour scheme, current and past leaders, candidates, policies, and overall record. A party brand generates emotional responses and loyalties and facilitates voter decision making. See also *branding* and *partisanship.*

permanent campaign: Electioneering throughout governance, which often involves leveraging public resources. This is more prevalent with fixed-date election legislation because all political parties maintain a state of election readiness that builds as the election approaches. Non-stop campaigning is most pronounced in the final year of a four-year cycle, during by-elections, and during the uncertainty of minority government when the possibility of a sudden election campaign is ever-present.

personal brand: All information that an individual has on a public figure, including her or his name, physical characteristics, attire, mannerisms, career path, political views, accomplishments and gaffes, and personal life. This includes impressions about, and feelings toward, a politician's image. See also *branding* and *personalization.*

personalization: The self-disclosure of private and personal details by politicians and the increased attention from the news media on the private lives of politicians, such as their family.

politainment: The media's treatment of politics as entertainment to stimulate audience interest. Market-oriented journalism is pressured by audiences' changing news habits and penchant for simplicity, which has evolving implications for news production.

political communications: The role of communications in politics, including the generation of messages by political actors (political organizations, non-profits, citizens, the media) and their transmission as well as reception.

political marketing: The application of business marketing concepts to the practice and study of politics and government. With political marketing, a political organization uses business techniques to inform and shape its strategic behaviour, designed to satisfy citizens' needs and wants. Strategies and tools include branding, e-marketing, focus groups, GOTV, internal marketing, listening exercises, opposition research, polling, public relations, segmentation, strategic product development, volunteer management, voter-driven communications, voter expectation management, and voter profiling.

political symbols: Visual icons that act as cognitive placeholders and simplify complex information, such as flags or colours.

press gallery: An organization composed of journalists accredited to cover the activities of the legislature, notably the Ottawa-based Canadian Parliamentary Press Gallery.

priming: Communications activities that seek to influence the criteria that journalists and citizens employ when evaluating subject matter.

product oriented: An approach to the marketplace guided by the assumption that audiences want a product or service simply by becoming aware of it and recognizing its value. Little consideration is given to gathering and using market intelligence to design or promote what is offered. See also *market oriented* and *sales oriented*.

professionalism: Refers to the media's treatment of political actors' communications as a proxy for political prowess.

propaganda: The subversive use of political communications to generate public support for an agenda or course of action. Propaganda is manipulative because it methodically exploits socio-psychological levers, often through controlled images that provoke strong emotional responses.

pseudo-events: Events coordinated for no other reason than to maximize publicity by providing the media with something to report. See also *information subsidies* and *media logic*.

pseudo-scandal: Exuberant media treatment of controversy as though it is a major outrage or crisis.

public opinion research: The collection of intelligence from a sample of the population designed to measure the public's views on issues, policies, leaders, and parties. The most common forms are opinion surveys and focus groups. See also *market intelligence*.

public relations: PR involves the strategic use of communications tools and media relations techniques to optimize interactions between an organization and its stakeholders.

publicity: The use of media relations and/or other communications to generate public awareness of a subject or topic.

relationship marketing: The use of marketing to build customer relationships and long-term associations sustained through commitment, loyalty, mutual benefit, and trust.

sales oriented: An approach to the marketplace that uses research data to design strategies for selling products to targeted audience segments. Emphasis is placed on research for advertising and message design, and on publicity and even propaganda that stimulates an emotional reaction. See also *market orientation* and *product orientation*.

segmentation: Division of electors into new groups to allow more efficient targeting of political resources and creation of new segments, such as ethnic minorities or seniors, as society evolves. Segments can be targeted by policy, communication, or GOTV, as well as to encourage greater volunteer activity. See also *microtargeting.*

social media: Internet-based applications in which users create and share content. Includes applications such as social networking (Facebook, Flickr, Instagram, Pinterest), blogs, microblogs (Tumblr, Twitter), online videos (YouTube, Vine), wikis (Wikipedia), and social bookmarking (Digg). They are also known as Web 2.0.

sound bites: The reduction of public remarks to short audio clips, usually from seven to fifteen seconds. This conditions public speakers to repeat their core messages and deliver quips in interesting ways. See also *image bites* and *media logic.*

spin: The framing of information to reflect a bias favourable to the sender, ideally without receivers noticing.

strategy frame: The tendency of political journalism to report news through a strategy lens and to treat punditry about strategy as newsworthy in itself. This includes reporting on PR attempts to manipulate the media and speculating about the strategic implications of a political actor's options. See also *game frame* and *politainment.*

whole of government: WOG is an umbrella approach to government that seeks to unify the disparate departments and agencies into a cohesive agenda.

Notes

PREFACE

1 CBC (2005a).
2 Wherry (2015).
3 Liberal Party of Canada (2015b, 2).
4 Liberal Party of Canada (2015b, 5).
5 Trudeau (2014, 21). This method is far more the norm in the parliamentary system than caricatures of leaders suggest; see Esselment, Lees-Marshment, and Marland (2014).
6 Levine (1993, 37, 39).
7 Levine (1993, 65).
8 Dafoe (1964 [1922], 68 and 83).
9 Trudeau (2015b).
10 CBC (2015e). Missing televised *The National* content transcribed by the author.
11 Edwards (2015).
12 Urback (2015).
13 Curry (2015c).
14 Canadian Press (2016).
15 Geddes (2015).
16 Cheadle (2015a).
17 For example, Kellner (2016, 124).
18 For example, see Gollom (2016).
19 Part of the government's email transformation initiative. See Shared Services Canada (2015).
20 Rana (2015a).
21 Rana (2015b).
22 Rana (2015a).

23 For example, Trudeau (2015a). This borrows from a growing norm in provincial politics.
24 Prime Minister of Canada (2015). Guides were available during the Harper era, however this was not widely publicized.
25 Saunders (2015). For more on delivery units see Barber (2008, 2015). For information about delivery in Canada from a political marketing perspective, see Esselment (2012a, 2012b).
26 See Akin (2015).
27 Prime Minister's Office (2016).
28 Ryckewaert (2015).
29 Young (2015).
30 Liberal Party (2015, 10).
31 Harris (2015).
32 Bryden (2015).
33 Liberal Party of Canada (2015b, 4); Trudeau (2015a).
34 See Appendices 1 and 2; Adams (2012); Kerby and Marland (2015, 15).
35 Raj (2015), Scotti (2015).
36 Trudeau (2015a).
37 Liberal Party of Canada (2015c); Morneau (2015).
38 Ambrose (2015).
39 Curry (2015d).
40 Van Dusen (2015).
41 Adams (2012).
42 Treasury Board of Canada Secretariat (2011a).
43 Citizenship and Immigration Canada (2015); Curry (2015e).
44 Curry (2015f).
45 Prime Minister of Canada (2015).
46 Dinning (2015, 2).

ACKNOWLEDGMENTS

1 MacCharles and Benzie (2011).

CHAPTER 1: THE CENTRALIZATION OF COMMUNICATIONS IN GOVERNMENT AND POLITICS

1 LeDuc and Pammett (2014).
2 Naumetz (2011a).
3 For a comparative overview, see Eshuis and Klijn (2012).
4 Levine (1993, 153).
5 Petty (2007).
6 CTV Chief Political Correspondent Craig Oliver, quoted in Ryckewaert (2011).
7 Curry (2014).
8 Simpson (2015).
9 Martin (2010), M. Harris (2014), Bourrie (2015), and Whittington (2015), respectively.

10 Turner (2009) and Rathgeber (2014), respectively.
11 Simpson (2001).
12 For example, Lathrop (2003); Rose (2000).
13 Aucoin (2008, 2012); Aucoin, Bakvis, and Jarvis (2012); Eichbaum and Shaw (2008).
14 Thomas (2013, 69).
15 Kozolanka (2006, 360).
16 Hacker, Giles, and Guerrero (2003).
17 Mayer (2004).
18 Cosgrove (2007, 7).
19 Milewicz and Milewicz (2014, 255).
20 Baum (2011).
21 White House (2014).
22 BBC (2005).
23 Kavanagh and Seldon (2000, 254–57).
24 Rigby (2015); Ross (2015).
25 Mickey (1997).
26 Bachrach and Baratz (1962).
27 Thomas (2013, 79); also Thomas (2010).
28 Hood and Lodge (2006, 48).
29 Thomas (2013, 56); also Thomas (2010, 81).
30 Needham (2005).
31 Zaller (1999, 3).
32 Popkin (1991, 236).
33 Zaller (1999, 15).
34 Bekkers and Moody (2015).
35 Marland, Giasson, and Lees-Marshment (2012); Marland, Giasson, and Small (2014).
36 For instance, Riddell (2005).
37 Among them, Canadian Association of Journalists (2010); Canadian Science Writers' Association (2012).
38 Cappella and Jamieson (1996).
39 Cappella and Jamieson (1997).
40 Savoie (1999a, 1999b, 2003, 2010, 2013, 2015).
41 Poguntke and Webb (2005).
42 Schlesinger (1973).
43 Gould (1998).
44 Bakvis (2001).
45 White (2005, 172).
46 Lewis (2013, 800).
47 Kerby (2009, 2011).
48 Bernier, Brownsey, and Howlett (2005).
49 Dowding (2013).
50 Davidson (2011).

51 Chrétien (2008, 7); emphasis added.
52 Savoie (1999a, 95).
53 Savoie (2010, 87).
54 Savoie (2015, 43).
55 White (2005, 67).
56 Bernier, Brownsey, and Howlett (2005, 245).
57 Privy Council Office (2013c).
58 Grayson (2001). See also Canada Public Service Agency (2007a).
59 Shively (2013, 16).
60 Scammell (2007, 176).
61 Campbell and Szablowski (1979).
62 Thomas (2013, 78).
63 Goldenberg (2006) and Flanagan (2009a), respectively.
64 Gossage (1986) and Kinsella (2001), respectively.
65 McLean (2012).
66 Delacourt (2013).
67 Grabe and Bucy (2009) and Cosgrove (2007), respectively.
68 Rose (2000).
69 For instance, Azoulay and Kapferer (2003).
70 Scammell (2007, 181).
71 Fletcher (1977, 86).
72 Aucoin (2008, 29).
73 Delacourt (2013, 207).
74 Flanagan (2009a, 319).
75 Levine (1993).
76 Levine (2014).
77 Esser (2008); Grabe and Bucy (2009).
78 De Landtsheer, De Vries, and Vertessen (2008); Esser (2008); Grabe and Bucy (2009, 60).
79 Berg and Lune (2012, 329).
80 Butler (1958, 40–49).
81 Ibid., 30–31.
82 Ibid., 89.
83 Some interviews were the basis of research published in Marland (2012a); Marland and Flanagan (2013, 2015); Marland, Lewis, and Flanagan (forthcoming).
84 Ibbitson (2010b).
85 Savoie (1999a, x).
86 Nelson (1995).

CHAPTER 2: MARKETING AND BRANDING IN POLITICS

1 For more, see Delacourt (2013); Marland (2003).
2 For example, Keith (1960).
3 Ford (1905).
4 Fox (1984).

5 Ford (1945).
6 Ford (1974).
7 Ames (1911); Kline et al. (1991).
8 See, for instance, Paré and Berger (2008).
9 CBC (2005b).
10 For example, party staffer (GG) (2006).
11 Lees-Marshment (2001a, 232).
12 Lees-Marshment (2001a, 2001b, 2006). In one internal email, Flanagan (2002b) described Harper as wanting to lead a "market-oriented party." However, the expression referred to support for the free market (e.g., smaller government, lower taxes, deregulation).
13 McLean (2012, 144).
14 Gaber (2007, 221).
15 Lilleker (2010, 111–12).
16 Grabe and Bucy (2009, 5).
17 Lilleker (2010, 170).
18 Kozolanka (2014, 4).
19 Mayer (2004, 629).
20 de Chernatony and Riley (1998).
21 American Marketing Association (2014).
22 Canada Public Service Agency (2007a).
23 Hynes (2009).
24 de Chernatony and Riley (1998).
25 Wood (2000).
26 Baker et al. (1986).
27 Hoyer and Brown (1990).
28 Muniz and O'Guinn (2001).
29 Hutton et al. (2001).
30 Interbrand (2013).
31 Isaacson (2013, 460).
32 See, for instance, Firestone (1970, 26).
33 Chaiken (1980).
34 Esselment (2014, 24). See also Needham (2005).
35 Chambers (2015).
36 Conservative Party of Canada (2015c).
37 Eshuis and Klijn (2012, 13).
38 Nimijean (2014, 192–93).
39 Thomas (2013, 53).
40 Dahl (2005).
41 For example, Smith (1999).
42 Calculated from Parliament of Canada (2014).
43 Fekete (2014b).
44 Curry (2009).
45 O'Malley (2015).

46 D. Martin (2007).
47 Ryckewaert (2013).
48 Bowler, Farrell, and Katz (1999, 7).
49 Russell (2014).
50 Savoie (2013, 74).
51 McGregor (2012a).
52 Franks (1987, 104).
53 Kerby (2011, 607).
54 House of Commons of Canada (2015).
55 Chong (2015).
56 Blidook (2012, 121).
57 Innis (2008).
58 McLuhan (1964, Chapter 1).
59 Russell (2008, 101).
60 Brown (1987, 547).
61 Campbell and Szablowski (1979); Savoie (1999a). See also Dwivedi and Gow (1999, 80).
62 Thomas (2013, 67).
63 White (2005, 18).
64 Savoie (1999a, 244).
65 Aronczyk and Brady (2015, 168).
66 Speed, Butler, and Collins (2015).
67 Rose (2010, 257).
68 For information on this line of analysis, see Giasson, Jansen, and Koop (2014).

CHAPTER 3: THE TUMULTUOUS DIGITAL MEDIA ENVIRONMENT

1   Taras (2015, 3).
2   Library of Parliament (2004); Statistics Canada (2013).
3   Industry Canada (2008).
4   Google (2013).
5   Roberts, Yaya, and Manolis (2014).
6   Savoie (1999a, 133).
7   Coddington, Molyneux, and Lawrence (2014).
8   Albaugh and Waddell (2014, 108).
9   Brown and Lloyd (2014).
10 CBC (2014a).
11 Schudson (1989, 271).
12 Entman (2007).
13 Schudson (1989). For a summary of political biases, see Chapter 1 in Street (2011).
14 Berkowitz (1990).
15 Street (2011, 48).
16 Chadwick (2013).
17 Blumler and Kavanagh (1999, 221).

18 Chadwick (2013).
19 Soroka (2002).
20 Strömbäck and van Aelst (2013, 342).
21 Gaber (2007, 223).
22 Entman (2007, 164); Scheufele and Tewksbury (2007, 11).
23 Cobb, Ross, and Ross (1976); also Parmelee (2014).
24 CBC (2014b).
25 Entman (1993, 52); also Popkin (1991, 82); Scheufele and Tewksbury (2007).
26 Parmelee (2014).
27 Cheadle (2015b).
28 Naumetz (2014b).
29 CBC (2014c).
30 McQueen (2004).
31 Party staffer (RN) (2005).
32 Gandy (1980).
33 Boorstin (1992).
34 Liberal Party of Canada (2010).
35 Chase (2009).
36 Bricker and Ibbitson (2013).
37 Campion-Smith (2014a).
38 CBC (2010).
39 Canadian Press (2011a).
40 Levitz (2013b).
41 Marland (2012a); Marland (2014a).
42 Campion-Smith (2009); Marland (2012a).
43 Chase (2015a).
44 Boesveld (2013); Puzic (2013).
45 McKie (2010); Supreme Court of Canada (2011).
46 For a summary of politics as entertainment, see Chapter 3 in Street (2011).
47 Franks (1987, 157).
48 Comber and Mayne (1986, 17–18).
49 Underwood (2001); see also Waddell (2012).
50 van Zoonen (2005).
51 National Arts Centre (2009).
52 Rana (2009).
53 The other scrolling photos were public service messages encouraging Canadians to prepare for winter driving, urging them to consider being blood and organ donors, and showing the prime minister participating in pre-budget consultations.
54 De Landtsheer, De Vries, and Vertessen (2008, 220); van Aelst, Sheafer, and Stanyer (2012); van Zoonen (2005, 74).
55 Praxius Public Strategies (2005).
56 O'Neill (2006).
57 Smith (2011).

58 McGregor (2012b).
59 Rojek (2001, 17).
60 Ibid. (105).
61 Party staffer (WS) (2005).
62 Lazarus (2009).
63 Quill and Campion-Smith (2010).
64 Taber (2010b).
65 Johnson (2012).
66 Scammell (1999, 80).
67 Aalberg, Strömbäck, and de Vreese (2011, 167).
68 Pétry and Bastien (2013).
69 Kerbel, Apee, and Ross (2000).
70 Sherman and Schiffman (2002, 56). This includes pollsters' erroneous projec-
    tions of incumbent party defeat in the 2012 Alberta and 2013 BC provincial
    campaigns.
71 Matthews, Pickup, and Cutler (2012, 281).
72 Pétry and Bastien (2013, 22).
73 Kerby and Marland (2015).
74 Seymour-Ure (1982, 49).
75 Aalberg, Strömbäck, and de Vreese (2011).
76 MediaMiser (2005).
77 Laghi (2006).
78 Ibbitson (2010a).
79 See, for example, Bowler and Karp (2004).
80 Goffman (1959, 208–9).
81 Alphonso (2009).
82 Wells (2014).
83 Soberman (2005, 421).
84 Conservative Party of Canada (2005a).
85 See, for example, Kinsella (2001).
86 Brader (2006, 4).
87 Dovring (1959, 5).
88 Jowett and O'Donnell (2006, 17); also O'Shaughnessy (2004).
89 Rose (2000).
90 Pinkleton (1997).

CHAPTER 4: PUBLIC SECTOR BRANDS

1 Eshuis and Klijn (2012, 20–25) identify tangible goods, processes, organizations,
   people, and places.
2 Chiu (2007). This extends to museums; see Aronczyk and Brady (2015).
3 Rose (2010, 270).
4 Grayson (2001).
5 Nimijean (2005; 2006a, 69; 2006b; 2014).
6 Kennedy (2015a).

7 Nimijean (2006a, 78).
8 Potter (2009).
9 Department of International Trade (2005).
10 Potter (2009, 28).
11 For more on this, see Marland (2014b).
12 Hudson and Ritchie (2009).
13 Rantisi and Leslie (2006, 366).
14 Marzano and Scott (2009).
15 For example, Pasotti (2010).
16 Hudson and Ritchie (2009, 223).
17 Canadian Tourism Commission (2006, 32).
18 For example, Xing and Chalip (2006).
19 Canadian Olympic Committee (2013, 19).
20 Hinch (2006).
21 Cormack (2012).
22 CanWest News (2006). For more, see Scherer and McDermott (2011).
23 Souiden, Pons, and Mayrand (2011).
24 Innes, Kerr, and Hobbs (2010).
25 Wood and Somerville (2007).
26 Muzellec and Lambkin (2006).
27 Interbrand (2014).
28 McMullan et al. (2009).
29 Public Works and Government Services Canada (2011a).
30 For example, Campbell (2007).
31 Cudmore (2014).
32 Howlett (2009).
33 Pyles (2008, 446).
34 Popkin (1991, 102–7).
35 Kozolanka (2006, 344).
36 Prime Minister of Canada (2012).
37 Manning (1989).
38 Party staffer (JH) (1992).
39 Wesley's preferred descriptor. See Posner (2009) for more about the nexus between academics and practitioners.
40 Wesley and Moyes (2014, 77). See also McGrane (2011, 82).
41 CBC (2015a).
42 Diebel (2008).
43 Conservative Party (2015b).
44 Quoted in Lilleker and Negrine (2003, 60).
45 Panebianco (1988).
46 Hopkin and Paolucci (1999).
47 Carty (2004, 11).
48 Carty (2002).
49 For example, Woon and Pope (2008).

50 Karlberg (2002, 13).
51 Smith and French (2009, 212).
52 Smith (2009, 211).
53 Merolla, Stephenson, and Zechmeister (2008).
54 For more on this, see Marland and Flanagan (2013).
55 For instance, Needham (2005); White and de Chernatony (2002).
56 Lilleker and Negrine (2003, 60).
57 For instance, White and de Chernatony (2002, 50).
58 O'Shaughnessy (2009).
59 Ditchburn (2013a).
60 Chaney (2001); Guthey and Jackson (2005).
61 Lair, Sullivan, and Cheney (2005).
62 Speed, Butler, and Collins (2015).
63 Guzmán and Sierra (2009, 208).
64 Goffman (1959, 1).
65 Zavattaro (2010).
66 Javidan and Waldman (2003).
67 Adair-Toteff (2005).
68 Bligh and Kohles (2009, 484).
69 Ferguson and Ferguson (1978). See also Grabe and Bucy (2009, 202–11).
70 Lair, Sullivan, and Cheney (2005); also van Zoonen (2005).
71 Trimble and Everitt (2010).
72 Everitt and Camp (2009, 33).
73 Lalancette, Drouin, and Lemarier-Saulnier (2014).
74 Flanagan (2001).
75 Plamondon (2009, 410).
76 Blatchford (2015).
77 Chrétien (1985).
78 E. May (2009, 28).
79 Trudeau (2014).
80 Harper (2013).
81 Mulcair (2015).
82 Strictly speaking, this refers to a "product line extension" and treats Justin Trudeau as a lower-calorie version of the original Trudeau product. In marketing, a "brand extension" is created when a brand name is attached to a product in a different category, such as a food brand name being applied to a different type of food product or a non-food product. The brand extension analogy would involve Justin Trudeau leveraging his father's fame in a cognate area, such as a human rights lawyer.
83 Reddy, Holak, and Bhat (1994).
84 Munthree, Bick, and Abratt (2006).
85 Pullig, Simmons, and Netemeyer (2006).
86 Sullivan (1990).
87 Kim and Sullivan (1998).

88 Brown et al. (1988).
89 Cosgrove (2007, 4).
90 Bó, Bó, and Snyder (2009).
91 Camp (1982); Clubok, Wilensky, and Berghorn (1969).
92 Litt (2008).
93 Ibid., 51.
94 Levine (1993, 287–90).
95 Ibid., 290.
96 Campion-Smith and Whittington (2015).
97 Kitching (2012). For more on Justin Trudeau as an idolized leader, see MacNaughton and Stoney (2014).
98 Abacus Data (2015).
99 Bryden (2013b).
100 Chase (2013).
101 Ivison (2015).
102 Kennedy (2014).

CHAPTER 5: COMMUNICATIONS SIMPLICITY AND POLITICAL MARKETING

1 Gidengil et al. (2012, 14–18).
2 Quoted in Marland, Giasson, and Lees-Marshment (2012, xiii).
3 Baker et al. (1986); Hoyer and Brown (1990); Hutchinson, Raman, and Mantrala (1994).
4 Lazarsfeld, Berelson, and Gaudet (1948).
5 Ibid.; Campbell et al. (1960).
6 For instance, Butler and Peppard (1998); Sirgy (1983).
7 Himmelweit et al. (1981, 11).
8 Newman (1994).
9 Downs (1957).
10 Popkin (1991).
11 Lodge, McGraw, and Stroh (1989).
12 Stokes (1963, 373); Clarke, Kornberg, and Scotto (2009).
13 Stokes (1963, 373).
14 Clarke, Kornberg, and Scotto (2009, 285).
15 Gidengil et al. (2012, 61).
16 Ibid.
17 Grabe and Bucy (2009).
18 Mendelsohn (1994).
19 Bailenson et al. (2008).
20 Budesheim and DePaola (1994).
21 Rosenberg and McCafferty (1987); Rosenberg et al. (1986).
22 Sullivan and Masters (1988).
23 Popkin (1991, 38).
24 Cherulnik, Turns, and Wilderman (1990).

25 Stewart and Clarke (1992).
26 Gidengil et al. (2012, Chapter 7).
27 Keown (2007).
28 Gidengil et al. (2012, 105).
29 Taber (2011a).
30 For example, Popkin (1991, 28).
31 Chaffee and Frank (1996).
32 Blais et al. (2000).
33 Nadeau et al. (2008, 244).
34 Chaffee and Frank (1996).
35 Prior (2005).
36 Prime Minister's Office (2006).
37 Wells (2013, 251).
38 Harber (2013).
39 For instance, Finley (2004a).
40 For instance, Paré and Berger (2008, 47–48).
41 Party staffers (MC and PM) (2004).
42 Party staffer (PM) (2004).
43 Williams (1997).
44 Party staffer (PM) (2005).
45 To name some, Delacourt (2013, 199–200); Wells (2006, 155, 214).
46 Gould (1998).
47 Included as an appendix in Flanagan (2005a).
48 Flanagan (2005b).
49 Finley (2004a).
50 McGrane (2011).
51 Liberal Party of Canada (2011, 50).
52 Liberal Party of Canada (2012, 3).
53 Liberal Party of Canada (2014).
54 Flanagan (2004b, 2005f). Also respondent CS 7.
55 Wells (2013, 244).
56 Scammell (2007, 181).
57 Carty, Cross, and Young (2000, 178).
58 For example, Issenberg (2013).
59 Chamberlain (1962). See also Smith (1956).
60 Baines et al. (2003, 225); see also Newman (1994, 67–70).
61 Gandy (2001, 146); Flanagan (2009b).
62 Davidson and Binstock (2012, 21).
63 Health Canada (2005).
64 Vavrus (2007).
65 Busby (2012).
66 Conservative Party of Canada (2011). See also Lindgren (2014).
67 Privy Council Office (1966).
68 Huffington Post Canada (2013).

69 Bryden (2013a).
70 Barton (2015).
71 Some of this discussion on email marketing is expanded in Marland and Mathews (forthcoming).
72 Watters (2015a).
73 Liberal Party of Canada (2015a).
74 Conservative Party of Canada (c. 2007).
75 Naumetz (2012).
76 Chase (2008).
77 Peyton (2013).
78 For example, see Grönroos (1994).
79 For example, Ferraras (2015).
80 Berthiaume (2011).

CHAPTER 6: BRAND DISCIPLINE AND DEBRANDING

1 Davies and Mian (2010); De Landtsheer, De Vries, and Vertessen (2008).
2 For instance, CBC (2015b).
3 Watters (2015b).
4 As described in Flanagan (2005c), wherein Conservative Party elites responded to a Supreme Court decision on private health insurance.
5 Courtney (1978).
6 Katsanis (1994, 8).
7 Persky (1992).
8 Flanagan (1992).
9 Flanagan (2002a).
10 Flanagan (2005e).
11 For instance, party staffer (RN) (2005).
12 Party staffer (KB) (2004).
13 Flanagan (2005a).
14 Boswell (2011).
15 Clark (2006).
16 Taber (2011c).
17 Harper (2015).
18 For example, Flanagan (2005d).
19 Kidd (2008).
20 MacDougall (2014).
21 Foote (2014).
22 McGregor and Fekete (2014).
23 Conservative Party of Canada (2014).
24 Galloway (2010).
25 Finley (2004a).
26 Conservative Party of Canada (2005a).
27 Flanagan (2004d).

28 For instance, Liberal Party of Canada (2012).
29 Stone (2013).
30 Fitzpatrick (2013a).
31 Member of Parliament (RW) (2004b).
32 Member of Parliament (RW) (2004a).
33 Wilson (2015a).
34 Privy Council Office (2015).
35 Esselment (2012a, 136).
36 Rathgeber (2014, 85).
37 Wilson (2015a, 239, 243).
38 Lilleker (2010).
39 Ibid., 194.
40 Elliot (2011).
41 For a chronology of the scandal, see Canadian Press (2015a).
42 Wright (2013a).
43 Wright (2013b).
44 Wright (2013d).
45 Wright (2013g).
46 Wright (2013e).
47 Wright (2013c).
48 Wright (2013h).
49 Stewart-Olsen (2013).
50 Wright (2013f).
51 Bakvis (2001, 68).
52 Wynne (2014).
53 Savoie (1999a, 313).
54 Canadian Press (2011c).
55 CBC (2015d); Cowan (2015); Kennedy (2015b).
56 Clark (2006).
57 Ditchburn (2013b).
58 Campion-Smith (2014b).
59 Paré and Delacourt (2014).
60 Chase (2010).
61 Ivison (2007).
62 Galloway (2011a).
63 Fitz-Morris (2010).
64 Canadian Association of Journalists (2010).
65 Canadian Journalism Foundation (2014).
66 Member of Parliament (RW) (2004b).
67 O'Malley (2014).
68 K. May (2009b).
69 Akin (2008).
70 K. May (2009b).
71 CBC Radio (2013).

72 For example, party staffer (CO) (2005); Mulcair (2015, 135).
73 MacCharles (2011).
74 Office of the Information Commissioner of Canada (2013).
75 For example, Gingras (2012).
76 Party staffer (JR) (2001).
77 Flanagan (2004c).
78 For instance, Bruno and Lapointe (2013); Wells (2015).
79 MacNaughton and Stoney (2014, 76).
80 Brader (2006, 5); Lang, Newhagen, and Reeves (1996).
81 Finley (2004a).
82 Progressive Conservative Party of Newfoundland (1993, 48).
83 Jamieson (2000).
84 Harper (2001).
85 Bovée (1999); Daro (2015); Varoga and Rice (1999).
86 Zelizer (2010).
87 Taber (2004).
88 Canadian Press (2008).
89 MacKinnon (2014).
90 As with Harper's Canadian Alliance leadership campaign; see party staffer (JW) (2001a, 2001b).
91 Brennan and Benzie (2015).
92 Milewicz and Milewicz (2014, 241).
93 Bruno and Lapointe (2013).
94 De Souza (2013a).
95 Lavoie (2013).
96 Magnuson-Ford and Gibbs (2014).
97 *Nature* (2012).
98 Environment Canada (c. 2013).
99 Axford, Madgwick, and Turner (1992).
100 Curry (2010).
101 Taber (2010c).
102 K. May (2009a).
103 Taber (2011b).
104 Panetta (2009).
105 Whittington and Campion-Smith (2008).

CHAPTER 7: CENTRAL GOVERNMENT AGENCIES AND COMMUNICATIONS

1 Wilson (1887, 201, 208).
2 Tupper (2003, 233).
3 Treasury Board of Canada Secretariat (2008b).
4 Treasury Board of Canada Secretariat (2011a).
5 Ibid., 4–5.
6 Roy (2013, 22).
7 Aucoin (2012, 188).

8   Ibid., 189.
9   Ibid.
10 Davies (1998, 122); Van Dorpe and Horton (2011, 246).
11 Tupper (2003, 234); May (2013).
12 May (2015).
13 Mulgan (2007).
14 Treasury Board of Canada Secretariat (2008b, 2015).
15 Wilson (2015b).
16 Ryckewaert (2011).
17 Burgess (2014); Maher (2011).
18 Dwivedi and Gow (1999, 42).
19 Savoie (1999a, 319).
20 Aberbach, Putnam, and Rockman (1981, 260).
21 Hood and Lodge (2006, viii).
22 Treasury Board of Canada Secretariat (2012a).
23 Privy Council Office (1946).
24 Privy Council Office (1950).
25 Privy Council Office (1957).
26 Privy Council Office (1965).
27 The communications policy of the government of Canada is an important framework for the administration of communications practices in the federal government. Readers are encouraged to consult the latest version of the policy via the Treasury Board of Canada Secretariat website (www.tbs-sct.gc.ca).
28 Treasury Board of Canada Secretariat (2012a).
29 Ibid.
30 Beeby (2014a).
31 Wells (2013, 24).
32 Privy Council Office (2013b).
33 Doyle (2007).
34 Axworthy (1988, 259).
35 Savoie (1999b).
36 CBC Radio (2013).
37 Axworthy (1988).
38 Goldenberg (2006, 93).
39 Ibid., Chapter 5. See also Trudeau (2015a).
40 Campbell and Szablowski (1979, 68).
41 Public Works and Government Services Canada (2014a).
42 Brodie (2012, 33).
43 Ryckewaert (2014).
44 Leblanc (2015).
45 Bonoguore (2006).
46 Calculated from Thomas (2010, 131).
47 Beardsley (2012).
48 d'Aquino (1974, 59).

49 Savoie (1999b, 660).
50 Savoie (1999a, 131).
51 Blanchfield and Bronskill (2010).
52 Privy Council Office (2010, 2013a).
53 Savoie (1999a, 126).
54 Privy Council Office (2011, 45).
55 Treasury Board of Canada Secretariat (2011c).
56 Savoie (1999a, 251).
57 De Souza (2013b).
58 Treasury Board of Canada Secretariat (2012a).
59 Johnson (1971, 349).
60 Ibid., 362.
61 Veilleux and Savoie (1988).
62 Treasury Board of Canada Secretariat (2013a).
63 Treasury Board of Canada Secretariat (2012a).
64 Ibid.
65 Trudeau (2015a).
66 Johnson (1971).
67 Public Works and Government Services Canada (2012a, 1).
68 Public Works and Government Services Canada (2005, 29).
69 Ibid., 30.
70 Communication Canada (2002).
71 Communication Canada (2003).
72 Public Works and Government Services Canada (2005, 42).
73 Public Works and Government Services Canada (2014b).
74 Canadian Heritage (2014).
75 Fekete (2013).
76 Canadian Press (2014).
77 Canadian Heritage (2013). See also Appendix A in Treasury Board of Canada Secretariat (1990).
78 Finance Canada (2013a).
79 Finance Canada (2010).
80 Hewson Bridge and Smith Ltd. (2007).
81 Canada Revenue Agency (2008).
82 Canada Revenue Agency (c. 2008).
83 Canadian Wheat Board (c. 2012).
84 Leblanc (2013).
85 Radio-Canada (2013).
86 Surridge (2012).

CHAPTER 8: BRANDING IN CANADIAN PUBLIC ADMINISTRATION

1 This overview is based on Chapter 7 in Canada (1969b).
2 Balzer (2011, 7).
3 Canada (1969b, iii).

4 Firestone (1970, 193).
5 Canada (1969b, 160).
6 Ibid., 189–90.
7 Ibid., 193.
8 Donoghue (1993, 106).
9 Nelson (1995).
10 Clerk of the Privy Council (2007).
11 Canada Public Service Agency (2007a).
12 Advisory Committee on Senior Level Retention and Compensation (2008).
13 Canada Public Service Agency (2007b); Public Works and Government Services Canada (2008a).
14 Centre for Excellence in Communications (2014).
15 Centre of Excellence for Public Sector Marketing (2009).
16 Public Works and Government Services Canada (2008b).
17 Aucoin (1995, 2012); Hood (1991); Tupper (2003).
18 Treasury Board of Canada Secretariat (2014a).
19 Treasury Board of Canada Secretariat (2012a).
20 Environment Canada (c. 2010).
21 Treasury Board of Canada Secretariat (2012a).
22 Galloway (2009).
23 Spears (2012).
24 Treasury Board of Canada Secretariat (2014e).
25 Treasury Board of Canada Secretariat (c. 2012).
26 Naumetz (2011b).
27 CBC (2014d).
28 PR Newswire (2012).
29 O'Malley (2010).
30 Bradshaw (2014).
31 Public Works and Government Services Canada (2006, 2015a).
32 Burgess (2015).
33 Treasury Board of Canada Secretariat (2012a).
34 Rose (2000, 2).
35 News Canada (2014).
36 Canada Revenue Agency (2012a).
37 Smith (2014).
38 Treasury Board of Canada Secretariat (2014d). See also Public Works and Government Services Canada (2006); Treasury Board of Canada Secretariat (2012a); and Rose (2000, 80–84).
39 Canada Revenue Agency (2012c).
40 Phoenix Strategic Perspectives (2007b).
41 For example, Beeby (2014c).
42 S. Harris (2014).
43 Page (2006, Chapter 5).
44 Treasury Board of Canada Secretariat (2009a).

45 Redfern Research (2010, 11).
46 Canadian Press (2011b).
47 Cameron (1980).
48 Way (1993, 58).
49 Treasury Board of Canada Secretariat (2012b).
50 Public Works and Government Services Canada (2012b).
51 Treasury Board of Canada Secretariat (2010c).
52 Treasury Board of Canada Secretariat (2010b).
53 Treasury Board of Canada Secretariat (2008a).
54 Treasury Board of Canada Secretariat (2011e).
55 Treasury Board of Canada Secretariat (2006).
56 Opinion Impact (2007, 8).
57 Treasury Board of Canada Secretariat (2010a).
58 Treasury Board of Canada Secretariat (1990).
59 Treasury Board of Canada Secretariat (2000).
60 Ibid.
61 Treasury Board of Canada Secretariat (2013d).
62 Library of Parliament (2004); Small (2012).
63 D'auray (2003, 42).
64 Naumetz (2014a).
65 Treasury Board of Canada (2014).
66 Treasury Board of Canada Secretariat (2007, 2009b).
67 *Jodhan v. Attorney General of Canada* (2011).
68 Treasury Board of Canada Secretariat (2013b).
69 *Jodhan v. Attorney General of Canada* (2011, 11).
70 Human Resources and Skills Development Canada (2009a).
71 Department of National Defence (2011c).
72 Canadian Press (2013).
73 Canada Revenue Agency (2012a).
74 Small (2009).
75 Levitz (2013a).
76 Clement (2011).
77 Small (2012).
78 Privy Council Office (2012b).
79 Francoli (2011).
80 Treasury Board of Canada Secretariat (2011b).
81 Butler (2013).
82 Treasury Board of Canada Secretariat (2013c).
83 Treasury Board of Canada Secretariat (2014c).
84 Turner, Hall, and White (2015).
85 Beeby (2014b).
86 Rubin (2014).
87 Ibid.
88 Department of National Defence (2012a).

CHAPTER 9: POLITICIZATION OF GOVERNMENT COMMUNICATIONS

1 Aucoin (2008, 27); see also Aucoin (2012, 179); Aucoin, Bakvis, and Jarvis (2013).
2 Aucoin (2008, 28).
3 Powell (2011).
4 Treasury Board of Canada Secretariat (2011d).
5 Treasury Board of Canada Secretariat (2012a).
6 MacDougall (2015).
7 Privy Council Office (2013c).
8 Department of National Defence (2011d).
9 Davis (2010b); Martin (2010, 59).
10 Martin (2010, 94).
11 Campion-Smith (2008).
12 Delacourt (2010).
13 Blanchfield and Bronskill (2010).
14 Davis (2010a).
15 More information on the government of Canada's international communications can be found in Potter (2009).
16 Bank of Canada (2013).
17 The rules of committees are less formalized than those for other legislative proceedings. However, when props become a distraction, including through real-time social media commentary, the chair can ask that they be removed. See Galloway (2011b).
18 Foreign Affairs and International Trade Canada (2010).
19 Levine (1993, 324).
20 For more on this, see Marland and Flanagan (2013).
21 Lunn (2011).
22 Wallace (2011).
23 Canadian Press (2015b).
24 Department of National Defence (2011e).
25 Transcribed from CBC (2012a). I have changed the name of the donor.
26 Fekete (2014a).
27 Public Works and Government Services Canada (2015b).
28 Canadian Press (2012).
29 CBC (2012b).
30 Phoenix Strategic Perspectives (2007a).
31 Public Works and Government Services Canada (2015b).
32 Finance Canada (2013b).
33 Pugliese (2014).
34 MacGregor (2015).

CHAPTER 10: THE FUSION OF PARTY AND GOVERNMENT BRANDS

1 Gordon (2006).
2 Cheadle (2011a).

3 Department of National Defence (2012c).
4 Galloway (2007).
5 Beeby (2011).
6 Naumetz (2015).
7 Dehaas (2015).
8 Delacourt (2007).
9 Fitzpatrick (2013b).
10 Treasury Board of Canada Secretariat (2011g).
11 Treasury Board of Canada Secretariat (2011h).
12 Treasury Board of Canada Secretariat (2011f).
13 See Miljan (2011). For details about the coalition crisis, see Aucoin, Jarvis, and Turnbull (2011).
14 Finance Canada (2009a).
15 Finance Canada (2009b).
16 Human Resources and Skills Development Canada (2009b).
17 Finance Canada (2009c, 2; 2009d, 2).
18 Cheadle (2011b).
19 Aucoin (2012, 195).
20 Canada Revenue Agency (2012b).
21 Human Resources and Skills Development Canada (2009c).
22 Cheadle (2010).
23 Public Works and Government Services Canada (2011b).
24 Cheadle (2009a).
25 Fitzpatrick (2011).
26 Office of the Conflict of Interest and Ethics Commissioner (2010, 9).
27 Roman (2010).
28 Cheadle (2011b).
29 Cheadle (2011a).
30 Treasury Board of Canada Secretariat (2009c).
31 Cheadle (2011a).
32 Cheadle (2009b).
33 For example, Massicotte (2013).
34 Curry (2015b).
35 Stoney and Krawchenko (2012, 499).
36 Hall Findlay (2009).
37 Beeby (2013).
38 Curry (2015a).
39 CBC (2015c).
40 MacCharles (2014).
41 Brown and Lloyd (2014). Data are not strictly comparable; they are for illustrative purposes only.
42 Beeby (2015).
43 Leblanc (2011).
44 Chambers (2015).

45 Ibid.
46 Privy Council Office (c. 2012a).

CHAPTER 11: GOOD OR BAD FOR DEMOCRACY?

1 Lilleker (2010, 171).
2 Phase 5 (2006, 2007); Phoenix Strategic Perspectives (2005).
3 Strategic Counsel (2006).
4 CBC (2011).
5 Savigny (2008).
6 Kozolanka (2006, 344).
7 Pasotti (2010, 3).
8 Sauvageau (2012, 32).
9 O'Shaughnessy (2004, 2009).
10 Eshuis and Klijn (2012, Chapter 7).
11 Levitz (2015).
12 Gandy (2001).
13 Supreme Court of Canada (2015).
14 K. May (2009a).
15 Aucoin, Jarvis, and Turnbull (2011, 211).
16 Loat and MacMillan (2014, Chapter 9).
17 Chase (2015b).
18 Some of this thinking is based on material in Marland (2012b). As this book went to print Sheila Copps, the former deputy prime minister, penned an op-ed containing similar perspectives; see Copps (2015).
19 Albinski (1963, 391).
20 For example, see Angus Reid Institute (2015).
21 Supreme Court of Canada (2014).
22 See, for example, Lusztig (1995).
23 Russell (2008, 122).
24 Indian and Northern Affairs Canada (2007).
25 White (2005, 77).
26 Marland (2014c).
27 Frumin (2015).

APPENDICES

1 For instance, Bruno and Lapointe (2013).
2 Party staffer (JW) (2001c).
3 Flanagan (2004a).
4 Finley (2004b).
5 Flanagan (2014b).
6 Source: party staffers (MS and PM) (2004); abridged for length.
7 Source: National Defence (2011a); public servants' names have been altered.
8 Source: Department of National Defence (2011a); abridged for length; press secretary's name has been altered.

References

Aalberg, Toril, Jesper Strömbäck, and Claes H. de Vreese. 2011. "The framing of politics as strategy and game: A review of concepts, operationalizations, and key findings." *Journalism* 13(2): 162–78.

Abacus Data. 2015. "Party leaders are people too." February 4. http://abacusdata.ca/ party-leaders-are-people-too/.

Aberbach, Joel D., Robert D. Putnam, and Bert A. Rockman. 1981. *Bureaucrats and Politicians in Western Democracies.* Cambridge, MA: Harvard University Press.

Adair-Toteff, Christopher. 2005. "Max Weber's charisma." *Journal of Classical Sociology* 5(2): 189–204.

Adams, Thomas C. 2012. "DAR." US Department of State internal email, May 29. https://foia.state.gov/searchapp/DOCUMENTS/HRCEmail_NovWeb/295/ DOC_0C05797631/C05797631.pdf.

Advisory Committee on Senior Level Retention and Compensation. 2008. Ninth Report to the President of the Treasury Board, January. http://www.tbs-sct.gc.ca/ rp/0108-eng.asp.

Akin, David. 2008. "$45 million: The cost of a majority." *Ottawa Citizen,* October 15, A3.

–. 2015. "Hi: We're the new Liberal cabinet and we're taking questions – but we don't have any answers!" Sun Media blog. November 4. http://blogs.canoe.com/david akin/politics/hi-were-the-new-liberal-cabinet-and-were-taking-questions-but -we-dont-have-many-answers/.

Albaugh, Quinn, and Christopher Waddell. 2014. "Social media and political inequal- ity." In *Canadian Democracy from the Ground Up: Perceptions and Performance,* ed. Elisabeth Gidengil and Heather Bastedo, 102–24. Vancouver: UBC Press.

Albinski, Henry S. 1963. "The Canadian Senate: Politics and the Constitution." *Amer- ican Political Science Review* 57(2): 378–91.

Alphonso, Caroline. 2009. "N.B. publisher steps down over Harper error." *Globe and Mail,* July 29, A7.

Ambrose, Rose. 2015. "Resumption of debate on address in reply." Canada. Parlia- ment. House of Commons. *Edited Hansard* 148(3). 42nd Parliament, 1st session, December 7.

American Marketing Association. 2014. "Dictionary." https://www.ama.org/RESOURCES/Pages/Dictionary.aspx?dLetter=B.

Ames, H.B. 1911. "The organization of political parties in Canada." *Proceedings of the American Political Science Association*, Eighth Annual Meeting, 8: 181–88.

Angus Reid Institute. 2015. "Future of the Senate: Majority of Canadians split between abolishing, reforming the red chamber." News release, April 7. http://angusreid.org/wp-content/uploads/2015/04/2015.03.08-Future-of-the-Senate.pdf.

Aronczyk, Melissa, and Miranda J. Brady. 2015. "Branding history at the Canadian Museum of Civilization." *Canadian Journal of Communication* 40: 165–84.

Aucoin, Peter. 1995. *The New Public Management: Canada in Comparative Perspective.* Montreal: Institute for Research on Public Policy.

–. 2008. "New Public Management and New Public Governance: Finding the balance." In *Professionalism and Public Service: Essays in Honour of Kenneth Kernaghan,* ed. David Siegel and Ken Rasmussen, 16–33. Toronto: University of Toronto Press.

–. 2012. "New Political Governance in Westminster systems: Impartial public administration and management performance at risk." *Governance: An International Journal of Policy, Administration, and Institutions* 25(2): 177–99.

Aucoin, Peter, Herman Bakvis, and Mark D. Jarvis. 2013. "Constraining executive power in the era of New Political Governance." In *Governing: Essays in Honour of Donald J. Savoie,* ed. James Bickerton and B. Guy Peters, 32–52. Montreal: McGill-Queen's University Press.

Aucoin, Peter, Mark Jarvis, and Lori Turnbull. 2011. *Democratizing the Constitution: Reforming Responsible Government.* Toronto: Emond Montgomery Publications.

Axford, Barrie, Peter Madgwick, and John Turner. 1992. "Image management, stunts, and dirty tricks: The marketing of political brands in television campaigns." *Media, Culture, and Society* 14: 637–51.

Axworthy, Thomas S. 1988. "Of secretaries to princes." *Canadian Public Administration* 31(2): 247–64.

Azoulay, Audrey, and Jean-Noël Kapferer. 2003. "Do brand personality scales really measure brand personality?" *Brand Management* 11(2): 143–55.

Bachrach, Peter, and Morton S. Baratz. 1962. "Two faces of power." *American Political Science Review* 56(4): 947–52.

Bailenson, Jeremy N., Shanto Iyengar, Nick Yee, and Nathan A. Collins. 2008. "Facial similarity between voters and candidates causes influence." *Public Opinion Quarterly* 72(5): 935–61.

Baines, Paul R., Robert M. Worcester, David Jarrett, and Roger Mortimore. 2003. "Market segmentation and product differentiation in political campaigns: A technical feature perspective." *Journal of Marketing Management* 19(1–2): 225–49.

Baker, William, J. Wesley Hutchinson, Danny Moore, and Prakash Nedungadi. 1986. "Brand familiarity and advertising: Effects on the evoked set and brand preference." *Advances in Consumer Research* 13: 637–42.

Bakvis, Herman. 2001. "Prime minister and cabinet in Canada: An autocracy in need of reform?" *Journal of Canadian Studies* 35(4): 60–79.

Balzer, Timothy. 2011. *The Information Front: The Canadian Army and News Management during the Second World War.* Vancouver: UBC Press.

Bank of Canada. 2013. Internal event briefing book. Access to information file number A-2013-00131.

Barber, Michael. 2008. *Instruction to Deliver: Fighting to Transform Britain's Public Services.* London: Methuen.

–. 2015. *How to Run a Government: So that Citizens Benefit and Taxpayers Don't Go Crazy.* London: Penguin.

Barton, Rosemary. 2015. "Conservatives face questions about taxpayer-funded mailings." CBC News, February 16. http://www.cbc.ca/news/politics/conservatives-face-questions-about-taxpayer-funded-mailings-1.2959525.

Baum, Matthew A. 2011. "Preaching to the choir or converting the flock: Presidential communication strategies in the age of three medias." In *iPolitics: Citizens, Elections, and Governing in the New Media Era,* ed. Richard L. Fox and Jennifer M. Ramos, 183–205. New York: Cambridge University Press.

BBC. 2005. *The Thick of It.* Episode 2.2. http://www.imdb.com/title/tt0720702/quotes.

Beardsley, Keith. 2012. "Tory backbenchers rise up against the boys in short pants." *National Post,* October 5. http://fullcomment.nationalpost.com/2012/10/05/keith-beardsley-tory-backbenchers-rise-up-against-the-boys-in-short-pants/.

Beeby, Dean. 2011. "Baird's business cards." *Globe and Mail,* September 30, A9.

–. 2013. "Survey says 'Action Plan' ads fall flat." *Globe and Mail,* July 22, A5.

–. 2014a. "Records of Jean Chrétien's first cabinet meeting revealed." *Toronto Star,* February 3. http://www.thestar.com/news/canada/2014/02/03/records_of_jean_chretiens_first_cabinet_meeting_revealed.html.

–. 2014b. "Tangle of rules and procedures strangles federal government tweets." *Globe and Mail,* February 3, A2.

–. 2014c. "Canada Revenue Agency's annual ad campaign losing steam, internal report says." *Globe and Mail,* February 10. http://www.theglobeandmail.com/news/politics/canada-revenue-agencys-annual-ad-campaign-losing-steam-internal-report-says/article16775309.

–. 2015. "Stephen Harper's pre-election N.S. event cost public thousands: Documents." CBC News, August 16. http://www.cbc.ca/news/politics/stephen-harper-s-pre-election-n-s-event-cost-public-thousands-documents-1.3190284.

Bekkers, Victor, and Rebecca Moody. 2015. *Visual Culture and Public Policy: Towards a Visual Polity?* Abingdon, Oxon: Routledge.

Berg, Bruce L., and Howard Lune. 2012. *Qualitative Research Methods for the Social Sciences.* 8th ed. Boston: Pearson.

Berkowitz, Dan. 1990. "Refining the gatekeeping metaphor for local television news." *Journal of Broadcasting and Electronic Media* 34(1): 55–68.

Bernier, Luc, Keith Brownsey, and Michael Howlett, eds. 2005. *Executive Styles in Canada: Cabinet Structures and Leadership Practices in Canadian Government.* Toronto: University of Toronto Press.

Berthiaume, Lee. 2011. "Conservatives behind questionable phone calls to Liberal MP's Montreal riding." *National Post,* December 1, A11.

Blais, André, Neil Nevitte, Elisabeth Gidengil, and Richard Nadeau. 2000. "Do people have feelings toward leaders about whom they say they know nothing?" *Public Opinion Quarterly* 64(4): 452–63.

Blanchfield, Mike, and Jim Bronskill. 2010. "Tories staying on message." *Hamilton Spectator,* June 7, A1.

Blatchford, Andy. 2015. "Stephen Harper's children make campaign debut." *Toronto Star,* August 4. http://www.thestar.com/news/canada/2015/08/04/stephen-harpers-children-make-campaign-debut.html.

Blidook, Kelly. 2012. *Constituency Influence in Parliament: Countering the Centre.* Vancouver: UBC Press.

Bligh, Michelle C., and Jeffrey C. Kohles. 2009. "The enduring allure of charisma: How Barack Obama won the historic 2008 presidential election." *Leadership Quarterly* 20(3): 483–92.

Blumler, Jay G., and Dennis Kavanagh. 1999. "The third age of political communication: Influences and features." *Political Communication* 16(3): 209–30.

Bó, Ernesto Dal, Pedro Dal Bó, and Jason Snyder. 2009. "Political dynasties." *Review of Economic Studies* 76: 115–42.

Boesveld, Sarah. 2013. "#dayinthelife: Stephen Harper tweets his entire day, including breakfast with the cat." *National Post,* January 28. http://news.nationalpost.com/2013/01/28/dayinthelife-stephen-harper-tweets-his-entire-day-including-high-five-and-breakfast-with-his-cat/.

Bonoguore, Tenille. 2006. "The PM and his photographer." *Globe and Mail,* July 21, A10.

Boorstin, Daniel J. 1992. *The Image: A Guide to Pseudo-Events in America.* New York: Vintage Books.

Boswell, Randy. 2011. "Are MP's remarks like 2004 again for Harper?" *National Post,* April 21. http://news.nationalpost.com/2011/04/21/are-mp%E2%80%99s-remarks-like-2004-again-for-harper/.

Bourrie, Mark. 2015. *Kill the Messengers: Stephen Harper's Assault on Your Right to Know.* Toronto: HarperCollins Canada.

Bovée, John. 1999. "Opposition research." In *The Manship School Guide to Political Communication,* ed. David D. Perlmutter, 107–200. Baton Rouge: Louisiana State University Press.

Bowler, Shaun, David M. Farrell, and Richard S. Katz. 1999. "Party cohesion, party discipline, and parliaments." In *Party Discipline and Parliamentary Government,* ed. Shaun Bowler, David M. Farrell, and Richard S. Katz, 3–22. Columbus: Ohio State University Press.

Bowler, Shaun, and Jeffrey A. Karp. 2004. "Politicians, scandals, and trust in government." *Political Behavior* 26(3): 271–87.

Brader, Ted. 2006. *Campaigning for Hearts and Minds: How Emotional Appeals in Political Ads Work.* Chicago: University of Chicago Press.

Bradshaw, James. 2014. "Canada's Foreign Affairs department tries its hand at BuzzFeed." *Globe and Mail,* December 16. http://www.theglobeandmail.com/

technology/foreign-affairs-tries-its-hand-at-buzzfeed-with-putin-myths-post/
article22107544/.

Brennan, Richard, and Robert Benzie. 2015. "Tory candidates told to avoid debates, media during campaign." *Toronto Star,* August 26. http://www.thestar.com/news/ federal-election/2015/08/26/tory-candidates-told-to-avoid-debates-media-during -campaign.html.

Bricker, Darrell, and John Ibbitson. 2013. *The Big Shift: The Seismic Change in Canadian Politics, Business, and Culture and What It Means for Our Future.* Scarborough: HarperCollins.

Brodie, Ian. 2012. "In defence of political staff." *Canadian Parliamentary Review* Autumn: 33–39.

Brown, David, and Jeromy Lloyd. 2014. "What GroupM's report says about Canada's media market." *Marketing Magazine,* August 14. http://www.marketing mag.ca/media/what-groupms-report-says-about-canadas-media-market -122141.

Brown, Paul. 1987. "Decentralization and the administrative ecology of the national state in Canada." *International Review of Administrative Sciences* 53: 545–58.

Brown, Steven D., Ronald D. Lambert, Barry J. Kay, and James E. Curtis. 1988. "In the eye of the beholder: Leader images in Canada." *Canadian Journal of Political Science* 21(4): 729–55.

Bruno, Jessica, and Michael Lapointe. 2013. "PMO's 'enemies' list reveals tight management of cabinet, say former Conservative staffers." *Hill Times,* July 22, 1.

Bryden, Joan. 2013a. "Prime Minister Stephen Harper defends Conservative bulk-mail campaign against Justin Trudeau." *Toronto Star,* April 26. http://www. thestar.com/news/canada/2013/04/26/prime_minister_stephen_harper_defends _conservative_bulkmail_campaign_against_justin_trudeau.html.

–. 2013b. "Occasional gaffe part of being a genuine leader." *Victoria Times-Colonist,* December 12, A8.

–. 2015. "First ministers aim to rebrand Canada green." *Hamilton Spectator*, November 24. http://www.thespec.com/news-story/6132560-first-ministers-aim-to-rebrand -canada-green/.

Budesheim, Thomas Lee, and Stephen J. DePaola. 1994. "Beauty or the beast? The effects of appearance, personality, and issue information on evaluation of political candidates." *Personality and Social Psychology Bulletin* 20(4): 339–48.

Burgess, Mark. 2014. "Swelling of feds' communications staff reflects growing 'public relations state': Experts." *Hill Times,* August 11, 1.

–. 2015. "Feds' $75 million in ads move away from print as 'branding' better suited to TV, Internet." *Hill Times,* April 13, 1.

Busby, Robert. 2012. "Selling Sarah Palin: Political marketing and the 'Walmart mom.'" In *Routledge Handbook of Political Marketing,* ed. Jennifer Lees-Marshment, 218–29. Abingdon, Oxon: Routledge.

Butler, David E. 1958. *The Study of Political Behaviour.* London: Hutchinson and Company.

Butler, Don. 2013. "MacKay's office sparked probe into 'leak.'" *Ottawa Citizen,* June 3, A1.

Butler, Patrick, and Joe Peppard. 1998. "Consumer purchasing on the Internet: Processes and prospects." *European Management Journal* 16(5): 600–10.

Cameron, David. 1980. "The marketing of national unity." In *Macromarketing: A Canadian Perspective,* ed. David N. Thomson, Patricia Simmie, Louise Heslop, and Stanley J. Shapiro, 9–22. Chicago: American Marketing Association.

Camp, Roderic A. 1982. "Family relationships in Mexican politics: A preliminary view." *Journal of Politics* 44(3): 848–62.

Campbell, Angus, Philip E. Converse, Warren Miller, and Donald Stokes. 1960. *The American Voter.* New York: Wiley.

Campbell, Colin, and George J. Szablowski. 1979. *The Superbureaucrats: Structure and Behaviour in Central Agencies.* Toronto: Macmillan of Canada.

Campbell, Murray. 2007. "Reporters excluded from PM's visit to base." *Globe and Mail,* May 24, A18.

Campion-Smith, Bruce. 2008. "Mum's the word till message vetted." *Toronto Star,* May 26, A12.

–. 2009. "Harper gives seal of approval to hunt." *Toronto Star,* August 19, A6.

–. 2014a. "MP angles for 'million-dollar shot' at Israel holy site." *Toronto Star,* January 22, A3.

–. 2014b. "Top aide parachuted into troubled ministry." *Toronto Star,* December 2, A4.

Campion-Smith, Bruce and Les Whittington. 2015. "Nothing wrong with using 'Justin,' Stephen Harper says." *Toronto Star,* August 4. http://www.thestar.com/news/canada/2015/08/04/nothing-wrong-with-using-justin-stephen-harper-says.html

Canada. 1969a. *To Know and Be Known: The Report of the Task Force on Government Information. Volume 1: Panorama.* Ottawa: Queen's Printer.

–. 1969b. *To Know and Be Known: The Report of the Task Force on Government Information. Volume 2: Research Papers.* Ottawa: Queen's Printer.

Canada Public Service Agency. 2007a. "A framework for developing a brand for the public service of Canada." Internal document, October 17.

–. 2007b. "Status report on branding." Internal document, November 28.

Canada Revenue Agency. c. 2008. "The CRA corporate look: A graphic standards manual." Internal document.

–. 2008. "Branding in the CRA." Briefing to the AC, Public Affairs Branch. Internal document, July 14.

–. 2011. "Fw: For review: T1 comms synopsis, web tasks list draft, News Canada articles, overarching messages." Internal email, December 7.

–. 2012a. "For review: Input – commissioner's report to the Board of Management June 2012." Internal email, June 22.

–. 2012b. *Tax savings working for Canadians.* Video, February 12. http://www.youtube.com/watch?v=1QOpYW0c_GM.

–. 2012c. "Phase IV – tax relief measures advertising campaign creative brief." Internal document, August.

–. 2015. "General income tax and benefit guide 2014." Public document.

Canadian Association of Journalists. 2010. "An open letter to Canadian journalists." June 22. http://www.caj.ca/?p=692.

Canadian Heritage. 2013. "The arms of Canada." http://www.pch.gc.ca/eng/135946 9552514/1359469845405.

–. 2014. "Canadian Heritage: 2014–15 report on plans and priorities." http://www. pch.gc.ca/DAMAssetPub/DAM-verEval-audEval/STAGING/texte-text/rPP-2014 -15_1394035189315_eng.pdf?WT.contentAuthority=1700.

Canadian Journalism Foundation. 2014. "CJF j-talk in Ottawa: Does the press gallery matter?" Media advisory, Canada News Wire, April 3. http://www.newswire.ca/ en/story/1334113/media-advisory-cjf-j-talk-in-ottawa-does-the-press-gallery -matter-less-than-a-week-left-to-reserve-tickets.

Canadian Olympic Committee. 2013. "2013 annual report." https://cdnolympic. files.wordpress.com/2014/06/coc_ar2013_en.pdf.

Canadian Press. 2008. "Lack of media budget sends Liberals to YouTube." *Marketing Magazine,* April 27. http://www.marketingmag.ca/brands/lack-of-media-budget -sends-liberals-to-youtube-14833.

–. 2011a. "Stephen Harper picks Twitter over 'official' channels." *Marketing Magazine,* February 2. http://www.marketingmag.ca/advertising/stephen-harper-picks -twitter-over-official-channels-22076.

–. 2011b. "Secret shoppers to rate government services at outlets across Canada." *Marketing Magazine,* August 2. http://www.marketingmag.ca/brands/secret -shoppers-to-rate-government-services-at-outlets-across-canada-33236.

–. 2011c. "Women ejected from Conservative rally a social media stumble, experts say." *Marketing Magazine,* April 6. http://www.marketingmag.ca/advertising/women -ejected-from-conservative-rally-a-social-media-stumble-experts-say-25589.

–. 2012. "Privy Council spending $463K on ethnic media monitoring." CBC News, November 15. http://www.cbc.ca/news/politics/privy-council-spending-463k -on-ethnic-media-monitoring-1.1218407.

–. 2013. "Environment Canada name stripped from weather website." CBC News, April 18. http://www.cbc.ca/news/politics/environment-canada-name-stripped -from-weather-website-1.1341863.

–. 2014. "Cost of 'Canada 150' commemorations comes out of military operations budget." CBC News, March 17. http://www.cbc.ca/news/politics/cost-of-canada -150-commemorations-comes-out-of-military-operations-budget-1.2572425.

–. 2015a. "Mike Duffy trial: Chronology of the Senate expense scandal saga." CBC News, April 6. http://www.cbc.ca/news/politics/mike-duffy-trial-chronology-of -the-senate-expense-scandal-saga-1.3022241.

–. 2015b. "Tories looking for vets to sing Stephen Harper's praises in campaign ads." CBC News, August 27. http://www.cbc.ca/news/politics/conservatives-looking -for-happy-vets-1.3205698.

–. 2016. "Trudeau family's Caribbean vacation splashed across the tabloids." CTV News, January 10. http://www.ctvnews.ca/canada/trudeau-family-s-caribbean -vacation-splashed-across-the-tabloids-1.2731532.

Canadian Science Writers' Association. 2012. "Prime minister, please unmuzzle the scientists." February 16. http://sciencewriters.ca/2012/02/16/prime-minister-please-unmuzzle-the-scientists/.

Canadian Tourism Commission. 2006. "2007–2011 strategic plan: Moving forward with vision." http://publications.gc.ca/collections/collection_2012/ic/Iu83-23-2007-eng.pdf.

Canadian Wheat Board. c. 2012. Advertising Standards Guide. Internal document.

CanWest News. 2006. "American strategist teaches Tories tips on keeping power." May 7. http://www.canada.com/reginaleaderpost/news/story.html?id=e0a004b7-31a1-4925-bb2c-dc34e911aceb.

Cappella, Joseph N., and Kathleen Hall Jamieson. 1996. "News frames, political cynicism, and media cynicism." Annals of the American Academy of Political and Social Science 546: 71–74.

–. 1997. Spiral of Cynicism: The Press and the Public Good. Oxford: Oxford University Press.

Carty, R. Kenneth. 2002. "The politics of Tecumseh Corner: Canadian political parties as franchise organizations." Canadian Journal of Political Science 35(4): 723–45.

–. 2004. "Parties as franchise systems: The stratarchical organizational imperative." Party Politics 10(1): 5–24.

Carty, R. Kenneth, William Cross, and Lisa Young. 2000. Rebuilding Canadian Party Politics. Vancouver: UBC Press.

CBC. 2005a. "Harper offers change to voters." November 29. http://www.cbc.ca/news/canada/harper-offers-change-to-voters-1.540961.

–. 2005b. "Harper vows to reduce GST." December 1. http://www.cbc.ca/news/canada/harper-vows-to-reduce-gst-1.554820.

–. 2010. "PM defends G8 fake lake pavilion." June 8. http://www.cbc.ca/news/canada/toronto/story/2010/06/08/g20-fakelake-costs.html.

–. 2011. "Harper campaign screening 'un-Canadian': Ignatieff." April 5. http://www.cbc.ca/news/politics/canadavotes2011/story/2011/04/05/cv-election-harper-ignatieff-rally-923.html.

–. 2012a. Penashue on spending. Video, August 14. http://www.cbc.ca/player/Shows/ID/2267142576/.

–. 2012b. "Transcript of Stephen Harper interview." The National, June 5. http://www.cbc.ca/thenational/blog/2012/06/stephen-harper-interview-transcript.html.

–. 2014a. "Journalistic standards and practices." http://www.cbc.radio-canada.ca/en/reporting-to-canadians/acts-and-policies/programming/journalism/.

–. 2014b. "Canada Job Grant ads cost $2.5M for non-existent program." January 13. http://www.cbc.ca/news/politics/canada-job-grant-ads-cost-2-5m-for-non-existent-program-1.2495196.

–. 2014c. "Vancouver MP claims Liberal Party promoting marijuana to kids." June 24. http://www.cbc.ca/news/canada/british-columbia/vancouver-mp-claims-liberal-party-promoting-marijuana-to-kids-1.2683052.

–. 2014d. "Stephen Harper considers U.S. request for further military help in ISIS fight." September 24. http://www.cbc.ca/news/politics/stephen-harper-considers-u-s-request-for-further-military-help-in-isis-fight-1.2776585.

–. 2015a. "Liberals issue talking points in confidential policy document." January 15. http://www.cbc.ca/news/politics/liberals-issue-talking-points-in-confidential-policy-document-1.2911875.

–. 2015b. "Typos in prime minister's office press pass induce mockery on Twitter." April 7. http://www.cbc.ca/news/canada/british-columbia/typos-in-prime-minister-s-office-press-pass-induce-mockery-on-twitter-1.3023977.

–. 2015c. "CRA's letter 'Conservative Party advertising,' Edmonton mom says." April 23. http://www.cbc.ca/news/politics/cra-s-letter-conservative-party-advertising-edmonton-mom-says-1.3045325.

–. 2015d. "Stephen Harper heading to Cumberland-Colchester for stop at secret location." August 12. http://www.cbc.ca/news/canada/nova-scotia/stephen-harper-heading-to-cumberland-colchester-for-stop-at-secret-location-1.3188706.

–. 2015e. "Behind the scenes with Justin Trudeau on his 1st day as PM." November 4, http://www.cbc.ca/news/politics/behind-the-scenes-with-justin-trudeau-on-his-1st-day-as-pm-1.3304860.

CBC Radio. 2013. "Politics, leaks, and the PMO." *The Current,* June 19. http://www.cbc.ca/thecurrent/episode/2013/06/19/politics-leaks-and-the-pmo/.

Centre for Excellence in Communications. 2014. "The challenges of public sector branding and positioning." http://www.comcec.com/public/challengebrand.html.

Centre of Excellence for Public Sector Marketing. 2009. "Guide to branding in the public and not-for-profit sectors." April. http://www.mikekujawski.ca/ftp/cepsm_branding_ebook.pdf.

Chadwick, Andrew. 2013. *The Hybrid Media System: Politics and Power.* New York: Oxford University Press.

Chaffee, Steven, and Stacey Frank. 1996. "How Americans get political information: Print versus broadcast news." *Annals of the American Academy of Political and Social Science* 546: 48–58.

Chaiken, Shelly. 1980. "Heuristic versus systemic information processing and the use of source versus message cues in persuasion." *Journal of Personality and Social Psychology* 39(5): 752–66.

Chamberlain, Edward Hastings. 1962. *The Theory of Monopolistic Competition: A Re-Orientation of the Theory of Value.* 8th ed. Harvard University Press.

Chambers, Bruce. 2015. "In advertising, the federal election has already started." CBC News, April 28. http://www.cbc.ca/news/politics/in-advertising-the-federal-election-has-already-started-1.3052084.

Chaney, David C. 2001. "From ways of life to lifestyle: Rethinking culture as ideology and sensibility." In *Culture in the Communication Age,* ed. James Lull, 75–88. London: Routledge.

Chase, Steven. 2008. "Tories toe Harper government's line." *Globe and Mail*, November 16. http://www.theglobeandmail.com/news/national/tories-toe-harper -governments-line/article1066007/.

–. 2009. "Harper makes donut run." *Globe and Mail* blog, September 22. http://www. theglobeandmail.com/news/politics/ottawa-notebook/harper-makes-donut -run/article4286299/.

–. 2010. "Why Harper wasn't asked about census." *Globe and Mail* blog, August 6. http://www.theglobeandmail.com/news/politics/ottawa-notebook/why-harper -wasnt-asked-about-census/article1664624/.

–. 2013. "Harper paints himself as outsider." *Globe and Mail*, November 2, A11.

–. 2015a. "PMO forced to admit security breach over videos of Harper visiting troops." *Globe and Mail*, May 6, A1.

–. 2015b. "Tory supporters launch HarperPAC." *Globe and Mail*, June 23, A4.

Cheadle, Bruce. 2009a. "Tory fiscal update came at hefty cost." *Toronto Star*, October 19, A4.

–. 2009b. "Tories deny deleting photos." *Chronicle-Herald* (Halifax), September 23, A1.

–. 2010. "No cash, no signs: Tories made stimulus funds contingent on erecting billboards." *Globe and Mail*, September 8. http://www.theglobeandmail.com/news/ politics/no-cash-no-signs-tories-made-stimulus-funds-contingent-on-erecting -billboards/article1379553/.

–. 2011a. "Harper's Economic Action Plan website got approval despite violating rules." *Whitehorse Star*, January 6, 8.

–. 2011b. "Big bucks: Harper government's ad buy costs taxpayers $26-million." *Marketing Magazine*, March 14. http://www.marketingmag.ca/brands/ harper-governments-ad-buy-costs-taxpayers-26-million-24288.

Cheadle, Bruce. 2015a. "Trudeau says image-making part of governing, not a popularity contest." *Winnipeg Free Press*, December 17. http://www.winnipegfreepress. com/business/trudeau-says-image-making-part-of-governing-not-a-popularity- contest-362839211.html.

–. 2015b. "Conservative government's anti-drug advertising blitz last fall cost $7 million." *Globe and Mail*, January 27. http://www.theglobeandmail.com/ news/politics/conservative-governments-anti-drug-advertising-blitz-last-fall -cost-7-million/article22667473/.

Cherulnik, Paul D., Laurie C. Turns, and Scott K. Wilderman. 1990. "Physical appearance and leadership: Exploring the role of appearance-based attribution in leader appearance." *Journal of Applied Social Psychology* 20(18): 1530–39.

Chiu, Belinda H.Y. 2007. "Brand USA: Democratic propaganda in the third social space." *Whitehead Journal of Diplomacy and International Relations* (Summer–Fall): 131–43.

Chong, Michael. 2015. "Reform Act, 2014 passes Senate, 38–14." News release, June 23. http://michaelchong.ca/2015/06/23/reform-act-2014-passes-senate-38-14/.

Chrétien, Jean. 1985. *Straight from the Heart*. Toronto: Key Porter Books.

–. 2008. *My Years as Prime Minister*. Toronto: Vintage Canada.

Citizenship and Immigration Canada. 2012a. "Working events list." Internal document, January 23.

–. 2012b. "Scenario note: Start-up visa." Internal document, April 18.

–. 2015. "#WelcomeRefugees." December 3. http://www.cic.gc.ca/english/refugees/welcome/.

Clark, Campbell. 2006. "Harper restricts ministers' message." *Globe and Mail,* March 17, A1.

Clarke, Harold D., Allan Kornberg, and Thomas J. Scotto. 2009. *Making Political Choices: Canada and the United States.* Toronto: University of Toronto Press.

Clement, Tony. 2011. @TonyclementCPC. February 2. https://twitter.com/TonyclementCPC/status/33003660573147139.

Clerk of the Privy Council. 2007. "Fourteenth annual report to the prime minister on the public service of Canada." April. http://www.clerk.gc.ca/eng/feature.asp?mode=preview&pageId=208.

Clubok, Alfred B., Norman M. Wilensky, and Forrest J. Berghorn. 1969. "Family relationships, congressional recruitment, and political modernization." *Journal of Politics* 31(4): 1035–62.

Cobb, Roger, Jennie-Keith Ross, and Marc Howard Ross. 1976. "Agenda building as a comparative political process." *American Political Science Review* 70(1): 126–38.

Coddington, Mark, Logan Molyneux, and Regina G. Lawrence. 2014. "Fact checking the campaign: How political reporters use Twitter to set the record straight (or not)." *International Journal of Press/Politics* 19(4): 391–409.

Comber, Mary Anne, and Robert S. Mayne. 1986. *The Newsmongers: How the Media Distort the Political News.* Toronto: McClelland and Stewart.

Communication Canada. 2002. "Public opinion research in the government of Canada: Annual report." http://www.tpsgc-pwgsc.gc.ca/cgi-bin/archived/pdf.pl.

–. 2003. "A year of review: Annual report on the government of Canada's advertising, 2002–03." http://www.tpsgc-pwgsc.gc.ca/cgi-bin/archived/pdf.pl.

Conservative Party of Canada. 2005a. "Literature catalogue." Internal party document. Flanagan fonds.

–. 2005b. "Advertising plan strategy." Internal party document. Flanagan fonds.

–. c. 2007. "CIMS and your campaign." PowerPoint presentation. Internal party document.

–. 2011. "Breaking through, building the Conservative brand: Conservative ethnic paid media strategy." Letter issued by the Office of the Honourable Jason Kenney, March 3. http://www.liberal.ca/files/2011/03/kenney-letter-and-presentation.pdf.

–. 2014. "Candidate nomination rules and procedures." February 8. http://www.conservative.ca/media/2014/02/Nomination-rules-14-02-12.pdf.

–. 2015a. "Where we stand." May 24. http://www.conservative.ca/where-we-stand/.

–. 2015b. "Iran and ISIS." Listserve email, June 26.

–. 2015c. "Protect our economy: Our Conservative plan to protect the economy." Campaign platform, October 9. http://www.conservative.ca/media/plan/conservative-platform-en.pdf.

Copps, Sheila. 2015. "Canada mimicking slash-and-burn tactics in American politics." *Hill Times*, June 29, 11.

Cormack, Patricia. 2012. "Double-double: Branding, Tim Hortons, and the public sphere." In *Political Marketing in Canada,* ed. Alex Marland, Thierry Giasson, and Jennifer Lees-Marshment, 209–23. Vancouver: UBC Press.

Cosgrove, Kenneth M. 2007. *Branded Conservatives: How the Brand Brought the Right from the Fringes to the Center of American Politics.* New York: Peter Lang Publishing.

Courtney, John C. 1978. "Recognition of Canadian political parties in Parliament and in law." *Canadian Journal of Political Science* 11(1): 33–60.

Cowan, Peter. 2015. "At this event, journalists were seen and not heard." CBC News, October 6. http://www.cbc.ca/news/canada/newfoundland-labrador/peter -cowan-stephen-harper-avalon-1.3258368.

Cudmore, James. 2014. "Army commander promises discipline against media leaks." CBC News, January 13. http://www.cbc.ca/news/politics/army-commander -promises-discipline-against-media-leaks-1.2495204.

Curry, Bill. 2009. "'I'm not Garth Turner.'" *Globe and Mail* blog, October 5. http:// www.theglobeandmail.com/news/politics/ottawa-notebook/im-not-garth-turner/ article4287873/.

–. 2010. "Pollster Frank Graves apologizes, denies anti-Tory bias." *Globe and Mail* blog, April 23. http://www.theglobeandmail.com/news/politics/ottawa-notebook/ pollster-frank-graves-apologizes-denies-anti-tory-bias/article4352832.

–. 2014. "Harper's rare advice for Republicans, conservative parties." *Globe and Mail,* September 25. http://www.theglobeandmail.com/news/politics/globe-politics -insider/in-rare-moment-harper-gives-advice-to-conservative-parties/article 20784184.

–. 2015a. "Tories plan $7.5 million ad blitz for pre-election budget." *Globe and Mail,* April 2, A4.

–. 2015b. "Poilievre video spurs fresh criticism." *Globe and Mail,* May 15, A4.

–. 2015c. "Adoring fans mob Trudeau at Manila economic summit." *Globe and Mail,* November 19. http://www.theglobeandmail.com/news/world/adoring-media -fans-mob-trudeau-at-manila-economic-summit/article27356563/.

–. 2015d. "Economic Action Plan taken off government websites." *Globe and Mail,* November 6. http://www.theglobeandmail.com/news/politics/economic-action -plan-taken-off-government-websites/article27155289/.

–. 2015e. "Liberals launch online ad campaign to promote refugee plan." *Globe and Mail,* November 26. http://www.theglobeandmail.com/news/politics/liberals -launch-online-ad-campaign-to-promote-refugee-plan/article27503813/.

–. 2015f. "Liberal red seeping into messaging on non-partisan government websites." *Globe and Mail,* December 10. http://www.theglobeandmail.com/news/politics/ liberal-red-seeping-into-messaging-on-non-partisan-government-websites/ article27707400/.

Dafoe, J.W. 1964. *Laurier: A Study in Canadian Politics.* 1922; reprinted. Toronto: McClelland and Stewart.

Dahl, Robert A. 2005. "James Madison: Republican or Democrat?" *Perspectives on Politics* 3: 439–48.

d'Aquino, Thomas. 1974. "The Prime Minister's Office: Catalyst or cabal? Aspects of the development of the office in Canada and some thoughts about its future." *Canadian Public Administration* 17(1): 55–79.

Daro, Ishmael N. 2015. "Is your online footprint clean enough to run for office?" *BuzzFeed News*, August 28. http://www.buzzfeed.com/ishmaeldaro/never-tweet.

D'auray, Michelle. 2003. "The dual challenge of integration and inclusion: Canada's experience with government online." *Journal of Political Marketing* 2(3): 31–49.

Davidson, Andrew. 2011. "Transcript: Stephen Harper: The Mansbridge interview (part one)." CBC blog, January 17. http://www.cbc.ca/newsblogs/politics/inside -politics-blog/2011/01/transcript-stephen-harper-the-mansbridge-interview-part- one.html.

Davidson, Scott, and Robert H. Binstock. 2012. "Political marketing and segmentation in aging democracies." In *Routledge Handbook of Political Marketing*, ed. Jennifer Lees-Marshment, 20–33. Abingdon, Oxon: Routledge.

Davies, Gary, and Takir Mian. 2010. "The reputation of the party leader and of the party being led." *European Journal of Marketing* 44(3–4): 331–50.

Davies, Morton R. 1998. "Civil servants, managerialism, and democracy." *International Review of Administrative Services* 64: 119–29.

Davis, Jeff. 2010a. "Bureaucrats chafing under 'unprecedented' PMO/PCO communications control." *Hill Times*, April 26, 1.

–. 2010b. "PMO communications control follows 'control freak' narrative, says Spector." *Hill Times*, May 3, 1.

de Chernatony, Leslie, and Francesca Dall'Olmo Riley. 1998. "Defining a 'brand': Beyond the literature with experts' interpretations." *Journal of Marketing Management* 14: 417–43.

De Landtsheer, Christ'l, Phillipe De Vries, and Dieter Vertessen. 2008. "Political impression management: How metaphors, sound bites, appearance effectiveness, and personality traits can win elections." *Journal of Political Marketing* 7(3–4): 217–38.

De Souza, Mike. 2013a. "Stephen Harper's government withholds details of $16-million PR campaign for oil industry." Postmedia Network, May 22. http://o.canada. com/technology/environment/stephen-harpers-government-withholds-details -of-16-million-pr-for-oil-industry.

–. 2013b. "Tories tried to massage media message." *Ottawa Citizen*, July 4, A4.

Dehaas, Josh. 2015. "Immigration minister calls Liberals 'the racist party.'" CTV News, June 11. http://www.ctvnews.ca/politics/immigration-minister-calls -liberals-the-racist-party-1.2417993.

Delacourt, Susan. 2007. "O Canada: Blue patriot love." *Toronto Star*, June 29, A5.

–. 2010. @SusanDelacourt, April 26. https://twitter.com/SusanDelacourt/ status/12875739718.

–. 2013. *Shopping for Votes: How Politicians Choose Us and We Choose Them*. Madeira Park, BC: Douglas and McIntyre.

Department of International Trade. 2005. "Evaluation of the Brand Canada (BC) program: Final report." Office of the Inspector General Evaluation Division. Internal government document.

Department of National Defence. 2011a. "MND speech: Historical designation." Internal email, August 8.

–. 2011b. "Noon PCO detect and correct re: historical designation." Internal email, August 16.

–. 2011c. "Re: web updates." Internal email, August 12.

–. 2011d. "Meeting debrief re: pending minister's announcement re: naming." Internal email, August 4.

–. 2011e. "PA update." Internal email, September 6.

–. 2012a. "Re: social media account request for CFRG." Internal email, February 15.

–. 2012b. "CDS CoC – DGMAE involvement." Internal email, October 1.

–. 2012c. "Rc: NR – brilliant exploits." Internal email, November 6.

Diebel, Linda. 2008. "Stephen Harper: Double-edged sword." *Toronto Star*, October 12, ID01.

Dinning, Jim. 2015. *Time for a reboot: Nine ways to restore trust in Canada's public institutions.* Public Policy Forum report, October. http://ppforum.ca/sites/default/files/Report%20-%20English.pdf.

Ditchburn, Jennifer. 2013a. "Trudeau's masculinity subtext of Tory attack ads." *Calgary Herald*, April 26, A4.

–. 2013b. "CIDA staff complained to Fantino about political control." *Globe and Mail*, January 31. http://www.theglobeandmail.com/news/politics/cida-staff-complained-to-fantino-about-political-control/article8030353/.

Donoghue, Jack. 1993. *PR: Fifty Years in the Field.* Louiseville, QC: Dundurn Press.

Dovring, Karin. 1959. *Road of Propaganda: The Semantics of Biased Communication.* New York: Philosophical Library.

Dowding, Keith. 2013. "The prime ministeralization of the British prime minister." *Parliamentary Affairs* 66: 617–35.

Downs, Anthony. 1957. *An Economic Theory of Democracy.* New York: Harper and Row.

Doyle, Simon. 2007. "Harper keeps a tight rein on lines of communication." *Daily News* (Halifax), December 24, 5.

Dwivedi, O.P., and James Ian Gow. 1999. *From Bureaucracy to Public Management: The Administrative Culture of the Government of Canada.* Toronto: Broadview Press.

Edwards, Peter. 2015. "'A cabinet that looks like Canada': Justin Trudeau pledges government based on trust." *Toronto Star*, November 4. http://www.thestar.com/news/canada/2015/11/04/new-government-to-be-sworn-in-today.html.

Eichbaum, C., and R. Shaw. 2008. "Revisiting politicization: Political advisers and public servants in Westminster systems." *Governance* 21(3): 337–63.

Elliot, Louise. 2011. "Alternate universe follow-ups." CBC blog, April 9. http://www.cbc.ca/newsblogs/politics/inside-politics-blog/2011/04/alternate-universe-follow-ups.html.

Entman, Robert M. 1993. "Framing: Toward a clarification of a fractured paradigm." *Journal of Communication* 43(4): 51–58.

–. 2007. "Framing bias: Media in the distribution of power." *Journal of Communication* 57(1):163–73.

Environment Canada. c. 2010. "Media relations handbook." Internal document.

–. c. 2013. Internal media lines. Access to information file number A-2013-01239.

Eshuis, Jasper, and Erik-Hans Klijn. 2012. *Branding in Governance and Public Management.* New York: Routledge.

Esselment, Anna. 2012a. "Market orientation in a minority government: The challenges of product delivery." In *Political Marketing in Canada,* ed. Alex Marland, Thierry Giasson, and Jennifer Lees-Marshment, 123–38. Vancouver: UBC Press.

–. 2012b. "Delivering in government and getting results in minorities and coalitions." In *Routledge Handbook of Political Marketing,* ed. Jennifer Lees-Marshment, 303–15. London: Routledge.

–. 2014. "The governing party and the permanent campaign." In *Political Communication in Canada: Meet the Press and Tweet the Rest,* ed. Alex Marland, Thierry Giasson, and Tamara A. Small, 24–38. Vancouver: UBC Press.

Esselment, Anna, Jennifer Lees-Marshment, and Alex Marland. 2014. "The nature of political advising to prime ministers in Australia, Canada, New Zealand and the United Kingdom." *Commonwealth & Comparative Politics* 52(3): 358–75.

Esser, Frank. 2008. "Dimensions of political news cultures: Sound bite and image bite news in France, Germany, Great Britain, and the United States." *International Journal of Press/Politics* 13(4): 401–28.

Everitt, Joanna, and Michael Camp. 2009. "Changing the game changes the frame: The media's use of lesbian stereotypes in leadership versus election campaigns." *Canadian Political Science Review* 3(3): 24–39.

Fekete, Jason. 2013. "Sesquicentennial fever rises." *Ottawa Citizen,* June 29, A3.

–. 2014a. "Federal government tracks opponents." *Ottawa Citizen,* September 24, A7.

–. 2014b. "Political leaders skip QP regularly." *Ottawa Citizen,* December 31, A1.

Ferguson, Stewart, and Sherry Ferguson. 1978. "Proxemics and television: The politician's dilemma." *Canadian Journal of Communication* 4(4): 26–35.

Ferraras, Jesse. 2015. "NDP nails April Fool's Day with dig at Senate expenses scandal." *Huffington Post Canada,* April 1. http://www.huffingtonpost.ca/2015/04/01/ndp-april-fools-day-senate-scandal_n_6986580.html.

Finance Canada. 2009a. *Canada's Economic Action Plan: Budget 2009.* January 27. http://www.budget.gc.ca/2009/pdf/budget-planbugetaire-eng.pdf.

–. 2009b. "Economic Action Plan advertising campaign proposals." Internal document, c. March.

–. 2009c. "Canada's Economic Action Plan: Visual style guide." Internal document, July.

–. 2009d. "Style guide: Project signage." Internal document, July.

–. 2010. "Update on retirement income correspondence." Internal memo, August 6.

–. 2013a. "Evaluation of the consultations and communications branch: Final report." https://www.fin.gc.ca/treas/evaluations/ccb-dcc-eng.asp.

–. 2013b. "Twitter overview." Internal document, March 14.

–. 2014. "Harper government prepares to consult on 'Made in Canada' branding campaign." News release, February 26. http://www.fin.gc.ca/n14/14-031-eng.asp.

Finley, Doug. 2004a. "Election 2004: Observations and recommendations." Internal party document, July 13.

–. 2004b. "Really distasteful conversations." Email, February 16. Flanagan fonds.

Firestone, O.J. 1970. *The Public Persuader: Government Advertising.* Toronto: Methuen.

Fitz-Morris, James. 2010. "Media have no flight plan on PM's plane." CBC Inside Politics Blog, January 29. http://www.cbc.ca/newsblogs/politics/inside-politics-blog/2010/01/media-have-no-flight-plan-on-pms-plane.html.

Fitzpatrick, Meagan. 2011. "Conservatives set for day of photo-ops." CBC News, March 14. http://www.cbc.ca/news/politics/story/2011/03/14/pol-pr-blitz.html.

–. 2013a. "Conservative MPs used like 'trained seals,' Rathgeber says." CBC News, June 6. http://www.cbc.ca/news/politics/conservative-mps-used-like-trained-seals-rathgeber-says-1.1314736.

–. 2013b. "Stephen Harper's jet gets red, white, and blue makeover." CBC News, June 7. http://www.cbc.ca/news/politics/stephen-harper-s-jet-gets-red-white-and-blue-makeover-1.1358276.

Flanagan, Tom. 1992. "Reform Party of Canada: Memorandum." Internal party document, August 17. Flanagan fonds.

–. 2001. "Fwd: An outsider's early view of Stephen." Email, September 21. Flanagan fonds.

–. 2002a. "Re: response to <reporter's name removed>'s comments." Email, January 9. Flanagan fonds.

–. 2002b. "Re: my whereabouts ... " Email, January 2. Flanagan fonds.

–. 2004a. "Fw: 'Demand better' alternatives." Email, March 23. Flanagan fonds.

–. 2004b. "Re: transition issues." Email, March 24. Flanagan fonds.

–. 2004c. "Re: facts." Email, March 26. Flanagan fonds.

–. 2004d. "Candidate pamphlet." Email, April 16. Flanagan fonds.

–. 2004e. "Re: OLO collective ten percenters – November." Email, November 23. Flanagan fonds.

–. 2005a. "Campaign manager's report and organizational recommendations." Internal party document, May 27. Flanagan fonds.

–. 2005b. "Pre-writ campaign plan for the period June 1, 2005 to February 1, 2006." Internal party document, June 1. Flanagan fonds.

–. 2005c. "Re:." Email, June 12. Flanagan fonds.

–. 2005d. "FW: Monday's release of party fundraising numbers for 2004." Email, June 30. Flanagan fonds.

–. 2005e. "FW: Urgent: For approval." Email, December 20. Flanagan fonds.

–. 2005f. "Please call me." Email, April 15. Flanagan fonds.

–. 2009a. *Harper's Team: Behind the Scenes in the Conservative Rise to Power.* 2nd ed. Montreal and Kingston: McGill-Queen's University Press.

–. 2009b. "Campaign strategy: Triage and the concentration of resources." In *Election,* ed. Heather MacIvor, 155–72. Toronto: Emond Montgomery Publications.

–. 2014a. *Persona Non Grata: The Death of Free Speech in the Internet Age.* Toronto: McClelland and Stewart.

–. 2014b. Email to the author, December 16.

Fletcher, Frederick J. 1977. "The prime minister as public persuader." In *Apex of Power: Prime Minister and Political Leadership in Canada,* ed. Thomas A. Hockin, 86–111. Scarborough: Prentice-Hall.

Foote, Andrew. 2014. "Peter Goldring retracts statement advising MPs to wear body cameras." CBC News, November 26. http://www.cbc.ca/news/politics/peter -goldring-retracts-statement-advising-mps-to-wear-body-cameras-1.2851472.

Ford. 1905. "Don't experiment – just buy a Ford." Advertisement. http://www. vintageadbrowser.com/cars-ads-1900s.

–. 1945. "There's a Ford in your future." Advertisement. http://www.vintagead browser.com/cars-ads-1940s/2.

–. 1974. "Ford Mustang II." Advertisement. http://www.vintageadbrowser.com/ cars-ads-1970s/2.

Foreign Affairs and International Trade Canada. 2010. "New directive: Backdrops and podium signs." Internal email, January 6.

Fox, Stephen R. 1984. *The Mirror Makers: A History of American Advertising and Its Creators.* Champaign: University of Illinois Press.

Francoli, Mary. 2011. "Embracing a new relationship with Canadians: Addressing barriers to new media adoption in Canada's public service." In *How Ottawa Spends 2011–2012: Trimming Fat or Slicing Pork?,* ed. Christopher Stoney and G. Bruce Doern, 280–96. Montreal: McGill-Queen's University Press.

Franks, C.E.S. 1987. *The Parliament of Canada.* Toronto: University of Toronto Press.

Frumin, Aliyah. 2015. "The new 2016 battleground: Instagram." MSNBC, September 6. http://www.msnbc.com/msnbc/the-new-2016-battleground-instagram.

Gaber, Ivor. 2007. "Too much of a good thing: The 'problem' of political communications in a mass media democracy." *Journal of Public Affairs* 7: 219–34.

Galloway, Gloria. 2007. "Foreign Affairs workers 'are just apoplectic.'" *Globe and Mail,* February 23, A1.

–. 2009. "It's a yes-or-no question." *Globe and Mail* blog, February 9. http://www. theglobeandmail.com/news/politics/ottawa-notebook/its-a-yes-or-no-question/ article782102/.

–. 2010. "Sandra Buckler's advice on dealing with media." *Globe and Mail* blog, August 23. http://www.theglobeandmail.com/news/politics/ottawa-notebook/sandra -bucklers-advice-on-dealing-with-media/article1378037/.

–. 2011a. "Well-travelled PM unveils volunteer awards." *Globe and Mail* blog, January 7. http://www.theglobeandmail.com/news/politics/ottawa-notebook/well -travelled-pm-unveils-volunteer-awards/article1861796/.

–. 2011b. "Why does Jason Kenney need props at committee?" *Globe and Mail* blog, November 24. http://www.theglobeandmail.com/news/politics/ottawa -notebook/why-does-jason-kenney-need-props-at-committee/article2247872/.

Gandy, Oscar H. Jr. 1980. "Information in health: Subsidized news." *Media, Culture, and Society* 2: 103–15.

–. 2001. "Dividing practices: Segmentation and targeting in the emerging public sphere." In *Mediated Politics: Communication in the Future of Democracy,* ed. W. Lance Bennett and Robert M. Entman, 141–59. New York: Cambridge University Press.

Geddes, John. 2015. "'It's not about image, it's about substance.'" *Maclean's,* December 16. http://www.macleans.ca/uncategorized/its-not-about-image-its-about-substance/.

Giasson, Thierry, Harold Jansen, and Royce Koop. 2014. "Blogging, partisanship, and political participation in Canada." In *Political Communication in Canada: Meet the Press and Tweet the Rest,* ed. Alex Marland, Thierry Giasson, and Tamara A. Small, 194–211. Vancouver: UBC Press.

Gidengil, Elisabeth, Neil Nevitte, André Blais, Joanna Everitt, and Patrick Fournier. 2012. *Dominance and Decline: Making Sense of Recent Canadian Elections.* Toronto: University of Toronto Press.

Gingras, Anne-Marie. 2012. "Access to information: An asset for democracy or ammunition for political conflict, or both?" *Canadian Public Administration* 55(2): 221–46.

Goffman, Erving. 1959. *Presentation of Self in Everyday Life.* New York: Doubleday Anchor Books.

Goldenberg, Eddie. 2006. *The Way It Works: Inside Ottawa.* Toronto: McClelland and Stewart.

Gollom, Mark. 2016. "Justin Trudeau's 'freewheeling' style of cabinet management not without risks." CBC News, January 4. http://www.cbc.ca/news/politics/justin-trudeau-cabinet-ministers-1.3382912.

Google. 2013. "Our mobile planet: Canada." May. http://services.google.com/fh/files/misc/omp-2013-ca-en.pdf.

Gordon, Sean. 2006. "Harper using the soft-sell approach." *Toronto Star,* January 18, A8.

Gossage, Patrick. 1986. *Close to the Charisma: My Years between the Press and Pierre Elliott Trudeau.* Toronto: McClelland and Stewart.

Gould, Philip. 1998. *The Unfinished Revolution: How the Modernizers Saved the Labour Party.* London: Little, Brown.

Grabe, Maria Elizabeth, and Erik Page Bucy. 2009. *Image Bite Politics: News and the Visual Framing of Elections.* New York: Oxford University Press.

Grayson, Timothy. 2001. "'Brand Canada' or branded Canadian?" *Policy Options* June: 47–49.

Grönroos, Christian. 1994. "From marketing mix to relationship marketing: Towards a paradigm shift in marketing." *Management Decision* 32(2): 4–20.

Guthey, Eric, and Brad Jackson. 2005. "CEO portraits and the authenticity paradox." *Journal of Management Studies* 42(5): 1057–82.

Guzmán, Francisco, and Vicenta Sierra. 2009. "A political candidate's brand image scale: Are political candidates brands?" *Journal of Brand Management* 17(3): 207–17.

Hacker, Kenneth L., Maury Giles, and Aja Guerrero. 2003. "The political image management dynamics of President Bill Clinton." In *Images, Scandal, and Communication Strategies of the Clinton Presidency*, ed. Robert E. Denton Jr. and Rachel L. Holloway, 1–37. Westport, CT: Praeger Publishers.

Hall Findlay, Martha. 2009. "Government communications." Canada. Parliament. House of Commons. *Edited Hansard* 144(118). 40th Parliament, 2nd Session, November 26.

Harber, Tyler. 2013. "Campaign forensics: Learning why you lost." *Campaigns and Elections* January–February: 52–53.

Harper, Stephen. 2001. "Re: research." Email, August 20. Flanagan fonds.

Harper, Stephen J. 2013. *A Great Game: The Forgotten Leafs & The Rise of Professional Hockey*. Toronto: Simon & Schuster.

Harper, Tim. 2015. "Sounds of silence from Tory candidates." *Hill Times*, August 31, 8.

Harris, Kathleen. 2015. "Justin Trudeau to meet premiers ahead of UN climate change summit." CBC News, November 12. http://www.cbc.ca/news/politics/canada-trudeau-obama-apec-g20-1.3315874.

Harris, Michael. 2014. *Party of One: Stephen Harper and Canada's Radical Makeover*. Toronto: Viking Canada.

Harris, Sophia. 2014. "Ottawa axes questions from post-advertising polls." CBC News, May 26. http://www.cbc.ca/news/business/ottawa-axes-questions-from-post-advertising-polls-1.2652475.

Health Canada. 2005. "Social marketing in health promotion ... the Canadian experience." Communications, Marketing and Consultations Branch. Internal government document.

Hewson Bridge and Smith Ltd. 2007. "Canada Revenue Agency brand strategy." Internal document, June 18.

Himmelweit, Hilde T., Patrick Humphreys, Marianne Jaeger, and Michael Katz. 1981. *How Voters Decide*. London: Academic Press.

Hinch, Thomas D. 2006. "Canadian sport and culture in the tourism marketplace." *Tourism Geographies: An International Journal of Tourism Space, Place, and Environment* 8(1): 15–30.

Hood, Christopher. 1991. "A public management for all seasons?" *Public Administration* 69: 3–19.

Hood, Christopher, and Martin Lodge. 2006. *The Politics of Public Service Bargains: Reward, Competency, Loyalty – and Blame*. Oxford: Oxford University Press.

Hopkin, Jonathan, and Caterina Paolucci. 1999. "The business firm model of party organization: Cases from Spain and Italy." *European Journal of Political Research* 35(3): 307–39.

House of Commons of Canada. 2015. Bill C-586. Parliament of Canada, 41st Parliament, 2nd Session. http://www.parl.gc.ca/.

Howlett, Michael. 2009. "Government communication as a policy tool: A framework for analysis." *Canadian Political Science Review* 3(2): 23–37.

Hoyer, Wayne D., and Steven P. Brown. 1990. "Effects of brand awareness on choice for a common, repeat purchase product." *Journal of Consumer Research* 17(2): 141–48.

Hudson, Simon, and J.R. Brent Ritchie. 2009. "Branding a memorable destination experience: The case of 'Brand Canada.'" *International Journal of Tourism Research* 11: 217–28.

Huffington Post Canada. 2013. "Trudeau attacks: Peter MacKay won't send controversial mailouts, spokesperson says." May 8. http://www.huffingtonpost.ca/2013/05/08/justin-trudeau-peter-mackay-attack-ad-mail_n_3238839.html.

Human Resources and Skills Development Canada. 2009a. "Re: wrapper on form downloads from the Service Canada forms site." Internal email, April 6.

–. 2009b. "EAP branding." Internal email, August 19.

–. 2009c. "Re: in response to your question on EAP signage." Internal email, September 22.

Hutchinson, J. Wesley, Kalyan Raman, and Murali K. Mantrala. 1994. "Finding choice alternatives in memory: Probability models of brand name recall." *Journal of Marketing Research* 31: 441–61.

Hutton, James G., Michael B. Goodman, Jill B. Alexander, and Christina M. Genest. 2001. "Reputation management: The new face of corporate public relations?" *Public Relations Review* 27(3): 247–61.

Hynes, Niki. 2009. "Colour and meaning in corporate logos: An empirical study." *Brand Management* 16(8): 545–55.

Ibbitson, John. 2010a. "Michael Ignatieff and the vanishing cigarette." *Globe and Mail* blog, October 5. http://www.theglobeandmail.com/news/politics/ottawa-notebook/michael-ignatieff-and-the-vanishing-cigarette/article1744326/.

–. 2010b. "Harper pondered appeal to queen over prorogation." *Globe and Mail*, September 30, A7.

Indian and Northern Affairs Canada. 2007. "First Nations communications toolkit." Public Works and Government Services Canada. https://www.aadnc-aandc.gc.ca/DAM/DAM-INTER-HQ/STAGING/texte-text/ai-bc-fna-cnc-pub-fnct_1332273776283_eng.pdf.

Industry Canada. 2008. "Cellphone services: Recent consumer trends." Fall. https://www.ic.gc.ca/eic/site/oca-bc.nsf/vwapj/FINALCell2008Info-Apr21-eng.pdf/$FILE/FINALCell2008Info-Apr21-eng.pdf.

Innes, Brian G., William A. Kerr, and Jill E. Hobbs. 2010. "A private-public strategy for international marketing through collective brands: Canada Brand foods." *Journal of International Food and Agribusiness Marketing* 23(1): 72–87.

Innis, Harold A. 2008. *The Bias of Communication.* 1951; reprinted, Toronto: University of Toronto Press.

Interbrand. 2013. "Interbrand releases 14th annual best global brands report." September 30. http://www.interbrand.com/en/news-room/press-releases/2013-09-30-d355afc.aspx.

–. 2014. "Best Canadian brands." http://interbrandfilehosting.com/bestcanadianbrands/2014/Interbrand-Best-Canadian-Brands-2014.pdf.

Isaacson, Walter. 2013. *Steve Jobs*. New York: Simon and Schuster.

Issenberg, Sasha. 2013. *Victory Lab: The Secret Science of Winning Campaigns*. New York: Random House.

Ivison, John. 2007. "Tories manage brand, not crises." *National Post*, June 23, A1.

–. 2015. "New Tory attack ad targets Liberal leader despite poll showing NDP ahead." *National Post*, May 25. http://news.nationalpost.com/news/canada/canadian-politics/new-tory-attack-ad-targets-liberal-leader-despite-poll-showing-ndp-ahead.

Jamieson, Kathleen Hall. 2000. *Everything You Think You Know about Politics ... and Why You're Wrong*. New York: Basic Books.

Javidan, Mansour, and David A. Waldman. 2003. "Exploring charismatic leadership in the public sector: Measurement and consequences." *Public Administration Review* 63(2): 229–42.

Jodhan v. Attorney General of Canada, [2011] 2 FCR 355.

Johnson, A.W. 1971. "The Treasury Board of Canada and the machinery of government of the 1970s." *Canadian Journal of Political Science* 4(3): 346–66.

Johnson, Brian D. 2012. "Brian Adams still sings straight from the heart." *Maclean's*, April 16, 90.

Jowett, Garth S., and Victoria O'Donnell. 2006. *Propaganda and Persuasion*. 4th ed. Thousand Oaks, CA: Sage Publications.

Karlberg, Michael. 2002. "Partisan branding and media spectacle: Implications for democratic communication." *Democratic Communiqué* 18: 1–18.

Katsanis, Lea Prevel. 1994. "The ideology of political correctness and its effect on brand strategy." *Journal of Product and Brand Management* 3(2): 5–14.

Kavanagh, Dennis, and Anthony Seldon. 2000. *The Powers behind the Prime Minister: The Hidden Influence of Number Ten*. 2nd ed. London: Harper Collins.

Keith, Robert J. 1960. "The marketing revolution." *Journal of Marketing* 24(3): 35–38.

Kellner, Douglas. 2016. "Barack Obama, media spectacle, and celebrity politics." In *A Companion to Celebrity*, ed. P. David Marshall and Sean Redmond, 114–34. Chichester, West Sussex: Wiley.

Kennedy, Mark. 2014. "Foot in mouth? Trudeau vows more 'discipline' over off-the-cuff remarks." *Ottawa Citizen*, October 17. http://ottawacitizen.com/news/politics/foot-in-mouth-trudeau-vows-more-discipline-over-off-the-cuff-remarks-with-video.

–. 2015a. "'No election win (is) worth pitting Canadians against Canadians': Trudeau says of niqab debate." *National Post*, October 7. http://news.nationalpost.com/news/canada/canadian-politics/no-election-win-is-worth-pitting-canadians-against-canadians-trudeau-says-of-niqab-debate.

–. 2015b. "Tories end gag order on people who attend Stephen Harper's events." *Ottawa Citizen*, August 10. http://ottawacitizen.com/news/politics/tories-end-gag-order-on-people-who-attend-stephen-harpers-events.

Keown, Leslie-Anne. 2007. "Keeping up with the times: Canadians and their news media diet." Statistics Canada Catalogue 11-008. http://www.statcan.gc.ca/pub/11-008-x/2006008/pdf/9610-eng.pdf.

Kerbel, Matthew R., Sumaiya Apee, and Marc Howard Ross. 2000. "PBS ain't so different: Public broadcasting, election frames, and democratic empowerment." *Harvard International Journal of Press/Politics* 5(4): 8–32.

Kerby, Matthew. 2009. "Worth the wait: Determinants of ministerial appointment in Canada, 1935–2008." *Canadian Journal of Political Science* 42(3): 593–611.

–. 2011. "Combining the hazards of ministerial appointment and ministerial exit in the Canadian federal cabinet." *Canadian Journal of Political Science* 44(3): 595–612.

Kerby, Matthew, and Alex Marland. 2015. "Media management in a small polity: Political elites' synchronized calls to regional talk radio and attempted manipulation of public opinion polls." *Political Communication* 32(3): 356–76.

Kidd, Kenneth. 2008. "How Harper let it slip away." *Toronto Star,* October 18, ID01.

Kim, Byung-Do, and Mary W. Sullivan. 1998. "The effect of parent brand experience on line extension trial and repeat purchase." *Marketing Letters* 9(2): 181–93.

Kinsella, Warren. 2001. *Kicking Ass in Canadian Politics.* Toronto: Random House Canada.

Kitching, Chris. 2012. "Poll: Trudeau-led Liberals find strong support in T.O." CP24, October 1. http://www.cp24.com/news/poll-trudeau-led-liberals-find -strong-support-in-t-o-1.978589.

Kline, Stephen, Rovin Deodat, Arlene Shwetz, and William Swiss. 1991. "Political broadcast advertising in Canada." In *Election Broadcasting in Canada,* ed. Frederick J. Fletcher, 223–302. Ottawa: Royal Commission on Electoral Reform and Party Financing; Toronto: Dundurn Press.

Kozolanka, Kirsten. 2006. "The sponsorship scandal as communication: The rise of politicized and strategic communications in the federal government." *Canadian Journal of Communication* 31(2): 343–66.

–. 2014. "Introduction: Communicating for hegemony." In *Publicity and the Canadian State: Critical Communications Perspectives,* ed. Kirsten Kozolanka, 3–22. Toronto: University of Toronto Press.

Laghi, Brian. 2006. "How Harper fashioned his lead." *Globe and Mail,* January 7, A1.

Lair, Daniel J., Katie Sullivan, and George Cheney. 2005. "Marketization and the recasting of the professional self: The rhetoric and ethics of personal branding." *Management Communication Quarterly* 18(3): 307–43.

Lalancette, Mireille, Alex Drouin, and Catherine Lemarier-Saulnier. 2014. "Playing along new rules: Personalized politics in a 24/7 mediated world." In *Political Communication in Canada: Meet the Press and Tweet the Rest,* ed. Alex Marland, Thierry Giasson, and Tamara A. Small, 144–59. Vancouver: UBC Press.

Lang, Annie, John Newhagen, and Byron Reeves. 1996. "Negative video as structure: Emotion, attention, capacity, and memory." *Journal of Broadcasting and Electronic Media* 40(7): 460–77.

Lathrop, D.A. 2003. *The Campaign Continues: How Political Consultants and Campaign Tactics Affect Public Policy.* Westport, CT: Praeger.

Lavoie, Judith. 2013. "DFO censoring federal scientists with research rules, critics say." *Victoria Times-Colonist,* February 16, A4.

Lazarsfeld, Paul F., Bernard Berelson, and Hazel Gaudet. 1948. *The People's Choice: How the Voter Makes Up His Mind in a Presidential Campaign.* 2nd ed. New York: Columbia University Press.

Lazarus, Eve. 2009. "Marketer of the year." *Marketing Magazine,* December 10. http://www.marketingmag.ca/advertising/marketer-of-the-year-12446.

Leblanc, Daniel. 2011. "Opposition blows gasket as PM jets to Canucks-Bruins game." *Globe and Mail* blog, June 8. http://www.theglobeandmail.com/news/politics/ottawa-notebook/opposition-blows-gasket-as-pm-jets-to-canucks-bruins-game/article2051914/.

–. 2013. "CBC's French service ditches 'Radio-Canada' for 'Ici.'" *Globe and Mail,* June 6, A1.

–. 2015. "A snapshot of how federal leaders frame their image." *Globe and Mail,* June 12, A10.

LeDuc, Lawrence, and Jon H. Pammett. 2014. "Attitudes toward democratic norms and practices: Canada in comparative perspective." In *Canadian Democracy from the Ground Up: Perceptions and Performance,* ed. Elisabeth Gidengil and Heather Bastedo, 22–40. Vancouver: UBC Press.

Lees-Marshment, Jennifer. 2001a. *Political Marketing and British Political Parties: The Party's Just Begun.* Manchester: Manchester University Press.

–. 2001b. "The marriage of politics and marketing." *Political Studies* 49(4): 692–713.

–. 2006. "Political marketing theory and practice: A reply to Ormrod's critique of the Lees-Marshment market-oriented party model." *Politics* 26(2): 119–25.

Levine, Allan. 1993. *Scrum Wars: The Prime Ministers and the Media.* Toronto: Dundurn Press.

–. 2014. "Control freaks and dictators." *Winnipeg Free Press,* January 4. http://www.winnipegfreepress.com/opinion/analysis/control-freaks-and-dictators-281262871.html.

Levitz, Stephanie. 2013a. "Questions being raised about how Stephen Harper uses Twitter." CTV News, June 3. http://www.ctvnews.ca/politics/questions-being-raised-about-how-stephen-harper-uses-twitter-1.1309392.

–. 2013b. "Flaherty to tweet next budget as part of new social media strategy." CTV News, March 4. http://www.ctvnews.ca/canada/flaherty-to-tweet-next-budget-as-part-of-new-social-media-strategy-1.1201466.

–. 2015. "Canada 150 ad costs rising but no plans in sight." CBC News, January 4. http://www.cbc.ca/news/politics/canada-150-ad-costs-rising-but-no-plans-in-sight-1.2889551.

Lewis, J.P. 2013. "Elite attitudes on the centralization of power in Canadian political executives: A survey of former Canadian provincial and federal cabinet ministers, 2000–2010." *Canadian Journal of Political Science* 46(4): 799–819.

Liberal Party of Canada. 2010. "Speakers announced for Canada at 150: Rising to

the challenge." News release, February 25. http://www.liberal.ca/newsroom/
news-release/speakers-announced-for-canada-at-150-rising-to-the-challenge/.

–. 2011. "Building a modern Liberal Party: A background paper for discussion among
members of the Liberal Party." http://convention.liberal.ca/files/2011/12/
BuildingaModernLiberalPartyFinal.pdf.

–. 2012. "Ottawa 2012: Consultations on the resiliency of the Liberal ideal." Internal
party document, January 13. https://convention.liberal.ca/files/2012/02/Ottawa
2012conventionroundtablesreport_bil.pdf.

–. 2014. "Visual identity standards manual." https://www.liberal.ca/files/2014/04/
Liberal-Style-Guide.pdf.

–. 2015a. *Justin Trudeau's Top 3 Volunteer Tips*. Video, April 9. https://www.youtube.
com/watch?v=TEmOsR0lLoc.

–. 2015b. "Real change: A fair and open government." Election manifesto. https://
www.liberal.ca/files/2015/06/a-fair-and-open-government.pdf.

–. 2015c. "We'll fly you to Ottawa." Party listserve email. November 27.

Library of Parliament. 2004. "Government on-line." July 15. http://www.parl.gc.ca/
Content/LOP/ResearchPublications/tips/PDF/tip122-e.pdf.

Lilleker, Darren. 2010. *Key Concepts in Political Communication*. London: Sage.

Lilleker, Darren G., and Ralph Negrine. 2003. "Not big brand names but corner
shops." *Journal of Political Marketing* 2(1): 55–75.

Lindgren, April. 2014. "Toronto-area ethnic newspapers and Canada's 2011 federal
election: An investigation of content, focus, and partisanship." *Canadian Journal
of Political Science* 47(4): 1–30.

Litt, Paul. 2008. "Trudeaumania: Participatory democracy in the mass-mediated
nation." *Canadian Historical Review* 89: 27–53.

Loat, Alison, and Michael MacMillan. 2014. *Tragedy in the Commons: Former
Members of Parliament Speak Out about Canada's Failing Democracy*. Toronto:
Random House.

Lodge, Milton, Kathleen M. McGraw, and Patrick Stroh. 1989. "An impression-
driven model of candidate evaluation." *American Political Science Review* 83(2):
399–419.

Lunn, Susan. 2011. "Harper goes for new look on stage." CBC blog, March 28. http://
www.cbc.ca/newsblogs/politics/inside-politics-blog/2011/03/harper-goes-for
-new-look-on-stage.html.

Lusztig, Michael. 1995. "Federalism and institutional design: The perils and politics
of a triple-E Senate in Canada." *Publius* 25(1): 35–50.

MacCharles, Tonda. 2011. "A man of many, many words: Database of Harper's quotes
charts the evolution of a politician." *Toronto Star,* April 30, A14.

–. 2014. "Feds spend plenty of dollars for your two cents." *Toronto Star,* July 26, A9.

MacCharles, Tonda, and Robert Benzie. 2011. "Tory strategist's firing rankles party."
Toronto Star, April 28, A10.

MacDougall, Andrew. 2014. "How the Internet hurts political reporting and breeds
spin." CBC blog, April 28. http://www.cbc.ca/news/politics/how-the-internet-hurts
-political-reporting-and-breeds-spin-1.2623876.

–. 2015. "A (sort of) day in the life of Stephen Harper's director of communications." CBC blog, February 18. http://www.cbc.ca/news/politics/a-sort-of-day-in-the -life-of-stephen-harper-s-director-of-communications-1.2960032.

MacGregor, Roy. 2015. "Inside Stephen Harper's 'strange fishbowl.'" *Globe and Mail*, October 9. http://www.theglobeandmail.com/news/politics/inside-stephen -harpers-strange-fishbowl/article26765304/.

MacKinnon, Leslie. 2014. "Agents provocateurs nothing new, probably not unethical, says former Tory strategist." *Hill Times*, September 15, 1.

MacNaughton, Craig, and Christopher Stoney. 2014. "Justin Trudeau and leadership idolization: The centralization of power in Canadian politics and political parties." In *How Ottawa Spends: The Harper Government – Good to Go?* ed. G. Bruce Doern and Christopher Stoney, 66–79. Montreal: McGill-Queen's University Press.

Magnuson-Ford, Karen, and Katie Gibbs. 2014. "Can scientists speak?" https:// evidencefordemocracy.ca/sites/default/files/Can%20Scientists%20Speak_.pdf.

Maher, Stephen. 2011. "Stephen Harper's PR obsession is fostering paranoia and paralysis in public service." Blog. *Province* (Vancouver), December 2. http://blogs. theprovince.com/2011/12/02/stephen-maher-stephen-harpers-pr-obsession -is-fostering-paranoia-and-paralysis-in-public-service/.

Manning, Preston. 1989. "Strategic directions, 1989." Internal party memo, March 25. Flanagan fonds.

Marland, Alex. 2003. "Marketing political soap: A political marketing view of selling candidates like soap, of electioneering as a ritual, and of electoral military analo- gies." *Journal of Public Affairs* 3(2): 103–15.

–. 2012a. "Political photography, journalism, and framing in the digital age: The management of visual media by the prime minister of Canada." *International Journal of Press/Politics* 17(2): 214–33.

–. 2012b. "Yes we can (fundraise): The ethics of marketing in fundraising." In *The Routledge Handbook of Political Marketing*, ed. Jennifer Lees-Marshment, 164–76. London: Routledge.

–. 2014a. "The branding of a prime minister: Digital information subsidies and the image management of Stephen Harper." In *Political Communication in Canada: Meet the Press and Tweet the Rest*, ed. Alex Marland, Thierry Giasson, and Tamara A. Small, 55–73. Vancouver: UBC Press.

–. 2014b. "If seals were ugly, nobody would give a damn: Propaganda, nationalism, and political marketing in the Canadian seal hunt." *Journal of Political Marketing* 13(1–2): 66–84.

–. 2014c. "The brand image of governing parties and leaders." In *First among Unequals: The Premier, Politics, and Policy in Newfoundland and Labrador*, ed. Alex Marland and Matthew Kerby, 100–20. Montreal: McGill-Queen's University Press.

Marland, Alex, and Tom Flanagan. 2013. "Brand new party: Political branding and the Conservative Party of Canada." *Canadian Journal of Political Science* 46(4): 951–72.

–. 2015. "From opposition to government: Party merger as a step on the road to power." *Parliamentary Affairs* 68(2): 272–90.

Marland, Alex, Thierry Giasson, and Jennifer Lees-Marshment, eds. 2012. *Political Marketing in Canada*. Vancouver: UBC Press.

Marland, Alex, Thierry Giasson, and Tamara A. Small, eds. 2014. *Political Communication in Canada: Meet the Press and Tweet the Rest*. Vancouver: UBC Press.

Marland, Alex, J.P. Lewis, and Tom Flanagan. Forthcoming. "Governance in the age of digital media and branding." *Governance*.

Marland, Alex, and Maria Mathews. Forthcoming. "Friend, can you chip in $3? Canadian political parties' email communication and fundraising." In *Permanent Campaigning in Canada*, ed. Alex Marland, Thierry Giasson, and Anna Esselment.

Martin, Don. 2007. "Tories have book on political wrangling." *National Post*, May 17, A1.

Martin, Lawrence. 2010. *Harperland: The Politics of Control*. Toronto: Viking Canada.

Marzano, Giuseppe, and Noel Scott. 2009. "Power in destination branding." *Annals of Tourism Research* 36(2): 247–67.

Massicotte, Louis. 2013. "Omnibus bills in theory and practice." *Canadian Parliamentary Review*, Spring: 13–17.

Matthews, J. Scott, Mark Pickup, and Fred Cutler. 2012. "The mediated horserace: Campaign polls and poll reporting." *Canadian Journal of Political Science* 45(2): 261–87.

May, Elizabeth. 2009. *Losing Confidence: Power, Politics, and the Crisis in Canadian Democracy*. Toronto: McClelland and Stewart.

May, Kathryn. 2009a. "Independent PS unravelling: Experts." *Ottawa Citizen*, November 30, A1.

–. 2009b. "Critics blast government's budget 'spin.'" *Ottawa Citizen*, January 24, A1.

–. 2013. "Public service fails MPs: Page." *Ottawa Citizen*, March 16, A1.

–. 2015. "Rise of the rude: Public service executives urge 'civility' policy." *Ottawa Citizen*, June 21. http://ottawacitizen.com/news/politics/rise-of-the-rude-public-service-executives-urge-civility-policy.

Mayer, Jeremy D. 2004. "The presidency and image management: Discipline in pursuit of illusion." *Presidential Studies Quarterly* 34(3): 620–31.

McGrane, David. 2011. "Political marketing and the NDP's historic breakthrough." In *The Canadian Federal Election of 2011*, ed. Jon Pammett and Christopher Doran, 77–110. Toronto: Dundurn Publishing.

McGregor, Glen. 2012a. "A mighty wind: Bob Rae tops analysis of most talkative MPs." *Ottawa Citizen*, December 1, A4.

–. 2012b. "Thomas Mulcair has remortgaged his home 11 times since 1980s." *National Post*, May 27. http://news.nationalpost.com/2012/05/27/mulcair-has-remortgaged-his-quebec-home-11-times-since-early-1980s/.

McGregor, Glen, and Jason Fekete. 2014. "Inside the controversial questionnaires the Tories, Liberals, and NDP use to screen would-be nominees." *National Post*, May 2. http://news.nationalpost.com/2014/05/02/inside-the-controversial-questionnaires-the-tories-liberals-and-ndp-use-to-screen-would-be-nominees/.

McKie, David. 2010. "Behind the numbers: The Conservative government tries to suppress records they fought for in opposition." CBC Inside Politics blog, October 8. http://www.cbc.ca/newsblogs/politics/inside-politics-blog/2010/10/behind-the

-numbers-the-conservative-government-tries-to-suppress-records-they-fought -for-in-oppositi.html.

McLean, James S. 2012. *Inside the NDP War Room: Competing for Credibility in a Federal Election.* Montreal: McGill-Queen's University Press.

McLuhan, Marshall. 1964. *Understanding Media: The Extensions of Man.* New York: McGraw-Hill.

McMullan, Kylie, Pinder Rehal, Katy Read, Judy Luo, Ashley Huating Wu, Leyland Pitt, Lisa Papania, and Colin Campbell. 2009. "Selling the Canadian Forces' brand to Canada's youth." *Marketing Intelligence and Planning* 27(4): 474–85.

McQueen, Rod. 2004. "Remembering Robert Stanfield: A good-humoured and gallant man." *Policy Options* February: 8–11.

MediaMiser. 2005. "Media analysis report: Conservative Party of Canada summer ad campaign." Internal party document, October 14. Flanagan fonds.

Member of Parliament (RW). 2004a. "Caucus focus group." Email, March 10. Flanagan fonds.

–. 2004b. "Re: E/R for caucus." Email, March 30. Flanagan fonds.

Mendelsohn, Matthew. 1994. "The media's persuasive effects: The priming of leadership in the 1988 Canadian election." *Canadian Journal of Political Science* 27(1): 81–97.

Merolla, Jennifer L., Laura B. Stephenson, and Elizabeth J. Zechmeister. 2008. "Can Canadians take a hint? The (in)effectiveness of party labels as information shortcuts in Canada." *Canadian Journal of Political Science* 41(3): 673–96.

Mickey, Thomas J. 1997. "A postmodern view of public relations: Sign and reality." *Public Relations Review* 23(3): 271–84.

Milewicz, Chad M., and Mark C. Milewicz. 2014. "The branding of candidates and parties: The U.S. news media and the legitimization of a new political term." *Journal of Political Marketing* 13(4): 233–63.

Miljan, Lydia. 2011. "Television frames of the 2008 Liberal and New Democrat accord." *Canadian Journal of Communication* 36: 559–78.

Morneau, Bill. 2015. "Dinner?" Party listserve email. December 2.

Mulcair, Tom. 2015. *Strength of Conviction.* Toronto: Dundurn Press.

Mulgan, Richard. 2007. "Truth in government and the politicization of public service advice." *Public Administration* 85(3): 569–86.

Muniz, Albert M. Jr., and Thomas C. O'Guinn. 2001. "Brand community." *Journal of Consumer Research* 27(4): 412–32.

Munthree, Shantini, Geoff Bick, and Russell Abratt. 2006. "A framework for brand revitalization through an upscale line extension." *Journal of Product and Brand Management* 15(3): 157–67.

Muzellec, Laurent, and Mary Lambkin. 2006. "Corporate rebranding: Destroying, transferring, or creating brand equity?" *European Journal of Marketing* 40(7–8): 803–24.

Nadeau, Richard, Neil Nevitte, Elisabeth Gidengil, and André Blais. 2008. "Election campaigns as information campaigns: Who learns what and does it matter?" *Political Communication* 25: 229–48.

National Arts Centre. 2009. "Oct 3 / special addition to NAC program." Internal email, October 1.

Nature. 2012. "Frozen out." Editorial. *Nature* 483: 6.

Naumetz, Tim. 2011a. "PM Harper should be more open to media on campaign hustings: Forum Research poll." *Hill Times,* April 7. http://www.hilltimes.com/news/2011/04/07/pm-harper-should-be-more-open-to-media-on-campaign-hustings-forum-research-poll/27836.

–. 2011b. "Conservatives using 'branding' to try and win over ethnic voters." *Yahoo! Canada News,* March 4. http://ca.news.yahoo.com/conservatives-using--branding--to-try-and-win-over-ethnic-voters.html.

–. 2012. "Voter identification 'massive job.'" *Hill Times,* March 6. http://www.hilltimes.com/news/politics/2012/03/06/voter-identification-massive-job-central-conservative-campaign-gives-voter/29964.

–. 2014a. "Conservatives painting government of Canada website blue." *Hill Times,* March 19. http://www.hilltimes.com/news/politics/2014/03/19/conservatives-painting-government-of-canada-website-blue-organizing-by-themes/37894.

–. 2014b. "Health Canada says it would have given 'full control' to doctors' groups over content of anti-marijuana ad campaign." *Hill Times,* September 18. http://www.hilltimes.com/news/politics/2014/09/18/health-canada-would-have-given-full-control-to-doctors-groups-over-content-of/39639.

–. 2015. "Hill construction hiding former PM Pearson statue." *Hill Times,* May 26. http://www.hilltimes.com/news/hill-life-people/2015/05/26/hill-construction-hiding-former-pm-pearson-statue/42313.

Needham, Catherine. 2005. "Brand leaders: Clinton, Blair, and the limitations of the permanent campaign." *Political Studies* 53(2): 343–61.

Nelson, Michael. 1995. "Federal information policy: An introduction." *Government Information in Canada* 1(3). http://library2.usask.ca/gic/v1n3/nelson/nelson.html.

Newman, Bruce I. 1994. *The Marketing of the President.* Thousand Oaks, CA: Sage Publications.

News Canada. 2014. "About us." http://www.newscanada.com/en-About.

Nimijean, Richard. 2005. "Articulating the 'Canadian way': Canada™ and the political manipulation of Canadian identity." *British Journal of Canadian Studies* 18(1): 26–52.

–. 2006a. "The politics of branding Canada: The international-domestic nexus and the rethinking of Canada's place in the world." *Mexican Journal of Canadian Studies* 11: 67–85.

–. 2006b. "Brand Canada: The brand state and the decline of the Liberal Party." *Inroads* 19: 84–93.

–. 2014. "Domestic brand politics and the modern publicity state." In *Publicity and the Canadian State: Critical Communications Perspectives,* ed. Kirsten Kozolanka, 172–94. Toronto: University of Toronto Press.

Office of the Conflict of Interest and Ethics Commissioner. 2010. "The cheques report: The use of partisan or personal identifiers on ceremonial cheques or other props for federal funding announcements." April 29. http://ciec-ccie.parl.gc.ca/

Documents/English/Public%20Reports/Examination%20Reports/The%20 Cheques%20Report%20-%20Act.pdf.

Office of the Information Commissioner of Canada. 2013. "Report on plans and priorities 2013–14." http://www.oic-ci.gc.ca/eng/report_on_plans_and_priorities -rapport_sur_les_plans_et_les_priorites_2013-2014.aspx.

O'Malley, Kady. 2010. "Ministerial spin watch redux: Over to you, Wayne Wouters." CBC blog, January 29. http://www.cbc.ca/newsblogs/politics/inside-politics -blog/2010/01/ministerialspinwatch-redux-over-to-you-wayne-wouters.html.

–. 2014. "Copyright exception for political ads mulled by Conservatives." CBC News, October 9. http://www.cbc.ca/news/politics/copyright-exception-for-political-ads -mulled-by-conservatives-1.2793758.

–. 2015. "Opposition day motions tilt toward campaigning, away from oversight." CBC News, February 3. http://www.cbc.ca/news/politics/opposition-day-motions -tilt-toward-campaigning-away-from-oversight-1.2940300.

O'Neill, Juliet. 2006. "Harper's aides vow to be more open about his health." *Ottawa Citizen,* January 28, A1.

Opinion Impact. 2007. "Stakeholder consultations on the Federal Identity Program: Final report prepared for the Treasury Board Secretariat." Internal government document.

O'Shaughnessy, Nicholas. 2004. *Politics and Propaganda: Weapons of Mass Seduction.* Ann Arbor: University of Michigan Press.

–. 2009. "Selling Hitler: Propaganda and the Nazi brand." *Journal of Public Affairs* 9: 55–76.

Page, Christopher. 2006. *The Roles of Public Opinion Research in Canadian Government.* Toronto: University of Toronto Press.

Panebianco, Angelo. 1988. *Political Parties: Organization and Power.* New York: Cambridge University Press.

Panetta, Alexander. 2009. "Mulroney troubles tear apart the Tories." *Toronto Star,* April 6, A1.

Paré, Daniel J., and Flavia Berger. 2008. "Political marketing Canadian style? The Conservative Party and the 2006 federal election." *Canadian Journal of Communication* 33: 39–63.

Paré, Daniel J., and Susan Delacourt. 2014. "The Canadian Parliamentary Press Gallery: Still relevant or relic of another time?" In *Political Communication in Canada: Meet the Press and Tweet the Rest,* ed. Alex Marland, Thierry Giasson, and Tamara A. Small, 111–26. Vancouver: UBC Press.

Parliament of Canada. 2014. "Sitting days of the House of Commons by calendar year." http://www.parl.gc.ca/parlinfo/compilations/houseofcommons/Sitting Days.aspx.

Parmelee, John H. 2014. "The agenda-building function of political tweets." *New Media and Society* 16(3): 434–50.

Party staffer (CO). 2005. "Re: comm call." Email, January 20. Flanagan fonds.

– (GG). 2006. "Re: GST on new homes (don't worry ...)." Email, January 18. Flanagan fonds.

– (JH). 1992. "Policy, strategy, and communications: New directions." Reform Party of Canada, internal party document, August 28. Flanagan fonds.

– (JR). 2001. "Analysis of PC-DRC unity report unveiled today." Email, December 12. Flanagan fonds.

– (JW). 2001a. "Discussion points, 10/08." Email, August 9. Flanagan fonds.

– . 2001b. "SWOT meeting." Email, August 22. Flanagan fonds.

– . 2001c. "Re: Stephen Harper's e-mail." Email, September 10. Flanagan fonds.

– (KB). 2004. "Memorandum: Election post mortem." Internal party document, July 12. Flanagan fonds.

– (PM). 2004. "Memorandum: Liberal advertising – campaign 2004." Internal party document, July 22. Flanagan fonds.

– . 2005. "The Victory by Pamela Williams." Email, March 20. Flanagan fonds.

– (RN). 2005. "Re: pool cam." Email, December 7. Flanagan fonds.

– (WS). 2005. "Re: Corner Gas." Email, November 3. Flanagan fonds.

Party staffers (MC and PM). 2004. "Memorandum: Lessons learned – campaign 2004." Internal party document, July 9. Flanagan fonds.

Pasotti, Eleonora. 2010. *Political Branding in Cities: The Decline of Machine Politics in Bagotá, Naples, and Chicago.* Cambridge, UK: Cambridge University Press.

Persky, Stan. 1992. "The ghosts of racism that haunt Canada's past." *Globe and Mail*, August 15, C16.

Pétry, François, and Frédérick Bastien. 2013. "Follow the pollsters: Inaccuracies in media coverage of the horse-race during the 2008 Canadian election." *Canadian Journal of Political Science* 46(1): 1–26.

Petty, Kathleen. 2007. "The House." CBC Radio, June 9.

Peyton, Laura. 2013. "Conservative campaign database fiasco costs party millions." CBC News, October 23. http://www.cbc.ca/news/politics/conservative-campaign -database-fiasco-costs-party-millions-1.2187603.

Phase 5. 2006. "Treasury Board Secretariat government on-line research panel: Results from the on-line focus groups. Final report." Treasury Board Secretariat, internal government document.

– . 2007. "Treasury Board Secretariat government of Canada Internet research panel: Ninth online survey – results." Treasury Board Secretariat, internal government document.

Phoenix Strategic Perspectives. 2005. "Summary of public opinion research related to government on-line." Prepared for Public Works and Government Services Canada, internal government document.

– . 2007a. "Final report: 2007 electronic media monitoring (EMM) user survey." Prepared for Public Works and Government Services Canada, internal government document.

– . 2007b. "Final report: Review of the advertising campaign evaluation tool." Prepared for Public Works and Government Services Canada, internal government document.

Pinkleton, Bruce. 1997. "The effects of negative comparative political advertising on candidate evaluations and advertising evaluations: An exploration." *Journal of Advertising* 26(1): 19–29.

Plamondon, Bob. 2009. *Blue Thunder: The Truth about Conservatives from Macdonald to Harper.* Toronto: Key Porter Books.

Poguntke, Thomas, and Paul Webb, eds. 2005. *The Presidentialization of Politics.* New York: Oxford University Press.

Popkin, Samuel L. 1991. *The Reasoning Voter: Communication and Persuasion in Presidential Campaigns.* Chicago: University of Chicago Press.

Posner, Paul L. 2009. "The pracademic: An agenda for re-engaging practitioners and academics." *Public Budgeting and Finance* 29(1): 12–26.

Potter, Evan. 2009. *Branding Canada: Projecting Canada's Soft Power through Public Diplomacy.* Montreal: McGill-Queen's University Press.

Powell, Chris. 2011. "Government seeks agency partner to update its brand image." *Marketing Magazine,* August 25. http://www.marketingmag.ca/brands/government-seeks-agency-partner-to-update-its-brand-image-34827.

PR Newswire. 2012. "Multimedia content drives nearly 10 times more visibility than text, PR Newswire study confirms." November 27. http://www.multivu.com/players/English/59124-pr-newswire-visual-pr/flexSwf/impAsset/document/4226241f-2b92-43b3-b1ff-18e5d214c1ab.pdf.

Praxius Public Strategies. 2005. "Memorandum: Peterborough focus group." Internal party document, December 21. Flanagan fonds.

Prime Minister of Canada. 2012. "PM celebrates marketing freedom for grain farmers in western Canada." August 1. http://www.pm.gc.ca/eng/node/21973.

–. 2014. "Public event for February 27, 2014." Media advisory, February 27. http://pm.gc.ca/eng/news/2014/02/26/public-event-february-27-2014-0.

–. 2015. "Open and accountable government." Government document. http://pm.gc.ca/eng/news/2015/11/27/open-and-accountable-government.

Prime Minister's Office. 2006. "Creating effective visual messaging." Internal document.

–. 2013. "Prime Minister Stephen Harper participates in a question and answer session with the Ivey Business School." Photo release, November 8. http://www.pm.gc.ca/eng/media/prime-minister-stephen-harper-participates-question-and-answer-session-ivey-business-school.

–. 2014a. "PM announces support for paid internships in high demand fields during his visit to Fanshawe College." Photo release, May 2. http://pm.gc.ca/eng/node/35897.

–. 2014b. "PM departs for Ukraine, the Netherlands, and Germany." Photo release, March 21. http://www.pm.gc.ca/eng/node/35477.

–. 2015a. "PM attends Kingston Frontenacs hockey game in Kingston, ON." Photo release, January 10. http://www.pm.gc.ca/eng/media/pm-attends-kingston-frontenacs-hockey-game-kingston.

–. 2015b. "Prime Minister Stephen Harper meets with Kathleen Wynne, premier of Ontario." Photo release, January 5. http://www.pm.gc.ca/eng/news/2015/01/05/prime-minister-stephen-harper-meets-kathleen-wynne-premier-ontario.

–. 2015c. "Livestream." Listserve email, June 18.

–. 2016. "Media advisory." Listserve email, January 11.

Prior, Markus. 2005. "News vs. entertainment: How increasing media choice widens gaps in political knowledge and turnout." *American Journal of Political Science* 49(3): 577–92.

Privy Council Office. 1946. "Cabinet conclusions." Library and Archives Canada, September 5.

–. 1950. "Cabinet conclusions." Library and Archives Canada, April 18.

–. 1957. "Cabinet conclusions." Library and Archives Canada, June 24.

–. 1965. "Cabinet conclusions." Library and Archives Canada, September 15.

–. 1966. "Cabinet conclusions." Library and Archives Canada, March 29.

–. 2010. "Communications and consultations." http://www.pco-bcp.gc.ca/index. asp?lang=eng&page=secretariats&sub=comm&doc=comm-eng.htm.

–. 2011. "Accountable government: A guide for ministers and ministers of state – 2011." http://www.pm.gc.ca/grfx/docs/guidemin_e.pdf.

–. c. 2012a. "Modernizing government communications: Branding." Internal document.

–. 2012b. "Action requested: Government of Canada social media inventory." Internal email, June 27.

–. 2013a. "Privy Council Office: 2012–13 departmental performance report." http:// www.pco-bcp.gc.ca/docs/information/publications/dpr-rmr/2012-2013/docs/ dpr-rmr-eng.pdf.

–. 2013b. "A drafter's guide to cabinet documents." http://www.pco-bcp.gc.ca/docs/ information/publications/mc/docs/dr-guide-eng.pdf.

–. 2013c. "A drafter's guide to cabinet documents." http://www.pco-bcp.gc.ca/docs/ information/publications/mc/docs/guide-eng.pdf.

–. 2015. "Memorandum to cabinet (July 2014)." http://www.pco-bcp.gc.ca/docs/ information/publications/mc/docs/mc-eng.doc.

Progressive Conservative Party of Newfoundland. 1993. "A party destined to govern: PC campaign organization manual." Internal party document.

Public Works and Government Services Canada. 2005. "Who is responsible? Summary." Commission of Inquiry into the Sponsorship Program and Advertising Activities. http://epe.lac-bac.gc.ca/100/206/301/pco-bcp/commissions/sponsorship -ef/06-03-06/www.gomery.ca/en/phase1report/summary/es_full_v01.pdf.

–. 2006. "Renewal in action: Annual report on government of Canada advertising activities, 2004–2005." http://publications.gc.ca/collections/Collection/P100-2 -2005E.pdf.

–. 2008a. "Public service branding." Internal email, May 14.

–. 2008b. "Positioning PWGSC within the government of Canada brand." Internal document, September 30.

–. 2011a. "2009–10 annual report on government of Canada advertising activities." http://www.tpsgc-pwgsc.gc.ca/pub-adv/rapports-reports/documents/rapport -report-2009-2010-eng.pdf.

–. 2011b. "Economic Action Plan signage update." Memo to the minister, internal document, March 10.

–. 2012a. "2012–13 departmental performance report." http://www.tpsgc-pwgsc. gc.ca/rapports-reports/documents/rmr-dpr/2012-2013/rmr-dpr-2012-13-eng.pdf.

–. 2012b. "2010–2011 annual report on government of Canada advertising activities." http://www.tpsgc-pwgsc.gc.ca/pub-adv/rapports-reports/2010-2011/tdm-toc -eng.html.

–. 2013. "2011–2012 annual report on government of Canada advertising activities." http://www.tpsgc-pwgsc.gc.ca/pub-adv/rapports-reports/documents/rapport -report-2011-2012-eng.pdf.

–. 2014a. "Government of Canada: Government electronic directory services." http:// sage-geds.tpsgc-pwgsc.gc.ca.

–. 2014b. "Public Works and Government Services Canada: 2014–15 report on plans and priorities." http://www.tpsgc-pwgsc.gc.ca/rapports-reports/documents/ rpp/2014-2015/tpsgc-pwgsc-rpp-2014-2015-eng.pdf.

–. 2014c. "2012–2013 annual report on government of Canada advertising activities." http://www.tpsgc-pwgsc.gc.ca/pub-adv/rapports-reports/documents/ rapport-report-2012-2013-eng.pdf.

–. 2014d. "Communications management: Introduction." http://www.tpsgc-pwgsc. gc.ca/biens-property/sngp-npms/ti-it/plncomm-commpln-eng.html.

–. 2015a. "2013–2014 annual report on government of Canada advertising activities." http://www.tpsgc-pwgsc.gc.ca/pub-adv/rapports-reports/documents/rapport -report-2013-2014-eng.pdf.

–. 2015b. "Social media monitoring (EN578-141760/B." April 20. https://buyandsell. gc.ca/procurement-data/tender-notice/PW-CY-007-64441.

Pugliese, David. 2014. "If you protest, expect government to be spying." *Ottawa Citizen*, June 5, A1.

Pullig, Chris, Carolyn J. Simmons, and Richard G. Netemeyer. 2006. "Brand dilution: When do new brands hurt existing brands?" *Journal of Marketing* 70(2): 52–66.

Puzic, Sonja. 2013. "Harper live-tweets his day, including breakfast with the cat." CTV News, January 28. http://www.ctvnews.ca/canada/harper-live-tweets-his -day-including-breakfast-with-cat-1.1133192.

Pyles, Nathan. 2008. "Building political will." *Nonproliferation Review* 15(3): 441–58.

Quill, Greg, and Bruce Campion-Smith. 2010. "PM gets hip with a little help from his friends." *Toronto Star*, May 19, 1.

Radio-Canada. 2013. "Branding: Radio-Canada corrects the record." News release, June 7. http://www.cbc.radio-canada.ca/en/media-centre/2013/06/7/.

Raj, Althia. 2015. "Adam Scotti, Trudeau's photographer, captures the PM like no one else." *Huffington Post*, December 23. http://www.huffingtonpost.ca/2015/12/23/ adam-scotti-justin-trudeau-photographer_n_8864408.html.

Rana, Abbas. 2009. "PM's Beatles singing gets nearly 500,000 YouTube views in one week." *Hill Times*, October 12, 1.

–. 2015a. "PM instructs cabinet to attend all caucus meetings." *Hill Times*, December 7, 1.

–. 2015b. "Cellphones barred from Liberal caucus meetings, Goodale says Grits don't want any distractions." *Hill Times*, December 14, 1.

Rantisi, Norma M., and Deborah Leslie. 2006. "Branding the design metropole: The case of Montréal, Canada." *Area* 38(4): 364–76.

Rathgeber, Brent. 2014. *Irresponsible Government: The Decline of Parliamentary Democracy in Canada.* Toronto: Dundurn Press.

Reddy, Srinivas K., Susan L. Holak, and Subodh Bhat. 1994. "To extend or not to extend: Success determinants of line extensions." *Journal of Marketing Research* 31(2): 243–62.

Redfern Research. 2010. "Internal stakeholder assessments of the communications branch at Citizenship and Immigration Canada 2010: Final report." Prepared for Citizenship and Immigration Canada.

Riddell, Peter. 2005. "The rise of the ranters: Saving political journalism." *Political Quarterly* 76(s1): 70–79.

Rigby, Elizabeth. 2015. "Australian election guru keeps UK Tories on a tight leash." *Financial Times,* March 13. http://www.ft.com/cms/s/0/454aa29e-c8b2-11e4 -b43b-00144feab7de.html#axzz3aRqWdMNf.

Roberts, James A., Luc Honore Petnji Yaya, and Chris Manolis. 2014. "The invisible addiction: Cell-phone activities and addiction among male and female college students." *Journal of Behavioural Addictions* 3(4): 254–65.

Rojek, Chris. 2001. *Celebrity.* London: Reaktion Books.

Roman, Karina. 2010. "Tory logo on cheques goes too far: Ethics chief." CBC News, April 29. http://www.cbc.ca/news/canada/story/2010/04/29/ethics-cheques. html.

Rose, Jonathan W. 2000. *Making "Pictures in Our Heads": Government Advertising in Canada.* Westport, CT: Praeger.

–. 2010. "The branding of states: The uneasy marriage of marketing to politics." *Journal of Political Marketing* 9(4): 254–75.

Rosenberg, Shawn W., Lisa Bohan, Patrick McCafferty, and Kevin Harris. 1986. "The image and the vote: The effect of candidate presentation on voter preference." *American Journal of Political Science* 30(1): 108–27.

Rosenberg, Shawn W., and Patrick McCafferty. 1987. "The image and the vote: Manipulating voters' preferences." *Public Opinion Quarterly* 51(1): 31–47.

Ross, Tim. 2015. "Secrets of the Tories' election 'war room.'" *Telegraph,* May 16. http:// www.telegraph.co.uk/news/politics/11609570/Secrets-of-the-Tories-election -war-room.html.

Roy, Jeffrey. 2013. *From Machinery to Mobility: Government and Democracy in a Participative Age.* New York: Springer.

Rubin, Ken. 2014. "PCO's new gig, as a central social media agency." *Hill Times,* January 20, 16.

Russell, Meg. 2014. "Parliamentary party cohesion: Some explanations from psychology." *Party Politics* 20(5): 712–23.

Russell, Peter H. 2008. *Two Cheers for Minority Government.* Toronto: Emond Montgomery.

Ryckewaert, Laura. 2011. "PM Harper takes communication strategy to next level." *Hill Times*, November 21, 1.

–. 2013. "Some Hill staffers foregoing raises, refusing to sign gag order." *Hill Times*, December 16, 1.

–. 2014. "QP prep a consuming task for cabinet, PMO staffers, say Conservative sources." *Hill Times*, October 6, 1.

–. 2015. "Hill media, Liberals settle on cabinet 'outs.'" *Hill Times*, December 14, 19.

Sauvageau, Florian. 2012. "The uncertain future of news." In *How Canadians Communicate IV: Media and Politics*, ed. David Taras and Christopher Waddell, 29–43. Edmonton: Athabasca University Press.

Saunders, Doug. 2015. "How the Liberal dream machine will work." *Globe and Mail*, October 23. http://www.theglobeandmail.com/news/politics/crafting-a-blueprint -that-aims-to-transform-liberal-promises-into-real-lifepolicy/article26950746/.

Savigny, Heather. 2008. *The Problem with Political Marketing*. New York: Continuum.

Savoie, Donald J. 1999a. *Governing from the Centre: The Concentration of Power in Canadian Politics*. Toronto: University of Toronto Press.

–. 1999b. "The rise of court government in Canada." *Canadian Journal of Political Science* 32(4): 635–64.

–. 2003. *Breaking the Bargain: Public Servants, Ministers, and Parliament*. Toronto: University of Toronto Press.

–. 2010. *Power: Where Is It?* Montreal: McGill-Queen's University Press.

–. 2013. *Whatever Happened to the Music Teacher? How Government Decides and Why*. Montreal: McGill-Queen's University Press.

–. 2015. *What Is Government Good At? A Canadian Answer*. Montreal: McGill-Queen's University Press.

Scammell, Margaret. 1999. "The model professionals? Political marketing in the United States and the prospects of Americanization of global campaigning." *Journal of Euromarketing* 7(2): 67–89.

–. 2007. "Political brands and consumer citizens: The rebranding of Tony Blair." *ANNALS of the American Academy of Political and Social Science* 611: 176–92.

Scherer, Jay, and Lisa McDermott. 2011. "Playing promotional politics: Mythologizing hockey and manufacturing 'ordinary' Canadians." *International Journal of Canadian Studies* 1(43): 107–34.

Scheufele, Dietram A., and David Tewksbury. 2007. "Framing, agenda setting, and priming: The evolution of three media effects models." *Journal of Communication* 57: 9–20.

Schlesinger, Arthur M. 1973. *The Imperial Presidency*. Boston: Houghton Mifflin.

Schudson, Michael. 1989. "The sociology of news production." *Media, Culture, and Society* 11: 263–82.

Scotti, Adam. 2015. adamscotti. December 14. https://www.instagram.com/ adamscotti/.

Seymour-Ure, Colin. 1982. *The American President: Power and Communication*. New York: St. Martin's Press.

Shared Services Canada. 2015. "Email transformation initiative." http://ssc-spc.gc.ca/pages/mlobj-crrlobj-eng.html.

Sherman, Elaine, and Leon Schiffman. 2002. "Political marketing research in the 2000 U.S. election." *Journal of Political Marketing* 1(2–3): 53–68.

Shively, W. Phillips. 2013. *The Craft of Political Research.* 9th ed. Boston: Pearson.

Simpson, Jeffrey. 2001. *The Friendly Dictatorship.* Toronto: McClelland and Stewart.

–. 2015. "Tories reign as master of the message." *Globe and Mail,* May 15, A11.

Sirgy, M. Joseph. 1983. *Social Cognition and Consumer Behavior.* New York: Praeger.

Small, Tamara. 2009. "Still waiting for an Internet prime minister: Online campaigning by Canadian political parties." In *Election,* ed. Heather MacIvor, 173–98. Toronto: Emond Montgomery Publications.

–. 2012. "E-government in the age of social media: An analysis of the Canadian government's use of Twitter." *Policy and Internet* 4(3–4): 91–111.

Smith, Gareth. 2009. "Conceptualizing and testing brand personality in British politics." *Journal of Political Marketing* 8(3): 209–32.

Smith, Gareth, and Alan French. 2009. "The political brand: A consumer perspective." *Marketing Theory* 9(2): 209–26.

Smith, Jennifer. 1999. "Democracy and the Canadian House of Commons at the millennium." *Canadian Public Administration* 42(4): 398–421.

Smith, Joanna. 2011. "Message scandal rocks Layton." *Toronto Star,* April 30, A6.

–. 2014. "And now, the news – brought to you by the Tories." *Toronto Star,* December 20, A1.

Smith, Wendell R. 1956. "Product differentiation and market segmentation as alternative marketing strategies." *Journal of Marketing* 21(1): 3–8.

Soberman, David. 2005. "The complexity of media planning today." *Brand Management* 12(6): 420–29.

Soroka, Stuart N. 2002. *Agenda-Setting Dynamics in Canada.* Vancouver: UBC Press.

Souiden, Nizar, Frank Pons, and Marie-Eve Mayrand. 2011. "Marketing high-tech products in emerging markets: The differential impacts of country image and country-of-origin's image." *Journal of Product and Brand Management* 20(5): 356–67.

Spears, Tom. 2012. "Simple question led to bureaucratic snowstorm." *Ottawa Citizen,* April 17, A1.

Speed, Richard, Patrick Butler, and Neil Collins. 2015. "Human branding in political marketing: Applying contemporary branding thought to political parties and their leaders." *Journal of Political Marketing* 14(1–2): 129–51.

Statistics Canada. 2013. "Canadian Internet use survey, 2012." November 26. http://www.statcan.gc.ca/daily-quotidien/131126/dq131126d-eng.pdf.

Stewart, Marianne C., and Harold D. Clarke. 1992. "The (un)importance of party leaders: Leader images and party choice in the 1987 British election." *Journal of Politics* 54(2): 447–70.

Stewart-Olsen, Carolyn. 2013. "Re Senate report." Internal email, March 1.

Stokes, Donald E. 1963. "Spatial models of party competition." *American Political Science Review* 57(2): 368–77.

Stone, Laura. 2013. "Conservative MP who set off backbench revolt finally set to speak about abortion." Global News, May 7. http://globalnews.ca/news/540917/conservative-mp-who-set-off-backbench-revolt-finally-set-to-speak-about-abortion/.

Stoney, Christopher, and Tamara Krawchenko. 2012. "Transparency and accountability in infrastructure stimulus spending: A comparison of Canadian, Australian, and U.S. programs." Canadian Public Administration 55(4): 481–503.

The Strategic Counsel. 2006. "CIOB – next generation public services/service policy: Final report." Treasury Board Secretariat, internal government document.

Street, John. 2011. Mass Media, Politics, and Democracy. 2nd ed. Basingstoke: Palgrave Macmillan.

Strömbäck, Jesper, and Peter van Aelst. 2013. "Why political parties adapt to the media: Exploring the fourth dimension of mediatization." International Communication Gazette 75(4): 341–58.

Sullivan, Denis G., and Roger D. Masters. 1988. "Happy warriors: Leaders' facial displays, viewers' emotions, and political support." American Journal of Political Science 32(2): 345–68.

Sullivan, Mary W. 1990. "Measuring image spillovers in umbrella-branded products." Journal of Business 63: 309–29.

Supreme Court of Canada. 2011. Canada (Information Commissioner) v. Canada (Minister of National Defence), 2011 SCC 25.

–. 2014. Reference re Senate Reform, 2014 SCC 32, [2014] 1 S.C.R. 704. https://scc-csc.lexum.com/scc-csc/scc-csc/en/item/13614/index.do.

–. 2015. "Speeches." http://www.scc-csc.gc.ca/court-cour/judges-juges/spe-dis/index-eng.aspx.

Surridge, Grant. 2012. "Brands of the year: CBC lives everywhere." Strategy, September 28. http://strategyonline.ca/2012/09/28/brands-of-the-year-cbc-lives-everywhere/.

Taber, Jane. 2004. "All aboard the 'truth tour.'" Globe and Mail, May 28, A5.

–. 2010a. "Harper has 'something to hide,' Liberal ads say." Globe and Mail blog, January 10. http://www.theglobeandmail.com/news/politics/ottawa-notebook/harper-has-something-to-hide-liberal-ads-say/article1425825/.

–. 2010b. "Exercising with Obama, jamming with Nickelback." Globe and Mail blog, December 23. http://www.theglobeandmail.com/news/politics/ottawa-notebook/exercising-with-obama-jamming-with-nickelback/article1849132/.

–. 2010c. "Tories blast 'agenda-driven' CBC gun-registry coverage." Globe and Mail blog, September 22. http://www.theglobeandmail.com/news/politics/ottawa-notebook/tories-blast-agenda-driven-cbc-gun-registry-coverage/article1719143/.

–. 2011a. "15%." Globe and Mail, January 27, A5.

–. 2011b. "Tories heap scorn on budget watchdog's 'lapse in judgment.'" Globe and Mail blog, October 12. http://www.theglobeandmail.com/news/politics/ottawa-notebook/tories-heap-scorn-on-budget-watchdogs-lapse-in-judgment/article2198935/.

–. 2011c. "Tories scramble to contain damage over family-planning group." *Globe and Mail,* April 22, A5.

Taras, David. 2015. *Digital Mosaic: Media, Power, and Identity in Canada.* Toronto: University of Toronto Press.

Thomas, Paul G. 2010. "Who is getting the message? Communications at the centre of government." Public Policy Issues and the Oliphant Commission: Independent Research Studies. Public Works and Government Services Canada.

–. 2013. "Communications and prime ministerial power." In *Governing: Essays in Honour of Donald J. Savoie,* ed. James Bickerton and B. Guy Peters, 53–84. Montreal: McGill-Queen's University Press.

Treasury Board of Canada. 2014. "Canada's action plan on open government." http://data.gc.ca/eng/canadas-action-plan-open-government.

Treasury Board of Canada Secretariat. 1990. "Management guide to corporate identity: Federal Identity Program manual." http://www.tbs-sct.gc.ca/fip-pcim/documents/man_1_0__p1.pdf.

–. 2000. "Canada wordmark study." http://www.tbs-sct.gc.ca/fip-pcim/pol-can-eng.asp.

–. 2006. "Re: draft speaking points for briefing deck." Internal email, February 8.

–. 2007. "Common look and feel standards for the Internet, Part 4: Standard on email." http://www.tbs-sct.gc.ca/pol/doc-eng.aspx?section=text&id=25439.

–. 2008a. "Service Canada sign." Internal email, November 3.

–. 2008b. "Public servants on the public service of Canada: Summary of the results of the 2008 public service employee survey." http://www.tbs-sct.gc.ca/pses-saff/2008/report-rapport-eng.asp.

–. 2009a. "Procedures for planning and contracting public opinion research." https://www.tbs-sct.gc.ca/pol/doc-eng.aspx?id=16491&section=text.

–. 2009b. "Common look and feel standards: Exemption requests." Presentation to the Policy Oversight Committee. Internal government document, April 9.

–. 2009c. Letter of reply drafted for the president of the Treasury Board, Vic Toews. Internal government document, c. September 25.

–. 2010a. "Re: follow up on signage." Internal email, February 26.

–. 2010b. "Re: interpretive signage – approval from funders requested." Internal email, May 6.

–. 2010c. "Re: approval of a logo." Internal email, October 20.

–. 2011a. "Values and ethics code for the public sector." http://www.tbs-sct.gc.ca/pol/doc-eng.aspx?section=text&id=25049.

–. 2011b. "Guideline for external use of Web 2.0." http://www.tbs-sct.gc.ca/pol/doc-eng.aspx?id=24835&section=text.

–. 2011c. "Policies for ministers' offices – January 2011." https://www.tbs-sct.gc.ca/pubs_pol/hrpubs/mg-ldm/2011/pgmo-pldcm-eng.asp.

–. 2011d. *Canada's Performance 2010–11: The Year in Review.* Report of the president of the Treasury Board of Canada. http://www.tbs-sct.gc.ca/reports-rapports/cp-rc/2010-2011/cp-rc-eng.pdf.

–. 2011e. "Re: branding program." Internal email, November 8.

–. 2011f. "FW: Open Government – Beta site for review." Internal email, March 10.

–. 2011g. "Re: Open Government – Beta site for review." Internal email, March 10, 4:42 pm.

–. 2011h. "Re: Open Government – Beta site for review." Internal email, March 10, 6:11 pm.

–. 2011i. "Re: Open Government jpegs 2." Internal email, March 16.

–. c. 2012. "Public affairs procedures: Media calls." Internal document.

–. 2012a. "Communications policy of the government of Canada." http://www.tbs -sct.gc.ca/pol/doc-eng.aspx?id=12316&section=text.

–. 2012b. "1998 Treasury Board decisions on the Federal Identity Program." http:// www.tbs-sct.gc.ca/fip-pcim/pol-dec-eng.asp.

–. 2013a. "The programs of the secretariat." https://www.tbs-sct.gc.ca/tbs-sct/abu -ans/tbs-sct/paa-aap-eng.asp.

–. 2013b. "Standard on web usability." http://www.tbs-sct.gc.ca/pol/doc-eng. aspx?id=24227&section=text.

–. 2013c. "Standard on social media account management." http://www.tbs-sct.gc.ca/ pol/doc-eng.aspx?id=27033&section=text.

–. 2013d. "Procedures for publishing." http://www.tbs-sct.gc.ca/pol/doc-eng.aspx? section=text&id=27167.

–. 2014a. "Government communications." https://www.tbs-sct.gc.ca/communications/ index-eng.asp.

–. 2014c. "Guideline on official use of social media." http://www.tbs-sct.gc.ca/pol/ doc-eng.aspx?id=27517&section=text.

–. 2014d. "Treasury Board approvals to fund the government-wide advertising plan (2013–2104: Quarter 3)." https://www.tbs-sct.gc.ca/communications/adv-pub/ alloc_1314_q3-eng.asp.

–. 2014e. Email to the author, December 2.

–. 2015. "2014 public service employee survey: Summary report." http://www.tbs-sct. gc.ca/pses-saff/2014/dr-rd-eng.pdf.

Trimble, Linda, and Joanna Everitt. 2010. "Belinda Stronach and the gender politics of celebrity." In *Mediating Canadian Politics,* ed. Shannon Sampert and Linda Trimble, 50–74. Toronto: Pearson.

Trudeau, Justin. 2014. *Common Ground.* Toronto: HarperCollins Publishers.

–. 2015a. President of the Treasury Board of Canada mandate letter. http://pm.gc. ca/eng/president-treasury-board-canada-mandate-letter.

–. 2015b. "Before I put the kids to bed." Party listserve email. November 3.

Tupper, Allan. 2003. "New Public Management and Canadian politics." In *Reinventing Canada: Politics of the 21st Century,* ed. Janine Brodie and Linda Trimble, 231–42. Toronto: Prentice-Hall.

Turner, Garth. 2009. *Sheeple: Caucus Confidential in Stephen Harper's Ottawa.* Toronto: Key Porter Books.

Turner, Tony, Andrew Hall, and Chris White. 2015. "Harperman song project." September 6. http://harperman.ca/.

Underwood, Doug. 2001. "Reporting and the push for market-oriented journalism: Media organizations as businesses." *Mediated Politics: Communication in the Future of Democracy,* ed. W. Lance Bennett and Robert M. Entman, 99–116. New York: Cambridge University Press.

Urback, Robyn. 2015. "Brace yourselves – four more years of PM PDAs." *National Post.* November 11. http://news.nationalpost.com/full-comment/robyn-urback -justin-trudeaus-pdas-are-making-things-uncomfortable-for-some-of-us.

van Aelst, Peter, Tamir Sheafer, and James Stanyer. 2012. "The personalization of mediated political communication: A review of concepts, operationalizations, and key findings." *Journalism* 13(2): 203–20.

Van Dorpe, Karolien, and Sylvia Horton. 2011. "The public service bargain in the United Kingdom: The Whitehall model in decline?" *Public Policy and Adminis- tration* 26(2): 233–52.

Van Dusen, Julie. 2015. "Justin Trudeau mobbed by federal civil servants." CBC News, November 6. http://www.cbc.ca/news/politics/trudeaudionduncancivilservants cheeredpearson1.3308271.

van Zoonen, Liesbet. 2005. *Entertaining the Citizen: When Politics and Popular Culture Converge.* Lanham, MD: Rowman and Littlefield.

Varoga, Craig, and Mike Rice. 1999. "Only the facts: Professional research and message development." In *Handbook of Political Marketing,* ed. Bruce I. Newman, 243–56. Thousand Oaks, CA: Sage Publications.

Vavrus, Mary Douglas. 2007. "The politics of NASCAR dads: Branded media paternity." *Critical Studies in Media Communication* 24(3): 245–61.

Veilleux, Gérard, and Donald Savoie. 1988. "Kafka's castle: The Treasury Board of Canada revisited." *Canadian Public Administration* 31(4): 517–38.

Waddell, Christopher. 2012. "Berry'd alive: The media, technology, and the death of political coverage." In *How Canadians Communicate IV: Media and Politics,* ed. David Taras and Christopher Waddell, 109–28. Edmonton: Athabasca University Press.

Wallace, Kenyon. 2011. "Conservative candidate asks for 'ethnic costumes' for Harper photo op." *Toronto Star,* April 13, GT2.

Watters, Haydn. 2015a. "Conservative app puts voter identification in campaign workers' hands." CBC News, June 12. http://www.cbc.ca/news/politics/conservative -app-puts-voter-identification-in-campaign-workers-hands-1.3104470.

–. 2015b. "Conservatives use photo of wrong type of salmon in campaign ad." CBC News, August 24. http://www.cbc.ca/news/politics/salmon-photo-conservatives -harper-atlantic-pacific-1.3201726.

Way, Alan. 1993. "The government of Canada's Federal Identity Program." *Design Management Journal* 4(3): 55–62.

Wells, Paul. 2006. *Right Side Up: The Fall of Paul Martin and the Rise of Stephen Harper's New Conservatism.* Toronto: McClelland and Stewart.

–. 2013. *The Longer I'm Prime Minister: Stephen Harper and Canada, 2006–.* Toronto: Random House Canada.

–. 2014. "This time, it's personal." *Maclean's,* September 8, 16–18.

–. 2015. "Of shields and swords and elections." *Maclean's,* April 20, 12–13.

Wesley, Jared J., and Mike Moyes. 2014. "Selling social democracy: Branding the political left in Canada." In *Political Communication in Canada: Meet the Press and Tweet the Rest,* ed. Alex Marland, Thierry Giasson, and Tamara A. Small, 74–91. Vancouver: UBC Press.

Wherry, Aaron. 2015. "What's really behind the niqab poll results?" *Maclean's,* October 2. http://www.macleans.ca/politics/ottawa/whats-really-behind-niqab -poll-results/.

White, Graham. 2005. *Cabinets and First Ministers.* Vancouver: UBC Press.

White House. 2014. "This is an infographic about millennials." October 8. http:// www.whitehouse.gov/share/millennials.

White, Jon, and Leslie de Chernatony. 2002. "New Labour: A study of the creation, development, and demise of a political brand." *Journal of Political Marketing* 1(2–3): 45–52.

Whittington, Les. 2015. *Spinning History: A Witness to Stephen Harper's Canada and 21st Century Choices.* Ottawa: Hill Times Books.

Whittington, Les, and Bruce Campion-Smith. 2008. "Puffin poop ad leaves stink." *Toronto Star,* September 10, A16.

Williams, Pamela. 1997. *The Victory: The Inside Story of the Takeover of Australia.* Sydney: Allen and Unwin.

Wilson, R. Paul. 2015a. "Minister's caucus advisory committees under the Harper government." *Canadian Public Administration* 58(2): 227–48.

–. 2015b. "A profile of ministerial policy staff in the government of Canada." *Canadian Journal of Political Science* 48(2): 455–71.

Wilson, Woodrow. 1887. "The study of administration." *Political Science Quarterly* 2(2): 197–222.

Wood, Emma, and Ian Somerville. 2007. "Public relations and corporate identity." In *The Public Relations Handbook,* 3rd ed., ed. Alison Theaker, 104–23. London: Routledge.

Wood, Lisa. 2000. "Brands and brand equity: Definition and management." *Management Decision* 38(9): 662–69.

Woon, Jonathan, and Jeremy C. Pope. 2008. "Made in Congress? Testing the electoral implications of party ideological brand names." *Journal of Politics* 70(3): 823–36.

Wright, Nigel. 2013a. "Re: Senate – residency and expenses." Internal email, February 11, 1:51 p.m.

–. 2013b. "Re: Senate – residency and expenses." Internal email, February 11, 8:51 p.m.

–. 2013c. "Re: Duff at 613-." Internal email, February 11.

–. 2013d. "Re: residency." Internal email, February 16.

–. 2013e. "Your letter." Internal email, February 19.

–. 2013f. "Re: Senator Duffy." Internal email, February 22.

–. 2013g. "Re: urgent: Senator Duffy." Internal email, March 1.

–. 2013h. "Re: Duffy." Internal email, March 21.

Wynne, Kathleen. 2014. "Letter to Prime Minister Stephen Harper." Government blog, November 19. https://www.ontario.ca/blog/article.php?post=298-premier_wynne_requests_meeting_with_prime_minister&Lang=EN.

Xing, Xiaoyan, and Laurence Chalip. 2006. "Effects of hosting a sport event on destination brand: A test of co-branding and match-up models." *Sport Management Review* 9: 49–78.

Young, Leslie. 2015. "Climate change a low priority for most Canadians: Ipsos poll." Global News, November 29. http://globalnews.ca/news/2366032/climate-change-a-low-priority-for-most-canadians-poll/.

Zaller, John. 1999. "A theory of media politics: How the interests of politicians, journalists, and citizens shape the news." Unpublished monograph.

Zavattaro, Staci M. 2010. "The implications of a branded president." *Administrative Theory and Praxis* 32(1): 123–28.

Zelizer, Julian E. 2010. "Gotcha politics gone wild." CNN Opinion, July 5. http://www.cnn.com/2010/OPINION/07/05/zelizer.gotcha.moments/index.html.

Interviews

Generic job titles have been assigned for comparability purposes and to shield the identities of most respondents. A communications strategist and communications messenger were differentiated based on my informal assessment of a respondent's prevailing role in the organization (i.e., some strategists and messengers straddle both worlds).

COMMUNICATIONS PRINCIPALS (CP) – PARTY LEADERS

CP 1: John Lynch-Staunton, former interim leader of the Conservative Party of Canada; former Conservative senator. April 5, 2012.

CP 2: Preston Manning, former leader of the Reform Party of Canada and the official opposition. June 22, 2012, and August 9, 2012.

CP 3: Stéphane Dion, member of Parliament; former leader of the Liberal Party of Canada and the official opposition; former cabinet minister. November 5, 2012.

CP 4: Stockwell Day, former leader of the Canadian Alliance Party of Canada and the official opposition; former Conservative cabinet minister. December 31, 2014.

COMMUNICATIONS STRATEGISTS (CS) – AGENTS WHO NEGOTIATE COMMUNICATIONS STRATEGY

CS 1: Election campaign research manager (Conservative). July 26, 2010, and July 5, 2012.

CS 2: Political advertising consultant (Liberal). July 30, 2010.

CS 3: Former communications director, Office of the Leader of the Opposition (Conservative). March 2, 2011, and May 25, 2012.

CS 4: Former communications manager, Prime Minister's Office (Conservative). March 14, 2011; April 19, 2012; and February 2, 2015.

CS 5: Doug Finley, senator (Conservative). October 17, 2011.

CS 6: Political advertising consultant (Conservative). March 27, 2012.

CS 7: Political advertising consultant (Conservative). April 12, 2012.

CS 8: Former communications manager, Prime Minister's Office (Conservative). May 4, 2012.

CS 9: Former communications manager, election war room (Conservative). May 28, 2012.

CS 10: Senator (Conservative). May 29, 2012.

CS 11: Tom Flanagan, former election campaign manager (Conservative). June 18, 2012.

CS 12: Media consultant (Conservative). July 6, 2012.

CS 13: Communications manager, Treasury Board Secretariat, government of Canada. July 10, 2012.

CS 14: Former communications manager, Prime Minister's Office (Conservative). July 19, 2012.

CS 15: Communications manager, Canada Post. September 10, 2012.

CS 16: Communications manager, Public Works and Government Services Canada. September 17, 2012.

CS 17: Communications manager, Canadian Heritage. October 5, 2012.

CS 18: Communications manager, Health Canada. October 18, 2012.

CS 19: Communications manager, Foreign Affairs and International Trade Canada. October 19, 2012, and November 12, 2012.

CS 20: Communications manager, Canadian Broadcasting Corporation. October 23, 2012.

CS 21: Tony Clement, president of the Treasury Board and member of Parliament (Conservative). November 14, 2012.

CS 22: Former communications manager, Prime Minister's Office (Conservative). November 21, 2012.

CS 23: Former communications manager, Prime Minister's Office (Conservative). December 20, 2012.

CS 24: Communications manager, Office of the Leader of the Opposition (New Democratic Party). February 13, 2013.

CS 25: Communications manager, Office of the Minister of Fisheries and Oceans (Conservative). December 4, 2014.

CS 26: Communications manager, Privy Council Office. December 5, 2014.

CS 27: Brad Lavigne, director of strategic communications and national election campaign director (New Democratic Party). December 5, 2014.

CS 28: Communications manager, Office of the Leader of the Third Party (Liberal). December 5, 2014.

CS 29: Former communications manager, Prime Minister's Office (Conservative). December 9, 2014.

CS 30: Former chief of staff, Prime Minister's Office (Conservative). December 12, 2014, and February 12, 2015.

CS 31: Former chief of staff, Prime Minister's Office (Conservative). January 6, 2015.

COMMUNICATIONS MESSENGERS (CM) – AGENTS WHO CARRY
OUT COMMUNICATIONS DIRECTIVES

CM 1:   Senator (Conservative). February 18, 2011.
CM 2:   Media pundit (Conservative). February 21, 2011, and July 19, 2012.
CM 3:   Senator (Conservative). March 1, 2011.
CM 4:   Senator (Conservative). March 15, 2011.
CM 5:   Political staffer, senator's office (Conservative). February 11, 2011.
CM 6:   Member of Parliament (Conservative). October 17, 2011.
CM 7:   Former political staffer, national party office (Conservative). October 17, 2011.
CM 8:   Former communications manager, national party office (Conservative). May 28, 2012.
CM 9:   Communications personnel, unspecified government of Canada agency. July 4, 2012.
CM 10: Advertising consultant (Conservative). July 5, 2012.
CM 11: Communications personnel, unspecified government of Canada agency. July 6, 2012.
CM 12: Communications personnel, Statistics Canada. July 19, 2012.
CM 13: Communications personnel, Public Works and Government Services Canada. September 17, 2012.
CM 14: Communications personnel, Public Works and Government Services Canada. September 17, 2012.
CM 15: Communications personnel, Canadian Heritage. October 5, 2012.
CM 16: Communications personnel, Health Canada. October 18, 2012.
CM 17: Executive staff, Department of Finance. November 9, 2012.
CM 18: Communications personnel, Canadian International Development Agency. November 11, 2012.
CM 19: Communications personnel, Aboriginal Affairs and Northern Development Canada. November 11, 2012.
CM 20: Executive staff, Citizenship and Immigration Canada. March 13, 2013.
CM 21: Executive exempt staff, Office of the President of the Treasury Board (Conservative). December 4, 2014.
CM 22: Former communications personnel, Privy Council Office. December 4, 2014.
CM 23: Former communications personnel, Privy Council Office. December 17, 2014.

COMMUNICATIONS INTERMEDIARIES (CI) – OUTSIDERS WHO
RECEIVE AND COMMUNICATE MESSAGES

CI 1:   News editor, *Toronto Star.* January 6, 2011.
CI 2:   Online journalist, *Calgary Herald.* January 7, 2011.
CI 3:   News editor, *Straight Goods News.* January 11, 2011.
CI 4:   Journalist, *NTV.* January 11, 2011.

CI 5:   News editor, *This Magazine*. January 13, 2011.
CI 6:   Journalist, Ottawa bureau, *Globe and Mail*. January 13, 2011.
CI 7:   President, Association of Electronic Journalists Canada. January 21, 2011.
CI 8:   President, Canadian Association of Journalists. February 15, 2011.
CI 9:   Journalist, *Embassy Magazine*. February 16, 2011.
CI 10: Photographer, Ottawa bureau, Canadian Press. February 17, 2011.
CI 11: Journalist, parliamentary bureau, CBC News. February 18, 2011.
CI 12: News editor, *Metro*. February 21, 2011.
CI 13: Columnist, Transcontinental Media. February 22, 2011.
CI 14: News editor, *South Asian Focus*. March 2, 2011.
CI 15: Nik Nanos, president and CEO, Nanos Research. July 16, 2012.
CI 16: Communications consultant, Delta Media. November 14, 2012.
CI 17: Campaigns director, International Fund for Animal Welfare. December 2, 2014.
CI 18: Susan Delacourt, Ottawa bureau journalist, *Toronto Star*. December 5, 2014.
CI 19: Jennifer Ditchburn, Ottawa bureau journalist, Canadian Press. December 5, 2014.

Index

journalism, 250, 374; and negativity, 190, 367; and pluralism, 191, 367; and political dynasties, 128; and political marketing, 32, 351, 358; and principles of, 45, 51; and public administration, 202–3, 205, 227; and public relations, 35, 361, 365; and segmentation, 152

Department of Agriculture and Agri-Food, 104, 109, 115, 244, 348(f)

Department of Canadian Heritage (PCH), 57, 109, 233–36

Department of Citizenship and Immigration, 84, 173, 329

Department of Employment and Social Development, 76, 255(f), 346

Department of Environment and Climate Change, xx, 196, 224, 250, 279, 284

Department of Finance, 54–55, 85, 326–42, 258(f)

Department of Fisheries and Oceans, 195, 269; seal hunt and, 105–6, 109

Department of Global Affairs, xxiii, 55, 104–5, 185, 247, 251, 329

Department of Health, 78–79, 266, 269, 282, 348(t), 385

Department of Human Resources, Skills and Development, 238

Department of Industry, 281, 285

Department of National Defence (DND), 111, 174, 244, 284, 304, 322, 323(f), 328, 333, 348, 395–400. See also Canadian Forces

Department of Natural Resources, 238, 348(t)

Department of Public Works and Government Services Canada (PWGSC), 54, 222(t), 230–33, 262, 263(t), 267, 270–73. See also procurement

Department of Trade and Commerce, 244

Department of Veterans Affairs, 185, 234

Destination 2020, 248

Diefenbaker, John, 22, 128, 192, 209, 330, 331

Digital media: blogs, 47, 65, 262, 276, 322, 406; BuzzFeed, 259, 355, 366;

Canada website, 115, 229, 264, 273–80, 302; candidate websites, 175; Combat Camera, 82, 111, 403–4; Consulting with Canadians, 228, 267; cyberbullying, 194, 279; department websites, 196, 270, 273–75, 279; Economic Action Plan website, xxiii, 90, 337–39, 342–47; email branding, xviii; Facebook, 62, 65, 73, 86, 184, 261, 272, 280 308(f); Flickr, 62, 65, 86, 115, 282; Google, 38–39, 62, 85, 261, 281, 322; Government On-Line, 274, 288; government standardization, 229, 273–78, 283–84, 343; Instagram, xxii, 62, 65, 366, 378; intranet, 264; justinoverhishead.ca, 132; media shock, 61–64, 71, 203, 286, 288, 355; media websites, 64–66, 71, 95, 261; MyBO, 8; Parliamentarian websites, 47, 115; party websites, 159, 198, 280, 342; prime minister's website, 86, 115; QR codes, 159; social media definition, 414; Twitter, 8, 62, 65, 71, 73, 85–88, 94, 115, 193, 272, 280–82, 285, 308(f), 322–23, 346, 403; Web 1.0, 40, 280; Web 2.0, 8, 40, 65, 248, 280, 283–84; website advertising, 154, 262, 331; White House website, 8; YouTube, 8, 62, 65, 67, 85, 89, 115, 192, 261(f), 282, 284–85, 298(f), 346. See also apps; 24 Seven videos

Dion, Stéphane, 127, 190, 192, 367; image framing of, 132, 198–200

Direct marketing, 40, 147, 155–64, 347; definition of, 407; direct mail, 63, 146–47, 151, 157, 347; postcards, 32, 175; robocalls, 67, 163–64, 187, 368; telemarketing, 165

Douglas, Tommy, 127

Dowding, Keith, 16

Downs, Anthony, 138–39

Duffy, Mike, 93, 341, 348; expense claims trial, 24, 180–82, 193, 198, 375, 381, 384

Economic Action Plan (EAP), xxiii, 25–26, 43, 52(f), 76, 90, 113, 221, 240, 258(f), 289, 335–49, 363, 367, 386

Communication, Strategy, and Politics

Thierry Giasson and Alex Marland, Series Editors

Communication, Strategy, and Politics is a ground-breaking series from UBC Press that examines elite decision making and political communication in today's hyper-mediated and highly competitive environment. Publications in this series look at the intricate relations between marketing strategy, the media, and political actors and explain how this affects Canadian democracy. They also investigate such inter-connected themes as strategic communication, mediatization, opinion research, electioneering, political management, public policy, and e-politics in a Canadian context and in comparison to other countries. Designed as a coherent and consolidated space for diffusion of research about Canadian political community, the series promotes an inter-disciplinary, multi-method, and theoretically pluralistic approach.

Other volumes in the series are:

Political Marketing in Canada, edited by Alex Marland, Thierry Giasson, and Jennifer Lees-Marshment

Political Communication in Canada: Meet the Press and Tweet the Rest, edited by Alex Marland, Thierry Giasson, and Tamara A. Small

Framed: Media and the Coverage of Race in Canadian Politics, by Erin Tolley

See also:

Canadian Election Analysis 2015: Communication, Strategy and Democracy, edited by Alex Marland and Thierry Giasson. Open access compilation available at http://www.ubcpress.ca/canadianelection-analysis2015/CanadianElectionAnalysis2015.pdf

Printed and bound in Canada by Friesens

Text design: Irma Rodriguez

Set in Univers Condensed, Sero, and Minion
by Artegraphica Design Co. Ltd.

Copy editor: Dallas Harrison

Proofreader: Dianne Tiefensee

Indexer: Laura Howells